# HOLMES-LASKI LETTERS

## VOLUME I

# HOLMES-LASKI
# LETTERS    VOLUME **I**

## THE CORRESPONDENCE OF
## MR. JUSTICE HOLMES AND
## HAROLD J. LASKI 1916-1935
## EDITED BY MARK DE WOLFE HOWE

ABRIDGED BY ALGER HISS FOR

# ATHENEUM    NEW YORK 1963

Published by Atheneum
Reprinted by arrangement with Harvard University Press
Copyright © 1963 by Atheneum House, Inc.
Copyright 1953 by the President and Fellows of Harvard College
All rights reserved
Manufactured in the United States of America by
The Colonial Press Inc., Clinton, Massachusetts
Published in Canada by McClelland & Stewart Ltd.
First Atheneum Edition

# PREFACE

In February 1949, Harold Laski gave to the Harvard Law School the original letters which Mr. Justice Holmes had written to him between 1916 and 1932. At the time when they were delivered to the School I undertook, at Mr. Laski's request, to have the letters transcribed and to supply him with copies, in order that he might publish some or all of them. As work progressed on the transcription I was told by a common friend that Laski had stated that I need feel no haste in completing the work since, under the pressure of other duties, he had abandoned, at least for the time, his original intention of preparing an edition of the Holmes letters. Work on the transcription continued, however, and was virtually completed when Laski died on March 24, 1950. At that time I reminded Mr. Justice Frankfurter of the fact that the Harvard Law School had in its possession all of the letters from Laski to Holmes which the Justice had preserved—nearly all which Laski had written to Holmes. On the suggestion of Mr. Justice Frankfurter, Mrs. Laski quickly and most generously consented to the plan of publishing the correspondence between the two men and indicated entire willingness that all editorial decisions should be mine. The publication of these volumes is the outcome of that willingness.

The kindness of Mr. Justice Frankfurter in providing a Foreword reduces to a minimum my responsibilities for setting the background of the correspondence. It may be well, however, if I state briefly what the principal editorial problems have been and how they have been resolved.

Some readers, feeling that the first responsibility of an editor is to discard superfluous materials, will complain, perhaps, that the publication of virtually all of the surviving correspondence of Holmes and Laski showed a lack of judgment. It may be urged that a selection from the letters would have sufficed to record the essentials of an extraordinary friendship and to mark the course of the intellectual pilgrimage of the friends. Time may justify the criticism, yet it seemed clear to me that the editor should not pretend to possess prophetic powers, and make judgments for later generations. If this correspondence is destined to become an important chapter in intellectual history it would be arrogance in its editor to cut the chapter to comfortable proportions determined by his own predictive interpretation of the history of ideas between 1916 and 1935. If the correspondence has the major importance which I believe it possesses, it is manifestly better to have the whole produced today than to leave to others the task of correcting this editor's well-meaning sins of omission.

This basic decision in favor of completeness involves one consequence which should be squarely faced. That consequence may, perhaps, best be phrased in terms of taste. In the letters as published there are many harsh comments, doubtless some unfair reflections on persons still living. Feelings are sure to be hurt by the publication of these statements and the taste of an editor who permits private criticism to become a matter of public knowledge is sure to be impugned. To this charge there is no plea in bar but there is merit, I believe, in a plea in confession and avoidance. Those critical comments which are published relate to people whose careers were conducted in public and whose names are familiar to their own generation and will probably not be unknown to later generations. Comment on such men is, therefore, criticism of their times. To spare the sensibilities of a few persons now living would have been to deny to later generations the benefit of contemporary judgment and, if you will, contemporary prejudice. Discretion by the editor might have developed his own reputation for good taste but it would have deprived the correspondence of much of its vitality and produced an artificial propriety hardly characteristic of the two correspondents.

This editorial problem was not unrelated to another. That was the question whether the editor, while disregarding the sensibilities of persons now living, should endeavor to protect the memory of the correspondents themselves. It would be less than honest to pretend that the exuberant, the passionate, and the controversial strains in Laski's character were loved and admired by all who knew him and his work. Among those who did not admire, some will be quick to seek in his letters to Holmes justification for their distrust. There they may find exaggeration, distortion, and falsehood. Had the editor felt it to be his duty to safeguard the reputation of either one of the correspondents he might have followed the easy course and omitted all passages which raised doubts in his own mind or he might have pursued the hopeless task of seeking to uncover the "true" version of all reported incidents. The hopelessness of following the second course ruled it out. The first alternative seemed unacceptable in the light of my conviction that the two men are larger than their failings and that the record of their lives and thought is a record of their times which should speak for itself in its entirety if it is to be heard at all. Presuppositions and prejudice could find easy confirmation in editorial censorship; when the whole correspondence is laid before the reader he will be empowered, as he should be, to form his judgment of the character of the correspondents upon the basis of all of the relevant evidence. The result was the decision to omit no passage in order to protect the name of its author from either justified or unjustified criticism. Those omissions which have been made are indicated by the conventional symbols and mark the spots at which either my judgment determined that the matter was of no appreciable interest to the public or where the limits of fair comment, as those limits are set by the caution of British publishers, seemed to have been passed.

In translating the informality of the handwritten originals to the formality of the printed page—and none of the originals was typewritten—I have taken liberties which purists may condemn. Paragraphing and punctuation have been added when they seemed manifestly called for; abbreviations have, for the most part, been eliminated. In all other respects the transcription is as accurate as my industry could make it, though I am sure that there are errors which other readers will discover. A particularly perplexing problem concerned the order in which the letters were to be printed. My general rule was to prefer that order which makes each letter responsive to its immediate predecessor over a sequence based entirely on a letter's date. I believe that this preference, aided by cross references, is justified, yet the reader may occasionally be troubled by its consequence. Perhaps it will be well for American readers to remember, in this connection, that it was Laski's habit to date his letters by numerals alone and that his practice was to give the day of the month before the month of the year. Thus his 9.X.24 stands for October 9, 1924, not for September 10, 1924.

With respect to the slight scaffolding which my annotations and biographical appendix provide I should perhaps add one word of explanation. It will be quickly seen that a series of somewhat arbitrary editorial judgments lie behind the footnotes and the Appendix. In the notes I have sought to provide the minimum aid which an informed Anglo-American reader of ordinary cultivation might find helpful. For his further assistance, and for the special benefit of any person who does not fit the measure of this imagined reader, the Biographical Appendix seeks to provide the relevant materials concerning persons who are referred to by the correspondents with some frequency and who are not such familiar figures as to need no identification. Doubtless a more scientific division could have been made between that information which is contained in footnotes and that which is to be found in the Appendix, yet I have felt that such allocations as I have made are better justified by instinct than by science. I should add, perhaps, that the relatively full annotation at the beginning of the volumes is reduced in the later correspondence. That reduction is based on the hope that the reader's familiarity with the materials, supplemented by the Index and the Appendix, makes editorial assistance increasingly superfluous.

M. DeW. H.

*Harvard Law School*
*September 1952*

# PREFATORY NOTE
## TO THE ABRIDGED EDITION

———

The decade which has passed since the publication of the two-volume edition of the *Holmes-Laski Letters* has naturally brought new interpretations of the two correspondents and their times. The letters themselves, of course, were kindling for reassessment. Now that I have looked into this skillful abridgment of the correspondence I have come to wonder whether I did not almost smother the flame of understanding by my extravagant use of kindling. In any case, I see in this selection self-portraits of Holmes and Laski no less revealing than those which appeared at fullest length ten years ago. I like to believe that a new generation of readers will find excitement in an extraordinary record of a remarkable friendship.

M. DeW. H.

# THE METHODOLOGY OF
# THE ABRIDGEMENT

---

It is appropriate to set out the criteria I have tried to follow in deciding upon the extensive excisions made necessary by limitations of space. First, I have sought to present without disfigurement the rich and varied contents of these widely-ranging, highly-civilized letters. Next, I have tried to preserve the tone of responsive dialogue which is the matrix for the self-portraits sketched by the two authors as they revealed to each other, through this prolonged correspondence, their personal tastes and traits.

With these major objectives in mind I have been guided by one further basic consideration. Justice Holmes's letters are an extraordinary historical and cultural heritage. As a boy he heard from his grandmother of the British entry into Boston. He thus spanned in his own lifetime and that of his familiars the entire history of our country. Brought up in a household of high culture, youthful officer in the Civil War, philosopher, eminent legal scholar and pre-eminent judge, he was a paragon without peer in American intellectual life. His letters are his major contribution to general literature, for his other writings ("The Common Law," judicial opinions, and collected legal papers and speeches) are principally concerned with legal subjects. Only the letters are fully accessible to the non-lawyer. And, despite the literary and intellectual power of his other writings, it was, naturally, in his letters that he most fully disclosed the style of his thought, the distinction of his personality, the mellow cultivation within which he was so fully comfortable, and the perceptive discrimination that had ripened during his long and privileged sojourn in the fairest fields of Western civilization.

Any conscientious editor, it seems plain, would want to preserve

intact the corpus of Justice Holmes's letters. I have done just this
with his letters to Harold Laski. The only excisions from Holmes's
letters that I have made are of a few sentences that refer without
expression of opinion to passages in Laski's letters omitted from
this edition. These deletions from Holmes merely avoid the distraction that would otherwise have resulted from unconnected, dan-
gling statements of no intrinsic quality.

My decision to make the required deletions almost exclusively
from Professor Laski's part of the correspondence was the more
easy to reach, and to adhere to, because the volume of his letters
was by far the greater. Despite the 540 pages of Laski's letters
that have been omitted, the representation of the two authors is
in this edition nearly equal in volume—Laski's share taking up just
under half the total number of pages. The Justice's frequent practice of restating Laski's points in replying to them has facilitated
abridging the Laski letters without undue loss of that quality of
interchange which characterizes notable collections of letters. My
excisions bear down most heavily on Laski's numerous lists of rare
works read, acquired or noted in dealers' catalogues, on conventional anecdotes, and on routine descriptions of scenery, paintings,
notables, and well-known or unimportant books. These omissions
do not, I hope, diminish the reader's opportunity to savor fully
Laski's warmth, his dedication as a teacher, his vast scholarship,
and the important part he played in the large events of his time.

One typographical point should be noted as to the Laski letters
retained in this edition. Deletions were sufficiently great in number and varying in length to call for a simplified method of noting
them in order to minimize interruption to the flow of the text.
Three dots represent each deletion, slight or extensive, and where
found at the beginning or end of a paragraph frequently replace
material that is separately paragraphed in the original letters.

Professor Howe's footnotes and biographical paragraphs have
been retained in view of their contribution to the general reader's
understanding. Wherever the footnotes I have added do not readily
disclose their authorship, by express reference to this edition, they
are marked with my initials.

Alger Hiss

*February 1963*

# CONTENTS

# CONTENTS

FELIX FRANKFURTER

# FOREWORD

The only justification for an extraneous foreword is the hope of drawing on one's good will with readers to secure their attention to an unknown author, or to assure them that a seemingly extinct volcano has again burst into flame. The crass absurdity that such could be the purpose of introductory remarks to the *Holmes-Laski Letters* precludes a misinterpretation of arrogance. When the public is offered two hefty volumes of correspondence neither revealing long-awaited secrets nor appealing otherwise to elemental curiosity, but preoccupied merely with things of the mind and the insoluble issues of man's spiritual quest, it may not be amiss to bear witness to the excitement these letters have stirred in one who has read every word of them.

This testimony is the more relevant since the public has already had two volumes of the *Holmes-Pollock Letters,* and since it comes from one who has read hundreds of unpublished letters of Mr. Justice Holmes and Harold J. Laski to other correspondents. How is it possible, we naturally suspect, that these *Letters* should not echo what we have already read? How can a correspondence so copious excite the mind from first to last? With full awareness of the treachery of superlatives, it becomes necessary to say that this correspondence surpasses all others from the pen—and it was the pen—of these prolific and extraordinarily endowed letter-writers.

One may ask in all soberness, was there ever another such correspondence? Consider its duration and continuity and range: high themes canvassed with enormous learning and a light touch, expressing deep convictions unmarred by intolerance, the exploits of two self-reliant adventurers in the world of ideas, passionately pur-

sued but with gargoylish humor. Added to all this, are the striking
differences between the two correspondents.

The outpour began with a bread-and-butter note from Laski, on
July 11, 1916, following the first meeting of the two in the Justice's
summer home at Beverly Farms, thirty miles north of Boston. This
opening letter and the prompt, longer reply by Holmes foreshadow
the essential characteristics of an exchange that lasted for close to
twenty years—the last letter written by Laski on February 17,
1935, about a fortnight before the Justice's death. They found
themselves drawn to one another at first sight by the magnetic attraction of two deep-ploughing minds full of disinterested zest for
the adventure of ideas.

Consider the situation of the two men who struck up at once
this deep, lasting friendship on that July day, 1916, at Beverly
Farms. By that time, through his writings—a famous little book,
a few essays, and his opinions—Holmes had powerfully changed
ways of thinking about law and had thereby rationalized law. A
few months earlier, his seventy-fifth birthday had been celebrated
as a national event. His fame transcended the boundaries of his
own country. He was acclaimed the preëminent judge of the
English-speaking world. Indeed, Judge Cardozo, no mean authority, was inclined to the view that Holmes was the profoundest intellect who had ever dispensed Anglo-American justice. The gifts
which nature had showered upon him—the handsome face and
distinguished presence, the noble voice and charming manner—
were accentuated by his long, dashing career which enveloped him
as though in a romantic aura.

Neither David Belasco nor Max Reinhardt could have contrived
a more dramatic contrast than Laski and Holmes when their friendship began. Facing one of the most impressive personalities of his
day was a frail stripling of twenty-three. More than half a century
separated them. Until he spoke, Laski was not particularly noticeable. But it was not the first time that Laski struck fire in an old
man who was the leader of his profession. When Francis Galton,
the famous geneticist, discovered that the author of an article
which had attracted his attention was "a schoolboy at Manchester,
aged 17!!" he wrote: "It is long since I have been so much astonished. The lad probably has a great future before him and he will
make a mark if he sticks to Eugenics . . ."

The lad did not stick to Eugenics after he went up to Oxford.
Probably through the influence of Sir Ernest Barker, then a don at
New College, the problems of politics, especially how liberty was
to be achieved, became for the rest of his life Laski's dominant
interest. He left Oxford at the outbreak of World War I. Having
been rejected for war service because of his physique, he spent two
years as a tutor at McGill. At the time of his visit to Holmes he

had just come to Harvard, an obscure junior instructor in the Department of Government, piecing out an academic pittance with which to support his wife and child (he had married at eighteen), by much writing during the summer, for Herbert Croly's *New Republic*.

Short as was his stay at Cambridge, only four years, the qualities in Laski that produced "the shock of recognition" between him and Holmes made a dent also on Harvard. Were there not a cloud of witnesses, competent and critical, it would not be credible that a young, unknown teacher could affect so deeply the life of a great university in so brief a time. For he taught his colleagues as well as his pupils as do all great teachers. In his case they were senior and distinguished colleagues. Professor Charles H. McIlwain, one of the glories of Harvard both as scholar and teacher, said of him: "His influence on students was greater than that of any other instructor I have ever known. His influence on me was profound . . ." One more bit of evidence must suffice. It is that of Professor Zechariah Chafee Jr., the eminent legal scholar and humanist: "There are few men with whom I have disagreed so often, and fewer still with whom I have passed so many happy hours and from whom I have learned so much."

It is not surprising that an ardent spirit with such diverse talents should have had his energy dispersed in many directions and his compassionate nature readily enlisted for all sorts of causes and individuals. But the main stream of his life was teaching. His central significance was that of teacher. To that calling he gave all he had—his learning (Holmes, writing to Pollock, called him "one of the very most learned men I ever saw of any age"), his eloquence, his imagination, his fantastic feats of memory, his dialectic powers, his ever-ready kindness and generosity, above all, what has been rightly called his "quite passionate interest in young people." There can be few countries in the world where there is not someone who will cherish for the rest of his days what Laski meant to him as a teacher. Not often can the function of teacher have been more completely fulfilled.

A temperament as swift as Laski's in reacting to any manifestation of injustice was bound, on occasion, to be betrayed by an excess of zeal on the side of the angels. He was not one of those, as R. H. Tawney said of him, who regard the omission from the beatitudes of "Blessed are the discreet" a regrettable oversight. The world suffers less from knight-errantry induced by a passion for liberty than from prudence dictated by self-regard. The letters of both men contain flippant and heretical passages that may offend some sensibilities. Judgments upon Holmes and Laski are bound to be drawn from these letters. But fair judgment can rest only on the correspondence in its entirety.

One more thing ought to be said. Good talkers are apt to embellish their tales and Laski's stories often gained in the telling. Indeed, at times he reinforced history by fancy. Some of his anecdotes remind one of Landor's "Imaginary Conversations," except that they are gayer and more illuminating. More often, however, when his accounts seems to transcend common experience they do so because things happened to Laski that lay outside the experience of less extraordinary people. And if he appears to indulge in some tall tales about the great, he was in fact the intimate of men like Lord Haldane and John Morley and Lord Chancellor Sankey and eminent men on the Continent, in the United States, and in Asia. He did move in the center of affairs as well as among the notables in the world of learning.

Holmes and Laski were obviously men apart. Much about them was calculated to keep them apart also from one another. But the factors of divergence—antecedents, age, preoccupation, geography —were absorbed by the confluence of their feeling for one another and by the intensity and range of their intellectual interests.

Thus it came to pass that when Laski announced to Holmes, in the early stages of their friendship, his return to England, the Justice wrote: "I shall miss you sadly. There is no other man I should miss so much." And toward the end, as Laski kept up his flow of gay and sustaining letters, his venerable friend wrote: "One of the greatest pleasures of my waning life is a letter from you."

*July 1952*

# HOLMES-LASKI LETTERS

## VOLUME I

# I

## 1916-1918

*The New Republic*
*New York City, July 11, 1916*
My dear Justice Holmes: That was the realisation of one of my dreams—and if I could write a fairy-story of the happiness men may hope for I should try to analyse the vigorous refreshment you gave to all I hold most dear.[1] I do not say 'thank you'—not merely because it is inadequate but because from one's master one learns that it is simply duty to receive. You teach our generation how we may hope to live.

I have sent you Sorel on *Violence*—perhaps it will pass some idle hour. The others you will have a little later and we shall want to hear what you think of them—perhaps the Morley will make you feel that the worship of Harriet still leaves her where Pius IX left Mary in 1854.[2]

I want badly to come again and I hope you will one day find room for me. Those hours cannot be too often lived.

I am sending you two little papers of mine which are perhaps not too dull for your acceptance.

I hope I may write sometimes and ask you questions.

*Very cordially yours, Harold J. Laski*

---

[1] On July 12 Holmes wrote to Sir Frederick Pollock telling him that Felix Frankfurter "the other day" had brought Laski to Beverly Farms, where Holmes spent his summers. 1 *Holmes-Pollock Letters* (1941) 237, 238.

[2] Laski had evidently undertaken to send Holmes a copy of Morley's *Notes on Politics and History* (1913) which Holmes read later in the summer of 1916; see, *infra*, p. 5. Morley's admiration for Harriet Martineau is referred to in subsequent letters; see, *infra*, p. 108. Pius IX in 1854, by the bull *Ineffabilis Deus*, proclaimed the dogma of the Immaculate Conception.

*Beverly Farms, Massachusetts, July 14, 1916*
*My dear Mr. Laski:* Your letter gave us great pleasure. You may be
sure that it was as much refreshment to me to see you as it can
have been to you to come here. As the second back (there have
been three) Judge Lowell [1] said in a case that I defended when
a man sued for salvage of a boat in which he had sailed some
thousand miles from a sinking ship, 'As the boat seems to have
saved him as much as he saved the boat I think that account
stands *in equilibrio*'.

Sorel came yesterday and I began it at once eagerly. I am not
yet ready with opinions—except that I do not share his following
of Bergson. (Did I mention the anticipation of B. in *Rejected Addresses,* 'Thinking is but an idle waste of thought'?) I was much
tickled with Santayana's rapier thrusts in *Winds of Doctrine.* Your
article in the *Harvard Law Review* came this morning. [2] I cut it out
to keep, I am very sure, in Washington, but I haven't yet read it.
I finished Beard's book, *Economic Interpretation of the Constitution,* without much profit. Personalty *vs.* Realty is suggestive—
but one didn't need evidence that Washington, Hamilton *et al* had
the opinions of the propertied classes, and the disclaimed insinuation of personal interest as a determining factor seems to me not
justified by the facts shown. I should think that Beard might have
read a far more amusing and cleverer book by Patten on *The
Development of English Thought,* in which P. searches the biographies of the leaders from Hobbes to Darwin to find the *aperçu*
that started them—system making coming later—with the conclusion that new lights in philosophy follow some economic change.

I wish I could remember the passage in Morley's letter in which
he so charmingly puts the mixture of flattered vanity and genuine
love for the young—it so exactly expressed my feelings. I had my
prolonged period of unhappiness and therefore think that I can
understand young men. And you chaps are so much more alert,
and take so much more for granted than the elders, that it makes
one young to talk with you.

I stopped here to read your article. It is brilliantly written—
but to indicate points of agreement and reserves would need talk.
I always have thought that most of the difficulties as to the *mens*

---

[1] John Lowell (1824-1897); great-grandson of John Lowell (1743-1802),
"the old judge," was successively judge of the United States District Court
for the District of Massachusetts and of the United States Circuit Court for
the first circuit. His cousin, Francis Cabot Lowell (1856-1911), also served
on the District and Circuit Courts from 1898 until 1911. A fourth member
of the family, James Arnold Lowell (1869-1933), was United States District
Judge from 1922 to 1933. The case to which Holmes refers is *Price* v. *Sears,*
Fed. Cas. #11,416 (1877).

[2] Laski, "The Personality of Associations," 29 *Harvard Law Review* 404
(February 1916).

*rea* was due to having no precise understanding what the *mens rea* is.[8]

I hope that you will come here again.

*Sincerely yours, O. W. Holmes*

*The New Republic*
*New York City, July 18, 1916*

*My dear Justice Holmes:* Your letter goes into my archives, and that superb honesty which returns my most precious hairbrush—I was poor-spirited enough to regret its natural inclinations to rest at Beverly Farms—wins my gratitude.

It is immensely interesting to have your comment on Beard. I found the book dull, and the considerations a little thin, but I liked his honesty and his serious attention to the documents. And it was a relief to get away from the revelation granted by God to Alexander Hamilton early in 1787. I do not know Patten's book—but I shall know it next week. I met him last year and found him as originally-minded as he was stimulating.[1] . . .

*Very cordially yours, Harold J. Laski*

*Beverly Farms, July 19, 1916*

*My dear Laski:* Your letter comes this morning and previously there came the other three books for which I must thank you—Morley and the two by Figgis.[1] I finished Sorel and wrote a few remarks to Frankfurter. His first principles are left to be divined I should suppose. A second myth: the sums withdrawn by capital —as if that meant anything but investment in something else—*i.e.* a direction of labor toward what the most competent prophet believed would be the demand six months ahead. I have put my belief into a few words at the end of my little volume of speeches —the last speech.[2] Sorel's myth formula is fine, but naturally I don't make much of his general conclusions. Morley is delightful as always. I have begun on Figgis, *Churches in the Modern State,* with much interest, but I am tempted to switch off on to the other book as I see that I shall find elucidation there of the views of Baldus—the man I quote in my opinion in *Kawananakoa* v. *Poly-*

---

[8] In the course of his article Laski had briefly discussed the problem whether corporations may be held guilty of crimes in which *mens rea* is an essential element. *Ibid.,* 415.

[1] Simon Nelson Patten (1852-1922) was Professor of Political Economy at the University of Pennsylvania from 1888 to 1917.

[1] Holmes's list of summer readings for 1916 includes John Morley, *Notes on Politics and History* (1914), and J. N. Figgis's *Churches in the Modern State* (1914) and *The Divine Right of Kings* (2nd ed., 1914).

[2] "Law and the Court," *Speeches* (1913), 98.

*blank,* 205 U.S. 349, as one of the precursors of Hobbes and Bodin, not knowing the theme had been studied (*Nemo suo statuto ligatur necessitative*). I suspect that you and Figgis are working the personality business a little hard, and drawing doubtful conclusions from it.[3] But to show you that the *de facto* limitations of sovereignty were not unknown to me a good while before I wrote *Cariño v. Insular Govt. of the Philippines,* 212 U.S. 449,[4] when I get at the *American Law Review* (while I edited it—vol. 4-7) I think I will try to give you some references.[5]

But I began this as a letter of thanks and I am beginning to preach if not to blow—so I will shut up. I have been so busy with books that I am behind now with the *New Republic* but I will not forget your recommendation.   *Sincerely yours, O. W. Holmes*

I reopen my letter for an imbecility. I early acquired an anti-Bergsonian conviction of the mechanical action of the human mind —by seeing the self-gratulatory smile with which man after man would say "Achilles" to me when I was wounded in the heel. Each thought he was being and manifesting a personality—all of which is a preface to asking how many you have heard apply the converse of the *New Testament* saying, and declare that you can't gather thistles from Figg's.

*The New Republic*
*New York City, July 22, 1916*

*My dear Justice Holmes:* Your letter was a challenge no less than an information. I am glad that Sorel did not disturb you. It always seemed to me that when we have so hard a task to get a little thinking into the world, it is a perfectly disastrous obscurantism to exalt mythology into a working hypothesis. But of course Sorel would now rejoice in the thought of how natural was his transition to Catholic Royalism.

Felix and I have serious complaint to make. We think it utterly unfair to assume that you are the only reader of your judgments. Felix sent me the sovereignty remarks in July, 1915. I have 'col-

---

[3] The pluralistic thesis of Laski and Figgis emphasized the reality and freedom of group and corporate personalities, and denied the omnicompetence of the state's sovereignty.

[4] Though Holmes in the *Kawananakoa* case had stated that "a sovereign is exempt from suit, not because of any formal conception or obsolete theory, but on the logical and practical ground that there can be no legal right as against the authority that makes the law on which the right depends" (205 U.S. at 353), in the *Cariño* case he had said that "when theory is left on one side sovereignty is a question of strength and may vary in degree" (212 U.S. at 458).

[5] Holmes had discussed problems of sovereignty in his article, "Codes and the Arrangement of the Law," 5 *American Law Review* 1 (October 1870).

lected'—I know you are an admirer of Ethel Sidgwick—the relevant remarks in *American Law Review* I-VII. I am under agreement with Croly[1] not to introduce your phrases more than twice
in any article and thrice in any number. Felix is teaching the growing youth—you make me feel that this is a contradiction in terms
—that cases like *Adair* v. *U.S.*[2] and *Lochner* v. *U.S.*[3] [*sic*] have
really got a philosophy within them.

I think your 'imbecility' had more truth than we like. If you
read the religious work Figgis has turned out since he started in
1911 to justify the ways of God to man, you would admit that it
is not only possible—Christ notwithstanding—to get thistles from
Figg's but even to find the Figg's nothing but thistles. I take your
comment on 'pushing personality too hard' to heart and mind. I
wonder though if the kind of polyarchy it politically represents
isn't as a fact the real salvation for democracy. It seems to me that
the groups—even if we have later to read them in a state context
—are simply basic and I am human enough to read sovereignty
in terms of their consent. Yale is publishing a little volume of
what, *à la* Spinoza, may be termed a *tractatus theologico-politicus*
in which I've tried to show the significance of this as a working
theory of the state.[4] Of course it will ask you to accept it—perhaps
you will put it next to Statham[5]—and to pull it into pieces.

If Figgis on Bartolus interests you, I would like to lend you a
book by a pupil of his on him which is tremendously good.[6] But
I don't want to overburden you with my hobby.

Will you tell Mrs. Holmes that by Washington Square the lilac
is in bloom and that it makes us think of her roses?

Every kind of good wish to you both—

*Very cordially, Harold J. Laski*

---

[1] Herbert Croly (1869-1930) had been editor of *The New Republic* since
its founding in 1914. He had written *The Promise of American Life* (1909)
and *Progressive Democracy* (1914).

[2] 208 U.S. 161 (1908). In this case a majority of the Court, with Holmes
and McKenna, JJ., dissenting, had held that an act of Congress prohibiting
railroads from discriminating against union workers was unconstitutional as a
violation of the liberty of contract.

[3] *Lochner* v. *New York*, 198 U.S. 45 (1905). A majority of the Court here
held that the New York statute establishing a ten-hour day in bakeries was
unconstitutional. Harlan, White, Day, and Holmes, JJ., had dissented.
Holmes's dissenting opinion contained his famous dictum: "The Fourteenth
Amendment does not enact Mr. Herbert Spencer's *Social Statics*." *Ibid.*, 75.

[4] *Studies in the Problem of Sovereignty* (1917).

[5] Among the oldest volumes in Holmes's library was a copy of Statham's
*Abridgement.* See Winfield, *The Chief Sources of English Legal History*
(1925), 210, footnote 1.

[6] Cecil N. Sidney Woolf, *Bartolus of Sassoferrato* (1913).

*Beverly Farms, July 28, 1916*

*My dear Laski:* Gelett Burgess's book comes this morning[1]—for which my thanks—but you worry me by spending your substance for my benefit although everything that you have sent has hit my liver one way or another. If I didn't hate to borrow books I should ask for the one about Bartolus—but it worries and bothers me to have other people's things. For God's sake don't take this as a hint that I want you to give it to me. I should be really mortified if you did. I got considerable nourishment out of Figgis. But apropos of him and your article in the *New Republic* July 22 [2] and your other writings I am led to a reflection or two. Admit what personality you like to the other groups inside of or overlapping the State—what of it? Man certainly is a personality but the Sovereign kills him when it sees fit and can. I take the proposition simply to be a counsel of policy—to tolerate and respect. I don't talk much of rights as I see no meaning in the rights of man except what the crowd will fight for. I heard the original Agassiz (Louis) say that in some part of Germany there would be a revolution if you added a farthing to the cost of a glass of beer. If that was true, the current price was one of the rights of man at that place. But I wonder whether toleration etc. is the lesson of the immediate future. Before the war it seemed to me that the trades unions and the trusts pointed to a more despotic regime. So long as efficiency is an ideal their tendency would seem to be enhanced by the war. I am not particularly in love with it, and if we are destined to blow it out, and as I once put it, to drop from Jim Hill to Aeschylus, I see compensations. But it isn't all one way.

I just have been reading some George Moore[3] and despite the intelligence of his criticism don't find his species of ignorant arrogance much more edifying than that of other sectarians. S. P. as to Bernard Shaw. I am somewhat moved by Moore to send for *Marius the Epicurean,* but barring some short early essays I haven't cottoned to Pater. I remember that one of his books years ago led me to say to someone: Hegel for the horizon, Spencer to lead you through the middle distance, and some body color from Carlyle for the foreground and there you are. I don't know whether I should stick to it now. Well, I started to thank you and have been betrayed into discourse—my choice of paper forbids my pretend-

---

[1] Probably *War: The Creator* (1916), which Holmes read in the summer of 1916.

[2] "The Apotheosis of the State," 7 *New Republic* 302 (July 22, 1916). Laski had there urged that men have responsibilities other than those owing to the state. He expressed vigorous dissent from the proposition that "in a crisis the thought and soul of the individual must be absorbed in the national life . . . ."

[3] Holmes's list of summer readings included Moore's *Confessions of a Young Man* (2nd ed., 1916).

ing surprise, however. If you see something that I ought to read just send a line suggesting that I buy it, as thanks to you I bought the *History of Contract in Early English Equity.*

*Sincerely yours, O. W. Holmes*

*The New Republic*
*New York City, August 1, 1916*

*My dear Justice Holmes:* Shall not a man do as he wish with his own? Let me have undisturbed a memory that means much to me —the thought that I gave you—and will yet give you—some not unpleasing hours. As to Bartolus—I note gladly your Aristotelian sense of property and respect you. The spirit of the καλὸs κἀγαθός is rare enough in our time.

Your reaction to (a) Figgis and (b) me reminds me of a story you tell in one of your papers of a young man who remarked that you would base your legislation on fears rather than hopes.[1] Granted that the sovereign may kill you or me, or even Felix, or the American Federation of Labor, what of it? Your scepticism comes, I venture, from a further doubt as to the worth of life; my pluralism comes from a certainty—you have yet to meet my wife —of its richness. And I see that richness so largely evolved out of the multiplicity of groups which are trying to think out some way of life, crudely and in ill enough fashion if you like, that where they conflict with the State, the reality, as I see it of their corporate mind, the intrinsic value of their real effort, makes me hesitate to say they must yield, *e.g.* the Roman Church was right as against Bismarck in the *Kulturkampf* and Rome as against Titus Oates. I want my variety validated in its freedom to make itself felt. I hope I am clear.[2]

I thank whatever Gods there be for one man who tells the truth about that incomparable apostate from intelligence, George Moore. You remember that Oscar Wilde asked him not to grow up in public. I would like him, just occasionally, to think his second-

---

[1] In "Ideals and doubts," 10 *Illinois Law Review* 1, 4 (1915); reprinted in *Collected Legal Papers* 302, 307 (1920).

[2] Writing to Felix Frankfurter on August 6, 1916, Holmes referred to this passage in the following terms: "I made some remarks to Laski about Figgis and his independent groups but by his answer infer that he did not appreciate the different point of view from which I wrote. I don't doubt the value of the groups or their independent origin, though I regard their personality as a figure of speech. I was thinking of their theoretical relation to the sovereign from a (sound) legal point of view—not of what it was desirable for the sovereign to do—but he inferred that at bottom I doubted whether life was worth living and said wait till you see my wife. I hardly should accept the inference, and doubt if anyone could make life richer than it has been made for me, so far as it does not depend upon oneself. But I liked to hear the lad say it because it made me believe that he too had struck it rich."

thoughts—though I doubt gravely if he has any. He's a man who lives on the intellect of his friends.

Walter Pater is not for me any more. At seventeen one is enthusiastic about him and goes about burning with all the hard gemlike flames his conclusion warrants. But at twenty-three it is pallidly esoteric—and I go back to the red blood of Huxley and Meredith and—if you will grant me leave—some of Oliver Cromwell's fighting letters. I can't sit with flowers in my hands and get exquisite pulsations. And of course they all become Romanists for the sake of incense and acolytes and swinging censers at the end.

I think in a choice between J. J. Hill and Aeschylus—I was brought up on Oxford logic—I should choose Euripides. Aeschylus, after all, got comfort from the heavenly galaxy; Euripides finely damned them and went his own way—*perversa quadam ratione inductus,* Cicero somewhere describes it; but that *ratio* is a fine big world. Of course I except some of the choruses in the *Choephoroe.*

Our British offensive thrills me[3]—I get word from my brother[4] of Lancashire youths marching into action with the old textile-folk songs of loom and mill and May-day on their lips. He tells me of one boy of eighteen whom he held in his arms as he died and the boy smiled and said (I can't reproduce the dialect) "Tell my mother I ha' lived a full life." And then people say we should give in. After all, we come from the Pilgrims' breed as well, and the whole of England is our Rock. You see that London has become my Zion and not even the attractions of New York will persuade my right hand to lose its cunning.

I will forward you a block of that foolscap paper if you will fill it for me. Phrases of yours make me inclined to say 'Nunc dimittis.' Americans—as I know them—are so inclined to think that all words take their stand on the first clause of the Declaration of Independence, but you thank God! were born an aristocrat of the pen.

Please salute Mrs. Holmes for me.

*Yours always, Harold J. Laski*

*The Association of the Bar of the City of New York*
*August 12, 1916*
My dear Justice Holmes: I have just read *Coppage v. Kansas*[1] as

---

[3] On July 1 and 14 British troops had made significant advances on the Somme.

[4] Laski's elder brother, Neville, at the time was serving with the 6th Lancashire Fusiliers.

[1] 236 U.S. 1 (1915). A majority of the Court, with Holmes, Day, and Hughes, JJ., dissenting, held a Kansas statute outlawing yellow-dog contracts unconstitutional.

the *New Republic* will show you²—for the first time. Please let me send a salute of thanks.

Apart from this, I write to suggest that amidst a vast sea of perverse irritations, you may greatly like two books I have just read—Zangwill on *The War for the World*,³ and Robert Michels' *Political Parties*. I'm a little dubious about the latter—but I think it will have a footnote of gratitude in the great man's book—when it comes along. Perhaps Graham Wallas will give that to us one day. The election suggests that it will be helpful.⁴ No one has wrung my spiritual withers as yet. Felix is for a bust-up and a new radical party, but I tell him that things do not happen that way. Are we like Alice when she lost the key to the garden door?

With greetings to Mrs. Holmes and yourself—

*Very cordially, Harold J. Laski*

*Beverly Farms, August 12,* [sic], *1916*

*My dear Laski:* Your letter came as if the answer to a Marconi¹— for I had been thinking to ask you to name some more books that interest you young fellows. I have read all that I had on hand, bar the books in the shelves and Tawney's *Minimum Rates in the Tailoring Trade*—as to which last the Chain Making Business seemed enough for the moment.²

I wrote to Frankfurter as to the last that he seemed to content himself with saying: You have got the goods, (improved conditions). And when I ask what is the bill, to expect me to be contented with that, going into the general charges at the end of the year—with no specified amount. F. replies, and I sympathize, that to improve conditions of life and the race is the main thing—but how the devil can I tell whether I am not pulling it down more in some other place. Faith doesn't seem to me an adequate thing to go on in questions of that kind.

You and I were not properly at issue on the sovereignty question—I was considering whether the legal theory of power was correct—you what it is desirable should happen—unless I am wrong. Your second letter came this morning and I have telephoned for Zangwill. I added Graham Wallas *The Great Society* and not your

---

² An unsigned editorial, "Neutrality in Strikes," included a quotation from Holmes's dissenting opinion in *Coppage* v. *Kansas*. 7 *New Republic* 28 (Aug. 12, 1916).

³ Laski reviewed the book in 10 *New Republic* 26 (Feb. 3, 1917).

⁴ In June Woodrow Wilson had been renominated as the Democratic candidate for President and Charles Evans Hughes had been nominated by the Republicans.

¹ The letter referred to is missing.

² In July, Holmes had read R. H. Tawney's *The Establishment of Minimum Rates in the Chain-Making Industry under the Trade Boards Act of 1909* (1914).

second book as you seemed wobbly on that. I am afraid I am a little overtrained—stale—for I find it hard to read novels without feeling as if I were wasting time—not normal to my earlier years. So I must have a touch of theory.

As you know I am not much on politics—but what the good of a radical bust-up and increasing Wilson's chances would be, I don't quite see—as I don't suppose Felix, any more than I, thinks it a duty to seek a Garrisonian (abolitionist) absolute, at all costs, every time.

The present moment is one that I have longed for when I have nothing particular on hand, and I ought to browse in *belles lettres* —but I doubt if I shall. I hope I shall see you again before the vacation ends.                    *Ever sincerely yours, O. W. Holmes*

> 1697 Cambridge Street, Cambridge, Massachusetts
> August 28, 1916 [1]

My dear Justice and Mrs. Holmes: I have interviewed gasmen, plumbers, grocers, butchers. I have bought furniture. I have seen in the nonfulfilment and misinterpretation of simple orders plainly given the real limits of human intelligence. I ought to feel angry and tired.

As a fact, I have a ceaseless chant of inward happiness. I have Frida and Diana coming to me tomorrow, and I have glorious things to tell them.[2] I can say how those wonderful new friends at Beverly refreshed me physically and stimulated me mentally. I can say that they have the unique power of setting even the humblest soul—I use the term as an algebraic bracket—on fire. And I can tell her that the big thing in this new life is to know you both and find enthusiasm and inspiration in the knowledge. Thank you deeply.

May I send you both my love? *Affectionately, Harold J. Laski*

> Beverly Farms, August 30, 1916

Dear Laski: You are a keen blade but you left another behind you. I enclose it in a box with a bit of glass for your wife—of no value but containing a bit of kingfisher's feather as a wish for your days in Cambridge.

---

[1] A short note from Holmes, dated August 17, suggesting that Laski might come to Beverly Farms on August 26, is omitted, as is another from Laski to Mrs. Holmes dated August 25, indicating that he planned to arrive at Beverly Farms in the afternoon of the next day.

[2] In January 1916, Laski had been appointed Instructor in History and Tutor in the Division of History, Government, and Economics at Harvard College, effective from September 1, 1916. During the academic year 1916-17 he was also enrolled as a first-year student in the Harvard Law School. Frida was his wife and Diana their baby.

I have read *The Dream of John Ball* and relished being transported to a land where all is oak and hand-made but was rather
unhappy to see Socialism recommended with such gaiety of heart
on such trivial grounds.        *Most sincerely yours, O. W. Holmes*


It was as much of a pleasure to me as it can have been to you to
have you here.


*Cambridge, Mass., August 31, 1916*
*My dear Justice:* I hope the Birrell will persuade you to try Hazlitt
again[1] —for I think him the least appreciated man of his time, and
certainly bigger than De Quincey whom I am emotionally not
disinclined to over-estimate. I finished *The Ambassadors*, and with
it all the Henry James for which I have time.[2] A second-class mind
dealing with fundamentally third-class material is hardly a necessity of life.

You will remember that I spoke to you of an unfortunate passage in Mr. Taft's book on the Presidency.[3] This is the relevant
quotation. ". . . in that case (*Warner Barnes & Co.* v. *U.S.*)[4] we
secured a majority of the court, Mr. Justice White pronouncing the
judgment in favor of the effectiveness of the ratification, and in
this way we defeated what I have always regarded as an inequi-
table claim. Of course those of us who were interested thought
that the last judgment was the deliverance of a Daniel come to
judgment. I do not say that there is any association between that
judgment and the fact that the judge who pronounced the majority opinion is now the Chief Justice of the United States; but
so it is." I suppose it is the *métier* of an ex-President to be genially
indiscreet.[5]

There is an exception I ought to have pled against our decision
*in re* Matthew Arnold. I think *The Scholar Gypsy* and *Empedocles*
really big stuff—so big that I have often been tempted to find a

---

[1] Holmes had recently read Augustine Birrell's *William Hazlitt* (1902).

[2] Holmes also had recently reread *The Ambassadors* (1903).

[3] William Howard Taft, *Our Chief Magistrate and his Powers* (1916), 99-103.

[4] 197 U.S. 419 (1905); 202 U.S. 484 (1906). The reference evidently intended by Laski was to *United States* v. *Heinszen & Co.*, 206 U.S. 370 (1907), in which White, J., wrote an opinion for a majority, upsetting the decision in the *Warner Barnes* case. The issues concerned the collection of duties on imports from the Philippine Islands. For Taft's irritation with Holmes's opinion for the majority in the first of the cases, see 1 Pringle, *The Life and Times of William Howard Taft* (1939) 267-268.

[5] In 1910 President Taft advanced Mr. Justice White to the post of Chief Justice.

Bacon for him. But he wrote his poems in the open air while his essays were done in the shadow of Balliol.

What does the railroad situation say to you about the orthodox theory of sovereignty?[6]

With every good wish to you both—

*Affectionately, Harold J. Laski*

*Beverly Farms, September 7, 1916*

*Dear Laski:* Just a word at this time. I am reading your Faguet[1] with much pleasure and general agreement, though why contract should found a right any more than existence he leaves to be explained. The truth I conceive to be that if we are talking law, contract rights depend upon and are created and limited by it as much as others—and others also are created. If we are talking morals, the like may be said.

As to Duguit I read one book of his, I think the *Transformations du droit public*[2] and found him suggestive but as I thought showing the usual continental or at least French feebleness in discussing fundamentals. My recollection is that by taking some intermediate provision that is only a wheel in a system he sought to invalidate what I think just as true today as ever: that all law means I will kill you if necessary to make you conform to my requirements.

I agree that the first class French books in French legal history and the Roman law are better than any similar German books I know. I doubt if any of them have the actuality of Ehrlich—but he is an Austrian, and Pound wrote a few—so that proves little.

I believe I did read Wells's *Modern Utopia*—he is a fangless Socialist, it seemed to me.

. . . One thing that gave me much pleasure in your talk was that you had not an easy optimism and didn't believe that universal bliss would ensue if the world would only get a move on and obey when the *New Republic* says Hocus—Pocus—Presto—Chango, and God knows I have as deep a respect as anyone for

---

[6] On August 29, President Wilson had delivered a special message to Congress, calling its attention to the railroads' stubborn insistence that outstanding issues with the brotherhoods should be submitted to settlement by arbitration, the refusal of the brotherhoods to accept that proposal, and the threat that a strike would occur on September 4. The principal request of the President was that Congress should enact an eight-hour law for railroad workers. On September 2 Congress followed Wilson's recommendation and adopted the Adamson bill, establishing the eight-hour day.

[1] Émile Faguet, *Le libéralisme* (1902). Faguet was there largely concerned to establish that it was error to speak of the rights of man as if they possessed an independent existence. He sought to show that their one source and whole origin was in contract.

[2] The volume appears among Holmes's list of readings for 1912.

the ability of Croly and Lippmann.[3] I have ceased to try to improve my mind and am reading Faguet as literature.

*Aff'ly yours, O. W. Holmes*

*Cambridge, Mass., September 9, 1916*

*My dear Justice:* I am so very glad that Faguet gave you pleasure. To me he is by far the biggest of modern French critics—and he did not surrender to the Gods like that wretch Brunetière. I like his ceaseless flow of intelligence and his capacity for analysis. If you happen not to have read his *Politiques et moralistes* you can spend some very happy hours with them.

It was immensely interesting to have your comment on my lack of optimism. I think I might have yielded to the perfectibilists before the war. But that surely demonstrated our humanity. I am a Darwinian, and Croly, Lippmann *et al.* seem to me really theologians—for they believe either in goodness or in sin as original and they have what I take to be a pathetic trust in environmental change. It seems to me so useless to be confident when again and again we are given proof that only the inbred qualities of men really count, and that you spread those by selecting them for survival, and not by building Polytechnics or starting settlements in the slums. I don't deny that an equalisation of opportunity would do much to improve the character of our thought. But my university experience, for example, has been that a very large number of the students are simply unfitted for university work in any real sense of the word. That is why I cling to the ideal of Oxford; for if it was too narrow, it had a high rate of productivity, and the people who were selected, largely fulfilled their promise. Here, I think there is too great confidence in the power of men to do anything to which they turn their attention. I often tell Felix that while Hamilton triumphed in his federal ideas, Jefferson was the man who supplied the mental atmosphere under which they went into operation. It's a silly theory to think that the brains of men are distributed on the same principle as the brains of sheep. So that while I am hopeful, I have to safeguard myself by scepticism.

The socialism of Wells's *Utopia* was not, I think, the ordinary economic brand. It appealed to me because he made (as I thought) a really effective plea for plan in policy instead of the blind and haphazard meandering you see in Wilson's railroad legislation.

You rejoiced my heart with your comment on French legists. F. P. [*sic*] Girard and Viollet, for instance, have always been two

---

[3] Walter Lippmann at this time was on the editorial board of *The New Republic*. He had already published *Drift and Mastery* (1914), *A Preface to Politics* (1914), and *The Stakes of Diplomacy* (1915).

of my heroes. I like to think that had Maitland lived he would have done for English history what Viollet did for French. I know the merits of Brunner and Gierke but they seem to derive their value rather from the artillery they mass than from the shells they actually fire. Ehrlich, of course, is every inch of him Jewish—a certain geometry of mind makes that plain. I wish you would one day suggest to Wigmore that a translation of his volume would be efficacious. Kohler and the rest seem small beer relative to him.

I have been reading two capital volumes of correspondence between the first Lord Granville and his aide between 1781-1821— too expensive to buy but good for the bedroom table. As soon as I have finished reviewing them, I will send them to you.[1] They will pass some idle hours very happily for you. Incidentally they give one a more clarifying vision of the real technique of government than fifty descriptive treatises.

But I must go back to Lamennais and the Catholic Reaction![2]
Our love to you both—                   *Yours always, Harold J. Laski*


                              *Beverly Farms, September 12, 1916*
*Dear Laski:* Unless they already are started don't send the volumes of Lord Granville's letters. I have so little time left that it is doubtful if I could read them and they are rather off my beat. I have just resumed Faguet who has been interrupted by *The Woman in White* and Belloc's account of the battle of the Marne[1]—the latter to make up for not reading the newspapers. He does his job well—like a good jury lawyer—recurring to main propositions, restating them, illustrating them by simple plans and fixing the main facts in your mind, whether his emphasis is the true one or not. Pursuing my sometimes profitable dodge of uniting disparates I combine Faguet's remark that man is born homicidal, adding Bernard Shaw's that he is born cowardly—in short that he is like other animals—and W. Collins's that he wants a story. I educe the conclusion that in the recent soft period of culture the crude facts at the foundation have been forgotten, and the result has been tea-table talk of pacifism and psychologic tales of insignificant scruples over unimportant events. Faguet in his main points seems like a French edition of H. Spencer's *Social Statics*—speaking from ancient memory. I don't care much more for theoretic limits to his function of government when based on the grounds for a static existence, than when based on an abstract axiom that I don't be-

---

[1] Laski's review of *Private Correspondence of Lord Granville Leveson Gower, 1781-1821* (1916) is in 9 *New Republic* 190 (Dec. 16, 1916).
[2] The third chapter of Laski's *Authority in the Modern State* (1919) was concerned with Lamennais.
[1] Hilaire Belloc, *The Elements of the Great War: The Second Phase* (1916).

lieve. With the tendency of both books I rather sympathize, thinking that the present swing toward government activity is exag-
gerated—that it expects too much, and will lead to things being
worse done. But the only limits that I should fix are practical, not
logical. Faguet however is a pleasure to read, and his side-shows
in the form of incidental remarks are worth the price of admission.
I have received this morning two volumes of Hazlitt, *Winterslow*
and *Table Talk,* which await the conclusion of Faguet. I shall
expect to send you a further word before I go on to Washington.
My compliments to your wife.

*Ever sincerely yours, O. W. Holmes*


*Cambridge, Mass., September 13, 1916*
*My dear Justice:* I hope it was only a re-reading of *The Woman
in White* which, with the exception of *The Moonstone,* is still my
favourite detective story—though I have a secret affection for a
nauseous volume called *The Mystery of a Hansom Cab.* Did you
ever take that journey?

Faguet I take to be in spirit a liberal of the Restoration, very
like in temper to Royer-Collard whom he admired greatly. That
meant that the Charter of Louis XVIII was the beginning of wisdom and I suppose it is almost the fullest statement of an *a priori*
theory of government. I know that you make much more of Herbert Spencer than I do; to me it seems always that he merely says
obvious things in pompous language. But Faguet is worth reading
for the luxuriant profusion of his ideas. I have just read a volume
of his on Anti-clericalism simply full of good things. It was fascinating to note the implicit pragmatism of your attitude to government. I, of course, with an English training in elasticity
couldn't feel otherwise; and that your experience leads you to that
conclusion means a great deal to me. But I am very worried over
the future of representative government. The complexity of social
problems seems to have outrun rather woefully the possibilities of
the parliamentary system; and while I believe that government by
administrative commissions can do much, still I feel we are going
to discover its limitations also and for the rest I can't help wondering whether the slow play of economic forces won't actually
give us the best adjustment. I feel, for instance, that most government work in industrial disputes results only in interim settlements
which are the jumping-off ground for the next scuffle. I take it
that the interests of capital and labor are irreconcilable in fundamentals—there's a sum to divide and each wants more than the
other will give. So that government intervention really neglects
the paramount issue which is the control of industrial management.
I wonder how you feel to this anarchical doctrine.

I have been working steadily at De Bonald for my book on the
political thought of the Catholic reaction in France, and amidst
much dissimilarity, I have been struck by certain integral likenesses
in him to your theory of law. He sets out by saying *"La justice
est un combat"* and phrases like *"Les lois humains ne sont que
les déclarations publiques d'intolérance"* are not unfamiliar to the
visitor at Beverly Farms. But you will have enough of this when
I write the book. He was a big man who only needed a little
feeling to be a great man.

I await your comments on Hazlitt. Our love to you both—

*Very cordially yours, Harold J. Laski*

When do you go to Washington?

*Beverly Farms, September 15, 1916*

*My dear Laski:* Your article[1] and your letter suggest more things
than I shall have time to say. The former is a lucid and interesting
account of a matter I knew nothing about—I even thought it
prudent to look out Erastianism in the dictionary. I take its excellence for granted sufficiently to make one or two criticisms. I
should drop pragmatic and pluralistic.[2] Perhaps I am the more
ready to say so because after honest attention I don't think there
is much in either of those parts of W. James's philosophy. But in
any event, though Pound also talks of pragmatism, the judging of
law by its effects and results did not have to wait for W. J. or
Pound for its existence, and to my mind it rather diminishes the
effect, or checks the assent you seek from a reader, if you unneces-
sarily put a fighting tag on your thought. So as to the other word.
As to the thing last involved I don't know that I could do more
than repeat what I have said or implied before. The scope of state
sovereignty is a question of fact. It asserts itself as omnipotent in
the sense that it asserts that what it sees fit to order it will make
you obey. You may very well argue that it ought not to order

---

[1] "The Political Theory of Disruption," 10 *American Political Science
Review* 437 (August 1916); reprinted in Laski's *The Problem of Sovereignty*
(1917) 27. The essay dealt with the Free Church of Scotland and the
cases which came to the Scottish and English courts concerning its secession
from the Established Church of Scotland.

[2] In his essay Laski had spoken of the "brilliant dissenting judgment of
Lord Jeffrey" in the Scottish Court of Session in *Earl of Kinnoul* v. *Ferguson,*
5 Session Cases 1010 (1843), 2 Buchanan, *The Ten Years Conflict* (1850)
380. In describing the opinion of Lord Jeffrey that the civil courts could not
disregard the determination of ecclesiastical authority, Laski had said that
Lord Jeffrey had adopted "a pragmatic test," and that his argument was "a
valuable contribution to that pragmatic theory of law of which Professor
Pound has emphasized the desirability." 10 *American Political Science
Review* at 462. Laski had concluded his essay with the suggestion that a
wise separation of secular and ecclesiastical authority "may connote a
pluralistic world."

certain things, and I agree. But if the government of England or
any other first class European power, or, under a changed Constitution, the Congress of the U.S., does see fit to order them, I
conceive that order is as much law as any other—not merely from
the point of view of the Court, which of course will obey it—but
from any other rational point of view—if as would be the case,
the government had the physical power to enforce its command.
Law also as well as sovereignty is a fact. If in fact Catholics or
atheists are proscribed and the screws put on, it seems to me idle
to say that it is not law because by a theory that you and I happen
to hold (though I think it very disputable) it ought not to be.

With which I pass to the kindred theory of Faguet and Hazlitt.
The last half of the former pleased me vastly, as he got into detail
and away from his first principles—and I was struck by how
parallel were the reflections of Hazlitt on Party Spirit.[3] All my life
I have sneered at the natural rights of man—and at times I have
thought that the bills of rights in Constitutions were overworked
—but these chaps remind me if I needed it, and I am not sure
that Croly doesn't, that they embody principles that men have
died for, and that it is well not to forget in our haste to secure
our notion of general welfare. The claims of the Interstate Commerce Commission in *I.C.C.* v. *Harriman,* 211 U.S. 407, made my
blood and [*sic*] boil [4] and it made my heart sick to think that they
excited no general revolt. The soft period of culture that I spoke
of the other day tended to oblivion of the fighting significance of
guaranties.

Turning to your letter, I hadn't been aware of a difference between us concerning H. Spencer but if I should take you literally
should feel quite sure that you didn't do him true justice. I think
myself that he was something of an originator, but at all events
his great influence as a *vulgarisateur* may not be realized by you,
coming after the accomplishment of the results. A great many
things that he said were very far from commonplace when he said
them, although I have no doubt they would seem pretty thin now.
When I remarked that concerning *The Scarlet Letter* to W. James
he replied, of course it does—it was an original book.

I have read *Winterslow* with great pleasure—Hazlitt says things
that W. James might have read in 'Belief Whether Voluntary' as
well as those that I have thought parallel to Faguet. If I may
illustrate—*obscurum per obscurius* (in my memory) I should think

---

[3] Among the essays in *Winterslow* (1850) were "On Party Spirit" and
"Belief Whether Voluntary."

[4] Holmes, writing for a majority of the Court in *Harriman* v. *Interstate
Commerce Commission,* in 1908, had denied the I.C.C. the broad powers of
investigation which it had sought to exercise, not in the enforcement of
existing statutes, but in determining what further legislation was desirable.

Hazlitt might be compared to Gregg [*sic*] of a later day.⁵ Not
quite possessed of charm, not quite genius in the narrow sense of
a discoverer of disconcerting phrases, he had an insight penetrating
enough to mark him as superior to most of his time—whether you
will call it genius or not is a question of degree.

*Ever sincerely yours, O. W. Holmes*

*September 21, 1916*
*Dear Laski:* Just a line to tell you that a clever woman—the
mother of Charley Curtis in the Law School¹—said to me the
other day that she thought your review in the last *New Republic*
of a book about Africa was the best review she ever read in Eng-
lish.² (I am not sure that even the last two words were added—
but *ex majori cautela* put them in to be sure I give you no more
than was said.) Apropos of your last letter³ I think I remember
hearing at one time that H. Spencer had great vogue at Oxford.
Bradley naturally wouldn't attribute any importance to him. Many
first-rate Frenchmen have cited him with respect as I have noted
from time to time—I think Faguet does in his volume I had the
other day. All this simply to insist that *de facto* he has been an
important influence.

I am keeping out of doors in this fine weather, but I have passed
into a second volume of Hazlitt—*Table Talk*. I may add to my
former appreciation that under eighteenth century forms his talk
on art—(not on Sir J. Reynolds lectures but on *e.g.* a landscape
by N. Poussin)—is really eloquent, perceptive, and full of noble
passion. That on Vulgarity and Affectation would be a good school
lesson for both England and America. *Yours ever, O. W. Holmes*

*Washington, D.C., October 7, 1916*¹
*Dear Laski:* Your letters are a constant pleasure to me and I shall
be glad if I get them here—but I can't give *quid pro quo* as I
have almost no time to write. You must not think it neglect or
indifference but simply a case of impossibility. Before we left
Boston my wife and I unexpectedly found ourselves in Cambridge.

⁵ W. R. Greg (1803-1881), author of *Essays on Political and Social Science* (1853) and *Literary and Social Judgments* (1873). See 3 Morley, *Critical Miscellanies* (1886) 213.

¹ Mrs. Charles P. Curtis was an intimate friend of Holmes's. Her son Charles P. Curtis, Jr., author of *Lions under the Throne* (1947), was at this time a third-year student at the Harvard Law School.

² Laski reviewed W. Walton Claridge's *A History of the Gold Coast and Ashanti* (2 vols., 1916) in 8 *New Republic* 172 (Sept. 16, 1916).

³ Omitted from this edition.

¹ A brief note from Holmes of October 6, 1916, is omitted.

We tried to find your house and to call on Mrs. Laski and you but I had not the address with me and after inquiring at a number of houses gave it up—I think coming within a door or two. It was most aggravating. . . .

Coming down I read Abel Hermant, *Confidences d'une biche*— a vivid picture—decidedly he is a knowing chap—and then reread some of A. de Musset's short stories. The first of them that I read seemed thin and I thought that they verified my formula that everything is dead in 25 years—but a focus [?] still was charming, and as I read on I still further succumbed to him. He is like the flowering of an apple tree and hardly lives beyond the moment of copulation, but I can't believe that knowing, but essentially second rate, R. de Gourmont that we now know that A. de M's phrase is empty.[2] Charm is one of the few things that survive. I am still in much confusion and have so many things to do that I don't answer your letters in detail. I am not likely to read any books for a good while. I can simply send you my love and await your orders.                              *Aff'ly yours, O. W. Holmes*

*Washington, D.C., October 22, 1916*
*Dear Laski:* A spare quarter of an hour gives me a chance to send you a line. They are damned rare, for a breathing space is sure to be occupied by a call, as yesterday afternoon by our beloved Felix, and perhaps this p.m. by him and Hackett.[1] If you are studying corporations let me mention one or two things that I have among my pamphlets, an article I thought good when I read it, by R. L. Raymond, "The Genesis of the Corporation," XIX *Harv. L. Rev.* No. 5, reprint dated 1906, Michoud, *La notion de personalité morale, (Extrait de la Revue de droit public et de la science politique en France et à l'étranger,* nos. 1 & 2 Jan. & April 1899).

F. Pollock in the *Festschrift* for Gierke wrote "Has the Common Law received the Fiction Theory of Corporations?" a short piece. Bound up with it I find Freund on *The Legal Nature of Corporations,* University of Chicago Studies in Political Science, 1897. I know nothing of the worth of this. I do not remember it. I have also P. Viollet, *Les corporations au moyen ages, (Nouvelle revue historique de droit Français et étranger,* no date) the French are damnable in that way. A note says it is a chapter in the third volume of his *Histoire des institutions.* This also I don't remember about. The first two are the things.

---

[2] See 1 *Holmes-Pollock Letters* (1941) 102.
[1] Francis Hackett (1883-1962), subsequently the author of *Henry the Eighth* (1929), *The Story of the Irish Nation* (1930), and *Francis the First* (1935), was at this time an editor of *The New Republic.*

I have read Santayana on *Egotism in German Philosophy* with less pleasure than *The Winds of Doctrine* but always with keen pleasure. I remember after reading and rereading Hegel's *Philosophy of Law* saying that still I don't believe the King of Prussia was God. The Germans generally perhaps—I mean the philosophers—have not clearly performed my first great act of faith and decided that they are not God.

I won't borrow trouble till it comes and therefore will not speculate as to Pound's book. Saleilles I have no notion about—I don't remember if I have read anything of his. I must off.

*Yours always, O. W. Holmes*

*Cambridge, Mass., October 23, 1916*

*My dear Justice:* Blessings on that quarter of an hour! Two of your references are new to me, and one, the Viollet, is invaluable. That, for two reasons, as it gave me due cause to embark on his book which I had long meant to do. . . .

I will be insolent and send you a quotation from a letter to me of a man who has the right to judge. "I envy you meeting Justice Holmes. When I think of America and its thought it is Hamilton and Holmes whose names I couple together. Marshall had too big an opportunity for us to separate ability from good fortune. But Holmes has been consistently progressive on the basis of an intelligence which has never swerved from the path in which intellect leads him. He fulfils the canon of D. F. Strauss.[1] He is the Huxley of America." I will tell Mrs. Holmes one day who wrote that, and we shall rejoice together.

I want you, if you will, to devote your next quarter of an hour to telling me what you think of Mr. Brandeis.[2] I hear that he is impressed by the greatness of the work and Justice Clark [*sic*][3] by its difficulty. . . .

Our love to you and Mrs. Holmes—

*Yours affectionately, Harold J. Laski*

---

[1] David Friedrich Strauss (1808-1874), German theologian and biographer; author of *Das Leben Jesu* (1835-1836; translated by George Eliot, 3 vols., 2nd ed. 1893). In his *Life of Jesus* Strauss made it his ruling objective to examine the gospels scientifically, and to distinguish myth from historical reality. His basic point of view was well expressed in his maxim: "The true criticism of dogma is its history."

[2] The nomination of Mr. Justice Brandeis to the Supreme Court had been confirmed by the Senate on June 1, 1916, and he took his seat on the bench on June 5, 1916.

[3] Mr. Justice Clarke, who had been appointed to fill the vacancy which had resulted from the resignation of Mr. Justice Hughes, took his seat on the bench at the opening of the October term, 1916.

*Washington, D.C., October 25, 1916*

*Dear Laski:* Your letter in what it quotes frightens me more than it encourages, even, for it makes me wonder if I hadn't better stop before anything happens to shake the kind opinions of the relatively few who know anything about me. However, there is no use in being cowardly and I shall crack ahead until a crack comes in my head or the machinery fails in some way or I feel more tired of it than I now am.

As to your inquiry what I think about our new accession, I might hesitate to express it if I had any new view, but in fact I have not had any new light or seen anything that would modify the impression accumulated during thirty and more years. Indeed as yet I have seen very little of him in the specific judicial character except as sitting in the row on the roost where I also sit. The time for discussions of any length is just beginning.

I am nearly mad with work at this moment and have to scribble off a line in Court pending a reargument on which I have made up my mind. I look forward to seeing you later. I won't undertake to determine beforehand whether I can put you up.

I wonder if old Viollet is still alive—he sent me the thing I mentioned. His history of French law I thought most admirable, though Brissaud? (translated in Wigmore's Series)[1] seemed to be above all others in showing the successive reactions between life and the law—a wonderfully good book, poorly translated, I think. I wonder too what has become of the writer of the most admirable book I have read on the Roman Law—Girard—unless my memory is wrong on the name.

I would rather talk to you than to listen—but I must turn back to the droolers.                                *Yours ever, O. W. Holmes*

*Cambridge, Mass., October 30, 1916*

*My dear Justice:* I did not mean to terrify you; and so long as you give to us the same thrill of eager determination to understand, I think you can keep the machinery going. I know that you have made an epoch in my life and that I am proud of your friendship.

Viollet and Girard are both dead. I am *in medio* Viollet and full of deep admiration. I wish he had not spent his Sundays worshipping the Sacred Heart; but I suppose that it is inevitable that we should allow a man of his calibre his hobbies. You made me happy by your praise of Girard. His *Manuel* first made me realize something of the breadth and sweep of Roman law. Then I think

---

[1] Jean Brissaud's *Cours d'histoire générale du droit français public et privé* (1904) was published in two volumes of the Continental Legal History Series, the first in 1912, *History of French Private Law*, as Volume III in the series; the other, *History of French Public Law* in 1915 as Volume IX.

he has a breadth and delicacy of touch which are lacking in most Germans—though I'd gladly except Mommsen's monograph on the *Collegia*.[1] Do you know the fine volume of texts he got out as an illustration to his manual? That was veritably a model text-book.[2]

My corporation is gradually getting registered—that is to say I am getting away from a discussion of hazy collectivism into the real guts of the subject. It is wonderful to see for how much the king and the church were responsible; they really constitute the key to things. I shall leave off at Coke when the concession theory is fully born.[3]

We are having an immensely happy time here. For the first time since I left Oxford we are pretty free from financial cares; and though we can't yet buy books still we can draw up the lists of them ready for the time when I blossom into a full professorship. I like the law work hugely, though I am eager to be done with the grind and to get into the thinking. Sometimes (*entre nous*) the natural folly of men coupled with the polite graces of the teacher combine to make the case-system a weapon of torment. One needs rather too frequently the incisive blandishments of the C. J. to intimate that argument has proceeded far enough.

Do you know a Frenchman named Hauriou? I should like you to lay up against your vacation his *Leçons sur le mouvement social* and his *Droit administratif et droit public*. He is a fellow with a genuinely first-rate mind. He sets out for me things I had long wanted to have said clearly by a big mind.

I wish the election were over. I don't think Mr. Hughes ought to win and I hate the idea of a Wilson victory. Sometimes there is much comfort in making Utopias and praying that if Mr. Wilson *is* re-elected he will be generous and bold and make Mr. Hughes the tenth justice of the Supreme Court.[4] But I must not write these speculations to you.

Santayana's book seemed to me to mark a decline in power of mind. Much of it gripped me, of course; but I often felt the sensation of an easy cynicism and a determined misunderstanding. There is a point of view in which Kant is not an egoist, just as there's a point of view in which Hegel is not entirely unreasonable —and one can't take them and stretch them out on the Procrustes' bed of Santayana's personal hatred. One needs an objective slide-

---

[1] Theodor Mommsen (1817-1903), *De Collegiis et Sodaliciis Romanorum* (1843).

[2] Girard, *Textes de droit romain* (3rd ed., 1903).

[3] Laski, "The Early History of the Corporation in England," 30 *Harv. L. Rev.* 561 (April 1917); reprinted in *The Foundations of Sovereignty* (1921), 171.

[4] In the impending elections Woodrow Wilson was the Democratic nominee for reëlection and Charles Evans Hughes, who had resigned as an associate justice of the Supreme Court in June 1916, was the Republican nominee.

rule in these matters. When I read Green's *Political Obligation*[5]
I am really grateful to Kant.

Our love to you both—                         *Yours always, Harold J. Laski*

*Washington, D.C., November 1, 1916*

*Dear Laski:* A line in neglect of my duties. There *was* a Hauriou
who wrote a history of scholasticism in two volumes that I read
before you were born—but probably he is not the man. I looked
to see if I had not the book you mention, having an impression of
familiarity (with the outside) but didn't see it. The sinister thought
has risen in my mind whether you young fellows were ironically
trying how much the old man could stand in the way of flattering
things, but of course I rejected it. In former days my friends
amused themselves with getting a rise out of me (on things in
general) but it was too easy. As to favorable comments I can
stand a good lot—it is a privilege of age—and a fact of human
nature—but I hardly need say that I believe in and reciprocate
the affection that I get from men like you and Frankfurter too
sincerely to have any real doubt. My remark is just like writing
D. V. to show that you recognize the possible irony of fate. I'm
sorry you wobble on Hughes. I won't say what I think of the
others[1]—but I do think he has qualities of character that would
make him far superior to the present incumbent.

Your remarks about Santayana reinforce the impression I had.
I am off to Court to witness the operation of some patents at 10:30.

My love to you and my homage to Madame.

*Yours ever, O. W. Holmes*

Penitential Postscript

On second thought, I am very sure that the man I read was
*Hauréau*[2] not *ou*. I am ashamed of such mistakes.        *O. W. H.*
November 2, 1916

*Cambridge, Mass., November 7, 1916*

*My dear Justice:* The letter and the penitential postscript make
me feel that when you come to the leisure of next vacation I shall
be firmly fixed in your affections; for assuredly you will think

---

[5] T. H. Green (1836-1882), *The Principles of Political Obligation,* was
published posthumously in Volume II of his *Works* (Nettleship, ed., 1889).
Green's metaphysics were founded in German idealism and his politics in
English utilitarianism. He was a strong advocate of state regulation based on
moral objectives and will, not on force.

[1] The Socialist candidate for President in the 1916 election was Allan L.
Benson (1871-1940).

[2] Barthélemy Hauréau (1812-1896), author of *Examen critique de la
philosophie scolastique* (1850).

highly of Hauriou. I have permitted myself the purchase of his
works—one that I have just finished on centralisation is superb;[1]
and it fits in very happily with the to me admirable doctrine laid
down in *Noble State Bank* v. *Haskell*[2] which perhaps you know.
I am tempted greatly to set down some thoughts about your finely
empirical conception of federalism. I have to write a little paper
on the other side of Christmas for a Canadian law review and
that would be a useful centre of discussion.[3] The opinion thrills
me the more often I re-read it—particularly the remarks which
come, if memory serves me aright, on p. 110 of the volume.

I do and re-do corporate history. I get more convinced that if
I can do any useful work one day the field of state-theory must be
my confine. The legal aspect of it throws me again and again into
a perspiration of mental excitement. I grow to love the law; and
I can even get excited about certain things in procedure—which
is saying much. The Law School justifies all my theories of corporate personality; for it has a soul about it which not even the
interposed irritations of those on the Faculty I do not like can
destroy. And I have big ties there. Kales[4] and Arthur Hill[5] are
splendid people, eager and generous-hearted. Felix of course is
a world in himself and he lights up the dark places that come to
me too often—come because most of me is in Europe aching to be
fighting there and feeling a poor, stupid nonentity because I can
only watch and hope when the youth of my generation are giving
up their lives with so supreme an idealism.

To talk of Felix reminds me to put some thoughts to you. I
think he badly needs some kind of settling influence. He is always
nervously restless, dashing here and there in a kind of creative fertility that drives me to despair. I don't find him able to sit down

---

[1] Presumably *Étude sur la décentralisation* (1892).

[2] 219 U.S. 104 (1911). For a unanimous Court Holmes had written the
opinion sustaining the constitutionality of an Oklahoma statute by which all
banks in the state were required to make payments into a Depositors'
Guaranty Fund. At p. 110, Holmes had written as follows: "Many laws
which it would be vain to ask the court to overthrow could be shown, easily
enough, to transgress a scholastic interpretation of one or another of the great
guarantees in the Bill of Rights. They more or less limit the liberty of the
individual or they diminish property to a certain extent. We have few
scientifically certain criteria of legislation, and as it often is difficult to mark
the line where what is called the police power of the states is limited by the
Constitution of the United States, judges should be slow to read into the
latter a *nolumus mutare* as against the law-making power."

[3] No such paper was published in Canada. See, however, Laski's "The
Problem of Administrative Areas" (IV *Smith College Studies in History*);
reprinted in *Foundations of Sovereignty* (1918), 30.

[4] Albert Kales (1875-1922), distinguished teacher and writer in the field
of real property, was Professor of Law at Harvard, 1916-17.

[5] Arthur D. Hill (1869-1947), Boston lawyer and intimate friend of
Holmes and Laski, was on the faculty of the Harvard Law School from
1915 to 1919.

solidly to a single thing. He wastes the time that ought to be given to the permanent work that is in him in writing fine letters to antiquated New York lawyers with doubts about the Constitution. I wish he were a little more concentrated—and I get afraid for his health. To New York three times in one week is a drain I wonder whether even he can stand. I wonder what you think of this?

From Hazlitt I have passed—for bed-reading—to Coleridge; and his *Friend* and the *Aids to Reflection* strike me as simply first-class political thinking. I wonder how that attitude in him has escaped the critics; but I suppose that they are so pre-occupied with style as to miss—Leslie Stephen apart—the significance of the matter. That fellow just breathed mind of the very highest quality. He seems to have read everything and to have gone with a poet's sureness of touch to the great things in what he read. I get simply wild with the talk of men like M. Arnold about him. He wasn't a man to be dealt with in the pretty-pretty style of Mary Ward.[6]

Our love to you both—and a hope that you will not over-work.

*Yours always, Harold J. Laski*

*Washington, D.C., November 19, 1916* [1]

*Dear Laski:* What an admirable number of the *New Republic* and how A 1 among A wonders is your notice of Treitschke.[2] It warms my gizzard, my son, and I am proud of you. . . .

I am afraid I don't quite sympathize [with] F. Hackett's, I suspect, rather prepossessed glorification of Lindsay, and of Sandburg some numbers back.[3] Knowing those poets only from him I prefer his writing to his quotations in the critiques. I trust that Frankfurter received my telegram at your house—I sent it according to order. I grieve at Valentine's death as a public loss.[4] I saw him but two or three times. What I did see impressed me much.

Don't work too hard.                    *Yours ever, O. W. Holmes*

---

[6] Mrs. Humphry Ward (1851-1920); British novelist, best known for her *Robert Elsmere* (1888).

[1] A brief note from Laski, dated November 8, 1916, is omitted.

[2] Heinrich von Treitschke, *Politics* (2 vols., 1916), was reviewed by Laski, 9 *New Republic* (Nov. 18, 1916, part II) 20.

[3] Francis Hackett had reviewed Carl Sandburg's *Chicago Poems* (1916) in 8 *New Republic* 328 (Oct. 28, 1916) and Vachel Lindsay's *A Handy Guide to Beggars* (1916) in 9 *ibid.* (Nov. 18, 1916, part II) 6.

[4] Robert Grosvenor Valentine (1872-Nov. 14, 1916), Indian Commissioner under Taft and Roosevelt, industrial and labor relations counselor, had been an intimate friend of Felix Frankfurter. See 9 *New Republic* 84 (Nov. 25, 1916).

I reopen this to say ditto to above about your Disraeli[5] which I
had not come to when I began this. Also on rereading I relent and
hesitate about Hackett's poet for this week. . . .


                              *Cambridge, Mass., November 20, 1916*
*My dear Justice:* Forgive my silence; but poor Valentine's death
upset me greatly. We had known each other only a little time, but
we had become the closest of friends. I felt that he was one of
the most creatively-minded people I have known and that he was
just gaining that maturity of vision which puts a man among the
big forces of our time. Then I loved him for the romance he em-
bodied, his high courage and his singleness of purpose. It is hard
to lose a friend like that. You know how dear he was to Felix;
and I think you will like to know that your telegram to Felix
helped him enormously on a bitter day. It was a characteristic act
of kindness on your part.

I am so drowned in work that I have been seeking relaxation in
what is the one book I can never tire of—Boswell. Really it is a
glorious cross-section of humanity, the little man's jealousy of Gold-
smith, his sneaking belief that there may be good in Scotland
despite the doctor, and Johnson's big, loveable curiosity about life,
even his healthy dogmatism. What a wonderful judgment of Burke,
"his stream of mind is perpetual." I hope you are an admirer at
this shrine.

I don't know how much time you get for the *New Republic*
these days; but you must read Francis Hackett in the supplement
this week—really a masterpiece.[1] Really I don't think there can
be any doubt that Francis really has more intuitive rightness about
his judgments than any critic writing in English. It's the same
brisk knack for psychology I suppose that you emphasise in W.
James. I wish he would let his mind play more freely, and on a
larger scale. And I wish Walter Lippmann would forget Freud for
a little—just a little.[2]

I have taken a big step lately about which I'd like your after-
approval. My old tutor offered me a professorship at Sheffield with
£600 and four assistants to lecture on political science. I thought
it over and after a struggle, refused it. I thought (a) that at twenty-
three my future was too uncertain to make it right for me to
saddle myself on a great new venture (b) that I ought—though
I am very uncertain about this—to finish the Law School (c) that

5 Laski reviewed Volume IV of G. E. Buckle's *Life of Disraeli* (1916) in 9
*New Republic* (Nov. 18, 1916, part II) 30.
    1 See p. 27, *supra*, note 3.
    2 Under the title "Trotter and Freud," Walter Lippmann had reviewed
W. Trotter's *Instincts of the Herd in Peace and War* (1916), 9 *New Repub-
lic* (Nov. 18, 1916, part II) 16.

while you & Felix & Francis [Hackett] give me such inspiration I
must not deprive myself of it and (d) that I ought not to use
Harvard as a jumping-off ground. I hope this is right because
while England is very attractive it doesn't look so near to my duty
as Harvard. Please tell me what you think.

Is Mrs. Holmes willing to borrow the sequel to Buchan's *Thirty-
Nine Steps*?[3] It is equally thrilling and splendid.

Our love to you both—                           *Yours always, Harold*

*Washington, D.C., November 25, 1916*
*Dear Laski:* Only now has it been possible for me to answer what
I should have liked to answer at once. I have been in the mad-
ness of writing decisions with a touch of dentist and extraneous
immediacies thrown in. As to your decision it seems to my necessarily imperfect judgment a wise one for reasons that I won't go
into at length—though there is no length to them, they being
mainly that I should suppose you had a better outlook here. I
don't quite see any duty to Harvard College unless you have some
express or implied engagement that I know not of. I feel a sort of
caution too against your letting yourself be too much influenced
by the first enthusiasm of new friendships. This is a really detached suggestion—for you like Felix have walked deep into my
heart—but whatever my hopes, you must remember that my life
is an uncertain speculation and I wish I felt more confident that
the other two would not wear themselves out before their time.
Selfishly I rejoice of course.

I am interested by what you say about what my sister used to
call Boreswell's *Life of Johnson*. It is not a standby with me but I
remember I used to say when I read Macaulay's belittling praise
that there was a Velasquez, explaining to you from time [to time]
as he put in a touch how he was painting a portrait—like the great
master that he was—and then a man comes along and patronizes
him as if Velasquez didn't know what he was about.

Hackett's worship of Lincoln is to me moving.[1] Some of his
other admirations seem to me more personal or more the result of
circumstance—though the same personality and experience tells in
his love for L. In these last two notices of poets that we have
spoken of, in which he so outshines them both—I can't help suspecting that it is mainly negations that he admires, they are not
aristocrats, they are not &c, &c, and he does the rest—but all I
know is the extracts he gives.

I had a call from Lippmann and a friend on Thursday and I

[3] *The Power-house* (1916).
[1] This had colored passages in his review of Vachel Lindsay's *Handy
Guide to Beggars, supra*, p. 27.

talked too much. The next time I will draw on him like a mustard plaster to make him do the bigger share. I feel so foolish afterwards.

Nov. 26 You speak of a sequel to *39 Steps,* or as you more elegantly and deliberately write *The Thirty-Nine Steps.* You don't mean *The Power House*—do you? I think I have the title right. That we had at Beverly Farms. If there is another I must get it. Don't overwork. I always am afraid you will push the machine too hard.                                   *Aff'ly yours, O. W. Holmes*

*Washington, D.C., December 13, 1916*

*Dear Laski:* You speak of reviving your intelligence by some happy days of reading.[1] I can't get them now and as I told Miss Noyes (the heroine of our Monday afternoons)[2] the only thing I could do would be to take a guitar and sing to her some little gem of a decision. For the like cause I can't write. I know *Martin Chuzzlewit* and have some favorite quotations from it as well as infinite delight in Bailey Junior *et als.* I think your bringing up in England must account for certain respectable and unhurried tastes that you have—like Hazlitt and Macaulay. I reasonably share them.

Your reflections on the crowd and popular government etc. are very near to things I have been thinking. There are some advantages, *non obstant* all the drawbacks so keenly realized today, in having gentlemen at the top. You can't get the last curl to the moustache any other way, so far as heard from. And oh how I should like to see our people more intent on doing their job than on pointing out grievances—and oh how little I care for the upward and onward trend. I must say "trend" that the *banalité* of the word correspond to the fact, of our legislation to make other people better, with teetotalism and white slave laws that make felons of young men (unless our court decides they don't) for crossing a state line with a girl,[3] and that manifest the sacredness of Woman. I think I must be an old Fogey and proud of the title. Goodnight—my love to you. It is more blessed in you to write than to receive.                                   *Yours, O. W. H.*

---

[1] Laski's letter to which this refers has been omitted from this edition.

[2] Frances Noyes (1890-1943) was the daughter of Frank B. Noyes, President of the Washington *Evening Star* and of the Associated Press. Later she married Edward H. Hart (see, *infra,* p. 249) and continued the literary career which had begun before her marriage.

[3] *Caminetti* v. *United States,* 242 U.S. 470 (1917), was at this time pending before the Supreme Court. Holmes concurred in the opinion of a majority of the Court (McKenna, J., White, C.J., and Clarke, J., dissenting), holding that the Mann Act was applicable to the interstate transportation of a woman for immoral purposes, though pecuniary gain was not a motive.

*Cambridge, Mass., December 21, 1916*

*My dear Justice:* . . . mutter on my behalf a hearty damn about Mr. Wilson. This note of his, I suppose, will do no harm in the end;[1] but its tacit assumption of equality in aim between the Allies and Germany, its insulting advice, and above all its smug complacency, do make one wonder where the materials of spiritual kinship between England and America are to be found. There were virtues in Mr. Hughes. I do not like the purchase of immortality on these terms.

I have been reading much Roman history since I rediscovered Mommsen and one book especially has fascinated me—Dill, *Roman Society in the Last Century of the Empire*; 'tis scholarly and human and vastly illuminating. I don't know if you ever read Ferrero's works[2] but it has often struck me that there is much to be said about his parallel between the last two centuries of the Empire and the condition of modern America. It would be a real help to me if I could discover in this country some widespread and continuous passion for intellectual effort. I suppose you don't have the opportunity to encounter the lighthearted ignorance which appalls me. But I get very certain that Socrates' definition of virtue was right and that we are losing ground because we give our intelligence soporifics and trust blindly to what we call the instinctive rightness of democracy. There is a certain detachment about great moral issues among people who should know better, a toleration of ignorance, which amazes me. And I am often bewildered at things like Pound's conviction that the typical French institution is the *Folies Bergères*—that learning is confined to Germany, that England's day is past and so forth. Even a great scholar like Haskins[3] thinks Pastor a greater historian than Creighton because he has read more manuscripts.[4] One feels that this efficiency business has really played itself out. I would like to

---

[1] Following Germany's proposal of December 12 that peace negotiations should be opened, President Wilson, on December 18, issued a note to the belligerents outlining proposals which seemed to him equitable. In the note he stated that "the objects, which the statesmen of the belligerents on both sides have in mind in this war, are virtually the same, as stated in general terms to their own people and to the world." *President Wilson's State Papers and Addresses* (Shaw, ed., 1917) 343, 345-346.

[2] Guglielmo Ferrero (1871-1942), author of *The Greatness and Decline of Rome* (5 vols. 1907-09).

[3] Charles H. Haskins (1870-1937), author of *The Normans in European History* (1915) and *Norman Institutions* (1918), was Professor of History at Harvard, one of the departments in which Laski was Instructor and Tutor.

[4] Ludwig von Pastor (1854-1928) was historian of the papacy and author of the sixteen-volume *Geschichte der Päpste seit dem Ausgang der Mittalters* (1899-1933). Mandel Creighton (1843-1901), ecclesiastical historian and Bishop of London, was author, *inter alia*, of *The Age of Elizabeth* (1899); *The Life of Cardinal Wolsey* (1903); *History of the Papacy during the Reformation* (5 vols., 1882-94).

condemn this generation to read certain chapters in Mill's *Liberty*, and to know Zimmern's *Greek Commonwealth* and what Homer meant by *aidos*. But I am too entirely medieval to be of use in a practical world. I was probably made to be a rural dean or a private secretary to another sceptic—anything but an instructor of history in the best organised & equipped of American universities.

My love.                                    *Affectionately, Harold*


*Washington, D.C., December 26, 1916*
*Dear Laski:* Your letter makes my heart ache a little. I well know (by memory) a solitude worse than any that you are experiencing, I am pretty sure. Also without knowledge except a divination or a guess I am gloomy in every way about the state of the country. I haven't even read Mr. Wilson's note—I have read very few words of his—but I am very confident that, to put it with moderate caution, I can not admire either his intellect or the moral nature of one who writes as he does. And when the general of an army is flabby the army is. I should like to have you expound to me and to let out my own scepticisms and bitternesses of heart so far as articulate—but I should like it still better if I could do or say something to keep up your heart.

I have been working madly, and at 4 p.m. today I sent my last ms. to the printer and really think I shall have time to read a few pages. If I do I shall first polish off Hannis Taylor's *Cicero*. I cannot believe that he is capable of unplagiarized merit but the book to my moderate knowledge is interesting and instructive. Also I must look through Beveridge's *Marshall*—which he sent me and I believe really well done—so I dunno if I shall get a whack at any of those things that sting us both. Some of your respectable English historians whom you venerate are not in that category. As I probably have told you—I hope so, that I may know you wouldn't abjure me for it—I don't care much for literary history. A history of Economics—Law or Philosophy, *bon*—but the works of literary gents in the general field are too unquantified in premise and conclusion to suit me. My notion of literary history is "Gallants staked whole estates upon a single cast of the die"—that is my unverified recollection of a line of Green's *Short History*—temp. Eliz.[1] I suppose he had read of one case and it became a generalization. (Mrs. Green, who I hear is not generally popular, is a great friend of mine—I noted something of the same in her book on Ireland).[2] You have me up a stump on Haskins and Pastor

[1] Everyman's Edition, vol. I, p. 375.
[2] Alice Stopford (Mrs. J. R.) Green (1848-1929) was author of *Irish Nationality* (1911), *The Making of Ireland and its Undoing* (1908), and *Town Life in the Fifteenth Century* (1894).

—should I blush? You remind me that there is a street between us
and the station at Beverly Farms, (parallel to the RR), that I
call the street of the unknown illustrious. Also of a notice that my
wife preserves of the death of Miss ———, say in Brockton, the
distinguished flower painter, "She was a pupil of Titcomb." The
greatest funeral procession I ever saw in Boston was of a man
whose name I never had heard, eminent I believe in fire circles.
However it may be with truth, certainly fame is relative. Let us
smile when we can't help ourselves—and try to hold as much of
life in solution as we can.                    *As ever yours, O. W. H.*

*Cambridge, Mass., December 28, 1916*
*My dear Justice:* Our correspondence is to me a kind of moral
katharsis. Your letter of this morning moved me greatly, and I
wish I were on hand to tell you many of the things it made me
want to say. I wish, too, that you could have spent Christmas with
us. We had Francis Hackett and S. J. Rosensohn[1]—whom you must
know for one of the finest fellows God ever made—and in two
ecstatic days we talked the world over. Francis was in glorious
form, lively, tender and incisive. I was glad to see the coincidence
of our attitudes to you, and he was really thrilled by some sentences about himself that I read him from one of your letters.

Your remarks on Mrs. Green are interesting. I have never met
her except formally, but that was enough to make me anxious to
know her really well. I have always had a real suspicion that had
she started early enough she would have been as big as Mary
Bateson.[2] Her *Town Life* is a really creative book; that on Ireland
I judged a little intemperate and—to coin a much-needed word
—pamphletic (*i.e.* splenetic on paper) but I imagine justifiably
so. Someday a great man will write Ireland's history in the grand
style and take account of its structural changes. P. W. Joyce has
done something of this in his *Social History of Ancient Ireland*;
but he writes badly and 'tis caviar to the general. . . .

I can't even write about Mr. Wilson, except to tell you an
amusingly curious story Francis Hackett brought that Walter Lippmann was at the bottom of this peace note. Really I am sick and
tired of benevolent amateurs and peace leagues and birth-control
and all the other means by which the reformers are going to make

[1] Samuel J. Rosensohn (1880-1939), Law School roommate of Felix
Frankfurter, was intimately associated with him in handling labor problems
in the War Department. After World War I he had a distinguished career
at the New York bar.
[2] Mary Bateson (1865-1906), historian and Fellow of Newnham College,
was author of *Medieval England* (1904), and editor of *Borough Customs*
(vols. XVIII and XXI of Selden Society Publications) and *Cambridge Guild
Records* (1903).

the tough discipline of life sufficiently tender for a generation
which likes even to read its classics in translations. A woman recently asked me to talk here to a society on English foreign
policy in the last thirty years 'provided you accept the ideas of
the woman's peace party.' The number of substitutes for fine and
clean thinking the world provides positively gnaws at one's
vitals. . . .

Our love and a thousand greetings to you both.          *Harold*

*Washington, D.C., December 31, 1916*

*Dear Laski:* You are a dear and your letters give me great pleasure
—but even an acknowledgment has to be written at a gallop as
there always is some demand upon my time hopping in—just now
it was 17 pages of opinion that I don't agree to. I grin with raging
envy when you speak of a week's reading. Apropos of the books
you mention, the life of Marshall is easy and interesting. H. Taylor
I think of as you do, the interest such as it is is in Cicero, of
whom I know less than I should. It did those chaps a lot of good
to live expecting some day to die by the sword. . . . But indeed
I never have heard of most of the people you mention, *e.g.* Ker's
*Dark Ages*—(mem. for future inquiry). I have a secretary[1] who
has socialistic velleities, though with a very rational nature, and
I see in him the tendency common to the time to believe in regulating everything—against which I am as prejudiced as you are
—not *a priori* but because I don't have sufficient respect for the
ability and honesty of my neighbors to desire to be regulated by
them, and because, though I don't believe in H. Spencer, I do
believe in *The Fable of the Bees.* I must go out to luncheon, and
send you my love. I wish I could write peaceably and at length.
I told my sec'y that there was no injustice in death or in being
born a toad rather than an eagle. I added that I desired to stand
as the upholder of the respectable and commonplace.

There is no short cut to fame or comfort and all there is is to
bore into it as hard as you can. But many of our friends seem to
believe that they can legislate bliss. I have been so busy that I
haven't opened even last week's *New Republic*—

*Aff'ly yours, O. W. Holmes*

*Cambridge, Mass., January 2, 1916* [sic]

*My dear Justice:* . . . Your letter came with its usual stimulus to
a million things I must try not to say. W. P. Ker is an Oxford man
who is a great philologist in Icelandic matters. His *Dark Ages* is

---

[1] Shelton Hale (1884-1920) was Holmes's law clerk at the time. He had
graduated from the Harvard Law School in the previous June.

a big book because he is one of about half a dozen men who can use literature as the basis of acute social analysis. Dill and Wilamowitz[1] do the same thing well; and I who am always troubled by the years between 476-919 find him a wise and sane guide.

I like what you say about the sword of Damocles hanging over those Roman fellows. Certainly it stimulated men like Seneca to take relief in philosophy, and if we could modernize stoicism we would do great good to our time. The trouble is that death is only a good penalty for great men. It matters not a whit to the meagre souls. I am glad you have no admiration for Hannis Taylor. . . .

You mean that Shelton Haile [sic] is a pupil of Felix. I suppose American worship of regulation has two main roots (1) the natural reaction from the late period of *laissez-faire* (2) an admiring imitation of the success of centralisation in Germany. I feel that the whole thing is going much too far though certain large principles—like the regulation of hours of labor—I agree with heartily. But I get much comfort from the thought that history is full of these excessive swings of the pendulum and that each swing deposits a little progress with it. The main fear I have is that our age (largely through Mr. Brandeis) is romanticising the simple beauty of the masses in a way that reminds me rather painfully of the days when Jeremy Bentham and John Mill thought they could bring about the millenium [sic] with a mechanic's Institute. The plea that short hours are justified by the place of leisure in a fine citizenship doesn't impress me; for I feel that leisure for ninety percent of people is consciously unproductive and that they neither have nor want to have the tug at the heart which impels a few in each generation to examination of and speculation about human experience. And when they say that the universalisation of the Gary system or Montessori up to the age of ninety will change the face of the world I can only throw up my hands. It's like the optimistic ethnology of Exeter Hall. . . .

The heartiest greetings to you both for 1917—and our love.

*Affectionately, Harold*

In my paper in this last *New Republic* 'patriotic' should be patristic.[2]

*Washington, D.C., January 8, 1917*

*Dear Laski:* There are a few minutes left before I must go to Court and begin my routine again. Unlike your interruption mine

---

[1] Sir Samuel Dill (1844-1924), classical scholar and historian; author of *Roman Society in the Last Century of the Western Empire* (1898) and *Roman Society from Nero to Marcus Aurelius* (1904).

Ulrich von Wilamowitz-Möllendorf (1848-1931); classical scholar and Greek philologist; commentator on Euripides, Homer, and Aristotle.

[2] See, *infra*, p. 39, note 2.

brought me no leisure and a chance to read. I read the *Cicero,* not because I differ a whit from you as to the author, but because it offered me some information I wanted. My final reflection was that our civilization is really far more Ciceronian than Christian. We don't believe sell all thou hast and give to the poor, or Love thy brother as thyself. Cicero is more like a Unitarian parson in his creed and I suppose monogamy as a doctrine comes from Rome. I have managed to tuck in a book about Prehistoric Art by Parkyn —a good intelligent manual—copiously illustrated—but mainly by sketches, which make you fear that possibly the draughtsman may have given the final touch of *chic.* I have been so interrupted every time that I hoped for a moment of peace that I haven't read the last 2 or 3 *New Republics,* but I have them and shall look for your initials.

On the economic side I am mighty sceptical of hours of labor and minimum wages regulation, but it may be that a somewhat monotonous standardized mode of life is coming. Of course it only means shifting the burden to a different point of incidence, if I be right, as I think I be, that every community rests on the death of men. If the people who can't get the minimum are to be supported you take out of one pocket to put into the other. I think the courageous thing to say to the crowd, though perhaps the Brandeis school don't believe it, is, you now have all there is—and you'd better face it instead of trying to lift yourselves by the slack of your own breeches. But all our present teaching is hate and envy for those who have any luxury, as social wrongdoers.

I eagerly await your article in the *Yale L. J.*—agree with you as to the futility of the optimistic ochlosebosis—to coin a word— also, so far as I can judge, concerning F. Hackett and I gather from your story that you are slow in sending the article that I expect.                                                       *Aff'ly, O. W. H.*

*Cambridge, Mass., January 10, 1916* [sic]
*My dear Justice:* Your last letter raises so many questions that I hardly know where to begin; but even if these comments are spasmodic I imagine they will be something of a relief after the Adamson argument.[1] The report in the papers suggests that the Court mainly spent its time in discussing John Stuart Mill's *Principles of Economics.*

When you speak of prehistoric archaeology you floor me completely. I admire but I do not emulate. What you suggest *in re*

---

[1] On January 8, 9, and 10 argument in *Wilson* v. *New,* 243 U.S. 332 (1917) had been heard. The issues concerned the interpretation and constitutionality of the Adamson Law of September 1916, establishing an eight-hour day on the railroads.

Cicero intrigues me much. Boissier's masterpiece I suppose you know[2]—it has always been one of my favorites. He and Cumont (the Mithras fellow)[3] are the people to whom most of the admiration I have for classical scholars goes. I want in my 150th work to assess the debt of Christianity to Rome. There's a lot of political theory in the Apostolic age which is straight theft ("indebtedness" the theologians call it) from Stoicism. Which reminds me to tell you that I am giving a course on the French Church under the Revolution and Empire to finish off a man's lectures which might be called "nine lectures in disillusionment." They expected theology and they get political theory. They find the Church treated as a substantial political institution without any divinity and it does them ever so much good. It will be glorious to have the later comments of the Faculty of Divinity. A great pope was lost in me. I have the dogmatic instinct.

I know the feeling that underlies your economic comments. I have certain scepticisms. I doubt if our productivity is at anything like its maximum simply because so much energy is diverted into wholly useless channels. If we stopped making chalices and copes and crosses boots would be cheaper, *i.e.* your 'stream of products' has many cross-currents in it capable of wise diversion. Then I had rather stand with the liberals in this venture than with Root or Gary or N. M. Butler who head the conservative brigade. I agree that the bitterness of today is really formidable—what I wonder is if it is not also cleansing. It puts the issue squarely instead of wrapping it up in charity and social welfare and the thousand other palliatives which enable ignorant men to hawk their cheap nostrums about the country. The haunting fear I have about democracy has a different emphasis. I'm clear that it has the right to a certain minimum basis of civilised life. But I feel uneasy about the utilitarian direction thought seems to be taking. The word "practical" is a net to conceal hell. Because I want to do fine thinking, or like to collect books, or hate crowds, or feel that I am unusually uninterested in business men, I get told that I am unrelated to the modern world. The things I want to reach don't show a quick enough return to be considered really profitable. And a university in this country seems to me less a thinking-shop which it ought only to be than a place for the manufacture of degrees which are really tickets to enable you to learn on what subject the holder has been given enough facts to enable him to pass an examination. The tragedy is that democracy seems perfectly content that this should be the case. It doesn't ask the questions it should or undergo any continuous self-criticism. In fact I

---

[2] Gaston Boissier, *Cicéron et ses amis* (1865).

[3] Franz Cumont, *Les mystères de Mithra* (3rd ed., 1913).

get to feel that 'democracy' has become a phrase like 'socialism' to be used lightly where real argument is wanting. That is one of my main intellectual difficulties with Mr. Wilson. The 'new freedom' is simply old dogmas wrapped up in new and greasy paper to keep the rain out. It is a distressing spectacle. I miss in American life the tonic quality of Oxford where men sit down to examine great things greatly. It is so worth while to say frankly to the crowd that some people can't do other people's work; that merely by education John Smith won't become Adam Smith. But I doubt whether the argument looks convincing to most people.

Still, I have read some great books lately. Hauriou's *La souveraineté nationale* is by far the best discussion of that I have ever read—it goes with a sweep and a vigor that are simply exhilarating. Faguet's *L'anticléricalisme* has all the best qualities of his work in it, and an analysis of the French temper which takes my breath away. And, above all, Brunetière on Bossuet which is superb— the kind of criticism which hews out an effigy in the solid marble of mind. That is a book to give you joy.

Let me end on a note of scepticism. Why is your obviously right decision in the Webb-Kenyon case (please send me a signed copy) left so lonely? [4] And why, oh why in that Adamson argument must Mr. Justice Pitney ask questions which even to a callow youth like myself betray a dubious familiarity with economics? I wish I had seen something of what you asked and my test of a God's existence will be whether in his infinite mercy he gives you the opportunity to explain to the railroads and the Bench what the Commerce clause really means. Of course Frankfurter should have argued that case for the government.

You will have noted my promptitude in sending you that Yale paper. My father is a thinking fellow.

My love to you both. I hope you will rest after these last strenuous days.                                     *Affectionately, Harold*


*Washington, D.C., January 13, 1917*
*Dear Laski:* I must write a line to you but hasty as usual, if only to disclaim the honor that you seem to do me of having been the writer of the Webb Kenyon decision. On the contrary I dissented in that case, being of opinion that the statute should not be con-

---

[4] *Clark Distilling Company* v. *Western Maryland Railway Co.*, 242 U.S. 311 (Jan. 8, 1917). A majority of the Court, giving effect to the Webb-Kenyon Act, by which Congress divested liquor moving into dry states of its "interstate character," permitted West Virginia, which forbade the manufacture and sale of liquor, to enjoin the importation of liquor for the personal use of the consignee. Holmes, with Van Devanter, J., concurring, dissented without opinion.

strued to simply substitute the state for Congress in control of
interstate commerce in intoxicants—*i.e.* to permit a state to say
although the purpose of the shipment (personal consumption) is
one that we permit, we forbid the shipment in interstate commerce—the unlawfulness by state law thus consisting solely in the
element of interstate commerce. And the Act of Congress was
further construed to adopt any such regulation in advance—at
least an extreme exercise of power. I thought the act did not mean
more than to say that if on other grounds the shipment would be
illegal but for the want of power on the part of the state over
interstate commerce, the fact of I.C. should not interfere. I did
not intend to dissent but so disliked the C.J.'s opinion that I got
stirred up—though I endeavored to assure myself that I was not
dissenting solely on that ground.[1]

I can't recite very well on this case as other things have driven
it from my head but I believe I give you the short point—*entre
nous* & Felix of course.

I read your article on Kidd [2] and liked it, as usual. That on
Vicarious Liability not yet. I should expect to find that we agree
that the justification is to be found rather in those cases where
the public pays the bill than in all, and that there should be a
limit to be found in the values to the public of the life, limb, or
what not damaged. As to the Adamson Law I humbly think that
an hour to a side was all that was needed—but we had some old-
fashioned roaring. You make me sad by your contrast between
Oxford and Harvard College. I think that possibly you exaggerate
it, and the war may have intensified the seriousness there, but at
bottom it is the echo of the fact that England is a more educated
and more civilized country than any part of the U.S. and that you
could have found 100 men there to 10 or 1 here who knew the
preliminaries for civilized talk. It takes time to make an educated
people or a turf. Now my blessings upon you—and I turn to my
agenda.                                                        *Aff'ly, O. W. H.*

---

[1] Writing to Felix Frankfurter on January 13, 1917, Holmes made this
further comment on his position in the *Clark Distilling* case: "I didn't write
anything, and have regretted that I didn't either say a few words or shut
up. I thought the law should be construed more narrowly to avoid awkward
doubts and as it seemed to me to express its probable meaning. But I had
intended not to dissent, and at the last minute was stirred to do so by
dissatisfaction with the opinion—thinking as I did the result also wrong."

[2] "A Sociological Romance," 9 *New Republic* 235 (Dec. 30, 1916). The
article critically reviewed the sociology of Benjamin Kidd (1858-1916),
author of *Social Evolution* (1904) and champion of religion in its struggle
with reason.

*Cambridge, Mass., January 15, 1916* [sic]
*My dear Justice:* I have nothing but dislike for the Supreme Court.
I had great hopes of hearing Felix argue and twinkling privately
to you from the background; and instead I must stay here and
teach youths and maidens and embryo clerics.[1] Is that fair? But you
will please tell me how he behaved and if we may be proud of
him.

It was your dissent from the Webb-Kenyon decision I applauded.
What the C.J. said seemed to me a masterpiece of casuistry but
not to touch the fundamental issues involved. He did not touch
upon what seemed to me a questionable feature of such legislation.
The fact that the uniformity he predicates on p. 10 of the opinion
is not real and that prohibition generally touches upon such vast
issues as to make hesitation the only right policy. Do you know
Archdall Reid's forcible little book on alcoholism? It is very impressive. I note your sentence on the Adamson argument with joy.

I don't want to overestimate the value of the atmosphere in
Oxford. I am sure that here there is a real eagerness for scholarship
and an enthusiasm for the play of the mind. But, if you know
what I mean, it isn't *en plein air;* it has to be organised and nursed
carefully; it has to be estimated in books and papers; and it doesn't
interact with the college life. But I agree that age counts with
colleges, just as with wine and I see in some men signs of the
change I care passionately about. Felix and Pound give it to the
Law School. Lake[2] and Haskins and McIlwain[3] to the college. But
the younger men seem to want breadth of mind. They limit themselves to 'fields' and 'departments.' It is a big advance that next
year they divide up my mentality among several parts of the
University.[4] But I want them to learn that one may read Maitland
and still be keen on Balzac. And that is true of every college I
have seen on this side. To be able to talk reasonably on the commonplaces of culture ought not to mean a reputation for pro-
digious width of view. I fear this sudden passion for the scientific
training in England may take a similar direction. People will be
authorities on elliptic integrals or internal combustion engines or
aniline dyes and they'll banish Dickens in order to read a German
monograph. Life isn't the algebraic formula they want to make out.

I have had a debauch of books this week in the intervals of
making an index to my book. One *The Stewardship of Faith* by

---

[1] On January 18 and 19 Felix Frankfurter participated in the argument
of the Oregon ten-hour day cases; *Bunting* v. *Oregon,* 243 U.S. 426; *Stettler*
v. *O'Hara, Simpson* v. *O'Hara, id.* 629 (1917).

[2] Kirsopp Lake (1872-1946), English-born theologian and historian, was
Professor of Early Christian Literature in the Harvard Divinity School.

[3] Charles Howard McIlwain was Professor of History and Government.

[4] Laski in the academic year 1917-18 was Instructor in History and Tutor
in the Division of History, Government, and Economics.

K. Lake is a brilliant examination of Christian origins and a polite
bowing out of the Church at the front door. Then to Duchesne
on the early history of the Church—poor on doctrine but very fine
on organisation. Church history is a great field so long as you have
Christianity on the other side of you. I think it is gloriously dead
intellectually and I think the French Revolution killed it. But the
real job is its analysis as the belief of a society which ran the
normal course of other associations and died because like them it
couldn't learn the new tunes. From this I went to Wicksteed's
*Dante and Aquinas*—a beautiful book full of much curious learning that you would, I think, enjoy. Now I am in the midst of a
tract of Hauriou's on Duguit[5] which is very satisfactory. He is
really a great man with his own ideas and therefore unperceived
by Pound who thinks that all roads lead, legally at any rate, to
Berlin. But Pound has a paper in the January *Law Review* about
which it is permissible to feel unadulterated enthusiasm.[6] And I am
not sorry to see a tilt at Sir Henry Maine. I never made anything
out of Maine's theories when I got back to their texts. I always
liked his fling at Popular Government though, and thought Morley
a little unfair.[7] I am more and more convinced that we have got
to restate all our ideas on representative government and work out
a theory as to state-action of a very different kind. But it would
go beyond a letter to enlarge on this. One day in the next month
I hope to run down to Washington and talk to you about it.

This is only an interim letter. I shall have more to say later in
the week.                                          *Affectionately, Harold*


*Cambridge, Mass., January 21, 1917*
My dear Justice: If you and Mrs. Holmes can have me from next
Friday (Jan. 26) until the Monday morning, I am your man. I
should get there in the evening and leave reasonably early in the
morning. If the court sits on Saturday, so much the better, as I
shall then come and listen.

Arthur Hill brought back the report that you were giving Felix
a run for his money. I shall be glad to have relief from the suspense. He wrote cheerfully about the judicial machine-guns, and
that you were both in great form.

I have had a revolutionary week. I have given up the Law School

---

[5] Maurice Hauriou, *Principes de droit public* (2nd ed., 1916), Appendix.
[6] "The End of Law as Developed in Juristic Thought, Part II, The Nineteenth Century," 30 *Harv. L. Rev.*, 201 (January 1917).
[7] In his *Popular Government* (1885) Sir Henry Maine had, by implication
at least, indicated considerable skepticism with respect to the virtues of
popular government. John Morley in England (*Studies in Literature*, 1891,
103) and E. L. Godkin in the United States had written critical replies
to Maine's thesis.

and planned my work in college for next year. The Law School was
giving me a great course in business jurisprudence where I wanted
a course in politico-legal theory; so it became clear that I must
stop. Next year I hope to have a happy time in college. But all
this is matter for talk rather than correspondence. . . .

I am very excited at a paper by a colleague of mine, McIlwain.
It is on Magna Charta and Common Law and I think a pretty
fundamental thing.[1] But what has excited me in it is the fact that
he really is on the line of showing that Roman imperial jurisprudence has through canon law been of decisive importance in
English constitutional history. The paper ought to be published
soon; and it will corroborate many of your scattered dicta from
other fields. But it makes one feel that those who want legal
separatism or who think that Bracton used Roman terms to give
a literary flavor to his work are completely wrong.

My love to you both,                         *Affectionately, Harold*

*Washington, D.C., January 23, 1917*
*Dear Laski:* Alas—I don't think it will be well for you to come
here on Friday. I have had and have the grippe—the real thing
—that made me miss Court yesterday and will again today. I hope
that I shall be in tolerable shape in a day or two but when I consider how important it is that you should not be ill I am afraid to
let you come into the place. Since I wrote the last word the doctor
has been here and he says ditto. I am very sorry.

*Yours, O. W. H.*

*Cambridge, Mass., January 24, 1916* [sic]
*My dear Justice:* . . . I have a fortnight's complete leisure now,
while the students prove the value of the examination system.
Next week I go to Ottawa to comfort Loring Christie[1] whom each
presidential note sends into a more abysmal gloom. I do not blame
him. I hate an anxiety to evade moral issues by a profusion of
cheap and easy sentiment. I wish that Mr. Wilson understood the
grim realities of *welt-politik*. . . .

For the moment silence—for examination papers are not an
inducement to speech, at least to intelligent speech. But I will ask
you some questions towards the end of the week.

My love and all kinds of impatience for your validation—
*Affectionately, Harold*

---

[1] "Magna Carta and the Common Law," in *Magna Carta Commemoration Essays* (Malden, ed., 1917), 122.

[1] Loring Christie (1885-1941); Canadian diplomat; graduate of Harvard Law School; legal adviser to Department of External Affairs, 1913-1923, 1935-1939; Canadian Minister to United States, 1939-1941.

*Washington, D.C., January 29, 1917*
*Dear Laski:* Better late than never. Can't you come here on Friday,
February 9? We have a small dinner party on the 10th which if it
doesn't amuse you won't take more than 2½ hours of your time.
It will be bully if you can—as we shall be adjourned. I go back
to work this morning in fair though languid shape.

*Aff'ly yours, O. W. Holmes*


*Cambridge, Mass., January 30, 1917*
*My dear Justice:* It is fine to know that you are back. Please guard
against the aftermath of that pestilential beast.

I shall come *maximo cum gaudio* on February 9th. It will round
off a world-holiday in which I see Ottawa, Montreal, New York,
Washington. And that recess will make it doubly pleasurable.
Thank you. . . .

It was curious to read of Cromer's death in the newspapers without a ripple of real interest.[1] I remember a talk with him once in
which he outlined what he really understood by the governance of
subject races. It was magnificent but it was not human. One gets
some sense of him in that best of his books on *Ancient and Modern
Imperialism*. Which somehow reminds me that there has been published a brilliant little book by a great friend of mine, R. W.
Livingstone, *A Defence of Classical Education* which I am quite
sure you would enjoy. Perhaps you read his volume of the *Greek
Genius*.

My love to you both.                         *Affectionately, Harold*


*Cambridge, Mass., February 13, 1917*
*My dear Justice and Mrs. Holmes:* You treated me like a king. I
felt happier than I have done in months and I came back with
the sense you always give me of the joy of staying firmly at one's
post. It was a breath of Elysian fields and I am refreshed. I do not
thank you; for that is the function which makes you both our inspiration. And that you cannot help, so that we who receive take
it as the great compensation. But if there *was* (which I deny) any
place in my heart you had not won, assuredly it is yours now.

I was glad that you liked the 'vicarious liability.' In a later paper
on *respondeat superior* I shall eat a leek and show that the doctrine goes back via the Canon Law to Rome.[1] That I suppose was
a last flicker of inherited Germanism. . . .

---

[1] Evelyn Baring (1841-1917), first Earl of Cromer, diplomat and colonial
administrator, was British representative in Egypt from 1883 to 1907.
[1] No such article was published by Laski.

Those whom the gods love may die young, but they visit 1720 I street first.

Please note, both of you, that I have a front name. My love and a thousand thanks,                         *Affectionately, Harold*


*Washington, D.C., February 16, 1917*

*My dear Alaskus:* In spite of your suggestion of your front name! I always thought it would be normal after getting to the *ut de poitrine* with a girl to pause and ask: "By the by—what is your name?"

Your letter delights me with the assurance that you enjoyed being here as much as we did having you. . . .

I have just about got all my ends tucked in but I have done nothing yet to inform my mind beyond reading your *Poe*.[1] I am not like you able to fill as I run, as I believe steam engines do—and yesterday when lamenting that I hadn't kept the book on *Caste,* I turned to reread *The Freudian Wish,*[2] in the hope of getting more nourishment out of it than I did the first time. I went to sleep. The Poe gent gives a charming picture of the Alhambra—but some believe that all great things require anguish for their production, from Phidias to even Michel Angelo, and I rather think some pretty good ones have been done without getting drunk. No doubt Poe and Walt Whitman are the best this country has done in poetry but you can't persuade me that the Baudelaire lot come into the same class with the men with adequate nerves and guts.

On vicarious liability I hope you haven't forgotten the possible strand of frankpledge 154 Mass. 332 [3] *Fitz. Abr. Corone pl. 428.* I envy you with all your books. I wish I had one here that would give me a boost.

My love to you.                    *Affectionately yours, O. W. Holmes*


*Cambridge, Mass., February 19, 1917*

*My dear Justice:* Then please let me send you some books. I can genuinely recommend:

Ferraz: *Histoire de la philosophie en France au XIXme siècle* which is in three small volumes, and, I think, really excellent.

---

[1] In Holmes's list of readings for 1917 appears Hanns Heinz Ewers, *Edgar Allan Poe* (Lewisohn, tr., 1917).

[2] Edwin B. Holt, *The Freudian Wish and Its Place in Ethics* (1915).

[3] *Dempsey* v. *Chambers,* 154 Mass. 330 (1891). At p. 332 Holmes had written as follows: "It is hard to explain why a master is liable to the extent that he is for the negligent acts of one who at the time really is his servant, acting within the general scope of his employment. Probably master and servant are 'fained to be all one person' by a fiction which is an echo of the *patria potestas* and of the English frankpledge. *Byington* v. *Simpson,* 134 Mass. 169, 170. Fitz. Abr. Corone, pl. 428."

Bouglé on *Caste* lies idly on my shelves not to be used for long. W. Trotter on *Instincts of the Herd* you may remember from a review by Lippmann in the *New Republic*.[1] Russell Smith on *Harrington and his Oceana* might give you some gay persiflage for an opinion. Breathe the word romance and I shall reply by return of parcel post.

Free from the burden of the Law School I am far happier. My work is just right; I have time to read and time to make my book slowly evolve itself from a chaos of ideas. The Yale book I am very anxious should be ready in time for your birthday. That is the intention. But a publisher's wheels grind almost as slowly as God's, so if it is a little late you will respect the ambition.

Your comment on Poe lightened my heart. I am dismayed by the frequent assumption of our modern critics that only nervous degenerates can really write. Sometimes I wonder if there can be an American literature until the more exotic Russians have been shipped back to the stews of Petrograd. I doubt if I could summon up one of those who make of *le pis aller* a profession as really essential to life. Gautier, Flaubert, Wilde pass away an idle hour. But mind in the sense that say Fielding or Meredith had mind I utterly deny. We chuckled over your remarks—which will delight Francis Hackett.

I have to look up your two references on Vicarious Liability. There are things in that paper I would take back now if I could. But so far as its main idea is concerned I presume it is the only possible doctrine so long as we run the state on the present lines. Have you ever dabbled in the history of that economic federalism which takes its rise from Proudhon? It gives me most furiously to consider and I am going to run a paper on *Fonctionnairisme* in the French book.[2] If you ordered Paul-Boncour *Le fédéralisme économique* now you would be certain of a happy summer vacation. . . .

Our love to you both: please *please* have no nerves anent book-borrowing. You can make Hale your conscience.

*Affectionately, Harold*

*Cambridge, Mass., [February 24-26, 1917]*
*My dear Justice:* You will of course buy the engraving.[1] In the first place it is cheap; in the second place such external self-indulgence is really sufficiently objective to be social; in the third you really want it more than most people which is the true title to artistic property.

---

[1] See, *supra*, p. 28.

[2] See Chapter V, *Authority in the Modern State* (1919).

[1] The letter from Holmes to which this is responsive is missing.

Well! I will send you no books. Though if you had re-read a third time *The Freudian Wish* I would have sent you, willy-nilly, some genial stimulants. The Ross[2] I share much of your keenness about; with the added comment that it is the only reasonably competent book he has written. But I suppose he was the first academic fellow to realise the significance of Tarde, and for that he deserves much. But the style is an insult to God.

I am in the midst of some brilliant French speculation on the state—more especially in relation to administrative regulation. Leroy[3] and Cahen[4] are two names I would like you to inscribe in the Positivist Calendar of fine spirits to whom is due the homage of critical and admiring disagreement; but of a disagreement which vanishes at the really fundamental things. More and more I get to believe that Hobbes was right in his view of the state but wrong in his view of its necessity. Duguit in a little book on *Le droit individuel et le droit social* has said some things on paper that so crowd my mind now as to make me wish to tempt thought out of you.

Please get time to read Francis on the "Fiction Factory" in this week's *N. R.*[5] That seems to me criticism at its best—hard and clean and joyous—the right kind of pleasure in killing a man because you have the swift realisation that he simply is not fit to live. That boy has the stuff of genius in him. He drops ideas as a cuckoo drops eggs.

We have Sam Rosenson here this week-end and talk fit for the Gods. I am going to bring him to Beverly this summer for he will thrill you. And he is glorious indeed about the war.

Our love to you both—                          *Affectionately, Harold*


*Washington, D.C., February 27, 1917*
*Dear lad:* Your letters drive me to despair at the thought of all the good things that I am missing—one never can tell that it is not *the* message of salvation that is escaping one. But as I have said so often one has to bet one's soul every half hour. To choose A is to give up B—(even to your lightning voracity). However, one gets what one can. For instance I saw Bergson a moment at the French Embassy yesterday p.m. and then hurried home and chattered nonsense with the boys and girls of Monday afternoon. Before I went I took up Ovid for a few minutes. I don't know him at all and was surprised to see how many lines were quotable. But

[2] Holmes had recently read E. A. Ross's *Social Control* (1901).

[3] Maxime Leroy (1873-1957), author of *Les transformations de la puissance publique* (1907) and *La coutume ouvrière* (2 vols., 1913).

[4] Georges Cahen, *Les fonctionnaires: leur action corporative* (1911).

[5] A review of Henry T. Baker, *The Contemporary Short Story, a Practical Manual* (1916), 10 *New Republic* 108 (Feb. 24, 1917).

to be sure you can find quotations anywhere if you know how to use them. Still I was more than usually struck by what I mention and still more to find what I had supposed to be a specially Christian doctrine that repentance might mitigate or do away with punishment. *Epistulae ex Ponto* 1-1.

Saturday was a most heavenly day. As you rightly divined, I bought the etching in the morning—and revived the enchantments of more than 50 years ago when I used to talk with Theis[1] who made the Gray collection, (Harv. Col. Art Museum) and with an old fellow who made up in volume for the omission of the most expensive prints. I used to sit up to all hours with him in Harrison Avenue at the South End and have a book of poems by him of which I seem to remember the lines: "He who dog or cat can love, loves God in that." Then in the afternoon (I mean of last Saturday) we drove and in the tangle by the riverside off the War College we, that is, my wife, of course, found the first green leaves open. In the evening we went to a splendid entertainment at the Russian Embassy, which gave pleasure from its adequacy. I like the Ambassador[2] and had some encouraging talk with the Vice President,[3] who has a good deal of good sense—disguised when he first came by his not knowing the tone or what was expected.

I had read Hackett's piece and agree with your superlatives about him, as you know.

This morning I mean to telephone to the print department of the Cong. library to see if I can come down and compare my etching with their copy. The telephoning is done. I shall go before long. How delightful is the mixed emotion half noble, aesthetic—half fishy—that of the collector, with which one turns to ancient things, in portfolios, with a history. So Goodbye, my son, for the moment. My homages to your wife.          *Aff'ly yours, O. W. H.*

*Cambridge, Mass., March 3, 1917*
*My dear Justice:* . . . You conquer me *in re* Ovid. I know only and know only to dislike the *Fasti* which have doubtless anthropologic merit from the point of view of religious interpretation but from the standpoint of a schoolboy were incurably dull. I will look into the Epistle with your remarks in mind. I was as a fact always glad he went into exile.

I have had two tremendous joys this week. *Imprimis,* I have begun to write my book on the French Catholics,[1] and I found a

[1] Louis Theis, curator of Gray Collection of Engravings, Harvard University, 1862-1870.
[2] The last Czarist Ambassador was Giorge Bakhmeteff.
[3] Thomas R. Marshall of Indiana.
[1] *Authority in the Modern State* (1919).

joy in the labour of composition which has thrilled me. Really there is a splendour in the company of great men that compensates for everything. They seem to live by the mere chance of transferring them to the printed page; and when I meet Lamennais in a better world I shall astonish him by my knowledge of his intimate thoughts. Then I have begun to read *Don Quixote* and I vote it the best bedbook in the world. He seems to me so like a modern social reformer aiming at great things in order to have whimsical mishaps. There's a gloriously frantic grotesqueness about him which is superb. And I couldn't help reading into Sancho Panza the amiable outlines of Mr. Taft. . . .

You have been exulting in a print. Please share my joy in a superb two-volume Gibson's *Codex,* (1731) as new as the Clarendon Press turned it out, with a thousand ideas tickling the palate on every page.

Our love to you both—              *Yours affectionately, Harold*

*Cambridge, Mass., March 6, 1917*

*My dear Justice:* I believe in the divine right of birthdays; and yours has a special significance for me.[1] I had hoped greatly that I could have sent you a copy of my book[2] as my freewill offering; but in these days of trade-unionism one has to let the printer have his way and that must be deferred. But all that my love and respect can wish for you I do wish. You are so much moulding all I think and write that in many ways these months since last July have been the happiest I have known. And certainly two of the great landmarks have been the days I have spent with you. You teach us all to dare greatly. You set us the example. I only am eager that we who are your pupils will not prove unworthy of our master.

When I think of you it is not of a Justice of the Supreme Court nor of the author of *The Common Law* that I draw for myself a picture. It is rather of a gallant gentleman who knows that the one thing worth while in life is the passion for fine thought; who gives even to the youngest of his company the opportunity to march with him on his journeying. I think of one who, as Maitland said of Acton, was 'in truth a very spendthrift of his hard-earned treasure and ready to give away in half an hour the substance of an unwritten book.' But what above all I cherish is the thought of your insistence on untramelled thinking, your gift of generous friendship, the way in which you turn for us the sunset of your achievement into the sunrise of our hopes.

---

[1] On March 8, Holmes was to be seventy-six.

[2] *Studies in the Problem of Sovereignty* (1917).

My love to you—and a greeting the warmer because it is but in thought.                                                    *Affectionately, Harold*

*Washington, D.C., March 8, 1917*
*Dear Laski:* Your beautiful and charming letter goes to my heart and emphasizes my wish to write at length—but I am so balled up with work that must be done as to make it impossible for me to do more than send you my thanks and my love.
*Affectionately yours, O. W. Holmes*

*Cambridge, Mass., March 14, 1917*
*My dear Justice:* I have been silent overlong; but there have been a host and a half of new students to fit in the scheme of things. They have taken time, wasted time, and shown themselves incredibly eager to be nursed and fondled. So that I have had my hands full with a vengeance.

I have also had a deep regret. I wanted badly to be at your party last Thursday, but time and health and things equally irrelevant but obviously demanding forbade. All I can do is to picture you bowered amid the beauty of Washington, and wreathed in the forget-me-nots of another world than law. . . .

I have had my comfort. I have bought an exquisite little Vergil, well-bound, well-printed and good to the eye, which yet has succeeded in filling my pocket. So I can revive ancient memories. For the eighth eclogue and the fourth Georgic I have vivid enthusiasm. The first *Aeneid* disappointed me somewhat but the sixth is really more than worth all the highest praise. Now I am going back to Lucretius for the contrast. One line in the 12th *Aeneid* I must set down in the context of America. '*Arma citi properate viro! quid statis?*' . . . '*Non haec humanis opibus, non arte magistra proveniunt.*'[1] For the rest I have been working at my book on the French very slowly but with a realisation that the plan as a whole gets ever clearer. And I have been dipping into the book of Boissier *La fin du paganisme* which seems to me as near exquisite as anything I have recently ventured in the classical world. There are really no thrills like those where intelligence drags affection in its train. I am trying to summon up the courage to adventure Grote. But it looks a vacation book every time I gaze at its 12 thick volumes.

You will realise that my own book arrived just too late to come when I would have wished it. But it comes none the less with a love of which I do not need to tell you the profundity.

Our love to you both—                                    *Affectionately, H.*

---

[1] " 'Quick! bring him arms! Why stand ye?' . . . 'not by mortal aid comes this, not by masterful art. . . .' " (H. Rushton Fairclough, translator.)

*Washington, D.C., March 15, 1917*

*Beloved lad:* The book arrived yesterday and your letter this morning. I read the first chapter last night with very great pleasure and of course with substantial agreement.[1] Possibly there is an implication of a slightly different emphasis from my own. I am reminded of what I said at Langdell's dinner—that continuity with the past is not a duty it is only a necessity.[2] It seems to me rather a necessity than a duty for sovereignty to recognize its limits—its own limits. It very well may recognize the limits of another sovereignty. I forget whether I ever called your attention to *Cariño* v. *Insular Govt.* 212 U.S. 449, 458. Probably I did. I hardly need to tell you how pleased and flattered I feel at your preface and quotation.[3] I suppose that I see from what I have read and the titles of the other chapters the scope of your understanding and I have no doubt that the book deserves and will bring you great credit.

The birthday was a great surprise and a great pleasure to me—but I would not have had you come on for a thousand dollars (payable to me). I couldn't have put you up and I should have been most anxious. . . . I should like to follow your steps in Virgil, (I stick to the old fashioned spelling), but there is not much chance. If there are any crevices your book will fill them for the present. I am not a slow reader but I can't read a page or even a paragraph at a glance like you, and moreover although I take a few spoonsful of the classics now and then I never can get rid of a feeling that I am wasting time when there is much new to be read—witness the dazzling stream of names that you fire off at me—perhaps to keep me in my place as a worm. To be sure such reading as I have done—*e.g.* the *Banquet* of Plato a few years ago, or the *Oedipus* last summer, or a little Homer—has given me interesting reflections, but the interest is apt to be more in the reflections than the thing. I am somewhat subdued to what I work in, I want to read what bears in a general way on my path and I feel the want of a certain tension. I don't read as many novels as I used to and I care less for them I think. Now I am sketching possible dissents in various directions—sometimes with, sometimes against my brother B. It is a fine sport as one is freer and more

---

[1] The first chapter, "The Sovereignty of the State," developed Laski's theory of pluralism, and criticized the monistic theory of the State.

[2] "Learning and Science," *Speeches* (1913), 67, 68; *Collected Legal Papers* (1920) 138, 139.

[3] In Laski's Preface he expressed the hope that he had learned "the lesson to be learned from the constitutional opinions with which Mr. Justice Holmes has enriched this generation." From Holmes's *Speeches* (1913) he had quoted this passage: "Your business as thinkers is to make plainer the way from something to the whole of things, to show the rational connection between your fact and the frame of the universe."

personal than when one is speaking for others as well as for oneself.
To them I return. My love to you and homage to your wife.
*Affectionately yours, O. W. H.*


*Cambridge, Mass., March 20, 1917*
*My dear Justice:* It was worth writing the book to have had your
letter; and I feel pretty certain from some dicta of yours in a new
decision Felix showed me yesterday that on the main heads we are
in substantial agreement.[1] I don't think sovereignty is anything
more than a balance of forces and I am anxious to stay the implicit
theocratising of any other attitude.

Your sly comments on the peregrinations of your mind are more
fascinating than I can say. I think as a fact that there are certain
fellows, Aristotle, Plato, Thucydides, whom one cannot read even
today without continuous enlightenment on modern problems. The
others give one—Euripides is a good example—an occasionally
priceless *aperçu*, and an amount of pleasure that with me at any
rate doesn't diminish. As to fiction—well I find that my dose de-
clines. There isn't time to read the romance of other people's lives
if you study properly the spider's web of your own. I am clear
that in reading one ought to have two rules—(a) to know one
subject inside out and (b) to have an eye to what the rest of the
world is doing. I mean, to take myself, that I ought to be able to
recite on Duguit or Austin or Maitland in detail and hear say J. J.
Thomson tell a good story about Jean Perrin without feeling a
cool breeze of ignorance.[2] And of course while I listen to Sir J. J.
I want also to have an intimate conviction that my subject is much
more fascinating and important, (as of course it is).

The Adamson decision was a relief and yet disturbing.[3] I did not
think it possible for Day, J. to be in the minority on any ground.
If you could steal for me a copy of it I would be pleased. In fact if
Hale could send me the offprints of your opinions it would give
me a great amount of pleasure.

[1] The reference is probably to Holmes's opinion in *McDonald* v. *Mabee*,
243 U.S. 90 (March 6, 1917), in which Holmes, after stating that "the
foundation of jurisdiction is physical power," indicated that the tradition
of the common law and standards of due process made a cautious exercise of
power appropriate.

[2] Sir Joseph John Thomson (1856-1940) was the distinguished British
physicist who was Professor of Physics at Cambridge University and Master
of Trinity College.

Jean Perrin (1870-1942), French physicist and author of *Les atomes*
(1914).

[3] *Wilson* v. *New*, 243 U.S. 332 (March 19, 1917). White, C.J., wrote the
majority opinion sustaining the Adamson eight-hour law. McKenna, J.,
wrote a concurring opinion. Day, J., wrote a dissenting opinion as did
Pitney, J., with Van Devanter's concurrence.

I have just finished a thrilling book. S. Reinach of the *Cultes* has written an *Orpheus* which is a general history of religions. It is simply absorbing. It goes down to date and in grasp of detail and breadth of perspective it is masterly. I wish you would note it for the summer. The Putnams publish it at $3. The chapter on early Christianity is one of the most illuminating syntheses I have read.

We had an exciting week-end with Francis Hackett here. One thing he revealed which I think you would like to know. He is very anxious to have an autographed portrait [sic] of you, but too shy to ask you for one. He was in great form and I felt again that he understands criticism in the French way, big and generous stabs at the heart of life.

My love to you both.                                *Affectionately, Harold*


*Washington, D.C., March 29 [23?], 1917*

*Dear Laski:* A moment snatched for a word or two of answer. *Imprimis*—Joy to be ahead of you on any book. Unless the *Orpheus* is a recension I had it years ago, recommended it to others, and I doubt not have it on my shelves. 2. I send the Adamson opinions by this mail. They are all together. I thought Day's dissent wrong but the most rational.[1] My own opinion goes the whole hog with none of the C.J.'s squeams—but I don't care to say more than is necessary. As I put it after the argument, I think if Congress can weave the cloth it can spin the thread. 3. Why did you call Ross a bad writer (in *Social Control*)? I thought it had considerable literary power. 4. I was delighted at your compliment to Peter Plymley.[2] There is a cheap ed. of this at Beverly Farms and I remember being much impressed by their power and their style. 5. Why use the word pragmatist unless you adhere to W. J.'s philosophy on that matter.[3] I never could make anything out of his or his friends' advocacy of his nostrum except either that in motives depending upon human conduct effort affects the result—which we

---

[1] Mr. Justice Day, acknowledging that Congress in regulating interstate commerce might fix the hours and wages of railroad workers, considered that the due process requirements of the Fifth Amendment had been violated in that provision of the Adamson Law which directed that the wages previously paid for ten hours of work should for an indeterminate period be paid for eight hours' labor. Pitney and Van Devanter, JJ., denied that the law was a regulation of interstate commerce and also condemned it under the Fifth Amendment.

[2] Sydney Smith's *Letters of Peter Plymley* (1808) had wittily and vigorously done much to encourage and hasten Catholic emancipation in Great Britain and Ireland. Laski had referred to them with commendation in his chapter "The Political Theory of the Catholic Revival" in *Studies in the Problem of Sovereignty* (1917) 121, 126.

[3] The word was used by Laski with some frequency in his *Problem of Sovereignty, supra*.

have heard—or that by yearning we can modify the multiplication table, which I doubt. His whole attitude—on the will to believe &c presupposes something that we can't change as the basis for recommending the will. Otherwise he has no answer if I say, "I don't want to." But I think as little of his philosophy as I do much of his psychology. He seems to me typically Irish in his strength and his weakness. 6. Which lastly reminds me of what you say of Francis Hackett. Of course I should be proud to have him really want a photograph of me (Oh Laski dear you said "autographed photograph" a vile phrase) but I never supposed he would care a damn for me, my ways, works, or machinery. So I am open to command but need a little reassuring. His and Wells's remarks led me to get Joyce, *Portrait of the Artist as a Young Man*,[4] of which I have read a part. Certainly a singular picture—on the whole not carrying me away—but worth reading. Many pages are impressionist blots—you have to stand two rooms off to see the solid intended. Homage to madam and love to you.

*Aff'ly yrs., O. W. Holmes*


*Cambridge, Mass., March 24, 1917*
*My dear Justice:* Your letter gave me some real thrills. *In re* Reinach I bow the head. But of course it was a great book and to assume that you had perhaps not read it was the fine impudence of youth which always believes that vision is identical with discovery. I'm so glad you like it—because to me there is something immensely attractive about that Voltairean scepticism and to know that you share my liking does my heart good.

*In re* Francis Hackett, I confirm and Felix confirms. He mentioned it to us, but he has a curiously shy feeling that he has little to give you for what is to him as to us a very precious possession. Write on it that he has given you happy moments and I think you will give him an immense impetus to life. (O God— autograph photograph—I will go to Holy Communion and partake of the Lord that I may be cleansed.)

Your phrase on the *Adamson* case was a real contribution. But one remark made *obiter* by the Courts on strikes in public utilities hits me in the midriff.[1] I think it comes up against the worst

---

[4] Francis Hackett had reviewed the *Portrait* in 10 *New Republic* 138 (March 3, 1917) and H. G. Wells had a brief essay on Joyce in the issue for March 10, 1917 (*ibid.*, 158).

[1] In the course of his opinion for the majority in *Wilson* v. *New*, White, C.J., had said that such rights as employees in a private business might have to strike for higher wages were "necessarily subject to limitation when employment is accepted in a business charged with a public interest." 243 U.S. at 352. With Laski's criticism of this passage compare his comments on Hauriou's opinions on the same matter, *Authority in the Modern State* (1919) 352-353.

dogmas of the modern time—really implies the fetish of state-
divinity which I hate as the successor of the medieval church.
But I take comfort in the thought that law after all depends on
the consent of men.

Your view of Joyce was interesting. I have got to the stage
where I just don't believe that realism and physiology are the same
thing. I have definitely decided in favour of the romantics. One
has enough in a newspaper (which you have the courage not to
read) of what these fellows make novels out of. I like the big
swashbucklers like D'Artagnan or Don Quixote—or else the epic
of man à la Meredith and Balzac.

I have been reading Michel's *Idée de l'état*. It is big and fine
analysis. You get a sense of what De Tocqueville meant to the
world when you read the books of his tradition. And I read Brunetière on Bossuet which is superb as criticism and utterly damnable on philosophy.

I want to think over your strictures on the use of 'pragmatic'
before I talk of it. I am not a Jamesian by any means—and now
I would go much further along the lines of a guarantee of individual apriorisms than I would a year ago. But I want to think
this out without replying offhand.

I love *Peter Plymley*—and he was a New College man which
doubles my affection.

My love to you both—                          *Affectionately, Harold*

*Washington, D.C., March 31, 1917*

This is to my friend Mr. Harold J. Laski
I am *quite* sure that anywhere *il n'y en a pas qui*
More than he have the encyclopaedical pass-key.
      'How sweet an Ovid was in Murray lost.'
So far I had written when your incursion into the language of
scriptures and the Moabite stone[1] was handed to me and strikes
a different note. It makes me chuckle. But I thought I helped the
prophet a little by the phrase territorial club—for nation[2]—and
admirable as are his lucubrations I don't think he establishes any
duty by pointing out the independent origin of the Catholic
Church—Trades Unions and Thieves Clubs. It is a question of
policy and power how far the strongest will stand the others. Just
now I do think it most desirable to strengthen so far as one can
the cohesion of the territorial bond—i.e. patriotism—(as a living
force—against 4th of July oratory and the decay incident to 50

[1] Laski had sent Holmes a light-hearted memorandum (omitted from
this edition) in mock-Biblical language contrasting various of Holmes's legal
concepts with his own thesis of plural sovereignty.
[2] Cf. 2 *Holmes-Pollock Letters* (1941) 27-29.

years of polite conversation). I don't know but we shall have to lock up the prophet for a time, as in theory, although not in practice (I stop for my secretary—he thought it was S—I thought it *C* —to look it out—I never can keep in mind which is verb and which is noun)—practice, as I was saying, an anarchist and under our statutes hardly ought to have been admitted into the country. However I shall not inform against him or proceed *ex officio judicis*. And since I wrote the last word I have finished your book. It is a wise and good one, and I am proud of you.

I expect Frankfurter to dine with us tonight and Richard Hale[3] to luncheon in a few minutes. I wonder what you refer to in your 'remarks by the Court on strikes in public utilities.' If I become articulate upon a case that is before us I am strongly inclined to say that any man who prefers the success of his private club— trades union or other—to the public welfare, *e.g.* by a general railroad strike, is a public enemy, which seems to me almost an identical proposition. Do I gather that you are the other way inclined?                                    *Aff'ly yours, O. W. Holmes*

I stick to my criticism of pragmatic. Unless you are ready to accept the philosophy, don't use its lingo, I say. Just as I thought it worse than bad taste for Bob Ingersoll[4] to talk of 'our calvary' & otherwise borrow the phraseology of a rejected creed.

*Cambridge, Mass., April 5, 1917*

*My dear Justice:* This is to be a long letter; and the responsibility for that is on your own head. For what you wrote me in reply to my Moabitish efforts stirs me to make some comments. . . .

*Imprimis,* I was wrong about pragmatism. I should not use the word because (to adopt your phrase) I do not believe that wishing can change the multiplication table. But I want a word to express the fact that we cannot be certain as to the truth of certain things. We adopt hypotheses about them and if they work we call them true. We say, for example, that the ultimate constitution of matter is atomic even though we do not know it is atomic save from the fact that the assumption helps us to explain a number of things otherwise inexplicable. I mean I see two kinds of truth (I) axiomatic—the dogmas from which we can't escape, and (II) the necessary—the hypotheses we are compelled to assume. I used pragmatic to cover the second kind. It's subjective and it's to that division that I conceive James to have made a real contribution.

---

[3] Richard Walden Hale (1871-1943) was a Boston lawyer and personal friend of Holmes's.

[4] Robert G. Ingersoll (1833-1899); American lawyer whose rhetoric and whose heart were dedicated to an interminable assault on Christianity.

Where he went wrong was to think that what he said of this part applied also to the first.

I turn to the philosophy of the State. You evidently (with the amiable perspiration of horror) think me next door to philosophic anarchy. Why! So I am, Hamlet, but the door is tightly closed. If you will define patriotism as a loyalty to the nation I am with you probably as far as you want to go—so far, for instance, as hating the enemies of England & loving its friends as an act of faith. But I distinguish between the nation and the state. The state seems to me just a great public service corporation and no more entitled (though its power enables it to receive) any more loyalty than a church or labor-union. Everything depends on the way in which it fulfills its function. I can't but believe that its shareholders have very different privileges and that since their interest in its activities has such different results those who do not share in the preferences have a right to seek ways and means of obtaining [them]. Surely the reason for the development of labor unions lies exactly there. Congress has not the utility for labor that it has for capital. It seems to me very clear that as a fact what we call the interest of the public is little more than a phrase. We invoke it against labor in a situation like that in the threatened railroad strike but when the roads ask for a 15% increase in rates we are singularly quiet about it. Once accept the postulate that political power is the handmaiden of economic power—which seems to me a historical truism—and I think it follows that the state which manipulates that power is also a capitalist institution. The fight between labor and capital of which the railroad strike was only a glaring instance seems to me part of a historic process which one day will take us out of the capitalist system just as in the sixteenth to the eighteenth centuries we got away from the feudal system. I don't think feudalism took thought for the interests of the public any more than capital, because I think that the idea of social justice as it was expressed *e.g.* by Holmes, J. in *Coppage* v. *Kansas*[1] is a new idea born in any widespread fashion from the shock of the French Revolution. If this is all true, then probably the neglect of the state of which you complain is a necessary incident in a historic process. I think that the declining belief in a representative system of government is really part of the same problem. The nation apart —the true bonds of allegiance are economic and not political; and representative government put its money on Congress (or Parliament) as the mirror of the nation. What we have to do is rather to make our political system mirror the sectional economic interests within itself and try to work out a harmony therein. Talk of any inherent agreement between the welfare of labor and of capital

---

[1] See, *supra*, p. 10, note 1.

seems to me as idle as between the state in Germany in say 1873 and the theoretic ideals of the Roman church. And I think that probably there results much good from the consequent demand to the state to justify itself by what it performs. (Holmes, J. *privatim* "I like the lad! but oh! what a hell of a mess.")

Of course your territorial club was the basis of my Rosetta Stone —but a great man is obviously he who makes proper use of other people's ideas. It makes me remember with a smile that one day at Beverly Farms you criticised to me the robust *étatisme* of a certain brother of yours—and behold—thou also art among the prophets. I take comfort in the thought that my next book[2] is bound to convert you—for it will make a most intimate appeal to your best (the C. J. would say your worst) emotions—it will have a fine flavour of thorough-going atheism about it. No one can read Catholic books and still believe in God—the thing is too utterly puerile to fit a big world like this.

I have just recommenced Gibbon—what a stately fellow he was! I played dishonestly and read my favorite—the 44th chapter— first with a renewed sense of amazement at its splendour. And I have just finished a great book on Montesquieu by Dedieu which you would like—very much on the lines of Ehrlich's article in the *Harvard Law Review*.[3] And then a scrumptious novel of Dumas, *The Forty-Five*—a good old hair-raiser of the old style which did me good. Sometimes a bathe in blood like that can change the world. Please tell that to Shelton Hale.

I am in the clouds *in re* the international situation[4]—and with a certain justifiable emotionalism. I like to feel that the country of Felix and O. W. H. is fighting for the ideals of my country.

My love to you both— *Affectionately, H.*

*Washington, D.C., April 12, 1917*
*Dear Lad:* Your letter and article[1] deserve an attention I can't give them just now as my work takes all my time—(daytime—I don't work or write at night). I won't bother on your hobby, though I am not quite sure whether we are in substantial agreement or enemies to death (as to state and nation). I read 9/12 Gibbon with reference to the day [of] judgment. I thought him obviously a great man. I thought he had a real power to tell an interesting tale and was easy reading—and I didn't find that he said a thing

---

[2] *Authority in the Modern State* (1919).

[3] Eugen Ehrlich, "Montesquieu and Sociological Jurisprudence," 29 *Harv. L. Rev.* 582 (April 1916).

[4] On April 2 President Wilson had delivered his War Message to Congress, and on the 4th and 5th the War Resolution was debated in the Senate and House.

[1] Not identified.

that I cared a damn to hear. Characters that I don't believe, of
persons to whose characters I am indifferent, wanderings of tribes
and movements not to be followed without an atlas in hand, super-
seded accounts of the Roman law, &c &c. He illustrated to my mind
how the emphasis had changed from his time to mine. Yet mind
I am perfectly sincere in saying that at once he struck me as a
great man. There are few books more than 25 years old, except
sources, that I much enjoy.

Isolated questions: Do you think my brother would be pleased
if I should speak of his voluable discourse or opinion? . . .

Is not *The Forty-Five* one of that Valois series? If so I stopped
just short of it, having got pretty well fed up with his two others
—summer before last. Alas, Dumas and even Balzac have paled to
me since my youth.

Did you ever read my little essay on Montesquieu? [2] an introduction to what I supposed was going to be a scholarly edition—and
that had pictures in it! A race in the circus and God knows what.
I never saw but one copy of the book beside the one sent to me.
I gave Felix or the Harvard Law School my last spare exemplar
of my part. I have awaiting examination three numbers of a new
magazine of art—*The Soil*. It looks like the aesthetic brother of
*The Masses* if you know that sheet. Also an unfinished volume of
that most delightful blackguard George Moore.[3] He simplifies the
steps to copulation as Raphael does the mountain in the Trans-
figuration. Also I have in my hands a Catholic book for the young
that fully parallels the otherwise incredible lectures on Hell in
Joyce's *Portrait of the Artist*. It does strike me as childish yet
horrible—and a kind of thing that only men out of the proportion-
ing experiences of active life could have worked out in such a
nasty way. I must stop. . . .                        *Aff'ly yours, O. W. H.*

*Cambridge, Mass., April 18, 1917*
*My dear Justice:* . . . *The Forty-Five* is a Valois romance—is
there anything you have not attempted? Your attitude to fiction I
know is right—even to the extent of making me distrust the
younger novelists. I mean that I'd rather Wells wrote a formal
treatise on the prospects of the XXth century than take refuge in
novels which only hide the need for perspicacity. . . . I have just
read Bardoux's little volume on Guizot which has some brilliant
pages and a volume of essays by Paul Bourget, *Sociologie et*

---

[2] Holmes contributed a critical and biographical introduction to a reprint
of *The Spirit of the Laws* (1900); it is in his *Collected Legal Papers* (1920),
250.

[3] Holmes's reading list for this period includes George Moore's *Memoirs
of My Dead Life* (1906).

*littérature* which is diabolically clever. One essay in particular *"La politique de Balzac"* I thought almost infernal. He brings out very well how these Catholic fellows find democracy a tough nut to swallow despite all their pretensions. What astonishes me much is to find that with most of them Renan is the high priest of a better day. There's a clever little book by Guy Grand, *Le procès de la démocratie* which shows clearly how all manner of impossible people are combined in the service of the traditionalist cause. But I hope that my next book will win your interest in these things.

I hope that you will have a chance to talk over life with Mr. Balfour.[1] *Inter arma Wilsoniana* he will need a touch of intellectual scepticism. I know the virtues of the τὸ γενναῖον ψευδῆμα but I confess I would feel a little happier if the statesmen generally did not promise us a heaven after peace. I can't help remembering the talk in '89 and '48. It's well to go into these things with open eyes. The difficulty is that our democrats go in with an open mouth. Meanwhile we must, each in our own way, follow the President's advice, *cultiver nos jardins!*[2]

My love to you both—                                        *Harold*

*Washington, D.C., April 20, 1917*

*Dear Laski:* . . . I think Wells is best employed on stories. His thought does not seem to me important—but he knows the emotional concomitant of a situation—just as presumably Shakespeare wouldn't have been a statesman or great king but can give you the feeling of a statesman or great king. I am not surprised at what you say of Bourget—30 years ago I was similarly impressed by his *Essais de psychologie contemporaine.*

As to Renan I read all but one or two of his religious historical books—mostly aloud, translating, to my wife. I even verified the references to the Bible in the first volume or two of his *History of Israel*—or whatever it is called—and used to wish that he might have to publish one volume every six months while I lived—for my intellectual amusement.

Did I mention having seen a real Catholic book for children published in this century that talked about Hell just as did the preacher in Joyce's *Portrait of the Artist?* It led me to wonder whether the world would not be better off if we never had invented the notion of *sin* and had contented ourselves, as I imagine

---

[1] Arthur James Balfour (1848-1930) at this time was British Foreign Secretary and was in Washington as head of the British Commission.

[2] In an address to the American people President Wilson, on April 16, had urged farmers and everyone "who creates or cultivates a garden" to increase the stock of agricultural supplies. *State Papers and Addresses by Woodrow Wilson* (Shaw, ed., 1917) 387, 391.

the Japanese do, and am told that the Russians do more or less,
with recognizing legal and social transgressions as such, dealing
with them as such—and no more. It makes me sick at heart, when
one thinks what automatic dolls we are, to hear poor little devils
told that what they thought were good actions were bad, because
they had a thought of reward or punishment and did not do it
simply for Christ—and the next minute to hear a puke in an apron
trying to scare them stiff with a picture of the Hell they are likely
to be sent to—and yet, I suppose from the preceding, ought not
to think of! As I was saying the other day I don't believe men who
took an active part in ordinary life could or at any rate would
have invented such mean and dirty spiritual tortures. But it is
time for me to shut up and go to Court.        *Aff'ly, O. W. Holmes*

*Cambridge, April 23, 1917*
My dear Justice: . . . Your Catholic reflexions pleased me mightily. But I doubt whether any tale you could tell equals the record
of low and mean intrigue the Jesuits compiled to break the heart
of Lamennais.[1] If ever I doubted the hollowness of religion what
I have learned since I began to study these French problems would
have completed the process of scepticism. God is like a cork in a
wine-bottle—used to see that only the right people drink. It is a
mean business. Which reminds me of the plausible tale that Benedict XVI [*sic*] was elected pope because after the first twenty-four
hours he was the only cardinal in the Conclave whose opinions on
the war were not known.[2] The whole atmosphere of clericalism has
about it the air of exotic untruth. . . .

Your thrill for Renan went to my heart. I love him as one loves
the romancers tinged with scholarship. Did you ever read his two
really permanent books—the one on Averroes and the other on
Philip the Fair? They are my especial favourites. . . .

I must not forget to say that on the way to Rockport[3] we stopped
off at Beverly Farms that my wife might see where you lived. I
had quite a proprietary air about it.

Our love to you both—                        *Affectionately, Harold*

*Cambridge, April 25, 1917*
My dear Justice: . . . Last night Frida and I saw a wonderful
play of Galsworthy's, *The Pigeon*—surely the most admirable com-

---

[1] See Laski's *Authority in the Modern State* (1919), Chapter III.
[2] Benedict XV had been elected Pope on September 3, 1914, as successor
of Pius X.
[3] Laski spent the summers of 1917, 1918, and 1919 in Rockport on Cape
Ann, some fifteen miles from Holmes's summer place at Beverly Farms.

ment on the principles of what sociologists term 'social effort' that
has thus far been written. I hope you will read the play which
makes good reading and is separately obtainable. It is a great thing
to read aloud. I am tempted to the thought that the dictum of
Bernard Shaw is correct and that the 'drunken bestiality' at 25/ a
week is 'fine spirits' at £5000 a year; a vagabond at one wage is
a romantic traveller on a private income. Did you ever read Veblen
on the Leisure Class—if you did what did you make of it?

But I have to lecture and Voltaire is the subject. So to him.

*My love, Harold*

*Cambridge, Mass., April 29, 1917*

*My dear Justice:* A few words about a new enthusiasm. I have
discovered Proudhon and I want you to share the joy. Really he is
immense and he has all the virtues. He is clear-headed, far-sighted,
anti-religious and his theory of the state satisfies all my anarchist
prejudices. I got on to him in the course of searching out the origins of the decentralising ideas of today in France—and I started
with a brilliant little book by Bouglé, *La sociologie de Proudhon*
and one on him in his most masterly fashion by Sainte-Beuve. He
seems to me to have anticipated most of Karl Marx and to have
said it better. He realises the necessity of safeguarding the rights
of personality, and at the same time he is not afraid of collective
action. He fits gloriously into the scheme of my new book and I'll
make him a peg for a bundle of observations. But the main thing
is that he will give you some pleasant hours this summer if you
can be so tempted.

For the rest I am like a washed-out rag. I can still read and
write, so that I am ⅗ alive, but physical exertion is difficult and
with Felix away there is no one to talk to sensibly. I have lost the
closest and dearest of my Oxford friends—I send you a little note
about him from the *Times*—and I feel as though I'd give all I
possess to be in France. One can take refuge within oneself for
a long way on the road, but I wish that the good God had made
it possible for me to be with my brother in France. When I see
these pupils of mine able to make a sacrifice withheld from me,
it seems that the business of thought can sting as well as illuminate. But I must not write down these internal moanings. . . .

Please be very sure to read Francis on Billy Sunday.[1] Much love
to you both—                                    *Affectionately, Harold*

---

[1] Francis Hackett, "Billy Sunday, Salesman," 10 *New Republic* 370
(April 28, 1917).

*Washington, D.C., May 5, 1917*

*My dear Laski:* But a word—I have been frantically busy and now at 6 p.m. Saturday must go out for a few minutes to stir my blood after a long day's work. I hope to fire off two cases on Monday[1]—writing one of which in the time taken was rather a *tour de force* that left me tired. . . .

I have read the Ste. Beuve and a more elaborate German book, A. Mülberger on Proudhon, but nothing at first hand. I am pleased to think he thought K. Marx a charlatan and a humbug. I think he himself with real insight bit off more than he could chew and wasn't the man to reconstruct society.

I sympathize with you on the loss of your friend—I have lost most of mine and so many that I seem hardened. The Montesquieu is not worth bothering about. It was published by D. Appleton & Co. in 1900—I thought it was to show scholarship—it did show illustrations! Prayer of Gustavus Adolphus before the Battle of Lutzen! A Roman Slave Market! etc. What else it shows I know not. My little essay is in the Harvard Law Library, I presume, bound in red morocco with other works of mine if I don't misremember Adams,[2] to whom I sent a copy to that end. Adieu, adieu.                                                                      *Aff'ly, O. W. H.*

*Cambridge, Mass., May 7, 1917*

*My dear Justice:* . . . The days here pass—a little lamentably without Felix but full of work. I was on the whole content with your sentence on Proudhon. Certainly he bit off more than he could chew, but only, I think, in the sense that any man who tries to sum up the ills and remedies of his age is bound to appear a little scatterbrain. I suppose we gain in efficiency by the narrowness of our experts; yet if I had to make a decision as to what our age does most require I think I would on the whole ask for a half-dozen first-rate critics of life like Proudhon. As to Marx, I wouldn't say *vox et praeterea nihil* as you seem inclined to do. A man who lines up so many alongside his thought must—if there be sense in Aristotle—have something in him. But I think he flung two great generalisations down and left us to find out their limitations—and one of them he cribbed from Proudhon, and the other he learned from Thomas Hodgskin.[1] He had one great prevision—the value

---

[1] On May 7, 1917, Holmes delivered the Court's opinion in *The Kronprinzessin Cecilie*, 244 U.S. 12, and *Chicago Life Insurance Co.* v. *Cherry*, *id.* 25.

[2] Edward Brinley Adams from 1913 to 1922 was Librarian of the Harvard Law School.

[1] Thomas Hodgskin (1787-1869); social theorist and journalist; co-editor of *Mechanics Magazine;* author of *Popular Political Economy* (1827), and advocate of something very similar to Marx's labor theory of value.

of labour solidarity and he deserves a blessing for that. But like so many Jews, he is never absolutely first-hand either in thought or research. . . .

I send you a note that one Hugh Elliott [*sic*] has written a good if somewhat patronising life of H. Spencer[2] which I think you would like. Did you ever know that the Italian Chamber of Deputies adjourned at the news of his death and that the London *Times* published a furious attack on him? But I must not summarise the good things of the book. One other good thing I adventure is a perfectly admirable little *Life of Guizot* by Bardoux. It almost made me forgive his wretched mistakes to read what an admirable old fellow he was.

Well! This is 10:15 and I have to lecture at twelve and I still have to write the notes of the lecture.

My love to you both—                              *Affectionately, Harold*


*Washington, D.C., May 8, 1917*

*Dear Laski:* I must write a word to correct a misapprehension, though as usual I have no time. I didn't say that I thought Karl Marx a humbug but that Proudhon seems to have thought and declared him to be one. It seemed to me that Marx had come on the idea of evolution probably not from English but from Hegelian inspiration and that, as Henry Adams, I believe, said to me, united the inconsistent attitudes of a philosopher and a proscribed man. He recognizes the inevitable, yet is bitter about it. I read him a second time in order that I might state to myself articulately the points at which I thought he became fallacious. It seemed to me that he could have avoided what I thought his errors if he had fixed his eye on the stream of products. I also thought that he tacitly shifted his desideratum to suit his argument—from the welfare of England to that of the world and *vice versa*. But I couldn't give chapter and verse—for my impression. My case was the *Kronprinzessin Cecile* which I fired off yesterday. It was a *tour de force* only in the sense that I did it at high pressure in a short time, with the consciousness that perhaps the House of Lords has shown a contrary tendency in a case that has not yet come here,[1] and with our Court very evenly balanced, though only Pitney, Clarke dissented. Brandeis has darkly intimated that I have neglected principles that he heard me lay down 30 years ago but as yet I know not what. I will try to send you a copy when I get some.                                             *Aff'ly, O. W. H.*

I come down from my dark suspicions, and apilogize—*i* is a diminutive. I used to think that epistles were young apostles.

---

[2] Hugh Elliot, *Herbert Spencer* (1917).
[1] *Mitsui & Co.* v. *Watts, Watts & Co.,* [1917] A. C. 227.

*Cambridge, Mass., May 15, 1917*

*My dear Justice:* I was glad of the correction on Karl Marx. I wonder if it was not rather that Marx thought Proudhon a humbug (*Misère de la philosophie*) than vice-versa.[1] K. M. learned more than he liked to admit from England, as the extraordinary preface by Foxwell to the English translation of Menger's *Right to the Whole Produce of Labor* would show you. As to Marx himself I always feel that his intuitions are right but that the applications are somewhat scatter-brain. He can't think organically. I would dearly like a word with you on the stream of products.[2] How far do you conceive your hypothesis to be modified (a) by inventiveness in substitutions during the war (b) by improved organisation (c) by a more rational incidence of productive activity? I think we have to revise a lot of notions we previously held dear. At least I have. . . .

My love to you both—                                    *Affectionately, Harold*

*Washington, D.C., May 17, 1917*

*Dear Laski: Imprimis*—apologies for not having acknowledged the book,[1] for which 1000 thanks—and the horizon is opening a chance to open it—but I have been more frenzied with a case than I can remember having been. There was strain in swiftly turning off the case sent to you, which I trust is not reflected in the written words —this one was a rate case, with endless tables and a terminology that drove me up a stump for two days. Then I came down and the mysteries began to vanish—but head and guts feel the strain.[2] The other work I had was easy and I have sent my last (for the present) case to the printers.

As to the stream of products I don't quite get your point. My use of that thought is simply to get to hard pan and think straight —to ask myself, do I want any and what changes in the nature of the stream or in its distribution, &c. It is not a proposition that the stream flows unchanged—of course it is changing more or less all

---

[1] Marx in his *La misère de la philosophie* (1886) had replied to Proudhon's *Système des contradictions économiques, ou philosophie de la misère* (2 vols., 1846).

[2] Holmes's economic theory, in which he made much of the "stream of products," was most fully developed in a short piece, "Economic Elements," first published in 40 *Cosmopolitan Magazine* 397 (1904) and reprinted in *Collected Legal Papers* (1920) 279. See also "Law and the Court," *id.* at 291.

[1] Franz Cumont, *The Oriental Religions in Roman Paganism* (1916). See, *supra*, p. 37.

[2] Presumably *Rowland* v. *St. Louis & S.F. R.R. Co.*, 244 U.S. 106 (decided May 21, 1917). On the same day Holmes delivered the Court's opinion in *Du Pont Powder Co.* v. *Morland, id.* 100, and *Nevada–California–Oregon Ry. Co.* v. *Burrus, id.* 103.

the time. I say it is a great help to straight thinking. For instance, take taxation—if you stop with preliminary machinery you think of breaking up great estates and old families by an inheritance tax or of cutting down great profits by an income tax—if you pass by means to ends you see that any form of considerable taxation means withdrawing so much of the stream to feed, clothe, and house those whom the Government elects to feed, clothe, and house—and that the rest of the crowd must have so much less. (The possibilities of increased effort, intelligent saving, &c. &c has nothing to do with the proposition). *Sat verb. sap.* I won't develop. My preoccupations are many and my lassitude considerable.

Presumably I go to luncheon with W. Phillips[3] and may have some talk with Balfour. In truth my interest in him is social rather than philosophic. He is a friend of my friends and has the ways of the great world. His book[4] seemed to me rather one to please the ladies and those who like W. James want like the devil to get a particular result—say truth is fluid, but you *ought* to want what they do.                                          *Yours ever, O. W. H.*


*Cambridge, Mass., May 22, 1917*
*My dear Justice:* I note your economic trouncings; clearly we have to fight it out, for I do not think I quite understand the drift of your remarks and you must tutor me by talk. Your conception helps me, but I want to append a warning as to its static character. That is my difficulty. It gives me an added reason for wanting to see you again.

. . . Did you ever read *Janus* in the old days?[1] That still strikes me as one of the most powerful polemics in history—better than Junius by far, and in the long run not less efficacious. This new book seems to shape itself well and the writing of it helps more than I know until I look back at it. . . .

I am glad your vacation approaches. You must have had the hardest year in your experience.

My love to you both—                              *Affectionately, Harold*


*Cambridge, Mass., June 4, 1917*
*My dear Justice:* A pathetic silence! But I have [been] at sea on the unending ocean of French Restoration theology, trying to find

---

[3] William Phillips, American diplomat, at this time was Assistant Secretary of State.

[4] Probably *Foundations of Belief* (1895); see 1 *Holmes-Pollock Letters* (1941) 59.

[1] The *Letters of Janus* (*The Pope and the Council*) were written by the German church historian Johann Joseph Ignaz Döllinger (1799-1890). Their principal concern was to deny the Papal claim of infallibility.

out where Lamennais got his ideas from and I have only just escaped drowning. But if anyone wants proof that it is unlikely that the study of theology will prove productive I feel more or less competent to proffer an opinion. But one thing I did learn. Education that is not secular and compulsory is not education. The fight for the schools in 19th century France revealed more dishonesty, more trickery, and more falseheartedness than anything of which I thought man could be capable.

However, I have read some other things—mindful of your remark that sources are the real meat of life. I have read every discussion of the making of a constitution in England or its colonies since 1815 and I found it fascinating. It's immensely interesting to see how the tone of the House of Commons declined after about 1886. Before, there do seem to have been real principles at stake about which men felt deeply. Afterwards, economic issues becloud the situation. It drives me back to my fundamental thought that representative government is really unfitted to deal with the economic organization of the state. We need new methods—not because our problems are new, but because the emphasis of our response has become so different. See my *Principles of Politics* (1923).

With Felix centred at Washington, Cambridge has departed this life. He attracts everyone there and none will come, far less stay, in this grave of youthful hopes. I fester on, in a curious effort to get outside the war and to believe that it is honest to go on thinking when others are dying to make it possible for me to think. Really, I want more than anything just now to be in Russia where the real political issues are being settled. Pound and I have had some great talks—and his plans for the Law School strike me as splendid. I wish he would extend it widely enough to rope in the study of government. Then I could migrate there and find a sense of comfort. But there's a friendliness about books which compensates for men. I wish, though, that you were near at hand.

My love to you both—      *Yours affectionately, Harold J. Laski*


*Washington, D.C., June 9, 1917*

*Dear Laski:* This is my first breathing moment, if it is one. Although I have had only a case a week or so and a little bit of dissent,[1] the last weeks of the term keep everyone's hands full. I have not quite finished preparing for the last conference—tonight —but I am in good shape. Total result I do not attempt to reply to the matters you have started.

I have managed at odd minutes to read about half of Cumont's

---

[1] On May 21, 1917, Holmes had delivered his famous dissenting opinion in *Southern Pacific Co.* v. *Jensen,* 244 U.S. 205, 218.

*Oriental Religions*—with much pleasure. I expect to finish it next week after the adjournment, for I suppose we shall remain here about a week after that event, relaxing and humanizing and waiting for Beverly Farms to get ready for us.

The Confederate gathering here[2] was not without its emotional value—amusing, touching, recalling my youth—and perhaps also a shrewd indication to other countries concerned that we are united.

I was more pleased than you would have been at one broad sign displayed

> *Damn a man who ain't for his country right or wrong.*

But I am not available yet to do more than *receive* general reflections. *Aff'ly yours, O. W. Holmes*

---

*Cambridge, Mass., June 18, 1917*

*My dear Justice:* This must be the merest word; for I have six books on hand to review for Francis Hackett, and I am always nervous until I have them off. One of them, on the technique of diplomacy, by Sir Ernest Satow, is immensely interesting;[1] and one *Europe Unbound* by March Phillips[2] is the best discussion of liberalism I have met during the war.

But the real purpose of this note is to ask you when you will pass through Boston so that I may pay my homage at the station. Twice a year to the lord's court did his vassals go and place their hands between his, and swear to be his men and do him faithful service as a man owes to his lord.

My love to you both, *Affectionately, H. J. L.*

---

*Cambridge, Mass., June 24, 1917*

*My dear Justice:* It was a joy to see you both even for that brief moment, the more so because now my wife can share in my hills of satisfaction. You made her very happy, and I am grateful. There is nothing like the sharing of such a possession as your friendship.

When you settle down to reading I want to lend you a very remarkable pamphlet of Saleilles—*Le domaine public à Rome*—that perhaps you have not read. There's an amazingly brilliant analogy worked out between the recognition of *dominium* and that of personality which thrilled me greatly. Of all continental jurists I put

[2] In the first days of June the United Confederate Veterans held their annual reunion in Washington.
[1] Sir Ernest Satow's *Diplomatic Practice* (2 vols., 1917) was reviewed by Laski in 12 *New Republic* 80 (Aug. 18, 1917).
[2] 12 *New Republic* 195 (Sept. 15, 1917).

68 )                                                      ( 1916

him first. I have another volume you might like by Geny—which
discusses the *systematische jurisprudenz* of Stammler, Duguit,
Kohler, Hauriou *et al* and orientates one admirably.[1] But you
shall decide if you want them.

I am spending happy days at my book. I lecture here at the
summer school until August 11, then I'm going to aid the *New
Republic* until the middle of September. I plan to spend two
week-ends with you—if you'll have me—one in July and one in
September. It will be glorious to have continuous talk again.

My love to you both—and welcome.

                              *Yours affectionately, Harold J. Laski*

(I) I have seen to the *New Republic*.

(II) I hope Mrs. Holmes got her flowers.


                                          *Beverly Farms, July 2, 1917*
*Dear Laski:* Telephone to me by Wednesday of the week you
would like to come and if the place is not bespoken you will be
welcome, I need not say. As yet we have no definite engagements
only imminences. I am reading a big book (sent to me) on *The
Value of Money*, B. M. Anderson Jr., Asst. Prof. Econ. Harv. Univ.
Until I have broken the back of that I don't want anything else
serious—but after that welcome Saleilles. The volume by Geny (?)
excites more doubt, yet perchance I might like to see it. You must
put a civilized edge on to me in some way—as I have thought
little but law during the term.            *Aff'ly, O. W. H.*
I reopen this (1) to thank you for the charming flowers—we
didn't know whom to thank—(2) to to [*sic*] utter a feeble squeak
of protest against *static* and *dynamic*. You young fellows of the
*N.R.* are constantly getting some word that becomes slang, and
that has little fitness for its use. I observe my value of money
man also is talking static and dynamic.[1] The minute a phrase becomes current it becomes an apology for not thinking accurately
to the end of the sentence.


                                          *Beverly Farms, July 8, 1917*
*Dear Laski:* Now, if you see fit to send on Saleilles, or any other

---

[1] Volume II of François Geny's *Science et technique en droit privé positif*
(4 vols., 1913-24). When Holmes read the volume in the summer of 1918
it stimulated him to write his essay "Natural Law," 32 *Harv. L. Rev.* 40
(November 1918); *Collected Legal Papers* (1920) 310. See, *infra*, pp.
121-122.

[1] In reviewing Willoughby and Lindsay, *The Financial Administration of
Great Britain* (1917), Laski suggested that the authors would have done
better had they discussed their subject "dynamically instead of statically." 11
*New Republic* 251, 252 (June 30, 1917).

book, not too big, that combines amusement with instruction I shall be your willing pupil—*not* memoirs or French Revolution, etc. but matters savoring more of abstraction, looking more in the direction of philosophy, literature, sociology or law. I like to feel that in a general way I am widening the channel or increasing the flow of the stream of my dominant interests. As I imply I have finished the book on *The Value of Money* and I also have got [rid of] various botherations that beset me at the start and now feel as if vacation really were beginning.   À *bientôt, O. W. Holmes*

No German—I read it with too much difficulty.

*Cambridge, Mass., July 13, 1917*
*My dear Justice:* Mine has been the silence of absorption and not of negligence. I have been buried in my book, which goes finely and is a source of unadulterated joy. I have had the chance of a real whack at the foundations of the Catholic Church and it has been a great joy to give it. This is the last of my ecclesiastical adventures and I am taking advantage of it; henceforth my plans send me back to politics, impure and complex. *Facilis descensus et hinc illae lacrimae!* I agree with Bob Barlow[1] who said that apart from theology and sex there is really nothing to talk about.

I know you'll like the Saleilles and the Faguet; the Brunetière I regard as more problematical. But though he was hopelessly committed to a wrong & (thank God) losing side, still I feel that one can't mistake the power of his mind and some of those essays (especially the one on Montesquieu) I thought showed a masterly ability in the handling of ideas. I don't think he has the ideological profuseness of Faguet, and certainly not Sainte-Beuve's genius in re-creating a man, but he doesn't conduce to boredom and that's the main thing.

Apart from writing I, have been buried in administrative law.[2] The French stuff is very impressive and I am absolutely amazed at Dicey's muddleheadedness about it. The rule-making rights of a French prefect are full of fascinating opportunities, & it's very striking to notice how in this crisis the administration here and in England have virtually adopted its principles. Hauriou's *Droit administratif* is one of the most suggestive books I ever read. I want to recommend to you a most brilliant performance by Ashley—*The Economic Organization of England*—it covers the whole space from 1066-1914 in eight crisp lectures & is suggestive at all points.

---

[1] Robert Shaw Barlow (1869-1943), Boston lawyer, partner of Arthur D. Hill, and friend of Holmes.
[2] See Laski's "The Responsibility of the State in England," 32 *Harv. L. Rev.* 447 (March 1919); reprinted in *The Foundation of Sovereignty and Other Essays* (1921), 103.

If you say the word I can bring it down next Friday. It can be read in two hours.

My love to you both—      *Yours affectionately, Harold J. Laski*

*Beverly Farms, July 14, 1917*
*Dear Laski:* By all means bring along the Ashley—I know him and like him and have read a good book by him on the Coal & Iron Industry.[1] I have read Saleilles[2] with some surprise at your enthusiasm. I am half through Faguet's *Rousseau* with unmixed pleasure—and have read two of Brunetière's with considerable though less.[3] The Montesquieu I think deserves your praise and the first in the book (Hardy) interested me the more that I had been reading Rolland's book that I have mentioned,[4] which touches the same themes. I have on hand also borrowed from a neighbor Gyp, *Napoleonette,* and another book of Faguet's *En lisant les beaux vieux livres*—which I think I have read, as I look into it.

We will talk of all these and more.           *Yours, O. W. H.*

*Cambridge, Mass., July 19, 1917*
*My dear Justice: Te deoque volentibus* I shall arrive at Beverly Farms tomorrow at 5:09, thus, with true appreciation of the laws of health, avoiding a train in the heat of day. I am very eager to see you both.           *Yours ever affectionately, Harold J. Laski*

*Cambridge, Mass., July 23, 1917*
*My dear Justice & Mrs. Holmes:*
*Halcyonii dies. . . .*
*Haec olim meminisse juvabit.*
They were indeed halcyon days. I do not try to thank you, not only because it is impossible enough, but because one does not thank Maitland for being Maitland. One simply drinks at the fountain. But if it was possible for my affection for you to go deeper into my heart (which I doubt) that you certainly achieved. . . .

My love & my gratitude to you both—
           *Ever yours affectionately, Harold J. Laski*

[1] In 1903 Holmes read William James Ashley's *The Adjustment of Wages; a Study in the Coal and Iron Industries of Great Britain and America* (1903).

[2] See, *supra,* p. 67.

[3] Holmes's reading list includes Ferdinand Brunetière, *Études critiques sur l'histoire de la littérature française* (4th series). It included essays on Alexandre Hardy and Montesquieu.

[4] Holmes had recently read Romain Rolland's *Some Musicians of Former Days* (1915).

*Beverly Farms, July 30, 1917*

*Dear Laski:* This accompanies the return by post of the two books you lent me. I am glad to return them as it bothers me to have other people's books. The next time please recommend a purchase by me. Ashley was as good as you promised.[1] The other has an Oxford don, discreetly religious, belief in the upward and onward, fortifying itself with the word Evolution.[2] It more edifies than instructs. The one on science strikes me as being as good as any. The philosophic note seems to be that of helping God to a victory over his own by-products and nonentity. I am contented with a humbler battle cry. I don't doubt the progress of the last 2000 years but have no convictions as to its indefinite continuance. I see sufficient reasons for doing my damnedest without demanding to understand the strategy or even the tactics of the campaign. The attempt to lift up men's hearts by a belief in progress seems to me like the wish for spiritualism or miracles, to rest on not taking a large enough view or going far enough back. I see no stay or support short of the universe as a whole (using the word whole with reservations), and I don't think that is helped very much by getting it into a beard and wrinkles (of finite thought). It is so hot this morning that I shall not walk to the p.o. but letter and books will go together.                          *Yours ever, O. W. H.*

*Beverly Farms, August 6, 1917*

*My dear Laski:* Your man Berth seems to me to have sucked other people's candy—Hegel's, Bergson's, Sorel's, Marx's, Proudhon's —until he drools.[1] Anyone who is contemptuously cocksure warrants a contemptuous retort. Hegel's trilogies when applied to concrete events in time may here and there furnish an amusing or even a suggestive synthesis at the hands of the original master, but applied by Berth, aided by Bergson, to transcending the concept and getting into life they make me puke. Pray what is Berth but an intellectual—a parasite of concepts? Transcending the concept has no meaning to my mind except thinking a little more accurately. If it is getting outside of thought then it has no validity except for the one who experiences it and I hope that for my time the policemen will be able to take care of the transcenders. The way in which Berth talks of the producers, as if only those produced who were in manual contact with the product would be enough to make me sure that I had no use for him. What is production? Man does not produce matter or force, to use popular

---

[1] See, *supra*, p. 69.

[2] *Progress and History*; essays arranged and edited by F. S. Marvin (1916). Among the essays in the volume was "Science" by the editor.

[1] Édouard Berth, *Les méfaits des intellectuels* (1914).

terms. All that he does is to determine the direction of a force—and every one who has shared in the determining of direction from the time the seed went into the ground to the time when I eat the bread or wear the shirt has shared in producing that which I consume. The architect produces more than the brick layer because he determines motion on a larger scale—and in a hundred years Descartes or Kant produces more than either.

I have finished the book since the last sentence and my opinions have not changed. I do not believe with him that man is a little God over against the universe. I do not believe that either Berth or Bergson has a supraconceptual vision that entitles them to bully me or gives authority to the Catholic Church. I might go on—but I must close in order to walk to the village. I busted a hot water bottle in my bed last night and so had to take to the couch, *per quod* I slept late and now at 4 pm have not yet gone out. I shall enclose the volume in a huge tobacco box—or rather my wife has —& shall post it with this. When I go to town, thanks to Berth and others I shall try to get Pascal & some volume of Proudhon.

*Aff'ly yours, O. W. H.*

I reopen this letter to say apropos of your English socialists—that while I hold myself open to giving open-minded consideration to all attempts by society to deal consciously with its destiny as a whole, I never read a socialist yet from Karl Marx down, and I have read a number, that I didn't think talked drool. Nor do I expect to hear anything better from anyone who hopes to regenerate society via property. And I believe myself able and hold myself ready at all proper seasons to give the reasons for my faith.

*O. W. H.*

Some essays by the great Webb in Fabian days I thought were slobber, if that is worse than drool. . . .

*Cambridge, Mass., August 7, 1917*

*My dear Justice:* I am behindhand in my comments—but I have been (a) hot and (b) absorbed as a colleague fell ill and threw his work on my none-too-broad shoulders. Wherefore I could not even imitate Balaam's ass and prophesy.

I am in accord with your remarks on progress. I think we are mistaking material advance for spiritual enrichment. The number of people who contentedly believe that we grow better as the clock slips by is really appalling. I suspect the fact is that unless you are willing to cultivate an intellectual detachment you grow into that lazy optimism as an excuse for the facts. I can *see* real progress in scientific achievement but though it's added to the comfort of the world I doubt whether as yet it has directed the desires of men and women into socially productive channels and that's all *I*

care about. Until we go beyond the stomach stage of civilisation
I think the less we talk about progress the better.

I knew Berth would touch you up. Really I think it's a more
significant book than you say, even while I grant its inconsistencies, confusions, and syntheses of alien ideas. But it cleverly presents a point of view which is, I think unfortunately, gaining increasing acceptance: namely that an intellectual class cannot really
be of use to the working class of a community, that the security of
the latter will lie not in the intelligence they can muster but in the
fused impulses for which they stand. It teaches those who will
listen that mind doesn't really matter, that if you hit a forge with
a hammer you are *eo nomine* one of the elect and it asks you not
to mind that the avenue of the intellect is closed to you since all
great action really springs from the passions. There is a sufficient
atom of truth in that to win the approval of those who won't see
that the only real sin is ignorance and the only real path of advance, the conquest of knowledge. Of course a Descartes really
effects more than Marconi; but when a sufficiently pinchbeck
Descartes tells the poor Jacques Bonhomme that it isn't so, with
a real charm of style and the pleasant flavour of vituperation which
makes a book readable, Jacques is going to listen; and it doesn't
seem to me that one ought to neglect the merchants of popular
opinion merely on the score of disagreement. When we know the
springs of thought we know the springs of action & I think that
the penalisation of intelligence is a real characteristic of our time.

I'm glad you are going to attempt Proudhon. I recommend (a)
the *Principe fédératif* and (b) the *Justice dans la révolution* as
the fundamental things. He is a great and misunderstood man.
Sainte-Beuve wrote a delicious life of him.

I was glad of that too-short glimpse of you both.

*Yours ever, Harold J. Laski*


*Beverly Farms, September 2, 1917*

I have assumed that if
you wanted to come you
would let me know.

*Dear Laski: Tempus fugit.* On Monday September 24 at the latest
we leave here. There is a dame coming Tuesday who may stay
over Sunday next though I doubt it. My nephew & his wife have
asked themselves here, I think for the 13th & 14th—and my last
Sunday (23$^d$) before leaving hardly will be available. The rest of
the time I believe is free. I suppose you are busy with your book
&c. but I should be sorry not to see you again.

*Yours, O. W. Holmes*

*The New Republic*
*New York City, September 5, 1917*

*My dear Justice:* I wish indeed that I had been at work on my book; but instead I have for the last three weeks been slaving away here on what, in rarely optimistic moments, I like to think is the formation of American policy. In real fact I think it could not be so dignified; but to write three notes and two leaders each week, together with a book review, must be very like writing an opinion.[1] The result is extreme doubt on my part as to whether I have a mind any longer. I have gone home o'night and read Balzac and his like in complete defiance of the rigid rules of civilised existence.

Well! There have been compensations. A visit to Felix in Washington last week-end convinced me of two things. (a) Washington is not Washington without you. I paid my bow to 1720 I. Street but I would fain have had it occupied. (b) John Chipman Gray was right when he said that the real rulers of a society are undiscoverable.[2] Mr. Wilson has charge of foreign policy and Felix seems to sponsor the rest of the government. To my certain knowledge he directs the War Department; Mr. Baker is the pale wraith that Felix casts before him in his progress. I saw that he has almost annexed the Shipping Board; there are similar rumours from the Department of Justice. And with it all, he is light and debonair, purposive and a skilful administrator. I would like a little more articulation in the joints of his ideas; but I feel very proud of him.

. . . Of course I am coming down to see you, and I am trying, as I hope my wire will be able to tell you, to bring F. Hackett along. To persuade that shy genius that you have tastes for conversation outside the frolicsome Felix and the inspired Walter Lippmann and me, the dolorous, will be marked on my grave as an achievement.

My love to you both.     *Yours ever affectionately, Harold J. Laski*

*Beverly Farms, September 6, 1917*[1]

No. 2

*Dear Laski:* Your letter was handed to me as I posted an answer to your telegram which was telephoned to me. I add that Hackett will be welcome if you can get him, though generally I think a *tête à*

---

[1] The anonymous notes and leaders by Laski have not been identified.
[2] This was one of the fundamental theses of Gray's *The Nature and Sources of the Law* (1909).
[1] A brief note from Holmes, dated September 5, 1917, is omitted. It contained a favorable response to Laski's telegraphed suggestion that he might call on Holmes on September 15 with Francis Hackett.

*tête* is better than a conversation of three—which is a reflection *not* a discouragement. I just have sent to a Britoness his review of Gilbert Murray which pleased me and I hoped would pain her.[2]

The lady who formerly praised a review of yours[3] the other day wrote me that she thought you wrote the best reviews that were to be found in English.

That part of the *N. R.* that shapes our destinies I generally skip and so can't recite on your performances in that line. Deal gently with us as you determine our future.          *Aff'ly yours, O. W. H.*

> *The New Republic*
> *New York City, September 7, 1917*
>
> *My dear Justice:* Hackett can't get away, so I travel alone (not unwillingly). There is much to be said and I am eager for talk. He was very happy with your remark about his review. . . .
>
> I am tired wherefore silence becomes me. My love to you both.
>                              *Affectionately, Harold J. Laski*

> *Beverly Farms, September 9, 1917*
>
> *Dear Laski:* On Friday next—14th—I expect to go to town returning by the 4:27 p.m., a good train. I assume that this will not interfere with you as I think you probably would not come earlier —but the early word gets the worm. I see much jaw ahead.
>                              *Aff'ly yours, O. W. H.*

> *The New Republic*
> *New York City, September 11, 1917*
>
> *My dear Justice:* You and I will both travel on the 4:27 on Friday —for that is the train I planned to take. . . .
>                              *Affectionately, H. J. L.*

> *Cambridge, Mass., September 17, 1917*
>
> *My dear Justice:* It was an Olympian banquet and if I do not utter thanks it is because I merely helped you to realise your destiny. You gave me great thoughts to ponder and I felt very proud that my own ideals should reflect even so palely the splendor of your own. You have made this a great summer for me. *Forsan et haec olim meminisse juvabit.*
>
> If you do not make an engagement with some cherished friend

---

[2] The review (12 *New Republic* 138) was of Gilbert Murray's *Faith, War and Policy* (1917). Mr. Hackett found the "English self-praise" of Murray's essays thoroughly distasteful.

[3] See, *supra*, p. 20.

of the past, let us see you as you pass through. We are free and eager.

I append the books of which we spoke:—

C. Delisle Burns. *Greek Ideals.*

Guy-Grand. *Le procès de la démocratie.*

Russell Smith. *Harrington and his Oceana.*

I will write during the week. This is merely a salute in passing. My love to you both—                                *Affectionately, H. J. L.*

*Beverly Farms, September 19, 1917*

*Dear Laski:* It is a great pleasure to get such a charming letter from you and to believe that you enjoy our conversations as much as I do. With regard to seeing you on our way through Boston I am inclined to think we had better give it up. We probably shall have a number of things to attend to and in such circumstances I am hurried, worried, and cross. I am very sorry to miss seeing your wife again, but with you it is only a postponement as you will be in Washington.                        *Aff'ly yours, O. W. Holmes*

*Cambridge, Mass., September 29, 1917*

*My dear Justice:* Silence has many and good motives; the term began with a plethora of irritating duties and I imagined that you, too, would like to be free from correspondence until you had settled down. But I want this to arrive in time to wish you both the best of luck for the year.

I am really back in harness again. The main business is political theory with graduates—too many of them for the individualism I like but a subject which permits the expansion of my anarchic gospel. Today I hinted at some of your scepticisms about Plato with good effect; but an eager Ph.D. wanted to know where you had printed them and I collapsed.

I have read some great things recently about the way in which the *Conseil d'État* has worked out a theory of state-responsibility. . . . Bertrand Russell's new book made me half-angry and half-amused.[1] *La vie du droit* by one Cruet has many ideas well-stated without the scaffolding a German would leave behind. For the rest, I have written some speculations on the Presidency in this week's paper which I hope you will have time to read;[2] and I have started a new chapter of the *magnum opus.* . . .

*Yours affectionately, H. J. L. . . .*

---

[1] *Political Ideals* (1917).

[2] An anonymous leader, "The Future of the Presidency," 12 *New Republic* 234 (Sept. 29, 1917), emphasized the increasing tendency to transfer national power from the legislature to the executive.

*Washington, D.C., October 1, 1917*
*Dear Laski:* Your letter is doubly welcome because I was compelled to miss seeing you in Boston. You already excite my envy
for there is little more reading books for me. . . . I was kept in
a stew till Saturday night by the non-arrival of my trunks with
clothes, checkbooks &c. but they have come and I am beginning
to get into order. My wife & I opened, sorted, threw away, or put
away about 1 y$^d$ x 2y$^{ds}$ cube of books & pamphlets accumulated
during the summer—as my secretary also was late. He is a fresh
youth of somewhat explosive speech but time will tame [him],
coupled with such quelling power as I may possess.[1] I perceive
that it is time for me to be off for the opening of Court, call on
the President, &c. I fear that I shall be a bad correspondent, not
for want of will.

I will try to send you any decision that seems interesting that I
write—but won't make promises as I am rather balled up in that
direction.                                    *Aff'ly yours, O. W. Holmes*


*Cambridge, Mass., October 13, 1917*
*My dear Justice:* You will forgive my silence; for our little girl has
been very ill and that has occupied all my thoughts.
    . . . The Law School is one-third its size.[1] College has lost some
thousand students. But I think on the whole that there is more
seriousness about things than last year and it may well be that
people will come to see that education is a way of life and not the
collection of information. . . .

I saw the *bas-relief* of you the other day.[2] I think the girl has
been really successful. There are one or two touches I do not understand—but it is a real interpretation with a very human and
strong execution. Wherefore I had her cast it speedily that I might
add to my photographs.

My love to you both—         *Yours affectionately, Harold J. Laski*


*Washington, D.C., October 14, 1917*
*Dear Laski:* There is just time to write that I haven't time to
write. I haven't seen the articles you mention in the *New Republic*
because since I left B. F. I haven't received it, so far as I know,

---

[1] Holmes's law clerk in the October term, 1917, was Vaughn Miller.
[1] Laski served as Book Review editor of the *Harvard Law Review* in the
issues published between November 1917 and June 1919. His influence
was evidently important in other departments of the *Review*. See Chafee,
"Harold Laski and the *Harvard Law Review*," 63 Harv. L. Rev. 1398
(June 1950).
[2] Bashka Paeff (1893-    ), Russian sculptress, had recently been engaged in doing a bronze *bas relief* head of Holmes.

though I wrote changing my address. I am sorry, especially as to your defence of scholarship. I don't think so much of Duguit & Co. as you seem to—though I quite admit that Duguit is a thinker and an original man. I vainly tried to get B. Russell's *Philosophic Essays* before I left. You slightly surprise me by what you say about Sidgwick's book though I never read it. I had a great notion of him—I knew him slightly—but I confess that to the best of my recollection I was not stirred to the depth by his *Method of Ethics*. . . . I am busy as the devil in a gale of wind so no more at present from                          *Yours ever, O. W. Holmes*


                               *Washington, D.C., October 15, 1917*
*Dear Laski:* Your letter crossed a letter from me—I add one line more to say that I am very sorry that your child has been ill and hope, as I infer from your 'has been,' that she is better now. I am relieved to hear that you like the relief. Can *La loi* by LeRoy? be had in your parts? If so and it does not cost more than $5 will you please order it to be sent to me *with the bill?*
                               *Affectionately yours, O. W. H.*


                               *Cambridge, Mass., October 21, 1917*
*My dear Justice:* Enquiry among the foreign booksellers reveals the regrettable fact that Leroy's *La loi* must be ordered from France. I can therefore either send you my own copy, or order one to be procured for you. It costs about two dollars. You will issue your commands and I will obey them. I don't see why you should not borrow my copy—your nerves notwithstanding. But I am ever your dutiful servant. . . .
  My love to you both—    *Affectionately yours, Harold J. Laski*


                               *Washington, D.C., October 24, 1917*
*Dear Laski:* Many thanks for your offer—I will order Brentano to get the book for me, and not trouble you. I am glad the little girl is all right. The strain here has not stopped—but I have just sent my only opinion to the printer[1] and expect to have everything cleaned up and to be at leisure very *anonly*. I also have had a brisk little lumbago from which I now am happily recovered. No reading of course, except petitions for *certiorari* and some pretty light matters that my wife has read to me at night.
  We still are fed by venal ravens but the servants even now I

---

[1] At the sitting on November 5, 1917, Holmes delivered the Court's opinion in *Fidelity & Columbia Trust Co.* v. *Louisville*, 245 U.S. 54.

presume are steaming toward Washington—with them *adieu* freedom.

It makes me feel quite cultivated even to read the titles of the books that you report reading. If I get a peek into one I shall be proud. I am glad and relieved that you like the *bas relief*. Would that I could write more but I can't.     *Aff'ly yours. O. W. Holmes*

*Washington, D.C., November 7, 1917*
*Dear Laski:* Your looked for letter[1] at once relieves and increases my anxiety. I am always afraid you run your machine too hard. We all feel that *we* are exceptions to the ordinary rules, but it is dangerous to yield to the illusion. 'In the vulgar herd there is one more than each of us suspects.' 'If you can't be good, be careful.' I read no books (except a detective story) but you make me want to see Marsiglio of Padua—I shall inquire at the Congressional Library. I haven't received the *Harvard Law Review* which they used to send to me. Oh yes—I have read *Le feu*—by Barbusse— the most vivid picture of trench life. I believe that like other Frenchmen he exaggerates the facts in order to give a true impression of the unimaginable. I feel that I have known things like in kind though less in degree—as when I nearly died of the cold in front of Fredericksburg. However, I mention him for a different matter which made me think of you. Not only does he share what I think the illusion of the passion for equality that makes (Faguet?) think it an injustice of nature that men should be born with diverse talents or lack of them—but like (I think) the *Méfaits des intellectuels*[2]—he insists that truth is simple—the implication being that all the complexities of the economists and philosophers are cobwebs woven in paid defence of things as they are. I think this the most ominous and dangerous humbug ever offered to the Crowd. Let the mass of men once believe that, as a religion, and reason is powerless and anything may happen. He treats those who don't admit it as knaves or fools—and I return the compliment.

I also have been under the weather—first with lumbago, then with a violent cold that kept me in the house two days and then seemed to depart as suddenly as it came. I don't believe in remedies, especially for colds—there are too many—but I am half convinced that there is something in a simple one, ½ teaspoonful (15 drops) aromatic ammonia, ½ teaspoonful bicarbonate of soda, in

---

[1] In this letter, omitted from this edition, Laski wrote that he had had "a slight attack of pneumonia" and that Marsiglio of Padua's *Defensor Pacis* is one of the great books of the world.

[2] See, *supra,* p. 71, note 1.

½ tumbler of hot water. As usual I must content myself with a bulletin as I have a lot to do. I am thankful that you are all right —but again beseech caution. . . .     *Aff'ly yours, O. W. Holmes*

I hope that your wife has not been too tired by the successive illnesses? Remember me to her, please—

*Cambridge, Massachusetts, November 11, 1917*
*My dear Justice:* . . . Your remarks on Barbusse leave me a distinct sense of pleasure. I have not read it—I have not read any war-book since *Britling* splurged a new God on the world. My mind simply refuses to waste itself on these pronouncements that A and B and C have come to grips with reality and either prophesy that *they* will be made new men or that the world will be made different because of it. Whether it's *Le feu* or Wells or Sorel, I get from the facts only one certainty and that's the simple one that they are so damned complex that no phrase will resume them. My good-hearted colleagues seem to imagine that after the war the lion and the lamb will lie down together. The clergy seem to expect that the second coming is at hand after the first great allied victory. And I, being an optimist, still preach that Darwin was [like ?] and that Nature is not saltatory. I believe that the world could be organised far more wisely than it is but I add to that the corollaries (a) that I couldn't do it and (b) that most people are content. No one adequately realises how the state bases itself on the inertia of men. Even those who are most full of change have not thought out what will happen on the morrow of the Revolution. Russia shows it admirably; for there I take it you have a middle-class *bourgeoisie* playing the Gironde to an *ouvrier* Jacobin Club.[1] It's a natural enough struggle, but it shows how little agreement there is on what the good to be aimed at actually is. I wouldn't define it as Bishop Laurence [*sic*] would do;[2] and I expect that your ideal is incompatible with that of Benedict XV. And certainly until we all violently desire the same thing there is no room for formulas to Paradise. Until then I am satisfied to go on attempting diagnosis.

Your law review will come; but it will not be published until Monday or Tuesday. I think it's the best number in some years (perhaps because I have written in it). But seriously Duguit seems to me to have done the most effective piece of analysis since Ehrlich's *Grundelung* and that is saying a great deal. . . .

---

[1] On November 7, the Bolsheviks, having secured control of the Petrograd, Moscow, and other soviets, carried through a *coup d'état* in Petrograd, and on the 8th Kerensky fled, and Lenin became chief of the new government.
[2] William Lawrence (1850-1941), Episcopal Bishop of Massachusetts, was a leading son of Harvard and representative of orthodox good will.

I have read three books with deep pleasure recently. (I) Boissier's *La fin du paganisme* you probably know. If not, it will give you some very happy hours. (II) Cuq, *Manuel des institutions juridiques Romains*—is *à la* Girard, but at every point striking and original. The part on contract I thought particularly good. (III) Esmein's *Mariage au droit canonique*. This is specialised, but ever so fine.

My love to you both.           *Yours in the best of health, Harold*

*Cambridge, November 20, 1917*
*My dear Justice:* I hope you will get a chance to turn over the pages of Morley's *Reminiscences*—especially the first volume.[1] . . . I hope you have paid your due entrance-fee and bought the new volume of Sherlock Holmes (*His Last Bow*). . . .

My love to you both—           *Yours ever, Harold J. Laski*

*Washington, D.C., November 22, 1917*
*Dear Laski:* The billows of the week begin to subside. I have written two cases and shall distribute the last of the two tomorrow.[1] We don't have a conference till Monday morning and then I believe adjourn for a fortnight. Saturday will give me time to get ready to recite so far as I am not now prepared. So I begin an answer to yours of the day before yesterday this evening, just for the pleasure of realizing that there is intellectual intercourse still left in this world. I wrote to some one, I think in England, in apology for buying an engraving the other day, that if we ceased to be interested in philosophy and art the war became a fight of swine for swill. I don't know that I have read a word since I last wrote—but I have got about half through Marsilius (*Defensor Pacis*) and now appreciate the grounds for your enthusiasm. Also I actually got a touch of amusement out of him—where he mentions an argument *vs* elective monarchs that they will be arrogant like the *nouveaux riches*—fancy *nouveaux riches* of 1320. As to reminiscences of Morley and the like—*pas a preesong*—as we say in German. Nothing that doesn't smack of abstraction except Sherlock Holmes, which I shall order forthwith. I do own the French book on the Law that you recommended—and ὡς ταχιστα I shall faithfully study the *Law Review*. . . .

For you must know that not having our official at homes on Monday we like the young ones to come in quietly on Thursday

[1] Laski reviewed the volumes in 13 *New Republic* 286 (Jan. 5, 1918).
[1] On November 26 Holmes delivered the Court's opinions in *Wear* v. *Kansas*, 245 U.S. 154, and *Day* v. *United States, id.,* 159.

and so today G[eorge] R[ublee] [2] and his wife, Miss Noyes, and some others—as well as Tommy Barbour,[3] who has spent a night or two here—enlivened your venerable and rather headachey and dyspeptic friend on his return from Court. I rejoice at what you say good about Pound as I prefer to and do believe in him, and he has been more or less attacked I think. I shall have dyspepsia if I write more tonight, so I adjourn to solitaire and a tale read by my wife downstairs.

November 23. I am converting misfortune into a source of satisfaction. For some years I have had trouble with my teeth on the left side of my mouth and I remember that as long ago as when I was in the Law School when I was getting up my first case to argue before old Parker,[4] being much excited and having got a case for a skiandhu with which to stick the enemy in the guts, I had a violent neuralgia in the same side of my face. My wife tells me that the doctor had told her that the disturbance of a great nerve by my wound at Antietam, when I was shot through the neck and for some weeks couldn't get my left arm away from my body, sooner or later would be likely to give me this sort of trouble. So I at least can pretend to myself that my discomforts came from that source—and inwardly swagger. Tommy Barbour has gone, a delightful creature and model guest. There was something that I had in mind to tell you about him last night but I can't think what it was. It shall go hard with me in the next fortnight if I don't have time to finish the *Defensor* and to read you and Duguit in the *Law Review*. I don't see possible work ahead sufficient to take away all leisure. At present the *New Republic* of the last weeks lies unopened on my table. Before you write the last word on the political theories of Christ won't you have to study the Talmud? Perhaps already in your omniscience you are familiar with that work. Well I must go to work. Remember me to your wife.

*Aff'ly yours, O. W. Holmes*


*Cambridge, Mass., November 28, 1917*
My dear Justice: . . . My brother, who has just been invalided out of the army, already begins to write to me (1) as a crotchety old colonel—he is twenty-seven; (2) as a professional strategist

---

[2] George Rublee (1868-1957) graduated from the Harvard Law School in 1895, during World War I was associated with government agencies in Washington, and was for many years a member of the Washington firm of Covington, Burling, Rublee, Acheson & Shorb.

[3] Thomas Barbour (1884-1946), friend and neighbor of Holmes's in Beverly Farms, Professor of Zoology at Harvard; related by marriage to Holmes.

[4] Joel Parker (1795-1875), after serving as Chief Justice of the Supreme Court of New Hampshire was Professor of Law at Harvard from 1848 until 1868.

of the old school who critically approves of the new methods; and (3) as the expert soldier who feels, damn it! that the thing oughtn't to be in the hands of the civilians. It's so gloriously English—the more so because he hasn't a drop of English blood in his veins. . . .

My love to you both—

*Yours ever affectionately, Harold J. Laski*


*Washington, D.C., November 30, 1917*

*Dear Laski:* You are a splendid young enthusiast and make me feel more alive. Your letter finds me in a happy humor to receive it for my work is done, for the moment. I have sent round an opinion in which I take three pages to say what should be said in a sentence, but which Brandeis thought ought to be put in solemn form because of its importance.[1] It is hard to dilate upon the obvious even when one is in a bare majority and may by one's efforts turn it into a minority. Also I have finished Marsilio and in a few minutes expect to return it to the Library (I hate to have other people's books) whither I am going, to compare the etching over which I am hesitating—Van Dyck—3ᵈ state—with the first state or reproduction of the same. I expect to find that it has lost nothing by the additions and that the work is as fresh as when it was born —I can't believe that it could be more vivid. That done, I recur to the *Harvard Law Review* and your article in the Fall Literary Review of the *N. R.* on *The Literature of Politics.* I sympathize with the young as you know, but I have the foibles of the old. It riles me to note the air of having it all for the first time that is so common in the contributors to that noble sheet.

*Later:* It is done—the book returned—the etching compared— your article and some others in the *N. R.* read. Yours to my mind the only good one of the first four. Even F. H. seems to me to have bit off a little too much.[2] You I think are open to a slight criticism for airy references to things that you know damned well your readers don't know about. Do you know anything about Prof. Goodnow's 'Splendid book on Social Reform & the Constitution'

---

[1] The case has not been identified. It is not improbable, however, that it was a draft opinion in *Hitchman Coal and Coke Co.* v. *Mitchell,* 245 U.S. 229 (delivered Dec. 10, 1917). Among Holmes's papers are copies of two dissenting opinions which he prepared in that case. In the end, however, Holmes delivered no opinion but, with Clarke, J., concurred in Brandeis's dissent. The majority, in an opinion by Pitney, J., held that officers of the United Mine Workers union might be enjoined from approaching the plaintiff's employees seeking to persuade them to join the union when those employees had signed yellow-dog contracts at the time when they secured employment.

[2] The Fall Literary Review (13 *New Republic,* Nov. 17, 1917, part II, 1) included an essay by Francis Hackett, "With Malice Toward None." It was an attack on the chauvinistic condemnation of all things German and all things Prussian.

(Beard p. 4)?[3] It sounds as if I ought to read it. I hoped to dilate
more at length but I must go back to my print seller—with my
etchings under my arm and buy (one or both?) and otherwise
bustle, but I would give one dollar and twenty-five cents for a
comfortable jaw with you about nothing in particular this afternoon. You delight me by your reference to Hobbes in your letter.
I think you seem to overrate Figgis[4]—who seemed to me a useful
worm rather than a flyer.

À bientôt.                                                      Aff'ly, O. W. H.


*Washington, D.C., December 3, 1917*
*Dear Laski:* Now Duguit in the *H.L.R.* is read—with the anticipated result.[1] The account of previous doctrines is good—and his
own I presume will have practical effects as an emotional stimulus
and a text accepted by many. As theory I don't get much nourishment from it, my own views being simple and brutal. I don't care
whether you use or discard the word sovereignty. I agree that although the lawmaker cannot admit that anything that it enacts is
not law, there is a large margin of *de facto* limit in the common
consciousness that various imaginable enactments would provoke
a general uprising. But that is an extralegal fact of uncertain
boundaries. The only limit that I can see to the power of the lawmaker is the limit of power as a question of fact. I don't think
Duguit's criterion is any better in *genere* than Herbert Spencer's
—indeed it is less definite.

When I talk of law I talk as a cynic. I don't care a damn if
twenty professors tell me that a decision is not law if I know that
the courts will enforce it. (Of course—when I speak of the law-
making power I mean concurrence of all the necessary organs in
putting the enactment into execution.) And I understand by human
rights what a given crowd will fight for (successfully). Old Agassiz
(Louis) once said that in some part of Germany if you added a
farthing to the price of a glass of beer there would be a revolution.
If that was true, to have beer at the current price was one of the
rights of man in that place.

---

[3] In Charles A. Beard's essay "Political Science in the Crucible" (*loc. cit.
supra*, p. 3) he had thus referred to Frank J. Goodnow's *Social Reform and
the Constitution* (1911).
[4] In his essay "The Literature of Politics" Laski had praised Figgis for
bringing historical perspective to political inquiry.
[1] "The Law and the State," 31 *Harv. L. Rev.* 1 (November, 1917). The
problem discussed by Duguit was whether there exists "a jural principle
(*une règle de droit*) superior to the State, which forbids it from doing certain things and commands it to do others." 31 *Harv. L. Rev.* 1, 2 (1917).
To this question Duguit gave an affirmative answer. The bulk of the article
was made up of a critical examination of German and French theories of
the state which had prevailed in the nineteenth and twentieth centuries.
Duguit himself denied both the personality and the sovereignty of the state.

It seems to me all fact—and this endless jaw the blowing of soap bubbles—but I think he brings out the thinness of the Hegelian theory uncommonly well. While I think it impossible to put the German practise in a logical hole, my objection to it is one that admits that there is no superior arbiter—it is one of taste—but when men differ in taste as to the kind of world they want the only thing to do is to go to work killing.

If Duguit's criterion is a new bill of rights to be enforced by the Courts it adds nothing to juridical theory on the fundamental problem. If it is not, then it is merely a counsel of perfection that if accepted might stimulate a revolution at a different point. But the question when and where you will *revolve* is a question of how a given crowd feels at a given time—not a juridical question at all. These again in haste.

I bought both Van Dyck and a rather expressive Whistler—the latter in guise of a Xmas present for my wife.     *Aff'ly, O. W. H.*
*La loi* has come.


*Cambridge, Mass., December 8, 1917*
*My dear Justice:* I spent four delirious days (and nights) at Smith College—hence your letters have only just been found. Chiefly, they made me realise the inadequacy of any save spoken words, for in your comments on Duguit, I pine for definitions and precise connotation and, above all, for argument. But some remarks I must adventure to save myself from bursting.

You seem to me to stop before Duguit (I do not swallow him, or anyone else, whole) begins. You say that what the courts pronounce is law. So it is; but it is not less important to know the sources whence it derives. Now I take it that one of the main changes of the last thirty years—you are partly responsible for it —is the addition of new elements to its determination—*e.g.* the considerations you had in mind in *Coppage* v. *Kansas*[1] could not have been even understood by your brother Field in the old days. Duguit says that more and more the courts will have to pronounce a law that takes into account the modern disposition of economic forces as, I think, (under correction) the Supreme Court did when it decided the constitutionality of the Adamson Law.[2] I think there that the chief and McKenna, J. would have had real difficulty if they had not been statesmen enough to let political necessity colour the direction of their mind. The thing means, I take it, that courts will more and more find that their sovereignty is going to be bound by the nature of their decisions. Three more decisions

[1] See, *supra*, p. 10.
[2] See, *supra*, p. 52.

like that of the majority in the *Lochner* case[3] would, after the war,
paralyse any organ or organs that attempted its enforcement. The
truth is that we are witnessing a revival of 'natural' law and
'natural' is the purely inductive statement of certain minimum conditions we can't do without if life is to be decent. The working-class
today won't accept decisions or statutes that are not based upon
the acceptance, voluntary or not, of these standards—and law and
everything else has got to shape itself to their determination. That
means the end of the *bourgeois* state—and we head fast for what
I don't think will be pleasant, the transference of economic and
political power from the mercantile to the working-classes. I agree
heartily that where there is difference of taste there can't be compromise on conduct—but the extermination is going to be the destruction of things like *laissez-faire* and the like *i.e.* anything that
does not correspond to the ideas that are becoming increasingly
dominant of what justice means in cash terms. It means a state
with limited powers simply because (thank God) the greatest discovery of the war is the relentless bureaucracy involved in state-
socialism and its utter incompatibility with liberty. The things the
crowd will die for will be the democratic control of industry, the
control of prices and profits, a graduated income tax and the like
—and because the crowd *will* die for them, as you say they are
natural rights. But I also think—what you omit—that they represent a bigger thing than the nineteenth century understood—the
movement towards the inductive realisation of these 'natural' rights
into a generalised social scheme in which a broad happiness (as
the Utilitarians would have put it) will be realised after a hell of
a row to get to it. Russia has started a movement of which the
evolution is still only at the beginning. I hope to see the best years
of it—first lean and hungry and then a larger fulfilment, because
they will have the epic proportions of the sixteenth and early
seventeenth centuries. But all this is talk for when I impinge on
the Washington horizon late next month. And I ache to talk of
it. . . .

I hammer at Figgis *et al.* for a definite (and noble) cause. I am
eager to get politics taught historically instead of descriptively and
I think that to push home the weakness of the second method and
the strength of the first is the one way to do it. I never realised
so much the pathos of analytic explanations of history until I took
down again T. H. Green on *Political Obligation* and saw how
little he had to say of first-rate significance on Hobbes & Locke &
Rousseau simply because he hadn't grasped their historic perspective. Figgis does that and I know no one else apart from Maitland
(*Coll. Papers* III. "The Body Politic") of real originality who does

---

[3] See, *supra*, p. 7.

and writes in English. And I carefully mentioned no book in that article that I didn't either like or hate greatly.

. . . I think on the whole that it really is doubtful, once you regard liberty as a process and not an emotion, whether Rousseau didn't do more harm than good. . . .

My love to you both—      *Yours affectionately, Harold J. Laski*

*Washington, D.C., December 15, 1917*
*Dear Laski:* Even on Saturday p.m. I must be brief. I enclose a letter from my N. Y. friend [1]—as to whom I never am sure whether he has a big piece of the future in his belly or only is riding his hobby hard. I have had striking *aperçus* from him but on his main points the wave swells with mighty portent and then so far as I am concerned sinks away without breaking. I have little to disagree with in your last letter, though I don't get much nourishment from Duguit or have much sense of novelty. I am more impressed by LeRoy, *La loi,* which I have managed to finish. I should have to take more time than I have to reduce any criticism that I might make to the articulate. The main point that is articulate with me now is that the very interesting statement of the change that he makes ends even in its latest phase in change *through* the courts and so subject to the sovereignty that can abolish the Courts. But it is nonetheless interesting and suggestive—it makes me think however that law has developed more serenely and with fewer superfluous hitches in England and here where people have been less bothered by sweeping and inadequate generalizations. 199 U.S. 401, *411.* [2]

As to whether Rousseau did more harm than good, might you not have the same doubt as to any great historical cause of later effects—when a thing has happened that is the way this universe came out and I shut up—not being a cosmic critic. Good and bad seem to me phrases for the future—that we sometimes apply to

---

[1] Franklin Ford (1848-1918), Director of the "General News Office" in New York, utilized that agency and an active pen to spread his gospel that the news system of the nation and the banking system of society must be utilized and organized as the central instruments of political and economic authority.

[2] *Carroll* v. *Greenwich Insurance Co.* (1905). In the course of an opinion for the Court, sustaining an Iowa statute prohibiting rate combinations by insurance companies, Holmes at 411 had written as follows: "Therefore the act in question does little if anything more than apply and work out the policy of the general law [as to acts in restraint of trade] in a particular case. Again, if an evil is specially experienced in a particular branch of business, the Constitution embodies no prohibition of laws confined to the evil, or doctrinaire requirement that they should be couched in all-embracing terms. It does not forbid the cautious advance, step by step, and the distrust of generalities which sometimes have been the weakness, but often the strength of English legislation."

the past but justifiably only as a means of helping to bring about
the future we desire. . . .

Hannis Taylor only submitted a brief on the Draft. Reading
some of his anarchist manifestos in one of the cases, I relieved my
mind to my neighbor Vandevanter by whispering "I do despise a
martyr. He is a pigheaded adherent of an inadequate idea"—and
then I felt better.

Now I must shut the dam—and visit the handfooter—χειροποδ
—with a brief drama from a letter from Mrs. Dow of Beverly
Farms—

Two old friends meet—"What are you doing now?"—"I'm in
the legislature but don't tell my dear old mother. She thinks I'm
a bartender."                                              *Aff'ly, O. W. H.*

*Cambridge, Mass., December 18, 1917*
*My dear Justice:* This is a letter I intended to write three days ago;
but I got into complications trying to finish a paper on the Conciliar Movement for the American Historical Association[1] and I
have had no leisure. It is a nuisance that people can't have dinners
and luncheons except to the accompaniment of dull papers on
duller subjects; and I had so many better things to do.

However, the interval introduced me to Franklin Ford and
Nicholas Murray Butler. Ford sounds a really interesting person
and I will try and look him up in New York next week. Butler's
review of my book is superb.[2] I spoke rather frankly about him in
the *N. R.* some months back[3] and this, I take it, is the answer. He
says, (1) I don't understand anything about (a) politics (b)
philosophy. (2) my book is only fit for the waste-paper basket.
(3) I had better read the "classic" works of J. W. Burgess. (4)
European thinkers have never understood that distinction between
state and government which is a commonplace of these United
States. I don't know whether to commit suicide or write another
book. I think it will be the latter. Anyhow, I shan't decide hurriedly.

[1] The paper was read at the annual meeting of the Association in Philadelphia. See 23 *American Historical Review* 513 (April 1918).
[2] Butler reviewed Laski's *Studies in the Problem of Sovereignty* (1917) in
54 *Educational Review* 513 (December 1917). Though he commended "a
certain agreeable scholarship such as Oxford, and apparently Oxford alone
can give," he described Laski's pluralistic theories of sovereignty as "grotesque." Butler ascribed the "philosophical frame" in which Laski's scholarship was set to "the author's very superficial knowledge of political theory,"
and suggested that Laski should "read, mark, learn, and inwardly digest
the first 183 pages of the classic work of Professor Burgess entitled *Political
Science and Constitutional Law.*"
[3] Perhaps the unsigned review of Butler's *World in Ferment* (1917), 12
*New Republic* 251 (Sept. 29, 1917).

*In re* Ford, I regret that he is cursed with the belief in the practical man. My own experience has been that nowhere do you find a being so tortured by an unconscious metaphysic and psychology as you do in the business world. As to centralisation I would urge *him* to read the 8 reports of the recent Industrial Unrest Commission in England [4] in which he will discover how many of the ills that have occurred have been due to the inherent vices of a centralised system. But I am glad he reads Jhering and Duguit.

It is with texts and texts that I have been concerned since I last wrote you, save for a piece on Dilke and one on Morley in the *N. R.* . . . Nick of Cusa I liked and Gerson I liked while I was doing that Conciliar paper—but the real prize was the letters of Aeneas Sylvius who became Pius II.[5] A real *succès de scandale*—titillating to one's natural love of the veiled indecencies of natural man and a perfect picture of the *nouveau riche* in ecclesiastical politics. He never told a lie simply because he found that no one ever believed the truth! You get a first-rate liking for him despite the harm he did. If you can stomach the Latin I expect you'd get some real amusement from this. . . .

My love to you both—                          *Yours affectionately, H. J. L.*


*Washington, D.C., December 26, 1917*
*Dear Laski:* All good wishes to you and yours. Mr. Ford has sent me the enclosed for you as you will perceive. I doubt if he is under illusions as to the practical man—and I feel bound to say that although the major premises of successful men of affairs are apt to be inarticulate—they are likely to be profound. And when once in a while you meet a man who can both do things and tell how he is very illuminating. I insist on this to myself as well as to you because I have no instruments but reason and such insight as I possess—and often have to regret my ignorance of business.

I have not had a minute to read your articles that you mention, but I presume that they are on my table and I shall expect to before this week is over. Meantime of course every instinct of mine is with you in your faith in reason. Reason among other things means the facts—and those who disregard it are likely to get a bump before they finish. But as I grow older I realize how limited a part reason has in the conduct of men. They believe what they want to—and although liable to shipwreck they very generally

---

[4] *Command Papers* #8662-8669.
[5] Enea Silvio de Piccolomini (1405-1464) was Pope Pius II from 1458 to 1464; conspirator against Eugenius IV; active in conciliar movement; author of plays and novels. His *Commentaries* was a work of autobiography and history.

get off with a hole in the bottom of their boat and stick an old
coat into that. When I read Malthus I thought he had ripped the
guts out of some humbugs—but they are as alive as ever today.
Humbugs have no guts—and live all the better without them. Now
I am off for business.                    *Aff'ly yours, O. W. Holmes*

*December 28, 1917*

*Dear Laski:* Many thanks for the book[1] which looks very amusing
but which as yet I can do no more than glance at. I found one of
your articles in the *N. R.* on Waldstein's book—which tickled me.[2]
The other I fear has disappeared into the *Ewigkeit*. I have been
too busy for pleasure and still am. Hill has just left us for N. Y.,
and later hours and early rising have added a straw to an overburdened Isaachar. I can do no more than send you my thanks
and love.                                             *O. W. H.*

*Cambridge, Mass., January 1, 1918* [1]

*My dear Justice:* May this be the happiest of your years. You will
help greatly to make it among the happiest of mine.

I ought to have written before; but I have had a week in New
York and Philadelphia[2] and it has not been the right atmosphere
for the written word. And my return was coincident with a domestic catastrophe (the pipes emulated the weather) and I have been
busy preventing the efforts of my wife from leading her to an
early grave. However, I have at least collected some things I want
to say.

To Philadelphia I went for professional purposes; and if there
is anything more pathetic than an academic congress I have yet
to meet it. I saw four hundred professors and met about fifty; and
I thought them almost all narrow and illiberal, and too many of
them ill-read. Such dicta as that White C. J. is the greatest judge
who ever sat on the Supreme Court; that Lowell is the greatest
student of government since Tocqueville; that a theory of sovereignty can usefully neglect all ethical, political and psychological
considerations; that Lippmann's *Preface to Politics* is too irreligi-

[1] Not identified.
[2] In 13 *New Republic* 155 (Dec. 8, 1917) Laski had reviewed Sir Charles
Waldstein's *Aristo-Democracy* (1917). The review contained reflections on
contrasts and similarities between English and American institutions. See
further Laski's later communication in response to a protest from Sir Charles:
14 *New Republic* 57 (Feb. 9, 1918).
[1] A brief message of New Year's wishes from Holmes is omitted.
[2] At the annual meeting of the American Historical Association. See, *supra*,
p. 88.

ous to be "safe" for the undergraduate—these are a few of the
things seriously told me in a tone of importance. I came away
quickly lest I should think myself a great and learned man. New
York restored my perspective. Hackett and Lippmann and I had
some good talk. . . . Hackett has a collection of reviews almost out
of the press;[3] and I think his foreword on criticism one of the
ablest short pieces even he has done. Lippmann (whom I hadn't
seen in months) I found vastly improved by homely pleasures; and
I imagine that the wife is as sensible in friendship as she is wealthy
in looks.[4] *Quid magis?* . . .

I have read Mr. Ford's pronunciamento but I find it difficult as
yet clearly understanding it; and I find real impedence [*sic*] in its
hyperbolic terminology; but I will re-read and digest. On business
men in general I don't share your enthusiasm. I have seen them
doing commerce and government and I have met able men. But
I did not see that they had—as a class—any light not elsewhere
vouchsafed. I should agree that an able mind would profit from
business experience but only as it would profit from any other.
I should largely deny that there is any real validity in the distinction between theory and practice. What business seems to do is to
give its practitioners a certain set of rules-of-thumb rarely thought
out, usually ill-digested and often highly questionable; as well as
a series of ethical principles which are only Hobbes without the
logic. I should say of them what I say to people who compare
your opinions with those of your colleagues that your superiority
consists in the emphasis you give to what is universal in the facts
at issue. The business man deals with particulars and he does not,
as a rule, rise above his special experience. F. W. Taylor, the
scientific management fellow,[5] is a shining example—so are Charles
Schwab[6] and Theodore Shonts.[7] Tupper[8] summed up their philosophy and they have a quantity-theory of life and of values, a pathetic belief in utilitarian ethics, which seems to me the merest
nonsense. Obviously this is food for thought and talk between us.
I would like to fight vigorously on the issue. . . .

[3] Francis Hackett, *Horizons* (1918).

[4] Walter Lippmann had married Faye Albertson in May 1917.

[5] Frederick Winslow Taylor (1856-1915) organized management in important steel companies; he was the author of *Principles of Scientific Management* (1911).

[6] Charles M. Schwab (1862-1939), self-made steel magnate who became
successively President of Carnegie Steel, and United States Steel, and Chairman of the Board of Directors of Bethlehem Steel Company.

[7] Theodore Perry Shonts (1856-1919), railroad executive and director.

[8] Martin Tupper (1810-1889), poetic champion of Victorian ideals; disappointed aspirant for the poet laureateship for which Tennyson was chosen;
author of *Proverbial Philosophy* (1838-1842).

For your trivial hours I hear great things of Somerville & Ross: *Irish Memories*, (Longman).

My love to you both—

> *Yours ever affectionately, Harold J. Laski*

*Cambridge, Mass., January 5, 1918*

*My dear Justice:* Fate has a grudge against me just now. We had no sooner solved our domestic issue than Diana had to have an operation which, though relatively slight, was really nerve-racking. . . .

I read Ford on Roosevelt[1] with real pleasure and I thought it a sane and well-balanced criticism. On the other hand, I do not share his enthusiasm over the possibilities of news and banking. The apotheosis of news seems to me more likely to result in Hearst and Northcliffe than in Croly or Massingham. It is less what is true than what sells; and though clearly the distribution of intelligence is bound to affect the future of organisation I think Ford is seriously confronted by the problem of adequate safeguards. One can, after all, so tell a story as to imply a thousand innuendoes—as where Northcliffe was wont to report Mr. Balfour as that "antiquated septuagenarian." I think he has to relate his news-office to the educational systems of the country and adapt its functions to the varying standards and demands and needs he will encounter. That, I think, means the federal system of which he seems to me unduly sceptical. So, too, with his banking and credit theory, the important thing to my mind is not either the systems or their programmes, but the use to which they are put. A banker, for instance, like Rothschild[2] appears to me not less a public danger than a public benefit. A man like your friend Paul Warburg[3] appears to me the system at its very best—cultured, eager, and genuinely interested in the universal aspects of his profession. But how much does he hear of or grasp the half-hidden movements that are stirring popular minds on the East side in New York or in the mountain ranges of Nevada? That astute old fellow Sully[4] once wrote something that has oddly but happily stuck in my memory (I think Burke quotes it in the *Present Discontents*): "*Les Révolutions qui arrivent dans les grands états, ne sont point un effet du*

---

[1] Franklin Ford's comment on Roosevelt has not been located.

[2] Alfred Charles de Rothschild (1842-1918), partner in Messrs. N. M. Rothschild & Sons; director of the Bank of England.

[3] Paul M. Warburg (1868-1932), partner in Kuhn, Loeb & Co.; member of Federal Reserve Board, 1914-1918.

[4] Duc de Sully (1560-1641); adviser, minister, and *confidant* of Henry IV. The quotation is from 1 Sully's *Memoirs* 133. Laski was, of course, right in believing that Burke quoted the passage in his "Thoughts on the Cause of the Present Discontents," 2 *Works of Edmund Burke* (Rafferty, ed., n.d.), 8.

*hazard, ni du caprice des peuples. Pour la populace, ce n'est jamais
par envie d'attaquer qu'elle se soulève, mais par impatience de
souffrir."* I feel very deeply that this describes a state of mind it
is becoming more and more possible to distinguish in its serious
beginnings; and I think that it will mean a discussion of government in other terms than Ford suggests. This is all great matter
for talk on the longed-for day when I can repeat my heresies from
the hearth-rug of your study. . . .  *Yours affectionately, H. J. L.*

*Cambridge, Mass., January 13, 1918*
*My dear Justice:* . . . I had a great talk in New York with Hackett
on Wednesday and his superb review of Sherman's book gave me
a new lease of life.[1] Please be sure not to miss it. It abounds in
unforgettable phrases. (Issue of Jan. 12).

. . . And as an appendix Pound & I agreed yesterday that if
you could hint to Brandeis that judicial opinions aren't to be
written in the form of a brief it would be a great relief to the
world. Pound spoke rather strongly as to the advocate in B. being
over-prominent in his decisions just as in his general philosophy.
This, of course, merely by way of a comment you may like to
have. . . .

And I have had some glorious reading. (I) Zeiller—*Politique de
S. Thomas,* a sober, careful and weighty analysis. (II) Picavet, *Histoire de la philosophie médiévale*—a superb book. (III) Bosanquet, *Philosophical Theory of the State*—watered Hegel but good
water. (IV) Gretton, *Modern History of the British People*—a
joyous two-volume gossip. (V) Trevelyan's *Charles Fox* which
never has and never will tire me. One hour with that fellow would
be worth half a hundred lives—beyond about ten people the only
thing worth the candle is the ideas in books. The real need is eight
hours free time a day and a pound of chocolate biscuits. In other
words I am a frank materialist.

Of importance is the fact that between February 1st and February 10th I have a holiday. Are you & Mrs. Holmes prepared for
a week-end debauch within that time? If so, I'd of course love to
come. And, if you feel up to it, I think Hackett would give his
soul to occupy the other bed. . . .   *Yours affectionately, H. J. L.*

*Washington, D.C., January 16, 1918*
*Dear Laski:* First as to your proposed visit. I need not say what
a delight it would be to me but at present I must hold it in suspense. If the weather in February should be what it is now we

[1] Reviewing Stuart P. Sherman, *On Contemporary Literature* (1917), 13
*New Republic* 318 (Jan. 12, 1918).

simply could not keep the upper rooms warm enough to make
them habitable. You know the difficulties as to coal. To them are
added others as to gas, so that at this writing I can't prophesy
what will be our condition next month. We will keep our eyes on
the weather and on the other matters and bring the matter up
again when the time draws near.

I wish I could answer your two delightful letters adequately,
but, as I warned you long ago, times come when it simply is impossible. Not working at night or even writing letters, which I
find advisable, makes my day-time so crowded that it is hard for
me to get a space of half an hour. What you say about the form
of Brandeis's opinions had been remarked on by me to him before
you wrote, if you refer to the form in a strict sense—the putting
in of headings and footnotes—and on one occasion I told him that
I thought he was letting partisanship disturb his judicial attitude.
I am frank with him because I value him and think he brings
many admirable qualifications to his work. In one case when he
wrote a long essay on the development of employers' liability[1] I
told him that I thought it out of place and irrelevant to the only
question: whether Congress had dealt with the matter so far as to
exclude state action.

Oh, how I envy your reading—not merely the leisure that gives
you the chance for it, but your knowledge of where to find the
books and your power of swift assimilation. I cannot get rid, however, of the apprehension that you are running your furnace (natural image in present circumstances) too hard. . . . By your suggestion I read Hackett's piece on Sherman. I am not quite as
warm as you—because I suspected that his book had more merit
than H's passion for Go as you please would let you believe—but
it certainly is brilliant.

My difficulty in writing about business is that all my interest is
in theory and that I care a damn sight more for ideas than for
facts. So it is really a discipline to myself that leads me to insist
on what I believe, that business men get a judgment generally, as
I said before, on inarticulate major premises, that can't be got
elsewhere. I know Pater but little—I didn't care much for most
that I read of his—but generally I agree with your contrast of
Berenson—I once spoke a few words on the difference between
knowing only the emotional result and knowing the causes—between qualitative and quantitative knowledge.[2]

Have I praised your review of Morley to you? It was admirable

[1] Dissenting in *New York Central* v. *Winfield*, 244 U.S. 147, 154 (1917).

[2] "The growth of education is an increase in the knowledge of measure.
To use words familiar to logic and science, it is a substitution of quantitative
for qualitative judgments." "Law in Science—Science in Law," *Collected
Legal Papers* (1920) 210, 231.

I thought. That on Dilke I have had no time for yet. I must shut
up. My love to you.                        *Aff'ly yours, O. W. Holmes*


*Washington, D.C., January 18, 1918*
*Dear Laski:* Whenever one says anything, one wants to explain
that one sees the other side. Of course I know that ideas are
merely shorthand for collections of the facts I don't care for. It is
the eternal seesaw of the universe. A fact taken in its isolation (to
quote myself) is gossip.[1] Philosophy is an end of life, yet philosophy is only cataloguing the universe and the universe is simply
an arbitrary fact so that as gossip should lead to philosophy, philosophy ends in gossip. This by way of postscript to yesterday.
                                                       *Yours, O. W. H.*


*Washington, D.C., January 25, 1918*
*Dear Laski:* By some mistake difficult to explain except that it got
hidden by other papers your letter of January 5 never was opened
by me till this morning. It is just as well I learn of your troubles
with Diana only when they are over.

I am just back from the funeral of my dear George Harrison's[1]
mother. It brings up that I recently have been thinking how rational men who have not merely accepted their environment without question can be Christians. It is like the justification of conventions—I respect a tall hat or the cult of monogamy not from
the internal self-justification of the accidents of space and time but
from the consideration that the inward necessity of man to idealize
must express itself in inadequate and transitory symbols of no
value in themselves but reverent for the eternal movement of which
they are the momentary form.

Well—the universe may be contemplated in two ways—one our
usual one, at the point of contact where it is finite, measurable,
predictable—the other as a whole, as an inexplicable mystery
which one can help oneself to realize by thinking that a roomful
of men would take us back to the unknown. If one dwells on that

---

[1] "The Class of '61," *Speeches* (1913) 95, 96: "I learned in the regiment and in the class the conclusion, at least, of what I think the best
service that we can do for our country and for ourselves: to see so far as
one may, and to feel the great forces that are behind every detail—for
that makes all the difference between philosophy and gossip, between great
action and small. . . ." See also "Speech at Brown University Com-
mencement," *Collected Legal Papers* (1920) 164, 166.
[1] George Leslie Harrison (1887-1958), was Holmes's secretary in 1913-
1914. He later became governor and president of the Federal Reserve Bank
of New York and president and chairman of the board of the New York
Life Insurance Company.

and becomes emotionally possessed by it one very well might accept any cult that he found at hand never troubling about its finite fallacies but taking it as the momentary expression of the eternal wonder.

You know my expression for it—as a bettabilitarian. A spontaneity taking an irrational pleasure in a moment of rational sequence.

I must be off.                                      *Aff'ly yours, O. W. H.*

*Cambridge, Mass., January 31, 1918*
*My dear Justice:* A bad cold and a heap of work have made correspondence difficult these last few days; but your footnote makes me want to utter a squeak at least of joyful agreement. So long as we have a veneration for reason and a scepticism in common there can be little ground for serious disagreement between us.

I have spent the week on Hegel—*The Philosophy of Right* and the *Phenomenology*. I began them in German, but, being human, I took refuge in my native tongue. I honestly thought them the greatest feat of speculative intelligence since the *Nicomachean Ethics*, and utterly unrelated to the life we live. Of course one can explain a world in that way, but it surely isn't our world; and I don't like *raison d'état* dressed up in Hellenic terms. None of his disciples, Bosanquet, McTaggart, Stirling[1] *et al* seem to realise that his equation state = society, while it may have been true in the Greek city-state, isn't true in a world so complex as our own. I think it's a magnificent piece of consistent thinking but when one interprets it in terms of function rather than programme, it clearly means that a state of 60 million people must act by delegates and delegates = Bismarck and not on my life will I give Bismarck the right to order me about until I have looked into the purpose behind his command. That's where I think most discussion of authority is invalid: it starts by accepting Aristotle's *Politics* Bk. 1, Ch. 2 about the τὸ εὖ ζῆν[2] and then fails entirely to see that in the modern state the term state as an operative fact is virtually equivalent to government and whether the acts of government are or are not in accord with the purpose of the state is very obviously a matter of opinion. But I am talking old stuff to you. Not that it's any the less true for that. . . .

My love to you both. . . .    *Yours ever affectionately, H. J. L.*

---

[1] James Hutchison Stirling (1820-1909), Scottish Hegelian; author of *The Secret of Hegel* (2 vols., 1865) and *Text-Book to Kant* (1881).

[2] In this book and chapter Aristotle had developed his thesis that the state came into existence after several villages had become united in a single community and that the continued existence of the state was justified for the sake of the good life.

*Washington, D.C., February 7, 1918*

*Dear Laski:* Now—today—has come the moment when I wish you would mention a book that I could get *right off* and that would feed the fountains of my soul. As to Hegel I never read the *Phenomenology*—I did the *philosophie* of *recht* more than once. The principal formula that it left in my mind was that I don't believe the King of Prussia was God, for all his talk—just as my critique on the *Logic* was that he couldn't persuade me that a syllogism could wag its tail. Like other philosophers it seems to me that his system is transitory and that his real contribution is a lot of penetrating *aperçus* that are quite independent of all his spider work. I say the same of Kant—and I daresay of everybody else who ever laid out life on an architectural plan. You remember Schopenhauer's remark that Kant's other categories besides cause and effect were blind windows. I have no doubt you see Hegel in a different light from that in which I do, but I think it would take some work to make me admire him on the grounds you mention.

Paul Warburg the other day told me that I was wrong when I bought a few etchings—that we should devote every cent to the production of tangibles, food, clothing, and the like. I don't know, but fear he is right, though I admit it unwillingly. Since the last word Miss Frances Noyes has been here for her usual Thursday call—do you know her? She is talking of going abroad on some job I don't approve of but, as in duty bound, I gave her a character in writing to help her to get the place. There were one or two artistic touches intended to give an impression of age and respectability that made me slightly smile. I don't quite know what you mean by your inquiry about Miss Paeff's *bas relief*—but I am greatly pleased that you speak so well of it. If you see her ever please give her my compliments. She seemed to me an attractive *Jeune mees* on the two occasions when I saw her. Everyone in relation with Felix seems to be or become attractive—perhaps by virtue of the relation. I now am expecting a call from the print seller who wanted to see my library & what few treasures I have —so I must shut up.                *Aff'ly yours, O. W. Holmes*

*Cambridge, Mass., February 10, 1918*

*My dear Justice:* I am ever so glad you are having a holiday; and herewith a list of recommendations.

1. Merz. *History of European Thought in XIXth Century.*
2. Hammond. *The Town Labourer.* (Longmans).
3. Gwynne & Tuckwell. *Life of Dilke.* (Macmillan).
4. G. P. Gooch. *History & Historians of XIXth Century.* (Longmans).

5. W. S. Ferguson. *Hellenistic Athens.* (Macmillan).
6. J. Chailley. *Administrative Problems of British India.* (Macmillan).

. . . I have done little this week except work and lie a-bed. For some unearthly reason I developed an abscess in that thing dignified by the name of frontal sinus and it has been giving me much pain; and I suppose I must have it out this week. . . . I read four volumes of Lecky with much enthusiasm and the feeling that his chapter on the French Revolution is the best thing in its compass in any language. Intermittently there have been large chunks of J. S. Mill whom to love is easy but whom to love greatly is impossible. . . .

It's wicked, but you never showed me Miss Noyes. You talk in superlatives, Felix casts his eyes to the ceiling, Mrs. Holmes relaxes; and all I know is that other people think her wonderful & you carefully conceal her from me. However, in April I shall drop in upon you and compel her production upon a bill in equity for specific performance.

My love to you both—                               *Affectionately, H. J. L.*

*Washington, D.C., February 12, 1918*

*Dear Laski:* If you are right and have to have an operation please let me know or tell some one to let me know as soon as you are through with it. I trust that there is nothing to be anxious about—but your careless and incidental way of mentioning the matter makes me suspicious—why not susponcious by inversion from *soupçon?* As to Miss Noyes I will do my best when you turn up —if a letter she got from me doesn't secure her a chance to go abroad before that time. I endeavored by a few happily chosen words to convey an untrue implication of middleaged dulness. She is a nice gal—and I like her very much.

As yet I am engaged upon a question of water rights as between 2 states[1] and have not reached the happy moment of irresponsible reading—No 4 vols. for me this Feb. I think.        *Aff'ly, O. W. H.*

*February 18, 1918*

*Dear Laski:* Your telegram was most thoughtful and a real relief to my mind [1] though I still am wondering as to the *vraie vérité* on the matter which you so casually intimated in British fashion. I should howl like King David over trouble with my teeth. Being

---

[1] Presumably *Arkansas* v. *Tennessee,* 246 U.S. 158 (March 4, 1918, opinion by Pitney, J.).
[1] The telegram is missing.

a little below par in that way I kept the house, except a visit to
the dentist a few doors off and after polishing what was to have
been an opinion into a dissent.[2] P[itney] as usual for the majority.
I began volume 3 of Merz—which I got at the Congressional
Library on Saturday. I took out 3 & 4 being the philosophical ones.
He knows what he is talking about and though I can't emulate
you I have read 125 pages. I doubt if he is very pungent—but
that is not necessary—and I infer that he would be down on our
scepticism as barren, which I don't think it is. Also I get fed up
with his antithesis of creative and critical moments. If any thought
is creative all fresh insights are. Sum total, I am pleased at the
chance to get a general view in place of my partial knowledge.

I must enclose in this a thing from Ford that I forgot until I
was clearing my table. I also compared a little Rembrandt that
hung in my father's study and was a feature in my earliest youth,
and found it to be an original—3[d] state, somewhat retouched. The
catalogue says *coarsely* or something of that sort, but the retouch-
ing hardly would disturb any one but a collector.

In this dissent I have to construe an ordinance which I say con-
ferred no rights—as it protests that it doesn't intend to. Do you
think it questionable taste to say "Perhaps an instrument could
be framed that 'whispering I will ne'er consent, consented' &c"[3]
going on to show that this is not such a case?

Well, dear boy, this is a bulletin in my uncertainty—with excursions based on the hopes raised by your telegram.

*Aff'ly yours, O. W. Holmes*


*Cambridge, Mass., February 22, 1918*
*My dear Justice:* The undersigned begs solemnly to affirm that he
never felt better in his life. He is lecturing with eager interest. He
is writing with solemn passion. And he generally feels inclined to
accept the universe.

Of news I have little enough beyond the fact of Felix's safe
arrival. That boy has the luck of the devil. He arrives just in time
to see an air-raid, and on his second day in England he hears a
full-dress debate in a full-fledged political crisis. If I could have

[2] *Denver* v. *Denver Union Water Co.*, 246 U.S. 178, 195 (decided March
4, 1918). The majority opinion was by Mr. Justice Pitney. Brandeis and
Clarke, JJ., concurred in Holmes's dissent. The majority of the Court held
that the preamble to an ordinance reciting that a local water company was
a mere tenant at sufferance and possessed no right or obligation to occupy
the City's streets or to continue to provide service was inconsistent with
the body of the ordinance which the Court found to be the grant of a
franchise. The water company was accordingly entitled to demand constitutional protection for its franchise.

[3] Holmes did not use the quotation in the published dissent. *Cf.* Jackson,
J., dissenting in *Everson* v. *Board of Education*, 330 U.S. 1, 19 (1947).

it in my heart to envy Felix I would envy him the breath of England. But he is pledged to a full report.

. . . I have been (as you have often been) to a Libby sale and bought one or two little treasures—Parsons, the old Jesuit, on the succession, and a volume of pamphlets about the French Revolutionary Clubs in England. I understand why they aroused Burke's indignation, for they are grotesquely naive. But they have some gems in them. One author does not think a drunken Prime Minister (Pitt) ought to rule England and someone has told him that Pitt and Dundas[1] have been drunk in the House of Commons. Wherefore this distich:

> I cannot see the Speaker, Pitt; can you?
> Not the speaker, Dundas? I see two!

. . . That is a great find—the Rembrandt. I have to choose between them and the books, and the books romp home. In pictures I am in the stage where I want my study crowded with portraits—in England I have a great Darwin and a superb engraving of Huxley—then Descartes and Newton and he who was once my god—to wit Laplace. I think they give a room an air—possibly spurious—that helps one. For instance, I get real joy out of that great Watts portrait of J. S. Mill; and a little medallion of Jeremy Bentham tells me to beware of 'Nonsense on stilts.'[2] It is at any rate an amiable weakness. . . .

My love to you both.                    *Yours affectionately, H. J. L.*

*Washington, D.C., February 26, 1918*
*Dear Laski:* Your letter is a great relief to my mind for I still was anxious. It would not have been or be amiss if you had or would vouchsafe[d] a few details. This morning I finished volume 4 of Merz (having skipped 1 & 2). How one hates a book while one is reading it! I got real good from the view of the different concurrents of thought—though I couldn't keep the details in my head. It is so instructive to see tendencies grouped and to see *aperçus* on which you have prided yourself or which have struck you in others appear as bubbles in a stream. Apart from cases that hit me personally I was much interested to see the notion of discontinuity which made me sit up many years ago in Newman's *Grammar of Assent,* and generalized idly on its recurrence in W. James, as com-

[1] Henry Dundas, Viscount Melville (1742-1811); Home Secretary and effective lieutenant in the Pitt government; forceful advocate of Britain's imperial power.
[2] In his "Anarchical Fallacies," which was concerned with the Declaration of the Rights of Man, Bentham had stated that *"Natural rights* is simple nonsense, natural and imprescriptible rights, rhetorical nonsense,—nonsense upon stilts." 2 Bentham's *Works* (Bowring, ed., 1843) 501.

ing from the desire for a chasm out of which the miracle would
emerge—whether of the church or of spiritualism—to see that
notion going back to DuBois-Reymond [1] and showing itself ever
since. So, to see pragmatism grouped with other voluntarist systems, &c, &c. The man's own philosophy or desire for one strikes
me as unimportant. The eternal demand for the superlative degree
—the unwillingness to accept less than being in on the ground
floor with God—don't impress me much, except as a fact in psychology. Why should we not be humble—why not willing to admit
that the primordial wiggle of the first churning of chaos came before our time? Not that I shouldn't like to have an angel about a
span long light on the top of my inkstand here and say, "God
directs me to tell you that it's you and He, that He made the
rest but you made yourself and He desires your friendship"—or
other encouraging message—that was warmer than the tepid concession of life as it is.

The opinion (dissent) of which I spoke already has dropped
the quotation from Byron—I put it in to pain the boys—and the
first who reported, Brandeis, shook his head. My reading ends with
this week. I think I shall reread Patten's *Development of English
Thought* to see how good a case he makes out for the origin of
each new system in some change of the environment—a healthy
skeptical corrective to Merz.

And my print man says he has some Claudes & Ostades coming
to him. There is a little Ostade that if I can get inside of $100 I
mean to have. It has the sympathy and more than the poetry to
be found in Millet—though not of course M's Michelangelesque
quality. Millet's etchings don't excite my desire very much—nor
does Zorn who is called superlative and fetches superlative prices.
It is astonishing how comparatively small a part of the day I can
call mine for reading—but Merz is a good dose of castor oil and
bitters. I am tempted to write a construction of the world of values
—with an excursus on sympathy. Did I ever tell you my theory of
the latter? It never impressed anyone—yet I believe has too much
in it not to be referred to some historic stream when stated. If so,
like Cambronne at Waterloo, I shall say Mer-z.[2]

*Aff'ly yours, O. W. Holmes*

---

[1] Emil DuBois-Reymond (1818-1896); German physiologist, renowned for
his studies of animal electricity; despite his early reputation as an exact
materialist, in two important lectures in 1872 and 1880 he developed the
thesis that beyond the reach of science lies the unknowable, laden with
insoluble questions.

[2] Vicomte Cambronne (1770-1842), commanding the Old Guard at Waterloo, had been credited with saying, as his force was surrounded: "La garde
meurt et ne se rend pas." Victor Hugo in *Les Misérables* varied the legend,
and as Larousse puts it, made the reply of Cambronne to the British demand
that he surrender *"beaucoup plus soldatesque"*: " 'Braves Français, rendez-
vous.' Cambronne répondit: 'M . . . !' "

*Cambridge, Mass., March 11, 1918*

*My dear Justice:* I have been literally bathed in boys for a fortnight. One of the history men was swooped down on by Washington and left things in a sad mess which I have been clearing up. So I have written little and read less; and the letter you sent me and the memory of your birthday[1] have been real oases in an endless desert.

. . . I am full of apprehension at the way in which Washington is rapidly becoming a kind of corridor in which the noisy promulgators of half-truths can easily mingle. That was why I attacked centralisation in the second appendix to my book.[2] I do insist that the fact of significant difference get governmental recognition; otherwise, as *Noble* v. *Haskell Bank*, pointed out,[3] a federal system isn't worth a tinker's damn. Dicey watches the progress of the American government just now and talks of federalism as a mere stage in the progress to nationalism.[4] That I fear greatly; but it's too long a theme to be embroidered. My one source of thankfulness comes from the realisation that the pendulum is swinging slowly back from this excessive confidence in monistic government.

I had a great adventure at a book-sale on Friday which I retail with pride; Godwin's *Political Justice*, 2 volumes 12c. Bolingbroke in five volumes for fifty cents. Milton's prose works in three exquisitely bound volumes for seventy-five cents. I nearly bought a Bolingbroke for you, for with all his perversity he is a damned readable fellow with several *aperçus* that I build on—but I thought you would rather have McIlwain's book[5] which is, accordingly, on its way to you. I am charging it in part to Felix, as he would not forgive me if he did not share in it. . . .

A brief note came from Felix full of eagerness and a cry of joy about the general sanity and foresight of Graham Wallas. I wish he were back. Did you read his very able report on the industrial situation?[6] It was a courageous document, messy in style but remarkable in substance.

My love to you both—          *Yours ever affectionately, H. J. L.*

---

[1] On March 8 Holmes was seventy-seven.

[2] Appendix B in *Studies in the Problem of Sovereignty* (1917) was entitled "Sovereignty and Centralisation."

[3] See, *supra*, p. 26.

[4] In an introduction to the eighth edition of his *Law of the Constitution* (1915) Dicey had devoted considerable attention to the disadvantages of federalism, and had indicated that when federalism has been successful it has generally been "a stage towards unitary government," and cited the United States as a federalism which was "tending to pass into nationalism." (*Id.*, p. lxxvi).

[5] Evidently Charles H. McIlwain, *The High Court of Parliament* (1910), which Holmes read in the spring of 1918; see, *infra*, p. 107.

[6] In February the President's Mediation Commission, of which Felix Frankfurter was counsel and secretary, had issued its *Report on Industrial Unrest*.

*Washington, D.C., March 15, 1918*

*Dear Laski:* You are a good angel and I thank you for many things
—including . . . McIlwain's book which I shall hope to read ὡς
τάχιστα—but I have ahead of it *Les sentiments de Critias* sent to
me (by way of loan) by Howland.[1] I must get that off my mind
and returned as soon as may be. Also I have rec'd from Dicey *The
Statesmanship of Wordsworth*—not to speak of one or two things
that have been lying on my table long—one, by the by, *The Battle
of the Somme* by John Buchan marked 'with the author's compliments' which I don't understand as to the best of my knowledge
I never met him—but I thought that I would read it in honor of
the author of the tales. In general if I have any time, which I
don't except in a rare case like a week or two ago, I avoid war
books. As I said to a neighbor of mine at dinner last night I see
no good in futile fidgeting—which she thought the President
should add to his alliterations. You may gather from this that I
dined out last night. It was at the House of Truth[2] with Lord
Eustace Percy[3] as host—2 dames and a lot of men all much
younger than I. They made me laugh consumedly. . . .

I can do no more than send a bulletin this time. Your letter
seems all right—but I wish you kindly would give me specific information whether you had to be operated on, or it was a false
alarm. What Major Pendennis's Morgan called these damned super-
sellious ways about your health don't suit me.

*Aff'ly yours, O. W. Holmes*

*Cambridge, Mass., March 24, 1918*

*My dear Justice:* I have had a delirious week. First three days at
Amherst where I gave something called the Beecher lectures. I
delivered myself of a hundred heresies and benefited both my
pocket and my soul.

And I have read some thrilling books. As you gaze on these
words please ring up Brentano's and buy *Sonia* by Stephen
McKenna. I think it is by far the biggest and finest novel I have
read in the last ten years. And I am sure you will think with me
that its picture of the *arcana imperio* of English politics is among
the big things of recent literature. Next and next best I have read
a book on *The Chartist Movement* by Mark Hovell (Longman).[1]

---

[1] Charles P. Howland (1869-1932), New York lawyer, and friend of
Holmes.

[2] The House of Truth was the name given to the house in Washington at
which a number of Holmes's younger friends, including Lord Eustace Percy,
then serving in the British Embassy, lived together.

[3] Lord Eustace Percy (1887-1958); diplomat, public servant and educa-
tionalist; he was President of the Board of Education 1924-1929, and later
became Rector of King's College, Newcastle.

[1] Reviewed by Laski, 15 *New Republic* 58 (May 11, 1918).

Its mixture of right and wrong, strength and weakness, are better displayed there than in any other book I know. I am sure you would like it for Beverly in the summer. . . . The last volume I have adventured is a very amusing book on the monarchy in English politics by J. A. Farrer.[2] It's like a good detective story—a little nauseating at times and irritating because it stops with Victoria where it ought to begin. But it confirms an old suspicion of mine that the monarchy in England is really a source of dangerous possibilities. I could write a great essay on triumphs of the English aristocracy during the nineteenth century and show how they maintained the substance of power by the enlargement of their categories on the basis of intermarriage with Lancashire cotton and Midland breweries. That reminds me that when I have met Percy the main impression he has left on my mind is a feeling that he resents the intrusion of the twentieth century on the feelings of a medieval cardinal with royal blood in his veins.

I am sure you will enjoy Dicey's very charming essay. I don't understand how he reconciles the ecclesiastical sonnets with the retention of a liberal creed. Buchan's book is an epic of the best. I hope he will be able to write one of today's offensive and say that the British troops held the line with a splendour like that of Leonidas three thousand years ago.[3] It makes me bow my head with shame to read the list of my dead friends and to think that my record of these years is on the whole one of happiness and certainly one of comfort. *Pro patria mori* rings out to me as a kind of clarion call; and all of them seem to me more living than ever before.

My love to you both—            *Yours ever affectionately, H. J. L.*


                                    *Washington, D.C., March 27, 1918*
*Dear Laski:* Obedient to your letter received yesterday my wife stopped on her way home from taking me to Court and got *Sonia.* She, however, stopped reading peremptorily when she came to the beating of a child—I suppose a boy. She has such a horror of it that she simply won't read any book that speaks of such a thing. I don't mind a reasonable amount of whacking and was not stirred as she was by the sight of birch twigs, witnesses of what had been, at Eton—(I think it was)—but I don't yet know when I shall have time to read it. All the rest must wait. I saw two generals on Sunday p.m. (English) who were wonderfully reassuring by their appearance and words of serene confidence, and I have heard

---

[2] James Anson Farrer, *Monarchy in Politics* (1918), reviewed by Laski in 65 *The Dial* 258 (Oct. 5, 1918).

[3] On March 21 the Germans near St. Quentin opened the first of four major assaults on the Western front. This first assault led to the repulse of the Fifth British Army.

other good things since—but one feels dreadfully nervous. Luckily two days in Court demand that one should forget such anxieties. I hope devoutly that we are not in the position of Leonidas and that a counterblow may be within our means, as is affirmed. If the Germans are stopped, one may doubt whether the move will not have cost them more than it comes to. Just before the move began I was tempted to one more extravagance—in a Méryon that I long have thought about. One of those things that on its face is a modern scene—a look through the arch of a bridge in Paris— but without your being certain whether he meant it—though you are certain that a shiver goes through it. The stains in the shadow suggest great bats—a man on a rope that mounts above the picture may be Baron Trenck escaping from his prison[1]—the people that dot a further bridge may be a foray returning to the *tourelles* at the end. Everything seems something else. I am almost ashamed to speak of it now, but we can't stay all the time at the superlative degree. As Poe noted in an essay on his writing "The Raven" that I haven't read since I was a boy—and as Swinburne forgets in his prose—getting you up to the high C in the first page, after which there is nothing left but to come down.

Another illustration is the *Père Duchêne*[2] published about the time of the Commune where the writer having let out all his dirty words and vehemence in the first article could only do it over again in the next, and soon, I should think, became a bore—showing also the advantage of letting people talk out.

It is time to go to Court—wherefore *adieu*—I assume that you are well, though you calmly ignore my inquiries.

*Aff'ly yours, O. W. Holmes*

*Cambridge, Mass., March 30, 1918*
*My dear Justice:* I can't say how sorry and stupid I feel about Mrs. Holmes and *Sonia;* her views therein quite slipped my memory though in fact I earnestly agree. But I wish she would persevere because the England of that book is the real England.

Your note on the battle warmed my heart, though today it looks as though the Germans will get Amiens.[1] I had a real sense of relief when I saw Foch's appointment.[2] It seems far more likely to

[1] Baron Friedrich von der Trenck (1726-1794), autobiographer, was successively a Prussian, a Russian, and an Austrian soldier. He met his end by the Paris guillotine on July 25, 1794.

[2] A newspaper published in Paris in 1871 by Eugène Vermersch (1845-1871).

[1] On March 27 the German forces had advanced to within fourteen miles of Amiens. The drive on that key rail junction, however, failed.

[2] The Allied War Council had recently designated Marshal Foch Commander in Chief of the Allied Armies.

result in a proper co-ordination of effort. Of course I know we'll
pull through; but one would like a quiet passage.

I was sorry to see Henry Adams's death. I think him on the
whole the first of the Americans who wrote specifically American
history. His book has the wrath and insight of a man who did not
merely write from documents but had something of his own to
say; and I think that the book on Mont S. Michel sets a model for
all future historians. It is worth ten years of life to have the re-
strained taste he invariably displayed. . . .

My love to you both—to Mrs. Holmes my regrets.

*Ever yours affectionately, H. J. L.*

I swear by Almighty God that I am as fit as a fiddle.


*Cambridge, Mass., April 7, 1918*

*My dear Justice:* I have finished my book and I feel alternately tri-
umphant and desperate. The triumph comes when I think of the
neat piles of manuscript devoted to the dissection of people and
ideals I do not like; but the desperation comes from losing an old
friend who really gave me much joy and from the kind of intellectual fatigue due to the release from a fit of energy. So I am like
a collapsed balloon and wait with eagerness the time and occasion
to begin afresh. My plan really can't get going until term ends;
though I want to submit it to the judicial mind *i.e.* to have your
criticisms. . . .

I wish something would happen on the Western front. The
German socialists seem to have been completely won over by the
attractiveness of Eastern victories and there is no help to be expected from that quarter. So it comes down to a military victory
and I could wish that Foch could show us that strategic insight is
not simply a German possession. One of the things that distresses
me much is the sense of deep suspicion of England in this country
from which even Harvard is not free; and I think that an allied
victory is essential to make it evident that we do not count on
winning the war merely by American lives. But neither in the
British nor the French governments do I see anyone with a real
insight into the morale of peoples; and it is yet very certainly upon
that basis alone that a settlement must be made.

I am longing to see Felix. . . . My love to you both—

*Affectionately always, H. J. L.*


*Washington, D.C., April 9, 1918*

*Dear Laski:* Another inspiriting letter from you reaches me today
as my labors have finished for the moment (unless I let Brandeis
egg me on to writing a dissent in advance, in addition to one that

I already have up my sleeve). I signalized the moment by beginning McIlwain[1] with much inward satisfaction. One criticism
or doubt has accrued already. On page 20 the council "*ubi termi-
natae sunt dubitationes judiciorum*" becomes in the text "where are
determined the doubts of the *judges*"—and the notion of the judges
feeling need of help etc. is developed on that and following pages.
I don't see why on its face it imports anything more than that
judgments were rendered there.

Also I read your *Sonia*. Do you know McKenna? Is he the son
of the public man of that name?[2] If so his mother, or the wife of
his father, let me out once from a private door, perhaps of the next
house, when I wanted to hook away unseen from an afternoon
party of the Asquiths in Downing Street. I should almost like to
write to her and compliment her son's work—though I hardly
should call it great. It is vivid and clever, and if you do know the
author I should think he took some traits of O'Rane from you—
*hein?* His remark that the Germans think other people like themselves without their excellence would apply to the English also I
should say, and perhaps to all mankind.

The first bad news about the German drive, contrary to my
boast, made me lie awake, have the dyspepsia and get a violent
cold now pretty much gone and, except when I have work to do,
there is a dreadful ache underneath that even the spring does not
make me forget—indeed rather it becomes an expression of the
inexorable.

Still since I wrote, I think, I have tumbled once more—to get a
Méryon that I have thought of for 20 years and never expected to
own. Not I think one of his most famous—not one of the expensive
—but as marked as any for Méryon's rather shuddery suggestion of
something else. I may have told you about it before and so stop
here. But I am just trying to snatch one of the moments that I envy
you in your recital and so shut up without expatiation.

                                    *Aff'ly yours, O. W. H.*


                                    *Cambridge, Mass., April 21, 1918*
*My dear Justice:* I nearly had a glimpse of you last week; for if
I had not been so tired and Francis Hackett could have got to
Washington I should have proved to you by word of mouth that
(a) *Sonia* is a much better novel than you are inclined to admit
(b) that I do not think I am like David O'Rane (c) that I am very
much alive. So what I did was to amble around New York book-

---

[1] See, *supra*, p. 102.
[2] Stephen McKenna (1888-      ), the novelist, is not the son of Reginald
McKenna (1863-1943) who was First Lord of the Admiralty, 1908-1911,
Home Secretary, 1911-1915, and Chancellor of the Exchequer, 1915-1916.

shops and then come home to spend 16 hours a day in bed. Now
I feel like Hercules and Ajax combined. . . .

Of course the one thing in all our minds has been the offensive
and Irish conscription. The first I don't understand except to feel
that a German victory is ultimately impossible and to pin my faith
to that. On Ireland F. Hackett expressed my sentiments exactly in
this week's N. R.[1] This Lloyd George government has lowered the
moral tone of English public life and I'd give five years of existence
to see it replaced by an Asquith-Grey combination.[2]

Well—my love to you both. I am glad your reading-time draws
near.                                        *Affectionately yours, Harold J. Laski*

*Cambridge, Mass., May 6, 1918*

*My dear Justice:* I am heartily ashamed of myself for being so
negligent; but I have been pathetically tired and I look forward
only to the end of the term. If we can manage it, we are going to
take a cottage for the summer at Rockport, where we can be cool,
and I shall be glad to have a holiday.

So, mainly, I have read bedbooks by the dozen, mostly memoirs.
I began with Harriet Martineau's *Autobiography,* a little grain amid
much chaff. I don't think I could ever dare to take myself quite
so seriously as she did, nor, at the end, did I follow from where
exactly the reputation came. The *History of the Peace* is good and
so is the condensation of Comte; but all else has been dead these
fifty years. Her attack on the false glitter of Edward Everett, and
her strictures on Macaulay (which Morley must have unconsciously used in his piece) are very interesting. . . . Tocqueville's
memoirs from which I lifted a first-rate motto for my book.[1] Really
he was colossal and I take my hat off to him. . . .

For the rest, I am pledged to read Beveridge's third volume[2] for
him, which I am not in the least competent to do; though I can
supply some most interesting references from out of the way
English memoirs. That somewhat reminds me that Harriet Mar-

[1] 14 *New Republic* 354 (April 20, 1918). Hackett vigorously opposed
the announcement of Lloyd George that the Irish would be compelled to
serve in the British forces.
[2] Since the fall of the Asquith government in December 1916, Asquith in
Parliament, and his foreign minister, Sir Edward Grey (1862-1933), in retirement, had been persistently, if discreetly, critical of the Lloyd George
government. Asquith had opposed Irish conscription.
[1] "I am tempted to believe that what we call necessary institutions are
often no more than institutions to which we have become accustomed, and
that in matters of social constitution the field of possibilities is much more
extensive than men living in their various societies are ready to imagine."
Quoted before Preface to *Authority in the Modern State* (1919).
[2] The third and fourth volumes of Albert J. Beveridge's *Life of John
Marshall* were published in 1919.

tineau treasured above all a picture of Colonel Shaw[3] sent after
his death by his mother as a mark of admiration. Was a memoir
of him ever published? . . .

For the rest, I am tortured by this offensive and all it means.
Two of my cousins, one a first-rate mind, died on one day and their
father a week after from the shock; and the Oxford lists are full.
I wish I could feel that in the White House every issue was being
carefully weighed and every step carefully measured. I shall go
home to an England full of ghosts.

My love to you both—        *Ever affectionately, Harold J. Laski*

*Washington, D.C., May 8, 1918*

*Dear Laski:* Your letter is delightful as usual but you make me
anxious about your being tired. You need exhortation as much as
Frankfurter though in a somewhat different direction. I am more
afraid in your case than in his that you will impair your capital
of health by blowing it out (or in) too hard. Don't. I haven't
written because I haven't been free to until now, but now my cases
are all written—all but one little fellow delivered [1] and the probability though not the possibility of any considerable burden has
ended with the end of the regular arguments. Let me say before
I forget it that I finished McIlwain's book and it left me greatly
admiring it as an altogether admirable piece of work. It also kept
me keenly interested from beginning to end. Other books have
I read none, as I don't count extracts from listenable things read
to me while I play solitaire. I am glad you are going to read
Beveridge's third volume. Make literary criticisms as well as others
if you see occasion. He takes them kindly. I should be surprised
if it were not a good piece of work. I never read memoirs when
I can help it, as I want all my limited time for books on the themes
nearest to my life—not that I can't imagine getting a good deal
out of them if my activities were in a different direction. This
apropos of what you have been doing. With the stopping of Court
I have got into gray clothes and soft shirts much to my comfort,
though I haven't given up thick shoes and winter drawers. Tonight
contrary to my habits I dine with Frankfurter. There is to be a
French officer there who I believe will tell of what he has seen of
Foch &c. I have been feeling more cheerful about the German
offensive and my hopes have risen—but one must expect ups and

---

[3] Robert Gould Shaw (1837-1863) was the young Bostonian who died in
the Civil War commanding the Fifty-Fourth Regiment of Massachusetts
Volunteers, made up of Negro troops.

[1] On April 29 Holmes had delivered the Court's opinion in two relatively
unimportant cases, *Dickinson* v. *Stiles,* 246 U.S. 631, and *Emery* v. *American Refrigerator Co., id.* 634.

downs in war. I take it that in what you say you are thinking more of the loss of friends. I have suspected that it may be part of Jewish bringing up to emphasize the cheerful view of things—at all events Felix always is comforting and he sees the powers that be at so much shorter range than I do that I value his intimations. Brandeis always has left me feeling happier about the world.

I hear that Knowlton, my successor as C. J. of Massachusetts is dead.[2] He was a very able man, lacking distinction and poignancy of style but taking penetrating views and capable at times of jockeying you with a cunningly devised question—begging phrases, if you didn't mind your eye. I had a great respect for him not uncoupled with occasional amusement or irritation. He was a pretty big chap —r. i. p. This last reminds me that I have attended two Catholic funerals, where high mass was said for South American diplomats, with the mixture of awe and amazement that grown men could do such things that I always feel. I thought I was original in saying that I didn't believe in Hell but was afraid of it until I saw it quoted in a newspaper from Madame de Staël. Our early impressions shape our later emotional reactions and when one adds the experience of having been cocksure of things that weren't so, I can't help an occasional semi-shudder as I remember that millions of intelligent men think that I am barred from the face of God unless I change. But how can one pretend to believe what seems to him childish and devoid alike of historical and rational foundations? I suppose such thoughts would be as likely to occur to you about Valhalla or the Mahometan hell as about this. Felix said so himself the other night—but I was brought up in Boston—and though I didn't get Hell talk from my parents it was in the air. Oh—the *ennui* of those Sunday morning church bells, and hymn tunes, and the sound of the citizen's feet on the pavement—not heard on other days. I hardly have recovered from it now. I am glad to remember that when I was dying after Ball's Bluff I remembered my father's saying that death-bed repentances generally meant only that the man was scared and reflected that if I wanted to I couldn't, because I still thought the same. The last is the point, for I see no virtue in being brave against the universe—against the source of the power that enables you to raise your defiant fist. Forgive this theological padding. It happened to come into my head—and is a self-revelation like anything else—and one end of letters is self-revelation. We shall meet I trust before July 1 and after.

*Aff'ly yours, O. W. Holmes*

―――――――――
[2] Marcus Perrin Knowlton (1839-1918). From 1887 to 1902 he was Holmes's associate on the Supreme Judicial Court of Massachusetts. In 1911 he had retired from the Bench.

*Cambridge, Mass., May 12, 1918*

*My dear Justice:* That was a glorious letter of yours for which I am
even more than ordinarily grateful. That I sympathise with your
theological reflexions, I do not need to tell you. If there is one
thing of which I become more convinced as I have gone on with
my work it is that religious convictions that are even remotely
orthodox stand in the way of any rational political system. They
always imply somewhere a lurking conviction that God has a hand
in the business, and that will come eventually to mean an insistence
upon the unreality of evil. I'm not indeed certain whether theology
is reconcilable with any philosophic system except idealism which,
for me, would be fatal to its acceptance. Did you ever read B.
Russell's rather striking piece of rhetoric—"A Free Man's Worship"
(*Mysticism and Logic*). I think that is the religion of all sensible
men.

I only half share your conviction about biography. I don't like
full dress portraits—but where I can catch a glimpse of the undress
mind and intimate thought of those who did the big things, I am
eager for the experience. For instance I read the other day a
memoir of Lord Hobhouse (of the Privy Council)[1] and from it I
got (I) a page of superb comment on Maine (II) an insight into
the technique of administration (III) a very valuable forecast of
the tendencies he saw implicit in the atmosphere of 1905—and
I took my hat off to him for his acuteness, his hard commonsense,
and his vigorous liberalism. I'd admit that there is much one feels
irritated about—*e.g.* genealogy, college training, etc. Then a book
like Pattison's *Casaubon* seems to me pure gold. It sets me all on
fire every time I read it, to think of that lonely fellow ploughing
through his manuscripts unwelcomed because one day the path
might be clear for the inspired genius to travel by. I have a selfish
reason too—for one of the books I intend to write is a history of
representative government in England and France in the XIXth
century—and I'm certain that the really valuable thing in such a
book would be the analysis of the general outlook of each class in
the community in the different stages of the century.

. . . The more I read of Bentham the bigger he stands out in
his age—and that means something where one rejects, as I do,
almost all his premises.

I hope you wrote on the Child Labour law.[2] I'd like to read you
on that. My love to you both,          *Affectionately, H. J. L.*

---

[1] Arthur Hobhouse (1819-1904), first Baron Hobhouse of Hadspen. The
book referred to is, doubtless, L. T. Hobhouse and J. L. Hammond, *Lord
Hobhouse, a Memoir* (1905).

[2] On April 15 and 16 *Hammer* v. *Dagenhart,* 247 U.S. 251, had been
argued. It was not decided until June 3, when a majority of the Court in
an opinion of Mr. Justice Day condemned as unconstitutional the Federal

*Cambridge, Mass., May 23, 1918*

*My dear Justice:* . . . I have been planning my new book. I think
I am going to call it (*à la* Newman) *An Essay in Aid of a Grammar
of Politics.*[1] It will begin by a discussion of the bearing of philosophy on politics and dismiss the idealistic canon of T. H. Green
and Bosanquet. Then it will go on to discuss the purpose of the
state (a) historically (b) in theory and show that (b) must, in
Aristotelian fashion, be derived from (a). That leads to the de-
fences, de Maistre, Austin, Burke *et al*, that have been made of the
state as the vital political unit. Chapter IV will treat of types of
states Greek, Roman, medieval and modern, and their internal organisation. Then a chapter on the relation of states and individuals,
singly or in groups and tries to work out criteria for the usual problem. Then the limitations of the state ethically, psychologically and
economically are considered. That leads to working out the relation
between the state and government. The rule of law is established
which involves a discussion of sovereignty. That leads to talk of
federalism and the separation of powers. We pass easily thereby to
the state and the official thence the theory of parliamentary democracy upon which grave note I conclude. It gives me a sense
of wild excitement to be on the threshold of a book, and especially
one where the data are not merely historical but also round about
us. I want badly to ask you many questions. . . .

My love to you both—                        *Affectionately, H. J. L.*

*Washington, D.C., May 25, 1918*

*Dear Laski:* . . . Your letter is a refreshment to me as ever—and
I need it after a high pressure week. Monday I purged myself of
all my opinions up to date—including one that rather pleased me
and seemed to please the other lads on a matter not without difficulty.[1] There came in on that day about 25 cases to be examined
more or less, applications for *certiorari* &c. On Tuesday the C. J.
asked me to take two cases which I done gone done and had them
distributed (I mean my opinion) on Thursday. On that day came

---

statute forbidding the transportation in interstate commerce of goods manufactured in plants employing children under fourteen years of age. Holmes
wrote a dissenting opinion in which McKenna, Brandeis, and Clarke, JJ.,
concurred. In 1941 the case was overruled: *United States* v. *Darby,* 312
U.S. 100.

[1] The title of the book when it was published in 1925 was simply *A Grammar of Politics.* The structure of the book varied substantially from that
outlined here.

[1] Of the three opinions which Holmes delivered on Monday, May 20
(*Erie R.R.* v. *Hilt,* 247 U.S. 97; *Carney* v. *Chapman, id.* 102; and *Western
Union Telegraph Co.* v. *Foster, id.* 105), the *Foster* case, involving problems
of interstate commerce, presented the nicest questions.

down an opinion that stirred the innards of Brandeis and me and
he spurred me to write a dissent. I read one to him that p.m. and
in consequence of his criticisms rewrote it and sent it to the printer
yesterday and now am awaiting the corrected proof to send round.
I incidentally printed another dissent in an important case in
which the opinion has not yet appeared and sent it to the writer
—that he might have my views before him—so altogether I have
been busy.[2]

I like your prospect of a book and only fear that you may run
your hobby a little hard. I think that it has become somewhat of
a prepossession and may be disproportionate if you don't mind
your eyes. Meantime what has become of the book you finished
the other day? Of course I have read nothing. I got half way
through Felix Adler's *Ethical Philosophy of Life* when Monday
came like Francesca's kiss. It is queer after my friendship with
Father Sheehan[3] now to get from an emancipated Jew a work
equally at the *ut de poitrine* of piety or above it almost to in-
audibility.[4] I haven't yet written to him—should I say my mind? I
should say, I respect your ideal. Idealizing is necessary to man—
and I can conceive his concentrating all his energies on sainthood.
But I also can conceive another man's saying with equal right I
would rather be Jim Hill or Rockefeller than any saint. Or I would
sacrifice a million lives for empire—or if I could come out on a
picture that should beat Rembrandt and Rafael I would consent
never to think of morality while I lived. There are a good many
ways of getting the superlative out of men—and I think it a parson's
prejudice that we all ought to be thinking of morals all the time
and giving all parts of it the right of way over everything. Adler
I should gather has lived the life of a sort of lay parson. I am told
that he is a real force in N. Y. and his book touches me, even while
I remain outside the fold. The dissent came in at this moment and
has been sent off. Silah—I begin to smell the salt breeze of leisure
—and I am ready for it—and shall be readier when it brings you.

                                        *Aff'ly yours, O. W. Holmes*

---

[2] On June 3 Holmes, with McKenna, Brandeis, and Clarke, JJ., concurring,
delivered a dissenting opinion in *Hammer* v. *Dagenhart*, 247 U.S. 251, 277.
On June 10, with Brandeis concurring, he delivered a dissenting opinion in
*Toledo Newspaper Co.* v. *United States, id.* 402, 422.

[3] Canon Sheehan of Doneraile (1852-1913) was an Irish priest, man of
letters, and friend and correspondent of Holmes's. See Herman J. Heuser,
*Canon Sheehan of Doneraile* (1917).

[4] Felix Adler (1851-1933), who had been brought up in the orthodox
Jewish faith, in later years founded the New York Society for Ethical Culture, and in his lectures and books developed a philosophical scheme built
on spiritual and ethical foundations.

*Beverly Farms, June 25, 1918*

*Dear Laski:* Here we are at last—and I hope before long to see you. Meantime send me a suggestion or two about reading. I don't want biographies. *The Rise of the Town Laborer*[1] sounds as it might be a bore—is it? Some one recommended Veblen's *The Nature of Peace.* Him also I suspect. I seek improvement without excessive *ennui.* Let me know where you are and your plans. Your last letter forwarded here leads me to direct to Rockport—though with doubt. Suppose that in about a week we shall feel settled. I remember a Hegelian book of Haldane's that I thought an echo.[2] Possibly I might repent as to biographies but I should be sorry to—and they generally cost a lot. I have no library to take from as I don't pay assessment to the Athenaeum. I would rather spend the money on purchases—These in great haste,        *Ever aff'ly yours, O. W. H.*

I had a good talk with Judge Hand (Learned) coming on which led to a characteristic and mighty good letter carrying on the talk.

*Atlantic Avenue, Rockport, Mass., July 5, 1918*[1]

*My dear Justice:* It was like meat and drink to talk with you again; and I am eager for next Friday when we can talk at length. Will you tell your wife how glad Frida will be to come with me and how much added pleasure that will give me?

The main purport of this is to make some comment on B. Hand's letter to you.[2] His thesis seemed to me acceptable in its result, but

---

[1] See, *supra,* p. 97.

[2] The reference which was presumably suggested by observations of Laski in a missing letter is probably to Lord Haldane's *The Pathway to Reality* (1903).

[1] A brief note from Holmes, dated June 28, 1918, is omitted.

[2] With the permission of Judge Hand (known to his intimate friends as "B" Hand) the following copy of his letter to Holmes dated June 22, 1918, is reprinted:

*"Dear Mr. Justice:* "I gave up rather more easily than I now feel disposed about Tolerance on Wednesday. Here I take my stand. Opinions are at best provisional hypotheses, incompletely tested. The more they are tested, after the tests are well scrutinized, the more assurance we may assume, but they are never absolutes. So we must be tolerant of opposite opinions or varying opinions by the very fact of our incredulity of our own. (This may be left for deductive demonstration in accord with the inexorable rules of formal logic by E.D.W., C.J., U. S. Sup. Ct.)

"You say that I strike at the sacred right to kill the other fellow when he disagrees. The horrible possibility silenced me when you said it. Now, I say, 'not at all, kill him for the love of Christ and in the name of God, but always realize that he may be the saint and you the devil. Go your way with a strong right arm and a swift shining sword, in full consciousness that what you kill for, and what you may die for, some smart chap like Laski may write a book and prove is all nonsense.' I agree that in practical application there may arise some difficulty, but I am a philosopher and if man is so poor a creature as not to endure the truth, it is no concern of mine. I

not in its method, and allowing certain difficulties to sneak round the corner instead of being boldly met. I take it that the history of ideas relative to toleration pass through three clear stages; (I) when the idea *eo nomine* is criminal and therefore meets persecution *e.g.* the early Christians; (II) when the idea itself is not judged criminal but inexpedient, and persecuted on that ground *e.g.* the Catholics under Elizabeth; (III) when the idea is regarded as having sufficient strength or weakness to be permitted survival. Hand seemed to me in the third stage about most ideas, and so am I. But is any government likely to adopt it? Isn't the normal government attitude necessarily (II)? I don't suppose that any logically-minded person could say, for instance, that the Sinn Feiners are criminal, but their attitude is judged inexpedient and persecution follows. I think myself it's a profound mistake, largely on the grounds urged by J. S. Mill in that admirable chapter of the *Liberty*. I mean that there are all kinds of theories *e.g.* Christian science, which seem to me stupid and wrongheaded, but looking at the natural history of such theories I don't think either their stupidity or wrongheadedness has a sufficient chance of survival to penalise the ideals themselves. The one case outside is when you get someone like the man in black in *Lavengro* who thinks toleration nonsense and is out to slay all who think differently. If he and B. Hand were the two last men in the world how could Hand secure the survival of toleration except by killing him? All of which surely means that there *is* something in Carlyle's ultimate question, Can I kill thee or can'st thou kill me? I ought to add that I am sure the real ground for toleration is the change of perspective. Burke, for instance, always talks of atheists as if they were moral lepers; Gladstone, I am sure, thought so; but he had to speak about Bradlaugh in a tone of hypocritical respect when the question came up in the House of Commons. There is an alternative hypothesis that toleration was a dodge invented by the physically weak to secure survival.

---

didn't make him; let the Galled Jade wince, speaking reverently of course.

"I sat under the Bo Tree and these truths were revealed unto me. Tolerance is the twin of Incredulity, but there is no inconsistency in cutting off the heads of as many as you please; that is a natural right. Only, and here we may differ, I do say that you may not cut off heads, (except for limited periods and then only when you want to very much indeed), because the victims insist upon saying things which look against Provisional Hypothesis Number Twenty-Six, the verification of which to date may be found in its proper place in the card catalogue. Generally, I insist, you must allow the possibility that if the heads are spared, other cards may be added under that subtitle which will have, perhaps, an important modification.

"All this seems to me so perfectly self-evident, self-explanatory and rigidly applicable to the most complicated situations that I hesitate to linger upon it, lest I should seem tolerant of any difference of opinion concerning it.

"I greatly enjoyed my good fortune in meeting you on the train.
                                    *"Faithfully yours, Learned Hand"*

I have been debauching upon a curious literary fragment which attempts to show that the positive character of the modern state has broken down the hypothesis of nineteenth century democracy. It is great fun; and I like to remind people that fellows like de Tocqueville really had vision and insight, *e.g.* he really did anticipate the decision in *Haskell* v. *Noble State Bank.*

My love to you,      *Yours ever affectionately, Harold J. Laski*

*Sunday, July 7, 1918*
*Dear Laski:* Just a line to say that I don't see where your quarrel with Hand is. It rather should be with me if either—but I don't see any quarrel. My thesis would be (1) if you are cocksure, and (2) if you want it very much, and (3) if you have no doubt of your power—you will do what you believe efficient to bring about what you want—by legislation or otherwise.

In most matters of belief we are not cocksure—we don't care very much—and we are not certain of our power. But in the opposite case we should deal with the act of speech as we deal with any other overt act that we don't like.

To be continued on Friday.             *Aff'ly, O. W. H.*

We are so glad your wife can come.

*Beverly Farms, July 16, 1918*
*Dear Laski:* Your letter gives me great pleasure in assuring me that your wife as well as you were happy here.[1] You gave as much pleasure as you got. I acknowledge the receipt of the stud—I thought you had forgotten it, but taking up the envelope I felt a nodule which turned out to be the article. As to the greatest man in the 19th century, I don't believe there is no sich animal. Like writing history it depends on your interests—where you will put the emphasis. Different gifts require incompatible qualities—some depend upon a relatively unstable nervous tissue—some on a relatively stable (to put it figuratively—for I do not speak as a man of science). You will put at the top the gifts that you like best. If greatest means the greatest number of human footpounds—reducing Shelley and Nansen[2] to a common denominator—probably the greatest was some cuss we never heard of. I think if I had to pick out one man from recent centuries I should take Leibnitz. Another would name Beethoven—and so on. Apropos of Karl Marx (who struck me in the book *Capital* as open to articulate demonstration of his fallacies) it really has an effect on one's reverence

---

[1] The letter referred to is missing.
[2] Fridtjof Nansen (1861-1930), Norwegian explorer of the Arctic and author of one of Holmes's favorite books of courage, *Farthest North* (1897).

to hear him serenely dismiss (*e.g.* Adam Smith, I think—at any rate) 'some of our most highly gifted men' as *bourgeois* intelligences. Proudhon who hates him and who also seems to me not above criticism, I think had more insight—though Marx had the force that any man gets who rides even a limping theory of Evolution.

I know nothing of DuVergier de Hauranne³ except his name. I stopped and went downstairs to look in the Everyman Encyclopaedia but didn't find him under either D or H. I did, however, find Claude Duval, the highwayman, of whom I used to read in my youth with secret rapture and his epitaph.

> Here lies Duval: Reader, if male thou art,
> Look to thy purse: if female to thy heart.

I am amused at what you tell of Story—a big chap, all the same. I dare say he may have given suggestions to De T[ocqueville].

I must shut up as it's time to walk to the village. My love to Mrs. Laski.                      *Ever aff'ly yours, O. W. Holmes . . .*

*Beverly Farms, August 10, 1918* ¹
Dear Laski: Just a word to say how I miss you. I have been absorbed in accounts that drove me nearly mad although a figure sharp from the Old Colony Trust Co. helped me to prove that I was not a swindler. My Heavenly Father never meant me to do sums. I have read all of Acton that I mean to²—as I shall omit in singing the chapters on Döllinger etc. I feel his learning, of course —and respect his impartiality about facts—but I [blank] his conclusions are the preferences of his religion and his class. I was instructed without delight—and turned with pleasure to Jules Lemaître.³ Alas, in these days books rarely give me the pleasure that so many seem to give you. Those that improve are generally dull —my appetite for novels has fallen off—and if a volume has charm I am likely to feel that I have not been improved. I cannot say as John Gray and Harry James did to me at different times that I thank God I have ceased to read for improvement. From the first two pages I do expect both that and pleasure from *The Town Laborer*—which as well as Lord Acton I carried away from Rockport. . . .

---

³ Laski's reference was probably to Jean Du Vergier de Hauranne (1581-1643), Abbot of St. Cyran, leader of the Jansenist movement, and bitter enemy of the Jesuits.
¹ A note from Holmes dated July 18, 1918, is omitted. Any letters written by Laski in the interval are missing.
² Holmes's reading list indicates that in Lord Acton's *The History of Freedom and Other Essays* (1909) he read pages 1-300 and 551-596.
³ The reading list includes Jules Lemaître, *Les contemporains*, volumes II and III.

I won't attempt to continue the argument over Veblen now. He
is remarkable and stimulating but I incline [blank] that you and
Hackett over-rate him—which may mean only that I am old fogey.
I see in Lord Acton and Figgis influences that seem to me to have
given an undue emphasis to your thought in certain directions. It
is odd that a Catholic and a high churchman should have succeeded in making you keen about a schism in the Scottish (or any)
church. The principle behind has assumed an importance in your
mind that I hardly think it would have but for the interest those
teachers inspired. . . .                          *Aff'ly yours, O. W. Holmes*


*Rockport, Massachusetts, August 27, 1918* [1]
*My dear Justice:* I am not easily moved; but I have a certain sense
of emotion beyond the written word in the thought that you both
have broken bread with us. Thank you.

I do not mind the extent of your reflections, but I want that piece
for the *Law Review*.[2] In me a great editor was lost, and, *me judice*,
(like the *[illegible]* the great man's learning comes out at every
point) I know a good thing when I see it. There are only two
things of yours that, at first sight, have moved me so much. One
is the 'Soldiers Faith';[3] the other the 1913 address to the Law Review [*sic*] Association.[4] And it is on a level with them both. Behind this, there is the full knowledge of how absurd it is for me
to estimate what you write. However, judgment is inevitable when
one loves deeply.                          *Affectionately, H. J. L.*


*Beverly Farms, August 29, 1918*
*Dear Laski:* Your letter moved me much—though when one has
shared the intimacies of thought I attach less importance to external facts. That does not matter to the effect of your words.

As to my little piece I have copied it in the attempt to secure
legibility for a cold world in which chirography seems to be an
almost forgotten art. I shall keep it a day or two to see if minute
tinkerments occur to me—as a few did on copying—and then send
it to you at Rockport. Have you any notion when it would appear?

You will notice that I say "shall send" not "will send"—so that
this sounds in prophecy not in contract—a distinction for which I

---

[1] Brief notes from Holmes, dated August 12, 19, and 24 are omitted.

[2] Holmes's brief article, "Natural Law," appeared in 32 *Harv. L. Rev.* 40
(November 1918); *Collected Legal Papers* 310.

[3] *Speeches* (1913) 56.

[4] Holmes's address, "Law and the Court," delivered to the Harvard Law
School Association, February 15, 1913, is printed in *Speeches* (1913) 98.

have to thank Bob Ingersoll but I am settled in my wish to put the little titman into your hands. . . .

*Affectionately yours, O. W. Holmes*

Your wife was beautiful on your sea-regarding piazza. My homage to her.


*Beverly Farms, September 18, 1918*

*Dear Laski:* Before your letter arrived[1] my wife had written to yours asking you to pass the night with us. We were celebrating Antietam,[2] where if the bullet had gone an eighth of an inch differently the chances are that I should not be writing to you. So, although after your letter came I saw that there was no chance, I waited until today. As to *Ju Toy*,[3] although I should be quite prepared to find that at that comparatively early stage I was more overawed by authority (which was pretty conclusive) than now, I don't see the trouble. We were answering questions which assumed that there was no abuse of authority, so that there was nothing to scrutinize. But let me add that you cannot argue from one exclusion proceeding to another. The nature of the case may make all the difference. The exclusion of aliens does not stand like the post office. Congress may exclude aliens as it chooses—and on a familiar principle if efficient exclusion requires the risking an occasional and not very likely wrong to a citizen that risk may be taken—even if it is a risk to constitutional right—(what the constitutional rights of a citizen who is outside of the country are to get into it I do not know). I suspect that your apprehension, which I more or less share, has led you not to notice the technical limits of the decision. On glancing it over it seems to me all right. I remember at the time Charles Adams wrote to me as if something ominous had happened, though in an (Adams) humorous vein.[4] I told him that you couldn't argue from one class to another in this kind of case.

I haven't read much. Curiously, I shrink from novels, which I used to devour. Did I mention after reading Glover's book on Virgil

---

[1] The letter referred to is missing.

[2] On September 17, 1862, Holmes was seriously wounded in the neck at the Battle of Antietam.

[3] In *United States* v. *Ju Toy,* 198 U.S. 253 (1905), Holmes for a majority of the Court, in answering a question certified by the Circuit Court of Appeals, held that an executive determination that a person returning to the United States after a temporary absence was not a citizen, had been made, and constitutionally could be conclusive on the Courts. The majority was persuaded that the spirit, if not the letter, of earlier decisions required this result. Brewer, Peckham and Day, JJ., dissented.

[4] Charles Francis Adams (1835-1915), man of letters, historian, railroad reformer, and brother of Henry and Brooks Adams.

that it seemed to me that one might say with some plausibility that
the triumph of Christianity really was the triumph of Roman
civilization as expressed in Cicero and Virgil, clothed in what Miss
Kingsley[5] called an oriental misfit? Our real thoughts are much
nearer to C. & V. than to those of the New Testament. I finished
B. Russell *Mysticism and Logic* without much profit. He seems to
me in the emotional state not unlike that of the abolitionists in
former days, which then I shared and now much dislike—as it
catches postulates like the influenza. Add to these, 3 books of the
*Odyssey* with more pleasure than formerly and reflections I don't
stop to repeat. *Othello* a rotten and repulsive play—and *Hamlet*
a bill filler—in which, much to their advantage, though to the
discredit of S.'s supposed dramatic quality, they all talk Shakespeare—words that sing to our ears perhaps more than Homer's
and almost as much as Dante's. 'Oh—one of our classics, we don't
read *them*' as a Briton once remarked to me. The mystery of the
universe—how it feels to be a king, and singing words—if I were
to sum up the bard in a sentence I think that would be it. And
I might repeat what I once said to a dame—an ounce of charm is
worth a pound of intellect. (But that depends.) I had a wonder
visit to the old graveyard that overhangs Marblehead yesterday—
which moved me as the old garrison house that we saw together
—but again I don't describe. Heaven guard you—

*Aff'ly yours, O. W. Holmes*

*Beverly Farms, September 24, 1918*[1]
*Dear Laski:* The *N. R.* came this morning and I have read your
piece with the usual pleasure.[2] Your remarks about the local magistrate remind me that I always have said it is harder to stay at the
bottom than to be at the top. When I think of the knowledge required by a police judge, I shudder and turn pale.

Yesterday I reread Chesterton's *Victorian Age in Literature,* a
delightful book—only his more than contemptuous speech about
Malthus, a good deal bigger man than C. with all the latter's epigrams and really delicate literary appreciation seems to me pre-
sumptuous insolence. It is due I suppose to his Catholicism and
his social views—to which it is disagreeable to admit the hard
truths that M. pointed out.

---

[5] Probably Mary Henrietta Kingsley (1862-1900), traveler, scientist, author
of *West African Studies* (1899); friend of Holmes.

[1] A brief note from Holmes, dated September 23, is omitted.

[2] In reviewing Lord Channing's *Midland Memories* (1918), 16 *New
Republic* 234, 235 (Sept. 21, 1918), Laski spoke of the significance, in
England, of the local bench and the Justice of the Peace.

It seems to me that every social improvement is immediately absorbed by an increase in the population.

However, I referred to C. in order to repeat if you have forgotten it the sentence of Lord Melbourne who always seems to have something that tickles one, when one gets a touch of him personally: "No one has more respect for the Christian religion than I have; but really, when it comes to intruding it into private life—"[3] Hein?

*Aff'ly yours, O. W. H.*

*Beverly Farms, October 1, 1918*
*Dear Laski:* Your letter comes as we are departing,[1] so this is but a word of *adieu.* I have been having a cold and being scared for fear it should come out grippe and stop us—but it hasn't. Plato and Aristotle struck me (in translations a year or two ago) much as they do you—Aristotle the universal wise man of all times. (Did you note that he has the government of laws and not of men— that I suppose John Adams may have got from Quesnay for the Massachusetts Constitution?) Plato, with a lot of the latter day beliefs in earlier form. I shall await your booklet eagerly.[2] You have added more than anyone to my pleasure this summer. I wish that we might have had more talks together, and am glad that I have begun to know your wife. I believe Mrs. Curtis has written to you. She was going to—to express her enthusiasm, in which I join, over your article, "A Province of England"[3] She thought it the very best ever—and so—goodbye for the present.

*Affectionately yours, O. W. Holmes*

*Cambridge, Mass., October 23, 1918*
*My dear Justice:* I enclose herewith the proof of your article.[1] When you have read it will you send it back to me here. The only suggestion I have to make is that you put in a note saying that it was Geny's book which gave rise to the article; I think that is a piece of information to which the reader is entitled. Frida is writing this for me, as I have been in bed getting over a rather painful inoculation against influenza.

Our love to you both.                     *Affectionately yours, H. J. L.*

---

[3] The passage was quoted by Chesterton, *The Victorian Age in Literature* (1913), p. 42, to illustrate the paganism of upper-class England at the opening of the Victorian Age.

[1] The letter referred to is missing.

[2] Presumably Laski's "The Problem of Administrative Areas," 4 *Smith College Studies,* no. 1 (1918); reprinted in *The Foundations of Sovereignty* (1921), 30.

[3] Reviewing Lord Channing, *Midland Memories* (1918); *supra,* p. 120.

[1] "Natural Law," 32 *Harv. L. Rev.* 40 (November 1918); *Collected Legal Papers* (1920), 310.

*Washington, D.C., October 25, 1918*

*Dear Laski: Imprimis* my sympathy over your bodily disturbance.
I hope all is well by this time. 2. As to the proof, I agree to the
reference to Geny but you must put it in as I have not the book.
How would a note do in this form: 'Suggested by reading volume
2 of Geny, [Title of book].'[1]

As I speak in less confident terms of the result of the war than
now would be natural is there any objection to putting 'August,
1918' at the end as I have. I leave that to you.

Your felonious retention of the MS has bothered me in places.
I have corrected some horrifying mistakes. . . .

As this is business I do not write on other matters even on a
heavenly two hours I had yesterday in the print rooms of the Congressional Library—the Library is shut but they let me in, and I
wallowed in potentialities some of which I actualized.

*Aff'ly yours, O. W. Holmes*

In the third paragraph I have misgivings whether the smile
accompanying the words 'poor souls' (inserted to indicate the individual's assumption of superiority) is sufficiently visible—but I
thought I would let it stand.[2]

I thought myself justified when quoting the language of my
youth to put it as I actually did and say 'lick'[3]—the wise will see
that I am not now using that word in sober speech—but the repetition of it further down is simply a printer's error which I have
corrected to 'kill.'


*Washington, D.C., October 28, 1918*

*Dear Laski:* Would that you were here. Then I would make you
tell me of some profitable book, as we adjourn again this morning.
But if I have the leisure I hope for and rarely attain I have stores
that I always can fall back upon. I almost wish I could attain
John Gray's and H. James's lofty position of no longer reading to
improve my mind—but I am a miser as to time and clothes. After
I had sent back the proof one phrase caused me some uneasiness
—'for the joy of it' which sounds to me like a reminiscence of

---

[1] The note as published was as follows: "Suggested by reading François
Geny, *Science et technique en droit positif privé*, Paris, 1915." The second
of Geny's three volumes was concerned primarily with the problem of
Natural Law.

[2] "But while one's experience thus makes certain preferences dogmatic for
oneself, recognition of how they came to be so leaves one able to see that
others, poor souls, may be equally dogmatic about something else." 32 *Harv.
L. Rev.* at p. 41; *Collected Legal Papers* at 311.

[3] "I used to say, when I was young, that truth was the majority vote of
that nation that could lick all others." 32 *Harv. L. Rev.* at p. 40; *Collected
Legal Papers* at 310.

Ruskin.[1] I loathe dropping into some ready-made expression—it shows that one is not living through the sentence. But as I said to my wife the officers in my regiment who went unwounded through a number of battles were apt to expect to be killed out-right—as some of them were—and a small spot on a cravat seems a guaranty against ruin. So I shall not attempt to recover this *levis nota infamiae* but rely upon it as a safeguard against greater miseries. I am talking away on the assumption that you are getting better by this time, as I devoutly hope you are. Our adjournments are made to avoid calling lawyers to this crowded and infected place,[2] and I daresay right, though my original impression, think-ing only of the possible danger to us, was the other way.

I saw a lot of Nanteuils at the print rooms of the Congressional Library and some more, two of which I coveted, at the print seller's. He always puts some Zorn before me and says that they will rise in value—but I don't buy prints as a speculation and despite Zorn's power of drawing naked women, omitting no detail, it seems to me that there is no great gift behind his technical one. I should like his Etching of Renan—which once I could have bought for $50 but had not the $50. So once I could have bought an adorable Corot for $500—but that was all the money we had. I daresay it is worth more thousands now. I must start for Court. This is but a reminder that I exist and a flight of good wishes. I sent the proof special delivery to the *Harvard Law Review* the day I received it. My love to your wife and you.      *Aff'ly yours, O. W. Holmes*

*Cambridge, November 3, 1918*
*My dear Justice:* This is to offer you the solemn assurance of my recovery. As you can see, I am not exactly in a condition to try odds with the ghost of Tom Cribb,[1] but I am to get up tomorrow and I have already shaved. Shaving and knives and forks are the real indicia of civilisation.

I have read nothing in bed but sheer rubbish—one extraordinarily powerful book called *Limehouse Nights* by Thomas Burke which suggests that the East End of London spends its time selling its daughters to Chinese sailors, which I take leave seriously to doubt. The magazines were superb. The heroine always succeeds, villainy is always punished, tuberculosis is always cured by two months in

---

[1] "We shall still fight—all of us because we want to live, some, at least, because we want to realize our spontaneity and prove our powers, for the joy of it, and we may leave to the unknown the supposed final valuation of that which in any event has value for us." 32 *Harv. L. Rev.* at p. 43; *Collected Legal Papers* at 316.

[2] The influenza epidemic of 1918 was at its height.

[1] English prize-fighter (1781-1848) who lost but one fight in his career.

Arizona. The editor gets letters to say that F. H. Shaw[2] is the greatest short-story writer ever, signed "Yours for success." He is asked to publish tales about motor cyclists, mechanics, railwaymen, and sure enough they turn up about six weeks later. It's a great profession. I also re-read Zimmern's *Greek Commonwealth* with acute pleasure. It's the only book I ever read except Demolins[3] which made me interested in geography.

This is a poor return for your two letters; but I promise you intelligence next week.

My love to you both.    *Ever affectionately yours, Harold J. Laski*
I thought Henry Adams's autobiography very poor and self-conscious.


*Washington, D.C., November 6, 1918*

*Dear Laski:* Your letter is the final relief from anxiety that I was feeling about you. I didn't suppose that it need be great but still I was worried until I heard good news. Please be careful to run no risks until you are solidly on your legs. Your Smith College performance is the next thing to be read.[1] It only came last night and therefore is virgin from my eyes. I have just read in the little interval due to our adjournment Lord Charnwood's *Lincoln*, an artistic work, to my thinking, Max Farrand's *Development of the U.S.* which strikes me as rather a masterly short summary of the deeper causes at work, and a translation (of Dent's publication) of Dante *De Monarchia* which sustains a deep conception by reasoning that seems rather childlike in its premises and amusingly scholastic in its syllogistic form. I have had it on my mind for years. So one is daily annoyed by some little corner that needs clearing up and when by accident one at last is stirred to do the needful, one wonders that one should have stood the annoyance so long when such a little effort would have done away with it. Moral: When in doubt, do it. I said that once at a Law School smoker talk and to my dismay in walking out afterwards found that some of the lads thought I referred to moral doubts, and, it would seem, recommended fishy conduct! Now we are off—the arguments have begun and for advanced cases have not seemed so far to present very difficult questions. But reading will be at an end, except records and briefs. How differently the recent events make one feel about life.[2] The horrible nightmare that has ridden us so long seems

[2] Presumably Frank H. Shaw (1878-1959), British author of stories of the sea.

[3] Edmond Demolins, *Les grandes routes des peuples* (2 vols., 1901-03).

[1] "The Problem of Administrative Areas," in 4 *Smith College Studies*, no. 1 (1918), and reprinted in *The Foundation of Sovereignty* (1921) 30.

[2] The German collapse and the Austrian surrender were the great events of the first days of November, leading to the Armistice on November 11.

driven off—though in dealing with the Germans eternal distrust seems necessary—or at least distrust till they are tied so tight that they can't wiggle. How much better is wiggle than wriggle at this point!

Well, dear boy, this is but a Halleluia over your news—I shout with joy.                                   *Aff'ly yours, O. W. Holmes*

Please give my love to your missus who kindly let me hear some good news before you wrote.


                                    *Cambridge, November 8, 1918*
*My dear Justice:* Your letter was ever so welcome. I am in the irritable stage of convalescence where I can't do anything and badly want something to do. But I have been out, and I could write a long tract on the philosophy of legs.

Your note on the *De Monarchia* is interesting. It always has impressed me as the prologue to a drama that was never acted. I don't think it would have had any importance if Dante hadn't written it. Of course the underlying conception is superb, but then so is the *Utopia* and the *City of the Sun*[1] and both seem to have been without any influence. Do you know the good edition by W. H. V. Reade in the Clarendon Press Series—bad print but an admirable introduction.

I see that you have some 'free speech' cases to listen to so that the next few weeks won't be without excitement.[2]

Life is very different since Germany began to break up. I confess that the prospect of Lodge as leader in the Senate is singularly uninviting. I do not, as you know, like the President; but Lodge seems to me assertive without knowledge and brutal without cause. He never seems to realize that some of us have to live in Europe after the war, and his idea of a peace dictated by America on the basis of English and French lives does not seduce me. But I hate the Republicans almost more than I do the Democrats and Lodge more than most Republicans.

I have been reading one or two joyous things this week—above all, Tacitus's *Annals* which struck me as intensely modern and not unlike Arnold Bennett's *Pretty Lady*. That led me to Dill's *Roman Empire* which, its praise of Christianity apart, struck me as admirable. I wonder if we realise enough how much there is to be

---

[1] Tommaso Campanella's *Civitas Soli* (1623) constructed an idealized communism—authoritarian, Platonic, and Christian.

[2] At the October Term, 1918, the Court heard arguments and reached decisions in three important cases involving issues of free speech: *Schenck* v. *United States*, 249 U.S. 47; *Frohwerk* v. *United States, id.* 204; *Debs* v. *United States, id.* 211 Holmes in each case wrote the opinion for a unanimous Court. In the first of the cases he formulated the "clear and present danger" test.

said for Gibbon's thesis that Christianity merely mangled a great
process of revival which Stoicism was accomplishing by perfectly
logical means. I, at least, never read Seneca without a sense that
he knew all that the Fathers had to say and preached it a damned
sight better.

I read with the same pleasure as yourself Max Farrand's book.
It was a real joy to get rid of the drum and thunder, the old stuff
about Hamilton and Jefferson and the character of Jackson and
have, instead, the play of the real historic forces. I read Charnwood some time ago and liked it greatly; but I think Lincoln was
dead wrong about Vallandingham[3] despite Charnwood's denuncia-
tions. Did I ever tell you that I wrote a life of Lincoln (300 pp.
*octavo*) when I was fourteen. It got burnt; but I have a suspicion
that it was probably an immortal work. I know that it justified
Sherman and Sheridan and urged that the South ought to have
been burned to bits.

My love to you both.            *Yours ever affectionately, H. J. L.*

*Cambridge, November 23, 1918*

*My dear Justice:* I am not really negligent; I have simply been
drowned in work. There have been lectures to make up, reviews
to write, students by the cubic ton to see, in addition to a vast
amount of necessary reading for my courses. I am sure you will
understand.

But the reading has been great fun. I have been lecturing all
this week on the political theory of the centuries from the sixth
to the tenth; and three of the writers, whom I have never studied
in detail before, seem to me really big men—Hincmar,[1] Gelasius,[2]
and Jonas of Orleans.[3] Hincmar and Jonas are more than big, they
are simply fascinating as they show so clearly what happened when
the Teutonic invaders met the Roman law. The amazing thing is
the clear shock that *Quod principi placuit* gets immediately it comes

---

[3] Clement L. Vallandingham (1822-1871), Ohio Copperhead, was arrested
during the Civil War and sentenced by military commission to imprisonment
for the War's duration. Lincoln, however, commuted the sentence to banish-
ment. From Canada Vallandingham conducted an unsuccessful campaign for
Governor of Ohio, later in the war returned to Ohio, and, without interference, continued his campaign for peace.

[1] Hincmar (c. 806-882), Archbishop of Rheims; in political science he
preserved the tradition of the Roman law that the maintenance of justice is
the central objective of government, yet rejected the maxim of Rome that the
law is the pleasure of the ruler. The dignity of kings was derived, in his
eyes, from the benediction of Bishops, not from earthly power.

[2] Gelasius was Pope from 492 to 496 and through his formulation of the
dualistic conception of the relationship between church and state contributed
much to political theory.

[3] Jonas, Bishop of Orleans (d. 844), like Hincmar, insisted that the King
was subject to law. His principal work on this theme was *De Institutione
Regia* (828).

into contact with the more democratic tribal traditions of the barbarians. . . .

My love to you—and tell HER that she lives in my inmost heart.
*Ever affectionately yours, H. J. L.*

*Washington, D.C., November 29, 1918*

*Dear Laski:* There is just time to write a line to tell you that I am not ungrateful for your letters but that since I was reassured as to your health I have been mad with work. First a stinker of a case that frightened me,[1] and then, as 500 times before, gradually shrank to the dimensions of a poodle, no longer diabolic except for the longwindedness and confused argument of counsel. Then came others and finally a dissent, I suppose it will be, touching the relative power of the U.S. and the States.[2] I have just put the last into an envelope for the printer—and with that I draw a long breath with nothing worse than the dentist for some trifling work ahead this p.m. Do not forget your aged friend in these necessary lapses of silence.                                    *Aff'ly yours, O. W. Holmes*

*Cambridge, December 1, 1918*

*My dear Justice:* Your letter was more than ordinarily welcome, for I had begun to fear that you were ill. Please do not overwork, even for the sake of the Constitution. I issue herewith a mandamus ordering a copy of the dissent.

I have just read over the *Law Review* piece. It is insolent in me to praise—but I do think it is splendid and I am proud that it came in the year that I have been trying to run the *Review*. Thank you over and over again. . . .

Reading has been mostly about eighteenth century politics with a good look at the *Defensor Pacis* thrown in. I took a shot at William of Ockham's *Dialogue*, but 60 pages folio satisfied me, and for the rest I contented myself with verifying Rietzler's [*sic*] references.[1] *In re* the 18th century there were one or two good

---

[1] Probably *Buckeye Powder Co.* v. *Du Pont Powder Co.*, 248 U.S. 55 (decided Dec. 9, 1918, after reargument on Nov. 13). The action was for triple damages under the Sherman Act, and the trial had taken five months.

[2] The reference is probably to *Ruddy* v. *Rossi*, 248 U.S. 104, 107 (decided Dec. 9, 1918), in which Holmes wrote a dissenting opinion, denying that Congress could constitutionally, or had sought by legislation to control state law with respect to lands which had once been owned by the United States but which had passed to private ownership.

[1] *Dialogus inter magistrum et discipulum de Imperatorum et Pontificium Potestate.* Ockham's political philosophy was carefully examined in Sigmund Riezler's *Die literarischen Widersacher der Päpste zur Zeit Ludwig der Baiers* (1874).

things. Brown's *Estimate*,[2] despite the sneers of Burke, struck me as an admirable protest against an age which had grown fat; and Law's letter to Hoadly in the Bangorian controversy[3] I thought quite the ablest pieces of controversial handling I have read in many a day. Hoadly really is utterly unreadable, though, damn him! he is full of commonsense. I have found it a most admirable policy to take Leslie Stephen's *18th Century*—a corking book— and read the writers (in Chapter X) in the order in which he deals with them. Which reminds me that I have just said in a review that his life of Fitz James is the best biography I ever read.[4] Does that at all disturb you? The only doubt I have is as to whether Maitland's *Life of Leslie [Stephen]* is not a better book. The one thing I'm certain about is that judgment goes for that family. . . .

Let us be political for a moment.[5] I am glad that the *Illuminé* decided to stay at home. The President is going to have an extraordinary time. I meet almost no one who does not resent his secrecy. The very experts who are going from here are not told what they are to attack and what defend. House & the State Department quarrel, so he lets House take one set of experts and Lansing another. And now it looks as though the Senate will send a third. But at least Mrs. Wilson will spend an exhilarating Christmas. How important it is—I think the observation is Heine's—to marry the right man the second time. On the other hand, does the end justify the means?

But I must go back to the 18th century. My love to you both—
                                        *Yours ever affectionately, H. J. L.*

[2] John Brown, *Estimate of the Manners and Principles of the Times* (1757), an unhappy protest against the vanity and luxury of English life in the eighteenth century. See 2 Stephen, *English Thought in the Eighteenth Century* (2nd ed., 1881), 195 *et seq.*

[3] Benjamin Hoadly (1676-1761), Bishop of Bangor, was the Whig theologian whose latitudinarian views led to the Bangorian controversy. Hoadly's most effective antagonist was William Law (1686-1761), a staunch nonjuror, maintaining the independence of the Church from secular authority. Of all the replies to Hoadly, Law's *Three Letters to the Bishop of Bangor* (1717) was the most effective. Laski wrote of the Bangorian controversy in Chapter VI of his *Political thought in England from Locke to Bentham* (1920).

[4] In reviewing H. Remsen Whitehouse, *Lamartine* (1918), 17 *New Republic* 287 (Jan. 4, 1919).

[5] In mid-November President Wilson had announced that he would personally attend the Peace Conference in Paris. On the 29th he announced, further, that the American representatives who would accompany him would be Secretary of State Lansing, General Tasker H. Bliss, Mr. Henry White, and Colonel E. M. House. The fact of Wilson's intention to go to Paris was not brought officially to the attention of Congress until he delivered his annual message to Congress on December 2.

*December 3, 1918*

*Dear Laski:* Your most welcome letter suggests two or three things that I must say right off. *Imprimis*—I am relieved to hear that you still like my piece and in return must tell you, what I omitted at the moment, that I admired your Smith College lectures[1] while I wondered how far your audience could follow you in your references to English problems that sometimes got me up a stump. I really wonder at your being able to turn out so much fine work— and when I add your voluminous reading I am simply flabbergasted. I can't help fearing that you are running the machine too hard and discounting future years, but you do easily what comes hard to most of us and I hope that you are discreet. *Secundo*—I am delighted at your praise of L. Stephen's *18th Century*. He was in labor with it when we mountaineered together[2]—and when he received *en route* a letter from his future first wife addressed to Reverend Leslie Stephen with the Reverend stuck out—as a bit of chaff on his giving up the fellowship. Then he married, his wife died, the book came out and I thought it a big thing and wrote to him—but everything then was dust and ashes to him. He had a great reverence for FitzJames (I never have seen the life you mention) but I thought his intellect was more original and penetrating than his brother's. That Stephen blood is a powerful one. It also accounts for Dicey. He certainly also is a big chap, but taking the Stephen manifestations *en bloc* while I greatly admire them, I think that as is apt to be the case with the voluminous, they sometimes miss the most exquisite *aperçus*. L. S. and Dicey seem to me the flowers.

. . . As to the journey to Europe I believe I may have written that, speaking as one of the ignorant, it seemed to me that if the prophet had transmuted the voice of the Lord from Sinai it perhaps would have had more effect than in his descending into the plain. The impression made on me by his speech yesterday, which I heard, was that, after a discourse as of any year, he said, and by the by I am going to Europe where they need my counsels—and left it there, only adding an implication that he would run things by the cables that he had taken over. I wonder if the Mrs. has anything to do with the job.

A whirlwind struck me in the middle of the last sentence—Tom Barbour's wife and sister, babies and servants arrived a little earlier

---

[1] See, *supra*, p. 124.

[2] In the summer of 1866 Holmes and Leslie Stephen had been on a climbing trip together in the Swiss Alps. Stephen, shortly before, had relinquished the Goodbehere Fellowship at Cambridge to which there were incidental clerical duties. In the summer of 1866 he was engaged to marry Thackeray's daughter, Harriet. They were married in 1867 and she died in 1875. Much of the friendship between Holmes and Stephen is recorded in F. W. Maitland's *Life and Letters of Leslie Stephen* (1906).

and now there is a descent upon me—for a lawyer to defend a suit, for the Secretary of State about a passport, &c, etc. *Que sçay je?* And I have been telephoning right and left. It has taken the [illegible] out of me—especially as when I can get calm I am catspawed by Brandeis to do another dissent on burning themes —and half an hour ago I was at peace! But those girls are wonderfully wonderfully handsome creatures and I should be proud to be their slave. So for the time being I suspend. My love to your missus.

*Aff'ly yours, O. W. Holmes*

# II

## 1919-1921

*Cambridge, January 12, 1918* [sic]
*My dear Justice:* I am horrified at the length of my silence, particularly when I think of your kindness to me in Washington. . . .

But I have had a harder fortnight than I have ever known. Look at it as a narrative. (a) I have corrected 380 pages of proof. (b) I have personally seen 150 new students who have come into my lectures. (c) I have comforted Ned Adams[1] who is on his back with a misplaced vertebra and much pain. The sins of the horses are visited upon their riders. (d) I have been to three committee meetings where long motions of my own were in debate. (e) I have written three book-reviews and innumerable letters. (f) I have been concurrently writing the lectures I have to give at the Croly School in New York.[2] (g) I have been continuing my education. This is what is called in poker a full house and there is no sign of release until Monday week.

The result is that whatever I have read has been strictly on business lines with certain trifling exceptions. The first was a joyful reading of Bentham's *Political Tactics* which for some unearthly reason seems to be the only discussion in existence of the theory of parliamentary procedure. It is certainly one of the best things he ever did—fresh and vivid and acute. I like that old fellow increasingly and I foresee that when my sabbatical year comes round it will be most difficult to avoid writing a book about him. And second I read Leslie Stephen's three volumes on the *Utilitarians* for the nth time with a sense that he there did an even bigger job than in his *Eighteenth Century*. The third thing was

---

[1] See, *supra*, p. 62.

[2] Herbert Croly was largely instrumental in establishing the New School for Social Research which opened in New York in 1919.

131

the confirmation of your discovery of Swift's *Polite Conversation*
—like all his things stamped with superb malignity and invaluable
for the total estimate of life. But I would like to have the opposite
side from Addison's gentle pen—something clinging and sweet on
the joy of being unutterably stupid. To read Swift is like being
locked up on a desert island with Napoleon in the capacity of
secretary. There is no prospect of relief.

I dined last night with Beveridge and heard from him a moving
account of Roosevelt's funeral.[3] What stirred me was his picture
of Root's dignity and Beveridge's sense that he alone there had
seized the perspective of things. I do not regret Roosevelt's death.
I think he had a rich and full life. He had made his mark; and for
the last decade he had spent his energies in comment instead of
observation. But if he could have given the present incumbent a
little of his stirring virility the world would be the better for it.

My love to you both. It was glorious to see you again.

*Ever affectionately yours, Harold J. Laski*

*Washington, D.C., January 25, 1919*
*Dear Laski:* Better late than never. This is the first chance since
hearing from you and is due to my cutting the conference as a
precaution for a very slight cold. Few intellectual events outside
of writing decisions and the routine. But I have got and have just
hung here an adorable Ostade that I have been on the watch for
for near two years. I think I showed you the reproduction in Hind's
book[1]—a peasant saying grace over his bowl of porridge—his little
boy to his right—wife and baby in the rear. It has the line of piety
that Millet got in his "Angelus"—but so simple, so unconscious,
so immediately sympathetic. I mean you don't feel that Ostade
was seeing himself sympathize.

Also controversy in various quarters over the superiority of the
oriental mind—I remember now that I mentioned the start with
Brandeis. Then came a visit to Mrs. Meyer[2] to see some early
Chinese paintings which she thought came from greater spiritual
heights than ever were reached by the west. I thought it hyper-
aesthesia on that theme. But before that I read a rather big little
book by Okakura on *The Ideals of the East*—taking similar views
to those of B and the dame but saying that Japan was It—which
the lady scorns. Let them fight it out. I stick to the world I know.

John M. Zane has been walking into me for believing that the
lawmaker is not bound by his own laws and that judges make law.

[3] Theodore Roosevelt had died on January 6.

[1] Arthur M. Hind, *A Short History of Engraving and Etching* (1911).

[2] Probably Mrs. Eugene Meyer, Sinophile and wife of the banker, public
servant, and publisher.

First near a year ago in the *Michigan Law Review,* now in the January *Illinois Law Review.*[3] He practises a dogmatism that I should not venture upon, but so far as he is not unconsciously using the word law in a different sense from that in which I use it, if he would state his view and not merely condemn—and if that should turn out as I dare say it would, really different from mine, I would take the contract to smash him. But he is great— he *ex cathedra* condemns wholesale all German philosophers and jurists from and including Kant to now, and thinks Bentham, Austin, and Hobbes little better than asses. In fact I don't know whom he respects in the higher walks of thought unless M. Arnold may be considered one! I ran my eye through Beale's *Bartolus*[4] with pleasure though I shouldn't think his work was very well done. I can't back up my impression without going through the book again. It is handsome and not a bad idea. This must do for a bulletin. My love to you both.                              *Aff'ly yours, O. W. Holmes*
The bronze relief of me is here and is to go up in the dining room. I expect I shall have to write to Mrs. Paeff for hooks—but I have forgotten her address.

*Cambridge, January 29, 1919*
*My dear Justice:* I waited until I had read Zane's paper in the *Illinois Law Review* before answering your letter. Now I am so angry about it that I hardly know how to write. It is not merely that the man is ignorant, he is also insolently ignorant. I talked it over with Pound, who is anxious, if you see no cause to object, to make some remarks on the general subject in the *Harvard Law Review.* I think I shall tilt at him in the *Yale Law Journal* and see to it that he gets properly pulverised.[1] As Cicero might have written to Atticus—what a stinker!

To more pleasant things. I have been writing a paper for the *Law Review*[2] and so unduly pressed; but it is off my hands and I breathe again. As to books, there have been some joyous adven-

---

[3] The articles by Zane were "German Legal Philosophy," 16 *Michigan Law Review* 287 (March 1918), and "A Legal Heresy," 13 *Ill. L. Rev.* 431 (January 1919). In the first of the two articles Zane criticized Holmes's proposition that "the law is a statement of the circumstances in which the public force will be brought to bear through the courts" (*American Banana Co.* v. *United Fruit Co.*, 213 U.S. 347, 356). In the second he elaborated his earlier incidental criticism of Holmes's "careless and debonair utterances" (16 *Mich. L. Rev.* at 349) in *Kawananokoa* v. *Polyblank,* 205 U.S. 349, 353, with respect to sovereignty.

[4] Zane in 16 *Mich. L. Rev.* at 348 had referred enthusiastically to Joseph H. Beale's *Bartolus on the Conflict of Laws* (1914).

[1] So far as has been discovered neither Pound nor Laski published comments on Zane's criticism.

[2] Probably his "Responsibility of the State in England," *supra,* p. 69.

tures. (a) McIlwain's edition of K. James's works—absolutely tip-
top; not a dull or needless line in 100 pages of scholarship. It is
a first-rate job. (b) I bought James Mill's Encyclopedia articles—
the ones Macaulay attacked [3]—in the private reprint. They struck
me as dry but astonishingly able, and I had the same insistent sense
I always have of how difficult Utilitarianism is to answer and yet
how impossible it is as a system. (c) I read Hobbes again with a
hopeless sense of despairing infirmity. The others in English theory
I would have a shot at equalling, but that old rascal leaves me
with a sense of how high above all others he is. (d) He took me
to Austin—and I re-read the whole jurisprudence. The result may
be usefully expressed in mathematical form.

$$\int_{John}^{Austin} \int \begin{array}{l} \text{lectures on jurisprudence} \\ \text{province of jurisprudence} \end{array} \text{ and all his followers} = 0.$$

Also some Bagehot. Please look at Volume VI of his *Collected
Works,* the essay on "The Metaphysical Basis of Toleration." I
don't know why he uses the word metaphysical; but his is certainly the most sensible discussion of that business I know. Also
in that same volume there is a superb paper on Gladstone and one
on Parliamentary reform that is worth its weight in gold. I have
begun re-reading Grote as a bed-book; but I'm not yet far enough
to have convictions.

Tomorrow we are off to Yale for the week-end. That blessed and
thrice-blest University has made me its Harvard lecturer for next
year—plenty of money and very little work. So we go this week-
end in order to show what nice manners we have. In fact strictly
between ourselves, next year the Laski family—supposing that it
survive so long—will be so financially comfortable that it will put
its hand in its pocket, pay an income-tax and support the deserv-
ing poor.

So you hit on the Eastern myth at the Meyers. She showed me
the Chinese paintings but they were so utterly alien from my experience that I remained in the valley and left her on the heights.
I like the fellows who tell you where they got their information
from. These damned mystics with a private line to God ought to
be compelled to disconnect. I cannot see that they have done anything save prevent necessary change.

My love to you both. Please look after the cold.

*Ever your affectionate, H. J. L.*

---

[3] See 1 *Miscellaneous Works of Lord Macaulay* (1880) 288.

*Washington, D.C., February 1, 1919*

*Dear Laski:* A few words in reply to your most welcome letter. I don't know about McIlwain's book but I should expect the first-rate from him—subsequent chance contacts with the matters he dealt with in his *High Court of Parliament* have enhanced my impression that he has handled that more profoundly than anyone else. I always thought James Mill a mighty able man from what I read in my infancy. I am glad too of what you say of Hobbes. W. James used to seem to me to speak coldly of him—which I didn't understand. He seemed to me a very big chap. I don't think you do justice to Austin though he writes as he were a conveyancer at his job. His wife and the wife of Adams on Equity always have touched me by their belief in their respective great men.[1]

As to Zane, if anyone takes the trouble to deal with him I think he should be handled lightly not wrathfully. A man who calls everybody a damn fool is like a man who damns the weather—he only shows that he is not adapted to his environment, not that the environment is wrong. As to the two points on which he falls foul of me, hitherto I have regarded those who doubted that the judges made law (interstitially, as I explained in the *Jansen* [*sic*] case),[2] as simply incompetent or else carried away by a hobby. On the matter of sovereignty also I can't see a question about the proposition as I mean it. Of course I am not speaking of origins and don't care how far it may have been derived from *princeps legibus solutus* or how far that formula needs qualification—nor on the other hand is it material that every ultimate repository of ultimate political power *de facto* has limits beyond which it cannot go because the people would fight—that is fact not law. I simply say that the ultimate source of law when you find it, is subject to such laws or resolutions only as it chooses to impose upon itself, from a legal point of view, and that therefore the State is not subject to legal claims except so far as it sees fit to submit itself to them—and I should think that that was obvious. Zane says the conclusion is right but it is simply a matter of convenience—who determines the convenience unless it is the mouthpiece of the State?

---

[1] Sarah Austin, the widow of John Austin, devoted the last years of her life to the revision of her husband's *The Province of Jurisprudence Determined* (1832) and its collation and republication with the manuscript of later lectures which her husband had delivered at the Inner Temple. The final result was published as Austin's *Lectures on Jurisprudence* (2 vols., 1st ed. 1863). Mrs. Austin, in her preface, expressed uneasy doubt whether her task had been adequately fulfilled: "What would have been the structure . . . had the Master been enabled to execute the plan he had conceived, is now left to melancholy conjecture." What part Mrs. John Adams played in connection with the publication of her husband's posthumous work, *The Doctrine of Equity* (1849), has not been ascertained.

[2] *Southern Pacific Co.* v. *Jensen*, 244 U.S. 205, 221 (1917): "I recognize without hesitation that judges do and must legislate, but they can do so only interstitially; they are confined from molar to molecular motions."

He seems to me to fall back on dogmatic dissatisfaction, and hardly to show his own hand if he has one—but I speak from a hasty reading and have not his articles by me. Of course I have nothing to say if any one wants to talk back, but I should think that Pound, without giving dogmatism for dogmatism, ought to consider himself on a different plane and to retain that position. So in your own case you are a scholar, while Zane, although I thought his "Renaissance Lawyers" a pretty piece of work,[3] makes on me the impression of the son of a *nouveau riche* who is very fashionable in his carriage but shows by little things that the high way is not in his blood.

I am delighted at what you say about Yale and as to the prospects of the Laski family.

Of course I agree with you as to those who tell you they are in on the ground floor with God. Did I mention Miss Spurgeon's *Mysticism in English Literature* that takes a different view?

To recur to Zane there is one other point that I forgot. He is patronizing to the errors of my *Common Law*. I don't know whether it has serious ones or how many—but I think the material thing to be that I gathered the flax, made the thread, spun the cloth, and cut the garment—and started all the inquiries that since have gone over many matters therein. Every original book has the seeds of its own death in it, by provoking further investigation and clearer restatement, but it remains the original and I think it already is forgotten how far that is true of the *C. L.*

*Aff'ly yours,* O. W. H.

*Cambridge, February 8, 1919*

*My dear Justice:* One of my learned masterpieces has gone to you by another post.[1]

I have had such a hectic week, that I hardly know whether I am on my head or my heels. First Yale then New York where I had some great talk with Walter Lippmann who is back for good and going straight to the paper. I thought he was in splendid form, and his attitude to things most eager and virile. Then back here with a ghastly amount of exam papers to correct, with only two real ones to lighten the task. But the joy of Felix's return here is over everything and I feel as though I am about to enter heaven—with the certainty that it will be heavenly.

I have read some books. The life of Grote by his wife was very amusing. She always speaks of him either as "Grote" or the "historian" and has one delicious remark of Lord William Bentinck

---

[3] 10 *Ill. L. Rev.* 542 (March 1916).

[1] Presumably his "Theory of Popular Sovereignty," 37 *Mich. L. Rev.* 201 (January 1919); reprinted in *Foundations of Sovereignty* (1921), 209.

the G. G. of India[2] who was anxious to meet an American. "Many came to Government House while I was in Calcutta, but of course I didn't speak to them." Next I read Gooch's *English Democratic Ideas in the XVIIth Century*,[3] a very scholarly book; and Michel's *Idée de l'état* which convinced me that when a Frenchman does a real job well he does it better than anyone else can do it. I read a volume of O. Henry, *Heart of the West* with certain critical kicks but with a sense that he had a right to his style and was a great story-teller.

I have talked to Pound *in re* Zane. He proposes to write a paper on the inarticulate major premise and explain what it really means and, as he puts it, to take the guts out of Zane in a footnote.[4] The man is really an ignoramus. While we are on the subject of these antagonisms can you tell me why Richard Hale is hostile to Felix? He was round at Ned Adams's the other day and launched a diatribe the mere report of which made me very angry. I thought Hale had common sense even if he lacked the finer perceptions.

I have had some interesting remarks about Wilson from Europe. One, from a person not to be mentioned, is too good to be lost. 'Wilson and Lincoln are both lonely men: but Lincoln's was the loneliness of humility and Wilson's the loneliness of arrogance.' And Mrs. Holmes will like to know that when Susie, Mrs. Wilson's negro maid, was asked what she thought of the gold plate at Buckingham Palace, she said it was not so good as that at Washington. 'Why, Susie,' said Mrs. Wilson, 'You know we have no gold plate at Washington.' 'I know, ma'am, but I wasn't going to let the United States down.'

But the work calls. I mainly want to send my love to you both and to wish there was a chance of talk.

*Ever yours affectionately, H. J. L.*

*Cambridge, February 23, 1919*
*My dear Justice:* There is so much to say and do that my days are a watch and a vision betwixt a bed and a bed. . . .

Mainly I want to remark that I have been rereading Maitland's *Leslie Stephen*, with the sense that apart from Leslie's own life of FitzJames it is the most perfect thing of its kind in existence.

---

[2] Lord William Bentinck (1774-1839) was Governor General of India from 1827 to 1835.

[3] Laski collaborated in the second edition of this book, published in 1927.

[4] In September 1919, Pound delivered an address to a section of the American Bar Association, "The Administrative Application of Legal Standards," 44 *Reports of the American Bar Association* 445, in which he discussed, without annotation, Holmes's dictum that decisions "depend on intuition too subtle for any articulate major premise"; *Lochner* v. *New York*, 198 U.S. 45, 76 (1905).

138 )	( 1919

I envy you the letters from Stephen, above all that supreme one
telling you of his engagement;[1] and there is a footnote about *The
Common Law* with an adjective which, from Maitland who was
sparing of adjectives, seems to me worth five hard years at one's
books.[2] I had only one judgment to dissent from—the *Utilitarians*
seem to me a far better book than Maitland admitted; even when
Halévy is borne in mind there is no work with the sweep and
insight of Leslie's; and that phrase of Meredith's "Phoebus Apollo
turned fasting friar"[3] is the kind of thing one would have liked
to have sponsored.

I had a joyous adventure yesterday—a sudden request to go to
Smith College and give an "oration" for Washington's birthday. It
was a moving thing—2000 girls all in white looking as charming
as nature and art can effect, the gorgeous robes of the academics,
and a choir that made even the national anthem sound a noble
thing. I talked for half an hour on the joy youth has in discovering
the possibilities of intelligence on the motto of Spinoza's—*omnia
praeclara tam difficilia quam rara sunt.*[4] If they enjoyed it as much
as I did they had a very good time.

I had some good talk with Walter Lippmann last week before
he left for a holiday. It pleased me greatly to find that the whole
process of statesmanship had left him with the conviction that the
real truths are in the great books of the world. I am eager for you
to see him again—he is more critical, less facile, and, to say the
same thing differently, with a deeper sense that you don't find
truth by skimming milk. Felix I had no chance to see before he
left.[5] I know he was happy to go, which makes me pleased he has
gone. But I'm very anxious that he should settle down and gain
the solid reputation which is the debt he owes to his intelligence.

My love to you both—	*Ever affectionately yours, H. J. L.*

*Washington, D.C., February 28, 1919*

Γε Λασκε: Smile, oh youth of learning—yet not too rashly—for the
dictionary gives 'γελάσκω, Anth.'[1] and unless I have forgotten more
even than I suspect ε is the imperative.

At last I get a pause—all too late; though I had a little one in

---

[1] F. W. Maitland, *The Life and Letters of Leslie Stephen* (1906), 310;
the letter announced his engagement to his second wife, the widow of
Hubert Duckworth.

[2] "Mr. Justice Holmes had not yet published his famous book on 'The
Common Law,'" *id.* at 298.

[3] The phrase was used by Meredith in describing Vernon Whitford, the
character in *The Egoist* (1879) of which Stephen was the prototype.

[4] "Everything excellent is as difficult as it is rare."

[5] For the Peace Conference in Paris.

[1] To laugh at or smile upon.

which I tucked in a book or two—but then came there a certain Judge and asked me to take a case, one that I hoped the Chief would give me, but which wrapped itself around me like a snake in a deadly struggle to present the obviously proper in the forms of logic—the real substance being: Damn your eyes—that's the way 'it's' going to be.[2]

The books I read are 1) Parodi—*Traditionalisme et démocratie* —an excellent smashing of the royalist catholic movement of Bourget *et Cie*,[3] but sounding from the remote past of 1909. 2) T. Davidson, *The Education of the Wage Earners*. I knew him young —full of Aristotle, Rosmini and the *perfervidum ingenium scolorum*—but he became an apostle.[4] Cohen sent me the books. Then I had a heavenly debauch over Coppier—*Les eaux fortes de Rembrandt*. He I should think has cut deeper than any predecessor —having studied history and dates and uniting the connoisseur with the bank note detector. He has studied the proofs and the original coppers that remain with the magnifying glass, and expounds methods and handwriting so to speak—and is altogether very satisfying. He gives a lot of reproductions, one of which shows that my "Faust" is a very good impression. He says it is not Faust but another man of (nearly) the same name known in R's time and a student of the Cabala. A little earlier I got some prosaic instruction from Charles Norton's *Church Building in the Middle Ages* at a moment when I had nothing to do—and, as perhaps I have mentioned, led by what you have said, I reread Mill on *Liberty*—fine old sportsman—Mill, and just now from a different way of thinking, but with somewhat similar atmosphere, T. H. Green's *Essay on Liberal Legislation* and *Liberty of Contract* and some other things of his. What strikes me in that one as in so many of the discourses of you who believe is that while he talks about what I would not waste breath upon—the possible moral disadvantages of compelling a man to be better than he is ready to be—he never bothers about the bill, the real, hard, concrete bill. If you require guards to machinery you say the detriment of increased cost to the public is less than that caused by the loss of certain fingers &c. If you say minimum wage you say those

---

[2] On March 3, 1919, Holmes delivered the Court's opinion in *Panama Railroad Co.* v. *Bosse*, 249 U.S. 41 and *Schenck* v. *United States, id.* 47.

[3] The contemporary "traditionalists" whom Parodi attacked were principally Ferdinand Brunetière, Paul Bourget, and Maurice Barrès.

[4] Thomas Davidson (1840-1900); Scottish-born philosopher, and, in William James's phrase, "knight-errant of the intellectual life," disciple of Rosmini and Aristotle. His peripatetic ways brought him to Boston in the 1860's and 1870's, and his radical idealism led him finally to establish a Bread-Winners' College on the lower East Side of New York; author of *The Philosophical System of Antonio Rosmini-Serbati* (1882) and *Aristotle and Ancient Educational Ideals* (1892). See Morris Cohen in 2 *Cyclopedia of Education* 255 (1911); 2 R. B. Perry, *The Thought and Character of William James* (1905) 731 *et seq.*

who can't get it must starve or be supported, and in the latter case those who get the wages must do the supporting. The only attempt to estimate the proportions of advantage and disadvantage that I remember reading is in Woodbury's *Social Insurance* that I read last summer. His general conclusion being, I don't know but I think it worth trying. Civilization is the reduction of the infinite to the finite. The realizing that there is so much forest, coal, etc so much even atmosphere—and no more. I wonder if it might not be possible that those who are withdrawing nitrogen from the latter might in time be found to be doing a deadly thing.

How I hate to borrow books. Since I began this I have had a funk because I could not find the book on Rembrandt in my drawer where I carefully put it—but sneaked in under others. Now it is returned and Cohen's are returned and my case has been sent round and I breathe freely once more. I will try to finish Green on the philosophy of Aristotle, expressing in a phraseology that I imperfectly understand, ideas that I don't believe. His ideas never are difficult—but the damned technical language of each new discussion keeps me in a fuzzle. It is all the same from Green's 'Universal' to 'L.C.L. freight'—I know what the latter is of late years. Adieu *poor lee presong*. Homage to your wife.

*Aff'ly yours, O. W. Holmes*


P.S. to yesterday's letter

*Washington, D.C., March 1, 1919*
*Dear Laski:* This is to say that your article on "The Theory of Popular Sovereignty"[1] seems to me admirable as opening both history and practical considerations. I don't know that you intend any specific conclusions to be drawn—or to do more than to make us realize the nature and conditions of the problem. I haven't a word of criticism upon your thought and was not conscious of any reserves. It is a good contrast to the generalities offered by popular oratory, and to all the isms accepted by cranks with an enthusiasm that causes me wonder and sorrow.          *Aff'ly yours, O. W. H.*


*Cambridge, March 5, 1919*
*My dear Justice:* The Yale University Press has given me an advance copy of this book,[1] so that I can send it to you for your birthday. I wish it represented more worthily what you and your

---

[1] 17 *Mich. L. Rev.* 201 (January 1919); *supra,* p. 136. Laski's emphasis in the article was on the antiquity and fictional character of the theory that the people, ultimately, are sovereign.

[1] The original of this letter is pasted in front of Holmes's copy of Laski's *Authority in the Modern State* (1919).

friendship mean to me; but you will find in it a sentence about friendship lying too deep for words and know what the book tries inarticulately to say. I do not need to tell you what love it brings with it. . . .

Your two letters gave me great joy. I envy you discovering Parodi, who overjoyed me when I read it. It's a great thing to dissipate as many shams as he does in that book. *Natürlich*, you guessed what I tried to do in that sovereignty paper and I'm glad you have no reserves. It's one of three or four I hope to do in the next year to show the entire lack of administrative meaning in some of the great popular phrases. I think it's a helpful job. Which reminds me that one book has recently given me especial pleasure —a life of Bismarck by C. Grant Robertson, well in the Lytton Strachey tradition. In another line, with much disagreement, I have enjoyed *Democracy at the Crossroads* by F. J. C. Hearnshaw (Macmillan $8.00), a restatement of Mill's *Representative Government* done in a finely controversial spirit. Also I have reread the *Federalist* with far more admiration than ever before—especially the parts on taxation and commerce.

But I don't want to say anything except an eager word of loving greeting to you both. Please remember that I sit by your side.

*Ever affectionately yours, Harold J. Laski*

*Washington, D.C., March 7, 1919*
Dear Laski: The book arrived this morning. I trust that I need not tell you how much I am surprised and moved.[1] Although I can believe little except your affection it makes me terribly proud that even for a moment I could elicit such an expression. I shall read the book as soon as I may be—not just yet I fear—and write to you about that. Meantime my thanks and love to you both.

*Aff'ly yours, O. W. Holmes*

*Washington, D.C., March 16, 1919*
Dear Laski: Your article was finished five minutes ago[1]—the first moment for reading that I have had. It commands my sympathy in its tendencies—but I must make one or two criticisms. At points

---

[1] *Authority in the Modern State* (1919) was dedicated "To Mr. Justice Holmes and Felix Frankfurter, The Two Youngest of My Friends."

[1] "The Responsibility of the State in England," 32 *Harv. L. Rev.* 447 (March 1919). The article touched upon the traditional immunity of the Crown from private suit, considered the limited liability of public officers, and regretted the immunity of government officials for the torts of their subordinates. Laski urged that administrative tribunals, analogous to those of the Continent, should be established, in order that public officers might be subjected to the rule of law.

it is obscure to a general reader because it takes for granted knowledge that he does not possess. An example would be reference to a case not stated, the bearings of which cannot be known, or to details of English government which I at least know only as you tell them to me (I don't say that this first is unjustifiable).

The main criticism would be that on the question of liability you do not distinguish between policy and logic. I am quite ready to accept the desirableness of government liability—subject to questions of details—but I have yet to see how it can be shown to be a logical necessity that the source of law should be subject to the law that it makes, unless it chooses to say that it will be. I don't know that I can add to the simple statement—but I may suggest that subject to law means I suppose subject to some sort of adjudication—and the adjudication I presume will come from some body of men that the source of law has seen fit to establish.

On the degree of responsibility I observe that you assume the principle *respondeat superior* as general and incontrovertible. I always had a good deal of sympathy with the English judge who spoke of the fellow servant doctrine as a bad exception to a bad rule. I have been inclined to believe that an empirical application of the principle in specific situations and with limitations in amount as in the more intelligent employers liability acts was about all that I could see clearly.

But I repeat that I sympathize with the general tendency of the article—with reserves in regard to torts.

I sent you yesterday some opinions in the *Debs* and other similar cases (and a queer one on the District Term [?]).[2] I greatly regretted having to write them—and (*between ourselves*) that the Government pressed them to a hearing. Of course I know that donkeys and knaves would represent us as concurring in the condemnation of Debs because he was a dangerous agitator. Of course, too, so far as that is concerned, he might split his guts without my interfering with him or sanctioning interference. But on the only questions before us I could not doubt about the law. The federal judges seem to me (again between ourselves) to have got hysterical about the war. I should think the President when he

[2] On March 3 Holmes had delivered the Court's unanimous opinion in *Schenck* v. *United States*, 249 U.S. 47, in which the defendant's conviction for participation in a conspiracy to violate the Espionage Act was sustained. In the course of his opinion Holmes formulated the "clear and present danger test" for free speech cases and had stated that "the most stringent protection of free speech would not protect a man in falsely shouting fire in a theatre and causing panic." On March 10 Holmes had delivered the Court's opinion in *Frohwerk* v. *United States*, id. p. 204 and *Debs* v. *United States*, id. 211. These cases also affirmed convictions under the Espionage Act. Debs's conviction was for obstructing the recruiting service of the United States in speeches opposing the war.

gets through with his present amusements might do some pardoning. I have been interrupted and so perhaps have been less coherent than I should have been.        *Aff'ly yours, O. W. Holmes*

*Harvard University, March 18, 1919*
*My dear Justice:* There are many and fascinating things of which I want to speak. Mainly, I want first of all to say how much happiness your note about my book has given me. I should not have been content if I could not have indicated, however inadequately, a little that you have brought into my life; and if that has given you a moment's passing pleasure I am amply repaid. It will not win the crowd; but I had rather please Cato.

I am grateful indeed for your criticisms about my *Law Review* article. I want badly sometime to develop a point I think you imply without expressly naming, and that is that sovereignty in law really means nothing more than that the ultimate source of immediate reference has spoken, where in politics we are dealing with the much less tangible factor of influences. By responsibility I simply mean that if the state injures X more than it injures the mass of men, unless a vital source of social interest is involved, the treasury ought to assist X; and if it doesn't probably the control over officials is relaxed dangerously—as *e.g.* where there is no control over the postmaster general his censoring privilege simply runks [*sic*] amok. I suppose that if you feel over-allusiveness in that paper I must plead guilty; it's the fault I suppose (really due to egoism) of thinking that everyone must be interested in the same materials as yourself.

I read your three opinions with great care; and though I say it with deep regret they are very convincing. The point, I take it, is that to act otherwise would be simply to substitute judicial discretion for executive indiscretion with the presumption of knowledge against you. I think you would agree that none of the accused ought to have been prosecuted; but since they have been and the statute is there, the only remedy lies in the field of pardon. Your analogy of a cry of fire in a theatre is, I think, excellent, though in the remarks you make in the *Schenck* case I am not sure that I should not have liked the line to be drawn a little tighter about executive discretion.[1] The Espionage Act tends to mean the prosecution of all one's opponents who are unimportant enough not to arise [*sic*] public opinion. Wilson has been utterly damnable in the whole business. . . .

Books! Get, steal, buy, Grant Robertson's *Bismarck*[2] and you

[1] See, *supra*, p. 142, note 2.
[2] Laski reviewed C. Grant Robertson's *Bismarck* (1919) in 19 *New Republic* 156 (May 31, 1919).

will bow the knee before me, in gratitude. I have been writing a paper on McIlwain's book and reading *tractati theologico-politici* for the past fortnight. But now it's done to the satisfaction of my editor and I'm luxuriating in a dozen or so of O. Henry as a relief from that and my New York lectures which are just over. Walter Lippmann told me of his visit to you, by which he was made very happy. A long letter from Felix turned up today full of sound and fury but signifying nothing except seasickness and satisfaction.

My love to you. I'd give a year of life for a talk.

*Ever yours affectionately, Harold J. Laski—*

*Washington, D.C., April 4, 1919*

Dear Laski: Enfingo vos—at last I get at you. I have just got through my work for the adjournment unless I am asked to take another case—and until now I have been a slave. My table is so piled up that I can't find your last letter till I clear for action, before we come in again. There is a stock of others remaining to be answered—and when they are done, there is a certain book. I wanted and wait until I can go straight through it. Every once in a while, faintly and vaguely as to you, a little more distinctly as to Frankfurter, I hear that you are dangerous men. . . . What does it mean? They used to say in Boston that I was dangerous. Have your writings as to sovereignty led people who don't read them to believe that you were opposed to law and order or what? I hear talk of Dorothy Brown[1] expressing extreme views but, again strictly between ourselves, I hardly think philosophical reflection her strong card. I confess, having had early experience with come-outers, to a general disbelief in them, as embodying the cock-sureness of semi-education.

I might say the same of a labor union that yesterday sent me a protest against the *Debs* decision, at once cocksure and hopelessly ignorant of all about it. Brandeis thinks character more important than intellect whereas I am wont to think I would rather have an able knave than a virtuous fool. Perhaps we are thinking of different cases and don't differ as much as we dispute.

Out of politeness, a Mrs. Hanna sent me her brother Rhodes's *History of the Civil War.* I did look into that at an odd minute and though I loathe reading about that time and generally do not read books of that class found it most interesting and well done. As to all else my mind is purged of everything but law—which for one sweet week I hope to abandon—and then to be able to report something.                           *Aff'ly yours, O. W. Holmes*

---

[1] Dorothy Kirchwey Brown, friend of Holmes and wife of La Rue Brown, Boston lawyer.

*Washington, D.C., April 8, 1919*

*Dear Laski:* The book is read—finished less than five minutes ago
—and read with enthusiasm. The combination of learning and
ability is very impressive to me—and to a very great extent I
follow you with agreement. We both are ideasts rather than thing-
sters and your attitude is what I should expect from that. There
is no doubt a slight tint of rose to you in what I should see blue.
You have some phrases that carry a suggestion I shouldn't accept
—*e.g. capitalist* regime as if socialism or any other ism wouldn't
have to be capitalistic or die. I don't mean by that of course that
mankind might not give up coordinated production on a large
scale—on the notion that it cost more than it came to—but when
such a self-denying ordinance as that is at hand perhaps society
would be ready to deal with life. I confess that to me any reconstruction that does not begin with that seems hopeless. I respect
your respect for the human soul while still doubting whether to
share it. The formula of life to great masses would be Feed—
*F-outre* and Finish, and I am not sure that it won't remain so. If
that should be true would there be ground for scruples (in the
contrast) to Pericles, Aeschylus and Aristotle? I confess that some
of the French conceptions of the equality demanded by justice
seem to me absurd. I don't quite understand the contrast between
a government for consumers and one for producers? The consumer
is the only man—a man may produce and be damned if the world
doesn't want his product. In the way of further criticism I think
your proofreading has not been very good. I have made a list of
places that seemed to need correction and you have a fondness for
certain words that I think could be used more rarely to advantage
—such are: equate—slay (very British)—basic—paramountcy—
tragic. But that empties my sack and the rest is all praise. If the
book does not bring you a lot of *kudos* among the competent I
shall be surprised—and even those who would fain have the conditions of society cast iron I should think would appreciate the
fairness of your decision. It is infinitely interesting to me and
opens new vistas. I have been much interrupted in writing—among
other things our cook is very ill here—I fear dying. So I haven't
said all I could wish to—but I hope enough.

*Aff'ly, O. W. Holmes*

*Cambridge, April 10, 1919*

*My dear Justice:* A word in the middle of a report for the government. Your letter went to my heart. I cared deeply for your judgment on my first principles and the measure of your agreement is,
for me, the measure of my success. I am possibly more optimistic
than I should be and too hopeful of the results of my teaching

upon men. But if I carry you along my path, even cautiously, I
feel that my work has a rationale that makes it worth while. My
debt to you, heaven knows, is already heavy enough. But a letter
like that makes me humbly grateful that you are alive. You are
one of very few who judge me on Menander's admirable principle:

> Μὴ τοῦτο βλέψῃς εἰ νεώτερος λέγω,
> Ἀλλ᾽ εἰ φρονοῦντος τοὺς λόγους ἀνδρὸς λέγω[1]

My deep affection to you both.        *Ever affectionately, H. J. L.*


*Cambridge, Mass., April 20, 1919*
*My dear Justice:* . . . One comment I am tempted to make because accident may give you the chance to say a useful word. Your
remark that some regard Felix as a dangerous person is at the root
of a real effort in Boston to make Felix's position here untenable.
From whom it ultimately derives I do not know, but so far as I
can gather it receives the most voluble expression from Richard
Hale with occasional assistance from Thomas Nelson Perkins.[1]
Hale is abominable. He actually sent for the editor of the *Law Review*
early in the year and warned him against Felix. Why he adopts
this attitude I do not know though Ned Adams suggests that it is
anti-semitism. The Pound forces in the school are generally having
a difficult time. There are three appointments to be made and
where Pound wants—and can get—real scholars they want to force
on him typical State Street lawyers whose success is doubtful.
Pound, of course, will stick by his guns, and his faculty is unanimously with him. But the animus against him (a relic of the
Brandeis affair)[2] is apparent at every stage. My own character is
less important. I've had no difficulties, though, of course, I have
enemies and to spare. But I have friends who would stand by me
and they are mostly those who have real standing among the
scholars. But on the main point if you ever get a chance to drop
a hint to Hale or Perkins you would do us all a great service.
My love to you both.        *Ever affectionately, H. J. L.*

---

[1] Unidentified minor fragment of Menander: "Have regard to this: not
whether I that speak am somewhat young, but whether I speak the words
of wisdom." Allinson Translation, Loeb Classical Library, *Menander* (1930),
p. 513.

[1] Thomas Nelson Perkins (1870-1937); Boston lawyer and Fellow of
Harvard College.

[2] In 1916 Dean Pound had supported Wilson's nomination of Brandeis to
the Supreme Court when leaders of the Boston Bar and of the Harvard community had actively opposed his confirmation.

*Washington, D.C., April 20, 1919*

*Dear Laski:* Some days ago a letter to you was begun but I chucked it into the fire as I did little more than repeat views with which you are familiar—the qualifications that I should feel to what seem to be your ideals in the social order. By the by the *New Republic* has a paragraph about Debs that seems to me exactly right although I suppose it would not be proper for me to say so publicly.[1] I wonder if Debs really has any ideas. What I have read of his discourse has seemed to me rather silly—and what he said about the judgment against him showed great ignorance, if as I am ready to believe he is not dishonest. Although we are outsiders I think we can agree that perhaps the greatest, most thrilling sentence that comes to us from ancient times is: Father forgive them; for they know not what they do. One who sees the inevitable everywhere has occasion to remember it pretty often. I told my fellow sportsmen yesterday they had done all they could to break an old man's spirit. 1. They adopted a dissent from an opinion I wrote and the dissent will go tomorrow as the opinion of a unanimous Court, although four of us think it wrong—but not a matter in which dissent is worth while.[2] 2. They granted a rehearing in a case I wrote—that is they will tomorrow.[3] 3. The C. J. hung up my this week's opinion to see what he would do about it.[4]

Yet, praise be to Allah, I am a merry bard. The rehearing is on some details overlooked, the emphasis being on a more general question (railroad) which will be left as it was decided (I was glad to have it granted)—and I doubt if the C. J. will shake the opinion of the others who agree with me, if he tries to. Also I don't care if he does. Of course all this is *entrissimus nous*—though I expect the results I mention will be public before you get this. I trust that your classic taste approves of my occasional excursions into linguistic innovations. I wish I had some *pièce de résistance* or lighter work to take up when there comes an hour of leisure, waiting for my assignment—as yesterday p.m. and this morning. Yesterday p.m. after walking home with Brandeis through the Botanic Garden at the foot of the Capitol and the Smithsonian grounds I toyed with books on etching and got a snooze. This

---

[1] "Eugene Debs has gone to the West Virginia Penitentiary to begin his ten year sentence. There is no doubt about the legality of his conviction. His Canton speech clearly violated the Espionage Act. But since that act ceases to have force when peace is declared, and since the emergency which might have justified it has passed, to let Debs serve his sentence would be both cruel and blind." 18 *New Republic* 362 (April 19, 1919). In December 1920, President Harding commuted the sentence of Debs.

[2] The case has not been identified.

[3] Probably *Central of Georgia Ry. Co.* v. *Wright*, 250 U.S. 519 (decided Oct. 27, 1919).

[4] Presumably *United Railroads* v. *San Francisco*, 249 U.S. 517 (decided April 21, 1919). This was the one opinion delivered by Holmes on April 21.

morning I actually have read most of the *New Republic.* Walter Lippmann sent me his essay in book form and I reread it with renewed admiration. You perceive that this letter is really a *dévergondage* of the spirit in default of your presence. *Inter alia* I looked at some of Goya's Miseries of War. They grow more terrible with familiarity. While I observe on the other hand that the poets like Browning and Swinburne who stirred me to the marrow when I was younger now move me less. Homage to the Missus.

*Aff'ly yours, O. W. Holmes*

*Cambridge, April 23, 1919*

*My dear Justice:* I sent you yesterday one of my extra copies of McIlwain's *James I.* It will fill up at least one gap in your leisure. I suggest that these books will tickle your palate. B. Russell, *An Introduction to Mathematical Philosophy* (Macmillan)—non-technical; L. T. Hobhouse, *The Metaphysical Theory of the State* (Macmillan); W. L. George, *Blind Alley* (Little Brown)—the best war novel I've read; F. S. Marvin, *The Century of Hope* (Oxford).[1] I would send them all but with a knowledge of your hatred of borrowing I await commands. Marvin in particular, please. . . .

*In re* Debs, I think most cool-minded people know that he is a well-meaning, obstinate mule—damnably sincere and a clear case for pardon. If the Court ever makes unofficial recommendations to the executive on this head, it has a great chance here to take the sting out of bad feeling. But no one I have met thinks the decision at all open to question—what was stupid was the act with the substance of which you weren't concerned. I don't believe in the C. J. so it's useless for me—also discourteous—to recite on him. He always leaves me in the air whenever he writes a case and I get no comfort from his attitude.

I agree heartily with your admiration of Lippmann's booklet. He has a mind like a knife and will be a great power one day. What you say of poetry intrigues me much. I get more and more the sense that the poets waste on form what substance more vitally demands—and I get my comfort from sources. I'd rather read Parliamentary debates than Wordsworth and a good decision than Herrick. But I put Goya among the documents—damn him, he makes my flesh creep as no one in the world and it seems as though his acids were the distillation of evil.

I've just read the report of the British military commission on conditions in Germany[2] with a sense that the Anglo-Saxon peoples

---

[1] F. S. Marvin's *The Century of Hope* (1919) was reviewed by Laski in 21 *New Republic* 30 (Dec. 3, 1919).

[2] *Command Papers* (Session of 1919) #52, 54, 208.

are, after all, the most fundamentally decent lot alive. No hate, no damned adjectives, simply a critical statement of the facts found, without extravagance or else but gravely and soberly set down. And they aren't trying to grab the earth like France and Italy and those blessed Balkan peoples. I could be an antinationalist in a fortnight if I were in Europe. As it is, I get moments when I appreciate even Lenin. And damn it, if I could take time off to write a gospel for atheists and tell them to come out against Church revivals and new theologies and higher thought and these blessed sciences that are neither Christian nor science it would be a moral katharsis to me.

I ache for the time when you'll be down at Beverly. We'll settle the world there in great shape.

My love to you both—it is good to have you alive.

*Ever affectionately yours, Harold J. Laski*


*Washington, D.C., May 1, 1919*

*Dear Laski:* First, accept my thanks for the noble volume, McIlwain's *James I.* I shall read the Introduction at my first leisure for McIlwain is first-class. The Monarch has changed places with his attendant and must play second fiddle. 2. I suppose it was the Debs incident that secured me the honor of being among those destined to receive an explosive machine, stopped in the Post Office as you may [have] seen.[1] It shows a want of intelligence in the senders. 3. In view of our past talks you don't surprise me by your attitude toward poetry, but I think you go too far. If poetry were mainly M. Arnold's Criticism of Life I might agree—but poetry in my opinion, although Royce was thought to have vanquished me in a discussion in Mrs. Whitman's studio many years ago,[2] has not the discovery of truth as its object—the great truths have not been discovered by the poets. Its function is to make us realize what we admit, to inspire, and to charm. I once told my father that I thought occasional poetry was more important than the great masterpieces, because in the mass it vocalizes the *milieu*—it brings home to the inarticulate the emotional and intellectual atmosphere in which they live. I may add incidentally that I don't suppose Shakespeare would have made a great king or a great philosopher (for his writing Bacon was a *tour de force*), but he knew how it felt to be a king or a Hamlet or Falstaff (Hamlet with more belly on a lower plane). 4. I have had a letter from Morrison and have

---

[1] See New York *Times*, May 1, 1919.

[2] Mrs. Henry Whitman (Sarah Wyman), Boston artist and friend and neighbor of Holmes at Beverly Farms. See *Sarah Whitman* (1904), p. 25, for Holmes's tribute to her memory. Josiah Royce, the Harvard philosopher, was among her friends.

answered it.[3] 5. Your speed in reading the *Odyssey* excites my envy. I put in a book or two in the summer but I don't find the Greek very easy in these days even with a pony alongside. I also found my enthusiasm cool as I went on. 6. I thought and think that Perkins was converted to Frankfurter by meeting him in Washington. I have hesitated about writing to Hale—and still hesitate. I can't imagine why he is stirred up—unless as you suggest it is an echo of the Brandeis row. You say you have enemies. I didn't know it and don't see why you should have—have you trod on toes? Ames[4] always wanted to pitch into me but he wasn't an enemy—he was almost a friend. By the by, when I read his collected works he struck me, as Gurney[5] years ago pronounced him, as a man of rather moderate faculties who had cultivated his garden. I am snatching a moment from duties and must shut up.

*Affectionately yours, O. W. Holmes*


*Cambridge, May 11, 1919*

*My dear Justice:* I seem to have been drowned in committees this last week—the more irritating because they did not in the result commit. But I am full of ideas as to the methods of organising discussion in small groups and in the summer I badly want you to tell me (if you will) how you organise the conferences of the Supreme Court and how far they are effective as an instrument of thought. If I had a really first-rate student I would put him on to studying the standing-orders of parliamentary assemblies to discover their efficacy in this regard.

What you say of poetry seems to me exactly just. I can see that at an epoch of crisis a poem (Lilliburlero, etc.) will have value for the mass of men; and I can see that normally any poem is individually priceless if you happen to feel that way about it. What I can't see is that the poetic exposition of experience is *per se* more valid than any other summary—that catching the glint of sunlight on a rose, or hearing the whirr of wild bird's unstreaked wings, or remarking that the morning is ivory-fingered means that the poet has deeper insights than other men or that I should learn more from Wordsworth's *Prelude* (which I can't read) than I should from *Tom Jones*. I like Shelley and Keats and Browning, but I

---

[3] Stanley Morrison (1892-1955) was to be Holmes's Secretary during the 1919-20 term of the Court. He later became Professor of Law at Stanford University.

[4] James Barr Ames (1846-1910), legal historian, was Professor of Law and Dean of the Harvard Law School, 1877-1909. His numerous essays were published as *Lectures on Legal History and Miscellaneous Legal Essays* (1913). He had crossed swords with Holmes on several issues, particularly on problems of the history of contracts in English law.

[5] Ephraim Whitman Gurney (1829-1886); Harvard classicist and historian, and Dean of Harvard College under President Eliot.

don't think their remarks justify or refute my beliefs, and that makes me suspect current emotions about the vital splendor of new poetic experiments or older assertions like that of Fletcher of Saltoun.[1]

Meanwhile I have been doing some jolly reading. Next week I have to lecture on the political theories of early socialism in England and France. I've been at the old books (which are the best books) with mingled feelings of contempt and admiration. Sismondi I put far higher than I had done in my Oxford days, and I thought that Saint-Simon and Fourier owed more to him than they admit. But the fellows I thought really superb were Hodgskin, Thompson[2] and Bray[3]—the early English socialists. Not, of course, in the fundamental surplus-value theory, but in their incidental remarks on the substantial content of the machine-technology, and I'm going, somehow, to get the money to reprint them or bust.

I understand your hesitation about writing to Hale and I am glad to have your remark on Perkins's attitude to Felix. The real truth is that there's a great fight on as to the future of the School and the older Tories are eager to make the place unbearable by Pound. He is a very great Dean and the students worship him and sooner or later the Law School Alumni Association has to step in and tell the world what Pound is counting for in scholarship and prevent this idle insistence on a *status quo* which has already lost its status. But I will tell you the inwardness of this when we meet.

Are you for a novel? Joseph Conrad's *Arrow of Gold* is superb. And please tell Mrs. Holmes that her friend Basil King has just published the worst novel ever written on this hemisphere. I am eager to hear if you read Freund in the *New Republic* of May 3rd and if you were at all influenced by his analysis.[4]

My love to you both.          *Yours ever affectionately, H. J. L.*

---

[1] Andrew Fletcher (1655-1716) of Saltoun was the Scottish politician and scholar who had observed in his *Account of a Conversation concerning a Right Regulation of Government* (1704) that he believed that "if a man were permitted to make all the ballads, he need not care who should make the laws of a nation."

[2] William Thompson (1783-1833); Irish economist and socialist, who passed from Benthamite Utilitarianism to Owenite socialism; author of *Principles of the Distribution of Wealth* (1824).

[3] John Francis Bray (1809-1895); American-born socialist and friend of labor; author of *Labor's Wrongs and Labor's Remedy: or the Age of Might and the Age of Right* (1839).

[4] "The Debs Case and Freedom of Speech," by Ernst Freund, 19 *New Republic* 13 (May 3, 1919). The article was critical of the decision and of Holmes's opinion in the *Debs* case, protesting that it allowed implied rather than direct, provocation as justification for a conviction for speech-making, and criticizing as inappropriate the analogy of crying "Fire" in a crowded theater. Freund also criticized the Espionage Act for the power which it appeared to confer upon juries to make arbitrary, nonreviewable findings that there is a psychological nexus between words and deeds.

[*May 13, 1919*]

*Dear Laski:* Yesterday I wrote the within and decided not to send
it as some themes may become burning. Instead I trust it con-
fidentially to you and it will answer your inquiry about Freund. I
thought it poor stuff—for reasons indicated within. As to Pound I
wish I could write something. I just have received notice of a
meeting of the Harvard Law School Association of which I believe
I am king (Log). They ask for suggestions. Could I say anything
to them? Answer quick. The letter comes from F. W. Grinnell,
partner of Richard Hale. The conference today hung up 2 of my
3 cases for dissent or further consideration[1]—the former I thought
absurd—the latter (as to a different matter and on suggestion of
Vandevanter) I thought wise—but all such things are irritating.
I have sent for the book you specially recommended. I forget the
name—*Century of Hope?*

I wonder if it would pay to read Aristotle (some parts) in Greek
this summer and if yea, why. I look forward to jaws.

                                              *Aff'ly, O. W. Holmes*

[Enclosure]

Supreme Court of the United States

*Private*                          *Washington, D.C., May 12, 1919*

*My dear Mr. Croly:* On Saturday Mr. Hard's article on Mr. Burleson, Espionagent, fell under my eye.[1] I do not know enough of the
details of public affairs to have opinions about Mr. Burleson's conduct of his office but the general aspects of the article so stirred my
sympathies that I want to express them. As long ago as 1908 when
I wrote *Harriman* v. *I.C.C.*, 211 U.S. 407 it seemed to me that we
so long had enjoyed the advantages protected by bills of rights
that we had forgotten—it used sometimes to seem to me that the
*New Republic* had forgotten—that they had had to be fought for
and could not be kept unless we were willing to fight for them.
Few can sympathize more than I do with Mr. Hard's general way
of thinking on the subject. As I spoke of it to my secretary and
of my inclination to write to you he called my attention to the
article on the *Debs* case which I had not seen. You had a short
paragraph in an earlier number that struck me as exactly right.[2]

---

[1] On May 19, 1919, Holmes delivered the Court's opinion in three cases:
*Schlitz Brewing Co.* v. *Houston Ice Co.*, 250 U.S. 28; *Coleman* v. *United
States, id.* 30; and *Sage* v. *United States, id.* 33. In the first of the three
cases McKenna and Pitney, JJ., dissented without opinion.

[1] 19 *New Republic* 42 (May 10, 1919). William Hard's article was
severely critical of the action of the Postmaster General in denying second-
class mailing privileges to periodicals of a "seditious tendency."

[2] See, *supra*, p. 147.

This article appeared to me less so if I understood its implications. The constitutionality of the act so far as the clauses concerning obstructing the recruiting service are involved was passed upon in *Schenck* v. *U.S.* and so all that was needed in the *Debs* case was to refer to that decision, and, given the finding of the jury, in my opinion it was impossible to have a rational doubt about the law. Freund's objection to a jury 'guessing at motive, tendency and possible effect' is an objection to pretty much the whole body of the law, which for thirty years I have made my brethren smile by insisting to be everywhere a matter of degree. In *Nash* v. *U.S.* 229 U.S. 373 the same objections were urged to criminal prosecutions under the Sherman Act in view of the interpretation of the Statute by the *Standard Oil* & *Tobacco* Cases[3]—but I answered p. 377 that 'the law is full of instances where a man's fate depends on his estimating rightly, that is, as the jury subsequently estimates it, from matters of degree,' and illustrated by murder and manslaughter— showing that a man might be hanged for consequences that he neither intended nor foresaw (apart from statute of course). I hated to have to write the *Debs* case and still more those of the other poor devils before us the same day and the week before. I could not see the wisdom of pressing the cases, especially when the fighting was over and I think it quite possible that if I had been on the jury I should have been for acquittal but I cannot doubt that there was evidence warranting a conviction on the disputed issues of fact. Moreover I think the *clauses under consideration* not only were constitutional but were proper enough while the war was on. When people are putting out all their energies in battle I don't think it unreasonable to say we won't have obstacles intentionally put in the way of raising troops—by persuasion any more than by force. But in the main I am for aeration of all effervescing convictions—there is no way so quick for letting them get flat. I always imagined a good illustration could be found in a little sheet published during the Commune, the *Père Duchêne,* although I never studied the work, after buying it in London. One would have trembled to know that now one was going to get it in the neck—with no reserves. Well, the writer let his heart out in No. 1—he could not get any higher in No. 2—and by No. 4 I suspect that he was a bore. I write this letter only to ease my mind, not to impose an answer on you.

*Very sincerely yours, O. W. Holmes*

Of course it is only for your private eye.

---

[3] Counsel had urged in the *Nash* case that because the *Standard Oil* (221 U.S. 1) and *American Tobacco* (*id.* 106) cases had held that the Sherman Act only prohibited combinations "unduly" restricting competition, the criminal sections of the Act had been rendered unconstitutionally vague.

*Cambridge, May 15, 1919*

*My dear Justice:* Only one word in very partial reply to a letter worth its weight in gold. If the Association would, *te movente*, record its appreciation of the way Pound kept the School going during the war it would help marvellously. That, *bien entendu*, if you felt so inclined.

My love and great gratitude for that letter.

*Ever affectionately yours, H. J. L.*

*Washington, D.C., May 18, 1919*

*Dear Laski:* The Post Office has shown intelligence for once. Your note directed to 421 West 21st Street, New York City, was forwarded to me. But stop—that is the *New Republic*. They probably sent it on. My address is always as above. Following your suggestion I have just written this note to Grinnell. "Your letter invites suggestion and I venture one. I have a very strong conviction of the value and importance of Pound who I think has done much to maintain the superlative reputation of the School. If it were possible to pass a resolution expressing our appreciation of the way in which he has kept the School going during the war, or giving him encouragement in such form as is deemed best I should be much gratified. Perhaps you will call this to the attention of the meeting." I shall post the letter along with this. As I shall not be present I did not put it as a motion made by me.

Talking with Brandeis yesterday (a big chap) he drove a harpoon into my midriff by saying that it would be for the good of my soul to devote my next leisure to the study of some domain of fact—suggesting the textile industry, which, after reading many reports &c, I could make living to myself by a visit to Lawrence. My last visit was as an undergraduate when I joined a picnic of the factory hands and on a visit to the factory next day with my classmate and host found that we were suspected to be responsible for the non-appearance of a girl that morning. I believe we convinced them of our innocence of any escapade. Well—I hate facts —and partly because of that am impressed by Brandeis's suggestion. It was good for me that instead of philosophy I was shoved into the law. I suppose it would be good for me to get into actualities touching spindles—immigration—God knows what—but I would rather meditate on the initial push and the following spin —(whatever the true translation) of ἴυγξ ἕλκε τὺ τῆνον ἐμὸν ποτὶ δῶμα τὸν ἄνδρα.[1] (Think not that I pretend to have been able to quote this without the book.) Meantime I have received at last *The Century of Hope* to which (at your recommendation) I turn from you.               *Affectionately yours, O. W. Holmes*

---

[1] Theocritus, Idyll II, "The Sorceress": "Turn, magic wheel, draw homeward him I love" (Calverley, tr.).

*Cambridge, May 20, 1919*

*My dear Justice:* That is a most generous letter of yours about Pound and on his account, as well as my own, I am very grateful. It will give exactly the kind of help that is needed. It raises the whole question in simple and direct form, and it makes the members realise that they must give support to a great adventure. I can't tell you how moved I am by your generosity.

Brandeis's remark to you is very interesting. Somewhere in Harnack[1] there is a sentence on the early nominalists to the effect that they were tired of abstractions and demanded contact with the hard and concrete facts. What you said the other day of socialism brings that vividly to my mind. I don't think anyone can read Thomas Hodgskin or William Thompson without a sense that their case against capitalism must be answered and that it is not easy to answer. If I may say so, you come into contact with men of property on their very best side—the lawyer of ability appealing to your intellect, the great business man describing some fine achievement, the wife of a millionaire asking you to share some deeply-felt aesthetic enjoyment, Paul Warburg making marvellously simple some vast technical complexity. You don't see the obvious evils that one gets contact with among the trade unions—the blindness to pain, the hard obstinacy, the relentless pressure, the unwillingness to experiment with the prospects of human nature. If you saw that Lawrence strike at first hand you would say (as I do) that almost any system must be better than one which gives some men economic power over others. I am not a socialist in a Marxian sense; but I am against the inheritance of great fortunes, against the refusal to allow labor a share in the control of business (an increasing share), the unwillingness to establish proper human conditions in the factory. I believe there is a real class-war and that progress towards a fuller development of human capacity comes out of the growing strength of the workers. What mainly impresses me under present industrial organisation is the wastage of capacity which for me is the worst sin. And we try to remedy by the second sin which is social reform—a name for multiplying the number of clerks and teachers and dethroning spontaneity for paternalism. The fact is that books like G. Wallas's *Francis Place* (I am sending it to you with my love) and Hammond[2] and Miss Hutchins on the factory system[3] destroy the hypothesis of a spirit for good in what, for want of a better phrase—one calls the master-

---

[1] Adolf von Harnack (1851-1930), church historian and theologian; author of *History of Dogma* (7 vols., tr. 1896-97).

[2] J. L. and Barbara Hammond, *The Skilled Labourer* (1919); *The Village Labourer, 1760-1832* (1911); *The Town Labourer, 1760-1832* (1919).

[3] B. L. Hutchins and A. Harrison, *A History of Factory Legislation* (1903).

class. You talk for an hour with Furuseth[4] of the seamen or Hillman[5] of the garment workers and you will realise how little we have done to use the brains at our disposal. But this is matter for talk and I leave it to prick you later on. . . .

Old Haldane wrote me a most kindly letter about my *Law Review* article which pleased me much and asked very sweetly after you. He is a generous-hearted fellow.

I wish to God that fellow Hawker had got across.[6] It makes one feel mean to know that men will risk their lives in adventure and end in the pathos of a lone obscurity.

My love to you both. It is good to know you are alive.

*Ever yours affectionately, H. J. L.*

Why I addressed you at the *N.R.* I know not.


*Washington, D.C., May 24, 1919* [1]

*Dear Laski:* While waiting for proof of an opinion in a case which the Chief asked me to take a few days ago although it is by no means certain that I can get a majority, your book, just arrived, and your letter call for my first activities. The book entices me because of the mention of Place, unknown to me before, in *The Century of Hope.* That I purchased, according to your directions, and am half through. I haven't had much time yet. I like to read an optimistic, hazardously generalizing book of that sort. Even though I can't follow it with entire belief, it stimulated hope. I rather like too the attitude toward man as a being of vast spiritual significance, which of course he must be for us, while I surmise that cosmically he is a case of animal like the rest. But I turn to your letter. What you say to explain my opinions, while it confirms what I have long said, fails to hit me. For a quarter of a century I have said that the real foundations of discontent were emotional not economic, and that if the socialists would face the facts and put the case on that ground I should listen to them with respect. I used to tell my wife or she used to tell me, it was a joint opinion, that the manner of the Beacon Street women toward their servants and employees did more than the women were worth to upset the existing order. My opinion, however, is based on the effort to think quantitatively not dramatically. I won't go over the old ground,

---

[4] Andrew Furuseth (1954-1938); President of the International Seaman's Union of America, and effective spokesman for American seamen.

[5] Sidney Hillman (1887-1946), energetic President of Amalgamated Clothing Workers of America and frequent representative of labor on governmental commissions.

[6] On May 18, Henry G. Hawker, and Lt. Com. McKenzie Grieve, of the British navy, started their unsuccessful transatlantic flight, by land plane, from Newfoundland. The plane came down at sea, and they were rescued on the 19th.

[1] A brief note from Laski, dated May 22, 1919, is omitted.

but to my mind the notion that any rearrangement of property while any part of the world propagates freely, will prevent civilization from killing its weaker members, is absurd. I think that the crowd now has substantially all there is—and that every mitigation of the lot of any body of men has to be paid for by some other or the same body of men—and I don't think that cutting off the luxuries of the few would make an appreciable difference in the situation. On the other hand I think that the ideals of men like Veblen besides cherishing illusions are ugly. No doubt I, like everyone, am influenced in my aesthetic preferences by my environment past and present—but I have intended to be detached. However, as the question at bottom is what kind of a world do you want, I, for whatever reason, do so far sympathize with the strug-for *lifeurs*, as the French put it, that in the ultimate necessary self-preference, I desire a world in which art and philosophy, in their use*less* aspect, may have a place. I say useless, to mark the point that they are ends in themselves. Of course I think them useful even in Veblen's world.——The proof has come, been corrected, and gone. Citations verified at Department of Justice. Now I am vacuous and can [illegible] before the robber. The moment work is done my natural bodily languor inclines me to stretch at full length and soon, *non obstant* literature, I snooze. I even have said that one should be able to go to bed at 11 a.m. to recover from the fatigue of getting up. I will try to read a little more of your optimist (Marvin) while waiting for the corrected opinion to return for distribution. There is a slight feeling of unreality in him as with others of the upward and onward—but as I have said he gives me pleasure. In the summer, if not before, you must remind me of Hodgskin and Thompson for I want to read whatever is thought best on that side. As I said those who have talked economics and whom I have read I think show yawning fallacies. I am glad that you heard from Haldane—I have had early and late encouragement from him but have not heard from him or known much of his doings for a long time. Also I have eaten good victuals at his house.                    *Affectionately yours, O. W. Holmes*

*Cambridge, May 26, 1919*
*My dear Justice:* This is to introduce Mr. H. W. Massingham, the editor of the London *Nation*. It would be insolent in me to praise him; but I want to say on paper that he represents for me all that is best and most generous in English life. And it is because I want him to see what I care for most deeply in America that I send him to you.

My love to you,          *Ever affectionately yours, Harold J. Laski*

*Cambridge, May 30, 1919*

*My dear Justice:* I have just been reading—as it is fitting I should read—not for the first time nor the last, your Memorial Day speech.[1] It made me even more proud of you than I am, for it has in it a beauty which this war has made thrice beautiful. The men of whom you write were my friends also and it matters nothing that they rest at Loos and Givenchy, on the Somme and at Vimy Ridge instead of Fredericksburg and Ball's Bluff and Antietam. I wish their mothers could read it and know from your warm yet moderate appraisal how they stand in our hearts also.

And I have been reading a very great book which shall be yours for the summer—if, by chance, it has escaped you. It is Benn's *History of Rationalism in the Nineteenth Century*. It's fine not only for its fine historic perspective but also because it gives one the courage that can come only from the historic demonstration that unreason contains the seeds of its own dissolution. I read also Maine on *Popular Government*—some clever predictions but the rest the typical product of a mind warped by Anglo-Indian experience. And that led me to a book which is, I think, the best I ever read on India. It's by William Archer[2] and on matters such as the supposed profundity of Indian philosophy, its supposed magnificent art, its bewildering pride in its genius for intuition, I think it is conclusive. I'd like you to read it and then, if you agree with me, to give it to Brandeis to read. It convinced me that metaphysical results, like those of science, are simply the result of dirt and sweat and that the idea that there's a royal road to truth through the intuition of a genie traveling on a lonely hillside is not merely nonsense but also dangerous nonsense. Which made me re-read friend Aristotle's *Ethics* with the conviction that no man ever lived more sane than he. I wouldn't exchange one book of it for all the volumes of all the Eastern philosophers there ever were.

I'm glad you liked *The Living Past*.[3] I've been trying it on my students to good advantage. Its mistake I think is to identify material advance with spiritual enrichment which is, I take it, the hang-over from Comtian days. I see a greater humanitarianism in these days than in the past and I value the determination that there shall be no avoidable pain. But for the rest I think the argument for progress is as yet unmade. I think there *can* be improvement. Education can make a bundle of sensual impulses into a man. But *that* education is too narrowly confined for us yet to boast of its influence. Marvin, I would argue, continually mistakes aspiration for accomplishment.

---

[1] *Speeches*, p. 1.

[2] Presumably William Archer, *India and the Future* (1912).

[3] Laski evidently interpreted Holmes's reference to F. S. Marvin's *The Century of Hope* (1919), *supra*, as a reference to the same author's *The Living Past* (1913).

I hope you will have the chance of real talk with Massingham, whom I ventured to send to you. He is the greatest of English editors. Fearless, honest, uncompromising, with fine perception and flawless taste. Perhaps a little too much the silent Englishman, but full of knowledge of events. He can tell you of Haldane, Asquith, Morley *et al* and he knows all about you. In other words we dined together.

My love heapily to you both,      *Ever affectionately yours, H. J. L.*


*Washington, D.C., June 1, 1919*

*Dear Laski:* . . . The Chief has suggested that I write a case of his and has done it in such a kind hesitating way that even if I could [have] hesitated otherwise, which I shouldn't have done, I can't now.[1] Hence I shan't be happy till I get (at) it—but your letter just arrived imperatively demands a word of agreement right off. It is apropos of Oriental insights. What I have been in the habit of saying is this. For fifty years it has been my business to know the movement of thought in one of its great expressions— the law—and my pleasure to try to know something of its movement in philosophy, and if anything is plain it is that during the period that counts—from Pericles to now—there has been a gradual advance and that our view of life today is more manifold and more profound than it ever has been before. When the Europe and Asia man said Europe has given us the steam engine, Asia every religion that ever commanded the reverence of mankind—I answered I bet on the steam engine. For the steam engine means science and science is the root from which comes the flower of our thought. When I have seen clever women who have read all their lives go off into enthusiasm over some oriental, pseudo-oriental, or spiritualistic fad it has struck me that all their reading seems to have given them no point of view—no *praejudicia*—or preliminary bets as to the probability that the sign turn to the left will lead to a *cul de sac*. If I follow Brandeis's suggestion I shall have little time for other things—but as my bet, on the strength of what I do know, is with Archer—bar reservations for the Taj Mahal, etc. that will keep.

I turn to another matter. I had a dear little letter from Pound expressing satisfaction at what I wrote to Grinnell but also saying that people there want to push Frankfurter out of the school. He says nothing about himself but I have been led to fear that the push extends to Pound. Two days ago I asked Brandeis if he thought it would be well for me to write to Lowell—he rather inclined yes. I still hesitate but probably should be writing to him

---

[1] The case has not been identified.

were I not writing to you. If the school should lose Pound and Frankfurter it would lose its soul, it seems to me. I hesitate because I know no details, but my conviction is strong. So far as Pound is concerned it is also disinterested, for I don't know his opinions except through his writings and so far as I know I never have come in for much credit in them. But there can be no doubt that he is a real focus of spiritual energy—and even if his presence has prevented subscriptions to the Law School I can't but believe that the spark of inspiration is worth more than dollars. By Jove, I think I'll say that to Lowell. I am worried—and all the more that without my foreknowledge I was put in as President of the Law School Association—of course merely as a figurehead—but I hate to feel King Log. With which I shut up as the barber is due to cut my hair. Does the movement threaten you? I am full of helpless anxiety.                    *Affectionately yours, O. W. Holmes*

*Beverly Farms, June 16, 1919*

*Dear Laski:* Your letter of the 12th¹ was forwarded to this place this morning where it finds us still somewhat pale from the Washington work and weather and the long journey—but on the upgrade. Apropos of Pound I wrote to Lowell and enclose his reply² which gives me a different impression from what I had feared. You may show it to Pound if you think it advisable (as I should). Please return it to me. I have the notion that Pound thought Lowell's attitude to be different from this, and it may cheer him up.

On the train I reread the greater part of Perry's *Present Philosophical Tendencies*—a clever book—but I think made a little obscure by professional phraseology. What do you know about him? It amuses me to see the philosophers laboriously getting back to

¹ This letter is missing, as are all others which Laski may have written to Holmes between those of May 30 and October 8, 1919.

² The letter from President Lowell to Holmes has not been found. With the permission of the President and Fellows of Harvard College the following copy of Holmes's letter to Lowell, dated June 2, 1919, is reprinted:

"My dear Mr. President: "Some days ago on receiving notice of a meeting of the Harvard Law School Association, of which I found I was King Log, I suggested a resolution recognizing Pound's services to the School &c which I hope would meet your approval. I should have consulted you had I not been taken rather suddenly. But I have a very strong feeling that Pound and in his place Frankfurter have and impart the ferment which is more valuable than an endowment, and makes of a Law School a focus of life.

"I venture while I am about it to suggest that Pound ought to have an LL.D. from Harvard as I believe he has from various other universities. He is one of the very few men whose work on legal subjects is referred to by Continental writers.                    *"Sincerely yours, O. W. Holmes*

"A. Lawrence Lowell, Esq.
"President, Harvard University"

very near the assumptions of the common man—that we are in
the universe not it in us—and I don't see that they improve much
upon my statement that we begin with a great act of faith by
deciding that we are not God, *i.e.* that we are awake and not
dreaming the world—which we never can prove. I have written to
Washington to see if I can get some of Brandeis's accursed recommendations in the way of reports.[3] The temptation is strong to say
that I am old enough to be entitled to leisure—but I suppose that
can't be while one is on the fighting line. Meantime I am amusing
myself with the *Essays of Elia.* . . .    *Aff'ly yours, O. W. Holmes*


                              *Washington, D.C., October 5, 1919* [1]
*Dear Laski:* A hurried line of thanks for your telegram. We got
on better than I dared hope and after two days rest at the Shoreham my wife has moved over here to our house. The worst feature
is the stairs to be mounted but she seems not to mind them.
Brandeis called and seemed to me transfigured by his experiences.[2]
He is in fine shape and talked most interestingly. I find great comfort in his companionship.

Coming on I read John Leitch *Man to Man* which seems to me
to deserve a puff in the *New Republic*.[3] It gave me more hopeful-
ness than anything I have read. He talks as one who has applied
his ideas and succeeded in making employers and employees work
together heartily. Also I read B. Shaw's last plays.[4] I don't care
much for him. He has an Irishman's wit, tenderness and insights
—but I see no correlating theory, only his dogma against the other
fellow's.

I have worked hard and made my secretary work harder in clearing up. Thank God or Prometheus for fire—even in the case of
books that have one's name printed on them so that they can't be
given away or traded, one or two cubic heaps alone remain.

I don't feel the usual glow in getting back to my books and
etchings. It hardly seems as if I had been away—whether preoccupation, age, or accident I don't know.

Tomorrow comes the plunge.

My love to you both,            *Aff'ly yours, O. W. Holmes*

---

[3] During the summer of 1919 Holmes's reading list indicates that he read
*Senate Document 870 of the 2nd Session of the 62nd Congress* on the strike
of textile workers in Massachusetts in 1912, and *Summary of the Condition
of Women and Child Wage Earners in the United States* (1915).

[1] Seventeen short notes from Holmes to Laski, written during the summer
of 1919, are omitted. They were concerned principally with matters of which
Holmes contemporaneously wrote in a similar manner to Sir Frederick Pollock.

[2] In the summer of 1919 Brandeis had been in Europe and Palestine.

[3] The book had been already somewhat critically reviewed in 19 *New
Republic* 361 (July 16, 1919).

[4] *Heartbreak House, Great Catherine,* and *Playlets of the War* (1919).

*Cambridge, October 8, 1919*

*My dear Justice:* . . . There is news and to spare; but I must
select. First, Felix is well, and I think, happy. The Law School
has a record attendance and Pound feels that the burden of the
struggle is past. And of Felix I hear enthusiastic accounts from all
the students who have met him. To me, of course, it makes a
world of difference that he should be here. My life is a whirl of
lectures and students and books. The Yale trip is a pleasant diversion. The Yale students have not the intellectual force of Harvard but they have all the irresistible charm of youth; and the
faculty has an intelligent *camaraderie* which stands out in contrast
to the isolation of Cambridge habits. . . .

I was glad indeed to hear your account of Brandeis; and it made
Felix very happy. I wish he could come in on this police strike.[1]
On both sides, it has become a silly question of prestige and the
real means of a solution get tucked out of sight.

My love to you both,          *Ever affectionately yours, H. J. L.*

*Washington, D.C., October 12, 1919*

*Dear Laski:* Your letter gave me great joy. I suppose I am growing
older. If I can keep the friendship of you and Felix and one or
two others to the end I shall be content. Since getting here, and
after two days of clearing up, I have gone through a stack of cases
and worked hard with success and satisfaction. The only things
read: two books sent to me—Waldstein's (now Sir Charles
Wal*ston*) on *Truth* sent by my friend Ly Askwith—and Mrs.
Clifford's *Miss Fingal.* The latter evokes less criticism on points of
taste than some of hers have and is, I think, imagined and really
*seen* by her—so I found it interesting straight through. I hardly
noticed a hint at mysteries.[1] I wrote to her that I take no stock in

---

[1] On September 9 the vast majority of the Boston Police Force had gone
out on strike, partly in protest against the discharge of nineteen officers and
men for organizing a labor union affiliated with the American Federation of
Labor, and also to secure improved salaries and working conditions. The
Commissioner of Police, Edwin U. Curtis, had stubbornly refused to seek a
compromise solution, and Calvin Coolidge, as Governor, had allowed matters
to drift until they were largely out of hand. At length the militia, buttressed
with Harvard teachers and students, had been called out. Throughout the
controversy Laski had publicly charged that Commissioner Curtis was principally at fault, and in showing more sympathy for the strikers than did the
majority of his articulate colleagues, had antagonized important elements in
the Boston and Cambridge community. The calculated effort of Coolidge to
establish the principle that "there is no right to strike against the public
safety by anybody, anywhere, any time" ultimately led the strikers to permanent discharge and Coolidge to the White House. Phases of Laski's position and the hostility which it aroused at Harvard are indicated in 22
*Harvard Alumni Bulletin*, 106 (Oct. 23, 1919).

[1] *Miss Fingal* (1919), by Holmes's friend Mrs. Lucy Clifford, involved
the theme that the soul of a dead friend lives on in the spirit of another.

possibilities that are such merely in the sense that you can't prove the contrary. I think they tend toward deliquescence. If you are going into such things I prefer to turn at once to my device for the relief of a bored God and think how many universes can be put into the same space without mutual interference so that where I sit there may be going on a deadly contest between a flamboyant demigorgon and an electric chimaera. The Society for Psychical Research I suspect would offer examples of what I deplore.

As to Waldstein's book I hardly think it contributes enough to justify printing, though it pointed out some defects in the English whom nevertheless he credits with being the most truthful race. I could but remember, as against his opening, the saying that a Frenchman wouldn't mind lying about facts on occasion but would think himself dishonored if untrue to his beliefs—whereas an Englishman who wouldn't misstate facts would equivocate about his beliefs. I suspect there is truth in it and that it points to the French being on a higher plane *quoad hoc*. Somehow I get more of an impression of simple straightforwardness from one of L. Stephen's books than I do from this one devoted to the theme. I wish I had a book this minute to dally with for an hour—and the worst is I know there are dozens around me that I want to read if I only could think what they were. I never read Plato's *Laws*—perchance I will take up the translation with an occasional glance at the Greek. The day of judgment grows nearer—and though not necessary, it would be becoming to have read that. Well, don't forget me till next time. Give my love to Mrs.

*Aff'ly yours, O. W. Holmes*

*Washington, D.C., October 16, 1919*

*Dear Laski:* If the project of printing some of my things has not been given up as a bore[1] (which it may have been and I shall not be wounded), I send you what may be of assistance in the form of suggestions—not insisting on anything. First a list[2]—intended to carry out what you said—and second a copy of my speech at Brown.[3] The earlier essays in *Harvard* [*sic*] *Law Review*,[4] so far as not taken up into my book on *The Common Law* are either young or transitory. Of the latter class are one on *Ultra Vires*[5] (I

---

[1] Among the omitted letters from Holmes written during the summer of 1919 is one dated September 1 indicating that Holmes and Laski had spoken of the possible republication of a number of Holmes's legal essays and speeches. The result, as subsequent letters indicate, was the publication in 1920 of Holmes's *Collected Legal Papers*.

[2] The list has not been preserved.

[3] *Collected Legal Papers*, at 164.

[4] The reference intended was to early contributions to the *American Law Review*.

[5] 6 *Am. L. Rev.* 37 (October 1871).

think the first time that this was made a distinct subject) and one
on grain elevators that had effect in its day.[6] If the project is serious
and under way I could help you unwillingly by sending to you in
confidence two volumes containing most of the things—but not
the Introduction to Wignore's *Continental Legal History Series*—
easily got however with their leave.[7] You said something about
some other speech. You would be free to use my volume. If the
scheme is given up please return the papers herewith enclosed. I
may add a trifle or two if you are going on.

*Aff'ly yours, O. W. Holmes*


*The Graduates Club, New Haven, Connecticut*
*October 17, 1919*
*My dear Justice:* Of course the plan has not been given up. The
difficulty has been that when I had compiled the list (I had all
you mention except the articles in the *Youth's Companion*[1]), I
found that back numbers were largely unavailable so that I had
to begin at once to copy them out for the typist and in a breathless
life that is a hard job. But your offer of the two volumes would
be like meat and drink to me. It would mean that I could get off
the MS to the printer by November 19th and have the book out
early in the New Year. Would you really lend them? That would
be very generous and I can give a guarantee that they will be
carefully treated and honorably returned. I should be ever so
grateful. . . .

My love to you both,    *Ever affectionately yours, Harold J. Laski*


*Washington, D.C., October 20, 1919*
*Dear Laski:* Herewith is handed to my secretary two volumes done
up and to be sent to you. One of them as you will see has all sorts
of fool memoranda relics of the past—but is precious to me on
that account. I have no time to do more than thank you for your
dear letter.                                    *Aff'ly yours, O. W. Holmes*
I haven't reread the *Youth's Companion* and don't know that those
pieces or either of them are worth reprinting—*et sic de similibus*.
I leave it all to you. Though nothing mentioned in my list is *not*
—I guess.

  [6] *Id.* 450 (April 1872).
  [7] 1 *Continental Legal History Series* (1912), Introduction; *Collected Legal Papers*, 298.
  [1] "The Bar as a Profession," 70 *Youth's Companion* 92 (February 1893); *Collected Legal Papers*, 153, 163.

*October 26, 1919*

*Dear Laski:* Your letter says parce*l*.[1] I trust you received two volumes sent separately. I didn't till this moment read your letter correctly and realize that it asked if I would write. I thought it expressed a regret but assumed that I couldn't—I can't—I am too much beleaguered with duties. I infer that you have had trouble, I hope not serious, because of your criticism of Curtis.[2] I gather from what I have seen that you didn't uphold the strike (which I think impossible) but pitched into Curtis's behavior, of which I know little but which I should think was at least open to discussion. I fear we have less freedom of speech here than they have in England. Little as I believe in it as a theory I hope I would die for it and I go as far as anyone whom I regard as competent to form an opinion, in favor of it. Of course when I say I don't believe in it as a theory I don't mean that I do believe in the opposite as a theory. But on their premises it seems to me logical in the Catholic Church to kill heretics and the Puritans to whip Quakers—and I see nothing more wrong in it from our ultimate standards than I do in killing Germans when we are at war. When you are thoroughly convinced that you are right—wholeheartedly desire an end—and have no doubt of your power to accomplish it —I see nothing but municipal regulations to interfere with your using your power to accomplish it. The sacredness of human life is a formula that is good only inside a system of law—and so of the rest—all which apart from its *banalité* I fear seems cold talk if you have been made to feel popular displeasure. I should not be cold about that—nor do I in any way shrink from saying what I think—but I can't spare the energy necessary to deal with extra legal themes. I just have declined once more on the same ground to deliver the Phi Beta Kappa oration—which if I had nothing on my mind I should like to do—but I expect to die without having done that or having been President of the Alumni.

*Aff'ly yours, O. W. H.*

*Cambridge, October 28, 1919*

*My dear Justice:* I should have said 'books.' We are having a grand time reading them, and the selection goes to the typist on Monday.

I have had a fight here, but am, I think, out of danger. Lowell was magnificent and I felt that I had a president in him I would fight for.[1] My protest in the police strike was against the stupidity

---

[1] The letter referred to is missing.

[2] See, *supra*, p. 162, note 1.

[1] For an indication that when the demand was made by some in authority at Harvard that Laski should be asked to resign because of his activities in connection with the Boston Police strike, President Lowell stated that "If the

of dealing in absolutes. It is useless to say you are *für oder gegen* the union. The problem is what conditions led to its formation? Could they have been remedied? Was an attempt made to remedy them? My insistence was that Curtis and Coolidge bungled the whole situation and the Republicans, naturally did not like it. But the atmosphere is clear again and I don't think there will be any difficulties over academic freedom in the future. That applies to Felix as well as to me. I am amazed at the barriers he has over-leaped. People meet him, and the adjective 'dangerous' melts as the snow before the sun. He is very happy—the students, *bien entendu,* are wild about him.

This is an interim letter only. But let me mention *Poor Relations* by Compton Mackenzie as a first-rate rib-tickler.

My love to you both,        *Ever affectionately yours, H. J. L.*


*Washington, D.C., November 3, 1919*
*Dear Laski:* Nothing to tell except the delightful visit of Frank-furter and his joyful news—I think it will be a good thing for him as well as for her.[1] I have had no, or only a few hours, time for reading. In them you couldn't guess what I have been looking at —Bishop Butler's Sermons! People sometimes say they are better than the *Analogy.* It is easy to see why Fitz James Stephen liked them. The old Bishop was a sensible Englishman and did not ignore the uses of resentment—but gave a British Bishop's account of the precept to love one [*sic*] neighbors. Rather a good old boy—and I think his discourses would have seemed about right to adults when I was in college though now they are as dead as Julius Caesar. Everything is regarded with the light of final causes and as ex-hibiting the skill and kindness of the artificer. You know the tale of the little boy who was told that God made everything. "Did he make elephants?" "Yes." "Did he make cows?" "Yes." "Did he make flies?" "Yes." "Fiddling work making flies, I should think." The same might be said of Butler's conception of the work of making man.

This is but to remind you that I live. The letter to the *Cosmo-politan*[2] or whatever magazine it was—or rather the private letter which I didn't intend to have published—was italicised by the

overseers ask for Laski's resignation, they will get mine," see Henry A. Yeomans, *Abbott Lawrence Lowell, 1856-1943* (1948), 316-317. Cf. Laski, *The American Democracy* (1948), p. 357: "President Lowell informed one of his faculty in 1919 that he himself would resign if dismissal was the penalty for utterance in a famous dispute of that year; but he also told the lecturer in confidence not to expect promotion from the university."

[1] In December 1919, Felix Frankfurter and Marion Denman were married.
[2] *Collected Legal Papers,* 279.

editor at his own sweet will and if I remember aright has misprints
in it that invert the sense. I hope that if the day ever comes I may
see the proof of that.                                 *Aff'ly yours, O. W. Holmes*

*Cambridge, 5.XI.19.*

*My dear Justice:* How comforting it is in a world of traps and
snares, of doubt and disillusion and constant economic torment, to
know that Felix is safe. It couldn't have been better if I had deliberately arranged it. She's wise and grown-up and good to look-
upon—a real companion. It's a great thing that he should be on
the threshold of that magic circle where only you and I really
dwell. And because we love him as few people can do ours is a
very special happiness.

I was glad to hear from him of how well you are, and of Mrs.
Holmes's gay perkiness. And he drew a picture of Brandeis which
suggested growth and sweetness and comradeship for you that
made me glad.

I have little news in Norman Hapgood's sense,[1] but much for
comment. I've started a paper on the origins of the modern state,[2]
trying to trace out the roots whence the Austinian notion derives.
It is really fascinating, and I'm glad, for the moment, to be out
of the realm of modern irritation into the peace of Leopold of
Babenburg[3] and Hincmar of Rheims whom I can flagellate without
treading on the toes of a single Back Bay republican. It's very
curious to note the slow beginnings of things—how difficult it is
for the medieval lawyer to get hold of the corporate idea. That I
suspect to be one of the main reasons why personal rule triumphed
so easily after the Reformation; the English distinction between
private and politic capacities still turned on a man.

The typing of the book goes merrily forward. I don't expect you
will want to be bothered with the legal stuff; but I'll send the
typescript of that economic note from the *Cosmopolitan* for your
approval. Then, when printing begins, you will of course have a
proof of the whole. I'm putting in the Marshall and the legal
speeches—especially the 1913 speech.[4] It's great fun doing this—
nearly as full of agreement as reading my own books. . . .

My love to you both—                                      *Ever yours, H. J. L.*

---

[1] Norman Hapgood (1868-1937); journalist and biographer; editor, successively, of Collier's *Weekly* and Harper's *Weekly*.

[2] Probably "The Pluralistic State," 28 *Philosophical Review* 562 (November 1919).

[3] Leopold of Babenburg, Bishop of Bamberg, author of the *Tractatus de
Juribus Regni et Imperii Romani* (1340); defender of the Emperor in
temporal conflicts with the Pope.

[4] *Collected Legal Papers,* 266, 296.

*Cambridge, November 12, 1919*

*My dear Justice:* In the midst of a feverish week, I want just to
say in so many words that amongst the many opinions of yours I
have read, none seems to me superior either in nobility or outlook,
in dignity or phrasing, and in that quality the French call *justesse,*
as this dissent in the Espionage case.[1] It is a fine and moving document for which I am deeply and happily grateful.

*Ever affectionately yours, H. J. L.*

Felix is like a radiant summer dawn.

*The Graduates Club, New Haven, Connecticut*
*November 14, 1919*

*My dear Justice:* I have just arrived here from a day spent with
Felix's young woman in Springfield. It was very pleasant. The girl
was positively radiant—bubbling over with a gentle, suffused happiness which made me feel how right all was. She looked like a
portrait by Luini. The general result on Felix goes straight to my
heart. He and I had one of those friendships compared to which
even Dooley and Hennessy hardly knew each other; now, within
a fortnight it seems to have gone deeper into more fruitful soil.
I won't say that this is the best of all possible worlds; but it's damn
near it.

I feel generally uplifted, in fact. (i) The government is going
to enquire into the university situation at Oxford and Cambridge;[1]
and as one of my best friends is to be on the Royal Commission I
hope to provoke some general enquiry through him into the preva-
lence of clerical control over endowments. That, as you can guess,
will come as balm to my soul. Even if I can't get Jews into Oxford
if I stop some mealy-mouthed parsons getting there it will be worth
while. (ii) I got a great letter from Sir Robert Morant,[2] easily the
best civil servant in England, asking me for ten copies of my 'Administrative Areas' for the use of the Cabinet. It almost made me
feel important until I realised that the cabinet wouldn't read it.
(iii) I'm just off on a weekend with Walter [Lippmann] and
Graham Wallas. That looks promising. Frida and the babe are in
Montreal just now and when I'm at home the house looks so
damned empty that I hate to be in it without them. I expect you
know the feeling.

---

[1] *Abrams* v. *United States,* 250 U.S. 616, 624 (decided November 10,
1919).

[1] *The Report of the Royal Commission on Oxford and Cambridge Minori-
ties* was presented to Parliament in 1922 (*Command Paper* #1588).

[2] Sir Robert Laurie Morant (1863-1920), Permanent Secretary to the
Board of Education, and a first secretary of the National Health Insurance
Commission; member, in 1917, of the Committee on the Machinery of Gov-
ernment.

And I have had a real dose of books lately. *Au fond,* all of them work books but some out of the way. First I read Trevelyan's *Life of John Bright,* one of the most moving biographies in the language. Then Marshall's new book[3]—a little timid I thought but an immensely able analysis of modern industrial organization, weak on the labor side but incomparably the best thing I've read on the unconscious principles of business men, and there is a little masterpiece tucked away on Adam Smith's Mercantilism in an appendix which is worth its weight in gold. The book ought to have been published ten years ago but it is really big stuff. . . .

This is vile writing. But the Graduate Club doesn't understand that pens have souls and that a bad soul is as easily chosen as a good. Even the ink clearly represents a period of inflated currency.

My love to you both.                          *Ever yours, H. J. L.*


*Cambridge, November 27, 1919*
*My dear Justice:* You must not think me negligent. For the past ten days Frida has been in bed with a sharp attack of dysentery and though the worst is over she still has a week more of bed. That, as you can imagine, has kept me both busy and a little anxious.

Nor have I been able to do much that might interest you. I did read with pride Croly's admirable piece on your dissent, with the feeling that vicariously its eulogy belonged to me as possessed of a lien on your affections. And I read in bed a brilliant little book by Carl Becker on *The Eve of the Revolution* (1776) which I thought quite the best thing on that issue I have seen—it made the proper allowances for *personalia,* the quarrel with Otis over Hutchinson's appointment as C.J., the curious mess of sour pottage that made up Samuel Adams's mind, Peyton Randolph turning up precedents to justify the expunging of the Virginia resolution No. 5 and so forth; also a deliciously-drawn portrait of Franklin. I wish you'd let me send you the book which can't be bought separately from a set. You can read it in a couple of hours and I think it would please you. Morris Cohen sent me his paper anent the pluralistic heretics and read me your comment.[1] I thought he did a

[3] Alfred Marshall, *Industry and Trade* (1919).

[1] Cohen's paper was "Communal Ghosts and Other Perils in Social Philosophy," 16 *Journal of Philosophy* 673 (Dec. 4, 1919); in substance included in Cohen's *Reason and Nature* (1931), Book III, Chapter III. Holmes's letter to Cohen, commenting on Cohen's criticism of Laski's theory of pluralistic sovereignty, was included in "The Holmes-Cohen Correspondence," 9 *Journal of the History of Ideas* 3, 17-18 (Jan. 1, 1948). In that letter Holmes had said: "I like your discourse immensely and I think there is not a word in

brilliant piece of logical criticism; but I thought also that he showed a pretty complete ignorance of history on the one hand and the psychology of administration on the other. But he is a damned clever fellow who is being wisely mellowed by time. His air of detachment amuses me a little—I doubt if it is more than a brilliant pose. Zionism makes him see red, Russia blue and General Leonard Wood [2] deep black. But every man has at least a natural right to his illusions.

I must not forget to tell you that Pound spoke to me with emotion about your dissent. He was certain that it would become a classic in the same sense as your *Lochner* case. He said he was writing to you to that effect; in case he did not, I thought you would like to know his feeling.

Felix is making this year quite the happiest I have had in Cambridge. He is so happy himself, and so appreciative of the nuances of one's outlook that it's a great joy to have him about. Nor must I omit the joy of talk with Wallas. I had a great week-end with him at Lippmann's. The talk was really good and I thought Walter had grown enormously. He read me the first two chapters of his new book which were really arresting without being original.[3] What he lacks is the historic sense. His world began about 1912 and the hundred odd civilisations that have gone to make American history leave him unmoved. But he has a real mind, agile, quick, incisive, and I wish I had his pen. He makes words talk of themselves.

My love to you both—            *Ever yours affectionately, H. J. L.*


*Washington, D.C., November 29, 1919*

*Dear Laski:* It is I who have been slow in writing but my mind has not been free till now. Today I expected to improve my mind with Ehrlich's *Die Juristiche Logik*—but as usual to such anticipations fate said nay. First an innocent little opinion of a page and

---

it with which I do not heartily agree. I always have told our beloved Laski that his are counsels of perfection not true theories of divided sovereignty." The influence which Cohen's paper ultimately had on Laski in persuading him that he "had lain under a dangerous spell woven, above all, by the exquisite charm of Maitland . . . and that bottomless pit of Gierke's leaning," is described with feeling in his essay on "Morris Cohen's Approach to Legal Philosophy," 15 *University of Chicago Law Review* 574, 577-582 (1948).

[2] Leonard Wood (1860-1927), physician who turned soldier and soldier who turned politician; Wood in war and in politics was one of Theodore Roosevelt's Rough Riders, and was a vigorous contender for the Republican nomination to the Presidency in 1920.

[3] Perhaps *Liberty and the News* (1920), reviewed by Laski, 110 *Nation* 594 (May 1, 1920).

a half came back with serious objections.[1] I had slipped in a little maggot of theory that I feared some sharp chap would spot and think better omitted—and so I had to put in some more washy stuff with more of the look of authority. Then in the p.m. Brandeis's lad, Atchison,[2] [*sic*] came in for a jaw and was here till 5. Then after finishing my work and perusing my favorite literature 'A Catalogue of Fine Old Books' just received, with little that interested, I was so sleepy, having been awake last night with a transitory dyspepsia, that I took a nap till dinner—just finished. I don't often read books merely for amusement off my beat—but I have had lying round *Letters of Susan Hale*[3]—and they have given me pleasure. I barely knew her and I suspect that in life she would have struck me as a type of cleverish Boston woman that did not open my soul—but she took life with gusto—as H. Higginson[4] did and H. Adams didn't—which is a gift to self and to others—and whether she is scrubbing up her house and washing her dishes or visiting the Pyramids or the Alhambra I find myself amused and with her. . . . I should like very much to see the Carl Becker book—especially if I could get it this coming week—I have needed your suggestions—though the Lord knows there are books enough around me that would repay reading or rereading. Atchison says Albion W. Small is Pound's great man and I shall try to get a whack at something of his'n.[5] Also I want to get a half day in the print room and I ought to go to be inspected by the dentist, but I shall leave most of these things undone I fear—when the opinions begin to come in—mine, only 2, are written. I want this to start as early as may be and therefore close tonight that the messenger may take it ere I wake. I am very sorry about your wife but hope she is all right now. I think she must be nearly so. Please give her my love.                                    *Aff'ly yours, O. W. Holmes*

---

[1] On December 8, 1919, Holmes delivered two brief opinions for the unanimous Court; *Liverpool Navigation Co.* v. *Brooklyn Terminal,* 251 U.S. 48, and *Chicago, R.I. and Pac. Ry. Co.* v. *Cole, id.* 54.

[2] Mr. Dean Acheson was Secretary to Mr. Justice Brandeis during the 1919-20 term of the Court.

[3] Susan Hale (1833-1910), Boston author and traveler.

[4] Henry Lee Higginson (1834-1919); Boston banker, founder of the Boston Symphony Orchestra, and Civil War veteran.

[5] Albion W. Small (1854-1926), sociologist; author of *An Introduction to the Study of Society* (1894), *Between Eras from Capitalism to Democracy* (1913), and *The Meaning of Social Science* (1910), which Holmes read at the end of 1919.

*Cambridge, December 9, 1919*

*My dear Justice:* Let me begin with an oath. Felix has just shown me your colleague McReynold's opinion in the Arizona case[1] and I did not conceive that such stuff could be got out from your court. Was it meant seriously? Is it just a bad joke? It is really an unbelievable thing from any point of view.

. . . I've been engaged on a big adventure. Did you ever read Newman's edition of the *Politics*—four hefty volumes. I made up my mind to go through them and the job is at last done. It's a monumental thing. You can tell every passage where there's a thin chance that A. might have had Plato or Socrates or Homer in mind. You can trace the relation of all the mss to each other. The introduction is that type of absolutely final analysis which makes you feel that the work need never be done again. It is really a great experience to plough through it. First it gives one a sense of humility and second it makes you feel better about your fellow-men. Both of them are very needful just now.

In bed I've skimmed Croker's diaries.[2] Did you ever peep at that slimy rascal? The great men are Peel, Wellington, and Lord Hertford, Thackeray's Steyne. He knows everything just twenty minutes after it happened from birth down to death. He believes *a priori* in kings, nobles, incontrovertible paper, a limited franchise and pocket-boroughs. The country is always just on the verge of disaster and only the advent of a Tory government can save it. Bright and Cobden are radical agitators of the lowest description, and Lord George Bentinck is a noble soul. Could you have lived in that atmosphere of faded velvet and patchouli?

Little enough to tell here. . . . I have a paper in the *Philosophical Review*[3] which I'll send along as soon as I get the reprints. Felix probably won't tell you the killing news that House has quarrelled with Wilson, the latter being now convinced that the Paris debacle is House's fault. Nor has he, I think, told you that

---

[1] The reference, presumably, is to the dissenting opinion of McReynolds, J., in *Arizona Employers' Liability Cases*, 250 U.S. 400 (decided June 9, 1919). A majority of the Court, with Holmes writing a concurring opinion, had sustained the constitutionality of an Arizona statute imposing absolute liability upon employers for injuries to their employees suffered in specified hazardous employments. In the course of his dissenting opinion, Mr. Justice McReynolds wrote as follows: "Until now I had supposed that a man's liberty and property . . . were under the protection of our charter and not subordinate to whims or caprices or fanciful ideas of those who happen for the day to constitute the legislative majority. The contrary doctrine is revolutionary and leads straight towards destruction of our well-tried and successful system of government." *Id.,* at 450-451.

[2] John Wilson Croker (1780-1857), whom Macaulay "detested more than cold boiled veal," was a Tory essayist and politician of Irish birth who held office as Secretary of the Admiralty under the Perceval and Wellington ministries. Croker's early devotion to Sir Robert Peel came to an unhappy ending in 1841 when Peel supported Cobden on the repeal of the corn laws. His *Memoirs, Diaries and Correspondence* was published in 1884.

[3] "The Pluralistic State," 28 *Philosophical Review* 562 (November 1919).

Smuts deliberately expressed his opinion that W. W. was an absolutely 2nd rate man. John F. Moors,[4] Ellery Sedgwick[5] and Mrs.
Wilson must be his only supporters by now. . . .

A rollicking English novel is *The Old Indispensables* by Edward
Shanks.

My love to you,                                   *Yours ever, H. J. L.*

*Washington, D.C., December 11, 1919*

*Dear Laski:* Your letters exhilarate me even when I am conscious
that I can make little return. I have but little chance to read here
—and my *pièce de résistance* is Ehrlich's *Die Juristische Logik*
with a dictionary—but dictionary food though sweet is not nour-
ishing—one doesn't get enough. Hearing that Pound thought Albion Small one of the greatest of his kind I got a book of his from
the Congressional Library and read it[1]—a good adult male with
something of the masculinity I noticed in a book by Sumner of
Yale that I read a year or two ago.[2] But he did not pretend to be
saying new things in this book and wasn't. We are in a sort of
chopping sea of important cases but I personally am serene for
the moment.

What Newman is it that edited the *Politics*? And is it Croker's
*Diaries* that you have skimmed? Upon my word your cuneiform
is hard to decipher at times. . . .

(Dinner) How did you and Walter Lippmann come by your small
handwriting? After court today I did a sad thing. I went to my
friend the print seller opposite the British Embassy to say good-
bye. His shop was empty (and marked with the odious "For Rent"
instead of "To Let") and he is about to leave and give up the
attempt to establish a business here. There is no sufficient market
for good things. I shall miss him and the place sadly. Admiral
Davis[3] and I have been wont to meet there on Saturdays at about
5 for an hour and turn over a portfolio and jaw—we called it The
Club—a club of two with Miss Biddle[4] often looking in and sitting
between us. If the Congressional Library were more convenient
the print room there would be in some respects a better substitute
—not only for its possessions but because of Professor Rice,[5] the
head, who really knows a lot and is a very pleasant creature. I

[4] Boston banker, liberal, and philanthropist.

[5] Editor of the *Atlantic Monthly.*

[1] See, *supra,* p. 171.

[2] Presumably W. G. Sumner, *Folkways* (1911).

[3] Charles Henry Davis (1845-1932); brother of Mrs. Brooks Adams and
Mrs. Henry Cabot Lodge.

[4] Miss Lydia Biddle of Washington and Warren County, Pennsylvania, was
an intimate friend of Holmes's.

[5] Richard Austin Rice (1846-1925), Director of the Print Department,.
Library of Congress.

spent three hours with him the other day but such chances are rare.
Give Felix my love. It is delightful to think of his being so happy—
and I hope he didn't think I had serious misgivings because I wrote
to him in rather a cautioning strain that martyrs were apt to be
damned fools. Also my homage to your dear Missus.

*Aff'ly yours, O. W. Holmes*


*Cambridge, December 22, 1919*

*My dear Justice:* Above all, our united good wishes for this season
to you both. If you have a tithe of the happiness we all want you
to have, all will be well. . . .

I've been reading one or two things of real distinction. Someone
gave me Bain's *J. S. Mill,* and I thought the *personalia* threw real
light on a man who sums up better than anyone I know the fears
and hopes of a complex century. In another line, I found H. J.
Ford's *The Rise and Growth of American Politics* (Macmillan), a
book full of first-rate comment on American institutions. I wish
you'd look at it; the admission price is only a dollar and it's the
best explanation of Congress I have so far read. Then a little
Bentham—the *Constitutional Code*—which as always gave old
thoughts new angles of richness. In the modern line I've read little
that was tempting. But I do commend to you the article by Keynes
in the *New Republic* for December 24.[1] There, I think, you have
psychological analysis at its best; and though less brilliant than
poor Weyl's masterpiece[2] I think it hits the bull's eye on the
whole peace conference. But the best thing I've read or re-read I
keep to the last. Need I say that it's Burke on the *Present Discontents* with that sentence "Whatever be the road to power that is
the road which will be trod" which I always feel is worth half a
library of formal treatises on politics. Surely in between himself
and Thucydides no one went as directly to the root of reality. And
I say that, though I disagree with all his fundamental assumptions.

For the rest, Felix is married and when he comes back all kinds
of new and interesting adjustments will be necessary. I feel that
it was right and wise; I don't know how in the least (if at all)
it is going to influence him. But he writes like a man with a vision
and I could ask nothing more.

My love to you both—

*Ever affectionately yours, Harold J. Laski*

---

[1] Maynard Keynes, "When the Big Four Met," 21 *New Republic* 103
(Dec. 24, 1919).

[2] Walter E. Weyl (1873-1919), economist; Associate Editor of the *New
Republic;* author, *inter alia,* of *The End of the War* (1918).

*December 27, 1919*

*My dear Laski:* A day or two ago came your as usual stimulating letter, and today I hear the song of the Thukydid. Perchance it shall lead me to penetrate that learned author from whose pages I have been repulsed with slaughter in the days since the compulsory Greek Reader. A moment of leisure seems at hand. I circulated all that I have to circulate last night and already have it back from three—one saying mark me dissenting, one I take no part unless necessary; in which case I should agree to the result with modifications, and just now a more cheering return from Brandeis, 'convincing.' My only other outstanding *opus* awaits a dissent from Pitney.[1] Yesterday I received an article on my dissent in the *Abrams* case—written in *The Review*[2] which my secretary tells me is a sheet intended to counteract the revolutionary influence of the *New Republic*. It is somewhat surprising to me that even under cover of the anonymous one should think it safe to give an off-hand condemnation of the work of a man who may be supposed to know enough of his job not to fall into obvious errors. He would not accuse me of being uncandid but he notes that I have omitted a most pregnant sentence quoted by Clarke. He seemingly does not note that the sentence was from another sheet not mentioned in the indictment whereas I was discussing the leaflet laid as an overt act. It was, I assumed, but I ought to have made it clearer, necessary that the overt act laid should be proved to be done with intent to forward a conspiracy to interfere with the war with Germany—and I thought it plain on the face of the document that it was written *alio intuitu*. On that question I thought what was said at other times immaterial. The whole piece seemed to me incompetent—and I don't think that my opinion depended at all on the article being adverse. (Another return of my opinion 'Please mark me as dissenting.' It looks shaky.) Beside the bracketed interruption I caught my wife just as she was going out and asked her to get Mr. Ford's *Rise &c of American Politics* and I have stopped also to read Keynes's piece in the *New Republic* —I quite agree to what you say of it. I don't suppose the President will read it, but he would not be happy if he did. At night when awake and coughing I have reread the French of *Baron Munchausen*. (Doré's illustrations, one inimitable—the fishes looking at the Baron's bottom plugging the hole in the ship.) I can't apply the 25 years rule to this. I don't see that it could be any better or

---

[1] On the next opinion day, January 5, 1920, Holmes delivered no opinions. On January 12 he delivered the opinion of a unanimous Court in *Birge-Forbes Co.* v. *Heye*, 251 U.S. 317, and announced the judgment of the Court and delivered an opinion in which White, C.J., and Brandeis and Clark, JJ., concurred, with Pitney and McKenna, JJ., dissenting in *The Mail Divisor Cases, id.* 326.

[2] "Justice Holmes's Dissent," *The Review* 636 (Dec. 6, 1919).

more amusing in its way if written now. My first exercise of leisure
will be to finish Frankfurter's well-written article in the *Yale Review*[3]—then the German book (Ehrlich), curious how he labors
over the obvious—excellent as the volume is. Then your Ford and
Thucydides.

But first I must read two opinions just sent in by Day, and so
*adieu* for the moment. I had a most delightful call from Wallas the
other morning, who gave me an amusing account of your playing
with the Corporation etc. on the question of your orthodoxy—but
he made me shudder with the thought that possibly you might go
back to Oxford. As D. Webster said on some historic occasion—
What is to become of ME?     *Affectionately yours, O. W. Holmes*

*Cambridge, January 4, 1920*
*My dear Justice:* . . . I'm glad you had a talk with Wallas. He is
really one of the best stimulants I know. I'm a little sorry he told
you that I was eager to go home. It's quite true. It's been borne
in on me these last months that I can't be useful in Harvard in
the way I hoped to be when I first came over. The Corporation
doesn't want me to have political views, partly because it doesn't
like my views, and partly because I am a foreigner. The Faculty
largely resents my constant sense that the majority of the pro-
fessoriate don't really give that sense of a great moral duty to the
student to their work. I conceive that a university has failed unless
the professor builds his life round his students. Here, he builds
them round his lectures; and protest is always taken to be 'Ox-
fordising' and therefore anathema. When I think what we could
do for the undergraduate in making him feel the glory of the intellectual life and the miserable pittance we dole out to him in
the form of courses, where knowledge is taken to be something that
has happened, it makes me want to weep. And so I told Wallas
to get me home. I think I can be more useful there and do better
work. But all this assumes that some English university will want
me, which I shall doubt until I have definite evidence.

We had a grand week-end last week with Walter Lippmann and
his wife. We talked the universe over and he made me very happy
by his patience and wisdom and insight. I rather gather that he
finds the paper a little difficult just now. Croly has the religious
bug very badly and Hackett is simply Sinn Fein with which Walter
doesn't sympathise. But he talked wisely and movingly of affairs;
and he is one of the few Americans I've met who realises that two
hundred millions are on the verge of starvation in Europe largely
because the Senate has gone back to its splendid and tragic isolation. I hope you'll read the letter of Zimmern in the *N.R.* of

---

[3] "Law and Order," 9 *Yale Review* (N.S.) 225 (January 1920).

January 7th,[1] which exactly represents my feeling; except that I
would add some unprintable remarks on the man in the White
House.

Pound lunched with me yesterday; and I wish you could have
heard his fury against that article in *The Review*. Of course the
definite object of that paper is to protest against all signs of intellectual liberalism; or else he and Felix would have written a
joint protest. But, as he said, no opinion you have written in years
has so profoundly moved the constituency of the court and it
makes a landmark of noble courage in an era of hysteria.

I've been spending the week on adventures in American history.
I loathe (i) Andrew Jackson, Jefferson Davis, Charles Sumner,
Thomas Jefferson. (ii) I stand by Hamilton, John Quincy Adams.
Have you read Henry Adams's *Degradation of the Democratic
Dogma*? Can you understand it?

Our love to you both,                                     *Ever yours, H. J. L.*

*Washington, D.C., January 14, 1920*
*My dear Laski:* Your confirmation of what Wallas indicated grieves
me, but does not surprise. I suspect that behind all that you mention you miss the thicker atmosphere of the old world. More civilized men to the square mile, more past in every environment.
Province Street, Boston, close to which in what now is Bosworth
Street, I was born, with its poor two centuries, or whatever, is
venerable, and sacred to me. How should I have felt if I had been
born under the shadow of a cathedral? I repeat my old aphorism
that everything is founded on the death of men—society, which
only changes the modes of killing—romance, to which centuries,
that is generations, of dead, or the memorial tablets of a great war,
are necessary. I won't borrow trouble till it comes but I shall miss
you dreadfully if you go away. . . .

I did read a book by Albion Small, *The Meaning of Social
Science* being told that Pound thought highly of him. Already
there remains but a faint perfume in my mind. He seemed an
adult male—but hardly struck me as revealing much. H. Adams's
book that you mention I have not seen. I am not so greatly at odds
with you about Charles Sumner—he showed me engravings and
some other interesting things when I was young—and asked me if
I knew what the cap on top of a flagstaff was, when I was a little
boy. I said a liberty cap—he said the Phrygian cap, my boy—
but the speech that led to the assault on him, was about on a
par with the assault and I suspect that an essay of his is largely

---

[1] 21 *New Republic* 17 (Jan. 7, 1920). The letter emphasized the disastrous economic plight of Europe and suggested that the disillusioned lips of
American liberals had other obligations than to murmur "I told you so."

responsible for an engraving of Pomponne de Bellièvre being called the *chef d'oeuvre* of Nanteuil [1]—a fine bit of ermine but the portrait is from a painting by Le Brun and to my mind almost anything that that marvelous creature *ad vivum delineavit* is better in its living flesh and very squinny of life—with no mannerism or tricks. His judgment, like his speech to me, seemed to me formal and priggish—not that of real sympathy and insight.

I am going through my usual experiences—a fever the first half of the week—then when I get my opinion distributed and the *certioraris* examined a lapse to comparative ease, though always there is some case requiring further examination. I received a pamphlet from the Jewrist Ehrlich on Bismarck, etc. which I shan't read but which gave me his address as I wanted to write to him. Also an essay of Effects of the War on Money Credit etc. in France and U.S. by B. M. Anderson (Carnegie Endowment for International Peace). I wonder if I had better read it? And what seems to me an unexpectedly interesting book by Scott on *Judicial Settlement of Controversies between States of the American Union* which I shall have no time to read. If I read anything I shall try to do the *Life of Marshall* out of friendship and because it ought to be instructive for my job. But I have no time to read *à presong* —and little to write.

Homage to the missus.                                 *Aff'ly yours, O. W. Holmes*


*Cambridge, January 14, 1919* [sic]

*My dear Justice:* Only you could have written that letter to the Harvard Liberal Club.[1] Felix and I chuckled with effervescent joy. That and Hughes's admirable protest[2] will tickle the ears of the groundlings.

Of news but little. Your mss is corrected and all the references verified and tomorrow will go off to the printer. It's been a great joy to me to re-read your things, partly because I like to know

---

[1] 14 *Works of Charles Sumner* (1883) 339-340.

[1] The Harvard Liberal Club on January 12 had called a meeting to protest against the excesses of Federal authority in curtailing freedom of speech. Holmes, asked to send a message to the meeting, had sent the following letter:

"For obvious reasons I should not care to speak upon your subject except as from time to time I have to.

"I see no impropriety, however, in suggesting the isolated reflection that with effervescing opinions as with the not yet forgotten champagnes, the quickest way to let them get flat is to let them get exposed to the air."

See *Justice Oliver Wendell Holmes, His Book Notices, and Uncollected Letters and Papers* (Shriver, ed., 1936), p. 137.

[2] Charles Evans Hughes had sent an open letter of protest to the Speaker of the New York Assembly when that body, at its opening in 1920, denied five duly elected Socialist assemblymen their seats in the legislature pending investigation into their qualifications and eligibility.

what you've done better than anyone else (the instinct of property), partly because I really enjoy educating myself. The greatest of them is the "Path of the Law,"[3] though there are touches in the 1913 speech[4] which make me feel mean and humble. It is great to have a man who takes his profession so greatly. Also I'm two-thirds through the proof of my Home University volume; it ought to be out by March 17.[5] I'll be eager to hear what you think. It doesn't read badly to me, and certainly it taught me some things in the writing. But you are one of about two people in America who will be willing to read it carefully enough to get what it is really about.

Felix and Marion are back and like two cooing doves. To see their anxiety for each other's proper protection against the snow etc. is charming. The boy is very happy. The girl is still rather reticent and shy so that I can't expound her much, but she makes him sing an unceasing song and I therefore add my tribute.

. . . I reread Thackeray's *English Humorists* and his *Four Georges* with joy unutterable. They are the best things he did—hit the mind just between wit and malice where wisdom dwells. And on the train to New Haven Meredith's *Beauchamp's Career* which I'd not read for five years. 'Twas very disappointing at second attack, obviously far-fetched and strained I thought. The human fellow writes down his gold unpurified—Meredith strains and strains until what is left is too pure for humble souls. Rather like his letters I thought—written with a sober nod to posterity.

My love to you both,          *Ever affectionately yours, H. J. L.*


*Washington, D.C., January 15, 1920*
*Dear Laski:* Your letter crossed one from me, but I must add a word. To begin with the end I am not surprised at what you say of *Beauchamp's Career*—though after I had read it I was interested to hear that it was based on his friend Admiral Maxse's experience,[1] as I used to be a friend of the latter's daughter, Ly Edward Cecil. I haven't seen her for ages but I put up at his place for a night or so once. (Note the erasure of the comma after friend before Admiral. It seems that one must say either friend's, A. M.'s or friend A. M.'s—Isn't that logical?)

I heard Thackeray deliver his *Lectures on the English Humorists*. My impression is that he was one-sided as to Sterne—whom I

---

[3] 10 *Harv. L. Rev.* 457 (1897); reprinted in *Collected Legal Papers*, 167.
[4] See, *supra*, p. 118.
[5] *Political Thought in England from Locke to Bentham.*
[1] Frederick Augustus Maxse (1833-1900); admiral and political writer, intimate friend of Meredith, who modeled the career and character of Nevil Beauchamp on that of Admiral Maxse.

always regard as marking a stage in the growth of the modern self-consciousness. I used to say *Hamlet—Tristram Shandy—Faust.*

I shall be eager for your book and am pleased to hear what you tell me about the collection of my things—and of course am set up by your kind remarks. I don't remember about the letter to the Harvard Liberal Club.

I was glad some time ago that you noticed the resemblance of Mrs. Felix to Luini's type—I always call her Luina.

Did I ever tell you of my last sight of Meredith? I called with Ly Pollock, who motored me out to his place. He had received some book inscribed to the *illustrissimo poeta*—at which he was cavilling—his attendant murmured (he being deaf), 'He likes it all the same.' But he said 'To me a (I am not sure of the adjective —say casual) novelist and puny whiffmajig poet'—which tickled me.                                                *Aff'ly yours, O. W. Holmes*


*Cambridge, January 26, 1920*

*My dear Justice:* . . . All the mss is with the printer and you will not be troubled until the proof-stage. I hope you will write some short preface—a kind of after-reflection. Walter Lippmann tells me that arrangements for its English publication are already make [*sic*]. You will believe me if I say that no literary work I have ever done has ever given me so much undiluted pleasure as getting these papers ready.

At the moment I am in the midst of exams which means a rest for a fortnight; also I have finished with Yale and so am a gentleman at large. And accordingly I have had some good reading. First and foremost, Keynes book.[1] If there is an answer to its overwhelming indictment of the peace I do not think it has been made; and written with the flexible strength of steel it bites into one's mind. I hope you will have a spare hour for its perusal. That is the outstanding piece of reading. Of lesser things just a novel about Harvard called *Peter Kindred*[2] which amused me because its obviously young author takes men here who seem to me worthless so very seriously as philosophers. Which somehow reminds me that Pound's Albion Small seems to me to represent exactly the worse side of Pound. Small belongs to that pedantocracy who doubts the value of ideas until he has fixed the boundaries of his methodology; who will give you six sentences of a dead authority which a living journalist could express in six words; whose conclusions look formidable until you realise that their vagueness doesn't conceal greatness but mist. It's the great tragedy

---

[1] Laski reviewed John Maynard Keynes's *Economic Consequences of the Peace* (1920) in 110 *The Nation* 174 (Feb. 7, 1920).

[2] Robert Nathan, *Peter Kindred* (1919).

of Pound's life that he can't see or be made to see that only some books are to be digested. His stomach must resemble an ostrich's and his own ideas are almost always clearer and more fruitful than those he cites, *e.g.*, compare that excellent paper of his on the administration of justice in a modern city,[3] where he has few authorities to rely on, with the cumbersome Juggernaut he rolls along in his papers on sociological jurisprudence. I think he believes in the natural right of every German to be quoted. I must not forget to ask you if you ever read Aristotle's *Rhetoric*? At the moment I am on fire with enthusiasm about it, and Cope's edition is well-nigh perfect. There's a very good translation by Jebb an hour of which would, I am sure, repay you. Like all that he wrote it is full of acute observation and those sudden flashes that make him, for me, the final criterion of sagacity—a quality incidentally that I think Bentham has next in order to him.

Two other things. Loring Christie writes me that a boss in his chief's district continually but uselessly bothered him for a job. Finally, the boss's brother wrote thus. "Dear Sir, I am sure you will be sorry to hear that my brother is dead. He died amid all the evidences of Christian piety. His last words were 'Sir Robert Borden is a son of a bitch.'[4] Yours truly."

And last of all—my old tutor, Ernest Barker of New College, Oxford is teaching for two months in Amherst (Mass.). Sometime next month he is going to Washington and I badly want him to meet you. If you feel like it, would you drop him a note to Amherst College and ask him to call? I should be very grateful. Our love in heaps to you both,    *Ever affectionately yours, H. J. L.*

*Washington, D.C., January 28, 1920*
*Dear Laski:* . . . Of course I am reading nothing until next month —but I did read "When the Big Four Met" with full accord to all your praise.[1] You relieve me by what you say of Albion Small. Do you know H. L. Mencken *Prejudices*? He I suspect would prove more or less a Philistine at bottom, but Lord with what malevolent joy do I see him smash round in the china shop—a pretty sound sense of real values as far as I have heard. (F. reads to me during solitaire). I am happy to note that he has a smash at Veblen which I haven't read and at Amy Lowell which I have. A pretty adult male, who, I infer, has had his share of alcohol and the amenities. Do you know Jules Romains, poet? Mrs. Brandeis

---

[3] "The Administration of Justice in the Modern City," 26 *Harv. L. Rev.* 302 (1913).

[4] Sir Robert Laird Borden (1854-1937), Canadian statesman, was Prime Minister of Canada from 1911 to 1920.

[1] The article by Keynes, *supra*, p. 180, was a chapter in his *Economic Consequences of the Peace* (1920).

says a star among the younger. I ran through his *Europe*—thought
Walt Whitman did it better—suspected him of loving his fellow
man *en bloc i.e.* preferring quantity to quality and respecting the
crowd, and generally hadn't much use for him, subject to the
admission that there might be exquisiteness that took a nicer
knowledge of French to appreciate, and that if he really were
somebody, probably one wouldn't like him at once and off hand.
I want to post this tonight and stop suddenly for the chance. I
asked FF to take you into his councils as to a young man for next
year. If I am alive and all goes well he will be at my 80th birthday
—in 1921. . . .

Love to you both,                                        *Aff', O. W. H.*

Being hurried I am sure that I am leaving out something that I
specially wanted to say. I wrote to E. Barker and sent the letter
off as soon as I read yours an hour ago.

*Cambridge, February 7, 1920*

*My dear Justice:* I have been shamelessly negligent of you; but you
possibly know that I have had my troubles here[1] and my main
temptation has been silence. But a long letter from Lippmann gave
me that thrill about you which makes my fingers itch and I go to
it once more. . . . I read the new volume of Veblen's essays; or,
rather, I began to read them but (tell it not in Askelon) I got
so damned bored with the first two essays that I contented myself
with the footnotes of the rest.[2] I read also a volume of essays, my
review of which (from the *Nation*) I enclose.[3] I think it is worth
while emphasising the stupidity of this negative liberalism. . . .
Felix and I dropped down to New York last Monday. On Croly's
desk there were two volumes—*The Christ within Us* and the *Inter-
Church World Movement.* Felix and I didn't know if it was tragedy
or comedy, but when we read the first two leaders in this week's
paper we decided that it was unmitigated tragedy.[4] Did I tell you
that Haldane had sent me his book *Before the War?* A very honest

---

[1] In January the editors of the Harvard *Lampoon,* abandoning their traditional assignment of publishing a humorous undergraduate magazine, brought
out a special issue, "exposing" Laski's radicalism and seeking through malicious ridicule to discredit Laski as a teacher and scholar.

[2] Thorstein Veblen, *The Place of Science in Modern Civilization* (1920).

[3] *Man or the State?* (1919), edited by Waldo R. Browne; reviewed by
Laski in 110 *Nation* 146 (Jan. 31, 1920). The volume consisted of selected
essays from Buckle, Spencer, Thoreau, and others. Laski's central plea in
his review was for a new liberalism which should no longer find its principal
concern in the conflict between the individual and the state but should put
its energy into the task of organizing the state and other agencies for the
benefit of the many.

[4] Two of the leading editorials in the *New Republic* for February 11, 1920
(vol. 21, pp. 303, 306) were concerned with the political responsibilities of
the Christian churches.

and convincing defence of his position I thought, with a reference to the 'inarticulate major premise' which pleased me.[5] And that reminds me to tell you that in an English case so far reported only in the press, it appears that the Court of Appeal has turned down the legality of a section of the Defence of the Realm Act on the ground that it conflicts with Magna Carta![6] So *Bonham's* case[7] wins its revenge; and Charles McIlwain walks about with his head in the air. I'd see judicial review in England without regret, tho' I should like to put Holmes, J. on the bench to train the judges into it. Oh! Nor must I forget to tell you that Eustace Percy has written a book. I read it and thought it very, very eloquent and very bad—but Zimmern thinks it very eloquent and very good.[8] The real masterpiece of these days is Keynes's book which I hope you will get time to read. I wonder if poor Walter Weyl's picture is quite so brilliant as the one Keynes has drawn of our lord and master.[9]

But I run on too long. My love to you both,

*Ever affectionately yours, Harold J. Laski*

*Washington, D.C., February 10, 1920*
Dear Laski: Your letter just read and I don't stop even for the accompanying print to write to you. I hardly heard of the *Lampoon* incident when Brandeis's secretary sent me a letter that he had received saying that the thing had proved a boomerang and had helped to put you up in the world. Later I received the paper and thought it such a childish and rotten little show as hardly to merit a second thought. It reminded me of the mock parts they used to give out from a Hollis (?) window—in which all the willingness to be anonymously smart at the expense of

[5] In his famous dissent in *Lochner* v. *New York* 198 U.S. 45, 76 (1905) Holmes had stated that "general propositions do not decide concrete cases. The decision will depend on a judgment or intuition more subtle than any articulate major premise." The phrase reëchoed an earlier formulation of a similar thought: "But although practical men generally prefer to have their premises inarticulate, yet even for practical purposes theory generally turns out the most important thing in the end." Holmes, "The Theory of Legal Interpretation," 12 *Harv. L. Rev.* 417 (1899); *Collected Legal Papers* 203, 209.

[6] The reference presumably is to *In re De Keyser's Royal Hotel*, [1919] 2 Ch. 197; affirmed, *sub nom. Attorney-General* v. *De Keyser's Royal Hotel*, [1920] A.C. 508. See Scott and Hildersley, *The Case of Requisition* (1920).

[7] 8 Rep. 115 (1610). It was in this decision that Sir Edward Coke suggested that acts of Parliament which contravened the fundamental principles of common law were void. Professor McIlwain in his *High Court of Parliament* (1910) had urged that Coke's thesis was constitutionally correct.

[8] Zimmern had written enthusiastically of Lord Eustace Percy's *The Responsibilities of the League* (1920) in his communication to the *New Republic, supra,* p. 177.

[9] See, *supra,* p. 180.

others expressed itself in rather witless fashion. I don't know whether you are sensitive about such things—(I was for a good while but have got somewhat hardened)—but that serpent seems to me a fangless one—however malignant in intent. I do hope that it hasn't cost you any worry.

I received your Duguit this morning.[1] I didn't know that you or rather Mrs. Laski had this up your sleeve. I shall read as soon as I have finished Beveridge's *Marshall*. Friendship and desire both required me to read it and I began it last Friday or Saturday. I have nearly finished volume 2 and expect to do the whole in a few days. It has repaid me better even than I expected. Beveridge seems to have put the most honest work into it. He has skimmed off with great success the banalities of which originally there were a few—and in the result I seem to get a better picture and more understanding of the time than I ever got before. I think B. also is a good story-teller—he keeps me interested right along. W. Lippmann and his wife dined with us the other night much to the pleasure of both of us (my wife and me). I hope we shall see them again before they go.

I am truly rejoiced that Veblen bored you. He takes an ungodly time to say the few things he has to say, that in my opinion amount to anything. I took malevolent pleasure in Mencken's *Prejudices* which devotes a chapter to speaking ill of him. Do you know that writer? With various foibles he has a sense of reality and most of his prejudices I share. He wiped off Amy Lowell in a way that seemed to me deserved; and he takes George Ade seriously which again I like. You will have gathered that I have leisure ahead. My letter writing is done. I have but two opinions, both awaiting dissent if anyone will take the trouble to write.[2] When I am going to dissent I almost always prepare my opinion at once —and then when the majority speaks, simply make such adjustments as bring our discussion *ad idem*—which I think is the decent way, but which is not practised. I don't know Haldane's book —do you mean that he used the phrase 'inarticulate major premise' or simply that that was what he had to deal with. I have read Keynes in the *N.R.* but not in a book. I pause to read—I have read—your review with the usual and expected pleasure. How much pleasure in how many ways you have given me!

*Aff'ly yours, O. W. Holmes*

---

[1] Leon Duguit, *Law in the Modern State* (translated by Frida and Harold Laski, 1919).

[2] Holmes delivered no opinions before March 1; he then delivered opinions in *The South Coast*, 251 U.S. 519, *Bates* v. *Dresser, id.* 524, and *Fort Smith Lumber Co.* v. *Arkansas, id.* 532. Dissents were noted, without opinion, in each of these cases.

*Cambridge, February 15, 1920*

*My dear Justice:* That was a grand letter and it gave me a real lift in the world. The *Lampoon* is off my mind now, though it makes me sigh for clearer skies.

I've been reading one or two things that I want very strongly to recommend. Hammond's *Skilled Labourer* is a real masterpiece,[1] and I think that few books of those I have recently read so admirably set the type of social history that I care about. Then Bryce sent me a lecture of his on World-History that gave me a deeply interesting *aperçu* of what a man who has looked over the whole field sums it up to be. On your advice I read Mencken, and with almost undiluted enjoyment. The piece on Veblen is grand— George Ade I do not know though I will adventure him in the next free space. And I read an excellent book by Ramsay MacDonald on the *Government of India*[2] which pleased me because it was the first labor book I have seen which recognised the complexity of that problem, though even he has some of what seems to me the sheer stupidity of a belief in the greatness of Eastern mysticism. . . .

I was glad to hear that Beveridge's *Marshall* gave you pleasure. I think he really has done a big job. It tails off a little to the end; and I doubt whether fellows like John Lowell[3] even to his own generation seemed as big as Beveridge says. Nor do I think that Aaron Burr would emerge from a fuller survey quite as stainless as Beveridge makes him out. But apart from minor criticisms like these the book unquestionably lives, though I would add the general remark that men less great than Marshall would surely have appeared great in that situation.

I never like to comment on your court or its technique. But I must say that in this Department of Justice case you warmed my heart.[4] I was, of course, deeply interested in the technique of your dissents. Did I ever tell you that Cardozo said to me in New York that he thought your opinions alone on the court just now bore the mark of proper and penetrating adjustment to the views of your colleagues—that the others tended to be essays largely written in a vacuum.

---

[1] Reviewed by Laski in 110 *The Nation* 594 (May 1, 1920).

[2] Reviewed by Laski in 22 *New Republic* 383 (May 19, 1920).

[3] John Lowell (1769-1840), lawyer and pamphleteer whose Massachusetts brand of Federalism made him more friendly to both Englands, old and new, than to the government in Washington. See, *supra*, p. 4.

[4] In *Silverthorne Lumber Co.* v. *United States*, 251 U.S. 385 (Jan. 26, 1920), Holmes had delivered the Court's opinion holding that the Department of Justice might not use information obtained through illegal search and seizure as the basis for charges of contempt. White, C.J., and Pitney, J., dissented without opinion.

The President's latest exploit seems beyond belief.[5] Morley said in the summer that he didn't believe Wilson ever knew what it was to lay his mind alongside someone else's. How government can be carried on if the President gets ill and the cabinet is not to meet I cannot for the life of me imagine. I should like a chance of doing a real essay on his thinking. He once spoke to me of being nourished on Burke and Bagehot, which I had to let pass; though I should like to have remarked on Burke's genius for friendship and Bagehot's insight into the psychological recesses of administration. Keynes, I think, measured him adequately—though I doubt whether Wilson is quite so simple as he suggests.

Walter L. wrote me a very enthusiastic letter about his dinner. You put heart and truth into him as, indeed, you do into us all. Walter is over effectively silent. But of all the *New Republic* bunch his mind is the wisest and most profound. Which reminds me that I hope you will take occasion to look into Croly's piece on Lincoln in the paper for February 18.[6] It needs more working out and I resent the entrance of Jesus Christ, but I think it has all the elements of a masterpiece.

I wish I could show you the exquisite copy of Bodin I have just bought—3rd edition in French folio, 1578. It is one of the finest pieces of printing I have ever seen and the cost was $7.50. I had Charles McIlwain to meet it at tea and was delighted to see him gnash his teeth in envy. I wish more people here had that proper possessive instinct *in re librorum*. Mostly they tend to be satisfied with the mausoleum Mrs. Widener erected,[7] which is, I think, a morally reprehensible attitude. Oh! and I bought for one dollar a gorgeous large paper copy of Adam Smith's posthumous essays with the memoir (a charming thing) by Dugald Stewart. So I am near to the Sixth heaven.

Our eager love,                           *Ever affectionately yours, H. J. L.*


*Washington, D.C., February 19, 1920*

*Dear Laski:* Your article on Keynes I had read,[1] with the usual and expected pleasure, before your letter came. I am waiting for the book. W. Lippmann asked me not to get it as he proposed to send it to me. If you look into George Ade read some of the *Fables in Slang.* I don't exactly understand who Beveridge's John

---

[5] In his illness President Wilson had refused to see or consult the members of his Cabinet, and was himself unable to make decisions. At length he dismissed Lansing, his Secretary of State, for disloyalty in holding informal meetings of the Cabinet during the President's incapacity.

[6] Herbert Croly, "The Paradox of Lincoln," 21 *New Republic* 350 (Feb. 18, 1920).

[7] The Harvard College Library.

[1] See, *supra,* p. 180.

Lowell was. I understood him not to be the judge. If I was wrong,
I remember my father telling me that my grandmother said that
the old Judge had brains enough to furnish three generations.[2]
You make me sick with your odious way of nabbing the books
that *nous autres* would like to have got—if we had the eyes to
see them. It is like my wife who will find a flower or something
that is beautiful in a vase where the rest of us see only a dirty
tangle. However, you are young and I am old and being old am
less keen than I should have been when younger to possess books
and engravings that reason tells me will soon be in the hands of
my executor. If I understand Cardozo's remark it indicates what I
may say without personal application that many American judges
cannot get very near to their insight in words. I always say in
conference that no case can be settled by general propositions, that
I will admit any general proposition you like and decide the case
either way.

My *New Republic* for the 18th hasn't come yet. Yesterday p.m.
my business affairs having been attended to and the books of
improvement on hand having been read—I sought a moment of
literary irresponsibility and took up at random a little volume of
Hugo's *Choses vues*—happening on a visit to the *Conciergerie* and
a mention of Louvel.[3] So I went to Larousse for Louvel and to
Paris guide books for the *Conciergerie* and had a delightful hour
in gossiping about places and people in Paris. I suppose it is the
*tourelles* of the *Conciergerie* that I see through the bridge in my
Méryon etching. I think one could spend months delightfully in
reviving literary and local gossip of this sort with regard to Paris
—and local with regard to London. I remember hearing of an
M.P. whom I knew slightly but whose name I have forgotten saying that after the adjournment he meant to devote two weeks to
London with a Baedeker. If it were not a principle that the joy
of life consists in the neglect of opportunities I could grieve that
I didn't make a point of seeing this and that in England. But after
all, as with the other parts of the globe, one has seen specimens
enough, and I do not share Bryce's desire to engollobate the whole
show. I must repeat another chestnut of mine that he who makes
the most of himself doesn't make much. Well—I leave you for
Victor Hugo once more.                    *Aff'ly yours, O. W. Holmes*

My compliments to the Missus on her translation which reads
well—bar the inherent obscurity of one or two phrases of the
author, especially his use of subjective and objective. One criticism
on the frequent use of *plea* to signify, as I understand, an *action*.

---

[2] "The old judge" (John Lowell, 1743-1802) was father of Marshall's
Federalist contemporary.

[3] Louis-Pierre Louvel (1783-1820); his hope that he might destroy all
Bourbons was only partially fulfilled when he succeeded in assassinating the
Duc de Berry.

It bothers a lawyer. May I venture to say that Duguit seems to me wanting in power of analysis—judging by the two books of his that I have read.

P.S. It sounded as if I were ending with a criticism and I kept my letter back this morning. I trust that I was too sensitive. I have a letter this p.m. Harcourt B & H with specimens. I stick to the original form and think it will be handsome. I mentioned to them that I believe I forgot a paper in *The Youth's Companion* back in '89. *Just the Boy Wanted: II in the Law*[4] but I don't think it worth bothering about. It ended with one sentence that I have quoted since—'The means by which the inevitable comes to pass is striving—'

I don't think I need say things about your value to me and my opinion of your value to the college.              *Aff'ly, O. W. H.*
I don't know that the other thing in *The Youth's Companion* was worth reprinting—I didn't reread it but left it to you.[5]

                              *Cambridge, February 18, 1920*
*My dear Justice:* There is only one moment in history where feelings comparable to mine just now may have developed—when the Holy Ghost knew that whatever Joseph did was too late because the incarnation had taken place. In simpler words, I have begun my new book and I feel lyrical about it. It's quite true that I have written only five pages in a week; but that misery of the first page is over, and vistas begin to open up. I've decided to call it *A Grammar of Politics* and the plan is somewhat (at the moment) as follows. It will open with a chapter on the historical foundations of the modern state in which I try to show how the modern state came into being and the consequences of the peculiar epoch in which it was born. Then I go on to show what psychological impulses a system of social organisation must satisfy if it is to be adequate. This leads to a discussion of the theory of parliamentary democracy with nasty remarks on legislative systems. It will follow that the essence of law is administration and chapter IV will study that. But the modern state is primarily industrial whence the interaction of politics and economics must be considered. Therefore chapters on the implications of capitalism, syndicalism, socialism and guild socialism follow—all of them having the honour of being rejected. This leads to a constructive chapter on the rights a social system must secure if it is to be enduring and to a final chapter on the meaning of freedom. It is quite wonderful to sit back and watch the cobwebs go out of my mind as I write. I really want to shout with joy. I know what I want to say

[4] 62 *Youth's Companion* 73 (Feb. 7, 1889).
[5] "The Bar as a Profession," *Collected Legal Papers*, p. 153.

HARVARD UNIVERSITY
CAMBRIDGE

Feb. 18, 1920.

My dear Justice,

There is only one moment in history where feelings comparable to mine just now may have developed — where the Holy Ghost knew that whatever Joseph did was too late because the incarnation had taken place. In simpler words, I have begun my new book and I feel lyrical about it. Its quite true that I have written only two pages in a week; but that means of the first page is over, and vistas begins to open up. I've decided to call it "A Grammar of Politics" and the plan is somewhat (at the moment) as follows. It will open with a chapter on the universal foundations of the modern state in which I try to show how the modern state came into being and the consequences of the peculiar epoch in which it was born. Then I go on to show it that psychological impulses a system of social organisation must satisfy if it is to be adequate. This leads to a discussion of the theory of parties — mediaeval democracy with nasty remarks on legislative systems. It will follow that the essence of law is administration and chapter IV will study that. But the modern state is primarily industrial whence the interaction of politics and economics must be considered. Therefore chapters on the implications of capitalism; syndicalism; socialism and guild socialism follow — all of them having the honour of being rejected. This leads to a constructive chapter on the rights a social system must secure if it is to be enduring and to a final chapter on the meaning of freedom. It is quite wonderful to sit back and watch the wheels go out of my mind as I write. I really want to shout with joy. I know what I want to say and it comes fun saying it — and incidentally I believe (entre nous) that I have a brand new hypothesis to explain the concurrent parts played by the theory of natural rights and the theory of sovereignty in the general run of events. Please shout loudly with me, for that's what I feel like doing.

And I've read a work which really tickled my innards — Lewis Melville's life and letters of William Cobbett.

*Laski to Holmes, February 18, 1920*

did you by any chance ever happen on it. Its like reading the history of Tom Cribb – if you don't agree with Cobbett you're a blackguard and he'll write a pamphlet against you. A really loveable blackguard – dead right on the main issue but so ludicrously impossible as to the manner of being right that half the reifers (there are hundreds of them) are wholly believable outside a Thackeray novel. I can only say that he made 165 speeches in 3 months in the House of Commons; that he moved for the chemise out of Peel for during to issue paper money; that he sent turnip-seeds weekly to his own in America; and you realise what a guy he is. Every an-imal is a wage, but he shouts for a week if one calls on him. He goes bankrupt on £10,000 a year. He goes poaching (very unjustly) to Newgate and engages wons there at twenty guineas a week, has most of his family there, and then belabors the tyranny of the government, isn't that grand. He took me to the memoirs of old Holyoake the secu-larist – full of good stories to read the clergy with. He tells one glorious story. In jail the chaplain thought it his duty to convert H. So H. was summoned to chapel and alone there was preached at for half-an-hour. After a short prayer the question came was Holyoake converted? No. Followed a second sermon and prayer. Was Holyoke con-verted? No. A third sermon and prayer. Any reach? No. Well, I have satisfied God and he gives Holyoake a shilling bible with the assurance that the means of salvation are therein. Could anyone on earth except Brother Huggins of Brick Lane have done that? Let me add in quite another connection that I have just read John Adams' Defense of the U.S. Constitution with a good deal of reverence for his learning.

Other things have put me in the clouds. My graduate class here has doubled and last night with the twelve of them I had the kind of discussion (on legislatures) which in the fairness of its give and take, its clarity, and its humility, made you feel that when the last word is said teaching is really the greatest job on earth. And in my undergraduate classes I would have had over 150 new students had conditions made their entrance possible. Add to all this that (a secret) Felix is going to write a book and you can see that my ideas get nourish-ment. He'll write on the 14 Amendment & that's the realisation of one of my most eager hopes. So that I feel as happy as a frog in a pond with an abundance of flies. Please share it all with me.

If of love to you both. I had to write this to get it off my chest.

Ever affectionately yours,

D.f.L.

and it is grand fun saying it—and incidentally I believe ( *entre nous* ) that I have a brand new hypothesis to explain the concurrent parts played by the theory of natural rights and the theory of sovereignty in the general run of events. Please shout loudly with me, for that's what I feel like doing.

And I've read a book which really tickled my innards—Lewis Melville's *Life and Letters of William Cobbett.* Did you by any chance ever happen on it? It's like reading the history of Tom Cribb—if you don't agree with Cobbett you're a blackguard and he'll write a pamphlet against you. A really loveable blackguard —dead right on the main issue but so ludicrously impossible as to the manner of being right that half the letters (there are hundreds of them) are hardly believable outside a Thackeray novel. I can only say that he made 165 speeches in 3 months in the House of Commons; that he moved for the dismissal of Peel for daring to issue paper money; that he sent turnip seeds weekly to his son in America; and you realise what a joy he is. Every aristocrat is a rogue, but he shouts for a week if one calls on him. He goes bankrupt on £10,000 a year. He goes wailing ( very unjustly) to Newgate and engages rooms there at twenty guineas a week, has most of his family there, and then belabors the tyranny of the government. Isn't that grand? He took me to the memories of old Holyoake the secularist[1]—full of good sticks to beat the clergy with. He tells one glorious story. In jail the chaplain thought it his duty to convert H. so H. was summoned to chapel and alone there was preached at for half-an-hour. After a short prayer the question came was Holyoake converted? No. Follows a second sermon and prayer. Was Holyoake converted? No. A third sermon and prayer. Any result? No. Well, I have satisfied God, and he gives Holyoake a shilling Bible with the assurance that the means of salvation are therein. Could anyone on earth except Brother Stiggins of Brick Lane have done that? Let me add in quite another connection that I have just read John Adams' *Defence of the U.S. Constitution*[s] with a good deal of reverence for his learning.

Other things have put me in the clouds. My graduate class here has doubled and last night with the twelve of them I had the kind of discussion ( on legislatures) which in the fairness of its give and take, its clarity, and its humility, made you feel that when the last word is said teaching is really the greatest job on earth. And in my undergraduate classes I could have had over 150 new students had conditions made their entrance possible.

---

[1] George Jacob Holyoake (1817-1906); Owenite missionary and father of secularism who in 1841 was imprisoned for six months on a charge of blasphemy, based on an offhand and novel interpretation of a Biblical passage. Author of *History of Cooperation* (2 vols., 1875-78) and *Sixty Years of an Agitator's Life* (1892).

Add to all this that (a secret) Felix is going to write a book and you can see that my ideals get nourishment. He'll write on the 14th Amendment and that's the realisation of one of my most eager hopes. So that I feel as happy as a frog in a pond with an abundance of flies. Please share it all with me.

My love to you both. I had to write this to get it off my chest.
*Ever affectionately yours, H. J. L.*

*February 23, 1920* [1]
*Dear Laski:* Your letter dated 18? posted 20 comes this morning. I shout with you—but cannot help worrying a little about your pace. I am afraid that you are spending capital in keeping at it so intensely—but there is no use in talking. We always are uneasy in seeing another stand on the edge of a precipice even if we would stand there ourselves with composure. I am very curious as to your theory of the part played by natural rights and sovereignty. You remember that Ehrlich has a good deal to say on their cooperation at certain moments—(in *Die Juristische Logik*). I can't help somewhat regretting the influence of Figgis—working for quite different ends—on your interests. I fear that it makes you tend to over-emphasise the supposed decay of sovereignty. But I have no doubt that whatever you do will be a gain to intelligent thinking on the subject.

I still amuse my leisure moments with Hugo's *Choses vues*— (new series). He is rather melodramatic and unreal even in details —but good reading with occasional references to Larousse. For this week I am in slack water and don't expect to do much except dawdle. Next week we sit again.

F. F. telegraphed to dine with us on Wednesday—and I look forward to a jaw with him.                    *Aff'ly yours, O. W. H.*

*Cambridge, Mass., 28.2.20*
*My dear Justice:* You need not have any fear about my gasworks. The engine works hard, but I have never been so well in my life as I am just now; and even if I had (which I have not) a tendency to overwork it, Frida is a stern and watchful guardian of its capacity. *Voilà.*

I am honestly grateful to you for your note of warning about Figgis. No one ever takes advice. I am conscious just the same that when you give me hints they become a part of my inner self in a way which would make you regard them as not thrown away. What I feel I owe to Figgis is threefold: (a) an understanding of

---

[1] A brief note from Holmes, dated February 20, 1920, is omitted.

the comparative lateness of the idea of a territorial state, or in terms of men, that Machiavelli in *Politik* and Bodin in *Staatslehre* are the beginning of the technique we can definitively call modern; (b) an understanding of the fact that the struggles of religious groups during the Counter-Reformation prevented what might otherwise (and disastrously) have occurred, namely the fusion of the sovereignty of legal dialectic with the sovereignty of political structures; (c) an understanding that the growth of religious toleration was what made possible the movement from an appeal to abstract right to an appeal to social utility, *i.e.,* when we leave out the command of God as the justification of our position we have arrived, for the first time, at a situation where such thoughts as those of Bentham become possible. What I deny in Figgis is above all his belief in the ethical superiority of the medieval world; next his *a priori* exaltation of ecclesiastical groups; thirdly his insufficient hypothesis as to the origins of modern liberties. That plural is important. He would have said 'liberty.' I think he was right in urging that religious warfare drove the state to make concessions to freedom. What I don't think he sufficiently saw is that (i) the concessions were always grudging because some religious group or other remained dominant and a religious group is *more suo* exclusive, (ii) that the concessionaire didn't care a damn about freedom for any of its rivals and, the Quakers apart, would probably have persecuted if it could, (iii) above all I don't think he grasped fully the value of the routine the state gives us, even if the routine is not yet wide enough to give the chance of creativeness to everyone who can make use of it. I hope I make myself clear. . . .

And while you have been ambling through Paris, I've been doing London. I got Muirhead's *Blue Book*—the substitute for Baedeker—and made up my mind what I want to see next summer. Incidentally I got a sense of the way London has grown that was delightful. Do you remember how Macaulay's Holly Lodge was in the country? Now it's a proper suburban residential district from which you throw a stone to Earl's Court. And to see a map on which the Cheshire Cheese and Dirty Dick's and the Hole in the Wall and Simpson's could be traced gave me deep emotions. Add to this the joy of (I hope) discovering a Lyndwood's *Provinciale* (1679) for ten shillings (dependent on a cable) and you'll know how I feel. Also I'm on the track of a set of Bentham for which I'd sell my soul but the democratic legislator's works have a habit of selling too quickly for the mail to be an adequate way of ordering. Eke a great novel—*Carnival* by Compton MacKenzie —to be bought by Mrs. Holmes and read aloud to you at solitaire.

My dear love to you both,

*Ever affectionately yours, Harold J. Laski*

*Washington, D.C., March 4, 1920*

*Dear Laski:* This is just a word of thanks for your admirable letter. You put your views so well that I only learn from them without a word of criticism. As to Duguit whom you don't speak of, but whom I dispraised, perhaps I might sum up my impression by saying that he seemed to assume that if a court upset a statute, that indicated a decay of sovereignty—as if a court means anything but a voice of the sovereign power—the dominant voice in the case supposed. For once I triumph in the matter of books. I have the handsomest Lyndwood I ever saw, printed by Bocard, 1501. If you get your 1679 it may be more correct but it won't look so fine. As Tennyson said to a girl who told me, others may have written better poetry but none wrote poetry that sounded better—or words to that effect (in which he erred, for Shakespeare beats him).

I got all my cases off on Monday (with dissents) to the relief of my mind—they were not specially interesting but I had been hung up until I was bored.[1] Between ourselves, I deeply regretted the situation of the Steel Trust Case—decided 4 to 3—without a majority of the whole court and with the probability that if the whole court could sit it would have gone the other way.[2] I could not change my opinion out of deference to that fact, but I have been in a minority of one as to the proper administration of the Sherman Act. I hope and believe that I am not influenced by my opinion that it is a foolish law. I have little doubt that the country likes it and I always say, as you know, that if my fellow citizens want to go to Hell I will help them. It's my job. I have one or more dissents on the stocks but am doubting whether I shall say more than a sentence in the one now in my mind. Perhaps if I say no more Brandeis will be led to expatiate as he was in another case, in which event I shall hand the reins to him.

I am comforted by what you say about Mrs. Laski's surveillance of you. I have great faith in her. Please tell her that I hope she will use the curb as well as the snaffle.

I shall miss you dreadfully this summer.

*Affectionately yours, O. W. Holmes*

---

[1] On March 1 Holmes had delivered the Court's opinions in *The South Coast, Bates* v. *Dresser,* and *Fort Smith Lumber Co.* v. *Arkansas, supra,* p. 240. He had concurred in the dissenting opinion of Brandeis, J., in *Schaeffer* v. *United States,* 251 U.S. 466.

[2] Holmes had concurred in the opinion of McKenna, J., in *United States* v. *United States Steel Corp.,* 251 U.S. 417, holding that the defendant corporation which had sought to achieve a monopoly and had succeeded in receiving economic power greater than any single competitor, had not violated the Sherman Act in so doing. Day, Pitney and Clarke, JJ., dissented. McReynolds and Brandeis, JJ., did not participate in the decision.

*Cambridge, Mass., 6.3.20*

*My dear Justice:* This letter ought to arrive on your birthday; and it really is a confession of failure for I simply don't have the words in which to tell you either of the depth of my love or the gladness with which I put it down on the day when it has a special meaning. But inarticulateness is the most articulate form that feeling can take and you will understand. I do hope the Hobbes arrived at the proper time.[1] You will guess what joy I had in finding it, and with what special pleasure Felix and I sent it along. I know you, like myself, have a special place in your heart for that best of ruffians. And it may even tempt you to think that the seventeenth century printers were not inferior to the sixteenth—Etienne [*sic*] alone excepted. (I mean Henry of the Thesaurus).[2]

Your letter was grand. I thought you would not mind my sharing the middle page with Felix—otherwise it is in the *arcanum imperio*. I'm glad you feel the stupidity of the Sherman Law. I don't doubt that many business operations are subject to the control of statute, but the ramifications with which that act tries to deal always seem to me to secure either inefficiency or dishonesty. Not that I liked the form of McKenna, J's decision[3]—I thought there were things in it that left dangerous loopholes to an acute lawyer like Sherman Whipple or Charles Choate.[4] But it may lead to a concentration of public opinion on the general question and that will be worthwhile. When one reads in the report of the Government committee on profits in England that a reel of cotton thread which cost 2d before the war now costs 10d—the normal cost at post-war prices ought to be 3½d—one feels that a serious consideration of the monopoly problem is due. . . .

My love to you both. Please have the happiest of birthdays.

*Affectionately yours, H. J. L.*

*Washington, D.C., March 6, 1920*

*My dear boys:* It is splendid and I am touched to the midriff with the joy of possession and gratitude—but you shouldn't do such things.[1] Your duty is to look out for number one and leave old fellows to eat what cake is left to them. I feel guilty. But a sense

---

[1] Felix Frankfurter and Laski gave Holmes an early edition of Hobbes's *Works* for his birthday, which was to be on March 8.

[2] Henry Estienne (1528-1598), of the famous French family of printers and scholars; his *Thesaurus Graecae Linguae* was printed in five volumes in 1566.

[3] *Supra,* p. 194.

[4] Sherman L. Whipple (1862-1930) was a prominent Boston lawyer, notably successful in trial and appellate work. Charles Francis Choate, Jr. (1866-1927) was the son and nephew of distinguished Boston lawyers, and himself prominent as counsel for important local and national interests.

[1] See, *supra,* p. 195.

of wrongdoing is an enhancement of pleasure and I am delighted. I think my next reading will be some of the things that I have not read—*e.g. Human Nature,* which I see in Allibone is called by some Hobbes's greatest work. (The homely old spelling Hobbs tickles one, like Cook for Coke) and what a fine portrait at the beginning. Oh decidedly, you know how to hit me where I live.

I am not thanking you adequately for I haven't got over my surprise but I will rely upon your knowing how I feel.

*Affectionately yours, O. W. Holmes*

*F.F. & H.J.L.*

*March 11, 1920*

*Dear Laski:* Your letter did arrive on my birthday. Need I say how much it moved me? I think you must have seen the delight I have had in your companionship. Such things are like the magnet, there can't be a North pole without a South pole. It has made my work easier and happier. It is a great fortune for an old fellow to have such intimacy with a young one, and your gifts have made it full of suggestion and instruction. You know all this, but one likes to say it and hear it.

Things are serene at this point for the moment. My case for this week has been written, distributed and returned approved by most of the lads. I was very sorry for the necessary turn taken by the *Steel Trust* case.[1] I couldn't change my position because I believed that if the other two judges could have sat the majority would have been the other way, but it is very unsatisfactory. Also I regretted the turn given to the opinion but I couldn't help it. I also regretted very much the decision as to stock dividends[2] but that also couldn't be helped. I hope that now we are in less troubled waters, but don't know, as there are other important matters ahead.

I wish I could sit down with my beautiful Hobbes. What a fine portrait—and no engraver's name. I wonder who could have done such a good piece of work in England—probably Rice (head of the print department, Congressional Library) can tell me—I shall ask him. . . . We have just read Turner's *A Place in the World.* One gets more fun out of the novels that are not great than out of the great ones. " 'Oh God,' she said, 'whatever that funny little man is asking you, please see he gets it.' 'That's a rotten prayer'

---

[1] See, *supra,* p. 194.
[2] In *Eisner* v. *Macomber,* 252 U.S. 189 (March 8, 1920), a majority of the Court, with Holmes, Day, Brandeis, and Clarke, JJ., dissenting, held that despite the Sixteenth Amendment Congress could not, without apportionment, tax as income a stock dividend paid to stockholders.

she added to herself" &c. You see I am not moving among the demigods. But I must turn back to work.

*Affectionately yours, O. W. Holmes*

My love to the missus.

*Cambridge, Mass., 21.III.20*

*My dear Justice:* . . . My reading in the past fortnight has been rather strictly along the lines of work. I did get a chance to race through a brilliant little book by Karl Kautsky, *The Dictatorship of the Proletariat,* which I thought the best critical analysis of Bolshevism I've yet seen—a big job neatly handled without malice or exacerbation. Then I read the two volumes of Lord Cockburn's *Examination of the Trials for Sedition in Scotland.* I wonder if you or any of your colleagues have by any chance read them. I know no more illuminating comment on this time than to see how a judge who as a boy knew the espionage atmosphere of his time sit [*sic*] down to insist how unbelievably stupid he was. If a man like Clark[e] J. could be persuaded to read them, I think *Pierce* v. *U.S.*[1] in the future would have three dissentients instead of two. Of other things I have read little of much interest. I must except Jeremy Taylor's *Liberty of Prophesying* which I thought very nearly as moving a piece as the *Areopagitica.* This is stately stuff in that seventeenth century stiffness.

Incidentally I have given W. H. R. Rivers a note to you. Probably he's the best living English anthropologist and a very delightful person. He knew Maitland and his scientific work is broad enough to make him see its bearing on law and history. I hope you will get a real chance to talk with him. He told me the great news that Russell has been reinstated at Cambridge,[2] which is the best evidence I have so far seen of the return of sense. Indeed if I may avow a private heresy to you alone, I have an uneasy suspicion that Cambridge is likely to meet the new age in a better and more awakened spirit than Oxford. Last night I dined with my old tutor[3] and what amazed me in him, a reputed liberal, was a refusal to admit that things like psychology have any recognised place in the university curriculum. He left me with a sense that I owe an incalculable debt to America for having (I hope) deprived me of insularity. He spoke of men with awe for

---

[1] 252 U.S. 239 (March 8, 1920). A majority of the Court there sustained a conviction under the Espionage Act. Brandeis, J., with Holmes concurring, had written a dissenting opinion, in which it was contended that the defendant's constitutional right of free speech had been infringed.

[2] In 1916 Bertrand Russell had been deprived of his fellowship at Trinity College, Cambridge, because of pacifist activities.

[3] Sir Ernest Barker; see, *supra*, p. 181.

being heads of colleges whom I knew to be heads through some
disreputable church intrigue. He spoke of appointments as always
made by merit. In fact he wanted me to accept Oxford as perfect
and change as the last sin. No man has a right to shatter one's
enthusiasms in that hard fashion.

I hope you will take a look at the article called "Precedents" in
the *New Republic* for March 24.[4] I put those together in the hope
that if by chance they come to the President's eye they would
cause him pain. Certainly they are apposite. It's interesting to see
how completely his house of cards is shattered. If you look at his
*History of the American People* (illustrated ed.) vol. ii p. 310, you
will find a perfect description of himself under the character of
Jefferson Davis even down to the 'feminine' quality of resenting
brilliant people near him. You remember the Latin proverb *Homo
extra corpus est suum qui irascitur.*[5] What a glorious job Lytton
Strachey would make of him!

Well! My love to you both. I am very anxious to talk again.

*Ever affectionately yours, H. J. L.*

*Washington, D.C., March 28, 1920*
*Dear Laski:* It has been a strenuous week at this end also, so that
I could not answer your dear letter at once. However we adjourn
on Tuesday, after some more arguments on the 18th Amendment
for the rest of the fortnight.[1] I have a case that interested me very
much and on which I worked fiercely.[2] It has a majority in its
favor but as two or three disagree I daresay that tomorrow morning they will want it to go over especially as the ever articulate
—— is one of them. I presume that your book (Home University
Series) is not yet out though I have heard rumors of notices.
Brandeis sent me your article in the *Manchester Guardian* as to
American and English universities—which I thought admirable.[3]
I had been struck myself or had got an impression at least that as
you say the English had a more intense and accurate use of their
intellects and our men a more general knowledge. I remember long
before you were born a man who had taken a double first or

---

[4] This anonymous piece consisted of quotations from Macaulay's *Chatham*
and Disraeli's *Coningsby*, pointing to the effect on government of executive
inaction.

[5] "A man who has lost his temper is a man outside himself."

[1] *The National Prohibition Cases*, 253 U.S. 350.

[2] It was not until April 19 that Holmes delivered any opinions; he then
delivered the Court's opinion in *Kenney* v. *Supreme Lodge*, 252 U.S. 408,
and *Missouri* v. *Holland, id.* 416. In the latter, the Court held, over the
dissent of Van Devanter and Pitney, JJ., that the migratory bird treaty with
Great Britain was constitutional and extended federal power to matters
traditionally of state concern.

[3] Manchester *Guardian*, Anglo-American Number, Jan. 27, 1920, p. 63.

double firsts, whichever is right, asking me if Swedenborg, whom
I happened to mention, was a professor at Harvard College. On
the other side it is enough to look at the work of American judges
and see how rarely they can get beyond some general proposition
—how unable they are to get close to their thought—or, better
perhaps, to think close to the case. . . . I am tickled at your dinner
with your tutor and your impression that America has done something for you. I spent a weekend with Lord Davey once (I forget
whether it is Davey, as I think, or Davy. No, it must be Davey)
wanting to talk about some legal questions and was struck with
the finality with which he said, "That is *not* the law of England."
I replied that I was aware of it, but was considering whether it
should not be the law of Massachusetts. He did not go beyond his
groove, although working very admirably and clearly within it.
I think I have noticed the same thing in other cases—at least I
remember suspecting it once with Jessel in his court and again with
the Chancellor, Lord Halsbury, in the P.C.—when, it is fair to add,
that I saw manifest signs that Davey felt the difficulties. I haven't
yet read your article in the *N.R.*, that you mention. I haven't had
a moment. Apropos of the President my wife told me of an article
to the effect that for some years we had been run by a woman as
Mrs. W. is supposed to determine whom the President shall see,
and to count for a good deal in what he does—I dunno. Will he
run again? . . .

As you say Lord Cockburn, I suppose it is the Scotchman who
wrote the book you mention—I never saw it. Your Rivers will be
welcome. I hope he will come pending the adjournment. As for
myself I am vacuous of all but law. Your letters even when the
heading is Ms always bear Harvard University so that I have to go
to my paper to verify the number of your house. I don't feel safe
with any other address. Is H. U. sufficient? I revere the ease with
which you tackle the stately, *i.e.* longwinded discourses of the past
—and I delight in all that you write—to me or to the world.

                              *Aff'ly yours, O. W. Holmes*


                              *Cambridge, Mass., 28.3.20*
*My dear Justice:* I do not know how to begin this letter. All my
abiding love for you comes tumbling to the end of my pen and
confuses the thoughts I want to express. The fact is this. I have
been offered a professorship at the London School of Economics
to begin next October. It offers me £700 a year, an amount of
teaching very much less than I now do, colleagueship with the
men who are the real masters of my subject, and, above all, England. I have talked it over with Felix, Lowell, Haskins, and my

colleagues in general; I have looked at it from the personal angle of Frida and my own people; and the conclusion is that I ought not, personally and intellectually, to refuse it. I have written my acceptance and so when I go in June it will be for good.

You will know what I mean when I say that my love for you and Felix is the one thing that holds me back. It is one of the two or three most precious things I have ever known and to diminish the personal contact that has lit up these last four years so much is not easy. Yet I think it has gone deep enough to make space, I do not say unimportant, but irrelevant. Wherever I am and whatever I do you would be one of the greatest joys I could have. If I end this American adventure will you believe me when I say that I end it only because what you have taught me has made it possible for others to think that I might be useful in what seems a career where I would exercise a larger influence than here. Wallas and Webb and Viscount Haldane were the people who urged my appointment. The school is the place above all where I have been anxious to teach. I can lecture there on the subjects about which I care most, and the work is almost entirely with graduate students. Then I have at hand the prospect of political work with the British Museum and the Public Record Office for materials nowhere else available. The income is not as large as I have here; but the time occupied by teaching leaves one a good deal more freedom both for books and such work as I have done these last four years in the *New Republic*. Felix and Lowell both emphasise their belief that the post is for my work, ideal. I feel that too. But I cannot be content until I know that the seal of your approval is on it.

And I want to say again that the thought of England makes me see how infinitely much I owe to our friendship. Not merely to the ideas you have given me—though they are the background of my thought, but above all to a generous affection which, I think, comes only once or twice in one's life and makes everything that has ever been bitter or hard seem petty and negligible. I want while I'm in England to try and fill for you the place Miss Chamberlain[1] had, to send you week by week comment and gossip and talk, but above all my love. If I could not do that I would not, of course, go. For I realise that the bigger thing is to contribute what I can to your happiness.

Please tell Mrs. Holmes this, for all that I say is for her equally with you. And give her, as yourself, my dear love.

*Ever affectionately yours, Harold J. Laski*

---

[1] Miss Beatrice Chamberlain (1862-1918); daughter of Joseph Chamberlain and sister of Sir Austen Chamberlain; intimate friend and correspondent of Holmes's.

*Washington, D.C., March 31, 1920*
*My dear Laski:* Your decision sounds right to me. Of course I
cannot judge with knowledge of all the elements—but it seems
plain that you will be in a better *milieu* for your work and that is
the first thing to consider so far as you are concerned. I gather
that your wife will like the change, or at least does not object to
it, and that being so, I should think the case was pretty clear. But
oh, my dear lad, I shall miss you sadly. There is no other man I
should miss so much. Your intellectual companionship, your suggestiveness, your encouragement and affection have enriched life
to me very greatly and it will be hard not to look forward to seeing you in bodily presence. However, I shall get your letters and
that will be much. I shall do my best to hold up my end of the
stick—though while the work is on here, as you know, it sometimes is hard to find time or to get free from the cramp to the law
—I should say, of the law, in the sense that one's mind after
intense preoccupation only slowly recovers its freedom—as the eye
only gradually readjusts itself to a new focus—especially with the
old. I feel as if I were good for some time yet—but I used to think
that the mainspring was broken at 80 and in any event as that
hour approaches one is bound to recognize uncertainties even if
one does not realize them—as I don't. If we should not meet again
you will know that you have added much to the happiness of one
fellow-being. Give my love to your wife.
                                        *Affectionately yours, O. W. Holmes*

*Cambridge, Massachusetts, April 2, 1920*
*My dear Justice:* Your letter overwhelms me a little by its affectionate generosity. It is good indeed to have it; for it makes me
feel that if I have added even a little to your happiness I shall
not have sojourned here in vain—I am glad you approve of my
decision. It brings Frida in range again of her people, which means
much to her. It gives me an endless amount of time. It brings (I
dare to hope) some very real political influence within my grasp.
I don't belittle the immense amount I owe to America; but I feel
that in these days a balance of utility lies on the other side. Incidentally, is it alright [*sic*] for me to come to Washington on
Tuesday, April 19th? I shall stay at the Shoreham and be round
at 1720 whenever you can have me. Then, too, I expect to get in
another week-end before I sail.

I spent this morning reading every decision you have written
this term. Pound had said to me yesterday, apropos of Wigmore's
piece,[1] that your work had never in his judgment been so richly

---

[1] Holmes's friend, the distinguished legal scholar John H. Wigmore, had
recently published a vigorous criticism of Holmes's dissent in the *Abrams*
case: "Abrams v. United States: Freedom of Speech and Freedom of Thug-
gery in War-Time and Peace Time," 14 *Ill. L. Rev.* 539 (1920).

profound and I was glad of the chance to verify it. Of course
*Abrams* v. *U.S.* hits me closest. I think that dissent will influence
American thinking in a fashion to which only your work in *Lochner* and the *Adair* case have rivalry. And I envy the clean straight
sweep of your mind, the ease with which it moves direct to the
point, and surveys the ground from an eminence shared by no
American judge whose work I know. Jessel seems to me to have
your directness, but he leaves his surfaces unpolished. Bowen has
your sense of the environment of the case but without your direct
march on its centre. It's a marvellous record and I'm proud that
its author should be my friend.

I have corrected half the galley proof of your *Essays*. I told
Harcourt that you were not to be troubled until the page-proof
stage was arrived at. Then I hope we'll tempt you into writing a
short preface. . . .

I've been reading two things with deep interest. The first is the
new edition of the Webbs' *Trade Unionism* which goes down to
1920. It is colossal—accurate, shrewd, penetrating, profound. What
I, being old-fashioned, like best is seeing the expert in armor on
the novelties—there are half a dozen pages in which guild socialism is dissected about as neatly as intellect can perform an operation. Then I have read the three volumes of evidence before the
Coal Commission. The *chef d'oeuvre* of the piece is Haldane's evidence on the organization of the civil service. I like to see a man
who throws overboard outright the whole system of mechanical
panaceas and takes the straight road on the old paths of initiative,
courage and knowledge as the roots of effective government. I read
too the brief of Leslie Scott; but I think, clever as it is, that in the
largest sense, it is at every point contradicted by the detailed mass
of evidence produced. Sankey J. did a wonderful job and in an
atmosphere of great bitterness kept everyone in calm temper.[2]
Outside of these I've mainly been finishing an historical piece on
the origins of sovereignty.[3] I've tried to show the circumstances
which led to the birth of the modern state from what I hope is a
new angle, *i.e.* the unity postulated for the internal organization
of the state is a necessary legal hypothesis deduced from the ex-

[2] See *Coal Industry Commission; Reports and Minutes of Evidence* (3
vols., 1919). Mr. Justice Sankey of the King's Bench Division of the High
Court was Chairman of the Commission constituted to inquire into the position and conditions prevailing in the coal industry. Lord Haldane's testimony
concerning the organization of the civil service put considerable emphasis
on the feasibility and effectiveness of university training for the service;
2 *id.* 1082-1085. In 1921 Haldane's testimony was published in pamphlet
form with an introduction by Laski and R. H. Tawney; see *The Problem of
Nationalization* by the Viscount Haldane of Cloan (1921). Leslie Scott, a
close friend of Holmes's, was counsel for the Royalty Owners and Mining
Association of Great Britain; his speech on behalf of his clients is in 3
*Reports and Minutes* 159.

[3] See the opening essay in *The Foundations of Sovereignty* (1921).

ternal unity which arose during the religious wars as a protection against the aggression of Rome. It sounds convincing and it would lead to the kind of wisdom which you will find in half-a-dozen pages of Leslie Stephen on Austin in the *Utilitarians.* Incidentally, my Home University Volume won't be out before the 15th of this month; as if, let me add, anyone should have a copy before you.

My love to you both. You give me more gladness than I know how to repay.          *Ever affectionately yours, Harold J. Laski*

*Washington, D.C., April 6, 1920*
Dear Laski: Your letter holds out a joyful prospect—you say *Tuesday,* April 19—Tuesday is the 20th—a patent ambiguity, in Lord Bacon's classification. On the 19th we come in again, so that I shall be less free than the week before—but probably I shall have no case to write that week. I can't ask you to put up with us—much to my grief—as things look now, but I shall do all that I can to see as much of you as I can of course. Yesterday freedom began and I made a codicil to my will and read in the Bolsheviki book.[1] I can't say that the theme is one for which I have any real predilection. I also have read with very different joy Hobbes on *Human Nature.* Every other sentence is an epigram that one wants to save for quotation in a dissent—of which I have been preparing one to be ready when the opinion comes out.[2] We talk about the truth and yet another man will say that he can see nothing in reasoning that seems to you conclusive. Truth is the unanimous consent of mankind to a system of propositions. It is an ideal and as such postulates itself as a thing to be attained, but like other good ideals it is unattainable and therefore may be called absurd. Some ideals, like morality, a system of specific conduct for every situation, would be detestable if attained and therefore the postulate must be conditioned—that it is a thing to be striven for on the tacit understanding that it will not be reached. How we elegantiate the past. Hobbes signed his dedication Hobbs—and Coke was Cook—but the time is not for discourse. I must go in 5 minutes to a conference of the JJ and therefore run down with a bump. I wish I could believe the kind things you say about my opinions. I am grateful however.          *Aff'ly yours, O. W. Holmes*

*Cambridge, April 11, 1920*
My dear Justice: I shall get to Washington on Tuesday April 20th. I am writing to the Hotel Lafayette for rooms. I shall stay until

[1] Étienne Antonelli, *Bolshevist Russia* (1920).
[2] The first dissenting opinion which Holmes delivered after April 6 was in *Knickerbocker Ice Co.* v. *Stewart,* 253 U.S. 149, 166 (May 17, 1920).

Friday morning when, as at present arranged, I go to New Haven. I hope that it is convenient for you. I don't need to tell you how eagerly I am looking forward to talk.

Of news I have little enough. Felix is away arguing a labor case in Rochester. I have had Rivers here for a week, and though his university lectures sadly interfered with talk we had a good time. What impressed me about him was the all-aroundness of his mind. A first-rate physiologist, an admirable psychologist, probably the best anthropologist in England. It gave his views a foundation of solid fact which was impressive. He told me what a happy hour he spent with you and spoke, as we all speak, of your illimitable youth. I got E. B. Holt[1] from his hermitage to meet him and we destroyed a goodly number of existing reputations; that always seems to me quite the most pleasing way of being malicious. . . .

My love to you both,                          *Ever yours, H. J. L.*

*April 14, 1920*

*Dear Laski:* This is merely to welcome you in advance and to hope that railroad troubles won't upset the programme. As I told you we shall be sitting on and after the 19th. My wife is still confined to her room with a cold. The doctor says she is normal but she remains weak. Her right hand, the faithful Annie, is in bed and worse off than my wife, though I expect she will be improving now. But D. V. we will eat and jaw. *Aff'ly yours, O. W. Holmes*

*Cambridge, May 7, 1920*

*My dear Justice:* I ought to be ashamed of myself for my delay in writing. But look what I have done since I left Washington: (i) three book reviews; (ii) a week-end in New Haven; (iii) two guests here for a week; (iv) finished my New York lectures; (v) sold all my surplus books; (vi) written endless letters about London arrangements. Now I can sit back for a week until my share in the Ph.D. exams—a task I loathe for it is like putting a man on the rack.

I need not tell you how glorious it was to have talk with you again. You are the one man in America of whom one can be certain that in talk there will be concentration on the essentials, and I really have no words to say how stimulating it is. I suppose there is no one I have ever met whose intellectual affections flow in channels so akin to my own and it's a heartening thing to find that the kind of work I want to do meets with your approval. Had

[1] Edwin B. Holt (1873-1946); Professor of Psychology at Harvard; author of *The Freudian Wish* (1916), *The Concept of Consciousness* (1914).

there been nothing else, these six years would have been precious
because they gave me your friendship.

I am rooting in books. I've decided to lecture on Congressional
Government and that gave me the right to experiment with American political theory. So I sold my surplus books and am buying
the works of Hamilton, Madison, Jefferson and John Adams. I
want like the devil to buy John Q. Adams diary which I think the
most revealing book on New England ever written; but Good-
speed's copy is seventy-five dollars and I let it go. Did you ever
read it? Really one of the most vivid portraits ever penned. I don't
know if I have ever said to you how deeply I admire the thinking
of that first generation. I put it with 16th century France and 17th
century England for sheer creativeness; and to have those fellows
at hand is a marvellous stimulus. Also I have picked up one or
two gems in the antique way—above all and especially Campanella's *De Monarchia Hispanica* which is one of the profoundest
things the Spanish fellows ever produced. And I have acquired
some interesting 17th century treatises, one by Grotius on the relation between *jus civile* and the church,[1] which are inconceivably
learned. Altogether, as you can guess, I am having a good time.

Felix seems to have done magnificently in these deportation
cases.[2] I have seen but little of him for the last ten days, but
Pound gives me a glowing account of his activities. Sassoon,[3] whom
I've told to call on you, is a dear—a shy poet, with all the medals
for bravery you want and *no* aestheticism. Could the heart desire
more?

My love to you both,     *Ever affectionately yours, Harold J. Laski*


*Washington, D.C., May 11, 1920*
*Dear Laski:* A dear letter came from you but this is business concentrated. I have gone over the proofs of the *Collected Essays* (qu.
and addresses?) and have made careful corrections—which I hope
may reach the printer but I am told to send to you—a number of
details deserve remark— . . .

The second half of the essay on Agency is omitted. I send it to
you to be included in the proper place. On the other hand, I have
struck out a few pages which are merely a newspaper abridgement
of an address given at length later. The Agency II can be printed

---

[1] Presumably his *Via et Votum ad Pacem Ecclesiasticam* (1642).

[2] During the first week of May, Felix Frankfurter had appeared as *amicus
curiae* before Judge Anderson in the Federal Court in Boston seeking the
release on *habeas corpus* of aliens held as radicals for deportation. In June,
Judge Anderson granted the writ; *Colver* v. *Skeffington,* 265 Fed. 17 (1920).

[3] Siegfried Sassoon (1886-       ); British poet, soldier, novelist, and autobiographer.

from direct. I don't want to keep it—it doesn't matter if it is destroyed. I think the corrections explain themselves—and mostly represent things I should be anxious about. I am a little wobbly about the title to books in foreign languages but incline to think it better to put them in Roman, as English titles in my opinion clearly should be. Let them be uniform one way or t'other.

I felt very gloomy when I first glanced at the proof but now am cheerful and am hoping to see the book. . . .

I tremble as I trouble you with this but the publishers sent me to you. The proofs will go by registered mail—if they will take them—the Agency by ordinary post as I could furnish yet another (I think) if that went wrong.

I believe that this is all for the moment, for I have been full of it for two days—but it is only a moment's suspense of other themes. . . .                                   *Aff'ly and gratefully, O. W. H.*

*No. 2, May 11, 1920*
*Dear Laski:* The letters went this evening but the P.O. branch was shut at 6 so the proof waits for tomorrow morning—also the Agency II. I add this P.S. to say that I grieve to come in on you when you are driven but bear witness that I ask nothing to hurry you.

I add that I did not read all the text of Equity or Agency but went over the notes with care. My secretary read what I did not. An author's eye misses obvious mistakes but sees things that others would not.                                          *Aff'ly, O. W. H.*
P.S. You have not put in the Introduction to Volume 1 of the Continental Legal History Series pp. xlv-xlvi (1911).[1] If you don't think it worth putting in, O.K., but it has what I think a good figure in it (the cathedral) and one or two thoughts—and if it were left to me I should put it in. My secretary is about to try to register the proofs for sending and if they can be I shall tell him to ask for a return card to save you the trouble of writing.

                                                                      *H.*

*Cambridge, Massachusetts, [May 15?, 1920]*
*My dear Justice:* All the papers came quite safely, and I will attend to the corrections. I had already noted the omission of the second paper on Agency, which was a stupid printer's blunder. Is it all right to print the piece on Continental Legal History? I wrote twice to Wigmore for permission without getting a reply.

Chiefly the news is that I have been writing a host of accumu-

---

[1] The essay was included in the collection as published; *Collected Legal Papers*, 296.

lated book-reviews; the one I enclose[1] I rather like and you may
not otherwise see it. But I think it's a useful thing to point out to
people that mere hysteria about the state is a vain and empty form
of amusement. The real problems of the world are, after all, problems of organisation; and wisdom suggests study instead of a
scream. But I've discovered that the first thing in which people
economize is thought and Bourne's book, with a good deal of
beauty, suffered badly from nerves and a sense of personal frustration. Otherwise I'm occupied in putting together a group of
papers for a little volume I shall publish this autumn;[2] except one,
an historical essay on the origins of sovereignty, you have read
them all. But they form a unity and I think it will be useful to
have them available in some such consecutive form.

Just now the atmosphere here is rather wonderful. I think the
boys are genuinely sorry I am going, and I agree daily to attend
some other dinner they are getting up as a farewell. It is very
moving to me because it shows how eagerly they repay even the
briefest interest in their intellectual well-being. If I had to make
up a creed for the professor I'm certain that its first article would
be "Trust undergraduates." They may be stupid, lazy, what you
will; but ninety-nine out of every hundred have a divine spark
in them somewhere which sympathy and enthusiasm is sure to
light. Really, it is leaving the undergraduates that cuts me most in
going from here. It's a wonderful thing to watch one's ideas take
root in a boy's mind and know that he will be different because
you have had contact with him. But I must not moralise.

Do let me tell you of one or two books that will interest you. (I)
*The New Germany* by George Young—by far the best thing on
the aftermath of war that I have read. (II) *Social Theory* by
G. D. H. Cole—a little too short for the substance but full of ideas.
(III) *The Non-Partisan League* by H. L. Gaston. The book is by
a sympathiser but it strikes one as fair and sane and it will, I think,
illuminate the background of your recent case.[3]

Here come the boys! My love to you. I observe that you are in
your happiest vein.                           *Ever affectionately, H. J. L.*


*Washington, D.C., May 20, 1920*
*Dear Laski:* Your letter gives the usual pleasure and your notice of
Bourne commands my hearty assent—although perhaps you respect

---

[1] Laski reviewed Randolph Bourne's *History of a Literary Radical and
Other Essays* (1920) in 1 *Freeman* 237 (May 19, 1920).

[2] *The Foundations of Sovereignty and Other Essays* (1921).

[3] In *Green* v. *Frazier*, 253 U.S. 233 (argued April 19 and 20, 1920,
decided June 1, 1920), the Supreme Court in an opinion of Mr. Justice Day,
sustained as constitutional North Dakota taxing statutes designed to make
possible the financing of public control of the manufacturing and marketing
of farm products.

the self-assertion a little more tnan I do. If I may quote my favorite author (as Thackeray says) with regard to his objections to treating a man as a thing—a means—and not as an end in himself, 'If a man lives in society he is liable to find himself so treated.'[1] I have no scruples about a draft or the death penalty.

As to the pages in 1 *Continental Legal History* I notice that the copyright is in Little Brown & Co. I am pretty sure that they have given leave but I sent the letters to the publishers. To save time I have interrupted this to write to L.B. & Co. asking them to write to you and enclosing a stamp to affect their conscience. I gave them your address.

My work is done for the moment but I have offered to take some cases and am awaiting the answer with the *malaise* incident to the imminence of the unknown. It is added to by an engagement with the dentist for tomorrow and some of the usual business arrangements to be made for the summer.

On Monday in a dissent I endeavored (as Rufus Choate put it about a witness who was seen amusing himself with a lady on a haycock) to mitigate the asperities of haymaking by inserting a protest that there were no special constitutional principles as to strong drink and by saying that so far as I know the fathers of the Constitution approved it.[2] I got a long anonymous letter in pencil (frequent in anonymous communications) this morning referring me copiously to the Old Testament and saying that A. Lincoln would have read his Bible and asked God about it before he gave it to the public—but A.L. was a great man and he guesses that men like me don't read our Bibles, &c.

Rum lot, the anonymous.

I was interrupted in *Oceana*—but have had a few minutes with *Les silences du Colonel Bramble,* by André Maurois, which is pleasant and rather funny.

Now I must go out to dine with my wife as I like to make sure that she gets a little air and light and change. She seems pretty well now but not able to do much.          *Aff'ly yours, O. W. Holmes*

I had a nice letter from Frankfurter that I haven't had time to answer before today—but hope to later today.

---

[1] The thought was developed, though the quoted phrase was not used, in "Ideals and Doubts," *Collected Legal Papers,* 303.

[2] *Knickerbocker Ice Co.* v. *Stewart,* 253 U.S. 149, 169. A majority of the Court held that Congress could not constitutionally authorize maritime workers to recover workmen's compensation under state statutes when their injuries occurred on navigable waters of the United States. Holmes wrote a dissenting opinion in which Pitney, Brandeis, and Clarke, JJ., concurred.

*Cambridge, June 2, 1920*
*My dear Justice:* My life at present is a long round of farewells;
to that and nothing else attribute my delinquencies. Three farewell
dinners from students and a fourth tonight; two farewell dinners
from colleagues; meetings of the division; talks to students in want
of parting advice. It has all been very moving, but also very tiring.
They gave me two presents you would like to see—from my colleagues a two volume folio (1702) of Milton's prose works, and
from the students a glorious Bayle (1735) in sixteen octavo volumes—both in beautiful condition. As you can imagine I treasure
them.

One blow-off I must do. I read Henry James's letters and if ever
God made a lame-cat James was the boy. Culture without perception, delicate to the verge of indelicacy, narrowly warm-hearted,
clinging to the margin of life—it all sounds to me like high middle-
class life described from the angle of a natural-born valet. Now
you knew him and I want badly to be told if I am all wrong. I
said to Felix today that I'd rather have your dissent in *Lochner* or
*Abrams* than all his damned novels put together. Those letters
make me vomit. . . .

We sail on the 19th and from the 12th I think we're to be in
New York. Please give me your travelling times so that I can
catch a glimpse of you in greeting. I heard from Hill how much
better she was and I rejoice with you.

My deepest love to you both—                    *Ever yours, H. J. L.*

*Washington, D.C., June 4, 1920, 4:50 p.m.*
*Dear Laski:* Your letter comes to me just as I return from a wearing
conference of the judges—a moment when one is cynical as to
one's fellow men. I had last Monday the recrudescence of an old
problem. Whether to dissent as to the judge's salaries being included in the income tax, was the occasion and the problem
whether to allow other considerations than those of the detached
intellect to count.[1] The subject didn't interest me particularly—I
wasn't at all in love with what I had written and I hadn't got the
blood of controversy in my neck. In fact I thought that Vandevanter put his side rather nobly. So when another (not he) suggested that I helped to make the position of the majority em-
barrassing—as deciding in their own interest, I hesitated. But I
reflected that if my opinion were the unpopular one I should be
but a poor creature if I held back—and that philosophically the

[1] In *Evans* v. *Gore,* 253 U.S. 245, a majority of the Court in an opinion
by Van Devanter, J., held that in computing the Federal tax on the net
income of a United States District Judge, his official salary could not constitutionally be included. Holmes wrote a dissenting opinion in which Brandeis, J., concurred.

reasons were the same when I was on the other side. And anyhow you get lost in morasses if you think of anything except the question, the answer, and whether the public interest is that both sides should be stated.

But this is simply the disorderly rush of reflections on the business I come back from. Your departure is more important and more interesting. I fear we shall not meet, from what you say. We go through to Boston on the 16th and it seems will just miss you. I venture a line of business. Is the book of my essays &c. finished —or has anyone charge of it, if not? I have been busy right along with court work and other matters incident to the time—so that even now my head whirls with conflicting pulls upon me. On Memorial Day I was encouraged—at Arlington I tripped on a damned little wire support of a bush and came a whacking header onto my arms and nose and nothing broke—whence I infer that my bones are not yet chalky as my pa used to tell me that old men's bones did.

Now, having galloped around the field in every direction I submit to harness and recur to your letter. I delight in all that the boys and the others have done and said in your honor. I grieve to have you go off without something worth while from me but I have little chance and less time to find it. I have told you how I shall miss you. I envy you even the smell of London. Lord, but I should like to get it once again. But I am gradually reconciling myself to the inevitable—as one notes the effects of age around one one comes finally to know that there are no exceptions. But I hope we shall meet again before I die. My love to you both.

*Aff'ly yours, O. W. Holmes*

*Cambridge, Massachusetts, 8.6.20*

*My dear Justice:* It looks as though we shall miss each other, but that only deepens my sense that it is impossible to say 'good-bye.' I'll come back, at least for a season, at the first opportunity, for the one thing that I shall miss in America is personal contact with the richest mind and the most generous friendship I can ever hope to know. You cannot even begin to dream what you have taught me—for my own sense of it is so much bound up with the limit of what vision I have as to be beyond my measurement. But at least I know that it is of the best stuff I have.

I can understand the difficulties of the salary case; but what would have irritated me infinitely more would have been the failure of the court to see the clear issues in the Seaman Workmen's Compensation case.[1] There I thought, if I may say so, that

---

[1] *Knickerbocker Ice Co.* v. *Stewart, supra,* p. 208.

you wrote one of the most convincing dissents even you have done this term.

Your book proceeds rapidly. I have told the publisher that after the 16th, he is to send page-proof to you to Beverly Farms. Do you want to write a little preface by way of postscript? I wish more than I can say that you would. It's been a perfect joy to me to have even so small a share in this book.

These last days are a mass of good-byes, exam books and packing. But I've had one glorious draught of new knowledge—G. P. Gooch, *Germany and the French Revolution* (Longmans), a really first-rate introduction to a phase otherwise, I think, untouched by English writers. Also I've read J. B. Bury's *History of the Idea of Progress*—a fine piece of historical suggestion with just enough Irish malice to make the narrative pointed.

This is merely an interim note. When I'm finished with papers I'll write at length.

Our love to you and her.

*Ever affectionately yours, Harold J. Laski*

*June 11, 1920*

*Dear Laski:* A word of *adieu* I suppose this is. I am so glad that you are to have this enlarged opportunity that I don't repine—but I shall when the summer comes and there is no Laski. 'Nor at the Farms nor in Rockport was he' as M. Arnold observes. I won't be solemn at this moment which must be dominantly one of joy for you.

As for me I have finished that damned *Oceana*—a curious mixture of Cromwellian style with fine and sometimes pregnant sentences. I suppose it sounds odd to you to hear a man mention finishing a book that you would devour in minus one hour and with joy—but my time has been very limited and compared with you I am a slow reader. I suppose you perhaps understood all his elaborate machinery. I got but a vague notion and didn't care for more. It is curious to note that rotation in office goes back to him. Knopf (I suppose) sent me *This Simian World*—by Clarence Day, Jr. It is quite a noticeable book—just and deep *aperçus* conveyed in wit. What kind of a world it would have been had the ants got the upper hand—or the cats—and the monkey traits in man. Also I had an hour or two with Rice at the Congressional Library and looked at a lot of Lalannes and other etchings &c. and went upstairs and lunched with H. Putnam,[1] the British Ambassador[2] *et al.* I left my "Sunset in Ireland," [3] my larger Whistler, and my Méyron

---

[1] Herbert Putnam (1861-1955), Librarian of Congress, 1899-1939.

[2] Since March 2 Sir Auckland Geddes had been British Ambassador in Washington.

[3] By Sir Francis Seymour Haden (1818-1910).

with him for the summer, to feel that the risk was divided—except the foregoing a few farewell calls, packing, and winding up business are all that I have to show for the last few days. I sat with Brandeis in Farragut Square (close to our house) and had a pleasant farewell talk while a catbird played the mocking bird overhead. In consideration of my age and moral infirmities he absolved me from facts for the vacation and allowed me my customary sport with ideas. Unless I err the assistant philosopher that I met *chez vous* (Englishman—son of man who had done work in or for India) has published a book that I mean to get when I reach Beverly.[4] I don't believe such books as a rule but they stir up the monkeys. Otherwise I must leave the future to chance. Well, my dear friend, I suppose this is the last word from me while you are on this side of the ocean—and the last word of the last words must be one of thanks and affection. You will be very often in my thoughts.

*Aff'ly yours, O. W. Holmes*

My love to your wife whom I admire.

*The Commodore, New York, June 21, 1920*
*My dear Justice:* In a little over twelve hours we shall be on board. My thoughts are curiously divided between a deep regret at the friends I shall miss and an eagerness to rebuild my home. But you are at the centre of all my thoughts. When I am inclined to despair about America I think of your achievement and find new comfort. When I am inclined to gloom about myself your friendship is a buckler in distress. I don't need to send you my love—you know you have it. And I hope you will not need my assurance that distance will not diminish its intensity.

My love, and Frida's to you both.

*Ever affectionately, Harold J. Laski*

I have ordered the last proof to be sent to Beverly F.

*Beverly Farms, July 10, 1920*
*My dear Laski:* Probably it will be some time before a letter comes from you giving your address, but I will start a reply in anticipation. I sadly miss you and for want of your suggestions *viva voce* I have a list of books that you mentioned in your letters. One, Cole, *Social Theory*, I brought down here and read.[1] I didn't care much for it. It took a good deal for granted that I don't believe. Of course I admit the value of the test of relevance to function that his school emphasizes, and I won't stop for the *buts*. Also I have read Hoernlé's *Studies in Contemporary Metaphysics*, on the assumption

---

[4] R. F. Alfred Hoernlé, *Studies in Contemporary Metaphysics* (1920).

[1] Laski had favorably reviewed G. D. H. Cole's *Social Theory* (1920) in 23 *New Republic* 154 (June 30, 1920).

that he was the gent I met *chez vous* in Rockport. He is a clever chap but struck me as expending language alternately upon the inexplicable and the obvious. These are confidential criticisms, as if I were giving my whole thought I should qualify and admit. In the main, so far, I haven't bothered about improvement. I read Pellico's account of his 10 years imprisonment with admiration for the sweet nature that triumphed over such embittering experiences, which even the tone of edification could not disguise.[2] Also *Vathek!* How the emphasis has changed since the Byronic time. One couldn't imagine anybody writing such a book now—yet not without its talent. Also Conrad's *The Rescue*—which combined with solitaire I found at times confusing—and I don't care much for the dame—nor for the matter of that a great deal for the hero. But of course he is a thriller. Also *The Moon and Sixpence*— (Maugham?) which Einstein[3] it seems to me rather overrated to me—but by no means bad reading. I bought it by the bath house on the beach at an itinerant van, run by two very presentable young women, I believe in the interest of some cause of holy Woman. It lit for a day at our shore. At this point my eye fell on your notice of Cole's book. I like it very much and recognize the detailed understanding to which I bow.[4]

                        *The London School of Economics*
        *Clare Market, Kingsway, London W. C., July 18, 1920*
*My dear Justice:* I have purposely waited for a fortnight before writing to you so that I might have some definite impressions to communicate; and merely to see London again was too lyrical an experience at first for sane commital to paper. We had a genial but slow voyage without casualties. Eleven episcopal bishops on board, but all were tame and one was a genuine liberal so that no mishaps occurred; though the temper of them *en masse* was hardly elevating intellectually. To see London again was thrilling; and ever since, I have wandered about like Haroun al Raschid, finding adventure at every street corner. My new post seems precisely what I wanted; and Sir William Beveridge, the Director of the School, is a charming fellow with all the qualities of the best type of civil servant. I had a good talk with Graham Wallas, who is full of the Royal Commission on Oxford and Cambridge, with Mansbridge,[1]

[2] Silvio Pellico (1788-1854), Italian dramatist whose most telling work was done not as playwright but as reporter of his sufferings in jail to which he was sentenced for political activities against Austria.

[3] Lewis Einstein (1877-1949); American diplomatist; intimate friend and correspondent of Holmes's; author of *Divided Loyalties* (1933) and *Historical Change* (1946).

[4] The balance of this letter follows, *infra*, p. 215.

[1] Albert Mansbridge (1876-1952); educator and leader in the movement for working-class education; from 1919 to 1920 he was a member of the Royal Commission on the Universities of Oxford and Cambridge.

who runs the adult education movement in this country and is
an eminently loveable person. A great lunch at the *Nation* with
Massingham, Brailsford, Masterman and such. Massingham was
vividly full of his visit to you in Eye Street and sent warm greetings. He really is a great editor. Lunch, too, with the Webbs whom
I like for their eagerness, their competency, and their direct march
upon what they want; and apart from a certain *brusquerie* of temper they really aren't nearly so difficult as their reputation. But
the great event was a long morning with Haldane, with whom I
dine again on Saturday next. I took to him at once. He talked
vividly of his crossing with you, of the dissent in *Abrams* v. *U.S.*,
the influence of *The Common Law,* the greatness of the Law
School, all with a mastery and interest which I liked hugely. Then
we agreed on most things which makes talk easy—agreed on the
civil service, the problem of educating the democracy and so forth.
Haig,[2] who should know, calls him the greatest secretary of war
we ever had; and it will be difficult to forget the accent in which
he said "I love the army." Also he arranged for me to spend an
afternoon with John Morley, of which I'll give you a full account
later on. And I went to a full dress debate in the House of Commons with the final impression that it was the worst legislature
England has ever known. I suppose that academic-minded people
like myself don't appreciate the business man as he should be
appreciated; but there they were *en masse,* and they talked, as I
thought, on a plane utterly unconnected with the world about us.
Let me add that Austen Chamberlain made an admirable speech;
that Asquith seemed to me clearly *passé*—no warmth, no eagerness, no incisiveness; and that I saw a labor member in the smoking
room finish up the half-drunk beer of another. The final note is
that I went to Manchester and saw my people for the first time in
nine years. I went because I thought I ought to show them that
there was a real eagerness on my part for the resumption of our
relationship. I don't think it did any good. They've become very
wealthy and my income and prospects are not on the plane which
interests them very greatly; and since I'm finding it impossible to
rent a house and cannot buy one under £3,000; and since they
must give us the £3,000 since I don't possess it, I am afraid we'll
have to live in S. James Park until they feel that Diana and Frida
can be palatable even though they were not born Jews. Do you
mind if I consign all religions to eternal damnation?

Felix and Brandeis, I needn't add, are great people here. Chancellors, Judges, Astors all vie for their entertainment. And I believe
they like it—Brandeis unbends delightfully. Felix, in his whirlwind ways, sees everyone and everything; and his wife looks on

---

[2] Earl Haig (1861-1928) had been director in the War Office (1906-
1909) while Haldane was engaged, as Secretary of State, in reorganizing the
General Staff.

in stately aloofness. Of course, I've been round the bookshops though their treasures are no longer three a penny. But they are undamaged by the war and I have picked up one or two pleasant things—Buchanan's *De Jure Regni apud Scotos,* the 1606 (Knolle) translation of Bodin's *De Republica,* and some modernities and the engravings make my heart faint with envy. There was a Rembrandt in Tregaskis—but I will not make you growl. All in all, England does not seem to have changed very much, at least in outward semblance. There is still the same servility for a two-penny tip. Still the same plethora of servants, the nursemaid still wears a uniform in which no self-respecting female would be found dead. But the life has a mature tone, an intellectual alertness, a sense of proportion, that is fitting for a people which has looked death in the face and emerged only with difficulty through its shadows.

My dear love to you both, and Frida's. I'd give much for a night's talk to straighten things out. From now on I'll write weekly.

*Ever affectionately yours, Harold J. Laski*

[*Holmes to Laski*]                                    [*Beverly Farms*]
*July 30.* Your letter has come and brings me joy. I will answer on this sheet begun so long ago[1]—just to show how my vacation began. It has kept on in much the same way. At your recommendation I read Gooch's *Germany and the French Revolution* with edification and pleasure—and also thanks to you I am just finishing the Webbs' *History of Trade Unionism*—the edition of 1911, alas, as that was the latest the Athenaeum possessed. It is a marvellously solid piece of work and I get instruction from it—but I believe that Webb's economics have a sentimental basis—though it is very bold for me to dare to say so—or would be if I didn't remember some of his earlier Fabian essays. I have no criticism for a given crowd's insisting upon maintaining a standard of living (at the expense of some other crowd) but when it is adopted as a thinking and not merely a fighting formula, I can but suppose that the writer believes in Croly's 'The sums now withdrawn by capital' which I think the emptiest humbug that ever was spawned. There seemed to me evidences in the book that the authors had not ceased to think dramatically. I didn't know that the Webbs were regarded as difficult. He struck me as far from exquisite but as a brilliant talker. The account I have heard of the way they laid out their life presented a marvel of system and *ennui* (not to them).

What you say of Brandeis and Felix gives me pleasure. The latter has an unimaginable gift of wiggling in wherever he wants to and I am glad that Brandeis should see more of England which

---

[1] See, *supra,* pp. 212-213.

when we last talked he admired beyond everything else—and I must admit (in spite of what I have said about the Webbs) that their book shows a respect for facts as against rhetoric in the working man that makes me envious. I wish I knew the later developments and present status of their movements. I don't think I agree with you about the nursemaid's uniform. Is it more than a cap? They look well in it. I should agree in disliking, except for the variety and amusement it gives to the eye, the rigging of men servants in a wholly different dress. It helps the stupid feeling of the employers that they are of a different clay. But it was more entertaining when you saw a lady driving with two outriders on horses matching those in the carriage. I saw in the Athenaeum that Ross who years ago wrote a good book, *Social Control,* had got out a big volume on sociology—which I thought that I either would omit or buy. I noticed with pleasure that he said that Malthus whose value had been depressed now stood at par. As you know, I wish his teaching in its substance were more taken to heart. (I bought the copy you mentioned to me in the 17th Street shop near my house.) The other day I ran through Blackie's translation of Aeschylus—and it led me to try to get the Greek (of course—I have it in Washington). I couldn't get a copy at Schoenhof's! So I took it from the Athenaeum—Aeschylus always has hit me harder than the others—and I think I must reread the *Agamemnon* and (especially) *Prometheus Bound,* the *ne plus ultra* of dramatic splendor.

I could run on I suppose for an hour but it is 11:20—I want to finish Webb and must walk to the P.O. before luncheon dinner at 1 and ∴ shut up. It gives me great delight to hear from you again. I had begun to feel uncomfortable. . . .

My love to you both—Oh am I glad to be with my playmate again!                                                  *Aff'ly yours, O. W. Holmes*

*London, July 28, 1920*
*My dear Justice:* My news is scattered and diverse but, I hope, not without interest. The real centre is a dinner with Haldane to which he had Brandeis and Sankey, J. I would like you to know the latter—strong clear mind, reading eagerly and keenly alive to events. Haldane himself talked superbly, particularly when he told us the story of how the British Expeditionary force was made. Then I spent a day in Oxford—whither I return tomorrow—and a week-end in Cambridge. Oxford, I think, disappointed me somewhat. The don, I take it, leads an oversheltered life and he gets wrapped up in the private, technical problems about him instead of the things the world outside is thinking about. Cambridge, very unpietically, I found much more alert. To begin with, I dined with Lowes Dickinson, who is in the thick of the ideas I care about.

And I stayed with Rivers (you remember him?) who is a first-rate fellow. And at Heffers' bookstore I bought for 2/6 a nice little 1663 *Utopia* with Isaac Newton's name written in it and what is surely the finest copy of Harrington (the folio of 1709) that is in existence. And I had a good long talk with Russell who sees the world very much with my eyes and not without the detachment that alone makes it intelligible. What is perhaps most important is that the goddess who presides over my destiny has found us a delicious little house. It's in S. Kensington about two minutes from the Natural History Museum and I think it can be made very attractive with our books and pictures. The address is 40 Onslow Gardens, S. Kensington and it's the ambition of my life to win you over to see it. Did I tell you that my father rejected my advances? The religious barrier was fatal and yet after nine years I found myself thinking that with you and Felix and one or two such there is no need for repining. When one has chosen the life of ideas the only thing possible is to stand by them. It means loss of means, but at least it's a gain in self-respect. Of other things, there's an enthralling book by the Webbs—*A Constitution for the Socialist Commonwealth of Great Britain*[1]—which is full of real insight. And oh! I mustn't forget to tell you that I've picked up a superb Bartolus—the folio of 1579—in the absurd way one does here. Really I'd give a year of my life for a chance to walk over the bookshops here with you. A friend of mine who keeps the Dunster House Bookshop in Cambridge, Mass.[2] (it's in Harvard Square just by Holyoke and Mt. Auburn Street, and you must go and feast your eyes on its treasures) bought the other day a first edition of *Sardanapalus* for threepence and a pile of Leslie Stephen's commonplace books for ten shillings. That in fact is what London is like—a desert redeemed by millions of unexpected little oases. Tomorrow I go down to Oxford to lecture and then to the sea for ten days. Then back here to the luxury of furnishing and the joy of getting into the house. Of other news but little, I fear. Felix I've seen, of course; but he flashes over London like a meteor. Morley I'm to see in the next fortnight. The political background is a huge chaos—men seeking to avert a revolution they do not understand with weapons they don't know how to wield. The great people are these working men who have realized the part that discipline of the intelligence must play in a democratic state and are devoting their lives to that end. But I find myself wondering if we have time. It isn't that English civilization is out-worn—there is more ability about than I have ever known —but that it has learned to know that things are desirable with-

---

[1] Reviewed by Laski, 24 *New Republic* 198 (Oct. 20, 1920).

[2] Maurice Firuski now owns The Housatonic Book Shop in Salisbury, Connecticut.

out an organization capable of reaching them within the due limit of time assigned. It's a great spectacle to watch.

My love and Frida's to you both. Tell me all you're doing.

*Ever affectionately yours, Harold J. Laski*

*Beverly Farms, August 11, 1920*

*Dear Laski:* A delightful letter from you this morning of July 24 [*sic*]. Is it *40* (I think) or 10 Onslow Gardens? My! but I'd like to go bookhunting with you—you would always get the treasures but I should have the fun and be allowed some crumbs. I am very sorry about your father as I had hoped I saw a *rapprochement* taking place. My reading is moderate. Tommy Barbour yesterday said that after motoring over to Cambridge, doing his day's work there and returning—he polished off a volume in the evening. It made me feel like a worm. The other day I came to Prothero— *The Psalms in Human Life,* sent to me years ago by my would-be evangelizing friend Kennaway of Devon.[1] To my surprise I found it a delightful little history of 2000 years in anecdote—the tales bound together by the hero's quoting the psalms before his head was cut off—or something of the sort. It reminded me of the Goncourt's *Les maîtresses de Louis Quinze*—backstairs stories given an air of philosophic significance which enables you to gossip without shame. Then the psalms themselves—with some surprises to see how very rudimentary the motifs and the life portrayed. Just before, I had labored through the *Prometheus* with a Greek dictionary for which I had to use a magnifying glass—and having to look out every fifth word. I spent two or three days last week in rereading my proofs. The last thing before that was the Webbs' *History of Trade Unionism* which I believe I spoke of in my last. You write as if something fundamental was going to happen. I am out of it, but hope that after talking fundamentals they will simply modify details. It seems to me that the waking up of the working classes is rather a change of dreams—with a general unwillingness to look disagreeable facts in the face. Also you speak of the time assigned as if people must look sharp or his axe would fall. I hope not—but again would like you to expound. I have the first half of Volume I (Charley Curtis, its apostle, when someone exclaimed against 10 volumes said there are only 8)—Marcel Proust, *À la recherche du temps perdu.*[2]

---

[1] Sir John Henry Kennaway, Bart. (1837-1919); barrister-at-law, M.P for Devonshire, 1870-1910; President of the Church Missionary Society.

[2] The balance of the letter is missing.

*August 18, 1920*

*My dear Justice:* . . . I read the correspondence of Hume with Strahan the bookseller. I hope you will get a peep at that. It is sheer delight—Hume at his very best, quick, easy, witty, perceptive and full of those acute flashes of insight such as he had above all people in the eighteenth century. . . . With pain and misery I read Einstein's little elementary book on relativity but apart from an occasional glimpse I don't believe I understood it. Have you any help to offer a hapless mortal to whom n-dimension space is entirely meaningless? Can you think beyond three dimensions? There have, of course, been pleasant diversions. I had a delightful dinner with Felix when we abandoned England and talked of you and the Supreme Court and McKenna's dissent in the liquor case.[1] Felix is in Germany now, full of vigor and as vivid as you can ever have imagined him. Then tea with Brandeis, who is, I expect, sailing just as I write this. He was fine and spoke very movingly of his affection for you. She, I thought, was very bonny—every remark a commonplace and most judgments out of perspective. I thought him infinitely more at ease when she retired and we talked alone. Then, too, a night at the House of Commons to hear the Polish debate.[2] Robert Cecil a great Englishman, Lloyd George infinitely clever and as infinitely shameless, Asquith a wreck of former talent. What impressed me was the absence of large views. There was improvisation but not statesmanship, cleverness but not depth—except from Robert Cecil and he, of course, ran his hobby of the League of Nations to the exclusion of all else. . . . Now one or two points in your letter. First, my objection to the nursemaid's uniform is that it's the travesty of a noble profession. The nurse has served her apprenticeship and she's a trained professional; the other's just a God-knows-what who apes the uniform without the technique. I admit contingent attractiveness, but I urge that much depends on the face inside the bonnet. . . .

My love and Frida's to you both.

*Ever affectionately yours, Harold J. Laski*

*Beverly Farms, August 30, 1920*

*Dear Laski:* Another letter from you has not come yet but this is the beginning of what I hope will be [an] answer before it is finished. For I must tell you without further delay that your book came since my last and that I read it with unmixed delight.[1] I think the Introductory Chapter truly masterly and the whole thing kept me enwrapped. My only criticisms are infinitesimal. One is

---

[1] *National Prohibition Cases, supra*, p. 198.

[2] The issue concerned the position which Great Britain should take on the war between Russia and Poland.

[1] *Political Thought in England from Locke to Bentham* (1920).

that you refer to things not generally known by your readers without explanation—a thing which inferior people do to *'épater les
bourgeois'* but you I doubt not simply because your own familiarity
with the facts makes you forget that others have not the same—
*e.g.* p. 19. 'Mr. and Mrs. Hammond have recently illumined' etc.
Why not a note referring to the book? I knew what you meant,
thanks to you, but my nephew whom I put on to your volume
didn't. The only other thing is an occasional slip in proof reading
—or of the pen . . . Cohen was here the other day and dazzled
me by his discourse. He added to the pleasure by sending or
causing to be sent to me Tourtoulon, *Les principes philosophiques
de l'histoire du droit*—which is a real enrichment to one's mind.
I could wish that you would read it. There is too much systematiz-
ing and distinguishing for my taste—as I wrote to Fred Pollock,
men's systems are forgotten, their *aperçus* are remembered, but he
reinforces every scepticism that ever I entertained and is the best
correction that I know to people who are astraddle of a formula,
like the Webbs or Cole (*Social Theory*). I suppose you would read
him in a day but I took five or so. Not having you on hand to keep
me up to the mark and send me the wherewithal, I took up one of
our books here—a collection of English Prose by Henley and
Whibley—which seems rather boyish—but why not, as well as the
*Golden Treasury?* I got considerable pleasure from it especially
in rerealizing that the old ones could write simple and forcible
English that agreeably contrasts with Milton when he does not
soar to a height, as of course he can. Now I am like Dr. Johnson's
dull boy hesitating between Dumas and *Don Quixote* while you
would have read both. On the whole I won't wait for your letter as
I want you to hear what you must have known, with that admiration I have read the *Political Thought.* My love to the lady.
*Aff'ly yours, O. W. Holmes*

*40 Onslow Gardens, London S. W. 7, September 8, 1920* [1]
*My dear Justice:* So much time has been occupied in the last ten
days in actually getting into our house that I have literally been
swept off my feet. There has been furniture to buy, decorators to
watch, books to arrange, and some twenty odd Harvard students
to entertain. However, it is all done except for such trifling episodes
as curtains and cushion-covers; and I am now at my ease in a
study which literally makes for work, on a desk beyond my wildest
dreams. My father came out a trump; for though he won't come
to see us, and persists in regarding my marriage as a crime, and
Diana as an illegitimate child (the happiest illegitimate you ever

---

[1] A brief note from Holmes, acknowledging Laski's letter of August 18,
is omitted.

saw) he offered to pay for the furniture, with the result that the house is supremely comfortable. I wish you could see it. I never dreamed that buying furniture could be poetic; yet so it is. The real triumph is the dining room which is all in chippendale; and I wish you could see the wine glasses which are long-stemmed and mauve and all of them 150 years old. I feel a ghastly capitalist; but at least it is workmanlike and I have been able to settle down to the normal routine.

The outstanding event of the last fortnight has been a visit to Morley. He is very old, but keen and vivid and wise. We talked the world round—you, Acton, Mill, Gladstone, Newman, Burke, Adam Smith. I found that he worshipped many of my gods; and I was glad to find him free from the cant of progress. He has a little outlived his generation, in the sense that the pure milk of the Cobdenite word remains pure even in the midst of changes. His library was superb—all I could ever want. And he had no blind admiration for Gladstone, admitted his indirectness and subtlety and the appalling depth of his Christianity. He retains a great liking for Asquith and told me that in 1908 when the latter made Lloyd George Chancellor of the Exchequer, he warned him of a stab in the back. I have had no like conversation since my days with you in Washington; and it led me to the observation that men are really divided into two groups, those with and those without the historic sense. If one's mind has ever ranged at all widely over the facts the notion of sudden improvement vanishes; and that clarity of disillusion Morley has in fine degree.

. . . As to reading, I have had some exciting adventures. First there is H. G. Wells's *Outline of History*—a little too eager, but, within its limits, I think a real masterpiece. A book I picked up is also a real find—*The Correspondence of Macvey Napier* who was Jeffrey's successor at the *Edinburgh*.[2] The joy of it is the correspondence with Lord Brougham who is even more remarkable than I have ever dreamed; only Lytton Strachey of the *Eminent Victorians* could do him justice. I have simply been reduced to tears of laughter over that situation. Then I read Raven's *Christian Socialism,* an account of Kingsley, F. D. Maurice *et al;*[3] but I do not, at the end, find myself convinced that Maurice was the great-

---

[2] Francis Jeffrey (1773-1850), Lord Jeffrey, Scottish barrister and judge, critic with strong Whig convictions, who was editor of the Edinburgh *Review* from its foundation in 1802 until 1829, when Macvey Napier (1776-1847) became his successor. Napier as editor was forced to take a position of vigor in standing up to the opposition of Brougham.

[3] Charles Kingsley (1819-1875), Frederick Denison Maurice (1805-1872), and John Malcolm Ludlow (1821-1911) were the leaders of the Christian Socialist movement in England, which blossomed briefly in the hope that social reform might be achieved through Christianity and coöperative production.

est thinker since Plato; the extracts given rather suggest a misty mind who speculates in a Christian vacuum. . . .

You will have seen that big events lie about us here, but I don't think there is much in the always too easy talk of revolution. Our government is incredibly stupid; they feed the Irish mayor to the Dublin police instead of to the populace.[4] They admit Deniken but not the Russian trade unionists;[5] they cajole the mine owners instead of the miners.[6] But any government which regards a crisis as a philosophy is bound to destroy its authority and the real problem in England is to find a possible prime minister and a working formula. There will be many tears before either. Maybe there will be blood, but I doubt it.

My love to you both. I hope my little volume came betimes.

*Ever yours affectionately, Harold J. Laski*


*Beverly Farms, Sunday, September 17, 1920*
*Dear Laski:* Another good letter for which I had been waiting comes this morning, and a prompt answer turneth away wrath. The general turn of your expectations or nonexpectations and feelings seem to coincide with mine. People talk fundamentals and superlatives and then make some changes of detail. I cannot believe that England or this country will repeat Russia. I went to town week before last to sit in a case where the statute requires 3 judges and having been shaky before was upset—insides and the lumbago—but it was all a small matter, only to be mentioned to account for rather an idle fortnight, in which I have looked at little more serious than *Cranford* and Walton's *Angler*. Fresh air and innocence are good if you don't take too much of them—but I always remember that most of the achievements and pleasures of life are in bad air. How rudimentary the life of the past seems from the *Psalms* to the *Angler*. No compound twists for them—they knew them not. But I have reread Maitland's *English Law and the Renaissance* and a book sent to me by Hale—*The World after the War*—by Roden (Man) and Buxton (Woman) with already forgotten instruction and the contemptuous rebellion I always feel

---

[4] Terence MacSwiney (1880-1920), the Lord Mayor of Cork, was at this time on his hunger strike following conviction for sedition. Despite great public protest Lloyd George refused to release MacSwiney, and he died of starvation on October 25.

[5] Anton Ivanovich Denikin had been the general commanding the White Russian forces against the Soviet armies. Following his defeat by the Soviets he had sought and been granted refuge in England. On September 7 the British government canceled the permission which it had granted in August to a Russian labor delegation to come to England.

[6] In the last days of August the miners had voted to strike; in early September negotiations between Union representatives, the owners, and the government were rather fruitlessly carried on. The strike at length took place on October 16 and continued until November 4.

when people talk of the exploitation of the many by the few. Also they quote Barbusse (of *Le feu*) with respect, whom from that book I thought a noxious animal. I wish I could have heard you talk with Morley—you speak of mentioning me, but I doubt if he even more than heard of me—though I saw him once at the White House with Roosevelt who absorbed his interest. Last Friday was Antietam (1920-1862) 58 years ago—and about 50 years ago I had a letter from Lieber saying that 50 years before he came out of the battle of Ligny with 16 men.[1] How hard it is to believe that L. then was as near to Waterloo as I now am to Antietam. How different the years before one's birth from those since. I hope you received my letter telling you how I delighted in and admired your book. Mine (due to Laski) is hoped for in October subject to trouble with printers &c. If I had had nothing else to do, I should have been tempted to add notes. There is no Index—but I don't see that it needs one. In a week we go to Boston and on the 29th to Washington. One reason for time going quicker is that all these things become routine. They used to be adventures.

*Ever aff'ly yours, O. W. Holmes*


*Beverly Farms, September 21, 1920*

Postscript to my letter of a few days ago—Canon Sheehan gave me the *McVey-Napier Correspondence* to read on my way home that last time I saw him. It is here somewhere. I remember that one gets an extraordinary picture of Brougham. For the moment I am glad you are not spurring me on to improvement as I have a chance to pick up odds and ends. After Walton's *Angler*—White's *Selborne*—volume 2. First volume with 15 letters missing here—but 2 volumes 2ˢ! I have it in Washington. Keen old boy and delightful. He says about earthworms what by popular report is attributed to Darwin's book. Last night I took up Landor's *Gebir*—a little confusing in details upon rapid reading but with fine lines—'Is this the mighty ocean! Is this all?' and a hundred others—sometimes emulating a little visibly Milton's majestic use of proper names. A few moments of leisure are good to pick up bits of literature that a gentleman should have read but generally hasn't. But why do I speak of gentlemen? Have I not always said that a philosopher couldn't be a gentleman or a gentleman a philosopher? The philosopher keeps all formulas fluid—the gentleman exists only on the footing that some are fixed—(those that concern his own personality).                                    *Aff'ly yours, O. W. H.*

---

[1] Francis Lieber (1800-1872); political scientist of German birth who had fought under Blücher in the Waterloo campaign, and came to the United States in 1827 as a political refugee; editor of the *Encyclopedia Americana* (13 vols., 1829-33); author of *Manual of Political Ethics* (2 vols., 1838-39) and *On Civil Liberty and Self-Government* (2 vols., 1853).

*40 Onslow Gardens, September 18, 1920*
*My dear Justice:* I am ever so glad that you liked the little book;
for you know how much I build upon your judgment. Your criticisms are justified and Frida agrees with you about elusiveness so
that, if there ever be a second edition, I will make some additions.
But the main thing is that it pleased you.

It has been a quiet ten days—mainly reading and writing. But
there were two joyous interludes. I went to Leicester to speak to
the trade unions on education. It was great fun; for I spent an
hour presenting a long case against democratic government, in
watching them look more and more gloomy and then urging that
all their gloom was due to a belief that there were short cuts to
knowledge instead of a willingness to realize the natural complexity of social organization and consequently to sweat towards
its understanding. I had a grand time and one genial soul, in
proposing a vote of thanks to me, suggested that I was a unique
combination of Jeremiah and Diogenes and wondered if I would
stand as labor candidate for Leicester! The other interlude was
lunch with Morley on Friday when we talked in that region of
inside knowledge about cabinet structure which is so valuable to
the outsider like me. I gleaned a sense that the cabinet is very
like a club, in which, as a rule, new members are to be seen and
not heard. He spoke with real enthusiasm about Balfour—his
courtesy, his charm, and his instinct for decency, but with not a
little contempt for Asquith, whose mainspring he regarded as
broken. Kitchener he thought *vin ordinaire*—a legend, not a fact.
Curzon was a flat failure both in the Lords and the Cabinet, mainly
through a consistent intellectual arrogance which influenced even
the *minutiae* of administration. We had a great fight about Gladstone whose honesty he maintained, even in the face of my argument that G. could not be honest and make the speech he did of
poignant regret at Dizzy's death.[1] And I was very moved at the
things he said of Chamberlain. 'We mustn't think of the later years.
He found radicalism a *vox clamantis in deserto* and gave it power
and organization. From 1870-1890 he was for every necessary
measure except Home Rule. He was clear-headed, direct and
generous.' A fine tribute. One interesting glimpse was his remark
that if he could have had his choice he would have liked to be
a great judge—men like Mansfield have the most enduring reputations. Literature depends so much on the choice of the moment in
lustre—politics on personal combination. But the law has a fine
impersonality which has always compelled his admiration.

Of books some great adventures. To begin with I had three

---

[1] Morley in his *Life of Gladstone*, 1904 (vol. III, p. 89) had stated that
Gladstone's tribute to Disraeli, in 1881, "cost him much searching of heart
beforehand, and was a masterpiece of grace and good feeling."

rather jolly finds. (1) Jeremy Collier's *History of Passive Obedience*. A first-rate anthology (1689) of all the important passages since the Reformation.[2] (2) Charles Leslie's *Best of All*—one of the very ablest of that fellow's tracts, and he was, Swift apart, the most brilliant pamphleteer of the generation; (3) a volume called *Essays on Reform* (1867) issued in reply to the Cassandra prophecies of Robert Lowe by Dicey, Bryce, Goldwin Smith, Harrison, Leslie Stephen *et al.*[3] Leslie Stephen particularly good and the whole thing a singularly arresting performance as stating with real insight the main difficulties of our own time. Reading has been mainly F. Stephen's *History of the Criminal Law* which I took at a solid gulp—manly and substantial I thought without Leslie's delicacy of touch and refinement of insight. And the memoirs of Colonel Repington—the war seen from the Carlton Hotel—which you must read—a *chronique scandaleuse* which will tickle your palate. The war for the exhibition of Lady Blank in nurse's uniform; the war leaves English life unchanged except for the decline in the number and quality of servants. . . .

*Ever affectionately yours, H. J. L.*

*Washington, D.C., October 3, 1920*
*Dear Laski:* Your letter of September 18, delightful as usual, comes this morning. It finds me with decks cleared for action and expecting a storm of work tomorrow or next day. We came straight through and after a day or so my wife came out smiling and relieved my mind from anxiety. Thursday and Friday got me into pretty good shape in the way of disposing of the summer's books and pamphlets and arranging the papers in unfinished cases (none of mine). Mrs. Brandeis sent over R. Rolland's *Liluli*—which as a lent book made me miserable until it was read and returned—a lot of clever touches—but by implication standing superior to the movements of mankind, and seeing the war a swindle of the workers by various humbugs, intellectuals, diplomats &c. which I think bosh. I had a delightful call from Brandeis who seemed to me wonderfully improved physically and in general feeling. He looked happier. It does a man good to be made much of. I think that possibly he is a little under the illusion produced by contact with good society in England until one's head has time to get

---

[2] The editorship of this anonymous book is generally ascribed to another nonjuring divine, Abednego Seller (1646?-1705).

[3] Laski was in error in his inclusion of Harrison (presumably Frederic Harrison, 1831-1923) among the contributors to the volume. Robert Lowe (1811-1892), Viscount Sherbrooke, who had shown reforming tendencies in his early political career, in 1866 led the opposition to Lord Russell's Liberal and mild reform bill. Leslie Stephen's essay was "On the Choice of Representatives by Popular Constituencies."

cold—but I am by no means sure that his impressions and judgments are not the final truth—not now pausing to define what
truth is. I add this last because my new secretary and I have been
continuing the jaw begun yesterday as to what law is and he has
been pressing for accurate conclusions. He came *non obstant* its
being Sunday. I am delighted with him. He is very polite and has
the flexibilities of the civilized man of the world and openness to
varied interests that make a good companion. He is so damned civil
that I look to see if there is a cat under the meal, i.e. a cold critic
in the garb of a disciple but I feel very sure that critical or not
he is a good fellow and will give me companionship. Day Kimball
is his name (I believe).[1] We feed for the present at the Powhatan
and do very well. This fact again is suggested by having gone
there for luncheon since the last sentence. Coming on I sacrificed
to Brandeis and more or less to you by reading part way through
the Interchurch report on the Steel Strike[2]—which seems to increase my prejudice against the Corporation's management, but
which does not charm me by its mode of presentation. Whoever
wrote it there is a clerical smack in its use of slang ('Hunkies' &c)
like clergymen trying to appear men of the world, and much repetition—I suppose in order to fasten the impression—but I only
read about 100 pp. when you would have finished it, even allowing yourself the slumber that I did. B. said you beat Frankfurter,
whom I had thought the end of the limit, in seeing everybody,
and I should not be surprised if he were right. I have got back
the etchings I left at the Congressional Library for the summer
and feel mighty happy in being in my own proper fur again. I
forgot whether I told you that I got a letter this summer from
Pound apropos of having heard that I wrote to Lowell that P.
ought to have an LLD. in which he surprised and pleased me no
little by some superlatives. When a man is going on 80 he has a
right to be pleased with a bit of praise now and then. I dare say
we all should be none the worse if we got more of it. My rambling
must stop for a drive with F. My love to you both. I do hope that
you won't get tired of writing to yours      *Aff'ly, O. W. Holmes*

                         *40 Onslow Gardens, October 5, 1920*
*My dear Justice:* . . . I've begun to write again. I begin with four
articles for Massingham in the London *Nation* on the constitutional
position here.[1] They're great fun to write—especially one on the

---

[1] Day Kimball had graduated from the Harvard Law School in the previous June. Later he practiced at the English bar and is presently a Justice of
the Supreme Court of Bermuda.

[2] *Report on the Steel Strike of 1919* (1920), by the Commission of
Inquiry of the Interchurch World Movement.

[1] "Mr. George and the Constitution," 28 *The Nation* 38, 124, 184, 269
(Oct. 9, 23, Nov. 6, 20, 1920).

cabinet where I'm playing with my private *fach* of administrative technique. I let most writing go for these three months and it did me immense good. Now I start with fresh courage and revivified ideas after much absorption of novel atmosphere. People, I've met in heaps. E. F. Wise, our best civil servant, who is conducting our trade negotiations with Krassin, the best type of Englishman, calm, collected, armed *cap à pie* in his facts.[2] The Webbs we dined with the other day and I had a happy time there explaining that if you have a written constitution the important thing is the way you choose the judges, *Jensen* v. *S. Pacific*[3] being a handy bomb in the discussion (I needn't add I mean the dissent). Also I visited a rather charming thing, the last cooperative workshop (brushmakers) which remains from the Maurice-Kingsley-Ludlow Christian Socialist time. They use no machines and can as a consequence talk as they work. To hear vivid and sometimes eloquent discussion as they threaded the brushes was a moving sight to me. I had also a charming note from Bryce—when would I go to see him, and had I news of you, quite in his kindliest vein. Haldane, let me add, never sees me without an inquiry about you. He's a dear fellow.

. . . If I don't, with Monday, Friday and Saturday free through the year, get a big book done I certainly deserve to fail.

My love to you both, and a special greeting from Frida.

*Ever affectionately yours, H. J. L.*

*Washington, D.C., October 19, 1920*

*Dear Laski:* Your letter as usual excites my envy at the description of your finds.[1] In my line I imagine finds would be more difficult —I mean etchings or engravings that weren't held at the highest market price—for I don't buy many books these days for a reason that equally applies to the other—no, I don't think it does—that I am too old to expect to use curious material. That does not apply to things that perform their function at once by being seen. The last word reminds me of what my wife was reading from a book that one looks into rather under protest, the recollections of James Huneker,[2] which I won't stop to characterize. Someone was talking about a performance of a female singer, I forget whom,

---

[2] During September and the first days of October trade negotiations with the Soviet representative Leonid Krassin (1870–1926) were carried on by British representatives, including Edward Frank Wise (1885–1933). The draft agreement of October 5 was ultimately modified and signed in March of 1921.

[3] *Southern Pacific Company* v. *Jensen; supra,* pp. 66, 135.

[1] The reference is to various rare books, listed in Laski's letter of October 5 but omitted from this edition, which Laski said he had bought in Oxford bookshops. Laski's comments on De Quincey and Carlyle have also been omitted.

[2] Probably James Huneker's *Painted Veils* (1920).

and said she was obscene but not heard. Also let me mention that
we dined out last Saturday to meet your ambassador[3]—and two
things amused or impressed me. The Ambassadress, whether she
knew that she was speaking of my wife or not I was not quite
sure, said I like to see an old lady like that with her white hair,
still dining out. It is sporting—and afterwards said much the same
to her. The other didn't seem to strike anyone but my wife and
me. We caught each other's eye. He thought that war was becoming impossible because they could drop a bomb that would poison
a quarter of a city or demolish a block. He said war has been
made by the crowds in the cities—but they wouldn't do it if they
knew that in five or six hours they would see a shadow. It seemed
to be imaginative and terrible. I have been working hard—a
swamping lot of *certioraris*—(applications for leave to bring a
case up) among other things. I distribute my first opinion this
morning—an easy one, but giving me a chance to put in a line,
if it is not stricken out, about that bastard notion *evading* a law[4]
—when it is evaded either it is broken according to its true construction and implications or care has been taken to keep on the
right side of the line. The very meaning of a line in the law is that
you may walk up to it if you don't pass it. I love your capacity
for enthusiasm over any damned thing that you are reading. I
shouldn't be surprised if you had glowed over *Oceana*. But I think
you are in the first flush in your talk about De Quincey. The last
time I read *Murder as One of the Fine Arts* it didn't hit me—
but perhaps I was off color at the time. His talk about a portrait
of Milton at the beginning of a book by —— which his daughter
said was the best, and which De Quincey said was also the best
portrait of Wordsworth[5] led me to suggest it to the Congressional
Library and they got it. I believe it is not dear, but the portrait
frequently is cut out. Indolence has prevented my trying to get a
copy. As to Carlyle there was a time within the memory of men
still living when my father asked me what book I would take for
a desert island, if I could have only one, and I said Carlyle's
*French Revolution*. I should not say so now. The last things I
read of his inspired something of the melancholy I have felt over
the dogmatisms of another great man, Tolstoi, which I did not

[3] Sir Auckland Geddes, supra, p. 211.

[4] *Western Union Telegraph Co.* v. *Speight*, 254 U.S. 17 (decided Oct. 25,
1920). The line to which Holmes refers was evidently stricken out. Writing
to Felix Frankfurter on October 24, Holmes spoke of the same opinion: "Also
I have a little case—whether it will go or not I don't know. As originally
written it had a tiny pair of testicles, but the scruples of my brethren have
caused their removal and it sings in a very soft voice now. . . ."

[5] De Quincey's *Recollections of the Lakes and the Lake Poets* in the essay
on Wordsworth (2 De Quincey's *Works*, 1862, at 144-145) contains the
anecdote concerning the portrait of Milton in Jonathan Richardson's *Explana-
tory Notes on Paradise Lost* (1734).

believe. Why melancholy? I can't explain, unless it is from the
fear that one is damned. I am in very good shape—buttermilk still
seems to have a wonderful effect in keeping me in good order
inside and to reduce my equator. I was a little taken down by
hearing the repetition of a remark of someone that it was pitiable
(or some other like adjective) to see those four old men still
hanging on to their places. But public men get hardened more or
less. The former Chief [6] used to say he was not to be paragraphed
out of his place. I wish success to the big book of the future that
you speak of. I have heard nothing of my little one since the
publisher wrote that they hoped to bring it out early in October.
The 21st is the anniversary of Ball's Bluff 59 years ago!

My love to you both.                    *Aff'ly yours, O. W. Holmes*

*40 Onslow Gardens, 1.XI.20.*

*My dear Justice:* My silence has been shameful; but when I tell
you that for the past three weeks I have been out on some kind of
business every night you can imagine how busy I have been. Some
of it has been interesting—especially a fine dinner with Haldane
when we wandered in talk over the universe, with special reference
to Mr. Justice Holmes as its focal point. . . . And I have had my
amusements this last week-end at a party got up by the Webbs
for Frida and me to meet the intelligentsia of the labour movement. Can you picture it? Webb taking me into a corner to tell
me that Cole is very able but his ideas completely fantastic; Cole
taking me to another corner to say that everyone must admire
Webb, but his ideas—pure fantasy. One man insists that everything depends on proper methods of propaganda. . . .

My best news I keep to the last. After negotiations that were as
agonising as they were absurd my family and I have made up the
ancient quarrel. Largely it's due to Frida's common sense and
courage—and to their amazed perception that I don't give a damn
for their money and had therefore better be left to my own vicious
views and a penniless career. The result is that my father has gone
to India happier than he has been for years, full of almost extravagant delight in Frida and me, and with copies of my books in his
trunk that he may talk to me of them when he comes back. It's
all very pathetic; for nine years ago the same thing could have
happened if he had cared for it. The main thing is that he feels
happy though puzzled at my refusal to accept £1000 a year from
him—puzzled, I suppose, on the theory that no son of a business-
man ought to live up to his principles. I'm very glad over it all, for
it brings Frida into her own. . . .

*Ever affectionately yours, H. J. L.*

---

[6] Melville Weston Fuller (1833-1910); Chief Justice, 1888-1910.

*Washington, D.C., November 17, 1920*
*Dear Laski:* Your letter came yesterday and gave me great joy.
Every letter does, but this most of all as it tells me that you have
made up with your family. I do immensely rejoice at that. Every
other item of your news is interesting but that is a weight off my
mind. For my part I have been rather mad with work—(I believe
Brandeis sends you our respective opinions.) The boys made me
emasculate one,[1] and Brandeis *inter alios* made me put in a passage
explaining a decision of Harlan's into one that I fired off Monday
that rather impeded the course of what I thought necessary but I
didn't care very much.[2] This week (it now is Wednesday evening)
I have distributed one that I dreaded and tried to shirk on to
Brandeis or Clarke as I had the assignment of it,[3] but it seemed
to go off pretty well, and I shall distribute another tomorrow
morning. So I am pleased as I have had many other things also
on my mind. And this week my book is out! You said it would
look well, but I had my doubts on the proofs—but now I am delighted. They said they should send one to you, so I economized
and didn't. I directed copies to be sent to Pollock, Dicey, Bryce,
Haldane, Leslie Scott and the British Academy (as I am a corresponding member of the last). I have read nothing but have on
my table Lowie—*Primitive Society*—I infer sceptical after my own
heart—my secretary knew I wanted it and gave it to me. Next
week or the week after I hope for a chance. . . . I don't see what
anyone can say if any notice is taken of my book except that they
are old chestnuts and the earlier of them dead on the author's
avowed principles. Yet I swear I am not ashamed of it. Although
an accidental congeries it touches some pretty remote points in
the circle of human interests. But I haven't had time to examine it
—if I ever do beyond reading the proofs sometime ago. I am glad
to gather up this little basketful before my 80th birthday, as I
was glad to get out *The Common Law* before my 40th. I hope
there is no illusion—writing opinions seems to me quite as easy
as it ever was and I think I write rather better English—but one
always is learning about that and I shudder to think that I do
something or other that I ought to know to be anathema. I hope
in dealing with the Webbs' noble piece of work you hint at the
sentimental character of their implied postulates. As to what you
mention about going on to the Bench—the law *stricto sensu* is a
limited subject—and the choice seemed to be between applying
one's theories to practice and details or going into another field
—and apart from natural fear and the need of making a living I

---

[1] The reference is probably to *Western Union Telegraph Co.* v. *Speight,
supra*, p. 228, note 4.

[2] *Northwestern Mutual Life Insurance Co.* v. *Johnson*, 254 U.S. 96 (Nov.
11, 1920).

[3] This case has not been identified.

reasoned (at 40) that it would take another ten years to master a new subject and that I couldn't bargain that my mind should remain suggestive at that age. I think I was right but there are many tempting themes on which it seems as if one could say something if one knew enough—I am glad on the whole that I stuck to actualities against philosophy (the interest of all actualities). Do you like Santayana's books? I do, though I believe Bill James didn't. Well—my thanks and love to you—and kindest messages to your wife. I am not surprised at what you say of her part.

*Affectionately yours, O. W. Holmes*

*40 Onslow Gardens, November 14, 1920*
*My dear Justice:* Behold me an M.A.—with a vote against the parsons in Convocation and a vote against the Tory for the House of Commons. It was otherwise a waste of twenty pounds, but a most amusing ceremony.

And I had a very jolly week. First, I met Wells and Arnold Bennett. Wells is rather fat, but astonishingly quick and eager, with a mind that dances like a Hottentot over a wide range. He told me that he is coming to America, and I extracted from him a pledge that you should have an evening. So please expect him. Bennett I liked very much. To begin with, he is essentially a craftsman, with the same pride in his art, *quâ* art, that men like Rembrandt must have had. Also he is whimsical, and add to that an ugliness which becomes gratifying and there is good food for talk. I dined also with Buckmaster, the ex-Chancellor,[1] whom I took a great affection for. We damned L-G; sorrowed over Asquith; and then spent an hour on the personalities of the court. Not to please you but as a matter of general interest you may like to have the order he put them in—Holmes, Brandeis, Van Devanter, Day, Pitney, White, McKenna, Clark[e], McReynolds. Then we talked constitutional law. He is a big-minded, generous man, with a very attractive forthright way of speaking. I'd like you to meet him one day.

. . . Mrs. Asquith I only skimmed [2]—but it impressed me as both less and more than the howl of indignation suggested—less in that it has really nothing of importance to reveal and more that

---

[1] Stanley Owen Buckmaster (1861-1934), first Viscount Buckmaster; Liberal in the House of Commons and the Lords; Lord Chancellor, following Haldane, on the reconstruction of the Asquith government from May 1915 to the fall of that government in December 1916; and subsequently distinguished appellate judge in the House of Lords and Judicial Committee of the Privy Council. Lord Dunedin, an opponent in politics, considered Buckmaster a sentimentalist—"unless he is sitting on his arse on the bench; there he is one of the most learned, one of the most acute, and the fairest judge I ever sat with." *Dictionary of National Biography, 1931-1940* (1949), 120.

[2] *Margot Asquith, an Autobiography* (1920).

it shows a woman of real feeling which is covered over by a cloak
of hardness demanded by the conditions of her social life. . . .

Well! Our love to you. I am anxiously awaiting the Collected
Papers of O. W. H.                  *Ever affectionately yours, H. J. L.*

*Washington, D.C., November 26, 1920*

*Dear Laski:* Every letter from you is a joy. I love to hear of your
acquisitions, your reading, your everything. I know not what M.A.
may signify with you—I believe it means something here now, as,
already years ago, my classmate Garrison[1] was given the modest
distinction of an honorary A.M. (I think that is our order in the
letters.) After I graduated you got it by living 3 years and paying
$5. As I preferred the $5 I think I never got the degree. As to your
talk with Buckmaster forgive me if I suspect that he was prompted
by his interlocutor—but I will hope not—though I take the marks
of your kindness with caution! This morning finds me in fine shape.
In excess of my hopes last Monday I was allowed to fire off (one
semi-castrated) the three opinions that I had, before adjournment
for a fortnight.[2] Only one new one was assigned to me and that
has gone to the printer. My other work is done. I telephoned to
see if I could go to the Congressional Library in a few minutes
from now to visit Rice and inspect new acquisitions—but aesthetic
swells come down late. I hope now to finish Lowie's *Primitive
Society* I believe I mentioned, and a book sent to me by Brandeis,
A. G. Gardiner *Prophets, Priests and Kings*—clear estimates of
public men, written I gather before the war—not quite first rate
but good. The books you recommend strike me as rather too far
off my beat. I think you quite right in your estimate of Mrs.
Asquith—judging from my old acquaintance—not the book. I
have been working so hard that I am glad of a breathing spell.
The C.J. who occasionally speaks to me as if I were unknown to
the world at large said that people thought I didn't work when I
fired off decisions soon after they were given to me. By the by, I
don't think Buckmaster's ranking does him justice. His faults are
obvious, but he has insights. I think, *e.g.* the credit is wholly his
of making the relations between the Interstate Commerce Commission and our court clear and putting the whole important business on a sound and workable footing. He is a big fellow, though
(strictly between ourselves) I should think built rather for a politician than a judge. I hope you have received my book. I paid for

---

[1] Wendell Phillips Garrison (1840-1907); reformer son of a radical father,
William Lloyd Garrison (1805-1879).

[2] On November 22 Holmes had delivered the Court's opinion in *International Bridge Co.* v. *New York*, 254 U.S. 126; *Horning* v. *District of Columbia, id.* 135; *Rock Island, Arkansas & Louisiana Rd. Co.* v. *United States,
id.* 141.

some supposed to have been sent to people here including one for me but have not received mine (of course I got an earlier copy) and another fellow told me he had not received his. The publishers seem amiable and as I told you I am delighted with the appearance of the volume. A purchaser sent a copy to me to write my name in it and as I couldn't say *from* OWH I wrote *Caveat Emptor* with my name. Also Frankfurter writes that he received his copy. So they have gone forth into the cruel world. You are such a hardened publisher that I may suppose (by fiction for we all really are sensitive) that you don't mind such a trifle as a bister [*sic*]—and this isn't even that—yet I feel a mild excitement at the rather old little boy going out in a new jacket and trousers.

My love to you both. *Affectionately yours, O. W. Holmes*

*40 Onslow Gardens, 28.XI.20*

*My dear Justice:* . . . Since I last wrote and as always an infinity of things seem to have happened. Above all, I had a glorious weekend in Cambridge with Rivers, meeting people, talking about books and work, in the way I had in America from you and Pound and McIlwain alone. Particularly I liked Sir Ernest Rutherford the physicist who talked of things beyond the atom with an easy elegance which quite won my heart. And I met a group of undergraduates there with an ability and a maturity that made one realise that there really is an intellectual renascence in this country. They were well-read and vivid and eager in a way that impressed me enormously. . . .

Of reading I have done little outside the line of work. But I did read and admire Hallam's *Literature of Europe* which, with some exceptions, I thought extraordinarily sane and balanced. And I read with much emotion a book on the negro by Dubois called, I think, *Darkwater*. It was very brilliant, but a hateful book—rather like, I felt, what the Southerner would write if he turned negro. And a great novel which you and Mrs. Holmes must read by Galsworthy called *In Chancery*. Also I re-read with deep pleasure George Eliot's *Scenes from Clerical Life*—outside *Middlemarch* I think it the very best thing she ever did.

We've been to some theatres too—particularly to *The Skin Game* by Galsworthy, a great play which only a great gentleman could have written and *The Whiteheaded Boy* by S. J. Ervine[1] which you *must* see if it comes to Washington—the most living picture of the Irish mind I can remember. And we went to an exhibition of etchings which would have made your mouth water —Zorn, Rembrandt, Ostade, Whistler so superbly arranged that the great points of each stood out very finely.

---

[1] Lennox Robinson was the author.

Work goes beautifully; and I have just enough of the political scene not to get immersed in it. Next week vacation looms on the horizon and I can settle down to a big draught of my book. Frida and I are very proud, by the way, of our daughter's ability to read.

Our love to you both,     *Ever yours affectionately, Harold J. Laski*

*Washington, D.C., December 17, 1920*

*Dear Laski:* Your letter November 28 brings me the usual joy. Mind that you keep on while I still creep. The only disappointment is that you don't mention having received my book. Of course this doesn't mean a demand for polite remarks but only that I want to know that it is in your hands. You are the first whom it should have reached. As I have said, I believe, I think its appearance very satisfactory—and the paper must be good for it is light for its size—a great point. I have no time for reading as the work has been hard. Last Monday I was in despair, thinking that if I ever got my case written it would take the approaching adjournment if not next summer. But as usual on Tuesday light began to gleam and grew brighter so that on Wednesday it was written, and it now is in the hands of the boys.[1] When I get a chance I want to read Santayana's new volume on *Character and Opinion in the U.S.* He generally hits me pretty near to where I live—even though one does not wholly like either him or his way of thinking. He is a philosopher very much after my own heart. Chafee's book on Free Speech is on my table—but I may not read that through as I have seen the preliminary extracts in *Harvard Law Review.* I believe it to be first rate. By the by your letter says that it is so long since you have heard from me, etc. I *always* write within a day or two of the arrival of your letter—even though I can make a most inadequate return. Let me know if you don't or do receive my letters. I have been so steeped in cases that I am good for nothing else, and shall send this off when in a few minutes I start for Court. Doesn't Brandeis send you his and my decisions? I understood with him that he would. I don't see much of him except in Court but he is a great comfort to me. You are in a thicker intellectual atmosphere than I am here. One has to manufacture one's own to a considerable extent. The secretary, Day Kimball, I find a very delightful companion. He is so damned polite that I suspected him at first but I think it comes from his nature and he gives me pleasure in all ways. He does his work rapidly and well and seems to like to walk with me when I get a chance. He has seen something of life and is open on many sides. There are tacit

---

[1] The case has not been identified. Holmes delivered no opinions until January 3, 1921.

reserves as to the President, whom he pronounced a gallant gentleman. He was with him in Europe. But he talks little of his experience and I ask him why he doesn't swagger more. Alas it is closing time. Accept this paltry scrawl as an expression of my affection for you. It has little other worth.

Love to you both,                          *Aff'ly yours, O. W. Holmes*

*40 Onslow Gardens, 14.12.20*

*My dear Justice:* First of all, our warmest good wishes to you both for Xmas and for 1921. I am delighted with the book. It looks dignified, it's easy to handle, and the type is excellent. I need not say that I re-read it at once; and I felt, what you will admit to be the real test of worth, that I would give much to have been its author. "The Path of the Law" still strikes me as the really great paper of the volume; after that "Early English Equity"; after that the speech to the Law School in 1886. But how impossible it is to choose where all make me doubly and triply proud of friendship. The only thing lacking in my copy is my name and you must please send me a slip to paste in.

First news of persons, then of books. It has been a rather quiet fortnight, for both Frida and I have had bad colds and gone out but little. But I had a lunch with F. Pollock and a dinner with Haldane both of which I enjoyed. Pollock I liked hugely, though I thought he had got very old and was mentally less alert than I had expected. He fired up when we talked of you but otherwise pitched his conversation in a low key. He was, I thought, unduly critical of Pound (learning without point) and unduly favourable to English jurisprudence. Haldane had a fascinating dinner—Sir William McCormick[1] who runs the research side of the Privy Council and Austen Chamberlain. It developed into a general fight upon the duty of the state to research—Haldane and I urging that you must provide careers for the brilliant young scientists the universities turn out and Chamberlain arguing that industry should take them up. I don't think we converted Haldane [*sic*] but we did at least convert McCormick, who invited me to talk to his Committee on the subject. Haldane spoke very charmingly of having received the book; and of his wish for a talk with you on some Canadian federal cases he's handling just now. Also we talked a little of Leslie Scott (I don't know him but sought information) and Haldane said he thought him quite the ablest conservative mind that appeared before the Lords. I hope, by the way, that Scott has

[1] Sir William McCormick (1859-1930) began his career as a literary scholar and ended it as an educational administrator, serving as secretary of the Carnegie Trust and in 1919 becoming chairman of the Treasury University Grants Committee.

sent you his volume on *A. G.* v. *DeKeyser's Hotel* [2]—a masterly
piece of work. . . .

My love to you both.        *Ever affectionately yours, H. J. L.*


*Washington, D.C., January 5, 1921*
*My dear Laski:* Another delightful letter from you. You never acknowledge mine but I presume that you receive the unworthy bul-
letins which are all that I can return. The recess is over and gave
me little of the leisure that I hoped for. I did manage to finish
re-reading Tourtoulon—*Principes philosophiques de l'histoire du
droit.* As with more famous men, e.g. Kant, Hegel—I care nothing
for the systems—only for the insights. Those delight me, all the
more that it seems to me I had had some of them and expressed
them before his day. I wish you might read him—not for that
cause but for his scepticism which seems to me most healthy. I
had one sweet hour of repose when all my jobs were finished and
divided it between another instalment of Marcel Proust—*Le côté
de Guermantes*—and the *Confessions of St. Augustine.* . . . Of
the two I would rather read St. Augustine. It is like a painting by
Morland set over an altar. Rum thing to see a man making a
mountain out of robbing a pear tree in his teens. On Monday I
got off 3 cases[1] but one went over for Brandeis—I have already
circulated a memorandum that my decision seemed to me wrong.
I don't know yet what I shall do with it. I am afraid you encourage
people to send me catalogues with false expectations. I don't buy
many books nowadays as it seems foolish at my age. If I were
younger I should be tempted to enlarge in directions and also to
get more etchings etc. I did get a fair Nanteuil sometime ago—
at the previous adjournment, and two little things. But I think the
catalogues the most delightful reading there is.

Hackett had a hard adverse review of Mrs. Asquith's book in
the *N. R.* a while ago.[2] It has a good deal of justice in it but a
slight touch of class feeling that made me sad. . . . I am very
glad at what you say about Scott. He sent me his book but I have
no chance to look at it at present. Cohen writes to me that he has
got his full professorship which I am very glad of, as I am sure
that he deserves it. As to your discussion with Haldane *et al.,* I
probably don't see the precise scope of it. One of the few endowments that I am not inclined to believe a misapplication of the
power of wealth is for the instruments necessary for scientific re-

[2] Leslie Scott and Alfred Hildersley, *The Case of Requisition: In re a
Petition of Right of De Keyser's Royal Hotel* (1920). See, *supra*, pp. 238-
239.

[1] *Erie Railroad Co.* v. *Public Utility Commissions,* 254 U.S. 394; *Southern
Pacific Co.* v. *Berkshire, id.* 415; *Atwater* v. *Guernsey, id.* 423.

[2] 25 *New Republic* 77 (Dec. 15, 1920).

search—they are costly and the scientific men can't afford them as a rule. They seem to me a good social investment irrespective of the promise of material results. But I wrote to Dillon[3] once when he sent me a speech of acceptance of a Carnegie library that such gifts on a large scale raised in my mind the only doubt I ever have felt as to the regime of private ownership.

Well, dear boy, I must shut up and go to work (it is Thursday morning now). I send you every good wish for the new year for you both and rejoice in the changed aspect of your affairs. . . . Love to you both.                                    *Aff'ly yours, O. W. Holmes*

*40 Onslow Gardens, 28.12.20*

*My dear Justice:* A very dear and welcome letter has just come from you and I sit down to answer it *instanter,* for you have been in my mind all day. A batch of your own and Brandeis's opinions came along this morning and I have been reading them with un-adulterated joy. Particularly first-rate, if I may say so, was *International Bridge Co.* v. *New York*[1] where you straightened out a complicated tangle with an easy brilliance that delighted me. The day your court will make me your colleague on the bench I'll come back to America for good and all. But the condition *sine qua non* is that I see you morning, noon and night.

Well, I have had my share of adventures since I last wrote and I must see if I can make them into a tale. First a lunch with Bryce, full of amusement and vivid interest. He mentioned the receipt of your book and said (I did not demur) that you and Bowen were the old [*sic*] two Common Law judges who wrote a style that was literature. Really the old fellow was astounding. He's eighty-five and, though a little shrunken, as lively as a cricket. He'd read all the latest books, as avid for all the latest gossip, damned Lloyd George up and down dale, fixed historians in their exact position like an examiner marking papers, and in short, gave me two entirely delightful hours. He never struck me as quite first-rate either in his reflections or in his comments. I rather judged that he'd made his reputation [more] by an extraordinarily active and alert mind than by one that had either depth or pene-tration. But it was an astonishing spectacle to see him so alive to the sweep and play of immediate forces. More thrilling still was a dinner (this between ourselves) with Haldane to meet Lloyd

---

[3] Presumably John Forrest Dillon (1831-1914); judge successively of Iowa Supreme Court and of Federal Circuit Court in Iowa; later practitioner of law in New York and Professor of Law at Columbia University; author of *Municipal Corporations* (1872), and *The Laws and Jurisprudence of England and America* (1894).

[1] 254 U.S. 126 (decided Nov. 22, 1920). The constitutional issues con-cerned the impairment of contract obligations, due process of law, and the coördination of state and national powers over international commerce.

George and Austen Chamberlain. The government has decided to
sidetrack educational reform and Haldane thought that coming
from an outside world an emphatic negative might make the Prime
Minister hesitate. It was literally amazing from start to finish. He
arrived with six armed soldiers to protect him from Sinn Fein and
two patrolled the House all the time he was there. I started in by
urging that we had, for good or evil, universal suffrage and that
the worst conceivable form of government was that of an un-
trained and ignorant democracy. Therefore the statesman who
devotes his energies to educating it would be the most venerated
a century hence. Haldane played up finely and then the P. M.
weighed in. I had hoped to be able to hate him and he gave me
ample cause. He literally doesn't know what principle means. I
had academic enthusiasm, could I teach him how to win elections?
Then two hours of brilliant, cynical persiflage—no ideals, no loyalty, no gratitude. It was Machiavelli's Prince turned *bourgeois*
solicitor—what means must I take to keep in office? Any means
—the bad Prime Minister is the man who loses offices. Full of
fascination, of course, unerring in his sense of this man's weakness
or that man's ambition—but the quality of rock you sense in the
greatest men, the ability to see beyond tomorrow, selflessness, generosity, of all these not a particle. And at the end, "You don't like
me, Laski?"—this with a dazzling smile, "I can't put my feelings
into such simple terms, Mr. Prime Minister." "Well, well, I daresay I shall discover the weak joint in your armour before long."
Austen Chamberlain I liked greatly—not an able man at all, slow,
a little puzzled, following Lloyd George's dazzling strides *longo
intervallo*—but patently honest and disinterested and in the few
minutes I talked with him alone an ardent worshipper of his
father in a way and degree that moved me greatly. Truly a memorable evening, and beyond it you must imagine the vast expanse
of Haldane's face wreathed in its smile broad as an Atlantic wave.
    . . . Frida and I have been having our first English Xmas since
1913—dining here, taking Diana to her first pantomime, having visitors by the hundred and trying in typical English fashion to eat a
Xmas dinner which secures repletion without exhaustion. Did I
remark to you that I am beginning to discover that there is a
genuinely English mind? I see that when I talk to Wallas, who is
full of real insights, can never concentrate on any subject, never
argue about it abstractly, is always driven to the use of a concrete
illustration, is rarely logical and about eight times out of ten
patently in the right. Well, say you, the life of the law has been
experience and not logic; but I think these English (I write with
the detachment of an outsider) specialise in subconscious processes
the implications of which they don't understand. To all of which
I am moved by some talk of Wallas yesterday on the civil service.

All he wanted was admirable and his reasons for wanting it would
have been equally applicable to the geodetic survey of Siam! So
he had his way and ended doubtful not of the arguments but of
their result. Do you wonder that such a people blunders into the
ownership of the world?

Well! My letter next time will carry a new milestone on its face.
We both want it to be happy for you both. It will be if love for
you can make it so.            *Ever affectionately yours, H. J. L.*

*Washington, D.C., January 12, 1921*
*Dear Laski:* An even more than usually delightful letter from you
came yesterday—(date 28th December). It told of a luncheon
with Bryce and a dinner with Haldane—which I mention on the
principle of a bit of cross-examination that Devens[1] used to recite:
'Merely to fix a date, your Honor—was this before or after you
were burnt in effigy by your neighbors?' But having mentioned it
I will add that your estimate of one of them seems to me correct,
if you add, most loveable and having a to me—probably not to you
—appalling omniscience. Industry is a dangerous virtue. I hardly
need add how tickled I was by your account of the dinner. If you
hadn't said between ourselves I should have read it to my wife
and my secretary. I think you know the latter—Day Kimball—
the politest and most agreeable of companions. I think having a
certain hardness of intelligence that makes him less sensitive to
atmospheric elements than to logic but doing his work as well as
his play with me in first-rate style. By repercussion that makes me
think of Landau[2] a former one whom you knew . . . He had few
goods in his shop window but gave one a good deal of spiritual
companionship—and that makes me think of Disraeli and the
affection that he inspired, and that makes me ask whether loveableness is a characteristic of the better class of Jews. When I
think how many of the younger men that have warmed my heart
have been Jews I cannot but suspect it, and put the question to
you. Brandeis, whom many dislike, seems to me to have this quality
and always gives me a glow, even though I am not sure that he
wouldn't burn me at a slow fire if it were in the interest of some
very possibly disinterested aim. I don't for a moment doubt that
for daily purposes he feels to me as a friend—as certainly I do to
him and without the above reserve. This, of course, *strictissime*
between ourselves. I pause to remark that I have a scarf pin that
gives me immense pleasure—it looks so like a cockroach hiding

---

[1] Charles Devens (1820-1891); Massachusetts soldier, judge, and statesman, whose service as Associate Justice on the Supreme Judicial Court of
Massachusetts from 1873 to 1891 was interrupted by service as Attorney
General of the United States in the administration of President Hayes.
[2] *Infra,* p. 338.

in a corner with a gleam of light upon his back. While interro-
gating you let me ask also whether you think as it sometimes is
said that the Jews always have No. 1 at the bottom more than
the rest of the world. I put these things to you as one capable of
detached opinions. I find it hard to imagine of Cohen, for instance,
who seems to me, whatever his foibles, to have a kind of holiness
about him. We are listening to arguments on all sorts of cases
rather more important than the average. The C. J. has been down
with a cold for a few days which makes it inconvenient in a number of ways. I think he will be up in a day or two now.

Must be off for Court in a moment now. At odd minutes I am
reading the *Confessions* of St. Augustine with much gusto. But I
ought to be spending the time I have taken to write this upon
some of the cases that have been argued: It is 'consumed in the
neglect of my duties.' I send you a thousand longing thoughts.

*Affectionately yours, O. W. Holmes*


*40 Onslow Gardens, 12.1.21*
*My dear Justice:* Work again is in full swing, and I am really
full of it. In addition to a new course on Federal Government,
I have to lecture on January 22 to the University of Wales on
Federalism, on January 25 to the Sociological Society on Parliamentary Government, and on February 4 to the Fabian Society on
Labour in America. There's a programme for you; and when you
add to it a genial little intrigue to persuade Lord Robert Cecil to
come over to the liberals (I being a member of the Labour Party)
you can see that I have my hands full. I wish you could sit in at
this last, for it's a great lesson in human nature. First there are
the liberals to be talked over. (a) Cecil is a natural Tory. (b) He
is a churchman. (c) He is a Cecil. (d) He'll never leave his party.
(e) A man who ruts is no use to us. (f) What will Asquith say?
(g) Well, will the country like it? (h) And so on. Then there is
Cecil himself who repeats a-f with additions due to a rather nervous temperament and a breeding a little too refined for this work-
aday world. But his union with Asquith is, I am convinced, the
one way to beat L-George at the next election,[1] so I go on pegging
away, giving dinners, going to dinners, hinting to some editors that
the game's afoot, and to others that it is a silly rumor and generally enjoying myself superbly.

And I have had some jolly dinners. The other day I went out
to the Reform Club and had a long talk with Buckmaster and
Massingham. And I learned one story that will amuse you. When

---

[1] There was no general election in 1921, and Lloyd George's coalition
government remained in office until October 1922.

the liberal government of 1906 was being formed² Lloyd George
conducted a long intrigue with Rosebery to keep Grey out of the
Cabinet. At last Asquith said he would not take office unless Grey
became foreign secretary; whereon L-George wrote to Lady Grey
and said he'd persuaded Asquith to withdraw his opposition and
that all would now be well. Then I went to the Webbs to lunch
and heard a great tale of Haldane. Webb is standing for a miner's
constituency in Durham and he asked Haldane on the score of
old friendship to come and speak for him. Haldane agreed on
condition that he should make only a semi-political speech. I
asked Webb what he talked about. He asked me to put the question to Mrs. Webb. She didn't seem very certain and referred me
to Mrs. Bertrand Russell who had been there at the time. Mrs.
Russell was not quite sure but thought it was about the second
part of Goethe's *Faust*. Can you imagine the spectacle of Haldane
addressing thirteen hundred miners just up from the pit upon
*Faust*. It must have been superb. Then I went to dinner to Morley
and met Rosebery and Birrell. Rosebery I thought very charming
and very pathetic. Birrell entirely delightful and astounding in the
amount of his literary knowledge. We fought over battlegrounds
you have trodden, why (*me dissentiente*) Cairns L.C.³ was a great
man, what makes Bryce not quite first-class, how long J. S. Mill
would live, why the slump in George Eliot (whom Morley and I
defended vehemently against the others). It was good talk such as
one rarely gets in a world obsessed by politics and economic
strife. . . .

Our love to you both,        *Ever affectionately yours, H. J. L.*


*Washington, D.C., January 31, 1921*
*Dear Laski:* A whirling letter from you has come and been read
this minute. The mysterious mode of dating intrigued me for a
while—12.1.20. I thought it had taken a long time from December 1. Then the correction of 20 to 21 illuminated me, though still
it seems long—but the post mark is January 5 or 15—I can't be
sure which. You give me delight as usual. My news is simple. This

---

² Following the resignation of Balfour in December 1905, Campbell-
Bannerman was asked by the King to form a government. The choice of a
Foreign Secretary lay between Asquith and Grey; Campbell-Bannerman's
final decision was to appoint Grey Foreign Secretary and Asquith Chancellor
of the Exchequer. Lloyd George joined the Cabinet as President of the Board
of Trade.

³ Hugh McCalmont Cairns (1819-1885), Earl Cairns, statesman and
clearheaded judge, was Lord Chancellor from 1868 to 1869 and from 1874
to 1880. Despite his conservatism in political matters he was an effective
participant in movements for law reform.

morning a Conference at 10:45. Then Court, opinions and adjournment for a month. I expect to fire off the only two that I have[1] and even if I get the longest cases to write I must have some leisure and wish I had you here to give me a hint on desirable books. I have a few on hand, however. The *N. R.* for February 2 (!) has a generous review on our book by Morris Cohen.[2] It pleases me greatly as there are few whose opinion I so value. It is the only one which I have seen except an early puff in the *Transcript* (Boston).[3] Also I have finished St. Augustine's *Confessions,* the only book that I have read while at work. Unless I mistake when he refers to the Scriptures he means the Old Testament, and I doubt, though I was not on the lookout, whether he cites others of the Apostles than St. John and St. Paul. He has the zeal of a convert which I suppose is largely responsible for this still lingering notion that mundane pleasure is *prima facie* at least sinful. I was interested to notice that Dante's line picked out by M. Arnold (Introduction to Ward's *English Poets*) *In la sua volontade e nostra pace* comes from the Saint: *In bona voluntate tua pax nobis est*—though not of course—the sweetness of the Italian verse. His rhapsodies move me, somewhat as Dante did, to feel what I do not believe. I said this to McKenna and he said, "Why don't you give yourself a chance?" To which I could only reply: "Because I believe neither the premises nor the conclusion."

For now the day is over. My opinions discharged—a tiresome conference ended—my throat painted with argyrol—jawing with the Monday afternoon callers performed—and the vacuum begins to yawn—I am ready enough for it. What bores people are who, when you tell them some fact that it is not likely they can have known, make it a point of pride to go you one better and to be entirely at home with the whole business. I have one or two connections who practice it and I get less than joy from their converse. On the other hand I saw some pleasant dames here, one of whom told me that my Secretary was warm as to his time here. Which I was glad to hear. His invincible politeness might cover a wonder of how much more of that damned old bore he had got to stand. Not that I thought so—but I didn't know how he felt. My small details are like the Vicar of Wakefield corresponding with the Prime Minister—but I tell you what happens to come up. We had a decision today from McKenna which avoided a 20 year sentence for Victor Berger on the ground that Landis J. ought to have left the bench on an affidavit of prejudice—the opinion was

---

[1] *Alaska Fish Co.* v. *Smith,* 255 U.S. 44; *Stark Bros.* v. *Stark, id.* 50.
[2] 25 *New Republic* 294 (Feb. 2, 1921).
[3] Boston *Transcript,* Dec. 4, 1920, p. 4.

not all that I could have wished.[4] A dissent by Day seemed to me irrelevant and feeble and another by McR. improper in its rhetoric. Landis always seems to make himself conspicuous in ways that I lament. I am rather a tired old bird for the moment and shall shut up—bidding you not to fail in writing—to give my love to your Missus—and not to run your machine too hard.

*Aff'ly yours, O. W. Holmes*

*40 Onslow Gardens, 1.2.21.*

*My dear Justice:* I have a delightful letter for which to thank you and the joy of knowing that the record of my English Odyssey does not bore you. But oh! for talk. One can't put the light and shade of these months on paper, and I think its most intimate substance is there. How to tell you, for instance, of a wonderful week-end with Zimmern in Aberystwyth from which I have just returned. It was not only the sanity and breadth of his talk and the joy of finding myself nine times out of ten in close agreement with his ideas. Together we dismissed the League of Nations; together we agreed that every social panacea is the prelude to social disillusion; together we travelled over the American continent, people and places, and found that we put you and Pound, Felix and Cohen, on much the same plane. The only person about whom we quarrelled was Kallen the philosopher[1] whom I thought a meddling nuisance and Zimmern a pathetic misfit in life. But it was the atmosphere of Wales and its university which was so enthralling. Imagine a town of seven thousand people with nineteen

---

[4] *Berger v. United States,* 255 U.S. 22. Holmes concurred in the majority opinion; Mr. Justice Day wrote a dissenting opinion in which Pitney, J., concurred, and McReynolds, J., wrote a separate dissent. Kenesaw Mountain Landis (1866-1944) at the time was judge of the United States District Court in Illinois. His talents secured more fitting recognition when he became High Commissioner of Baseball in November 1920. A majority of the Supreme Court considered that the Federal statutes required that when charges of personal prejudice were made, in proper form, against the trial judge, another judge should hear the case. McReynolds, J., dissenting, did not consider that Judge Landis's alleged expressions of vigorous hostility to German-Americans indicated prejudice—they simply bespoke an enlightened patriotism: "The indicated prejudice was towards certain malevolents from Germany, a country then engaged in hunnish warfare and notoriously encouraged by many of its natives who, unhappily, had obtained citizenship here. The words attributed to the Judge . . . may be fairly construed as showing only deep detestation for all persons of German extraction who were at that time wickedly abusing privileges granted by our indulgent laws. . . . a public officer who entertained no aversion towards disloyal German immigrants during the late war was simply unfit for his place. And while 'an over-speaking judge is no well tuned cymbal' neither is an amorphous dummy unspotted by human emotions a becoming receptacle for judicial power." 255 U.S. at 42-43.

[1] Horace Kallen (1882-      ); philosopher, journalist, and teacher who had joined the New School for Social Research in 1918 after an academic career principally at the University of Wisconsin, and who was a frequent contributor to the *New Republic* in its early years.

244 )                                                      ( 1919

chapels of various Methodist sects. Picture seven thousand people
to whom the main ambition in life after forty is to be deacon of
one of these chapels; with a younger generation coaxed into
church by the excitement of previous betting upon the number of
the hymn. And the university. I call God to witness that outside
of Liberia no worse intellectual organization goes by that name.
The Principal is mainly occupied with variations upon the sixth
commandment—so no male student must talk to a female student
after 6 p.m. save three times a term when written permission may
be obtained from the principal. Nine out of every ten professors
dictate verbatim notes to their students who have usually bought
the notes of the previous generation at a price varying from one
pound for first-class notes to ten shillings for a poor set. The professor of music confided to me (with the air of one daring greatly)
that his ambition was to put a gramophone in every home in
Wales. The professor of geography (by no means a dull fellow)
wants every student to study maps by compulsion. Everyone goes
to Sunday School, professors included. There has never been a
divorce in the town. No shop is open on Sunday and no trains run.
Zimmern is a living mystery to the inhabitants. He has mingled
with the great world—he can speak of Lloyd George as an acquaintance. So, as a student said to me, when you listen to his
lectures it is like a visit to London. I wish you could have seen
that town. Here is a people naturally gay, not inartistic, genuinely
interested in abstract questions, who about 1750 were caught in
the floodtide of the Methodist revolt and have ever since been
sternly repressed within its narrow and soul-destroying categories.
No one is contented under forty; and over forty the source of happiness is doing to the younger generation what was done to them
—with interest. Fie upon such a cattleyard of a nation!

    . . . I have been reading (*more meo*) a vast chunk of Guy de
Maupassant—sometimes bored but often as not, feeling the real
hand of a master. Especially in *Boule de Suif* which I hereby being
in my sane mind do declare to be the greatest short story in any
language. . . . Granted that Debs is silly, that his ideas are crude,
his propaganda muddle-headed—anything you like—no sane person would say there was an atom of cause now for his imprisonment, certainly not after your verdict in the *Berger* case. I wish, as
a court, you had the power to recommend pardon. That people
like the wretched Abrams should still be in prison is intolerable.
And that leads me to Chafee's book which I have just read.[2] It is
good and solid; but it suffers from the almost complete absence
of literary virtues and from a tendency to repetition which makes
it at times a little boring. This, I suppose, because it is reprinted
articles; but if one is going to write a book, one is going to write

[2] Zechariah Chafee, Jr., *Freedom of Speech* (1920).

a book. On the other hand, I read F. J. Turner's *Frontier in American History* which I insist you get—quite obviously the biggest contribution to the interpretation of America in my time—the book of a real master with a great thesis to maintain. . . .

But I run on too long. Tomorrow I lunch with the Asquiths and I'll send you a full account later. Our love to you both.

*Ever affectionately yours, H. J. L.*

*Washington, D.C., February 18, 1921*

*My dear Laski:* About the time when I begin to fidget and think that it is time for a letter a letter comes and makes me happy. This was 1.2.21. Oh, I can think it out in time. *Imprimis* as to *Boule de Suif.* I remember that many years ago Tom Perry,[1] (who knows or used to know all that could be known about novels especially French, I think,) said exactly what you say. If I had been left to myself I should not have had the will to detect its supremacy but it certainly is a masterpiece. Perchance I will, perchance I will not get Turner's book. It depends on my time. At present I am reading Wells's *Outline of History*, for which I fear you will turn up your nose at me. But he has the story teller's gift, and does at least two good things. He makes you feel vividly the continuity of prehistory and history—and he makes you realize that if you are talking about the world there are some pretty big spaces that are not covered by the tale of the Roman Empire and its heirs. Also he connects the scattered settlements of one's knowledge into a unity. I don't care about the degree of his accuracy and don't much mind the obvious judgment. I think he performs the function of an artist—to make you feel and realize, not to discover new truths. This is light reading—in spite of recess I don't have time for much. My heavy reading has been M. Proust, *Le côté de Guermantes*—being part 1 of *Tome* III of his *À la recherche du temps perdu*—a book with few paragraphs and not a chapter—with long complex closely printed sentences—taking half a page to say—bacillus—out jamesing H. James in his rotation of nuances. I didn't read it with the care that it demands to do it justice, stopping to visualize what he describes, and so at the end I don't know whether to say that this was the thickest yet about the Evanescent or that it was the talk of a little snob unduly attentive to his life—which last would be inadequate and unjust.

After one opinion I have had no writing to do. Except a short dissent upon a question of jurisdiction, which raised an interesting point—my convictions are categorical but I expect that almost everyone is of the opposite way of thinking.[2] Here I pause to go

---

[1] Thomas Sargeant Perry (1845-1928); man of letters and lecturer whom Dr. Holmes described as "the best read man I have ever known."

[2] McReynolds, J., concurred in Holmes's dissent in *Smith* v. *Kansas City Title Co.*, 255 U.S. 180, 213 (Feb. 28, 1921).

to the dentist, damn him * ** * which reminds me that I am
but a poor worm for the moment. Coughing at night beyond the
help of argyrol &c. But the downs give way to the ups as the ups
to the downs. I was deeply pleased by another notice in *The
Nation*—by Thomas Reed Powell—I think a professor at Columbia
and esteemed there.[3] So now I am expecting to be taken down in
that particular, probably about the moment when I cease to cough.
As I am a little seedy and as, if I post this now, I may catch a
Saturday boat I will shut up prematurely. I have to dine at the
Secretary of State's tonight,[4] which I suppose will mean a bad
night. My love to you.                            *Aff'ly yours, O. W. H.*

                                    *Onslow Gardens, February 11, 1921*
*My dear Justice:* . . . My main news, of course, is my visit to the
Asquiths which I enjoyed more than I can say. The other guests
were Masterman, a close friend of mine and an aforetime member
of the late liberal cabinet, and Sir Donald Maclean[1] who is Asquith's chief lieutenant in the House. I sat next to Asquith during
lunch and we had a fine talk. He gave me not an atom of suspicion of that indecisiveness of which his enemies speak. He
trounced Lloyd George in forthright fashion, spoke of the terrible
character of the government, all with the easy certainty of a man
who knows his own mind. I discovered in him a zeal for old books,
and a fragrant zest for scholarship which, as you can imagine,
pleased me greatly. We spoke of Oxford and its problems, he
there being more conservative of the present order than I liked.
He mentioned his old acquaintance with you and spoke of the
little volume of speeches you had given him years ago. He told
me one delightful story of Roosevelt in London in 1913. Grey gave
him a dinner to which Asquith and Bryce were the other guests.
T. R. started on the American Constitution and, said Asquith, made
such howlers about it that poor Bryce was perspiring with agony
but too overawed by the Rooseveltian vigour to dare to contradict.
After lunch I sat with Mrs. A. in her room and had a long talk
with her. She is an extremely vivid, eager person, absolutely fearless, gloriously indiscreet, and devoted to her husband in a way
that makes you feel that you also want to go into his service. She
remembered you very vividly and spoke of having shown you the
history of her horses many years ago. Do you remember that?
We must have talked over everything—the Labour Party, the possibilities of the next election, the way in which Asquith was turned

---

[3] 112 *Nation* 237 (Feb. 9, 1921).

[4] Bainbridge Colby (1869-1950) was Wilson's last Secretary of State.

[1] Sir Donald Maclean (1864-1932) was Chairman of the Liberal Parliamentary Party from 1919 to 1922 and a faithful political ally of Asquith's.
In 1931 he became President of the Board of Education.

out of power in 1916, her book and so on. It was all great fun, and I saw no sign, for instance, of the kind of qualities Francis Hackett assigned to her in his review of her book in the *New Republic*. On the contrary, I thought she was an essentially humble person, with a real sense in talk that the other man had a point of view and a disposition to listen which you can guess I found pleasing. Her personal judgments amused me greatly. Haldane was a 'sweet donkey'; Morley was a great soul, but in height rather than breadth; Rosebery was a spoilt child of fortune who had deceived his mistress. She used to know Bill James and had been reading his letters with great joy. Her daughter, by the way, has gone out to Washington as wife of the Roumanian minister,[2] and I promised her that you would look her up at the Roumanian embassy. Well—there's one epic for you; the other, I'm afraid, is by way of an anticlimax but still amusing. I spent Sunday morning with Haldane and talked over things. You know that when the first Coalition Ministry was formed Haldane went as the Tories would not sit in the Cabinet with him.[3] As a result, and not unintelligibly, he is very anti-Asquith and is conducting a twofold flirtation, in part with the Labour Party and in part with Lloyd George. So while I was persuading him that liberalism as personified by Asquith was not dead, because a party of moderation is the vital need of the hour, he laboured mightily to persuade me that labour was the true gospel or, alternatively, that if Lloyd George would listen to his advice (which he won't) the coalition government was the instrument the country needed. Then he switched off on to Einstein and outlined the two-volume work he has just finished on relativity. "H.J.L. (pathetically), Lord Haldane, I simply don't understand Einstein; Haldane (sternly), But I am explaining it to you!" You can imagine the completeness of my collapse. But Haldane is an old dear, though rather like a hippopotamus in his intellectual (and physical) movements. Let me add that he keeps far the best cigarettes in London.

. . . The last piece of news I have is that we have bought a house of our own and shall move there in April from this flat. It's a charming place—not large except for the room that is to be my study, but attractive for its old oak panelling and a delicious little garden. If you will only come over and stay we can offer you a suite of rooms to yourself, bathroom included. It will be a great joy to have the independence a flat [*sic*] offers.

Well—I must go off to lecture. My love to you and Mrs. Holmes and a strict injunction to *you* to rest.

*Ever affectionately yours, H. J. L.*

---

[2] Elizabeth Asquith was the wife of Prince Antoine Bibesco.

[3] The first Coalition Government had been formed by Asquith in 1915. Haldane had been Lord Chancellor until then.

*Washington, D.C., February 25, 1921*

*Dear Laski:* A letter from you this morning brings the usual joy.
(February 11). You tell of the Asquiths *et al.* As you know I
retain an affectionate recollection of Mrs. Asquith and an abiding
respect for her, *non obstant* her lamentable want of reserve to the
public. I hadn't read her book, but have seen extracts and/or subsequent communications to the papers. Wells's book (*Outline of
History*) I have not quite finished—interruptions have been constant—but nearly, and with profit in spite of his asm for isms. He
has the artist's gift. We don't go to artists for the discovery of
truths but that they should make us feel and realize. That I think
Wells does. He makes us feel, as I may have written, the continuity of history with pre-history, and feel the world as one. As
I draw near the end I find more dominant the tendency to expound
and illustrate his opinions which I don't care much for. I am indifferent to his philosophy of life. Cohen, who was here the other
day and delightful, was disgusted with his lack of appreciation for
the Greeks—and of Alexander the Great (Wells seems *ex industria*
to belittle all the most famous—Alexander, Caesar, Charlemagne,
Napoleon). Cohen discoursed most interestingly about what Greece
taught the orient and the Jews. Now the recess draws to an end
—with as usual less leisure than I hoped, but at least with the
dentist done with for the present and also with some pleasant
moments, though I haven't had a chance for a jaw with Rice, the
head of the print department in the Congressional Library. The
few days when it was possible my throat has been in such condition that to talk meant to cough at night. The Doctor came in
yesterday (summoned by my wife to look at me) and gave me a
sucker for my throat that really seems to do good. I had the best
night for a fortnight last night. Incidentally he inspected me as I
have puffed and panted more than I used to and said I was all
right in heart and lungs. These physical details are unpardonable.
Do you regard abbreviations in a letter as equally so? I don't. *The
Nation* had a very flattering review of our book—by a lawyer,
Professor Thomas Reed Powell of Columbia—and altogether I am
on the look-out for something that will take me down badly—for
P.L. also put in a little puff in the *N.R.*[1] (I have mentioned
Cohen's notice.) This egotistical excursus must be forgiven—if
one can't think about oneself a little as he reaches 80 when can
he? It makes me tired to read of the mellifluous days when it is
to be all SERVICE—and love of our neighbor and I know not
what. There shall be one Philistine, egotist, unaltruistical desirer
to do his damnedest, and believer that self, not brother, was the
primary care entrusted to him, while this old soldier lives. If A

---

[1] In Philip Littell's column "Books and Things," 25 *New Republic* 380
(Feb. 23, 1921).

lives for B and B for C and so on there must be an end somewhere.
Let's be Ends—you as well as I. I am proud of you.

*Aff'ly yours, O. W. Holmes*

N.B. I always have insisted that the above vaunted egotism makes
us martyrs and altruists before we suspect it.

*Washington, D.C., March 10, 1921*

*Dear Laski:* You seem to divide your time between the illustrious
and becoming so—as my uncle John used to say to me. You have
my approval. The birthday has come and gone—I caught Cohen,
who wrote a charming letter, speaking of my 80th birthday. When
a man is 80 he has had 81 such days. It was on Tuesday. On
Sunday my wife casually intimated that it would help the servants
if we lunched out and dined at home, reversing the usual order
and she got me to dress in honor of our last Sunday in the 79's.
I had a moment of suspicion which was dispelled and we went
down together a little after 8. The folding doors were opened and
there were nearly all my old secretaries and also Bissell [1] and Hart [2]
and his wife standing round the dinner table. She had made them
come in by the lower door via the kitchen—and it knocked me
silly. When presently we settled to work and champagne appeared
she says I gave a yell of joy. The waiter offered a choice of grape
juice to conscientious objectors, but I saw none. Well we had a
most affectionate, wholly delightful meeting and it melted my
heart. The next day Haldane's notice in the *N.R.* [3] put the *comble*
to my happiness. And on Tuesday came letters from those whom
I most value. Altogether I have been at the top of the tree but
I got pretty well tired out—to come home from Court and talk
(which makes me cough at night) till dinnertime and then scribble
off as many letters as I could in thanks for letters and flowers. I
have nearly finished now and expect a moment of repose. Luckily
I had no case to write this week. It is a great preservation to be
on the fighting line and to be anxious about the next thing. You
can't settle down upon the past. As no doubt I often have remarked, when a man is comfortably satisfied with himself he is
finished and I don't want to read my obituary yet. Naturally I
have read nothing else. We have been having some important cases

---

[1] Louis G. Bissell (1883-    ), graduate of the Columbia Law School,
at this time was a government attorney living with Felix Frankfurter and
others at the so-called "House of Truth"; subsequently he practiced law in
New York City.

[2] Edward H. Hart (1885-1951), living also at the "House of Truth"; his
later career was at the New York bar. In January 1921 he had married
Frances Noyes; see, *supra*, p. 30.

[3] Lord Haldane's essay was a warm tribute to Holmes as the best representative of American achievement and aspiration; 26 *New Republic* 34
(March 9, 1921).

including a new attack on the Shoe Machinery Co. with the inde-
fatigable Brown (who married Dorothy Kirchwey, you may remember) as protagonist against them and Choate and Fish for
the defence.⁴ The record reaches from the floor to my middle. How
I hate great cases. Brandeis does not sit in this one.

We had a call yesterday here—from Berenson (the great picture sharp) and his wife. W. Lippmann wrote to me about him
and I suspect was the cause of his call. He was very interesting
on several themes and exonerated the Germans from Rheims. He
says the trouble was that the French red tape delayed taking down
the scaffolding around the cathedral and that all the substantial
damage was done by that taking fire . . . that the German shells
accurately spared it. Also he made the suggestion that the failure
of the peace Conference was due to the inevitable preponderance
of the machinery of foreign offices over persons. I can remember
him in Boston standing in an aesthetic attitude like Dumaurier's
young aesthete and an aureol of hair above his upturned face. I
must stop, unwillingly before I reach an end of paper or discourse
just sending you my love and gratitude and all good messages to
your wife.                                    *Aff'ly yours, O. W. Holmes*


*16 Warwick Gardens, W. 14, 13.III.21* ¹
*My dear Justice:* Please, above all, note the new address. I don't
want any of your letters to be delayed. We don't move in until
next week, but we are there already in spirit.

Of news both much and little. . . . [M]y peregrinations yesterday . . . took me to lunch to Lady Astor. . . . [T]he simple vulgarity of the labour party as against the complex vulgarity of the
rich Tory seemed to me full of beauties I had not before known.
Today I spent the afternoon with the Secretary to the Cabinet²
one or two of whose tales I must repeat to you. We are now solemnly engaged in revising the peace of Sèvres with Turks three of
whom are war-criminals on the special list and one of whom distinguished himself during the war by massacring over 10,000 Ar-
menians. That seemed to me a little cynical. Oh yes! said my host,
but as the Prime Minister said, when it comes to making peace,

⁴ *United Shoe Machinery Co.* v. *United States,* 258 U.S. 451 (April 17,
1921). A majority of the Court, with McKenna, J., dissenting, sustained
a conviction of the defendant corporation for violating the antitrust laws.
La Rue Brown, Boston attorney and friend of Holmes, represented the government in the Supreme Court and Charles F. Choate, Jr., and Frederick
P. Fish, also of the Boston bar, were counsel for the company. Mr. Justice
Brandeis, who, while a practitioner, had been associated with United Shoe,
did not participate in the deliberation of the Court.
¹ A brief note from Holmes dated March 11 is omitted.
² Sir Maurice Hankey (1877-1963), later Baron Hankey; Secretary of the
Cabinet, 1918-1938.

we must not haggle over trifles. Then I asked him how Lloyd
George managed to keep a vigorous personality like Curzon[3] so
subdued. Quite simple, it appears. When he wants to settle a foreign issue, he settles it and leaves Curzon to find it out. A little
autocratic, I remarked. Well, said mine host, Lloyd George has
made the great discovery that it is easier to be autocratic under a
democracy than it is under any other system. And while I'm telling
tales, let me record one delightful anecdote of Haldane's. Frida
and he and I dined here *à trois* the other night and we got talking
of Margot Asquith. Years ago, he said, he went bail for John Burns
after the Trafalgar Square Riots[4] and when prison had made Burns
eminent Miss Tennant expressed a desire to meet him. So Haldane
arranged a dinner—Margot Tennant, Miss Beatrice Potter, (Mrs.
Webb), Mrs. J. R. Green, Asquith and Grey. When Burns arrived Miss Potter seized upon him and began to discuss the technique of trade union organisation. Miss Tennant waited a moment,
strolled across and remarked casually, Mr. Burns, what beautiful
eyes you have! Thenceforward, said Haldane, Burns talked to no
one else. Miss Potter sulked, Mrs. Green went home early, Asquith
tried to get in a word, but Margot Tennant and Burns sat on the
sofa by themselves with complete aplomb and he saw her home.
Isn't that the very definition of triumph?

Other things? First books. Mainly I've been spending my days
looking for Burke's letters in the odd places of the earth. I told
you, I think, that I'm going to edit a selection of his correspondence for the Oxford Press.[5] Grand letters they are, too, with every
quality you could want except humour; and certainly no letters of
any statesmen I have read exhibit such a generous insight into
political problems as that fellow had. He has his faults, of course.
He was a snob; and whenever a peer of the realm passes by, there
is Burke with his hat in his hand. But he cannot endure the in-
fliction of needless pain; and I think now that no other quality
counts for so much in social life. Burke reminds me that I have
just read Bill James's letters, too, I liked them enormously—a big
heart, a full mind and a generous temper. When I compare them
with the letters of Henry it makes me realise what an artificial
and meagre-souled person he was. And particularly I thought the
letter to Wells on his *Future in America* one of the wisest things
about America in small space I have ever seen. I wish I'd seen
Bill James—or rather I wish he had been alive so that I could
have had him as a colleague at Harvard for he cared about the
same reforms as I should have liked to introduce if I had had a

---

[3] Lord Curzon was Foreign Secretary at this time.

[4] John Burns (1858-1943) had been an energetic participant in troubles
in Trafalgar Square in 1885 and again in 1887, when he was sentenced to jail.

[5] *Letters of Edmund Burke; a Selection, Edited, with an Introduction, by
Harold J. Laski* (1922).

chance. He did at least see that teaching is not offering information but ideas—and—forgive the inference—this last is so much
the most difficult thing that it takes a first-rate person to decide to
tackle it. . . .

And that takes me to your book. I saw what Morris Cohen and
Powell wrote of it—both of them good, I thought, particularly
Powell; but the real gem is what I got Haldane to write for the
*New Republic* which I expect you've seen by now. I gave a spare
copy to Sankey, J. of the K. B. here and he overflowed with gratitude, picking out "The Path of the Law" as the best thing in it.
I had a letter from Harcourt the other day telling me that the first
edition (1200) was exhausted and that they are printing another
thousand. That seems to me remarkable; for, after all, much of it
is severely technical and I don't rate the discriminating public
very large. I have decided, by the way, that any royalties that
accrue I'm going to send to Vienna for the relief of the destitute
professors there. At present exchange even two or three hundred
dollars is such an enormous sum that it means the actual saving
of life and that, I am certain, is what you would care for most just
now. A great meteorologist committed suicide there the other day
for fear of starvation. One such death prevented would justify the
book. I hope, by the way, you'll be seeing Redlich one of these
days. The Austrian Ambassador told me he'd sailed for America
and he was eager for talk with you. Did I tell you of my joy in
your *Coca-Cola* decision? [6] I took it with me to *The Nation* lunch
last week and read it to the company. But, said Massingham, that
isn't law, it's literature!

Well, my love to you both. You'll be glad to have Hughes near
you again. [7]                   *Ever affectionately yours, Harold J. Laski*

*Washington, D.C., March 27, 1921*
*My dear Laski:* A more delightful letter than ever, if possible,
comes this morning and I turn from all duties to answer it at once.
As to business, of course you may do what you like with whatever
you may receive from the book. What you suggest as your intention seems generous and good. I don't know about the matter personally. The next thing, proceeding by the gossiping principle of
contiguity, is that I have seen Redlich twice with great satisfaction. He called the other evening and we had a few hours jaw
and yesterday he dined with us and we had more. He certainly is

[6] *Coca-Cola Co.* v. *Koke Co.*, 254 U.S. 143 (1920); Holmes's opinion, for
a unanimous Court, held that the earlier but subsequently abandoned decep-
tions of the plaintiff company did not disqualify it from securing injunctive
relief against defendant's unfair competition.
[7] On March 5 the Senate had confirmed President Harding's nomination
of Charles Evans Hughes as Secretary of State.

able, cultivated, and human (with a touch of Southern Europe's gift for saying flattering things—but he seems to me really a sincere nature). I was more delighted with him than ever, all the more that he spoke very appreciatively of you, only fearing as I do that you were working your machine too hard. But we both have confidence in the guardianship of your wife, whom I hope you obey like a good husband. Your remark about expatriated Americans has the sympathy of my prejudices rather than of my knowledge—but I regretted the occasion because from seeing her once or twice at dinner—no more—I had supposed that she was a free and generous spirit but the occasion was poor old Gordon McCabe's[1] when he was staying with me and he was a Virginian known to her childhood. Perhaps she would give to the South what she denied to mankind. You speak of Sankey J. I gather that he is a great man but I don't know his work at first hand. I have just been glancing over *The Mirrors of Downing Street* by a Gentleman with a Duster and am delighted to see that he gives Haldane (and Haldane alone so far as I have noticed) credit for just such ability and first rate moral qualities unqualified by any belittling, but I think that I wrote you what deep pleasure his notice in the *N. R.* gave me. But I didn't wait for that to believe in him. I thought his book has the signature of greatness—and also I have known him for a long time. I wonder what has become of Maxse who used to pitch into him.[2] At one time I knew M's sister Ly. Edward Cecil pretty well but I have not seen her for many years. L. Stephen came with me to M's to luncheon and I passed a night or two with the old Admiral years ago. All of which reminds me that Ly. E. met my scepticism about Jowett[3] by saying that his sermons showed his intellectual power—or something big. I tried vainly to get a look at them in the Congressional Library —in memory of the past. As I failed I remain a sceptic still. Your yarn about Miss Margot Tennant is very credible. I regret some things but feel my old affection for her. *"Quoique leurs chapeaux sont bien laids*—God damn—*j'aime les Anglais."* If you ever meet Ly. Desborough I should be curious to know your impressions. She was a niece of my dearest friend Henry Cowper—and while I know both sides I think, I have loved her since she was a little

---

[1] William Gordon McCabe (1841-1920); Virginia soldier, schoolmaster, and man of letters, whose verses and addresses were colored by a lifelong devotion to the Confederacy.

[2] L. J. Maxse (1864-1932); editor of *The National Review*; wholehearted imperialist and critic of the League of Nations; he was the son of Admiral F. A. Maxse (1833-1900), *supra*, p. 179, whose fame lives principally in the pages of Meredith's *Beauchamp's Career*. The Admiral's daughter Violet became the wife of Lord Edward Cecil.

[3] Holmes's path had crossed that of Benjamin Jowett (1817-1893), master of Balliol, clergyman, and translator of Plato's *Dialogues*, when Holmes first visited England in 1866.

girl.[4] In your "Recent Contributions to Political Science"[5] p. 91 (a mighty good little piece) you touch on what has struck me very much and gives me the feeling of unreality when I read Cole *et al.* What you call 'vicious intellectualism' which I dare say is as good a characterization as can be had. Latterly I have read nothing to speak of—but I have discovered (following the *Obiter Dicta* man[6]) Herman Melville. He used to live within ¾ of mile of us at Pittsfield and don't I wish that small boy as I was I had tried to get hold of the (if my memory is right) rather gruff taciturn man that I saw in my father's study. I doubt if he had read or could have been influenced by Borrow's nearly contemporary work—but he wrote in times of long peace and polite conversation with an actuality and first hand contact with life that I suppose hardly pleased my father's generation as much as it does me—and his manner reminds one of Borrow, a little. His talk about whale fishing in *Moby Dick* is A-1 and he talks about the sailors and mates and cannibals all with the same respect that the polite commonly reserve for men of political place. He gives one a new pride in one's country as he tells of the old whalers from Nantucket. It comes home to me the more as I used to have a little place near New Bedford—from which he shipped—Mattapoisett, while the echo of the old time of building whale ships still lingered—and I remember the tale of a respectable *pater familias* pursuing New Bedford lads with a harpoon when they came over to make their annual row. You can't realize that when I was a boy we burned only whale oil lamps— and that we had no water supply in Boston but pumps in our back yards. . . . But I must stop. My love to you—and may the letter come soon.                                    *Aff'ly yours, O. W. H.*

*16 Warwick Gardens, 1.4.21* [1]
*My dear Justice:* . . . today there has begun the worst of all our coal-strikes, bitter beyond words in both origin and possibilities.[2] Where it will end I know not—for it may spread to the railmen

---

[4] The Baroness Desborough (1867-1952), was granddaughter of the Sixth Earl Cowper, and intimate friend of Holmes. Her uncle Henry Cowper (1836-1887), M.P. for Hertfordshire, 1865-1885, became one of Holmes's most intimate friends when Holmes made his first visit to England in 1866.

[5] 1 *Economica* 87 (1921).

[6] Augustine Birrell, "Immortal White Whale: Herman Melville's *Moby Dick*," 308 *Living Age* 659 (March 12, 1921).

[1] A brief note from Laski, dated March 30, is omitted.

[2] Laski told of the issues in two articles in American periodicals: 46 *Survey* 18 (April 2, 1921); letter of April 4, "The British Coal Strike," 112 *Nation* 617 (April 27, 1921). The strike occurred when the government announced that government control, established in 1919, would terminate on March 31 instead of August 31. The miners, not unnaturally, saw this as the beginning of wage reduction. At the outset of the strike the probability was considerable that a general strike would ensue.

next week and it is the really unnecessary type of strike—owners taking advantage of commercial depression not only to attack wages but to shatter, if they can, the men's organisation. I think a mediator of Felix's talent could have settled it in two days negotiation—but there is no one who now commands sufficient general confidence to intervene.

. . . [One volume] which I did not even know existed—being grossly ignorant—namely an answer to Hobbes by Lord Clarendon —and a singularly interesting piece too, a full recognition of Hobbes's merits, a good deal of nervous irritation and a general spectacle of a really able fellow caught in a web of logic from which he sees no egress except temper. Also I have been reading Bryce's last lucubration[3] with much impatience. Ample knowledge, accurate description, and, if I may say so, evidence on every page of a really commonplace mind. I hope you get a chance to turn its pages, for I should much prize your verdict. In my judgment Bryce has written nothing first-rate since the *Holy Roman Empire*. *The American Commonwealth* was great journalism but not in the class of Tocqueville. I lunched with B. the other day and had pleasant talk—especially of you. He confided to me that he dreamed of a large tome on Justinian before he had done. I reminded him of Fontenelle who said, you remember, to the damsel of eighteen, "Ah! Madam, would that I were eighty once more." You who have never been more than twenty-five will not appreciate this.

I don't think I have told you of my first (I hope the last) visit to Lady Astor. . . . I found myself defending everything I loathe from free love to the Middle West. What amused me most was that the one American who had really penetrated her consciousness was Felix whose fascination seemed to have engulfed her among a million others.

. . . Apart from all this I have been ambling through Burke's letters, picking out the ones to print and liking him more each day. Sure I am that the essential thing in him is conservatism, the spurts about India, America and Ireland seem to me to spring less from doctrine than from sheer hatred of pain. He was a good bit of a snob, too, and if Chatham put his head between his legs at the sight of the King, Burke went on his knees when he smelt Lord Rockingham. And in the matter of reading, let me add that I made a gallant effort to read Parton's *Life of Jefferson*. Whether it was Jefferson or Parton I don't pretend to know but I found it so nauseating that I gave up at the end of the first volume; as compensation I dipped into the *Works*, but the *Notes on Virginia* apart, they seemed to me just frothy rhetoric with no meat to speak of, certainly not in the same universe of discussion with Hamilton. . . . [The Adams family] ought to reprint at a reasonable price

---

[3] *Modern Democracies* (2 vols., 1921).

the memoirs of J. Q. Adams. I read it in Cambridge with constant admiration, and discovered when I wanted it that it was out of print and seventy-five dollars. I think it a great manual for statesmen and the more widely it is known the higher J. Q. A. will stand. That would be a great *monumentum pietatis* for Brooks Adams in his leisure time. And that reminds me again that someone just sent me a piece by Henry Adams called a *Letter to Teachers of History*[4] which—with respect—I think one of the most astounding pieces of arrant nonsense that ever came from the pen of a strong intelligence. Muddle-headed would be a complimentary epithet—Did it ever come your way? . . .

*Ever affectionately yours, Harold J. Laski*

*Washington, D.C., April 14, 1921*

*My dear Laski:* Another delightful letter from you. I hope you realize what a joy they are to me and with what pleasure I follow you in your picking up of treasures and interviews with interesting people. Beginning with the beginning, has Lord Askwith[1] lost his skill in composing differences or been turned to other jobs? His talk conveyed to me the impression of a man highly fitted for what he used to do—successfully as I supposed. 2. Clarendon on Hobbes would be interesting but I should suppose an unequal contest. 3. Bryce sent me his book but I haven't had time to examine it since receiving it a few days ago. I can't help fearing what you indicate. He has been too industrious. A man can't have a stream going through his person all the time and send it out highly tinctured with his acids and deposits (not elegant but relevant I think). 4. Lady Astor you spoke of before—I believe you unwillingly—I am glad Felix made an impression. I pass the other matters except to say that I believe Brooks Adams has gone to South America and so removed himself *pro tem.* from exhortation. I never read J.Q.A. but always feared that I must admire his powers more than I want to. Did I mention my revelation, induced I believe remotely, by the *Obiter Dicta* man? Herman Melville and *Moby Dick*—an account of sperm whaling with a story superadded. Anyhow I have finished it now and can say more certainly than ever that, with *longueurs*, it is, yet, I think, a mighty book. Not Shakespeare had more feeling of the mystery of the world and of life. There are mountain peaks and chasms—and the whole is as thick with life at first hand now as the day it was written—as Hawthorne's *Scarlet Letter* seemed to me thin, 20 years ago. (W. James replied to me

---

[4] Originally published in 1910, the *Letter to Teachers* was included in *The Degradation of the Democratic Dogma* (Brooks Adams, ed., 1920).

[1] George Ranken Askwith (1861-1942), first Baron Askwith; barrister, public servant, and effective advocate of the settlement of disputes through arbitration; his wife, Lady Ellen Askwith, was a lifelong friend of Holmes's.

when I said so, Because it is an original book.) Incidentally, it
pleases me that he takes his fellow-sailors, a cannibal, an Indian,
a negro and old Nantucket mates and captain with the same unconscious seriousness that common men would reserve for Presidents and Prime Ministers. And my, but he nobly exalts the Nantucket Whalemen, the Macys, the Coffins and the rest. I don't want
to say too much but if you like George Borrow as I do I think this
is a bigger man. If I made a shelf of strong impressions of recent
years it would be an odd lot. *Moby Dick* beside Pearson's *Grammar of Science* or the best of Santayana or Lotze's *Microcosmos*.
Apropos of the obscurity of original ideas in their first appearance,
of which no doubt we have talked etc., (I doubt not I told you
my experience with Plato's *Symposium*) I have just finished a little
volume that Cohen sent me—*The Literature of the Old Testament*
which speaks of Hosea as starting the notion that God is Love.
Well, if you read Hosea in the English Translation with the similar-
ity of everything in the Old Testament to everything else in consequence of the language, like herrings in a box—I don't believe
you would realize that there was a new note. I think it required
the instructed eye or ear to catch the new tint or tone. Yet I am
perfectly willing to believe it. I vaguely remember that I thought
the H. Adams book you mention pretty rotten. Harcourt confirms
your account of the sale of the first edition of our book—I wrote
for four copies and couldn't get them because of a strike. I must
stop before I want to—as I must play solitaire and get to bed if
possible by 12:30 so as to go to the ear man tomorrow at 10:15.
The ear is bothering me, but I am well and cough less.

*Aff'ly yours, O. W. H.*


*16 Warwick Gardens, 13.IV.21.*
*My dear Justice:* Your delightful letter gave joy not only to myself
alone, but to three great Melville enthusiasts to whom *Moby Dick*
is part of life's essence. And it was an extra diversion in difficult
days when we count the hours until the outbreak of civil war. As I
write I hear outside the steady pat-pat of horses hoofs, as the
cavalry rides down to Kensington Gardens. I have seen the machine-guns in place in Whitehall, and the tanks collected at the
railway stations ready for action. The trade-union leaders all expect a great outbreak; I myself do not see how some sort of *émeute*
can be avoided yet pass by on the omnibus and you realize as in
no other fashion the stolidity of the Englishman.[1] Pass Hyde Park,

---

[1] It had been announced by the Triple Alliance that railwaymen and
transport workers would strike at midnight, April 12. Continued negotiations
of the coal dispute led to a postponement of the threatened sympathetic
strike until April 15. On the 15th, however, the railwaymen and transport
workers determined not to join the strike.

where there are thirty thousand troops, and he comments on the
beauty of the horses. Pass down Whitehall and he mutters that he
wouldn't like the Prime Minister's job. A miner's leader who had
just made a speech at Downing Street bitterly complaining (I
think wisely) of Lloyd George's trickery, then cursed the government for not providing a cup of tea at the conference. We live
from hour to hour just now. I think myself that the issue has been
deliberately forced by the Prime Minister to save a growingly impossible personal position; and when the *Times* acknowledges the
justice of the miners' case, I don't need to add my own personal
analysis.[2] But I am not going to add either political comment for
one of the great joys of writing to you is the freedom it affords
from the cares of contemporary speculations; and we shall have
our fill of those these next few days.

I had a great lunch with Morley last Thursday—Asquith and
Ramsay MacDonald being the others. We damned Bryce's new
book, Morley and I fought against old Bolingbroke who was defended by Asquith and MacDonald. We dissected Lloyd George's
naked soul and left him mangled on the further shore. It was great
fun and I think the old man was in great form. She also was there,
a little frail, but charming as ever, and as always, with the eager
word of Leslie Stephen who, of all their friends, seems to be closest
to their hearts. I was interested to hear Morley come out with a
quite wild attack on Gladstone's scientific ignorance, and some useful words to Asquith about the dangerous hold of the churches at
Oxford.

    . . . The only other thing I have read is the Adams' Civil War
Letters[3] which I thought just over the margin at which publication
is worth while. I liked Charles Francis Jr. better than Henry—the
latter is too self-conscious, too critical of events in which he had
no part, and (does this prick you) too contemptuous of an England
which, as its attitude to Italy showed, was just as capable as he of
appreciating a great moral issue. But I suppose an Adams is *sui
generis* and not to be judged by human standards. Beale,[4] who
dropped in unexpectedly the other day, was much more enthusiastic than I. . . .

    My love to you both,    *Ever affectionately yours, Harold J. Laski*

[2] In his letter to the *Nation, supra,* p. 254, note 2, Laski had written that
Lloyd George "had to choose between power and his honor, and, charac-
teristically enough, chose power."

[3] *A Cycle of Adams Letters,* 1861-1865 (2 vols., Ford, ed., 1921). The
volumes were constituted of the letters of Charles Francis Adams, Charles
Francis Adams, Jr., and Henry Adams written during the Civil War.

[4] Presumably Joseph Henry Beale (1861-1943), Professor of Law at
Harvard.

*Washington, D.C., May 8, 1921*

*My beloved Laski:* For once, four or five days, including a week-
end when I suppose a vessel sails for England, have gone by after
a letter from you before I answered. The reason is that I have been
in such a spasm over three interesting cases that I could do nothing
else till I finished them. The first was on the constitutionality of
an Estate Tax levied by Congress.[1] The next on the validity of conduct charged against a Reserve Bank as intended to compel the
plaintiffs—State banks—to come into the system—and collect and
remit the proceeds of checks from a distance without a charge.[2]
The cases took concentration to get them stated to my liking. After
these came an easier one that I took to relieve the C. J. on business
of retreating to the wall when defending one's life.[3] I finished that
this morning. I am pretty well satisfied with all of them and with a
recent one that I wrote upholding the constitutionality of the
Emergency Housing legislation enabling tenants to hold over.
McKenna shrieked over the downfall of the Constitution[4]—yet a
few days later he said something to me about everything being a
question of circumstances that showed that he understood the
business as well as anyone. But he not infrequently recurs to the
tyro's question: Where are you going to draw the line?—as if all
life were not the marking of grades between black and white. My
satisfaction does not mean any great conceit, but simply that I
watch myself to see if I am keeping up to the mark. No reading of
course. I got a copy of the original edition of *Moby Dick* in fair
condition at Lowdermilk's $3.50—as a tribute to Melville—and
my wife has sent for the French Gauguin's *Noa Noa* which is interesting in the illustrations and even in the translation. Gauguin
thought—I don't doubt sincerely—that in Tahiti he got back to
the classics and away from the degeneracy of civilization—I ain't
quite sure about it—and of course myself prefer civilization with
all its defects to Tahiti in all its glory—and that they did have
damned handsome women in those parts I devoutly believe especially remembering photographs that Stevenson many years ago

---

[1] *New York Trust Co.* v. *Eisner,* 256 U.S. 345 (May 16, 1921).

[2] *American Bank & Trust Co.* v. *Federal Reserve Bank, id.* 350.

[3] *Brown* v. *United States, id.* 335. The majority held that a Texan,
threatened with the "immediate danger of death or grievous bodily harm"
by an assailant may stand his ground and kill the assailant without being
guilty of murder. "Detached reflection," wrote Holmes, "cannot be demanded in the presence of an uplifted knife." Pitney and Clarke, JJ., dissented from the judgment.

[4] *Block* v. *Hirsch,* 256 U.S. 135 (April 18, 1921). The Chief Justice,
with Van Devanter and McReynolds, JJ., joined in Mr. Justice McKenna's
dissent. Writing to Felix Frankfurter on April 20, 1921, Holmes made this
further comment on the decision in *Block* v. *Hirsch:* "I was content with
my statement and made no changes after receiving the dissent, although it
criticized my opinion, which I think bad form."

sent to a friend of his and mine. Well, my lad, I am tired—more
than I ought to be—and so instead of duties or reading I mean to
stretch myself out and try to sleep. I think it tends to take me in
my innards when I get over-wrought. Your feeling of the imminence of civil war I trust was unwarranted. Who was the 'She' who
also was at the luncheon Morley, Asquith, and McDonald? Was it
Mrs. Asquith? I don't quite understand what follows "And as always with the eager word of Leslie Stephen who of all their friends,
seems to be closest to their hearts." I didn't know that Mrs. Asquith
ever knew L. S. which seems queer if your sentence means what
it seems to. Who is Beale? The Beale of the Harvard Law School?
I have just run my eye over a learned study of his on the law of
retreating to the wall.[5] It has a little more veneration for the texts
and for human life than I have but seems a good analysis of the
old law. Why should any remark about Adams prick me? My wife
gave me those two volumes but I have passed by on the other side
hitherto and intend to stay there. Now for a little rest.

*Yours as ever, O. W. H.*

*16 Warwick Gardens, 30.IV.21.*

*My dear Justice:* Do forgive me for this long silence. I have been
sitting for the past fortnight on the Miners' Publicity Committee,
and that has entailed two meetings a day lasting for four or five
hours. Now alack! it has ended, not because a settlement has been
reached, but because definitely bad government management has
resulted in a breakdown of negotiations which I had every hope
were going to be successful.

I wish I could sit with you for a couple of hours and tell you the
inside history of this strike. I don't know what human impulse
there is that it does not illustrate. Mainly, I think, two—fear and
the sense of prestige. Everyone I met was afraid of his fellow, and
owners, miners, and government alike all seemed most to dread
any step capable of interpretation as a surrender. When I last wrote
to you I dreaded revolution. My fear now is that the dispute will
drag into a stage where our industrial recovery will be jeopardised
for long. And all this because the Prime Minister does not realise
that men will not work with him or through him unless he offers
proof that his intentions are honorable. I saw him twice during the
negotiations.[1] Each time he left me with the same impression—a
man trying to dodge issues, not to meet them, and fundamentally
incapable of intellectual sincerity. He admitted three things to me
(I) the organisation of the industry was inefficient (II) the owners

---

[5] "Retreat from a Murderous Assault," 16 *Harv. L. Rev.* 567 (1903).

[1] For an account of an earlier meeting of Laski and Lloyd George, see
Henry W. Nevinson, *More Changes, More Chances* (1925), 330.

were impossible people to deal with (III) the wage-reductions
were absurd. Say those things in public, I said, and you can have
a permanent settlement tomorrow. But you cannot get him to
commit himself. He lives by momentary improvisations. He is ignorant of economics, ignorant of the working-class temper, and
so full of a kind of neo-Napoleonism as to be useless. And he is
surrounded by an adulation that gave me nausea.

Well—him apart I have had to see others. The person who
showed most sense in the crisis was by all odds Haldane. In fact
I think myself that he is the one person of high position who really
understands what the crisis is about. But he remains without influence. Asquith I talked with, but he was very disappointing. He
had not taken the trouble to acquaint himself with the facts with
the result that our talk was not discussion at all. One glorious
incident I must not omit—a Scottish miner M. P. asked me to
write a letter for him to the *Times*. He gave me his ideas and I
licked them into shape, adding a quotation from Burns to drive
home the point. The next day the *Times* commented on the letter
by saying that it showed "that national pride in poetic achievement
which has made for Scottish success in things of the mind." Do
you wonder that I am not unsceptical of editorial discernment.

. . . for a lecture at Toynbee Hall on Cromwell I re-read Carlyle's *Cromwell* and thought it very big work. It struck me rather
forcibly in going through it that what ultimately survives is the
picturesque. It's full of inaccuracies, obvious forgeries swallowed
whole, dates misplaced, documents misunderstood, yet Cromwell
living on the page as in no other book. I made it the text of a
talk to 300 Communists to show them that the makers of an event
never shape its ultimate destinies; that things are bigger than men
and that if they made a revolution in the name of freedom, the
stability they would inevitably search for would bring despotism
in its train. They took it very well save one fierce soul who said
we lived under a despotism now. What you mean, I said, is that
you prefer your despotism to theirs. . . .

I needn't tell you what joy your last letter gave me, and your
notes on Melville are cherished. Masefield the other day said to
me that he thought him derived from Borrow and was much interested in your remarks. . . .

My love to you both—          *Ever yours affectionately, H. J. L.*


                                   *Washington, D.C., May 12, 1921*
*Dear Laski:* Your letter of the 30th comes this morning—the long
gap was before I received the last one, which I answered a few
days ago. This as usual is adorable and stirs me with every kind
of interest. I am just recovering or recovered from the strain of last
week when I worked too fiercely. But I polished off two cases, my

own, that the boys have all agreed to and seemed to like.[1] I think myself they show no falling off. There was a third, a criminal case about the supposed duty to retreat to the wall (if there is one) before killing the assailant, which I took from the C. J. and which also is assented to by all but Pitney and Clark[e]. Beale wrote a learned discourse in the *Harvard Law Review*[2] upholding the rule —but I think it an instance of an early statement ossifying by repetition into an absolute principle when rationally it is only one of the circumstances to be considered with the rest in deciding whether the defendant exceeds the reasonable limits. I don't say all I think in the opinion. But law must consider human nature and make some allowances for the fighting instinct at critical moments. In Texas where the thing happened, but on U.S. post office ground, it is well settled, as you might imagine, that a man is not born to run away—and there are two decisions of our Court by old Harlan to this same effect. This is private, but I hope the decision will be announced before you get this, as neither P. nor Cl. retained my opinion as they naturally would if they intended to write. I assume that Brandeis will send you these with the other cases that he sends. I think your reply to the fierce Communist hit the nail precisely on the head. The reply, I suppose, is that a man has a right to follow his preference, if he understands the cost. The trouble is usually that he doesn't. I always used to say about the Sherman Act if you want to go to that show and have the money to buy a ticket I have nothing to say, except that I don't think you would want to if you did not entertain economic delusions. As to the unforeseen consequences of panaceas or supposed improvements to which you advert, my recollection is that a book I recommended, Tourtoulon, *Principes philosophiques de l'histoire du droit,* has admirable remarks.

This morning brings a surprise—I was notified some time ago that prepayment of tax by companies issuing bonds counted as part of my income and that a small additional tax was due from me for two past years. I wrote back that I should pay as soon as I received my bill and that I didn't know it made any difference that by the decision of our court (I dissenting) I had overpaid by some thousands, as my salary was taxed. Answer comes that if I apply for a refund of it I shall receive prompt attention—I don't quite know whether to or not. The wiley Brandeis has had overpayment credited on a tax, I believe.

I am delighted at what you say Redlich said about Felix (and pleased of course that he liked his visit to this house). As to Melville and Borrow (whom undoubtedly M suggested though I think M the bigger man) I had it in my head that the dates made M's

---

[1] See, *supra,* p. 259.

[2] *Supra,* p. 260.

indebtedness unlikely but I see from Allibone that some of Borrow's books were out some ten years more or less before *Moby Dick*. So I can only say as Lincoln did of Grant: that he wished he could give some of Grant's whiskey to the other generals. I like your airs of maturity. Child—chicken—have you yet hopped up to the perch of 30? When you look from the pyramid of 80 you may recognize the approach of eld. At 90 it is time to begin to learn golf and possibly to resume horseback riding—but the world is all before you.                                    *Ever aff'ly yours, O. W. H.*

*16 Warwick Gardens, 12.V.21.*
*My dear Justice:* Days of riding the whirlwind, but pleasurable, for all their excitement. The two most interesting events by all odds were a long talk with Milner[1] and a rather delicate negotiation over the coal strike. Premising that they were confidential, let me tell you the story. Our coal strike has reached the point where the main problem is how to bring the parties together without sacrificing their *amour-propre*. Could an intervention come from a big man whose impartiality would carry weight? Milner seemed the person and I got an introduction to him from the P. M.'s secretary. I liked him exceedingly. A little hard and gaunt—but not an ounce of superfluous intellectual fat. And I noticed with much interest that when I talked his eyes went through me like two gimlets; but when he spoke he kept his eyes closed so that beyond his actual words, I had no clue to what passed in his mind. Felix would call that good administration. Well! He cleared the ground for me by a frank and honest picture of the feeling in the cabinet. I took his view to Haldane, got his judgment upon it, digested it myself and then went over to the Miner's Federation. There I saw Hodges,[2] their secretary and a first-rate intellect. I put to him what I conceived to be the elements of a settlement and got his assent to five principles. My problem was, as you can imagine, to find a formula which government would accept as saving its dignity and would yet yield to the miners the substance of their demands. Well! after a two hours search with Hodges we got a plan. Then came the part where I was in real terror. I know liberals and labour men; Tories are out of my sphere. I couldn't go to the liberals for Lloyd George would take no plan from them. I couldn't go to labour for any advance from them the P. M. would interpret as a sign of weakness. Finally I got hold of a young Tory who was interested in Zionism. We talked of Brandeis, Felix *et al* and I then inno-

---

[1] Alfred Milner (1854-1925), Viscount Milner; statesman, imperialist, and colonial administrator; member of Lloyd George's War Cabinet; Colonial Secretary, from 1918 to February 7, 1921.

[2] Frank Hodges (1887-1947); author of *Nationalisation of the Mines* (1920) and *My Adventures as a Labour Leader* (1924).

cently asked if he would like a hand in settling the strike. He jumped at it, read my plan with enthusiasm, and asked where it came from. That of course I could not tell. But I offered to explain it in detail to his friends. He promptly got about forty members together and I analysed my scheme suggesting that it "might prove acceptable to the Miners." They formed a deputation to take it with their blessing to Lloyd George and he now proposes to call them together on that basis. It looks uncommonly like a settlement; and it's evidence, if that be needed, that disinterested good will can still play a big part in political affairs.[3]

All this, as you can imagine, has taken much both of time and thought. Public men in general do not possess the two great qualities of intellectual concentration and intellectual decisiveness. They are constantly occupied with the peculiar problems of their own prestige so that situations which are really simple become in the drift of events tangled and complex. . . . I have promised by the way to write a Fabian pamphlet on Karl Marx which ought to be good fun in the writing.[4] I am pretty sure that the Socialists won't like it; for (a) I propose to show that the surplus theory of value is nonsense (b) that it wasn't his own (c) that he was a great man by accident rather than design. But I find toying with his books very interesting and one pamphlet *The Civil War in France* is very well, even brilliantly, done.

But enough for today. My love, you know, comes with fullness to you both. I wish that distance were merely in the mind.

*Ever affectionately yours, Harold J. Laski*

*Washington, D.C., May 27, 1921*
Dear Laski: Your letter of 12 V. 21 (I can copy if I cannot emulate) came this p.m. too late for me to catch the boat that I still imagine to sail every Saturday. Your tale of negotiations was most interesting but I fear from what little I have heard or seen later that it did not succeed. With us the main event has been the death of the Chief Justice.[1] Poor man, he suffered long and bore up against it heroically—but life could not have been satisfactory longer, even if his pain had ceased. He had, beside the trouble of which he died, cataracts on both eyes and had grown very deaf. I cannot judge whether his delaying any operation was due to determination not to give the appointment to Wilson or to love of the office or to mistaken sense of duty—possibly all combined. For

---

[3] Laski's hope was not realized; misunderstanding, fruitless negotiation, and increasing hardship continued to prevail. Not until June 27 was a provisional settlement reached, with the miners returning to work generally on July 4.

[4] Published in 1922.

[1] Mr. Chief Justice White had died on May 19. The vacancy was filled at the end of June by the appointment of William Howard Taft.

I think he loved the office as an end in itself. There is a queer difference in people about that. The only thing that gives me appreciable pleasure is when people—the rare ones that I care about and whose judgment I respect—tell me that I have hit the *ut de poitrine* in my work. Then for half an hour I feel that the long struggle has been rewarded—and then comes again the doubt —will the next one do the trick. As I may have written, the last year or two has brought more of the feeling of reward than ever before—and I fully appreciate the part that you have played in bringing that about. Now people speculate as to who will take White's place—Taft is much mentioned. I would rather have Hughes but I think he doesn't want it. Hughes is very hard working. Taft is said to be indolent. He has been out of judicial place for 20 years or so—and though he did well as a Circuit Judge I never saw anything that struck me as more than first rate second rate. I have heard it said and denied that he is hard to get along with if you don't agree with him. I assume that the President will be impressed by political experience (which of course is valuable) and popular prominence. You may wonder if I am thinking of it. Not in any sense except that all possibilities occur to one and that no doubt a few here and there have named me. They would not appoint so old a man—and although I think I know my place with regard to the higher aspects of the law, I should not expect it of the appointing power. That is not the kind of thing that excites me much. I take it for granted that Brandeis's chance died with Wilson's departure. I wonder how many men are pulling wires now. I give you my word of honor that I am not. I don't even know what, if any, wires I could pull—I haven't lifted a finger. When White was appointed I told McKenna that I believed that he and I were the only justices who hadn't got a little boom of greater or less magnitude. *Quam parva sapientia regitur mundus.* The funeral was preceded and followed by garden parties at the White House. I went yesterday from a sense of duty and found it both pleasant and beautiful. I hoped I might meet the Princess Bibesco (Mrs. Asquith's daughter) whom I have not yet seen—but I didn't. The colors of some dresses and many ladies' faces were bright and it is always agreeable to see some one brighten up with a friendly look. I had a short talk with Cabot Lodge whom I hadn't seen for a long time. He looked tired. There are not many now with whom one has had a lifelong familiarity and he is ten years younger than I. Mrs. Gray[2] is here and the other day I took her out to my private show—Fort Stevens where I saw Lincoln when the big guns were firing and our skirmishers going up the opposite slope and the enemy got their nearest to Washington. It is a hidden spot that few know and I was posing as the last survivor in the little ceme-

---

[2] Mrs. John Chipman Gray, an intimate friend of Holmes's.

tery nearby when we met 3 80-year olders two at least of whom
I believe were there—and we held a little reunion that pleased
Mrs. Gray and them. My work is pretty nearly done. We expect
to go to Beverly Farms or Boston rather June 15, and oh, how I
shall miss you there.

Compliments to the missus.    *Affectionately yours, O. W. Holmes*

*16 Warwick Gardens, 6.VI.21.*

*My dear Justice:* A hectic life these last weeks, so hectic that I
have hardly known where to turn for the chance of leisure. First,
there has been the coal strike. I spent hours trying to put commonsense into the member of the Cabinet most closely concerned. He
agreed with my strictures upon the present system. He agreed with
my statistics. He had no alternative proposals of his own; and he
finally put my plan (which the miners agreed to accept) into the
waste paper basket. The result is a worse chaos than ever. Everyone is very angry and the faint hope of a trade revival has disappeared. If ever a government represented ignorant reaction it
is this government.

The compensations have been a great dinner with Morley and
some really glorious talk with the Asquiths. Morley was in fine
form; and though I really believe that at bottom he's a natural
*laissez-faire* Tory whose liberalism represents a hatred of pain,
he's a very loveable person. If I had to pick holes, I should complain that he was (like Mill his master) basically a feminine mind
with the difficult vanity of a brilliant woman. She is a dear, and
her kind sweetness has a glow about it that is very attractive. With
the Asquiths (this *entre nous*) I have been engaged in a pretty
little intrigue to get Haldane back to a basis of friendship with
them. Ever since L.G. became Prime Minister Haldane has gravi-
tated towards him, not, I think, on intellectual grounds, but just
because Asquith was morbidly conscious of unfairness in dropping
Haldane in 1915. So I set to work to rebuild the bridges. I discovered that Haldane's alienation was very largely hurt pride at
being left alone. He and the Asquiths love each other and I concluded that the impairment of a friendship was here sheer wastage.
So they've invited each other to dinner at my recommendation;
and I hope now that the breach will be healed. It's taken effort and
delicacy, but I'm very sure it's worth while. Mrs. Asquith I really
like hugely. She [is] brilliant, witty and generous. Her faults are
obvious enough—indiscretion above all and she is too easily influenced by her immediate environment. But she is amazingly
educable and I'm trying, through her, to get him to see that the
old industrial formulae will no longer work and that he must
move to broader ground. His faults are inertia and a tendency to
dwell too much on the virtues of the past and too little on the

dreams of the future. But he is entirely selfish, [sic] amazingly loyal and full of that deep steadiness of character which is, in the end, worth more than brains. He and I have reminiscences of you each time I go there. I'd like you (if you will) to send him the *Collected Legal Papers* of which I've been speaking to him. It would touch him greatly for he has real affection for you. Two remarks of his (*en passant*) I must quote. He told me that when he formed the Coalition of 1915 he said to Bonar Law that he would offer the Lord Privy Sealship to Curzon. Bonar Law: "He won't take it, it isn't big enough." Asquith: "Oh, yes, he will; it gives him precedence at all official dinners." And Curzon jumped at it. The other remark was of Winston Churchill. "He has," said Asquith, "all the qualities a statesman needs except unselfishness. He's so wrapped up in himself that he feeds upon his own vitals." I make no comment.

. . . I have picked up one or two jolly things. . . . Buchanan's works—this for the *De Jure Regni apud Scotos* which is I think the more brilliant the more often I read it. All of Rousseau is in it as clear as noonday without any of the mystical nonsense about a general will. My ambitions for a copy of the *Second Part of a Register* were rudely nipped in the bud. It brought £45 and you can imagine what quality of indignation I felt when I discovered that it was bought by Northcliffe's brother who couldn't read it but had decided to be a collector. . . .

My love to you both.                    *Ever yours, Harold J. Laski*


*Beverly Farms, June 21, 1921*

*My dear Laski:* Yours of the 6th has just reached me here and the moment I have finished it I take up my pen. You certainly are delightful and I fear that I shall make an inadequate return. I will direct Brace Howe & Co. by this mail to send a copy of my book to Asquith, although I cannot but suspect that your friendship exaggerates his remembrance of me. Mrs. Asquith's recollection you never mention, which makes me fear that time has dimmed it or that the unfavorable reactions to which perhaps she may be subject have prevailed. I always have been deeply attached to her. All my memories of him are agreeable but I didn't begin to know him as well as I knew her. Apropos of your work on the Coal Strike I got a statement of his views from Leslie Scott which seemed to me able, but I am too ignorant to have an opinion on the merits. Do you know him? I have the impression that you two have met. He is not brilliant but he is very thorough and has a high character, with what I should think non-conformist influences. I have a strong old friendship for him. Haldane sent me his book on relativity and I read 80 pages coming on in the train last

Wednesday and mean to finish it ὡς ταχιστα but we only got here
Saturday night and the first days admit no reading. Yesterday
evening to be sure, after completing my duties with solitaire, I took
up Pascal's *Pensées*. My expectation from old days was that they
would say little to me but I was surprised and delighted. I wonder
if he anticipated Malebranche as to the pursuit of truth; *nous ne
cherchons jamais les choses, mais la recherche des choses*—etc.
(Sect. 2, 135—Dent's ed. following Brunschvigg [*sic*]). His theology or something made him unphilosophical as to the inevitable
activity of man—which is S.P. as the kitten chasing its tail or the
dancing of the cover of a kettle on the fire—but how many living
intuitions this old beggar had! I can't imagine how I came to retain an impression that he spoke only to the good.

My notions of Morley are only from his books, though I saw
him once at the White House—preoccupied with Roosevelt. When
first I opened him I was enraptured but I do not regard Miss
Martineau as the Virgin Mary or Mill, much as I admire and like
him, as St. John. You excite me as to Buchanan. I don't know what
you mean by *Second Part of the Register*. My only Register is the
*Registrum Brevium* and I know damned little about that. Your
feeling is like mine as a young lawyer when Judge Gray[1] took
away from me at an auction of Kent's books the great edition of
the *Grand Coutumier*. He got it for less than it was worth but
more than I could afford—and promised to leave it to me which
of course he didn't. . . . I shall be very lonely here this summer
—you away and Mrs. Curtis going abroad. If you don't write
regularly I shall use my influence on high to have you damned.
But I shall hope to read something—even though I can't swallow
books like oysters. Felix and his wife were here on Sunday—after
many misadventures delaying them. It was good to see them. They
go to a quiet place in the country. Also I have had a perturbation
in being refused buttermilk because I didn't take my other stuff
from the place—but the Doctor issued his fiat and I am told that
I shall have it. I miss it more almost than I should tobacco. Have
I chronicled small beer sufficiently? My love to you both.

*Affectionately, O. W. Holmes*

*16 Warwick Gardens, 26.VI.21*
*My dear Justice:* Term is over at last; so I can sit down to three
clear months of reading and work. I have been frightfully busy
these last days—partly in pleasure, but mainly in business. The

---

[1] Horace Gray (1828-1902); learned predecessor of Holmes as Associate
Justice and Chief Justice of the Supreme Judicial Court of Massachusetts and
as Associate Justice in the Supreme Court of the United States; half brother
of Holmes's close friend, John Chipman Gray (1839-1915).

latter has chiefly consisted in an effort to get Asquith to make some statement upon the coal issue. So far I can't say I have succeeded; but I have brought him to the point of asking me to bring the miners' leaders round and I take that to be something of an advance. The Asquith situation is very complicated. I like her hugely —she is generous, impulsive, indiscreet, has, in fact, all the qualities that make for feminine attractiveness. But she doesn't in the least understand her husband's position. She thinks it is all due to intrigue and newspaper dishonesty. She doesn't see that he says nothing to the point in these days, and of course, helps one but little in bringing him up to fighting scratch. He is as sweet and charming as can be; but he is very self-indulgent and it's the very devil to get him to read the documents he ought to know without guidance. Both of them see admirably the defects of the labour party; but they don't see the defects of the liberals, and they seem very content to wait in the curious belief that weariness of L.G. will drive the country back to them. It's absurd doctrine; but as they move mainly among people who never contradict them they too rarely meet the other side. And he is so shy that when you indicate an obvious path to him, he hesitates, even when he thinks you're right, lest to occupy a position be deemed arrogant. I suppose that he hasn't recovered from the discovery of disloyalty in 1916; but he must be driven into statements if he is ever to be of significance again. So I'm occupied in driving. What I want eventually is a liberal-labour arrangement to get rid of George. Labour won't touch it now because Asquith has made no pronouncements on *their* specific problems. If he came out for a great program of industrial reconstruction they would, I think, leap at him.

Well! All that has taken time. But I have done some reading and found some books. . . . Then Morley's *Rousseau* which I had not read for years and found on reacquaintance very second-rate. It was a good personal study; I don't doubt that Rousseau as a man was very like what Morley makes him out to be; but Rousseau for the world is, after all, a book in breeches and the man over whose tomb Schiller and Hölderlin wept lyrical tears can't be dismissed as a meagre and vicious charlatan. . . . Then I have been wading my way through Gierke who leaves one despairing. If you are to watch life as well as books I don't see how the acquisition of such knowledge is possible. I have tested parts of the book; and he is every whit as good on any century as another up to say 1650. His one defect is a certain weakness when he touches books in foreign languages. Then he treats third-raters with a respect they don't deserve; and I suspect that agreement with the gospel as preached by Gierke is not unconnected with the appraisal. Lastly in the catalogue is Bertrand Russell's *Analysis of Mind*—beautifully written and very clever and profoundly un-

true—an attempt to prove that consciousness is an illegitimate inference from misinterpreted facts—a revival of the old doctrine of
the soul. . . .

My love to you both. I wish you were here.

*Ever affectionately yours, Harold J. Laski*

*Beverly Farms, July 12, 1921*
*Dear Laski:* Your longed for letter has come and the moment I
have finished reading it I begin my reply. You tell of pushing at
Asquith, getting rare pamphlets and preparing books—I have
nothing correspondent. I am fooling around, have prepared and
sent off accounts as trustee and for taxation, and am dabbling in
philosophy. Haldane led me to get from the Athenaeum Wallace's
translation of Hegel's *Logic*. I read it once—I mean Hegel's *Logic*
with French translation with no understanding—my only result
being as probably I have said before that H. couldn't make me
believe that a syllogism could wag its tail. Less metaphorically
having just finished Wallace's introduction, I still entirely fail to
grasp the transition from timeless logic to phenomena in time and,
I suppose like most other people have, I don't believe that Hegel
succeeded in his attempt to create the world out of nothing. I
wrote to you with enthusiasm when I was beginning Pascal's
*Pensées*—but the last half simply bored me. He is wholly governed
by assumptions from his antecedents and environment that he
thinks he has transcended and his treatment of the Bible seems
childish nowadays. . . . Admiral Sims's book *The Victory at Sea*
stirred my enthusiasm—which Lansing's[1] does not—the latter interests me mainly by confirming some impressions about Wilson.
Taft did not surprise me by saying (according to the papers) that
the CJ-ship had been the ambition of his life. I think I wrote what
I thought of that kind of ambition as against the aspiration to
touch the superlative in one's work. The last I do not expect (between ourselves) from Taft. I doubt if he can go higher than the
first rate second rate—but this is strictly private, and I may be
wrong. He did well as a judge. I haven't seen Beveridge for a
week or more. He was writing an address on the suggestion that
we should forgive the foreign debt arising from the war—putting
the two sides—but suggesting the conclusion that we should not[2]
—with which I incline to agree. I don't know whether he has gone
off to deliver it or what has become of him. You may like to know

---

[1] Robert Lansing, *The Big Four and Others of the Peace Conference*
(1921).

[2] Concerning Beveridge's political activities during the summer of 1921,
see Bowers, *Beveridge and the Progressive Era* (1932), 524 *et seq.*

that Nugent (who takes us out motoring) always inquires about
you. Evidently you made a deep impression upon him. I am in
very good shape—bothered a little by coughing but not enough
to complain about, except that I can't read aloud. At long intervals
I go to luncheon with a dame or two but my main companion
since your departure, Mrs. Curtis, has gone to Europe. I miss my
weekly call on her and I miss you every day. I am not surprised
by what you say of rereading Morley. When one first opens him
one thinks one has found *IT*—the superlative—but the impression
fades. I speak from ancient memory. My love to you both.

*Aff'ly yours, O. W. Holmes*

*16 Warwick Gardens, 6.VII.21*

*My dear Justice:* Crowded days! And I hardly know where to begin
telling you of people and things. But first a word about Taft's
appointment, for I must wreak my anger somewhere. I thought it
was a scandalous appointment. First it was so obvious that as a
matter of simple justice you should have been appointed; next,
after his attack on Brandeis of last October I should have thought
decency would have made him see that colleagueship was impossible.[1] I boil about it; for I fear that Taft's smiling exterior
really conceals a very malicious and petty nature. However I've
said my say and it's a katharsis merely to utter one's curses.

Well! First as to persons. Last Monday we had a jolly dinner
here, at which I sighed for you—Haldane, Birrell, Croly and
Massingham. It was mainly a political scrap—Haldane against
Birrell and Massingham on the issue of Asquith. Birrell particularly
was delightful. He has done with politics and speaks of it now as
a vague recollection. Haldane sighs for power and there was a
great fight as to the ways and means of getting back. . . . On the
Thursday evening we went to dinner to Wells and had good talk.
Let me list the things at which he tilted (a) the monarchy (b)
professors (c) universities (d) Carlyle (e) Arnold (f) governments
(g) socialists (h) Sinn Fein—always, let me add, with real verve
and gusto. He's a wonderfully agile mind, full of superficiality,
but so naturally and arrestingly intelligent that you can't *help*
liking him. I imagine that he is a solo player rather than a member
of an orchestra, but he certainly has the ability to make one think.
We saw his wife for the first time—a pale, negative sort of person

---

[1] On June 30 President Harding had nominated William Howard Taft as
Chief Justice, and the Senate had confirmed the nomination on the same
day. In the October issue of *The Yale Review* Taft in critically reviewing
the Wilson administration had included severe comments on "the new school
of constitutional construction" led by Brandeis and Clarke, JJ., which tended
to encourage "Socialist raids upon property rights." "Mr. Wilson and the
Campaign," 10 *Yale Review* (N.S.) 1 (October 1920).

who obviously represented the hard, lean days. She tried to keep up with him; but a drag-horse cannot pace an avalanche . . . *The Seconde Parte of a Register* is a Puritan tract which has 144 other tracts reprinted within—a great thing to possess, but blown sky high by collectors' fads. Let me by the way give you a true story of a bookseller here. I wandered in the other day and found he had a copy of a rather rare book, Languet's *Epistolae Politicae* —I offered to buy it, when he said that he hadn't seen a copy for ten years and wanted to sell it for use not profit. He'd let me have it if I translated it with fluency. So I sat down and translated a page, he following with great care and criticism. I remember vividly how I translated *"cuneatim"* "in wedge-like formation" and bless me if the old boy didn't look it up in Lewis and Short to see if I was faking. Well! I got the book, and liked the man for his determination. Did I tell you that I'm doing a pamphlet on Karl Marx for the Fabians? All the Marxians will rise up and call me cursed when it's finished.

My love to you eagerly—and to her.                *Ever yours, H. J. L.*

*Beverly Farms, July 21, 1921*
*Dear Laski:* A letter delightful as usual came last night—telling of a dinner *chez vous* with Haldane, Birrell *et al.*, your triumph with the bookseller for Languet and a dinner with Wells. As to the last I think the division of poets (artists) and thinkers holds good. He is an artist and I don't care what he thinks. I have seen how wonderfully clever he is and have been amazed at his talk on varied themes—but still when it comes to the depths I don't think he was born to philosophize but to tell stories—and when his *Outline of History* is taken in that way I think it a triumph. I don't care what inaccuracies, vague theories, or prejudiced judgments there may be. He makes you feel the continuity of the story in time and space, which it takes an artist to do. I forget whether I had finished Hegel's *Logic* when I last wrote. It is hard reading and many sentences displaying the movement of his dialectics I didn't fully understand. But I didn't bother on that as they are merely details of an attempt I don't believe in. Yet the old devil with all his charlatanry felt, if he didn't lead, as perhaps he did, the future of thought, and made a misty world poem in the form of syllogisms. Now I have Taylor's *The Mediaeval Mind*—I think you have mentioned it to me. I find it delightful and pretty big. I am glad to infer that he is an American for he seems to write with a first-hand learning unusual here. But it is astonishing, seeing that I am supposed to be at leisure how little time I get to read to myself. In the evening I don't like to turn my back and put my nose

into a book, so I play solitaire and F. reads to me—but that is
not the same thing. She has read a good piece of Col. Repington's
book which is entertaining.[1] I wonder what manner of man he is.
He raises doubts in my mind.

You and I never have had much abstract philosophical talk. As
against Haldane, Hegel *et al* I am still in the darkness of the *ding
an sich.* I believe that other people exist in the same sense that I
do—and therefore that there is a part of the universe outside of
my consciousness. When I get as far as that I bow my head.
Thought may be my ultimate but I don't see the warrant for
assuming that it is the cosmic ultimate. And I don't believe in the
infinite importance of man—I see no reason to believe that a
shudder could go through the sky if the whole ant heap were
kerosened. . . . As usual I am a little hurried and so send you
my love and wind up.                          *Aff'ly yours, O. W. Holmes*

                                      *16 Warwick Gardens, 17.VII.21.*
*My dear Justice:* The two main events of the week are the heat and
Ireland. Imagine a week's continuous temperature of 90° in London,
with the stolid changeless Englishman about as equipped to meet
it as he would be equipped to meet an iceberg. I leave off my
waistcoat, and become to my friends a kind of sartorial Faraday
full of novel and arresting ideas. One thing at least America taught
me, and that is the technique of countering hot weather. Of Ireland
I don't want to write too optimistically.[1] L.G. is the artful dodger
and Ulster is very sulky and spoiled, but it does look as though
there are real hopes of peace and as if some kind of dominion
settlement would finally end that misery.

Of people next. I went a week since to a lunch given in honour
of F. W. Hirst, the economist, a good fellow and a noble journalist
who is to call on you in Washington this autumn—you may remember that I lent you his life of Adam Smith. There were two
admirable speeches—one from the Lord Chancellor[2] who, his
natural blackguardism apart, is the best after-dinner speaker I have
ever heard, and one from John Simon who told me with what interest he had read the *Collected Legal Papers.* Then a little later

---

[1] See, *supra*, p. 225.
[1] In the opening days of July, negotiations, which were later successfully
concluded, were opened between Sinn Fein representatives and the British
government.
[2] Frederick Edwin Smith (1872-1930), first Earl of Birkenhead; after a
notoriously successful career at the bar, largely in criminal cases, Smith became one of the most spectacular figures in Parliament, where his conservatism in political matters had contrasted with his colorful tastes and
talents as orator; he had become Lord Chancellor in the Lloyd George
government, in 1919.

274 )                                          ( 1919

I took Croly to tea to Morley who was in great form and talked quite superbly. Really as a critic of life, he is, with all his defects weighed nicely, quite the first man in England. He said one admirable thing. "Rousseau only added false sentiment to Locke's theory of the state. I like my Locke without dilution." Last Wednesday I had a little dinner for Croly—Ramsay MacDonald, Nevinson the war-correspondent and some others. Croly interested me by feeling (as I do) that of all current politicians MacDonald has by all odds the soundest sense and certainly the deepest insight into the currents of present opinion. Like all Scotchmen he is very well read; and he has a turn for abstract principles which is wholly delightful. Nor must I omit a jolly dinner at Wells's to meet Shaw where we thoroughly enjoyed ourselves—Wells in great form and literally the topics were (I) God (II) boxing (III) Lamarck (IV) Socialism (V) Conrad (VI) Bennett (VII) psychoanalysis (VIII) America (IX) Lloyd George (X) S. Webb. Shaw was very gloomy over Dempsey's victory,[3] but cheered up when we told him that Dempsey greatly admired *Cashel Byron's Profession*. He told me two delightful stories I ought not to let you evade. He spoke of Frank Harris the journalist. "A loveable but impossible man. I had him to dinner twice. The first time he sat next to Sarah Bernhardt and spoke to her of the sinfulness of illegitimate children—she having three in that condition. The next time I put him next to a bishop's wife and he told her a story the nature of which I can only glean from the fact that in the middle of dinner she rose and said 'Charles, I think we had better leave.' " The second story was of Oscar Wilde. Harris was very disturbed at the criminal charge and urged Wilde to fly with him on a yachting tour round the world. Wilde as steadfastly refused. "Harris could not understand," said Shaw, "that compared to a yachting tour with himself, Wilde regarded prison as a pleasurable alternative." One other dinner and I have done. On Thursday I dined with Morley to meet a select company—Ramsay MacDonald, Sir Donald Maclean who leads the independent liberals in the house, Birrell and Lord Inchcape.[4] The latter is the typical first-class business man—solid in substance but quite incapable of imaginative effort. Birrell is, without exception, the best diner-out I have met. He and I struck up a great friendship and talked Hazlitt, Marvell, Adam Smith and Hume till the small hours. Maclean, too, is a nice fellow—buried in the house, but full of information and eagerly sincere upon it. Thoroughly enjoyable altogether and old Morley dealing out his

---

[3] Jack Dempsey had beaten Georges Carpentier by a knockout in the heavyweight bout on July 2.

[4] James Lyle MacKay (1852-1932), first Earl of Inchcape; his business career in India was followed by notable successes in the shipping industry in England.

genial aphorisms like the Fates well fed and tickled with a glass
of champagne. . . .          *Ever affectionately yours, H. J. L.*

*Beverly Farms, July 30, 1921*
*Dear Laski:* Your letter of the 17th comes this moment, is read
and as usual makes me at once start my answer. You mention the
Lord Chancellor's after dinner speaking—I remember him as a
most amusing man at dinner when there were no speeches. I went
to see him when I was with Leslie Scott whose understrapper he
once was—I believe. But I shouldn't think he was of the calibre
of the great chancellors. You never mention (or rarely) the receipt
of my letters but I suppose you get them. I have answered every
one of yours. As I have not your lightning capacity for gobbling
books I only yesterday finished *The Mediaeval Mind*—with continuing pleasure though I should think that the best part was in
the transitions to and his early part of the middle ages. The account
of the schoolmen seemed to me a little more mechanical and like
what anybody could do—except that I was interested in his impression of Roger Bacon. My recollection (very ancient) is that
Hauréau in his book on those men[1] didn't give much attention to
him. Incidentally I ran through the *Mabinogion,* suggested by
quotations in *Greeks and Barbarians,* as bearing on the natural
magic business. They liked bright colors. Peredur sees a bird that
had been killed by a hawk and on which a raven had settled and
he thinks that his lady's hair is blacker than the raven and her skin
whiter than the snow and her cheeks redder than the blood upon
the snow. So I remember opening in a book at Bryce's once (some
old Irish matters); "If the leaf of the forest had been gold and
foam of the water had been silver, Finn would have given them
all away." I quote from very ancient memory again. These are not
high social themes—but when the cat is away the mouse will play.
Brandeis on the one side and you on the other are not at hand
and so I wander at my own sweet will. Felix's speech[2] I hadn't
heard of, but I had a line from him the other day from Hadlyme,
Connecticut, a place unknown to me. I remember reading a book
in the Home University Library on Socialism by Ramsay Mac-
Donald and that I didn't think much of it, but I couldn't recite

---

[1] Barthélemy Hauréau, *Historie de la philosophie scholastique* (2 vols.,
1872-1880).

[2] At the recent Zionist Convention in Cleveland the unsuccessful efforts
of Judge Mack, Rabbi Stephen S. Wise, Felix Frankfurter, and others to
assure that the Palestine Foundation Fund should be systematically managed
and be applied to social services only and not to the financing of economic
enterprises led to the resignation of many leaders of the Zionist Organization
of America, including Judge Mack, Mr. Justice Brandeis, Rabbi Wise, and
Felix Frankfurter.

upon it now. I mustn't forget to thank you for the book on Conspiracy etc.[3] which I gather from your name pencilled on the
wrapper and the enclosures of reproductions of Méryon comes
from you. I shall have at it forthwith. I forget if I mentioned a
letter from Holdsworth saying he had finished his *History of English Law,* 7 volumes—and inquiring the problems as to sale here.
I couldn't say much—but should suppose libraries, of which there
are a good many, and scholars would buy it. I feel rather sadly
out of things. There is nothing that I want to change—as my job
is enough, but there are so many matters I should like to know
about and don't. Here, of course, I keep very quiet and avoid
society. Even Beveridge I very rarely see. He always has some iron
in the fire that he is full of. I rather think now an appreciation of
Roosevelt but am not sure. I return your exhortation not to work
too much which I fear and believe you do, and I send you my
love.                                      *Aff'ly yours, O. W. Holmes*

> *"Red Lodge," Parsonage Road*
> *Bath Road, Bournemouth, July 31, 1921*

*My dear Justice:* As you will notice, this indicates a holiday. It's a
charming little red-roofed cottage, out of the mainstream of Bournemouth, and yet near enough not to make you feel that life has
passed you by. We came here on Thursday and shall stay a month.
Then Frida and I go to Belgium for ten days with perhaps a side
glance at Paris.

We have had full days since my last letter. First an amazing
week-end with H. G. Wells at his place in Essex. He is a charming
host and improves hourly with acquaintance. He has a rapid, agile,
superficial mind, amazing in its capacity to sum up an argument,
light, easy, and full of unexpected turns. He's very sure, and
usually wrong, in personal judgments. He has no interest in scholarship and *expertise* has no meaning for him. But put up to him
some problem of your own and he is quite certain to see it from
all kinds of unexpected angles. His other visitors would have
amused you—by name Klisliko, the husband was assistant chief of
the Russian Soviet Bureau in London. The wife was English and
a bigger pair of snobs I have never met. They were no more communists than my boots unless communism means an amazing capacity for organised self-indulgence. A Rolls-Royce car of their
own, a chauffeur who was once the cherished possession of the
King of Spain, their main problem the question of how to have
their private armorial bearings engraved on their car, do you wonder that I felt the simple and unadorned ways of the *bourgeoisie*
instinct with a certain ascetic virtue of their own? . . .

[3] Percy Henry Winfield, *The History of Conspiracy and Abuse of Legal
Procedure* (1921).

And you? I don't need to say how eagerly I read your letter.
I understand the boredom with Pascal. But any mind that becomes
attuned to the harmony of an inner faith sooner or later becomes
a public nuisance. I was amused at your travail over Haldane—
I frankly tried the chapter on the state, found no nourishment
there and assumed that it was a good book for an ex-chancellor
and a bad one for a professional. I've read but little these last
days—though I must except a superb book on Shakespere by
Croce[2] the Italian which gave me very great delight. Eke I waded
through the two stout volumes of Ludendorf on the General Staff
and found them, with judicial skipping, very interesting. That says
much for the book, for as a rule, military essays bore me to tears.
Now I'm compensating mind for matter ( *i.e.* work for holidays)
by reading Karl Marx to write this pamphlet on him. On the whole
my regard grows less. A big man clearly—but apart from fire and
thunder little originality save in the mere mass of statements to
prove his thesis.

My love to you both. We're having rain for the first time in
three months.                                        *Ever yours, H. J. L.*

*Beverly Farms, August 11, 1921*
*Dear Laski:* A letter this morning—delightful as ever. I have still
debauched a little on philosophy. After that damned Hegel, Aristotle's *Metaphysics* in the Clarendon Press translation which seems
scholarly. I didn't regret not having the Greek as I don't read old
books for stimulus but for the history of thought. The profound
things one knew—the half devoted to laborious sophisms aren't
worth troubling about. But it always is wonderful to see how A
has made the world think in his terms for 2000 years. One sees in
this book also elements of Christian doctrine and roots of Hegelian
ditto. While waiting for the *Phaedrus* from the Athenaeum I read
Bergson's *Creative Evolution* for the third time. The first time I
felt as I did when I first saw an impressionist picture—the second
time it was difficult and I was controversial. This time it read like
a novel and I was through it in no time—I think he is churning
the void to make cheese, but I think he is very stimulating—somewhat revealing and the author of rather a great world poem. After
the *Phaedrus* I mean to cut philosophy. I think I spoke of the
other books that have counted, especially *The Mediaeval Mind*.
I don't think I mentioned that some time ago I followed your suggestion and sent my book to Asquith with a line telling him not
to bother about writing. I should like to see the book on the Bard.
I shall inquire for it. An English translation of Croce's *Aesthetics*
was given to me some years ago and impressed me at the time.

[2] Presumably Benedetto Croce's *Ariosto, Shakespeare and Corneille* (Ainslie,
tr., 1920).

I envy you your ability to read books that are only material for
your thought with gusto. Books like Hegel and Aristotle bore me
frightfully—I count the pages. The Aristotle wasn't paged—an
aesthetic abomination—so I went through it beforehand counting
and marking the $25^s$ and $100^s$. A. Hill and his wife were here last
night—both very amusing. I never saw a man more improved
than Hill as compared with before the war. His foibles had vanished and he talked like an able sensible humorous man. This
waited to the end of the day that I might get rid of a lot of duty.

Aff'ly yours, O. W. H.

"Red Lodge," Bournemouth, August 7, '21

*My dear Justice:* Here, it seems to be a place where nothing in the
world can happen. It is exquisitely peaceful and equally dull. The
other people provide a little amusement and deepen one's doubts
of the democratic hypothesis. They pick up my books as they lie
about and put them down with a shudder. They ask me whether
I don't find reading a very wearisome occupation. They have no
knowledge of anything except the satisfaction of unexplored desire.
And it is extraordinarily interesting to watch the people who
arouse their comment—A who has a large car, B who lives in
Park Lane, C who has come down here with a French maid. The
disinterested care for intelligence simply isn't existent amongst
them. One man expressed to Frida his astonishment at my occupation. "When I saw him playing tennis, Mrs. Laski, I said to my
wife that it was a pity he was wasting himself in those dull
studies." The main comfort has been the chance to get a good deal
of writing and reading done. Mainly I have been at Karl Marx
with less and less admiration as I go on. What is good is all taken
from Hodgskin and Thompson, the two early English socialists.
The rest has the powerful influence any book would have which
used effectively and for the first time those terrible blue books of
the forties and fifties on the employment of children. Otherwise it
is all phrases of part truth—with a series of semi-mathematical
formulae that are entirely worthless. I agree, mind you, that Marxian socialism is the only kind of socialism that moves men, but I
believe that it moves them less by any actual substance than because it promises a fight and a victory. What amuses me a good
deal is Engels' insistence on Marx's priority as the discoverer of
the labour theory of value. I could produce certainly twenty-five
precursors and show either from quotation or indirect quotation
that Marx had read half of them. Anyhow, I propose to attack
him in this Fabian tract and argue that reformism is by all odds
the safest road to tread. Outside of Marx I've read a good deal of
Hegel—never with comfort. He seems to me like a con-
jurer who produces poorly bred rabbits from a shabby hat. There's

a brilliant insight in the *Philosophy of History*. The *Phemonenology* [*sic*] I thought pure jargon. Altogether it's too damnable static a philosophy to suit a Heracleitan world. Novels, of course, I've read galore. One new adventure I must commend to you—though probably you have read it—*Phineas Finn* and its sequel, *Phineas Redux*. The best political novels anent the sixties that I have read outside of Dizzy. And they have the additional merit of ambling along quite quietly. In the sequel there is the best account of a murder-trial (an acquittal) that I have seen in print. Eke I read a book called *Women in Love* by D. H. Lawrence who, so Violet Asquith[1] told me, was a genius. But quite early in the book the girl hits the young man over the head with a leaden paper weight because physical proximity irritates her and I came to the conclusion that genius glowers too strangely for prosaic minds like mine. I must not forget to add that I have picked up some books here —two implying strange adventures. Months ago I bought T. Fitzherbert *Policy and Religion*, Part 1, 1606 which is, I think, the first considered English answer to Machiavelli. The second part was missing and I despaired even of seeing it separately as it's rare and a little expensive. But it was the first book I put my hands on here and the second was a first edition of Soto, *De Justitia et Jure*. Also the man sold me some first editions of Kipling which I promptly (not giving a damn for Kipling) resold to a London bookseller for fifteen pounds profit. But there is no other bookshop nearer than Exeter, though there is a printshop where I have spent some delectable mornings. I picked up there and sent on to Haldane a print of his grandfather, a Presbyterian divine of the thirties, extraordinarily like Haldane himself, save that his mildness is replaced by a grim flatness suitable to the Calvinist faith. Mainly the man specialises in views of places; but he had some judges (17th century) which I bought for my brother's chambers. One of Ellesmere, and one of Holt C.J. were particularly fine. But here I must stop, for I go off this afternoon for a couple of days to the Isle of Wight to meet Masefield. You shall have a full account. . . . Our love to you both.

*Ever affectionately yours, H. J. L.*


I shall not risk sending
to your temporary address.

*Beverly Farms, August 22, 1921*
*Dear Laski:* A letter from you this morning . . . I also have received within a day or two your *Foundations of Sovereignty, etc.* Some of the essays I knew already and have sung their praises to

---

[1] Asquith's eldest daughter, Lady Violet Bonham Carter.

you—the rest I will read ὡς τάχιστα. I also have received my
friend Einstein's *Tudor Ideals* which I should think that you
would wish to read. The first five chapters suggest to me that it
is a very interesting dealing with imponderables. I don't suppose
that Einstein knows nearly as much as you about the political and
economic side, but he does know about the art and I presume the
literature and I expect to be able to praise heartily the substance.
As to form, the writing disappoints me and I notice some repetition
as to the vagueness of the elements at work, etc. If you read it let
me know what you think. I am through with philosophy for the
moment. After Aristotle I read (3d time) Bergson's *Creative Evolution*—this time finding it as easy as a novel and stimulating
though I didn't believe it. Also Plato's *Timaeus* in the edition and
translation of R. D. Archer-Hind—with an introduction that
seemed to me quite remarkable, written before Bergson and making me wonder if he had read it. Do you know anything about
Mr. Archer-Hind? He seems an impassioned Platonist—and perhaps reads more into Plato than is clearly there but makes you
grateful. Since then I have read *The Story of a Style*—a scalding
criticism of Wilson from the style of his writing—which so far
gratified me. But having drawn and tasted blood Mr. Hale went
in to kill generally and I cared less the further I read. Also he
worked on rather a crude acceptance of Veblen and Freud. Also
a popular book Van Gennep, *La formation des légendes*—with
enough for a spare hour or two, but I haven't had as much time
as I wanted for reading.

I think there are other humbugs in Marx besides those you mention, but won't expatiate now. I agree with what you imply—that
Hegel's contribution was insights not systems (which always is
the case) and in having found more of them in the philosophy of
history than elsewhere. . . . I remember *Phineas Finn* with pleasure from many years ago. If I hadn't so many irons in the fire I'd
get *P. Redux*—but the vacation is flashing by. You have no idea
—really no idea—how fast time goes for the old. You surprise me
by not caring for Kipling. My love to you both.

*Affectionately yours, O. W. Holmes*


*Bournemouth, August 14, 1921*
*My dear Justice:* I need not tell you that your delightful letter was
welcome.[1] And very largely I agreed with what you said of Taylor's
*Middle Ages*. It's a good book, disfigured by inaccurate translation
and a little too much of the medieval love of tearfulness. He's
right about Roger Bacon, on whom you can read a quite excellent

---

[1] *Supra*, p. 275.

book edited by A. G. Little (Oxford). I don't think he understands
sufficiently how vital in the whole story is the conflict between
William of Champeaux and Abelard.[2] The more I go on the more
I realise that the main dividing line of life is between nominalists
and realists. One of the joys of medievalism is the keen perception
of that. Hauréau, whom you mention reminiscently is really excellent. Perspectives wrong at times but always sane and full of
real learning. What the study of the middle ages really wants is
that a man with Hauréau's learning and something of the personal
insight of Sainte-Beuve should take to them. I know very few
books which reach that standard—the nearest approach is Ker's
*Epic and Romance*—one of the books that impress you as a great
achievement the more you read it.

I have, as you can imagine, been having a very peaceful time.
The week-end with Masefield was interesting without quite filling
my expectation. He's a gentle quiet soul, full of unexpected *aperçus*
and a superb judge of letters. I like to hear him read which he
did in a fine sonorous voice that got, if I may make myself intelligible, the very pith out of words. Let me add that what he read
of other people's seemed to me finer than his own. He seemed at
times to be still in that crude stage where the artist believes that
he is true to life because he is painting ugly things. Him apart, I
have seen no one. I did step up to London, but only to find some
references to Karl Marx for my pamphlet. Now I have it well under
way, and he irritates me profoundly. If I were writing sixty thousand words instead of six thousand I should spend much time on
showing up his patent dishonesties. I think that a good deal of
him is really the internal mind reflected outwards as a universal.
He wants to be a great man of action—the times forbid; he
prophesies great action as a compensation, dreaming, as he writes,
that he is in the van of events. I can't extract from him a single
fundamental novelty; there's no history (except bad history), no
psychology, no perception that an economics entirely divorced
from ethics is likely to rebound upon itself. In general, I venture
the criticism that no revolutionist ever perceives what a dull thing
the average man is; he judges by his own enthusiasm and while he
may be ideally right, he is usually practically wrong. That's why
the successful revolutions of history are like that of Cromwell
where you fight for something that comes within the ambit of
every man's immediately personal experience. There, of course,
was Roosevelt's strength; his progressivism wasn't real in the sense

---

[2] William of Champeaux (d. 1121), Professor at Paris and, later, Bishop
of Châlons, was the teacher of Abelard. His pupil, however, abandoned the
extreme realism of Champeaux, developing the doctrine of conceptualism,
intermediate between the realism of Champeaux and the nominalism of
Roscellinus.

of implying basic change; but it was the kind of plea near enough
to your coachman and tailor to make them feel uplifted by it. . . .
I have re-read your *Collected Papers*. I say nothing of them save
this that I am proud indeed to have my name on the page. One
thing struck me—merely for information desired. In the paper on
Agency, you build a great deal on West's *Symboleography*. How
far should West be discounted as himself a civilian and therefore
having a *parti-pris?* I'm not, for I dare not, questioning but merely
eager to know.

A long letter from Lippmann this week telling me that he comes
over to England on September 13 and that he is leaving the *New
Republic* for the New York *World*. I don't know why and I'm
sorry. Daily journalism corrodes the soul; and I think he'll take
from the *N.R.* a vividness of quality that they can't replace in
their circle. I'm thinking for instance of that little birthday tribute
to you.[3] He is the one person of those around Croly who could
have written it. I presume he has good reasons, for he is capable
of infinite deliberation, and his wife's head is as wise as charming.
But Croly will have a bad time. I heard, too, from Felix who
tells me that Pound is coming to Europe next year. Of that, I'm
immensely glad for it seems to me that he needs the kind of
breadth travel confers to achieve his own soul. O! While I think
of it. I propose this winter to do a paper for the *Michigan Law
Review on Martial Law*.[4] Have you ever made any observations
upon it? I don't want to miss them and so give you the trouble of
answering. . . .

My love to you both. Writing's a meagre substitute for talk.

*Ever yours, H. J. L.*

*Beverly Farms, August 27, 1921*
*Dear Laski:* A heavenly letter from you—August 14, (visit to
Masefield, Lippmann coming to Europe &c.). L. will be a great
loss to the *N. R.* certainly. You ask what I know about Martial
law. I remember when entering the Law School ex-C.J. Parker[1]
asked me what I had read in the way of law and I answered with
some satisfaction Benét's *Court-Martial!* Since that time, nought.
All that I have come in contact with is an occasional question
whether a Court Martial was properly constituted under the
Statutes. As to Agency and West I can't say much after thirty

[3] The tribute was published on Holmes's seventy-fifth anniversary, 6 *New
Republic* 156 (March 11, 1916).

[4] No such paper by Laski seems to have been published.

[1] Joel Parker (1795-1875) had been Chief Justice of New Hampshire
before accepting the professorship at the Harvard Law School which he
filled from 1848 until 1868.

years.[2] I think the paper was a contribution because it stated the problem accurately—and it was the result of careful search. West and a note of Godefroi in the *Digest* gave the capstone and the start, but at the time I thought the evidence collected from the reports and statutes made the explanation the most plausible. Note that I referred to native institutions (frithborgh etc.) also. Now I don't know whether anything better has been shown to explain the way in which the doctrine was reconciled with or to legal thinking. Note also that I left open the field of modern law where R.R.'s, factories, &c. shift the expense to the public, so that it becomes a question of what burdens the public shall bear to get what it wants. I was writing and thinking solely of the principle as a principle wholesale—applying to you and me as much as to great business.

As I have written before, I received your book and reread most of what I had read before, and read for the first time, with unqualified pleasure and admiration, "The Foundations of Sovereignty"—I found not a word to criticize. It is so solid that I rather tremble for my friend Einstein if as I hope you look at his *Tudor Ideals*. He is not documented as you are. His faults of style are obvious—he repeats phrases and ideas—yet I hope that you will find insights in the book. I should be really sorry not to believe it a contribution. I think I asked you about Archer-Hind—(translated *Timaeus*—remarkable introduction). With my *adieux* to philosophy and after your book and Einstein's and a little *Life of Adam Smith* by Haldane I am vacant and yesterday was rereading (I have only a translation here) the *Père Goriot*—not quite finished. It makes me rather sick for the wholesome English air—but even in a translation it goes to great heights. The old man's talk about his love for his daughters is superlative. I expect to idle for a few days. I hurry to an end as I must go to the village and there will post this.                    *Aff'ly yours, O. W. H.*

*Hinton Court, Grove Road*
*Bournemouth, 25.VIII.21.*

*My dear Justice:* What a joyous letter![1] You made me take up the *Metaphysics* and I read it without profound emotion. Some brilliant *aperçus*, a good deal of just and hard commonsense and the

<hr>

[2] In his essays on Agency which were reprinted in the *Collected Legal Papers* Holmes in tracing the history of vicarious liability and the fiction that master and servant are one had found the sources in the Roman law of *pater familias* and the system of frankpledge, or Frithborgh, familiar in England at the time of the Conquest. Holmes did not appear to read the passage from West which he quoted as the restatement of a doctrine of the Roman law.

[1] *Supra*, p. 277.

rest (I thought) idle logomachy. Bergson I care nothing for,
though I heard him make a speech at Oxford last year that was a
miracle of graceful diction. But I distrust all these philosophers
who refuse to believe that the rabbit *is* produced from the con-
jurer's hat. B. is a stylist but he isn't a thinker; and metaphors
aren't metaphysics. I agree with your liking for Taylor's *Medieval
Mind* but I want you to read what is by all odds his best book,
*The Classical Heritage of the Middle Ages*. It shows why one suddenly comes upon Duns Scotus and Erigena with a bang and
realises that the dark ages were shot through with light. You'll
like Croce on Shakespere if you read it—in fact no book on him
has given me such undiluted pleasure since I read Bradley's *Shakesperean Tragedy* many years ago. That still seems to me by all
odds the best piece of Shakesperean criticism in the language—
an instance of the English mind at its best with just the dash of
French perceptiveness that adds mustard to the meat. . . .

For the past week the three of us have been staying here with
my people—their country place—and really enjoyed it. There is
much joy over returning as the prodigal and finding that the butler
has extra-special instructions as to the necessary courtesies. In the
result my trousers get pressed every night whether they need it
or no, the extra chauffeur hardly lets me use my legs in the zeal
with which he presses the car on me and, as Frida says, it only
needs their entrance into our room backwards to produce in us
the complete conviction that we are royalty. Winston Churchill
was here the other day and we had a good political scrap. . . .
I had not seen him at a long stretch for many years. Unquestionably he has real genius; but he lacks staying-power and the egoism of his utterance would be appalling if he were not so obviously just a grown-up child. . . . On Saturday I ran down to the
Asquiths for a day and had a long chat and a good dinner. I
thought him a little jaded, but she was as brilliant and tireless as
ever. I taught her a new game of patience and she said, "Mr.
Laski, you have given me one of 8 gifts I have received in my
life." I: "What is that?" She: "A new sensation." He's got a collection of the classics down there which makes my mouth water,
and he knows them too. I met the boy who has his mother's charm,
with a certain steadiness that is obviously the stout Yorkshire
stock of his father. That, I think, exhausts my news save that on
September 6 I go to Belgium for a week. Mainly Frida and I are
going to visit old friends, particularly Oleffe,[2] the painter, whose
work I expect you know, and partly to lecture to the Belgian
trade-unionists (in French) which frightens me a little. I expect
we'll drop down to Paris for a day and see if any books are to be
had. I've a fancy to pick up Mably and Morelly and see what

---

[2] Auguste Oleffe (1867-1931), distinguished Belgian landscape painter.

those XVIIIth century school of nature people are like; and it's ten
years since I was in Paris. Work begins again on October 2 by
which time I hope to have this damned Karl Marx pamphlet out
of the way. He keeps me awake o' nights for the more I get on
with the less admiration I can summon up. I'm sure that popular
praise comes from the width of his invective. I expect by now that
my little collection of papers has come to you and occupied you
for an hour. I needn't tell you what they owe to you, or how happy
the pupil will be if the master pronounce them not unworthy. But
at least they come with all my love.

*Ever affectionately yours, Harold J. Laski*


*16 Warwick Gardens, London, 9.IX.21*
*My dear Justice:* Two quite divine letters from you remind me
that the days since I returned have flown by and that I must
hasten to tell you the news. It is heavenly to be back in my study,
and I find myself patting the backs of familiar volumes with cor-
dial affection. Also I have done much work—arranged all my
courses at the university, written half a dozen book-reviews, finished my edition of Burke, and got all business affairs straightened
out. As a result though bankrupt I am happy; for not even the
misery of paying out one-third of my salary in income-tax has depressed me. Moreover, I find that from Wednesday to Sunday in-
clusive I have no lectures at the School and that opens up adorable prospects of research and writing. But first some details of a
book-hunt that will tickle you. I got a catalogue and marked down
five little items as my prey. I went off to the shop and discovered
to my misery that they were all sold. Well, said I, at least I'll
look round and see if I can find something else. But from the
cartloads of eighteenth [century] divines like Warburton nothing
at all arresting could be gleaned. So in despair I went out and
halted at the penny-box (You know that God-given English institution?) Item one was a dirty but complete copy of Brown's
*Estimate* (see my Locke to Bentham) which I was happy to have;
next turned up Wollaston's *Religion of Nature Delineated.* I had
already bought it in Bournemouth but this copy was once Thomas
Gray's and that gave me a little wiggle of joy. On the other side
was a twopenny box and thence came *Bellarminus Enervatus* by
Amesius (see McIlwain's *James I*) a very rare book and half a
dozen quite scarce leveller tracts including one by John Eliot of
New England Indian fame. I walked on air. I clean forgot two
Americans whom Frida had invited to tea. I forgot to put a rather
large cheque loose in my pocket in the bank. In fact the main
impression on my mind was the certainty that this really is heaven
and that talk of an after-life is largely irrelevant.

Then as to books I have read. First Einstein whom I have read twice. It's the book of a man with most solid knowledge and much perception who is, I think, stronger on the cultural than on the political aspect. I don't think you can satisfactorily describe Tudor politics in terms of abstract and imponderable formulae. The thing is more complicated than he makes out and he divorces the political side from the religious too much. Off-hand I should say that three Tudor political books refer to a state as such considered as *selbstandigkeit*—the rest have all a semi-ecclesiastical background. And in the result the book doesn't show clearly enough that an English political ideal came from the Reformation. I don't think he emphasises enough the growing import of Puritanism (1560-1600) and he makes a little too much of literary evidence. I miss names that I ought to see—Tyndale, Goodman, Edward Fox, Stephen Gardiner, Bekinsau. There ought to be estimates of certain special types like Robert Parsons who is the Renaissance bravo turned religious fanatic and at every point a typical Tudor. But it's a refreshing and stimulating piece of work, and from Parts II and IV I have learned a great deal. I will write him a special note of eulogy. I ought to add that I think he unnaturally divides his subject and so lends himself to unnecessary repetition. Archer-Hind of whom you write gratefully was father of a friend of mine killed in the war. He was a first-rate Cambridge don who did too much tutoring and too little writing and his name is in most Cambridge editions of classics as one who offered generous improvement. He was a loveable old fellow, rather crabbed, very dogmatic, very mystical at bottom and alive to nothing after the death of Polybius. I don't think he ever showed his full powers; but I imagine that he was the type of person who finds publication very difficult. . . .

My warm love to you both.                    *Ever yours, H. J. L.*

*Beverly Farms, September 7, 1921*

*Dear Laski:* Your letter delightful as usual was at once followed up by me—I went to town this morning and got from the Athenaeum Taylor's *Classical Heritage* and Bradley's *Shakespearian Tragedy* —Croce I didn't take as it was a 14 day book and although I should have read it long before that I don't like to be expected. Probably I shall buy it. Meantime I have been twiddling—since your book. I already have told you that I thought the first one (new, as I take it) masterly.[1] In that connection I have been somewhat worried. E. F. Gay for the N. Y. Evening *Post* asked me to notice the volume saying that the published comment on your work had been unsatisfactory &c. I wrote back that I was

---

[1] The first essay in *The Foundations of Sovereignty* (1921), bearing that title, had not been previously published.

distracted by affectionate friendship—but that I hadn't supposed that there had been any want of appreciation by the most competent. I declined on the ground that I decline all outside work and more especially that I didn't consider myself competent to criticise your social ideals without a study for which I hardly have an opportunity. You do not feel that I was wanting in friendly zeal I hope—I do not think so myself.

I said I have been twiddling—I made my first acquaintance with Sallust! And in a translation! that I found in the house. S. makes you wonder what the Catiline side was—especially when you notice that none of his men would split, although offered pardon and reward and that they all died in their tracks. I dare say we shouldn't care for either side much—on a fair statement. 2) Shelley's prose—new to me—*Defense of Poetry* a lovely rhapsody, and letters—good. I had hoped that S. was a dd fool—as it would be contrary to theory for the creator of his divine mists to be gifted in articulate thought. He is not a fool by a good deal, though the thought is not disconcertingly powerful. He was naturally followed by Byron's letters—which in small form I took to read in the cars—but now I must follow your lead. I don't know why it is that I have read so little—and yet have been busy all the time. Bryce comes here 13th-15th. On 24th to Touraine— 28th Washington.                               *Aff'ly yours, O. W. H.*


*16 Warwick Gardens, 26.IX.21.*
*My dear Justice:* First a word about that review. I need not tell you that I would rather have a good word about my book from you than from any other living person; but, almost equally I should be very angry with myself if I thought that I was even an innocent cause of adding to your burdens. What you wrote to me about it more than suffices for friendship and everything else. *Voilà.*

. . . last Tuesday I went to lunch with Morley who had Rosebery along and there was great talk. Morley and R. had a great scrap about Ireland and Morley laid down admirable dicta about liberty in the Actonian manner. He was also full of fine enthusiasm about Leslie Stephen whom he had just been rereading and you can imagine that I was adamant chorus. I horrified him by insisting that except for the *Areopagitica* Milton wrote intolerable prose; he thought that it had all along a profound majesty. And I said, Morley *dissentiente,* that he wasted time as Latin Secretary. M. has a curious fondness for the man of action, probably because he is himself so natural a doctrinaire. I dissent, for in long-term value, Aristotle or Bacon or Darwin, on the bad side Rousseau, seem to me worth fifty Napoleons. Rosebery was rather tragic—out of heart and touch with things, rather like fine faded velvet, miserable at events, and incapable of inner harmony. He's a beautiful person, with quite obvious gifts of leadership; but he was an immovable πoῦ στῶ and he is an irretrievable Mid-Victorian. . . . I have been writing first book reviews and then my piece on Marx, of which I have about half done—the difficult biographical part. It is great fun for I manage to smuggle in the criticism in asides and parentheses so that it almost appears as part of the doctrine. Really I loathe the fellow even while I recognise his powers. And I don't doubt that he really did want a tip-top revolution with all the blood possible. Also I plume myself on the discovery of some sweet little inconsistencies in the *Communist Manifesto*—hitherto, I think, unnoticed. At the beginning is a vast eulogy of the middle class with an emphasis on its tremendous achievements. Then follows an insistence that it has no brains, *quia* Marx wants the workers to slip in. All the communists of the world will arise and call me cursed when this appears. . . . I have read much in bed of Bayle, always with profound admiration. For the critical mind at its best, I think his proof that Languet wrote the *Vindiciae*[1] is as good in its way as Bentley's disproof of the Phalaris business.[2] Which reminds me to ask you if you ever read Volumes II and III of Sandys, *History of Classical Scholarship*. It really is a joy, particularly the sections dealing with the Renaissance and the 18th century. If you think the classics worth six dollars please plunge and let me hear the result. I have enjoyed it hugely.

Next week you shall have a real letter. Walter Lippmann comes tonight, and on Saturday Frida and I go down to H. G. Wells, to meet whom? You would not guess in your wildest dreams. 'Tis Charlie Chaplin. I think no better test of my Catholicity of temper could be offered than that Wells wants him to know me. I shall retaliate by sending him to see you in Washington—that is if he is as interesting as Wells declares he is. At any rate you shall have a full account.

Our united love and good wishes to you both. I heard from Brandeis yesterday. He spoke of his eagerness to be at work with you again.                              *Ever affectionately yours, H. J. L.*

[1] Pierre Bayle (1647-1706) in a supplement to his *Dictionaire historique et critique* (1698) elaborately supported the contention that the *Vindiciae contra Tyrannos* (1579) was written by Hubert Languet (1518-1581). Laski later wrote of the problem of the disputed authorship in the introduction to his edition of the *Vindiciae*, giving considerable credence to the contention of others that the true author was Duplessis-Mornay; *Defense of Liberty against Tyrants* (Laski, ed., 1924), p. 57 *et seq.*

[2] Richard Bentley (1662-1742) in his *Dissertation on Phalaris* (1697) conclusively established that letters previously ascribed to Phalaris, the tyrant of Agrigentum, were written by another, hundreds of years after the death of Phalaris.

*Hotel Touraine, Boston*
*Tuesday, September 27, 1921*

*Dear Laski:* This I fear will be but a poor bulletin *in transitu.* We have been here since Saturday and start for Washington straight through, tomorrow—if we are waked in time and nothing breaks. I am, you may remember, a nervous traveler in the matter of catching trains. Frankfurter and his wife dined with us Sunday evening, much to our pleasure, and last night Bob Barlow and we went to the movie of *The Three Musketeers* with great edification. In the main we are quiet. There are a lot of things I have had it in mind to speak about but shan't remember I fear. One was Bradley's *Shakespearean Tragedy,* which you put me on to—I thought it *too* thorough. I hardly can admire a man for such meticulous study, and then too it becomes a religion—and things loom too big. I can't feel that interest in the character of Iago for instance, or think the play *Othello* other than disagreeable. It is annoying to have a man say to the audience, "I am a villain," and then proceed with tricks which but for happy accidents, always on the villain's side, would come to manifest grief—to the end—inviting your attention to the machinery. I may have spoken of this before and if so I told you probably of the engraving by Visscher—of a full blood negro which he calls *The Moor*—a later illustration of the use of the word of the most convincing kind. One accepts the union of O and D, black and white, because one has been so accustomed to it. Otherwise it would disgust most of us. In short I shouldn't reread *Othello* except in connection with a criticism. Your account of your finds in the penny box &c. (I never heard of it before—of course rows of books marked with a small price are familiar) fills me with sympathetic delight. I must have mentioned Bryce's two nights with us I think—very pleasant and old timey. He is very alert and all round, but has out-lived his superlatives, I should think—which I think a loss. Perhaps I should rather say I doubt if he ever had them. Beveridge and his wife dined with us one night and B. talked well when Bryce questioned. Beveridge still is tormented by the choice—Senate or another book. I think he will be happier in politics—and whichever he chooses probably will repent it, at times.[1] He surprised me also by seeming bothered over the question of the future life. He asked me if I believed in it and if I was a Christian—two questions that astonished me—and when I said I saw no ground for believing in a future life—thought that then we were the victims of a cruel joke. I told him he retained a remnant of theology and thought of himself as a little God over against the universe instead of a cosmic ganglion

---

[1] Beveridge received the Republican nomination to the Senate in 1922 but was defeated by his Democratic opponent in the election.

—that any one was free to say I don't like it, but that it was like damning the weather—simply a declaration that one was not adapted to the environment—a criticism of self not of the universe —all of which commonplaces it seemed odd to find myself repeating.

Thinking that I remembered the *New Republic* speaking of Eliot, presently unknown to me, as the greatest going poet I, or rather my wife, after my refusal bought a little volume. It reminded me of Bill Hunt (the artist) to a pupil—"Oh, I see you want to do something damned smart right off." I am not prepared yet to say it is not pay dirt—but I suspect a good deal of watering will be needed to get any gold. How many try short cuts to fame—and there ain't none. I was pleased with the moral of an article in the *N.R. Plus de Jazz*.[2] I write with difficulties in an almost waned light—but this will take you my love—Till next time.

*Aff'ly yours, O. W. H.*

*Washington, D.C., October 9, 1921*

*Dear Laski:* Your letter of the 26th came yesterday and I snatch a moment of the relative repose of Sunday morning to answer— I thank you for your kind words about the review. It would have driven me mad to have it on my mind under the avalanche of work that is on us, but still I worried. We are fairly started—arguments after the usual call on the President last week and a conference yesterday from 12 to close upon 5 that left us pretty tired but disposed of a good lot of stuff. Taft I think will do well as CJ—the executive details, which, as I have said, are the matters upon which the C.J. most counts as such, will be turned off with less feeling of friction and more rapidly, I think, than with his predecessor, especially after he had become so infirm. As to opinions we shall see. I heartily agree with you about Milton's prose—and it wasn't simply the universal fact that no one had yet learned to write prose well. My recollection is that a fair number of people before M's time had done it—*e.g.* Ascham. I agree on the other hand with Morley in reverence for men of action. Jim Hill is my favorite type, not from knowledge of Hill but from a theoretic construction of what he must have been— probably my reason is similar to that of Morley. For when it comes to the question of effect I said in my book that I didn't think it absurd to say that Kant after a century counted for more than Napoleon.[1] But not being a man of affairs and affairs being half

---

[2] The article by Clive Bell, rejoicing that the age of jazz had nearly run its course (28 *New Republic* 92, 94; Sept. 21, 1921), had spoken of T. S. Eliot as "a poet of uncommon merit and unmistakably in the great line."

[1] In "The Path of the Law," *Collected Legal Papers* 167, 202.

at least of life I look up to those who have profound insights and
foresights and successfully act on them. Naturally however it is a
joy to me to see Aristotle put contemplation at the top. I know
not Sandys's *History of Classical Scholarship*—I trembled when
I thought I read in your ms. volumes 11 and 19 but concluded
that it is II and III and the price six dollars indicates that it is
not as long as the *Encyclopedia Britannica*. But no reading for me
at present, alas. Brandeis called on me the first afternoon and his
companionship is my great comfort. He said wise things that I
couldn't have said. Already we are in the field—a labor case that
has been argued 3 times and in which I prepared what then was
a dissent has now taken the form of memoranda by Pitney and me
—but I don't know how the boys will go—I only circulated mine
yesterday P's having been handed out two days before.[2] What I
had to say was nothing much—a repetition of the dissent in
*Vegelahn* v. *Guntner* 25 years ago[3]—noting the tendency in that
direction. By good luck a decision of the English Court of Appeals
—1921 3 KB 40 [4] has just come out in which Scrutton refers to
my opinion as one of the best statements and agrees with it. F.P.
had just sent me a note of his on it in the *L. Q. Review*.[5] I regret
to say that on quite a different matter Pollock has joined the vulgar
—he says 'I do confess that I divine rather than read the last part
of many words. *Desinit in piscem?*' [6] (apropos of my handwriting).
I never have seen Charlie Chaplin in a movie. Last night my wife
was noticing that there had been some show with him in it and
regretting our missing it. I shall be curious to hear about him. I
shall look with great interest for your essay on Marx. My recollection is that he has the usual confusion, of which S. Webb was guilty
in his earlier years, between ownership and consumption and also
that he skipped at will without notice from world welfare in a
narrow sense to English and back as it suited his argument. His

[2] The reference to these arguments indicates that the case was *American
Steel Foundries* v. *Tri-City Central Trades Council*, 257 U.S. 184 (Dec. 5,
1921). As finally disposed of, the majority opinion was by Taft, C. J.,
Brandeis, J., concurring in the substance of the opinion, and Clarke, J., dissenting without opinion. The Court there held that Federal courts could not,
under the Clayton Act, enjoin persuasion through peaceful picketing whether
by employees or by associated workers. On the same day in which final
arguments were made in the *Steel Foundries* case, reargument was also heard
in *Truax* v. *Corrigan*, 257 U.S. 312 (Dec. 19, 1921). Taft, C. J., for a
majority there held that a state statute depriving state courts of jurisdiction
to prohibit picketing was unconstitutional under the Fourteenth Amendment.
Holmes delivered a short dissenting opinion. More elaborate dissents were
delivered by Pitney, J., and Brandeis, J.

[3] 167 Mass. 92, 104 (1896).

[4] *Ware and De Freville, Ltd.* v. *Motor Trade Association.* The case was
not cited in any of the opinions in the *Steel Foundries* and *Truax* cases.

[5] 37 *L. Q. Rev.* 395 (October 1921).

[6] Ovid, *Metamorphoses*, IV, 727: "Cauda desinit in piscem": where his
tail being smallest ends in fish.

magnificent tone of patronage towards great names, as *bourgeois* intelligences, tickled me. You no doubt remember that Proudhon treated Marx as a charlatan. And my impression is that Proudhon had profounder insights than his rival. My love to you both. Your letters give me companionship and joy.    *Aff'ly yours, O. W. Holmes.*

*16 Warwick Gardens, 18.X.21*

*My dear Justice:* . . . I note your tinge of disappointment in Bryce. I think I have told you that I found him singularly wanting in the ultimate qualities—a third-rate mind with first-rate gestures. He has immense width, but not, I think, depth. I find that the people here for whom I have the most respect, Morley, Haldane, Birrell, all dislike him intensely; and Morley particularly emphasised to me his utter lack of adaptability when he found himself in the cabinet.[1] One incident is too precious to be lost. In 1906 they had a soldier before the cabinet to discuss the fortification of the Nile Delta. The soldier said it was practically unpassable. 'Nonsense,' said Bryce, 'it was crossed twice two thousand years before Christ.' The soldier, says Morley, was buried quietly next day.

My own news is scant because of full days. The chief incident was our week-end with Wells to meet Charlie Chaplin. Wells was in great form, as always down on the classics, eager to teach universal history to everybody, critical of all politicians, full of his American trip. I promised him, by the way, that you would have him to dinner. His Washington address will be % the New York *World* office. I am sure he will give you a most jolly and stimulating two hours. Chaplin was a complete surprise. In the first place he was as finished a gentleman as you could wish to meet. And unlike any other actor I have ever met, he had no desire to talk about himself. He was modest and simple and obviously sincere. He was full of ideas, and (since I largely agreed with them) very wise ideas. On the Saturday night he gave us a private show, and I have never come nearer to sheer death from laughter. It was pure artistry and of an exquisitely finished kind. That week-end apart, I have had lunch with Morley, mainly on Ireland, and dinner with Haldane. The latter is the most sane of all political people and he sees that the root of the mischief is an untamed democracy full of desires but with no realisation that there is no short-cut to universal prosperity. Like all of them he has an amiable vanity which takes the quite harmless form of a belief that his philosophical work is important; but otherwise he is as honest and realistic in his thinking as any I've met. My main disappointment, indeed, is Graham

---

[1] In 1906 Bryce was Chief Secretary for Ireland, a post which after considerable criticism, he surrendered to become American Ambassador in December 1907. Morley at this time was Secretary of State for India.

Wallas, who spent Sunday with us. He is very loveable and charming, but he seems to me totally without the creative instinct. I
expect you have read his last book[2]—plenty of shrewd *aperçus*
but nothing approaching a synoptic view. Yet he seriously thinks
that political salvation is in that volume and is quite incapable of
considering alternatives. Also I have seen something of Sankey J.
—always with great pleasure. He has a fine, incisive mind, great
power of penetration and a width of interest which (please pardon
me) is quite unusual in a judge. And outside Haldane he's the
one lawyer of importance I have met here who realises the vast
superiority of American legal education to our own. But law reform
must wait till Pound comes over this Christmas. Then I hope we
can start some real criticism.

Bookhunting very largely in suspense this last fortnight, through
work. But I did pick up a nice first edition (1607) of Cowell's
*Interpreter* for ten shillings and a goodly number of review copies
have come my way—one book, Buckland on *Roman Private Law*
—being really admirable. But Thursday week is the red letter day
of my life for I then bid at auction for a copy of Goldast's *Monarchia* and I am selling all I have to secure it. There's been no
copy on the market since 1889, and it has everything in that I
want. . . .                                    *Ever affectionately yours, Harold J. Laski*


*Washington, D.C., October 30, 1921*
*Dear Laski:* Your letter has come and has been read this moment
—just as I had my shoes put on after breakfast. I was beginning
to wonder whether your name should be pronounced Lazy or *Lasse*
—but find that your condition has been like mine. The work at the
beginning of the term with 100 *certioraris* to examine was considerable and this last week I was nearly mad over a case not in-
trinsically very difficult but made so by a chaos of a record without
index and briefs with inadequate references. However, all my work
is done, my two cases[1] distributed and returned approved by all but
Pitney, who always takes his time, and the C.J. who seems not
to have taken to heart what I said to him as to the duty of a
prompt return. Probably he has his hands full—but he has had
time to circulate his first opinion,[2] fluent and very sufficient without
poignancy—I think he will do very well. This week of adjournment
promises a little time for reading. How I wish I could have you

---

[2] *Our Social Heritage* (1921) had been reviewed by Laski in 29 *Nation
and Athenaeum* 60 (April 9, 1921).

[1] *Marine Railway and Coal Co.* v. *United States*, 257 U.S. 47; *Springfield
Gas & Electric Co.* v. *Springfield*, *id.* 66 (Nov. 7, 1921).

[2] On November 7, 1921, Mr. Chief Justice Taft delivered the Court's
opinion in two cases: *Yazoo & Mississippi Valley Rd.* v. *Clarksdale*, 257 U.S.
10; *Hildreth* v. *Mastoras*, *id.* 27.

here to tell me just what I need for salvation. I have finished Le Bon, *Les opinions et les croyances*, begun in the train, with some satisfaction—not the flash of lightning that he seems to think it but with enough good sense to make me wish that all educated persons might read it—also Boutroux—*Contingency of the Laws of Nature*, a translation sent to me by Cohen last spring—written a good while ago, I gather—difficult to follow in places because one does not know the sense in which words are used—but I should think probably reducible mainly to the proposition that you can't prove quantitative relations between the world of matter and the world of mind and that if you try hard you can believe in free will—Providence—God etc. Probably Cohen sent it because of its backing up, as far as it goes, his insistence that the invariability of natural laws and the persistence of force is a faith like another— which I am quite willing to accept. Yesterday p.m. Brandeis sent me in a lecture by Toynbee—*The Tragedy of Greece*—I think it was called. I have returned it. I read it twice—as I thought it had something quite big in its conception. He treats every civilization as a work of art—the Greek as the best to study, because it is finished and has left magnificent expression. He calls the whole history from 1000 B.C. to 800 A.D. that of Greek Civilization, as he regards the Roman Empire as part of it and he nails it by quoting great things. It is a Clarendon Press pamphlet well worth getting to my mind. I shall try for it if I don't forget. In your absence I don't know but I shall fall to gnawing some of the bones that we have always with us—*Hamlet* or some touch of Latin. As to Bryce and his anecdote, Mrs. Holmes and I incline to surmise that Bryce was trying a bit of Scotch wit on the boys and was taken seriously—*Hein?* My wife says he is a dear old grandfather who knows more facts than any man. He certainly gives openings to affection, however little he may have been available as a col- league. I am interested by what you say of Chaplin. Certainly I don't remember any actress who didn't want to talk about herself. I haven't seen many actors—and haven't wanted to—for the reason that you indicated. I shall see Wells no doubt if he comes to Wash- ington—as I did on his former visit. Many interruptions—the last my wife suggests that we can see a Charlie Chaplin movie tomor- row p.m.—to which I say yes. I never have seen him. Others—a dame from Seattle: "Will you dine with us at the New Willard tonight?" "Sorry, engaged." A younger dame: "Can I come this p.m. and bring the baby for you and Mrs. Holmes to see?"—"Sorry, I have to be out." Shade of Michael Wigglesworth I revere thee. He wrote a poem on infant damnation. It is hard to keep any thread with the telephone bell ringing every other minute. I am thinking of starting a new ideal—to live to 90 (*ninety*—not go), call the old job finished, and start this as a new one (continuing however to work on the bench, if only as a means of survival). It seems as if a man must reach 90 to be really old. But I guess it is pretty hard sledding to get there. Well, my delightful lad, I must leave thee—but with all good messages—and hopes for another word soon. My love to you both.        *Aff'ly yours,* O. W. Holmes

*16 Warwick Gardens, 29.X.21.*

*My dear Justice:* Woe is me! My precious Goldast was bought by Sir Leicester Harmsworth (who cannot read Latin) at forty pounds, I being the underbidder. Probably it was a good job for me, as I should have had to sell cherished possessions to make up my bid, but there is undeniable bitterness of spirit in being beaten by a Harmsworth. . . . did I, I wonder, tell you of the profound admiration I have conceived for the Spanish Jesuit legists of the sixteenth century—especially for Soto, Suarez, and Sanctarelli.[1] They have all the refinement and precision of a man like Challis[2] together with a wide philosophic sweep quite beyond the latter's ambition. And it's intensely interesting to watch how all their main propositions are destructive of Jesuitism and then to see how carefully little loopholes are left for the entrance of papalistic doctrine. Suarez is of course straight Dominican Aquinas, but touched with Renaissance fervour.

. . . I dined . . . with Haldane and gleaned from him a very good narrative of the war of 1914; Grey was there, very charming and not very well-informed, but with that faint aroma of the great Whig families clinging to him which I always find most attractive. On Tuesday I lunched with Asquith and we had a great scrap at the table over the future of Oxford. At bottom he likes things as they are and fought ardently against my insistence that there isn't a man in Oxford who knows how to teach (a) political philosophy (b) psychology (c) economics. But when I asked for names, what emerged was a complete bankruptcy, and I left with the feeling that he is living on his memories of the Jowett days which he finds satisfactory merely because he was himself successful. On Thursday George Young and his wife[3] (Ilbert's daughter) dined here. You remember him as a young *attaché* at our embassy in Washington. He is just back from Russia and was deeply interesting because he

---

[1] The reference is presumably to Antonio Santarelli (1569-1649), Jesuit theologian and author of *Tractatus de Haeresi, Schismate, Apostasia* (1625).

[2] Henry W. Challis (1841-1898), English conveyancer; author of a standard treatise, *Law of Real Property* (1885).

[3] George Young (1872-1952), later Sir George Young, in his early career had been an *attaché* in Washington and after his marriage to the daughter of Sir Courtenay Ilbert (1841-1924) returned as *chargé d'affaires* in 1906. From 1920 to 1924 he was an Expert Delegate on the British mission to Russia. Later he wrote a number of books on international problems.

is not only a very accurate observer, but is wont to take long views. He is impressed both by the ability of the Bolsheviks and by the fact that outside the towns the old motives of a dominantly agrarian civilisation defy all the devices of pressure and propaganda. He was very taken with Trotsky who has, he said, a Napoleonic flair for military organisation; and Lenin, he thinks, impressed him as the most obviously great man he had ever met. The rest, he thought, you could meet in any government—rogues, fanatics, able silent men, great orators without the habit of the desk. I wish you could have heard his talk.

I hope the Court flourishes. But from the list of causes I venture to foresee historic dissents.

My love and Frida's to you both.

*Ever affectionately yours, Harold J. Laski*

*Washington, D.C., November 13, 1921*

*Dear Laski:* Your letter telling of your disappointment as to Goldast came yesterday. It reminds me of one of my own on a much smaller scale as to price, though I now doubt if it was in value. When Gray J.[1] cut me out from the magnificent first edition of the *Grand Coutumier* of Normany [*sic*] (I forget whether it was spelt with an S.) I was a young lawyer and had no money. He said he would leave it to me, but of course didn't. Had I known what I know now I would have made him pay more for it. I am much interested in what you say of the Spanish jurists. When Canon Sheehan was dying he gave me Suarez whom he pronounced an original man—I thought of reading him one summer but was discouraged by the precious time it would take. I think it was while you were on hand to pump newer blood into me. Well, we have been having doings here that somewhat disturbed the even current. First came the unknown soldier.[2] I had been disgusted by the vulgarities of the bogus sentiment, the odious emptiness of reporters' talk that seems an echo of the popular mind. But when I saw the coffin borne into the great rotunda of the Capitol, which became beautiful and impressive in the dim twilight, and afterwards saw the miles of people marching through, three abreast, from early morning into the next day, I realized that a feeling may be great notwithstanding its inability to get itself expressed. I allowed representations of danger to the aged to persuade me not to go to Arlington and I am glad that I did although I was the only judge absent, as it would have been very trying to me. I had a fine view of the procession from the War Department. That was

---

[1] See, *supra*, p. 268.
[2] The burial of the Unknown Soldier of World War I took place in the Arlington Cemetery on November 11.

on Friday. Yesterday I went with the others and my wife to the opening of the disarmament conference, and was moved and delighted by the dignity with which Hughes did his part,[3] and by his proposition which, speaking as as [*sic*] an outsider, seems to show that we mean business. Then at 2 we went to our Conference and I hope that quiet will reign once more—I am bothered by not quite knowing what to do with various letters of introduction, but I shall manage them somehow. I thought I would wait until Wells gets here before trying for him.[4] To return to the unknown soldier I couldn't help thinking how on the one side was a little life, probably like thousands of others, and on the other the passion of a people, striving to meet, and stretching away into the infinite, eternally drawing nearer, but like parabola and asymptote never quite meeting—for he will never know and we shall never know.

I have read nothing but records since I last wrote—though I listened last night to some stirring passages from the life of a quasi-schoolmarm among the mountain people (in Tennessee?)—boys brought up like the old highlanders in an atmosphere of feuds and killing—and having their ballads too—and I have, to be sure, read the best reading there is—catalogues of things that make one's mouth water. But you are wrong to tell people to send their catalogues to me, much as I like them. In view of my age I almost never buy now. Age suggests to me what I may have mentioned— that I think of establishing a new ideal—to reach 90 if I can— call the job finished, though I shall keep on working. This last year has had such a series of notices as I never could have expected and seems to mark a wind up. But there is a chance to figure as a survivor. What think you? With which twaddle I close for the moment. My love to you both. You continue to give me great joy —and I am proud of you.                    *Aff'ly yours, O. W. Holmes*


                                        *16 Warwick Gardens, 23.XI.21.*
*My very dear Justice:* A long and delightful letter from you this morning reminds me of my recent negligence. But I have been overwhelmed with work—three university lectures, besides a host of public meetings—all on adult education—so that I seem to have spent most of my time these last days in trains. And I have had the very hard job of refusing four different requests that I stand for Parliament at the next election—hard because when a group of working men pay their own expenses to London to tell you that they want you for their member it is very difficult not to agree. But I weighed the agony of going to the House and finding myself

---

[3] Hughes at the time was Secretary of State and served as the Chairman of the Disarmament Conference.

[4] H. G. Wells was at the Conference as a press correspondent.

in a hopeless minority against the possibility of doing a really big
book on the theory of politics and I feel pretty certain that the
latter is at present more important. . . . there have been some
interesting dinners. One with Morley to meet Winston was amusing.
Morley very quiet, but Winston full of wild exuberance of spirit,
cursing those whom he dislikes—*e.g.*—L. George—with a carefree indiscretion which amazed me. Morley, when he had gone,
said to me that Winston was so hungry for fame that nothing stood
in the way of notoriety. He amused me by his heroics against
Russia. Property was sacred, a man with an income was an asset
to the country and so on . . . Then a dinner with the Webbs to
meet the Russian Soviet representative[1]—a most able fellow, full
of insight and with a most obvious flair for organisation. Webb is
really astounding. He has finished simultaneously a big book on
the Cooperative Movement and one on the history of the English
prison system. I have read them both in MS and I thought them
quite admirable.

. . . I have read (or re-read) Ian Hamilton's *Soul and Body of
an Army* which I think very brilliant, the best account of military
organisation I know. . . .

And, like all great dramatists, I reserve my titbit for the last. A
month ago I received £70 on account of O. W. H. *Collected
Papers* from Harcourt. As you know, I regard that as a trust and
looked round for the right object. I found a student who was the
sole support of a mother and young sister who was killing himself
to get a degree and keep them alive at the same time. Result
of course pneumonia. So I financed them in the convalescence,
sent him away for ten days, put him in for his exam and found
yesterday from the examiners that he'd got a brilliant first and
had done so well in banking that McKenna[2] had agreed to start
him at 400 pounds a year in the head office. So if you had not
stepped in vicariously the boy would have had to postpone his
finals and drag on miserably for another year. One good deed at
least to your account (this between ourselves). . . .

My love to you both.          *Ever affectionately yours, H. J. L.*


                                    *Washington, D.C., December 9, 1921*
*Dear Laski:* Your letter of '23 xi 21' (wondrous) came yesterday
and as always I go off bang when you pull the trigger. Of course
the first thing is the suggestion that you stand for parliament! It
may be that I am too timid and cautious, but I greatly rejoice that
you did not yield to the temptation. Of course I don't know the

---

[1] Leonid Krassin was the Chairman of the Russian Trade Delegation to
Great Britain.
[2] Presumably Reginald McKenna, *supra*, p. 107.

conditions but it seems to me that, for the present at least, you
are in the right place now, and that the big book is better both as
a contribution to the world and as a form of self-expression. I put
self-expression last out of deference to popular speech, but I think
it first. As you know, I think nature takes care of our altruism for
us, and that a man who thinks he has been an egotist all his life,
if he has been a true jobbist, (you remember my club?)[1] will find
on the Day of Judgment that he has been a better altruist than
those who thought more about it. I read your article on Christian
Socialism[2] with the pleasure I always get from your writing, but
with a touch of regret at the tone that you hint from time to time
that the existing order is wicked. The inevitable is not wicked. If
you can improve upon it all right, but it is not necessary to damn
the stem because you are the flower. As it seems to me that all
society has rested on the death of men and must rest on that or
on the prevention of the lives of a good many, I naturally shrink
from the moral tone. In short I believe in Malthus—in the broad
—not bothering about details. I believe that F. has sent for Ian
Hamilton's book—according to your recommendations. Wells dined
here the other night with the Japanese Shogun.[3] The latter left
early and Wells remained and talked as usual delightfully, sug-
gestively, and dramatically. I hope he enjoyed it half as much as
I did. Your Mr. Nevinson I expect will call next Sunday p.m. and
I have seen one or two others—but I have not bothered about the
illustrious who are in town. I haven't had a word with Balfour. I
don't feel as if he would inspire any great intellectual interest in
me—and as to lions—Foch, Briand &c.—I leave them to the lion
hunters. Some of the fashionable dames seem to like to show their
importance by saying that they have seen a good deal of A, B or
C or all of them. . . . I am glad to hear that you have received
some cash from the publishers and as to the disposition of it
regard it as your affair. I haven't heard from them but assume
from what you say and the exhaustion of the first impression that
the sale has been tolerably satisfactory. That book, coupled perhaps with my birthday last March, has brought out such a set of
notices that I feel that my life has had its reward—the only one
I care for—in the assurance from those voices I value that I have
more or less done what I desired but I did not dare to expect.
I so tremble at the thought, that I wish I could be declared
Emeritus—my job finished—and the rest an irresponsible appendix.

[1] For a fuller published description of Holmes's "society of the jobbists,"
see Shriver, *Justice Oliver Wendell Holmes, His Book Notices and Uncollected Letters and Papers* (1936), 178.

[2] A review of C. E. Raven's *Christian Socialism* (1921), 29 *New Republic*
49 (Dec. 7, 1921).

[3] Possibly Holmes's friend Count Kentaro Kaneko (1853-1942).

I believe I suggested a substitute ideal—merely to be a survivor and reminiscent—but alas there is no such pause possible—'Does the road lead [*sic*] uphill all the way? Yes—to the very end.' And one must still take one's chances.

I have to scrabble to an untimely end. I called last night on Princess Bibesco, daughter of Mrs. Asquith—of whom perhaps something hereafter. I was very glad to see her at last.

I note some further recommendations of yours and wish I could keep on.                              *Affectionately yours, O. W. Holmes*

*16 Warwick Gardens, 8.12.21.*

*My dear Justice:* You can imagine what a sense of relief we all have over the success of the Irish negotiations.[1] It's a load such as only the Armistice in my lifetime has taken off our minds. Two little pieces of secret history about it will (for your own consumption) interest you. For the last month I have been seeing Winston Churchill weekly about negotiations and urging as best I could the need of peace.[2] Last Wednesday he told me that things were likely to break down upon the problem of allegiance. So I talked at length upon this as a quantitative problem which need not be met in the formal way of the past. The real thing was to get the safeguards of function which came not from an oath exacted, but a conscience satisfied. He seemed impressed, and when I was going asked me to drop in the next day. When I arrived he had the Attorney-General[3] with him and asked me to repeat my argument. This I did with amplification, and for 1 and ½ hours we argued up and down. Finally the A-G asked if I could put my views (with which he disagreed) into a formula. I suggested an oath 'to the Irish State and the King in Parliament as the head of the British Commonwealth.' Churchill was very surprised and said it was a new approach. Then explore it, I said: but the A-G was very hostile and I left with a sense of hopelessness. On the Saturday I went to town and had a hurried summons from Winston who said that Lloyd George liked my formula and could I develop the

---

[1] The negotiations between the British Negotiations Committee and the Sinn Fein delegates had come to a successful conclusion on December 6 after settlement of disagreement concerning the oath of allegiance. The form of oath finally adopted for members of the Irish Parliament was as follows: "I, ————, do solemnly swear true faith and allegiance to the constitution of the Irish Free State as by law established, and that I will be faithful to his Majesty King George V, his heirs and successors by law, in virtue of the common citizenship of Ireland with Great Britain, and her adherence to, and membership of, the group of nations forming the British Commonwealth of Nations."

[2] Winston Churchill was among the British representatives at the Anglo-Irish conferences.

[3] Sir Gordon Hewart (1870-1943), later Lord Hewart, who was Attorney-General from 1919 to 1922, and Lord Chief Justice of England, 1922-1940.

point on paper. This I did, and got a note on Sunday saying that L-G would put an almost identical formula before the Cabinet on Monday. The Irish were stiff about it but in the end accepted it in return for a full free trade agreement. Yesterday as a result the Irishmen invited me to tea. They are very impressive people, especially Collins[4] who is obviously a statesman of high calibre. He told us some amazing stories of hair-breadth escapes in the days when he was in hiding from the British troops. Well, I expect all this has become history now; and I imagine that a new era will open for Ireland. For me not the least joyful fact is the certainty that this will greatly facilitate Anglo-American cooperation. And if our countries express in terms of common agreement their will to peace neither the folly of France nor the militarism of Japan can stand in their way. One other visit I must tell you of. On Friday I lunched with Rathenau,[5] the late German minister of reconstruction and the head of the Great German electrical trust. The details were all about reparations; but I must tell you how impressed I was by his imagination, his vigour and his idealism. If every country had half a dozen business men of his intelligence the commercial world would be in very different case. Beyond this, I think the most interesting thing has been a long visit from Bertrand Russell. As always, there is something almost impish about his mind, but in sheer perceptiveness and in mastery of phrase I do not know his equal. And he appals me by sheer width of interest. He meets me and talks learnedly of political science; he sees Whitehead and talks mathematical logic; he sees Bosanquet and talks philosophy. And in each case one can be quite certain that he will be full of originality and suggestiveness so that an hour's talk leaves you a little gasping. So much for men; though let me note that Walter Lippmann arrives here tomorrow and I am busily organising the legions on his behalf. He has been over half Europe, and must have vivid impressions to communicate. . . .

My love to you both.                          *Ever yours, H. J. L.*

*Washington, D.C., December 22, 1921*
*Dear Laski:* Your letter of 8. 12. 21 arrived yesterday, is a thriller. You certainly seem to wiggle in wherever you want to and I am glad to believe that the men in power know a good thing when they see it. I wish you had explained a little more about the oath, because I don't quite know what was the hitch. I hope the event is going to be as you expected when you wrote. Everything that you write delights me, including your final remarks about Mrs.

---

[4] Michael Collins (1890-1922); Sinn Fein leader in war and peace, who was murdered, in August 1922, by extremists of the Irish Republican Army.
[5] Walter Rathenau (1867-1922) was assassinated in June of 1922 while Foreign Minister of the German Republic.

Nickleby.[1] I used to tell my mother that Mrs. Nickleby was the
universal woman. But alas, how little have I to tell you in return
for all you say. I fired off two dissents on Monday.[2] Brandeis, and
in one of them Pitney, also writing separate ones. One of Brandeis
is a very elaborate study.[3] He said what is true that it was not
proper for a judicial opinion, ordinarily, but people are so ignorant
that it was desirable that they should know and I dare say he was
right. It was a boycott case in which the C.J. disappointed us
after a happy success in uniting the Court in an earlier one.[4] At
B.'s request I wrote a few words before I saw his and as he wanted
me to print I did. For the same reason I added a few words in the
other case under the Sherman Act. As Brandeis said it was a proof
of Pitney's intellectual honesty that having taken the former case
to work the other way after the first argument he changed his
mind on reflection. Well, after Conference and Court on Monday
from 10:30 to 4 I whisked home and landed in on a reception
where I jawed till 6 and then laid me down and slept like a dog.
I lit on an unknown dame, with a southern accent and the devil
set my tongue loose. I told her that abuses were the parents of the
exquisite, which vanished from the country with wine—that I
loathed most of the things in favor of which I decided and that
you couldn't have a people like the Greeks (*temp.* Pericles) except on a basis of some kind of slavery. Wouldn't that have made
some headlines if she had been a female reporter? There is nothing
like a paradox to take the scum off your mind. I have just sent an
opinion to the printer which contains a phrase or two that I have
some hopes will give pain—that there is no over-law to which the
United States must bow—and that legal obligations that exist but
cannot be enforced are ghosts that are seen in the law but are
elusive to the grasp.[5] I think the Chief's performance in the above-
mentioned case[6] is rather spongy—copious citation of generalities
become platitudes that don't bring you any nearer to the concrete
case. I always say that I will admit any general proposition that
anyone wants to lay down and decide the case either way. This
gossip sounds rather like *The Vicar of Wakefield* after your high
political effort—but I give this half—I can no more. I must add
that I continue pleased with the Chief's way of conducting busi-

---

[1] In a passage omitted from this edition Laski, speaking of rereading
Dickens, called Mrs. Nickleby "by all odds the greatest character-study
of all."

[2] *Truax* v. *Corrigan*, 257 U.S. 312, 342 (see, *supra*, p. 374, note 2);
*American Column Co.* v. *United States*, id., 377, 412.

[3] Brandeis's dissent in *Truax* v. *Corrigan* was largely devoted to an examination of the efforts of England, and of the state and Federal governments
in the United States to deal with labor problems.

[4] *American Steel Foundries* v. *Tri-City Central Trades Council*, 257 U.S.
184, See, *supra*, p. 291.

[5] *The Western Maid*, 257 U.S. 419 (Jan. 3, 1922).

[6] *Truax* v. *Corrigan*, *supra*, note 2.

ness—though at times a little too long-winded—which I dare say
he will get over.

I have read nothing to speak of—nothing beyond listening or
half-listening pending solitaire to what F. reads to me when her
eyes permit. I have been much bothered with coughing at night—
and on her insistence that smoking was at least part of the trouble,
have without admitting it to her—stopped all except the morning
cigar, and to my infinite chagrin the cough seems to be stopping.
I believe I have told you that Wells dined here the other night and
remained after the Jap Shogun had left and talked you know how
dramatically and interestingly. Also your man Nevinson has dined
and later spent an evening here, much to my pleasure. Zimmern
and Mrs. dine here Saturday—I don't bother about the illustrious
(as probably I have said but it seems to need an apology) unless
they have something to say to me which probably most of them,
including Balfour, have not. Did I mention calling on the Princess
Bibesco and her coming downstairs and helping me on with my
coat when I left? It was the most marked intimation of venerable
years that I have received. Unless when years ago Dorothy Kirchwey, as she then was, kissed me for a grandpa. I watch myself
somewhat but feel as if my vigor had not yet abated. A merry
Xmas and my love to you—I am proud of you.

*Aff'ly yours, O. W. Holmes*

*16 Warwick Gardens, 31.XII.21.*
*My dear Justice:* First of all, the best of New Years to you and Mrs.
Holmes. I think the fog of the world begins to lift just a little. I
can't help envying your friend Hughes his share in it. I don't think
his disarmament plan has succeeded; but he has put Anglo-American relations on a better footing than they have been this century.
That's a great deed. . . .

I have been fearfully busy this Xmastide. Item, a dinner with
Churchill. He was almost feverishly brilliant in talk, indiscreet and
vivid but utterly unsafe to follow. I like him *qua* man, and as
politician he is detestable. But I can't follow the modern method of
not dining with the man with whom you disagree. On the whole,
I get more stimulus that way. Item, a lunch with Morley. He was
very tired after the Irish affair, but he talked well and bravely in
the manner of Victor Hugo's great remark that amnesty was the
greatest word in our tongue. (I was glad to see Debs released.)[1]
He had Birrell there as usual and we had a good scrap over Peacock in whom Birrell delights. I find him unreadable, frankly, and
was visited by wrathful excoriation. But I stuck (and stick) to my

---

[1] President Harding had released Eugene Debs from imprisonment on
December 23, but had not restored him to citizenship.

guns. Also I urged, he and Morley dissenting, that the nobility of
Milton's prose style is based on a dozen famous passages and not
on all the body of prose work—that *e.g.* his stuff on divorce, however sensible, is unreadable, and I argued that Jeremy Taylor and
Hobbes just licked him hollow as prose-writers. Altogether one of
those entirely delightful bookish lunches that are so rare nowadays. . . .

Also I have read . . . *The Legacy of Greece,* edited by Livingstone. Do get this at all costs. The Oxford Press publish it. It's got
superb essays in by Gilbert Murray and Zimmern, besides most
interesting accounts of Greek medicine, science and mathematics. . . .

I end with a humble request. Will you send me such a statement
as I might use for a testimonial? I mean your feeling that I am not
feebleminded and have written not entirely disreputable books. I
have been asked to submit my name for a lectureship ( 6 lectures)
at Cambridge next year, for the which I want some testimony from
distinguished men. If it is a labour please do not bother; but if you
think you can in conscience I shall be very grateful.

Our joint love to you both, and very warm good wishes.

*Ever affectionately yours, H. J. L.*

# III

## 1922-1923

*Washington, D.C., Sunday, January 15, 1922*
*Dear Laski:* Your letter comes this morning and has just been read.
I was thirsting for it and beginning to say to myself that with your
multitude of interests you naturally would slack up, when the joy
arrived. First as to its contents. I am delighted to find that we
agree as to Peacock—(except the little verse, "The mountain
sheep are sweeter—But the valley sheep are fatter—We therefore
deem it meeter—To carry off the latter"—I quote from memory).
Many years ago there was discourse by Lady Desborough and, I
think, Asquith, who avowed themselves Peacockians. I grieved
but could not see it. She had him bound in purple morocco. Also
as to Milton's prose. Query if what you say might not be applied
to the Old Testament and *King Lear*. Next as to Nevinson. He
has dined here and called twice or thrice. He was here last night
with a young man from the N. Y. *Nation*. I delight in him. I told
him that in view of his having twisted the tails of elephants,
tickled the noses of crocodiles with a straw, freed slaves, &c, there
was no adequate thrill to be offered in this safe house—but it was
thought to be furnished by a little electric toy that made him
start the first time and to which he recurred last night—a bulldog
in a kennel—you speak sharply to it and it jumps out at you about
a foot. I have made no effort to see Balfour, but this chap goes
to my innards—I don't know exactly why, I will rather say, all
round. Wells, I didn't see again. I was rather surprised to hear
Nevinson say that he used to like Zimmern but not now—they
differed so radically in politics. He attributed to Zimmern more
pro-French and anti-English zeal than I have seen any trace of.
I think I have told you of Zimmern's visits here. The other chap
and I endeavoured to mitigate N's conviction. I too was glad at

the release of Debs—although I hardly can believe him honest
(not that that has anything to do with his being kept in or let
out). They sent me *The Legacy of Greece* and I have read it with
delight. The chapter on mathematics I didn't understand—but got
something from—and Inge on Religion didn't seem to me very
clear on a single rapid reading. It was the first thing that I had
read by Inge. Murray, Zimmern, and Toynbee I thought all admirable—and I got a good deal of pleasure from others. I have
just begun a little book by Lévy-Bruhl, *La morale et la science
des moeurs*—much recommended by a young French student P.
Lepaule[1] whom Frankfurter sent to me, but the beginning rather
disappoints me. Many words in getting—I suppose—to a point of
view that I expect I shall think a matter of course. Probably a
man writing in a Catholic atmosphere has to put out more labor
than you or I in getting to the surface of the ground. I sent you
the other day an opinion that I thought rather good and one of
several dissents that I have fired off lately. One of them was sup-
plementary to longer discourses in the same direction by Brandeis
and Pitney—a boycott case.[2] The C.J. disappointed us after a good
start, as it seemed, in what we think the right direction in an
earlier case.[3] I thought this performance rather spongy. As poetry
gets the magic touch of chance from the interruption of logical
sequence by the suggestions of rhyme—so my sequence is broken
up by alternate recollections of things of my own to tell and what
you say. I recur to the latter to remark that I always have understood that many of the long subsequent legal reforms were suggested in the Cromwellian days. I remembered the registry of
deeds *e.g.* I look forward eagerly to your publications and am
keen to see what you say about Marx. As you know, I read him a
second time in order to state articulately to myself what I thought
his fallacies—though I have forgotten all but some generalities.
Just now Brandeis and I are in opposition—as yesterday he held
up an opinion of mine in which five others concur to see if Pitney
or Clarke would not write a dissent. He seemed disinclined to
bother with it himself. It isn't a case that I care greatly about—
but I fondly hope there will be difficulty in smashing me.[4] I am
lingering in your delightful company longer than I should, for I
have a case assigned to me that I think may take some cunning

---

[1] Pierre Lepaulle was a graduate student at the Harvard Law School in
1921-22.

[2] *Traux* v. *Corrigan, supra,* p. 291.

[3] *American Steel Foundries* v. *Tri-City Central Trades Council, supra,* p.
291.

[4] Perhaps *Gillespie* v. *Oklahoma,* 257 U.S. 501 (Jan. 30, 1922). Holmes,
for the majority, sustained a claim that income from leases of Indian lands
was immune from state taxation. Pitney, Brandeis, and Clarke, JJ., dissented
without opinion.

penmanship to state convincingly and to keep away from rocks
and whirlpools. When such a thing is in the back of one's head
one strains to get at it—in spite of age, which was rubbed into
me the other day. It was icy and slippery and Clarke and Vandevanter, with whom I was, insisted on not letting me walk part of
the way home—I saw them (in my mind) saying, "The old gentleman ought not to be allowed to take the risk of a tumble."
Then I said to my wife I would go out for a walk—and she made
such a row that I gave it up. Then she handed me the N. Y. *Nation*
on the boycott case above-mentioned which referred to me as the
"wise old jurist" [5]—and I began to feel that there was no doubt
about it—that in Emerson's words "It is time to be old" &c. But
I don't feel so today. My love to you both,

*Affectionately yours, O. W. Holmes*

*16 Warwick Gardens, 22.1.22*
*My dear Justice:* . . . students in general are fascinating people,
and after seven rather full years of academic life, I find myself
in love with every aspect of it except the other teachers! Much
visiting, too, these days. A great lunch with Morley, when he and
Frida fought over my prostrate body as to whether I should enter
the House of Commons. It's the greatest platform of all he said,
and extolled the life of action. No, said Frida, the ultimate men
are teachers and thinkers whose work the statesmen turn into
rather ineffective legislation. . . . We went also to a jolly dinner
at the Webbs to meet Shaw. As always, he talked most brilliantly,
holding the whole table by power of the perfect phrase. But he
lacks the art of singing with the chorus—he is conductor and chief
tenor in one. And at bottom he is intensely an intellectual aristocrat to whom the common people mean only a vague vast lump
that he can't translate into Jones and Brown and Robinson. And
I must tell you also of one glorious political adventure. I went to
Lincoln to speak on education and the Dean of Lincoln[1] took the
chair. During the question-time a man asked me how I could expect a workman to be interested in education when his first interest was to get them earning so as to keep body and soul together in the home. I said that I agreed, and that there was no
hope for the working-class until the devastating torrent of children
was somewhere and somehow stemmed. Up, stentorian-like, jumped
the Dean. He begged most emphatically to dissent from this pestilential doctrine. He knew many working-class families which
had brought up six children in decency and comfort on thirty
shillings a week. It was our duty to follow the scriptural injunc-

---

[5] "Does Mr. Taft Want Direct Action?" 114 *Nation* 32 (Jan. 11, 1922).
[1] Thomas Charles Fry (1846-1930), Dean of Lincoln, 1910-1930.

tion and multiply as the sand upon the sea shore. Voice then floats
out from the audience, "Don't you fret, Mr. Laski, the Dean has
only two children himself." The dean left hurriedly amid roars of
laughter. Amid these *personalia,* let me add that I have seen a
good deal lately of Bertrand Russell, and always with pleasure.
He is essentially at bottom a Voltairean whig of the 18th century;
but he is so absolutely simple and fearless in straightforward in-
tegrity of mind and so detached from the men of formulae that it
is a sheer joy to talk things over with him. Also amid work of this
kind I have been reading. In a way I got most pleasure out of
Fitzjames Stephen's *Horae Sabbaticae.* I wonder if you have ever
read them? It's criticism with a bludgeon and poor Fitzjames
never knew that any other type of mind except his own existed;
obviously also he was ruined by taking too many walks with
Carlyle. But it is fine masculine vigour, with that profound commonsense which is so striking in all the Stephen clan from Leslie
down to Dicey. . . .

Last night we dined alone with Haldane—a very jolly dinner
with much secret history. One thing is, I think, too amusing not
to bear repetition. You know that Barrie was given the Order of
Merit—our one decoration that is still of solid worth. When L-G
proposed it to the King the latter wrote to Haldane and asked
him what he thought of the proposal. Haldane wrote back that
he did not think that Barrie was of the required standard and that
something ought to be done for F. H. Bradley who, write [*sic*]
or wrong, was, with Bertrand Russell, the one European figure in
our philosophy. But in the absence of Balfour there was no one
either in the *entourage* of the Cabinet or of the Court who had
heard of Bradley and it was not thought wise to confer so distinguished a ribbon on the unknown! We talked of Mrs. Asquith's
visit to your shores[2] with, I think, a common regret. It is the first
time that the wife of a Prime Minister has appeared on the platform as a public entertainer and it will do her husband great
harm. As Morley said to me, if he wants money he should go
back to the Bar. Anything is better than the loosening of a very
useful social standard. But I hope, at least, that you will have
some pleasant evenings from her adventure; then I shall regret it
the less. . . .

My love to you both.           *Ever affectionately yours, H. J. L.*


*16 Warwick Gardens, 4.2.22.*
*My dear Justice:* I owe you thanks for a delightful letter and for

---

[2] On January 21, Margot Asquith had sailed for the United States, where
she went on a lecture tour, later described in detail in her *Places and
Persons* (1925).

a most generous and valuable enclosure.[1] You comment on age. Simultaneously with your letter I had a note from Pound (from Italy) one of whose sentences runs: "I have just been reading a new batch of Holmes's decisions. If I read them as nameless productions I should ask what newly vigorous mind has been added to the Court." I agree. The way in which you adjust yourself to new situations in the light of a very consistent general philosophy is to me a source of perpetual admiration. I shudder to think what would happen to the Court if you resigned.

. . . Then Woodrow Wilson's *Congressional Government* in preparation for my lectures next term on Congress. I came out of this adventure with a very much higher opinion of W.W. than I had before. He has an imitative, stilted narrow mind. But he has a consistent intensity of gaze which gives him quite genuine *aperçus*, and he knows his Bagehot and Burke well enough to have selected wisely the points for which he ought to seek. Did you ever read it, I wonder? . . .

In the way of persons, little of note. I had a jolly dinner with Morley who was full of vigour, and Bryce who had just died, was allotted his position among the shades. . . . You didn't do more than mention Zimmern's visit, but I'm glad you saw him. . . . You will be amused, by the way, to hear of a request which now lies on my table from the Manchester *Guardian* that I write 1000 words on P. Vinogradoff[2] "for eventual use as an obituary notice!" Shall I? I don't know. I'd like to say in print that his most important work was to turn Maitland to the study of legal history and that after *Villainage in England* he didn't write anything of real value. But I don't like the notion, and I don't like Vinogradoff who is pompous and conceited. I note that you are snow-bound in Washington—I do hope it hasn't brought you discomfort. Here the weather is more like a mild summer than winter, though snow is foretold. Well! My love to you both—it is good to have you alive.                                    *Ever affectionately yours, H. J. L.*

*Washington, D.C., February 17, 1922*

*Dear Laski:* Another joy to me dated 4.2.22. You and I are like Dr. Johnson's clever and dull boys—while the latter is debating which of two books he shall read the former has read them both. I am at the hesitating point and as I said the other day may fall back on rereading *Faust*. Brandeis put into my hands Fraser [*sic*] (*Golden Bough* Fraser) on *Pausanias*, uncut. I cut and read it—

---

[1] The letter referred to is *supra,* p. 305. The enclosure was doubtless the letter to Cambridge University requested by Laski, *supra,* p. 304.

[2] Sir Paul Vinogradoff (1845-1925), legal historian, whose academic life was divided between Russia and England, where he held the Corpus Christi chair of jurisprudence at Oxford.

with not much profit. Also I ran through the *Kreutzer Sonata*
which I had not read—a rotten book I think. Then I took the
scum off my mind with Pound's *Spirit of the Common Law*—a
stimulating book. I distrusted some of the causes emphasized—
which seemed to me (subject to further thought when necessary)
cloud shapes. Also I felt as I have felt heretofore that his strength
lay in the broad view of wonderfully complete knowledge rather
than in a very poignant personal reaction. But his view is so much
broader than the common that if his book is widely read, as I hope
it will be, I feel as if it would be a gospel of enlightenment that
may do untold good. Speaking of being widely read—H. B. & Co.
wrote to me the other day, in answer to an inquiry of curiosity,
that, if I remember rightly, they had sold 1800 and odd copies of
our book. I should think considering that it is old stuff that was
satisfactory. What do you think? Yesterday we had a Conference
and my cases were passed. Thence I flitted to the dentist and
thence to a dame with whom I jawed till it was time to walk home
to dinner. And when I went to bed I coughed half the night. It
is a great bore—but I begin to fear that the cough will be my
companion for the rest of my life. It does not threaten existence
—only comfort, but it is damned uncomfortable. I have much the
same impression that you have of Vinogradoff and his writings—
but if I didn't show you the pleasure—real, deep, pleasure I always have in seeing Zimmern I did myself injustice. Your letter
opens the thought—I had forgotten it when I began. I will send
for Wilson's *Congressional Government*. I have meant to read it
for years. Oh—I forgot to add that I like Mrs. Zimmern. She
talked intelligently and read a little Racine aloud, well. I stopped
and telephoned to the Congressional Library for Wilson's book.
What a convenience. And now I must go out and get a little walk
before luncheon. The snow you speak of was terrifying from the
weight it put on roofs but it melts off comfortably. Now it is pretty
cold but the sun shines and life seems joyful once more.

*Affectionately yours, O. W. Holmes*

*Washington, D.C., February 7, 1922*
*Dear Laski:* Again there is gladness here because of a letter from
you—(22.1.22). I hope your 'except the other teachers' to your
joy in your work doesn't mean that you don't get on well with
them. It is worth an effort and some self-suppression to keep things
smooth wherever one is called on to cooperate with others. In fact
I think that is one of the lessons that it is valuable to learn. As to
your debate with Morley over the H. of C. I am on the side of
Mrs. Frida—as to the immediate present and also as to the ultimate kingship belonging to the man who starts fundamental ideas.

Such men never can be sure that they don't live in a fool's paradise but the dream is splendid and you get as much reassurance as is good for a man of your years from those you value. Later, circumstances may change—and I agree that a man of ideas well may want to test them by the hard contact of the immediate and with men who don't care for them. I don't attach much value to my opinion because I am too far from the facts—but I give you my bird's eye view. Of course, I am much interested by what you say of Bertrand Russell and Bernard Shaw, and tickled no little by your adventure with the Dean of Lincoln—I wonder if you met my kind hosts of former days Lord and Lady Monson[1]—or her young daughter whom I have larked with here—Miss Margaret Turnure. Fitzjames Stephen makes the same impression on you that he did on me. He gave me some of his early essays and I have bought others. I am afraid my opinion on the United States vessels found you rather cold.[2] There are petitions for rehearing in all the cases, where they patronize me on the fading of Austinian (Austinian!) doctrine, and, I inferred at the argument, thought that a man not familiar with navigation could not follow the mysteries of personifying a ship. They quote you, *inter alios,* to show that I didn't know what I was talking about—but I humbly apprehend that I did. Nevinson has gone—he came here a number of times and delighted me immensely. He entered into the warmest part of my gizzard and when he left, sent me a volume of his essays with a charming inscription that made me feel that the pleasure was mutual. I have read a few of them—not all, for I am just getting through my work—with great satisfaction. Yesterday we had to breakfast early to get to the last sitting of the Conference.[3] It was a moving moment—and while I am hopelessly ignorant of the details of the agreements, I hope and believe that they and meeting around a table will do a great deal of good. But such excursions are fatiguing to me. I told General Pershing when he came in the afternoon that I had said to myself while shaving that the greatest bores of life were world events and illustrious persons. Too late I regretted the last item as addressed to him—but we always talk so cheerfully—(I remember him as

---

[1] Baron Monson (1868-1940), of Benton Hall, near Lincoln, had married an American, the widow of Laurence Turnure of New York.

[2] In *The Western Maid, supra,* p. 302, Holmes in writing for a majority of the Court had refused to permit the fiction by which vessels are personified for purposes of *in rem* proceedings in admiralty to override the policies establishing governmental immunity in favor of the United States. In briefs and argument counsel had relied on Laski's "Responsibility of the State in England," 32 *Harv. L. Rev.* 447 (1919) to show that the principles of sovereign immunity should not be taken as sacrosanct.

[3] The Disarmament Conference had concluded on February 6, after agreeing on the terms of seven treaties to be submitted to the participating powers for ratification.

an understaffer at the White House) that I don't think it did any
harm. I frequently remark that I am paid to listen to people, and
that the notion of gratuitously going in search of that kind of
trouble is against my grain. In a few minutes I must try to get
hold of Brandeis and see whether he thinks it worth while for me
to utter a squeak on the matter of fraud orders by the post office
which raises doubts in my mind that never have been adequately
discussed.[4] The trouble is that it is perhaps too late in the day.
This is the moment when I specially need your suggestions—we
are adjourned until the end of the month and my cases are written—so I hope to read a little. I may resort to the old—the classics
or *Faust* or something—I dunno—I am not quite ready to begin.
I must see the dentist and do some business before I am really
free. One of my cases has a touch of fundamentals in it—that
Brandeis noticed as I hoped he would. One of those things that
seem obvious when stated but take some trouble to state. My love
to you both.                         *Affectionately yours, O. W. Holmes*


                                        *16 Warwick Gardens, 25.2.22*
*My dear Justice:* . . . I've read Gibbon with intense admiration.
I saw much more contemporary reference than heretofore but the
way in which the judgments have stood and the broad commanding sweep of the whole were, I think, superb. Maitland, I am
sure, would have done better work on the same canvas; but I can
think of no other English historian in the same universe of discussion. Then I took a big dose of Newman, beginning with the
*Apologia,* and ending with the *Grammar of Assent.* Style and temperament alike exquisite; matter and knowledge as a rule as third-
rate as the ingenuity was intensely clever. It revived all my sense
of his charm; but I thought him less significant than when I went
into him with care four or five years ago. Also I reread the *Wealth
of Nations* and was very interested to note how very much less of
*laissez-faire* there is in it than one is tempted to assume. Fertility
is the real word for that fellow's mind. He hasn't an ounce of
Hume's subtlety or depth. He is "knowing"; and the faculty of
abstract observation of things is intense. But he has the typical
Scotch tolerance of hardship; which leads him to underestimate
the harm done, as Aristotle long ago said, when you have a society in which great wealth and great poverty dwell alongside
each other. But I thought that the very longest bill of exceptions

---

[4] In *Leach* v. *Carlile,* 258 U.S. 138, 140 (Feb. 27, 1922), Holmes wrote
a dissenting opinion in which Brandeis, J., concurred, protesting that the
Federal statute authorizing the exclusion of printed matter from the mails,
had unconstitutionally deprived the sender of his right of free speech.

one could draw would still leave him far and away the biggest mind in the history of economic theory. . . .

Influenza did not help to see people but I have had some adventures. First I had lunch with Bernard Shaw that you would have enjoyed. He was interested and forgot all mannerism with the result that he talked like Swift—giving a kind of handbook of aristocratic dement with a brilliance that was appealing. I can't reproduce it, but I would have given much to have had you there. Then out to Morley to dinner—Birrell the only other guest. . . . Morley was very eager about my little *Marx,* and told me how he had informed Gladstone of K.M.'s death. Mr. Gladstone did not know who he was and when Morley explained opined that he was a survivor of 1848! Yet I imagine that Marx will outlive Gladstone and even Morley's hero worship could not quite stomach that.

. . . I imagine Washington has done something to check Japan in the Pacific—I don't give much for the rest. But it was a great gesture.

Well—my love to you both and the happiest of happy birthdays.                          *Ever affectionately yours, H. J. L.*

*Washington, D.C., March 11, 1922*

*Dear Laski:* Yours of February 25 came this afternoon to welcome and refresh me after the usual Saturday Conference. I am interested by what you say of Gibbon. I too was vastly impressed by his sweep and mastery and his power of telling a story. I doubt if one can say that Maitland could have made such a picture had he lived at that time. But what struck me was that he told me very little that I cared to hear. The emphasis has changed, as it always does, and apart from the fact that much more is known upon the subjects that we do want to hear about, such as Christianity and the Roman law—he takes time in giving characters that I don't believe and am indifferent to, and a thousand details of wanderings, incursions and alarums that I forget as soon as read, but gives me nothing of the rise and decay of institutions such as I could read about in Fustel de Coulanges.[1] I speak from a memory of about ten years ago. History has to be rewritten because history is the selection of those threads of causes or antecedents that we are interested in—and the interest changes in fifty years. Newman struck me—probably forty or 50 years ago—much as [he] does you—a tender spirit and a born writer arguing like a pettifogger —but I have only read the *Grammar of Assent* I believe. A fine

---

[1] Numa Denis Fustel de Coulanges (1830-1889), historian, whose scientific method had a more lasting effect on historiography than did his dogmatic convictions. He is best known for his *La cité antique* (1864) and *Histoire des institutions politiques de l'ancienne France* (1874).

start he makes in pointing out how much we must take for granted
if we would talk together. But I said to myself, accepting that
premise, if I put it brutally I think him an incompetent old ass—
and he would think me an impertinent young monkey. (I was
young then.) Adam Smith is about as far back as Newman. His
book seemed to me more like a treatise on life than political
economy in a narrow sense. I didn't think Karl Marx the size to
patronize him as a bourgeois intelligence, as I think he did. Your
pamphlet on K. M. delights me by its learning and many-sided
intelligence—although I hardly believe that he is so great as you
think him. The criticisms that remain in my mind from reading
him are the fundamental ones that he treats ownership and consumption as convertible terms—my universal criticism on most of
the writers who look for some great change with desire (possibly
at times even my beloved H.J.L.) and that he skips from world
welfare to England's welfare and back according to the exigencies
of his argument. I can't back up what I say from present memory,
but those things stuck out at the time when I last read him. I
certainly don't see why he shouldn't outlive Gladstone—or why
Gladstone should live at all as a figure in the history of thought—
which Marx well may. Gladstone was a great figure locally—so was
Jowett—but I hardly imagine that anyone out of England cares
for Jowett. I read W. Wilson's *Congressional Government* the other
day. It seemed to me sufficient to teach me things I didn't know,
which anybody can, but to owe its *élan* to Bagehot and not to be
big enough to found a reputation. Perhaps I told you that I wrote
a short dissent (Brandeis alone concurring) against the constitutionality of post office fraud orders.[2] It was too deeply settled to
be disturbed at once, but it has been on my conscience for years
and some day a dissent may bear fruit. Various pleasant letters
came to me on my birthday with flowers etc. and one or two
puffs in the newspapers. After 80 a man begins to be interesting.
As I wrote to Lady Desborough the *Comandatore* (qu. sp.?) has
stepped up another stair with a bang but I hope he will have to
climb some more before I feel his marble hand.[3] I had a lunch
with Mrs. Asquith as she flitted through and am telephoning now
to see if I can take her out to my private show of Fort Stevens—
where I saw Lincoln and the enemy nearer in to Washington than
they ever were again. My love to your Missus and you.

*Aff'ly yours, O. W. Holmes*

[2] *Leach* v. *Carlile, supra,* p. 312.
[3] The reference is to the appearance of the statue of the Commendatore
in the closing scene of *Don Giovanni.*

*16 Warwick Gardens, 11.3.22*

*My dear Justice:* . . . Then a week-end in the country to meet Hodges[1] (the miners' leader), Webb, and Arthur Henderson, the leader of the labour party. A very good time, and on my part a great increase of confidence in the quality of labour statesmanship. Some jolly secrets in the shape of Henderson's reminiscences of the War Cabinet[2] and of L-G's amazing shifts of opinion—particularly of how nearly he made peace in 1917. . . . While I am in the way of anecdotage I must record one other story. About forty years ago Mrs. Webb was travelling from Newcastle with Sir George Trevelyan. The latter told her how he had consulted his uncle, Macaulay, as to whether he should marry rank or money. "My boy," said Macaulay, "as a Trevelyan, you have all the rank you can want: marry money." Mrs. Webb thought this admirable and next night at Asquith's told it to Rosebery. R. went crimson and burst into hysterical laughter. Mrs. Webb then went to Asquith and asked him why Rosebery had received an amusing tale in so curious a fashion. "Oh," said Asquith, "you will see in the papers tomorrow the announcement of his engagement to Miss Rothschild."[3] I leave you to dissect Mrs. Webb's feelings.

I have been reading some jolly books about which you may like to know. . . . *The General Eyre* by W. C. Bolland—a most attractive little book. It's a study, mainly from the year books, of the Eyre as an administrative machine and it gave me the atmosphere of the 13-14 centuries as few books I have read. . . . Do take down your Bentham (I envy you its possession) and look up the essay on political tactics. For wise and considered ingenuity, I know few things to beat it, and I can't find anything superior since his day. What a glorious fellow he really was!

Nevinson has had two dinners with us in the last ten days and I have had really direct news of you. He was very happy in your friendship and full of Mrs. Holmes. And he insisted (to a willing hearer) that no man has ever made the splendour of the law more apparent than you have done in *Collected Papers*. Harcourt wrote me of its sale—an amazing achievement I think. But really even the technical papers have a special flavour that puts them on the

[1] Frank Hodges (1887-1947); Secretary of the Miners' Federation (1918-1924); civil lord of the admiralty in MacDonald's ministry (1924); author of *Nationalisation of the Mines* (1920); *My Adventures as a Labour Leader* (1925).

[2] Arthur Henderson (1863-1935) had been one of the five members in Lloyd George's original War Cabinet but had resigned in 1917 when the government's policy on Russia seemed to him mistaken.

[3] In 1878 Rosebery had married Hannah de Rothschild, who a year before had succeeded to the fortune of her father Baron Meyer Amschel de Rothschild.

plane of general philosophic interest (especially "Privilege, Malice and Intent") as well as that of jurisprudence. I'm more proud of having persuaded you to collect them than of most things I have done. But next I want the decisions. I shan't really be content until they are accessible in similar form.

But this is already too long. My love to you both. Please take care and see that the cough does not worry.

*Ever yours affectionately, H. J. L.*

*Washington, D.C., March 26, 1922*

*Dear Laski:* What a pleasure would depart from my life if I ceased to receive letters from you. The last, (11.3.22) delightful as usual came just too late for me to try to catch the boat, that, by *ante bellum* conviction that has remained unshaken since old days, I assume sails on Saturday. Also I have been pretty hard at work. Two cases this last week beside sitting and its incidents. They both will go tomorrow, one as to the liability (non-liability, I say), of a landowner for the drowning of children in a poisoned pool where it did not appear that the children had been in any way tempted to enter the land.[1] The pool was in an old cellar in which sulphuric acid etc. had accumulated from old works. Clarke writes a dissent, C. J. & Day accord, that seems to me sentiment and rhetoric of a kind that suits him. He is a very dear, affectionate creature and just now in great sorrow from the death of his sister who was his most intimate companion. I wish that his writing was more to my taste than I can pretend. There seems to be a tacit *rapprochement* between McReynolds and Brandeis of which I am glad. McR. doesn't do himself justice in his opinions. He often is acute in suggestion and has worked on useful legislation. In one case that I wrote last week my opinion seems to have convinced the majority of the contrary, so a dissent by Day, written after the disagreement was obvious, becomes the opinion and I write a few words of dissent, McR. and Brandeis alone with me.[2] It is not of much interest—a question as to the liability of a doctor for prescribing a lot of heroin etc. to an addict—to be taken without supervision—but, on the indictment the doctor acting in good faith. The brethren are a sure cure for a swelled head. We adjourn on Monday for a fortnight and so far I have only one case—(as to liability for an accident in the Cape Cod Canal)[3] so I hope for a

---

[1] *United Zinc and Chemical Co.* v. *Britt*, 258 U.S. 268. Holmes's other opinion, delivered on March 27, was in *Pacific Mail Steamship Co.* v. *Lucas, id.*, 266.

[2] *United States* v. *Behrman*, 258 U.S. 280 (March 27, 1922).

[3] *White Oak Transportation Co.* v. *Boston, Cape Cod & New York Canal Co.*, 258 U.S. 341 (April 10, 1922).

little leisure. I shall read at once W. Lippmann's new book—
*Public Opinion*—a chapter on guild socialism tickled me on a
preliminary peep—also a little book that Farrand sent me on the
*Fathers of the Constitution.* If I can (could) get to those you
mention, or at least *The General Eyre,* I shall (should) be glad.
I note too the reference to Bentham. I stopped to try to find it and
put in a mark but the Index and Table of Contents refer to ii 299
or 301 and I don't find it yet. My edition is bound in parts instead
of volumes and there is some hitch. I received the other day Sir
A. Quiller-Couch *On the Art of Writing*—a matter I always like
to read about, but so far as I have read it doesn't seem to me to
amount to very much. The distinction between the older direct
unconscious expressions of emotion and the philosophical expression is good but old, still, interesting as localized, or rather tem-
poralized. He gives a credit to Wyatt that is new to me.[4] Some of
his criticism seems to me to run into prejudice, *e.g.* I think he is
extravagant against the word *case.* But I have read next to nothing
—I must try to get a morning with Rice—of the Print Department.
I bought a few the other day—as I may have mentioned—one of
the Mantegna series but thought not by his hand and therefore
valued in tens instead of hundreds—and several others. Good old
Nevinson—give my love to him when you see him next. A young
good-looker that he brought with him once, appeared for a moment, afterwards, like Gilbert *au banquet de la vie,* and disappeared. I begged her to drop one word—I think it was *gesture,*
which has become a banality of the fleeting hour. There always is
some word that the leaders of opinion run hard for a time. Did I
ever take you to my little private show of Fort Stevens—the point
where the enemy made his nearest approach to Washington in '64
—and where I saw Lincoln *et al* and a brisk little fight? I wanted
to take Mrs. Asquith but it was no go. It is an old earth work
hidden behind houses, but rather interesting for a last survivor to
take a dame to. *Adieu* dear boy—pray don't overwork but keep
well. I turn to the Cape Cod Canal. *Aff'ly yours, O. W. Holmes*

*16 Warwick Gardens, 5.4.22*
*My dear Justice:* At last my vacation; and I'm enjoying a perfect
month free from any cares in the world. I have read and re-read
till I feel really in the swim again and feelings of weariness have
disappeared altogether. And I have seen a good many people—
most interesting of all Lord R. Cecil with whom I have had much

---

[4] Quiller-Couch considered Sir Thomas Wyatt to be "one of the heroes of
our literature" and commended the originality and natural directness of his
verses; *On the Art of Writing* (1916), 140-145.

talk. He's a fine fellow, human, quick to grasp things, and with a wider reach than most. He needs badly the sense of responsibility that comes from having a big party behind him, and he is, I think, a little overmastered by his high sense of tradition. But at least he knows that the old formulae have broken down; and he has the depth of character which makes you want to work with him. If the Labour Party only had half-a-dozen people like him life would be much simplified. Then I've had a very jolly dinner with Morley who was in great form. He surprised me much by saying that Rosebery was by all odds the most natural-born leader he had ever met, and after him Gladstone. Haldane, who was there too, bore it out and I with a picture of a very jaded and cynical old man who occasionally makes a brutal epigram was left with a sense of the importance of time in politics. We all agreed that Fox was the most loveable person English politics has known; and Morley added that in his view Peel was the greatest administrator.[1] Have you, I wonder, ever read Rosebery's monograph on Peel? A very charming and careful piece of work which you will find reprinted in his *Miscellanies*. Other dinners have been many, but not of great interest. I went to lunch at Haldane's to meet the Lord Chancellor and thought him ( *entre nous* ) very clever but an obvious cad. He posed, and talked as though he were a revivified Brougham—not a pleasant picture. But of his brains there's not a ghost of a doubt. It was amusing to hear his bitterness about Carson.[2] The latter is now the stormy petrel of the lords, and though I agree with Birkenhead that his political activities are intolerable in a judge, I must say that he adds to the spice of life.

. . . And on Saturday, Lippmann's big book[3] arrived and I read it through with great care. I thought it a brilliantly written book. There is a spare, nervous strength in his style that obviously reflects great mental power. And the diagnosis is admirable with an amazing ability to lift the curtain which conceals the intimate recesses of the mind. And yet and yet ° ° ° What does it say at the end? That truth will be easier to obtain if we have more objective measurement of facts. That this may be obtained by the multiplication of intelligence bureaux. I wonder! My difficulty is that the expert has no more ability at interpreting facts than the first-rate practical-minded amateur. Between the soldiers and Haldane, I choose Haldane without a tremor. I agree that the trained mind is important; I agree that facts need more careful sifting. But

---

[1] Laski later contributed an essay on Peel to *The Great Victorians* (Massingham, ed., 1932).

[2] Edward Henry Carson (1854-1935), Baron Carson; his fame as advocate and champion of Ulster will outlive his reputation as lord of appeal in Ordinary, 1921-1935.

[3] *Public Opinion* (1922).

I don't believe that these things get to the roots of social questions.
The book, in fact, seems to me to be supreme journalism, but not
of the class of mind which Felix instantly displays when he comes
to tackle a problem. What do you think? The best thing in it is
the admirable analysis of why Federalism declined and Jefferson
came out on top. But put alongside things like Tocqueville, it is, I
think, a disappointment. Also I have read Asquith's report on
Oxford and Cambridge, which is *very* bad.[4] It leaves everything as
it stands and where it alters, it touches only inessentials. The things
I care about *e.g.* the utterly inadequate provision for law and
political science it hardly touches at all, and they are very badly
done. A man can still go through Oxford today and leave thinking
that Aristotle, Hobbes, Locke and Maine represent the ultimate
fruit of political science. No psychology, no attempt to analyze the
political implications of law, no connection between politics and
economics. Asquith had a glorious opportunity and chucked it in
the street—through laziness I suppose. . . .

It was very distressing to have news of Ned Adams's death[5]—in
what circumstances I do not know. Few Cambridge memories of
mine are as sweet as the sense of his kindness and thoughtfulness
and his love of his work. And it will be very hard for that little
wife of his—a stranger in a very arid desert of stiff and unbending
Bostonians. I hope Arthur Hill will help her through.

Well! My love to you both. I expect to go off to Paris next week
on a hunt for books. If I do, I shall at least have adventures to
chronicle.                          *Ever affectionately yours, H. J. L.*


*Washington, D.C., April 22, 1922*
*My dear Laski:* Your letter of the 5th is as interesting and delightful as usual. I am interested by your impressions of people and
books that you give me in it—Lord R. Cecil whom (I think it
was Lord R.) I knew as a young lawyer many years ago. I used
to know Lady Edward Cecil quite well but haven't seen her for
ages. The Lord Chancellor whom I saw a number of times when
I was with L. Scott—a witty cove, but from reading one or two
of his political speeches I find it hard to believe him profound. Yet
I hear that his decisions show much study and mastery. I never
met Rosebery nor read his monograph on Peel. What you say
about Lippmann's *Public Opinion* impresses me. I too was struck

<hr>

[4] Asquith had been Chairman of the Royal Commission on Oxford and
Cambridge Universities. Its report was published in March 1922.
[5] Edward Brinley Adams (1871-1922), Librarian of the Harvard Law
School, had died on March 24. Arthur D. Hill wrote of Adams in 35 *Harv.
L. Rev.* 895 (June 1922).

by his not coming out anywhere—but much more by the intimate perception of the subtleties of the human mind and of human relations. What you say of the soldiers and Haldane reminds me of what Albert Nickerson,[1] a fierce philistine long dead used to say of the intelligence of English management, that had in each department a body of permanent experts and put an able man of the world on top. He made a fortune in the stock market—and said one day—"They talk of our leading the market. We only follow the procession ahead, like little boys. If we turn down a side street the procession doesn't." Which I thought showed size. You gave me the first news I had of Ned Adams's death. I was truly grieved—for him—for his wife—for the library. Almost the same day, Pollock told me of Dicey's departure. He was dear to my heart—and life seems appreciably more bare—but I am getting stripped very fast these days. The third edition of his *Conflict of Laws* arrived the same day. Personally I have been much bothered by coughing, etc. and really was relieved when the Doctor told me that I had a smart attack of asthma. I would rather be uncomfortable than an angel and I had felt bothered (not much—I don't worry about the end) by symptoms that if they were not asthma I couldn't understand. If I should die now before any changes in my fortune I should die happy—so far as I personally am concerned—for I should feel that I got out of it before any disappointment after the extraordinary—recognition sounds too confident a word—that has come this last year—the last a really charming notice in the *California Law Review* for March.[2] Francis Hackett wrote to me a moving letter on his leaving the *New Republic* &c.—Frankfurter and his wife have just been here for the night. He was as good as ever—but I have been in such a storm of occupations this week that everything interfered with everything else. I wasn't feeling very well but I got through an opinion that the majority seemed to like.[3] It awaits some words of dissent from the C.J.—J. Clarke with him. It concerns the question whether the Fleet Corporation can be sued or shares the immunity of government—I think you would like it—although I do not call it a shining star.

23rd. This morning brought a letter from Lady Bryce telling of

---

[1] Presumably Albert Winslow Nickerson (1840-1893), inheritor of the mercantile fortune of his father, Captain Joseph Nickerson. The son greatly increased the father's fortune and pursued a successful career in Boston as director of railroad companies, as entrepreneur of mining and industrial ventures, and as stock-market operator.

[2] A review of *Collected Legal Papers* by Orrin K. McMurray, 10 *California Law Review* 266 (March 1922).

[3] *Sloan Shipyards* v. *United States Fleet Corp.*, 258 U.S. 549 (May 1, 1922). Over the dissent of Taft, C.J., and Van Devanter and Clarke, JJ., Holmes wrote an opinion for the majority denying the Fleet Corporation's claim of sovereign immunity from suit.

Dicey's death and also news that the top of the New Willard is
burned. I have had a pretty good night's sleep and therefore take
life more composedly than yesterday p.m. when I was very tired.
My nephew and his wife come here tomorrow morning, but we
are pondering whether we ought to offer our room to somebody,
as there must be a lot of people turned out. I shall leave my wife
to meditate upon that and shall turn to my case, assigned last
night, on whether liquor can be transported from Canada through
this country to a foreign port or whether the treaty and a statute
were upset by the 18th Amendment. Also whether it can be shifted
from one English vessel to another in New York harbor—or something like that.[4] A week ago Saturday the doctor kept me at home
and I had a delightful irresponsible day part of which I spent on
Radcliffe, *Fishing from the Earliest Times* by an enthusiast in
fishing and the classics. It was sent to me or I never should have
seen it—little as I like compulsory loans I got much pleasure from
it—pictures from Egypt, Assyria, China and what not—discussion
of a text in Martial as indicating the artificial fly—which came
first—spear, net or line—and a thousand [illegible]—just the thing
for a sick room. I read it through, with which and my love to you
I stop. I must get my case started and the barber comes at 12. I
look forward to your book adventures in Paris.

                              *Affectionately yours, O. W. Holmes*
Kindest remembrances to your Missus (feminine in spite of the
termination).

                                        *16 Warwick Gardens, 17.IV.22*
*My dear Justice:* Little news out of the ordinary except that I go
off tomorrow morning to Paris for a week. I have a full programme
there; for I have to see Poincaré,[1] Caillaux[2] and Marc Sagnier[3]
among the politicians, and Anatole France and Aulard[4] among the
men of letters. Also I propose to go book hunting, and I have composed a list of three foolscap pages of antiquities ranging from

---

[4] *Grogan* v. *Walker & Sons,* 259 U.S. 80 (May 15, 1922). Holmes, for a
majority, wrote an opinion, holding that the Eighteenth Amendment and the
Volstead Act forbade the shipments in question. McKenna, Day, and Clarke,
JJ., dissented.

[1] Raymond Poincaré (1860-1934) at this time was Premier and Minister
of Foreign Affairs.

[2] Joseph Caillaux (1863-1944) had been Premier of France in 1911 and
minister of finance in the Doumergue cabinet in 1913. His pacifism during
the First World War led to his conviction and imprisonment for correspondence with the enemy. He was released from prison in 1924 and thereafter
continued to be an important and controversial figure in French politics.

[3] Marc Sagnier, Catholic democrat.

[4] François Aulard (1849-1928); distinguished historian of the French
Revolution; author of *Histoire politique de la Révolution française* (1901).

Jean Boucher[5] to Saint-Simon of things for which to look. I have
had some fine luck here this last week. Item, Roger [sic] Wiseman,
*The Excellency of the Civil Law* (1656), a book intended to show
that the real reform of the law is not the scheme contemplated by
the Commonwealth Commission, but the entire abrogation of the
Common Law and its replacement by the law of Rome. It's an
able essay, a little lyrical in places, and, of course, over-simple in
its claims. But it shows a real perception of the weaknesses of the
common law. Item, also a *Parte of a Register* (1590). This is very
rare. It was secretly printed and contains the Puritan attacks on the
English church during Elizabeth's reign. McIlwain, I think, had
never seen a copy. Item, a volume of pamphlets on the Wilkes
controversy which belonged originally to Woodfall, Wilkes' printer
and has some notes in by him. One is to the effect that Camden is
the greatest judge that ever was "and knows the burdens under
which we poor printers groan." [6] But my best find is really more
interesting than anything I have come across in the last few years.
It was a bundle containing thirty unprinted speeches delivered by
John Stuart Mill to the London Debating Society in his own autograph—on which society and its value to him, see the *Autobiography*. You will find there what a change in him was produced by
the reading of Wordsworth. I have the MS of a speech on Wordsworth in which all this is set out. There is an able, if Puritan attack
on Byron. You will find in the *Autobiography* a reference to an
impressive debate with Thirlwall the historian.[7] I have Mill's
original speech and his answer to Thirlwall's reply. All the others
are good stuff—on the Church, lawyers, radical reform, the use of
history, university education. What exactly I shall do with them I
don't quite know yet. The debate with Thirlwall I expect I shall
print in the *Economic Journal* [8] as it is historically important because of its attack on Robert Owen and its analysis of Malthus. It's
a pity that I haven't Thirlwall's own speech to complete the sequence. It's very amusing to note what a saving disposition Mill

---

[5] Jean Boucher (1540-1644) was the French theologian whose energies
were largely devoted to the Catholic League and who wrote a forceful
pamphlet justifying the assassination of Henry III, *De justa Henrici III
abdicatione* (1589).

[6] Charles Pratt (1714-1794), Lord Camden, as Chief Justice of the Common Pleas, had done much to preserve the constitutional rights of Wilkes;
after he was removed as Lord Chancellor, in the House of Lords, he effectively criticized the action of Lord Mansfield in the prosecution of Henry
Sampson Woodfall (1739-1805) for libel in publishing Junius's letter to the
King in the *Public Advertiser*.

[7] Connop Thirlwall (1797-1875), barrister, bishop, and historian, best
known for his *History of Greece* (8 vols., 1835-44). See Mill's *Autobiography* (New York, 1874), p. 125.

[8] See Laski's 1924 edition of Mill's *Autobiography* (London) and its
appendix.

had. Some of the speeches are written on the backs of letters from
George Grote, Charles Austin[9] *et al.* I sold two of them for two
guineas which was the price I paid for them all. The Oxford Press
wanted me to make a little volume of them to be called the early
speeches of J. S. M. but I have refused since he could have published them himself and evidently did not care to, and in any
case their interest is rather for a person to whom Mill is personally
attractive as he is to me than any general widespread importance.
But I shall have a jolly afternoon reading them to Morley when I
come back from Paris and reminiscencing on the Victorian age.
. . . I suppose you will have heard of Dicey's death. I enclose a
little paragraph of mine upon him which says what I feel.[10] I only
saw him twice after my return from America; and his deafness
made talk very difficult. But I think he was a great man, and the
position he had won for himself as a constitutional lawyer was
remarkable. I can think only of one instance where he used his
authority unjustly—when he tried in 1911 to argue that the Parliament Act was unconstitutional—he who had done more than any
living person to disprove the idea of unconstitutionality. But that
was the only lapse I can think of. He was very kind to me at Oxford, and very stimulating as a teacher; and he and Pollock were
the only two considerable lawyers I know who understood what
the teaching of law in England might be if we founded here a
Harvard Law School. . . .

My love to you both. I hope to send you some real news next
time.                                        *Ever affectionately yours, H. J. L.*


*Washington, D.C., May 3, 1922*
*Dear Laski:* By this time you are back from your Paris trip on
which you were starting when your letter came a day or two ago.
I am glad you gave an appreciation to Dicey—dear old chap—he
leaves a big blank behind him. I loved him personally and read
with pleasure all that he wrote. It was voluminous (in character)
yet not loose fibred. I mean by voluminous that it suggested that
he could go on like that for miles—yet never a page that one
wouldn't want to read.

Your purchases and discoveries made me gasp. I think you were
very right to refuse to publish the Mill speeches *en bloc*—indeed
I think it would be very wrong to publish them—as he didn't.

I have been hard at work—not feeling very well—as I had an
attack of asthma and still cough more or less at night—and at the

---

[9] Charles Austin (1799-1874), ardent Benthamite and for years a leader
of the English bar, where his financial successes equaled his oratorical
achievements.
[10] 31 *Nation and Athenaeum* 77 (Apr. 15, 1922).

same time having people, mostly relatives, in the house. Frankfurter and Mrs. were here for 1 night (or possibly 2) and gave me
joy only qualified by the limited time I had for them. Some others
whom I have met reminded me of what I read in the *Atlantic
Monthly* last summer that except for a brief moment in Greece
conversation has consisted in imparting information that the other
person did not wish to receive. People ought not to be trusted with
facts until they are warranted not to use them.

If I went on long you soon would see that I am tired. I think I
go to bed too late—and there has been a string of stuff. There is
still ahead of me a despairing case to fix the boundary line between
Texas and Oklahoma.[1] Private war between the states was immi-
nent when we put in a receiver. The sandy waste that no one cared
about a few years ago turned out to be full of oil and we have had
a polygonous fight between T., Okla. and the U.S. and many
private claimants. We have decided that Texas owns only to the
South bank of the Red River and also decided questions between
Okla. and the U.S. but the question remains where the South bank
is. The briefs are as long as the Bible—and the record susceptible
only of cubic measures. I wish they were to Hell. Taft continues
to give me great satisfaction as C.J. He delivered a decision last
Monday on the power of Congress to deal with commission merchants and dealers in the Stock Yards that had a kind of big
movement in it parallel to the interstate trade he sought to por-
tray.[2] Also he is amiable and comfortable.

I close my potato trap and seek a moment of repose before
going on.                    *As ever affectionately yours, O. W. Holmes*


*16 Warwick Gardens, 30.IV.22*
*My dear Justice:* . . . I had a very interesting time in France,
crowded with incident.[1] Let me begin with people and then go on
to less fleshly matters. I saw Poincaré the Prime Minister for half-
an-hour and disliked him exceedingly. He is obviously a first-rate
intelligence, but full of rancour and bitterness and the yearning
for revenge. He hates not only Germany and Russia, but England
and America and Italy. The only point of agreement we found was
a common admiration for his brother Henri.[2] But if the destinies of
France are for long to be entrusted to him, I don't think Europe
has much future. He sees everything in terms of the war. He isn't

---

[1] *Oklahoma* v. *Texas,* 258 U.S. 574 (May 1, 1922; opinion of Van
Devanter, J.).

[2] *Stafford* v. *Wallace,* 258 U.S. 491 (May 1, 1922).

[1] Laski wrote of his trip in "A Little Tour in France," 31 *Nation and
Athenaeum* 188 (May 6, 1922).

[2] Raymond and Henri Poincaré were cousins, not brothers.

large-minded enough to make the transition to peace. He seemed
to me exceedingly reckless in all his judgments, and to have no
first-hand knowledge of the economic situation outside of France.
But he knows what he wants, and he knows how to get what he
wants. If I were as certain about a single really grave problem as
he is about the solutions to all his problems I should feel that life
was very simple. We did little save attack each other; he spoke
with great feeling and eloquence; and I felt as an early Christian
must have felt when Nero spoke of the regretful necessity of sending him to the lions.

Then I saw Anatole France and he is unmitigatedly delightful.
He is old now, and a little fragile, but his mind is like a razor. He
is exactly a twentieth century Voltaire and his easy scepticism
combined with his passion for truth and contempt for organized
religion are very attractive. He knows old books from within and
they mean things to him as they do to us—his treasure being a
book that once belonged to Montaigne. Some of his epigrams may
tickle you as a connoisseur in these matters. "When I was young,
I wanted to enter politics, because I believed that the politicians
could do everything; when I was middle-aged I used to pray that
they would do something; now that I am old, I pray that they
will do nothing." "I never go to the Capitol at Rome without gazing at the statue of the Emperor Constantine and saying to myself
'Ah! Apostate!' " "I rarely meet a Jew who is not in practice a
Christian; I never meet a Christian who does not hate Jews." So it
went on in an unending stream of sheer delight; and I rather
enjoyed the way when the old man mouthed a particularly spicy
morsel he looked at me out of the corner of his eye to see that I
had really got the point. A third most interesting figure was Aulard,
the historian of the French Revolution. He is still a Jacobin of '93
and one of the two or three most impressive scholars I have ever
known. I asked him about the influence of Rousseau on the Revolution. He poured out a stream of comment, references to original
pamphlets, quotations from the debates in the convention, memo-
rials that had been unveiled between '89 and '94 all of them effort-
lessly and as though the stream of knowledge was perpetual. He
was liberal-minded in the best sense of the word—that type of
Frenchman to whom intelligence is really the great adventure of
life. These three, I think, were the pinnacles. I saw Duguit—a
rough diamond, some good ideas, but ( entre nous ) a good deal of
what Felix would call a faker. He quotes German in his books, but
I found that he cannot read it, and he has that shrill patriotism
which makes rhetoric a substitute for argument. Geny I saw—a
kind of lesser Pound; he was full of the widest and most accurate
knowledge, but he did not give birth to generalisations that were
worth the obviously high price of admission. To say, for instance,

that a legal system is the concerted effort to secure justice, and to
quote eight writers in three languages in support is really breaking
a butterfly on the wheel. I met, too, a host of younger men but
without much enthusiasm. They were mostly of the type of which
Lowell is a quite admirable specimen, accurate, mechanical-
minded, informative, but not arresting.

. . . I came back last Sunday to discover that Pound was coming to dinner. He was very amusing—so childlike, so eager, and
so full of misinterpretation. He has convinced himself that England
is militaristic—because of the regimental flags in cathedrals! He
does not think they do much work in Cambridge—because the
surroundings are so beautiful. He is full of knowledge, and always
with the right intentions. But he doesn't get the ethos of things—
or at least (perhaps more truly) I do not recognise his perceptions. We had B. Russell to meet him—the rapier against the
bludgeon. . . .

I am longing to hear from you. I heard that you had not been
well. Is that true? . . .              *Ever affectionately yours, H. J. L.*


*Washington, D.C., Friday, May 12, 1922*
*Dear Laski:* Your letters usually come just too late for me to catch
the imagined Saturday boats—whether they go on Saturdays as
*ante bellum* I never have inquired—but this one gives me hopes.
You speak of wanting to hear from me—I bear witness that *I
invariably answer at once* and always have done so. As to health I
am all right, bar a certain amount of coughing, which I expect has
come to stay. I told you I think, that I was pleased to be told that
I had an attack of asthma. I had tried to interpret symptoms in
that way long before but the doctors said no. Asthma is uncomfortable but not usually deadly—and as yet I have had none of
the severer incidents. I can feel time at work, little by little, but
his most serious manifestation is nothing more than the loosening
of an under tooth which I suppose will come out before long. On
the whole I am in very good shape. *Et toi?* I am always afraid that
you are working the machine too hard. Of course I am deeply
interested by what you say of the Frenchmen. Poincaré I knew
nothing about—not even that he was brother of the genius. I am
pleased at what you say of Duguit and Geny. It feeds my undog-
matic scepticism about them. Your account of Anatole France is
delightful. Aulard I know not of, to my shame—but you warm my
heart with your "to whom intelligence is really the great adventure
of the age." I have had a little—not much—leisure—outside law
and business—(there are always business matters to be attended
to for the summer). I read F. Hackett's *Story of the Irish People*
[*sic*]. It was sent by the publishers—and I don't quite dare to write

to them. The tale keeps you interested and rather horrified straight through—but one feels that there are counter reflections to be made, although they are not sufficiently articulate in me to find utterance. I should compliment the author with reserve as to the result. I told you, I think, what a charming letter he wrote to me when he was leaving the *New Republic*. *Treasure Island* again after many years. A book by Quiller-Couch, *On the Art of Writing* —suggestions and prejudices—worth the little time it took but not much more. Now a very ingenious *Philosophy of Speech* by George Willis, not finished, that is paying well. I should think he was a Briton with as stubborn prejudices as Coventry Patmore from his schoolmaster's platform dealing delightful, damaging whacks at English grammar and other godlinesses—such as reformed spelling —with counter reformations of his own—and tumbling all the languages in his lap like little puppies. He goes into fundamentals with the air of a master. When knowledge ends and very bold guessing begins I don't know enough to say. Just now I am at a breath stopping theory of the case of the substantives as all coming from a preposition postponed—*e.g., serve = servo-de = servod = servō* with the *o* lengthened on the dropping of the consonant and as *I* becomes *Ai* when we drop the *K* from *IK*. Here is a sample sentence "the '*bi*' in '*tibi*' = to thee, the '*bus*' in '*omnibus*' = for all, and the *by* in '*thereby*' would seem to be the same word." Does it pique you? Conference tomorrow and probably a few days work on Monday after our deliverance and motions—but I hardly think much for me. Final adjournment June 5. Boston June 7—Beverly Farms, I expect, on Saturday, the 10th. The Vice-President asked me to go to Amherst, I suppose for an honorary degree I think on the 19th which I provisionally accepted. If you would pick out from the books that you have mentioned a little list of suggestions for my summer reading you would be a benefactor.

*Affectionately yours, O. W. H.*

*16 Warwick Gardens, 15.V.22*

*My dear Justice:* Busy but interesting days. I'm now hard at it trying to get my colleagues to agree to a draft report of the Commission on settlements of which I have been chairman for the last five months.[1] Most of them have done social work for years, and it is very amusing to find that whereas the evidence shows quite clearly that, special individuals apart, the settlement benefits its workers much more than *vice-versa* still they don't like to face it. Then I've done a good deal of writing for the *Nation* and we've had some week-ends away. First we had a jolly dinner for Pound.

---

[1] Probably in connection with the First International Conference of Settlements; see *Settlements and their Outlook,* (1922), pp. 129-130.

Hirst the economist, Gooch the historian, and Nevinson. Much talk
of you, as you can guess, and most interesting questions from
Gooch as to where you, first of American lawyers, picked up the
notion of the historical examination of the common law. I couldn't
answer, neither could Pound, and I wish you would grow a little
autobiographical and tell us where that book came from. When did
you start it and where did the idea of comparative historical work
spring from: was it from reading (and meeting?) Sir H. Maine?
Pound was in excellent form and his learning and shrewd fund of
commonsense impressed everybody. Hirst was a great Hooverite
and the scrap between him and Pound thereon was quite excellent.
Then I had a very thrilling interview with Lord Robert Cecil
which gave me much insight into things. He has published a
manifesto on the present political situation[2] which agreed quite
largely with my standpoint and even more with Massingham's. So
we jawed over the whole field of politics, agreed in all save emphasis and detail. He told me things of L-G that made me gasp;
spoke quite warmly of House, but much less so of Wilson, thought
that the hope of the world lay in Anglo-American cooperation and
the determination of them both to stop by economic boycott any
recurrence of war. I can't reproduce the moral impression he made
on me except to say that I went out feeling cleaner by contact with
him. And I was so impressed that I set to work genially to intrigue
with the result that next week I have a little dinner here of him,
Haldane, Massingham, and some influential young M.P.'s to see
whether we can't arrange to give him the backing that will elevate
him to the leadership of the Liberals, Asquith being now generally
recognised as hopeless. I wish you were here for that for it will be
two hours' good talk and some port that my father gave me that
would tempt your palate a little. Then into the country for a week-
end with the Webbs and the Tawneys. . . . I came back to a
jolly dinner at Haldane's to meet some of the upper reaches of
the Civil Service. They are very impressive, cold, precise, extraordinarily well-informed and with a knowledge that is most illuminating of the source of government ideas. Yet they all clearly
had a certain curious class-bias—I mean the belief that the young
brain of England is concentrated in Oxford and Cambridge. But
they were liberal-minded and astonishingly alert; and even the
younger of them spoke with a width of experience that left me
with a sense of the most appalling immaturity. . . . Also I have
done much reading and some of it I would like to recommend for
Beverly Farms. (1) Webb on *Prisons and Local Government* with
a very brilliant preface by Shaw. I found this really thrilling and

---

[2] Lord Robert's anti-Coalitionist manifesto urged that the perilous appeals
of revolution and reaction must be resisted by a revived liberalism dedicated to the cause of freedom and committed to international peace and a
partnership, at home, between industry and labor.

treated historically it puts the whole issue on a much better footing for discussion than when one reads of it in the sentimental school. (II) *Clothing Workers of Chicago*—a fine volume and a credit to America which really shows what commonsense and good will can do to eliminate industrial disturbance if they are given a proper show. (III) G. B. Adams—*Constitutional History of England* which I thought very good on the earlier period but disappointing after 1688 where the best chance of research begins. . . .

My love to you both and insistence on great care,

*Ever affectionately yours, H. J. L.*

*Washington, D.C., June 1, 1922*
*Dear Laski:* Two, it may be three, days have gone by since I received your letter which mighty rarely happens before I answer. You ask me what started my book. Of course I can't answer for unconscious elements. I don't think Maine had anything to do with it except to feed the philosophic passion. I think the movement came from within—from the passionate demand that what sounded so arbitrary in Blackstone, for instance, should give some reasonable meaning—that the law should be proved, if it could be, to be worthy of the interest of an intelligent man—(that was the form the question took then). I went through much anguish of mind before I realized the answer to that question that I have often given since. I don't think of any special book that put me on the track—though the works that I cited such as Lehuërou helped.[1] I rooted round and made notes until the theory gradually emerged. I guess you have seen the MS book in which I collected texts and references on privity—the rights of a *res*—possession &c &c &c.

You mention for Beverly Farms, good God! Webb on this and that—and *Clothing Workers of Chicago*. My boy I mean to enjoy myself if I can—to get the unexpurgated Pepys—even read (going on) John Dewey's last[2] in a philosophical way or Pound on Law[3] but if you think that I am going to bother myself again before I die about social improvement or read any of those stinking upward and onwarders—you err. I mean to have some good out of being old. It seems to me very unlikely that even Brandeis will make me learned on the textile workers of New England and I mean to go my own way, read what gives me pleasure and leave the 'undone vast' for others. Those two words from Browning look a little like 'undone vest' (a word I never use) to be buttoned up by others. I must cut this short as I hie to the tavern for evening victuals. We

---

[1] Holmes concluded his Preface to *The Common Law* with a quotation from Julien Marie Lehuërou (1807-1843), historian of Carolingian and Merovingian institutions: *"Nous faisons une théorie et non un spicilège."*

[2] *Human Nature and Conduct* (1922).

[3] *An Introduction to the Philosophy of Law* (1922).

had the Lincoln Memorial show on Tuesday[4]—a wonderful sight
from the top where we were. I could not hear (because of inter-
vening pillars) what was said. So it is without personal application
that I wonder what makes the world throng to hear loose-fibred
and coarse-grained men drool. I am paid to listen and would not
gratuitously attend the preachment of an Apostle. I believe the
Honorable James M. Beck after his labors as Solicitor General is
to illume Gray's Inn on the Constitution of the U.S. He evidently
wanted to do something damned smart right off, as Bill Hunt used
to say, but I doubt if he has the patience to get to the bottom of
things. I wish I were not so scrabbled with things to be done on
these closing days but so it is.          *Aff'ly yours, O. W. Holmes*

*Beverly Farms, June 14, 1922*
*Dear Laski:* A letter from you arrived here with us the day before
yesterday and brought the usual joy.[1] The stinking pens of these
parts hinder all spontaneity as they hitch along the paper—and
these rotten little sheets are not fit for intelligent sceptics, but my
happiness in hearing from and writing to you may overcome the
obstacles. In one of my last I revolted from your Webbs and
Labor Conditions and indicated Wheatley's *Pepys*, two volumes
of which I have here. Your Bonar *Philosophy and Political Economy* I note and shall try for. On the way on and after I read John
Dewey, *Human Nature and Conduct*, a book that I find it hard to
characterize. It is like shavings of jade—subtle—sometimes epi-
grammatic—emancipated—seeing the world and man as fluid—an
immense advance upon any book there was when I was younger—
yet somehow not quite seeming to arrive anywhere—and not feeling to me quite as new as it is civilised. I seem to have known the
fundamentals before. Also he indicates emotional attitudes that do
not quite stir my sceptical mind. He talks of the exploitation of
man by man—which always rather gets my hair up. As I have said,
no doubt, often, it seems to me that all society rests on the death of
men. If you don't kill 'em one way you kill 'em another—or prevent their being born. Is not the present time an illustration of
Malthus?
   Enough of that—We had a hard journey on to Boston—hot with
the horrid Washington heat that gives you a fever—a jolting train
—an hour + late—our usual nice rooms at the Touraine but I
never feel well in a hotel. We stayed there from Wednesday
evening to Monday p.m. and then motored down here. I am just
beginning to feel normal, and wish I could be quiet for a month.

---

[4] The dedicatory exercises at the Lincoln Memorial in Washington had
occurred on May 30.
[1] The letter referred to is missing.

But next week I must go to Amherst if I can—motor I think—but I dread it. I have stipulated no speech. I read Felix's introduction to the Cleveland Book[2] with unmixed enthusiasm. It seems to me full of the scientific spirit. It did not seem to me too long, as I gather that it did to you.

I am excited at the thought of the big book you have promised to make. My only hesitation the eternal fear that you will run the machine too hard.

My head still feels a little woolly after the vicissitudes of travel, heat and cold—for it is cold here—so I shall shut up. As always my love to you both.                    *Aff'ly yours, O. W. Holmes*

*The Corey Hill Hospital*
*Brookline, July 7, 1922*

*Dear Laski:* Your letter[1] makes me realize that birds still sing outside—but I'm locked up while awaiting an operation. Just as I was going to Amherst for an honorary degree and as we would privately celebrate our golden wedding Fate intervened—2 days of catheter then here—pipe from my bladder—glass of water every hour and operation when the doctor says. I understand that the prospects are wholly cheerful. If not, I think I am philosophical—still such things are serious. Please keep on writing as usual and I will answer when I can. I am not good for much now.

*Your affectionate, O. W. Holmes*

*16 Warwick Gardens, 3.VII.22*

*My dear Justice:* . . . one really amusing job in getting H. G. Wells adopted as labour candidate for the university in place of Rivers. *Sacro egoismo* is a wonderful thing. I found him pining for political fame and curiously eager for the chance to fight the seat. I hinted at literary sacrifice but this was measured as worthless in the balance. . . .

People have poured in the last few weeks. Pound came in for a couple of days before sailing—full of ideas, often weird, but always interesting and effective. Haskins came also, a little ponderous and official, but very friendly. He obviously wanted me to comment on the Harvard trouble about the Jews,[1] and I was not less eager to avoid it, so we skirted round each other amusingly. . . .

My real news I keep to the last. Cambridge University has ap-

---

[2] *Criminal Justice in Cleveland* (Pound and Frankfurter, editors, 1922).

[1] Omitted from this edition.

[1] President Lowell of Harvard had recently suggested that an effective means of combatting anti-Semitism might be for all colleges to admit no more than a limited number of Jews.

pointed me a special lecturer in political science for two years. I shall go down two days a week, enjoy my own rooms in Magdalene College (a charming place, where the Pepsyian library is) and lecture (a) on the theory of the state, (b) on Political Thought from 1400-1789. It ought, I think, to be interesting; and I like, as an Oxford man, to be invited to the abode of sin. I need not tell you that a certain little note of yours was not devoid of effect.

My love to you both.          *Ever affectionately yours, H. J. L.*


*16 Warwick Gardens, 18.VII.22*

*My dear Justice:* You can imagine with what emotion I read your brief note from the hospital. To be away from you is hard enough; but to have you ill is bitter indeed. I shall venture to wire in the morning to know how you are; for operations need care. And I hope that Mrs. Holmes has been able to bear it all with her own steel courage. For you both, all my hopes and my love. It will be a happy day when I hear that you are about again.

But I will write news and not express fears. As to persons. We have had a hectic week lately going almost everywhere. First a dinner with Birrell, who was really delightful. He had dined with Taft at the Asquiths' and found him—I use his phrase—pleasant but comatose. He asked me how you and Taft got on intellectually, I said like Carlyle and Sterling.[1] "Ah," said Birrell, "I wish I had known that, for I should have told Taft that he was lucky in presiding over a court where he had Holmes, J. to follow." . . . On Thursday a jolly lunch at Oswald Mosley's—political gossip mainly, with one or two pleasant touches of malice. X.Y. becomes a trustee of the National Gallery, being a war-millionaire. Invited to present a picture by his fellow trustees, he indicates his belief that there are pictures enough there already and he would sooner keep his money in his pocket. He also buys a large country house, and hearing that decorated ceilings are fashionable, gets Charles Sims[2] to do him one. Guests pass the criticism that it is too lightly painted and X.Y. sends for the artist and suggests that he "darken in the background." I don't think any Chicago extravaganza went beyond these. . . .

Well—till next week. With Mrs. Holmes at your elbow I need not ask you to take care. Don't bother to write to me—a pencilled note from a maid to say that you improve is all I want. And may that golden wedding indeed be golden. You have known wonders that way as I have done, and she has always seemed to me as ex-

---

[1] John Sterling (1806-1844), English author whose name survives in literary history not by reason of his talent but because Carlyle was his biographer and friend.

[2] Charles Sims (1873-1928); British artist, known for the freshness of his talents as portraitist and muralist.

quisite in her sweet insight as anyone I have ever known. I salute
you both with all my heart, and I am to lay Frida's at your feet.

*Ever affectionately yours, Harold J. L.*

I address to B. Farms for safety.

*Beverly Farms, Saturday, August 19, 1922*

*Dear Laski:* Are you prepared for a renewal? A feeble one, I fear,
on this side, at first. We motored over here on Thursday p.m. and
on my arrival the doctor sent me to bed. Yesterday I idled and
gawped. I begin today with you. But I tell you what, it is easier to
get into one of these big things than it is to get out. The operation
was most successful and I recovered without hitch to the point of
being discharged. Now comes the time for recuperation and more
doctors. He says, before this I had noticed that the end of your
nose was white &c. That means that the reaction (the return kick
of circulation as I understand it) is not quite what it should be.
Otherwise you are in good shape—we must build that up—we can
—those pills—keep the nurse a few days—she will report pulse
etc. Meantime I lollup round upon my lounge—try to rejoice in
irresponsibility and having nothing to do, read a little Shakespeare
and snooze. Everything is encouraging but at this moment the
fact is that I am rather a feeble old man—who however is going in
for 90 if he can get it. I don't know whether you knew John
Palfrey? [1] An able chap whose only drawback is that he hasn't
goods in his shop window. He has been an angel—has helped my
wife through all the business of accounts and check drawing—
and insists on regarding it as if done for parents and not business.
Forgive the egotism of an invalid. It can't be helped. Have you
read Santayana's *Soliloquies* ('Soliquities' my nurse called them)?
His scepticism seems most akin to my own—his dogmas or preferences the results of a temperament and Catholic bringing up that
we have a perfect right not to share and I don't. When he speaks
of life as hideous I venture to see the Church rather than a free
aesthetic judgment. But I am not yet fit to talk as a thinking being
—though I am very fit to receive the talk of another—and as I
ought to be down I will shut up—but sending you my love.

*Aff'ly yours, O. W. H.*

*Grand Hotel, Belgium, 26.VIII.22*

*My dear Justice:* I am hoping that silence is the best of messengers.
But it will be a real joy to have definite news that you are about
again.

---

[1] John G. Palfrey (1875-1945), Boston lawyer, was the nephew of one of
Holmes's commanding officers in the Civil War and became over the years
his close personal friend and attorney.

. . . I do not write of politics. But I am glad you are away from the sense of impending doom that hangs over Europe just now. My friend Collins killed in Ireland; Rathenau's death taking from Germany its one great statesman[1]—and the fires of Russia slowly spreading. I am eager to get home, more eager still to talk with people above the hum of daily cares.

Our warm love to you both.     *Ever affectionately yours, H. J. L.*

*Beverly Farms, September 10, 1922*
*Dear Laski:* A letter just received from you in Belgium speaks of silence but I have answered—with poor little answers to be sure—every letter when it was received. I wish I had things to tell you in return but I am still on the monotonous road of slow convalescence. I still too am in Shakespeare (I wonder if I misquoted *A. & Cleop.* to you—if I did I know better.) Now it is the historical plays and there the word-fugues leave nothing to be said. Kings, I suspect, don't talk as Richard II does about death when in his circumstances—but a sympathetic angel does—in a higher sphere. So the dying Gaunt about England—all the later passion for England—Kipling—Brooke—recent war poems—a million other expressions, seem inspired by the bard. As I believe I said before one doesn't complain that Shakespeare can talk better than Macbeth. One's only reserve is *C'est magnifique mais ce n'est pas la vie.* It makes one remember Turner's reputed answer to one who said nature didn't look to him like that. "Don't you wish it did?" Law! how out of everything I am. Frankfurter sent me Morison's *Prologue to American History*—his Oxford Inaugural Lecture. I have read only a part but it seems very good. I believe he (Morison) is really a new literary light. But beyond this I believe I have not looked into a pamphlet or a paper or a new book.

Have patience with me for a while—I still feel rather sorry for myself. The Court looks as if it would have a shaky beginning of the term.[1] I assume that I shall be all right, but the papers treat Day's resignation as possible. I know nothing about McKenna—but fear that Pitney is far from well—and we shall have Sutherland *vice* Clarke. I didn't admire Clarke's rhetoric but he believed

<hr/>

[1] On the deaths of Collins and Rathenau, see, *supra,* p. 301.
[1] On September 1 Mr. Justice Clarke tendered his resignation from the Supreme Court. On November 13 Mr. Justice Day retired, as did Mr. Justice Pitney on December 31. On September 5 Senator George Sutherland of Utah was nominated and confirmed to succeed Clarke, J. The vacancies resulting from the retirement of Day and Pitney, JJ., were filled by Pierce Butler, who took office in January 1923, and Edward T. Sanford, who took his seat in February 1923.

it—which is something and I shall miss his affectionate companionship. If you are not discouraged in writing you can have no more appreciative reader of your letters. My love to you both.

*Aff'ly yours, O. W. H.*

*16 Warwick Gardens, 6.9.22*
*My dear Justice:* It was indeed delightful to find your letter[1] when I got here on Monday. And I can't find words to express my gladness at the swiftness and (I hope) completeness of your recovery. I dare not say that I am eager that your nose should be really red, but I shall be glad to know that it has become in, of course, a purely medical sense, roseate.

. . . Tonight we have Dean Acheson, whom you will remember as Brandeis's secretary, to dinner, on Sunday Ruth True,[2] who, from her letter, seems to be one of Felix's spiritual harem, and on Tuesday Roy Hack[3] a clever young professor of classics from Harvard. The Americans are here in shoals. On Monday night I saw House with Massingham, but though, as always, he was charming, I can't say that he had much of illumination to contribute. He prophesied hell for Europe; that we see. He foretold slow improvement for America; that we hear of. He expressed his opinion that Wilson is a misjudged man; to which I replied in Montaigne's wise sentence that all wise men know that men in high place are misjudged, but like so many statesmen, he mistook diagnosis of a disease for the relief of the trouble. He seemed to think that America was moving towards intervention in Europe, but I can't say that he was very convincing. . . .   *Ever yours, H. J. L.*

*Beverly Farms, September 22, 1922*
*Dear Laski:* Your letter of the 6th gives me the usual pleasure. Each letter is a literary event for me. Beyond that my only one is that I have finished the Bard—his plays I mean. As Barlow remarked to me the other day in other words, if a man does the trick he remains, and it doesn't matter how much other stuff he pours out! I wound up with *Othello, Lear* and *Macbeth* and one is inclined to be silent about them—they are so stupendous.

---

[1] *Supra,* p. 333.

[2] Miss Ruth True was a research worker in the Children's Bureau of the Department of Labor in Washington.

[3] Roy Kenneth Hack (1884-1944) was Assistant Professor of Classics at Harvard from 1918 to 1923. Subsequently he taught in the Graduate School of the University of Cincinnati.

*Othello* is disagreeable to me because his villain comes down front
and tells you he is a villain and what nasty things he means to
do, and chance favors him unfairly, but the talk is so tremendous
that you forgive that. As to Shakespeare generally, apart from the
superlative passages, as I believe I said the other day, he can talk
better than Richard II or Macbeth or any of the rest of them, and
he gives you his talk without too much regard to whose mouth he
uses. It is a transcendent echo of life rather than life. How far is
our pleasure in his language a matter of education and convention
like that in the language of the Bible or the French delight in snor-
ing tirades in Alexandrine verse which gives me no pleasure at all?
Tomorrow, (Saturday) we go to the Touraine, and on Tuesday
26th go on by night to Washington, where, for I hope few days,
we put up at the Powhatan while they complete an elevator from
the first to the second story of my house. It is a costly business—
a surgical operation and the consequences—if the elevator can be
called one. I am stronger on my legs and better than I was even
a week ago and feel as if I could stand any usual intellectual tax
—but Palfrey says that one is liable for months to a mental blank
that will frighten one while it lasts—and as the mind draws on the
same fund as the body I suppose one must be careful. I have had
warning from many—and an occasional suggestion that I should
drop the job and take my ease—but I want to produce as long as I
can and think that I shall be intellectually honest in judging my
condition and product. At least I am alert in anxiety not to deceive
myself. As you have seen we have Sutherland not L. Hand as you
wished. I should think he would be up to the average of the Court
but don't know much about it. I have lived in invalid isolation,
bar an occasional call, and have lost all relation with outside affairs
beyond a vague anxiety. Pray do you keep well.

*Aff'ly yours, O. W. H.*

My salutations to Mrs. Laski.


*16 Warwick Gardens, 13.9.22*

*My dear Justice:* . . . People begin to drift back slowly and I
have seen one or two. Yesterday I lunched with Asquith's chief
henchman in the Commons, Donald Maclean, whom I have liked
much. He gave me a melancholy history—Asquith devoted to
bridge and small talk, doing no real work, and leaving the party
leaderless. I gathered that they all want him to go, and see no
means of explaining to him how much he stands in the way. He
told me one delightful story of President Wilson. Morley met him,
and asked afterwards for his opinion said he was like a jealous
woman who regards interest in other ideas than his own as an

act of sexual aberration. There is a real truth in that, as Felix and Walter Lippmann could bear witness. . . .

My warm love to you both.                    *Ever yours, H. J. L.*


*Washington, D.C., September 28, 1922*

*Dear Laski:* It is likely to be long before you receive a letter from here that you honestly can say is worth reading for anything but affection. The work lies before me in cubic yards, but I shall not tackle it until tomorrow. We got here yesterday morning less fatigued than we expected. I did some very good sleeping—but was disgracefully wheeled in a chair from the car to the taxi. Which means that although I am in very good spirits and am not afraid of hard work, my body is still somewhat weak and easily is tired. The house except the back half of my library is chaos—for putting in an elevator from the first to the second story. So I expect to put up at the Powhatan for a fortnight. We have a wonderful suite on the 9th floor and can look on the Kingdom of the Earth.

Please make a note to let me know if you can without much trouble whether Professor John M. Morgan,[1] at one time professor of Constitutional Law in the University of London still lives and what his address [is]. I found on my table, as yet unexplained, a copy of the *19th Century* for November, 1910 with a letter from him of October, 1910 and an article of his. I may have seen them and answered but have no recollection of ever having seen them before. I have a warm regard for him. I am pretty sure that I have written to him since then. I think *pendente bello*. You would shudder to see in what levities I have been taking pleasure by a writer called Don Marquis—in his lower moments brutalizing (or almost) noble legends into farce—but having also an original vein. There are verses in a book with the unprepossessing name *Old Soak*, with a ditto picture of Old Soaks, that are funny and original in the superlative degree. Also a volume *Hermione*—the discourse of a rich young woman who takes up with her group of advanced and serious thinkers all sorts of things from the Cosmos and the Infinite to Trial Marriages—that I found very funny and hitting with legitimate exaggeration the pretences of many young women to serious thought.

And that is all. I just finished Shakespeare in the time that would have sufficed for you to read the last edition of the *Encyclopaedia Britannica,* and am largely preoccupied with the egotisms of an invalid—but that will be blown out of me next week.

---

[1] General John H. Morgan (1876-1955); author of *The House of Lords and the Constitution* (1910). The article referred to by Holmes was presumably his "The Constitution in Writing," 68 *Nineteenth Century* 765 (November 1910).

338 )                                                ( 1922

I can't do much stirring round. To put away the contents of the
one trunk I sent on from B.F. here was enough. When the secretary comes tomorrow he will undo and sort the packages from
the Clerk's Office and I will see what progress I can make. I shall
not worry if I can't recite on all the *certioraris* (applications for
leave to come up to us) with which we begin the Term—especially as the only difference would be that more may be let in. I
being rather Rhadamanthine on that. And so no more at present
from yours ever,                                        *O. W. H.*


                                *1720 I Street, October 22, 1922*
                                *Ball's Bluff 61 years ago, yesterday—*
*Dear Laski:* A letter[1] from you delightful as always came yesterday. I have just driven to this house from the Powhatan—I walk
very little—not at all as yet, down here, and the doctor says don't
walk uphill when I do. It is 12 and a former secretary is coming
to see me—but although I think I hear him downstairs I think
ere the day is over I shall have a chance to write. We adjourn on
Monday for 3 weeks and the breathlessness will let up for a time
—I expect to deliver an opinion (interrupted here) tomorrow that
I am not ashamed of.[2] One last Monday[3] was about on a par with
the *New England Primer*—and was saved from being worse by
my Secretary suggesting that I cut out a chunk. In this one my
brethren, as usual and as I expected, corrected my taste when I
spoke of relying upon the petty larceny of the police power, dele
"the petty larceny of." It is done—our effort is to please. But I
saved something that I really wanted by giving it a turn as if it
might have come from the Court below—no false representations,
only a slight ambiguity. My former secretary, Landau,[4] I doubt
if you knew him, made a very pleasant call. He shows an affection that I return. My present one, Benjamin,[5] also is a Jew—as
yet rather solemn but efficient. He hasn't had much of a chance

---

[1] In this letter, omitted from this edition, Laski said that J. H. Morgan
was lecturing at the London School of Economics on Constitutional Law.
[2] *Jackman* v. *Rosenbaum Co.*, 260 U.S. 22 (Oct. 23, 1922). In sustaining
a Pennsylvania statute, based on custom, permitting an adjoining owner to
destroy an old and rebuild a new party wall without liability for damages,
Holmes had said that if "from time immemorial, it has been the understanding that the burden exists, the land owner does not have the right to
that part of his land, except as so qualified and the statute that embodies
that understanding does not need to invoke the police power."
[3] *Knights* v. *Jackson*, 260 U.S. 12 (Oct. 16, 1922).
[4] Lloyd H. Landau (1893-1957) graduated from the Harvard Law School
in 1918 and was Holmes's secretary during the October term of the Supreme
Court in 1918-19.
[5] Robert M. Benjamin (1896-    ) had graduated from the Harvard Law
School in June 1922.

as yet in our confusion. I hope that in a few days I shall be allowed to sleep in the house, even if the cage isn't put into the
elevator—but they are afraid of my walking up the front stairs—
which, by direction, I do like a child, the same foot first all the
time—or stop halfway and change. Forgive these silly details—
they are put in as circumstantial confirmation of apologies. Taft
continues a very agreeable presiding officer—he is not brief—but
he carries things along with good humor and is disinclined to put
cases over—so we get work done—but we didn't finish our conference yesterday till 5:30 which is a pretty long pull.

Now it is 3 p.m. and I am going out for a drive with my wife.
How I wish I could counter your learned ac- and dis- quisitions
with a worthy equivalent—but that may not be *à presong*. Later
—but if I could picture to you the drive to Great Falls it would
be an equivalent, all the wonder shows of the autumn and of the
noble Potomac. Did you ever go up there? I am impressed to my
marrow whenever I do. I suppose Ball's Bluff is 30 miles more or
less further up—and if the Virginia side of the River is the same
in between as it is here and according to my dim memory was
there, it is one of the rivers of the world, and I am so pleased
with the old canal on this side with an occasional canal boat on
which I believe children are born, live and grow up. The result
is that it is dinner time and I have done no work—but I don't
care. It has been a wonderful day. If I had any visual memory I
should remember it always—as it is, it will fade, while your discourse remains.                          *Yours as ever, O. W. Holmes*


*16 Warwick Gardens, 30.X.22*
*My dear Justice:* I am living in a nightmare, for what with lectures and the general election[1] I neither read nor think. The only
merit is that it will be over in a fortnight. I escaped having to
stand by the skin of my teeth; Tawney's illness, (he's getting
better) fortunately enabling me to plead the duty of deputising
for him. So once a day I go down to Tottenham, address a meeting, and come home bewildered by democracy. It's very interesting, of course; but it's an unholy way of obtaining political power.
Above all, I note the appalling rate at which one makes generalisations, after a time not even attempting to put in finer shades. I
comfort myself by the knowledge that my invective against Lloyd-
George is reasonably accurate and that the rest is as god made
democratic government. I am speaking also for Bertrand Russell

---

[1] On October 19 the Lloyd George Coalition Government resigned; on the
23rd Mr. Bonar Law, Unionist leader, was appointed Prime Minister by
the King. On the 26th Parliament was dissolved and November 15 was fixed
as the date for a General Election.

—in fact such is my relief at not having to be a candidate that I would speak almost for anyone out of sheer sympathy. It's a queer election, in which I expect (i) to see the Tories returned (ii) a great increase in the number of labour members (iii) the virtual disappearance of L-George's party. When the show is over and I have time to breathe again I must write you the whole story of his fall—as dramatic an episode as there is in our annals. Meanwhile—this salute from the middle of a great fight and my love in heaps to you both.        *Ever affectionately yours, H. J. L.*

*1720 I Street, November 11, 1922*
*Oh, my dear Laski:* Your note tells of hurry and crowded hours. Mine also have been so, but with less noble exigencies. I have been shut up with a cold—and then have just moved back to this house, and the myriad nothings of adjustment tire me so that I hardly can sleep. Just now my secretary has been replacing St. Jerome, Ostade, and at this moment Van Dyke on the side of the slightly changed bookcase. (The elevator occupies the space of what was a closet in our bedroom and pushed out where the folios were as you entered the library if you remember.) I am gaining space by sending off (that is I intend to) the old *Encyclopedia Britannica* and Rees's *Cyclopedeia* to the Pittsfield Library which has a lot of my father's books, and may give them a place. Also I shall send back the Circuit Court of Appeals reports—superfluous duplication. Wouldn't you rather have an empty shelf than a full one? I gaze with rapture on some void spaces that I already have accomplished. There is still considerable to be done and we begin a four weeks sitting on Monday. Nasty letter files, books, photographs—framed things with no place for them—and the Lord knows what, waiting to be sorted out. Thank heavens for fire. I have burned a reasonable number of sacred relics, but always as you begin to breathe free emerges another mass of stuff, and I know that there are cubes out of sight in boxes and what not. Yet I have been considerate to my successors and haven't left a fraction of what I might have. At odd minutes I have read the 2nd volume of Warren's book on the Supreme Court. It is truly admirable. I incline to think better and more instructive than even Beveridge's *Marshall*—although I wouldn't say so publicly— especially just now as poor Beveridge has been defeated in his attempt to go back to the Senate. I feel some solicitude about him. I haven't seen him for a year but the Beverly doctor seems to think that he had been running his machinery very hard, and I am afraid his failure will cut him deeply—but perhaps not. Brandeis always thinks B. better fitted for literature than for poli-

tics, and hoped he wouldn't try to come back. Well dear boy, it is a worm that writes to you—but an affectionate worm that wishes you well. I expect to fire off three cases on Monday[1]—all I have— nothing much—but one perhaps is pretty good.

*Aff'ly yours, O. W. H.*

*16 Warwick Gardens, 29.XI.22*

*My dear Justice:* . . . The election was a thrilling affair. I made some fifty speeches in three weeks—mainly for Russell, H. G. Wells, Tawney and Webb. Only the last was successful, but generally we did very well and I think we have recreated a real opposition, which is the main root of a continued social peace.[1] I have been once to the new House since operations began and I like its spirit. The government is a series of Hardings—dull, rather bizarre, and without debating strength. So on the principle *populus credit quia impossible* I give it three years.

Meanwhile the normal course of work. Cambridge I have liked immensely. It has always been a weekly rest, and the joy of having half-a-dozen first-rate book shops to pillage has been an added attraction. I make certain observations. The intellectual level of the senior common-rooms is not very high. Talk tends to be chit-chat, and the state of the world what is gleaned from the morning's paper. The average don, too, is too much absorbed in the daily round to grasp the relation of research to his teaching. He cultivates his little garden; but I don't think he experiments enough with new seeds. The one joy I have had is in meeting R. H. Murray[2]—the author of *Erasmus and Luther*—a precious monument of learning. He's a scholar after my own heart, who knows his texts, takes the *genus humanum* with a smile and doesn't believe that Plato and Aristotle solved the problems of the universe. Some of the big men of science are attractive—especially Rutherford the radio-activity man. But most combine pleasantness in a very high degree with a pale intellectualism which is neither deep nor broad. I prefer London a thousand times—but I like peeping into Cambridge. . . .                    *Ever affectionately yours, Harold J. Laski*

---

[1] *Keokuk and Hamilton Bridge Co.* v. *United States*, 260 U.S. 125; *McKee* v. *Grotz, id.* 127; *Brown* v. *Thorne, id.* 137.

[1] In the General Election of November 15 the strength of the principal parties in the House of Commons was as follows: Unionist, 344; Labour, 138; Liberals, 60; National Liberals, 56. Laski wrote of the new House of Commons in 32 *Nation and Athenaeum* 308 (Nov. 25, 1922).

[2] Canon Robert H. Murray (1874-1947), historian of religion and political theory; author of *Political Consequences of the Reformation* (1926); *Life of Edmund Burke* (1931).

*Washington, D.C., December 14, 1922*

*Dear Laski:* Your letter came just after Zimmern and I had inter-
changed regrets at your silence which he explained by your electioneering activities. It makes up for the hiatus. It came just after
the 20th anniversary of my taking my seat here, the 8th, which,
to my surprise, some people remembered, with flowers and letters
—some very nice and moving ones. Tomorrow will be 40 years
from my going on the Bench of Massachusetts—a good long time
of judicial service. I will enclose with this my last opinion with
Brandeis's dissent—delivered last Monday.[1] It was a question of
degree, upon which people naturally differ but the lads were with
me, except B. If you read the document you will see that I do
not, as he suggests, rely upon average reciprocity of advantage as
a general ground, but only to explain a certain class of cases. I
am still writing—I have one case to be done—but we are adjourned
until January 2 so I hope for a little leisure. Zimmern told me that
you spoke slightingly of Douglas (and Orage) *Credit, Power and
Democracy.* It so happens that I sent for it a few days ago as the
widow of Franklin Ford thought it had the future in its belly. He
used to write to me occasionally and I never quite made up my
mind whether he was a genius or a crank. I gathered that this
book was in the line of his ideas. Until I hear otherwise from you
I think I shall let the book wait. I believe I told you that I lately
got Frazer's 1 volume edition of his *Golden Bough*—as I suspected
him of riding a hobby I had let the 7 volumes alone especially in
view of Lowie, *Primitive Society.* I think I mentioned this also. I
have Azo's *Summa*—but my recollection is that I paid old Quaritch[2] £10 for it. When I asked if he could get it for me he said
you can get anything, if you will wait, and pay for it. Which I
thought memorable. . . . The secretary works well. The little
fiend seems to have discovered an omission in my last income tax
return which will necessitate my sending a check for a hundred
and odd more dollars to the Collector. What with hospital and

---

[1] *Pennsylvania Coal Co.* v. *Mahon* 260 U.S. 393 (Dec. 11, 1922). A
Pennsylvania statute which forbade mining operations beneath improved
lands was found by the majority of the Court to be unconstitutional when
it was applied to owners who in conveying rights to the surface occupants
had reserved the right to mine as they saw fit, without regard to surface
damage which might result. Holmes, for the majority, said that the state's
action could be justified only if compensation were paid, as an eminent
domain. In distinguishing an earlier case in which the Court had held that
mining companies might be required to leave pillars of coal standing in the
mines, Holmes said that in that case the regulation "was a requirement for
the safety of employees invited into the mine, and secured an average
reciprocity of advantage that had been recognized as a justification of various
laws." *Id.* at p. 415.

[2] Bernard Quaritch (1819-1899), German-born dealer in rare books,
whose London store was established in 1847.

elevator this has not been a rich year. Among minor matters I have just received a letter from the great grand-daughter, I think it is, of the old woman into whose house I was put after Antietam. She suggests that her nursing saved my life. General Le Duc who put me there told me that he used some threats to force me upon an unwilling hostess.[3] I don't quite determine whether the letter was written for largesse. It won't get it unless I change my mind. These whiffs from sixty years since have a certain interest however.

Have I mentioned Owen Wister's *Neighbors Henceforth*? I haven't finished it as I have read nothing for weeks, but his account of his travels in France within a year of the war and his sympathetic alternative appreciation of French and Yankee have moved and pleased me. I hope to be more cultivated in, say, a week. I think that I grow stronger. I took something of a walk yesterday and was none the worse for it. The work so far as I can see doesn't hurt me at all—but I don't go about, dine out or give dinners—I think that we shall drop out of society. And now, to work!                    *Affectionately yours, O. W. Holmes*


                              *Washington, D.C., December 22, 1922*
*My dear Laski:* No news since my last recently sent—so my answer to yours of the 5th[1] received yesterday p.m. will be short. I found that Douglas and Orage *Credit, Power and Democracy* was short and I am through it without waiting for you. I didn't follow its reasoning clearly, but felt that I could see the outside limits of its use to me and so put it in the shelves. To free me from scruples, the same or the next evening your Mr. Martin[2] (clever chap) turned up and gave me an account of an evening with the authors at the Webbs with Bertrand Russell *et al.*—and brought peace to my spirit. The next evening he dined with us and I enjoyed talking with him very much, though I am far from sharing all his views. All manner of details present themselves as soon as one has a little leisure down to the clearing out of corners and making more room in one's bookshelves. My! I feel so clean—the result is that the days go by with little reading done. I have just past [*sic*] the middle of the one volume *Golden Bough*—the pages pitilessly snug with compact print—the ideas—I dare say to a considerable extent originating with Frazer—but familiar—the illustrations for

---

[3] The incident is described in *Touched with Fire* (Howe, ed., 1946), 65-66 footnote. See also "The Man who Rescued the Captain," 180 *Atlantic Monthly* 80 (August 1947).

[1] Omitted from this edition.

[2] Kingsley Martin, best known as editor of *The New Statesman and Nation* [A.H.].

the practice of the Bugaboos—the Wee Wees—the Beshitkas and manifold other savages—making as my father used to quote the Scotsman for saying about the calf's (sheep's) head—fine confused eating—the whole rather a reinforcement than an illumination—and heartbreaking to one who wanted to get through it—even though content to read. I can't bring my conscience to skimming—I have to read every word, though probably with no better result than if I just took the tips of the asparagus. So I shall be lucky if I have finished the damn thing by the time we go back to Court. You meantime will have eviscerated 100 pamphlets, and skun six folios, and eaten X octavos, all *en route* for a *magnum opus*. Fired by that thought I resume Frazer. My love and Christmas wishes to you both.          *Affectionately yours, O. W. Holmes*

I sent you a decision in my last. I enclose another according to your request[3]—one other rather interesting one I have no spare copy of. In this one I send I coined the formula 'average reciprocity of advantage' which I think neatly expressed the rationale of certain cases—not of all as Brandeis did vainly talk in his dissent that I sent you before.


*Washington, D.C., January 6, 1923*

*Dear Laski:* There is little to tell from this side in reply to a letter 23.XII.22[1] more delightful even than usual—and every letter is a delight. The Saturday conference is on. I came home with Brandeis who grew really eloquent on the evils of the present organization of society. When I repeated my oft repeated views as to the economic elements he told me they were superficial and didn't deal with the real evil, which was not a question of luxuries or victuals but of power. He was fierce and fine as [to] the men he knew who didn't dare say what they thought because of the power to which they were subject. He compared the Scotsmen who eat oatmeal, but stood up—men. Then said that I hadn't seen and knew nothing about the evils that one who had been much in affairs had seen and known. He bullies me a little on that from time to time. I didn't say more than that I thought that there might be an answer and that every society rested on the death of men—meaning that I surmised that the repressions and extinctions are the inevitable results of the situation. That they have been, I regard as sufficiently established by their occurrence. But that merely means that when I say my thought I apply the words good and bad only to the future—unless I hope to influence the future by rhetorical condemnation of something that has happened—and for all that Brandeis may be right as to the thing to be

---

[3] *Jackman v. Rosenbaum Co.*, 260 U.S. 22, 30 (Oct. 23, 1922).
[1] Omitted from this edition.

desired. I don't know what practical conclusions he would draw—
unless it might be a modified Sherman Act, not allowing a combination to go beyond a certain size.

Now that work has begun again I have read nothing more. After
*The Golden Bough* I reread F. Pollock's *Essays in the Law*—that
is I had read most of them when they first came out. I was impressed by his use of his learning, and his happy presentation.
Also May Sinclair—I think I have mentioned that—*Anne Severn
and the Fieldings*. I didn't care much for the echoes of Freud or
the felicities of the copulative conjunction. I was interested to read
it because I was told that F.P. said that she had written 2 good
philosophy books—and slightly because of hopes to blush that
were disappointed. The philosophy the bookseller didn't know
about—and wanted to send for it on spec. but I told him that I
read little in these days, that I preferred my own. But this morning I received from Cohen—Spinoza's *Ethics* with Introduction by
Santayana. I shall reread that ὡς τάχιστα—also *Doctors' Commons
and the Court of Admiralty*. Did you see that? Some one wrote
to me that he was going to send it and I can't remember who. It
looks an interesting little book. Have you any idea how many
copies of *our* book have been sold? I am ashamed to ask the publishers, and should like to know. I suppose scattering copies may
be bought still, while I remain on the Bench. There are many
themes for jaw could we meet. I would pay currency to bring it
about. I repeat all my good wishes for you and yours.

*Aff'ly yours, O. W. Holmes*
I had overlooked the flyleaf in *Doctors' Commons*. 1000 thanks.


*16 Warwick Gardens, 2.1.23*
*My dear Justice:* . . . Also a dinner with Morley . . . First some
grand talk on the French thinkers of the 18th century. He puts
Turgot first and Montesquieu second; Voltaire a bad third. I reversed the order and urged that Voltaire grows bigger the more
you go into the period, though I admit that Turgot is a noble
mind of quite the first order. I was impressed at his high estimation of Emerson who always struck my Philistine mind as a general Autolycus whose wares were pleasant and pleasantly displayed,
but quite without an original *aperçu*. Morley surprised me by saying that he and George Meredith and Leslie Stephen had found
deep comfort in him in the sixties. Was that your experience? I
remember only his superb *mot* to you anent Plato,[1] but I do not
recollect that he shifted your perspective. . . .

*Ever affectionately yours, H. J. L.*

---

[1] As an undergraduate Holmes showed a severely critical essay on Plato
to Emerson. When later Emerson saw the young Holmes he said: "When
you strike at a king, you must kill him."

*Washington, D.C., January 13, 1923*

*Dear Laski:* A letter (2.1.23) delightful as usual. Also your Fabian Tract—a remarkable discourse[1]—although I grieve to say I don't much believe its postulates (of possibility) and *therefore* its ideals. The time has come when, if ever, it is lawful for me to doubt as it is imperative for you to affirm. I fear that I am out of accord for the moment with my public-minded friends in another way. Frankfurter generally writes to me about any important opinions of mine and he has been silent as to the one I sent you in which Brandeis dissented;[2] probably feeling an unnecessary delicacy about saying that he disagrees. Of course, I understand the possibility of thinking otherwise—I could not fail to, even if Brandeis had agreed. But nevertheless when the premises are a little more emphasized, as they should have been by me, I confess to feeling as much confidence as I often do. I always have thought that old Harlan's decision in *Mugler* v. *Kansas*[3] was pretty fishy. But I am not going to reargue the matter now. I was not greatly impressed by Atcheson's [*sic*] support of his former boss in the *New Republic*,[4] except for the admirable politeness with which he expressed his difference. He thought B's view more statesmanlike—which is an effective word but needs caution in using it. I read your little book about *Doctors' Commons* with the amused pleasure you expected. I wonder if the writer is learned on the subject. And now when I have a moment, (I have had but two or three as yet) it is Spinoza's *Ethics* in Everyman's Library. Santayana's charming introduction made me feel as I did years ago, how much nearer my view of the world is to Spinoza's than it is to, I don't know but I may say, any other—leaving the machinery and the would-be mathematically conceived reasoning out. It is evening and I stopped here to carry up the birds in the elevator, which my wife can't be induced to use on her own account, saying that she should get it out of order in some way. I resume by getting out a case of which I had no spare copy earlier that I think may slightly entertain you—I will enclose it. I was told the other day

---

[1] *The State in the New Social Order.*

[2] *Pennsylvania Coal Co.* v. *Mahon, supra,* p. 342.

[3] Mr. Justice Brandeis in his dissent in the *Mahon* case had put considerable reliance upon the decision of the Supreme Court in *Mugler* v. *Kansas* 123 U.S. 623 (1887) in which Harlan, J., for the majority, had held that a state might constitutionally prohibit the manufacture and sale of intoxicating liquor and give effect to the statute, without payment of compensation, against a going manufacturing concern.

[4] An anonymous editorial in 33 *New Republic* 136 (Jan. 3, 1923) had discussed at length the opinions of Holmes and Brandeis in the *Mahon* case; it had included the statement that "Justice Brandeis's view seems the superior statesmanship." Holmes, presumably, had reason to know that the editorial was written by Dean Acheson, Brandeis's secretary during the 1919-20 term of the Supreme Court.

that the Professors at the Law School don't like to be called Professor and on the chance I change my direction to you to Esq. I am amused at your talk about Emerson which seems to me true, but not the whole truth. Emerson, I think, had the gift of imparting a ferment—I believe my father borrowed the phrase from me in his book about E. That gift is genius—and I think he was a real poet. As with other poets, I don't care what he thought—I don't care what Carlyle did. The poetical pole is the South to the philosophical North. The interests of explaining, and of realizing and feeling are antithetical and when I have made up my mind to which a given writer is nearer I don't bother much about his relations to the other. To my ear some of Emerson's sentences sing, or did when I read them, enchantingly. I glanced this afternoon through a few pages of Alice Meynell's prose. It seemed to me that her religion and her nature made an exquisite result— inadequate as exquisiteness must be when an ultimate, but charming when you don't ask all from one. I remember writing to Lady Desborough at the time of the Boer war that it would give England a chance to pay for some of its unearned exquisiteness. When the feeling that it is unearned becomes strong it becomes somewhat repulsive. I am with you on Smith's *Wealth of Nations*. I was staggered when Marx patronized him. He drove in my pickets —but was repulsed with slaughter at the second line. I never have read enough of Seneca to talk about him. I have meant to but so far have failed. As to Racine *et al.* my impressions are like yours but I don't value them as our aesthetic judgments are largely determined by our special experiences. I don't see but a Mussoo has as good a right to admire him as we to admire Shakespeare. To be continued in our next.                          *Aff'ly yours, O. W. H.*

*16 Warwick Gardens, 21.I.23*

*My dear Justice:* A delightful letter from you yesterday revived all my longings for a month in America. You say so much that I want to discuss and dispute—why Brandeis is indisputably right about the moral and economic rottenness of the present social order, why I think that, with all its charm, J. G. Frazer's *Golden Bough* is on the wrong methodological lines, why I have become convinced that the U.S. constitution is the worst instrument of government that the mind of man has so far conceived, and so forth. Well! I save a little against the day. But Massingham has been driven from the *Nation* under circumstances beyond print[1] and I,

---

[1] A syndicate of Independent Liberals purchased the *Nation and Athenaeum* in January and H. W. Massingham, the man who had since 1907 been editor and made the paper what it was, was retired. See 130 *The Spectator* 87 (Jan. 20, 1923). See also Massingham's last essay in the *Nation*, "Vale," 33 *Nation and Athenaeum* 106 (April 28, 1923).

in common with the rest of the staff, Nevinson, Hammond *et al.*
have resigned in protest. It may be, if we can get the capital, that
we shall start a new weekly, but until it gets going, most of my
extravagances must be cut off.

    . . . I undertook, whether wisely or not I can't say, to write a
pamphlet on the second chamber problem,[2] and on looking into
it, apart from the special needs of the federal state I cannot find
a single adequate reason for being in favour of a bicameral system;
and I am comforted to discover that Franklin and Tom Paine and
Sam Adams agree with me. . . .

                                    *Ever affectionately yours, H. J. L.*


                                    *Washington, D.C., February 5, 1923*
*Dear Laski:* The time is coming and now is—but only now—when
it should be possible for me to send a worthy reply to your 21.1.23.
I am wrong as to the now-is-ness of it because as yet I have only
looked upon the Promised Land. For when my work was done I
had at once to turn to loathed slabs of galley proof that had been
accumulating on my table to enable me to write an introduction
to one of Wigmore's enlightening collections.[1] He asked for it a
year ago—and though much has happened to me since, I didn't
like to back out. So first to read and then to write took my spare
time until today. But henceforth I shall fall back upon the excuse
—my wife thinks the necessary excuse—that I must keep all my
strength for my duties. So this morning after reading sympathetically a second part of what I may have mentioned before, a discourse of a young Chinaman, now in Berlin, who professes to think
highly of my legal philosophy and writes upon that theme for
publication here[2] and in Germany—I wrote to him that I could
not afford the energy to write a critical introduction to accompany
his essay. And all the day has passed in writing letters, two short
walks, and correcting the proof of the introduction—a brief three
pages—perhaps I should have said first in getting up late. I breakfast in my library alone where I am served by the gentle Annie
with my messenger in the background. And now perhaps I can
finish Spinoza's *Ethics,* cut untimely off by the end of the last
recess. You would read it in an hour and be able to recite on it.

---

[2] *The Problem of a Second Chamber* (Fabian Tract, No. 213; 1925).

[1] Professor Wigmore was Chairman of a Committee of the Association of
American Law Schools which was responsible for publishing The Modern
Legal Philosophy Series. Holmes contributed an Introduction, dated February
1923, to the first volume of the series, *Rational Basis of Legal Institutions*
(1923) by various authors.

[2] John C. H. Wu, "The Juristic Philosophy of Justice Holmes," 21 *Mich.
L. Rev.* 523 (March 1923).

Not so me. Perhaps I have said before that if you leave out his logic-shopping and theological machinery his view of the cosmos seems to me better than any other I know in the past. I wish that we could talk. You stir up the monkeys a little by your opening suggestions—they seem to me to savor of enthusiasm. I don't lie awake nights wondering at the inspiration of those who made the Constitution but your condemnation needs to be justified. I don't believe that the present social order is morally or economically rotten—and I have yet to hear Brandeis say that he thinks so, although he criticises it freely. If he did, I should think he proved that he was not infallible. As to Fraser [sic] I am not sure that I know what you mean—by his wrong methodological lines. If merely that you think his farrago of facts would need sifting and combing out before one could have confidence in anything more than some tendencies—I should agree, and if his latent purpose was to discredit the beliefs accepted by the Church I don't think the work worth the trouble—possibly it was when he began, though I know I wouldn't have done it if I could—not good enough. I never have had convictions on the Second Chamber problem—on the face it looks like a survival. I don't know that I care much for the three that you say agree with you. Why did you and Morley agree to condemn St. Augustine? That interests me. Is it as having led to the Calvinistic way of thinking? I make a note of Kennedy's *Canadian Constitution* and will inquire tomorrow. Somehow I feel as if you were getting a little exacerbated in your judgments. Are you working the machine hard? I am always afraid that you are working it too hard. If you insist upon finishing up in mid-middle age—wait at least till I am out of the way.                                         *Aff'ly yours, O. W. H.*

*16 Warwick Gardens, 1.II.23*
*My dear Justice:* A delightful letter from you on Sunday lit up the day. And before I forget I must answer your specific question. So far nearly 1800 copies of *Collected Papers* have been sold—an extraordinary record, I think, for a book of that kind. For I enquired the other day at Cambridge and discovered that in ten years they have only sold one thousand of Maitland's *Collected Essays*. I still have to receive the accounts of the last half year, which will, I expect, bring the total up to well over two thousand.

I have been unexpectedly busy this last ten days, mainly because Graham Wallas a little unexpectedly decided to retire in order to write and I have had to take over the headship of the department. It was extraordinary to find how great was the confusion in which a man who writes professionally on how to admin-

ister had left it. The records were non-existent; he had never urged
the claims of younger members of the department; he had never
enquired from them if and upon what they would like to lecture;
and he had never arranged conferences of the staff to talk over its
problems. So I had to go into all this most delicately, first so as
to avoid treading on his toes, and second to get some unity into
what was a mass of discrete atoms. But at last the thing is largely
done.

. . . an amusing lunch with Arnold Bennett who attacked all
living novelists except Arnold Bennett and tried to convince me
of the greatness of one Marcel Proust; but a short experience convinced me that he was small beer. . . .

Of reading less, I fear, than I should like. But one very remark-
able book which I hope you'll read at leisure—Schweitzer, *The
Quest of the Historical Jesus.* It's an essay on the history of New
Testament criticism since Reimarus;[1] and it puts better than any-
thing I have ever seen the way in which the critical treatment of
Christian origins has developed. I enjoyed it more than any book
I can remember in recent days. . . .

My love to you both.               *Ever affectionately yours, H. J. L.*

*Washington, D.C., February 15, 1923*
*Dear Laski:* At last just as the adjournment is ending I seem to
have a leisure moment—but I have been living in a cloud of mos-
quitoes most of the time, and even now shall not give a worthy
answer to your record of performances that delight me as usual—
(1.II.23). When my work was done . . . there came a lot of people, one after another, and a Conference and another case to write
—and income tax, and this and that, until only yesterday was I
free. At the happy moment came Pound's *Interpretations of Legal
History*—but I have not yet been able to read more than the first
two chapters—with great pleasure, that I expect will continue. I
have thrown in John Buchan's *Huntingtower*—for a thriller—and
had elegant extracts and *Bleak House* in the evenings. I wonder
if Pound has a little too much of the German professor about his
way of thinking. Somehow his subdivisions do not always give me
the feeling of life—to take the latest example in my mind, what
he says of political interpretations. Of course if he is rightly de-
tecting atmospheric influences he can't be expected to produce
anchors and chain cables. But the attribution of one set of phenomena to a theory of will and another to a tradition of relations
&c, while it amuses and interests me, does not convince. As I re-

---

[1] Hermann Samuel Reimarus (1694-1768); author of *Von dem zwecke
Jesu und seiner Jünger* (1784).

turn to my desk and go on with this I am met by a letter from the *Harv. Law Review* asking me to review Pound. I am glad to be able to say that I already had promised . . . never again to do any outside work. *Videbo eos damnatos prius*—as we learned to say. I meant to have a morning with engravings—but could only snatch a half hour. I saw however some most wonderful photographs in color, that seemed to reproduce the originals—a new thing. Rice wasn't expecting me and the only etching that even suggested purchase was a Waterloo.[1] But Waterloo never seems to get very high and the imperial potterer passéd on in miser meditation pocket free. Some of the virtuous under the call of E. Root and William Draper Lewis meet here next week to talk of the restatement of the law (I believe).[2] I declined to take part and was sceptical but Lewis writes rather begging me to look in on them. I will try to but I will take no hand and won't believe till they produce the goods. You can't evoke genius by announcing a *corpus juris*. I didn't know it but I see that I am tired and dull—never mind—I still pulsate responsive. I remember William Hunt saying I feel that some day I might wake up and be able to do as well as the Venetians—but they knew they could every day. Perhaps some day I shall write you as good a letter as you do to me every time.                          *Aff'ly yours, O. W. H.*
I tried for the book on the Canadian Constitution—they sent me a collection of sources—historical antecedents, etc.—which I thought evidently not what you meant—but the Congressional Library had not what I understood you to refer to. OWH


*16 Warwick Gardens, 11.II.23*
*My dear Justice:* Some happy days since I last wrote to you. First a glorious weekend with H. G. Wells at his country place. We talked the universe over, and I have never known him in better form. We agreed that, the *New Arabian Nights* apart, R. L. Stevenson is pretentious adolescence made pathetic by invalidism. We united in liking Hazlitt and putting him at the very top of the essayists' class. We thought Meredith first-rate in patches, but that he was continually walking to Manchester in order to get to London. Our one real fight was over Henry James. I urged that he

---

[1] Anthonie Waterloo (ca. 1610-ca. 1676); painter, engraver, and etcher, best known for his landscapes.

[2] The American Law Institute was organized at a meeting in Washington on February 23, 1923, under the energetic sponsorship of Elihu Root (1845-1937) and, acting as Chairman, William Draper Lewis (1867-1949), Philadelphia lawyer and Pennsylvania teacher. The purpose of the Institute was to reduce the complexities of American law by the publication of restatements of principal subjects in the law.

was a queer involuted soul much too morbid about his American
origins, and quite without the ability, especially as he grew older,
of writing a simple narrative. Wells, however, put him quite high;
and gave him a psychological flair which I have never detected.
He insisted, too, that his book on America[1] was full of real insight.
I read it later and thought two or three things perceptive, the rest
all twisted and out of tune. Then I spent a long day with Bertrand
Russell who talked like a god, with that superb Voltairean irony
which he and Anatole France seem to have. I was interested to
find that he thought Morris Cohen the most original mind in contemporary American philosophy but thought he wrote in too frag-
mentary a way to bring a wide recognition either for his views
or for his merits. I doubt whether you would have sympathised
with our general sense that civilisation now has a choice between
socialism and a rapid degeneration; but as we talked it out it
sounded to me like a set of axioms from Euclid. (I won't have
the retort that Lobatchewski has destroyed Euclid.) Really Russell's mind is amazing. It is like watching a really great fencer
handle his rapier to see him at work. . . . Then a long morning
with Haldane on a case he has. Zaghlul the Egyptian leader is
deported to Gibraltar and detained there by the Governor of Gibraltar. Can he sue out a writ of *habeas corpus* against the governor.[2] I say yes, on the ground that Gibraltar is a Crown Colony
and *habeas corpus* is incidental thereto. I found cases, and Mansfield has made remarks. But the thing is not as clear to Haldane
as it is to me. Have you any views?

In the way of reading, some pleasant things. (a) Carl Becker,
*The Declaration of Independence*. I thought this quite excellent,
learned, well-written, and well-balanced. I got a litte bored with
the too long discussion of the exact text, but I thought it more
than repaid scrutiny. (b) Keim, *Helvétius*. . . . One other thing
which I hated as doctrine and thought quite marvellous as a piece
of thinking was Bradley's *Logic* which I commend eagerly to you.
It is the English mind at its best; and I really don't think that
between Hume and our day there has been a piece of English
philosophic thinking that is quite in its class. I expect you will
have seen that Bosanquet is dead. I don't think he was a great
man, but it was a life of noble devotion to philosophy, and he
tried as few people try to make his ideas a recognisable and whole-
minded system. I liked him much; though politically his outlook

---

[1] *The American Scene* (1907).

[2] In the end, it was not found necessary to settle the legal question by
legal action; Saad Zaghlul (1860-1927), the leader of Egyptian opposition
to British rule, on grounds of health was released from his internment at
Gibraltar.

was that of charity organisation which I loathe. Still he was rare in this age of hurry and heedlessness, and we ought to be very grateful to him. Our lamps shine the more brightly because he bored for oil. . . .

I had a nice note from Brandeis the other day, speaking of you, as you will guess, with great warmth and admiration; and Felix writes me that he argues the Minimum Wage case before you at the end of the month[3] I envy him that; though I add that in a sane state the constitutionality of such an Act, granted the terms of industrial civilisation, ought not to be in doubt. . . .

*Ever affectionately yours, H. J. L.*

*March 1, 1923*

*Dear Laski:* Yours of 11.II.23 was slow in coming—but gives me the usual delight. I easily can imagine that it was a great pleasure to *parcourure* the universe, as a girl once said to me, with Wells— little as I am inclined to take seriously his philosophizing on social or metaphysical themes. I always thought H. James's drooling on the social relations of important Americans with the old world a trifle underbred. I never read his book on America. I think he was a pretty big chap who by rejecting all that didn't come within a narrow circle of taste wrote stories that generally I found dull. I am delighted at what you say Bertrand Russell thinks of Cohen— and heartily agree so far as I can speak. I can say nothing profitable on the *habeas corpus* question. Bradley's *Logic* I am inclined to send for—but I have little time to read, with my inveterate habit of solitaire after 9 o'clock. The time I waste on that gives me my only hope that I don't make the most of myself and thereby verify my axiom that those who make the most of themselves don't make much. I agree with you in not thinking Bosanquet (how do you pronounce his name?) a great man, but he was suggestive in what I have read of his writing.

February behaved like a naughty boy—overcast and ominous— but one knew that the spring had him by the slack of his breeches and that he soon would be dragged out. The tops of the elms begin to thicken with swelling buds—and there was a hint of sunshine today. Brandeis and I felicitate ourselves that the spring is drawing near. I am glad at what you say he wrote because he is a great comfort and help to me—and the way in which that cuss is loaded with facts on all manner of subjects leaves me gawping. We get a short talk together almost every day on the way homeward. I see almost no one out of court—but this p.m. Lord and Lady

---

[3] *Adkins* v. *Children's Hospital*, 261 U.S. 525, was argued on March 14.

Middleton[1] came in to tea and I got the C.J. to do the like and we had a very pleasant little general chat. The C.J. throws himself into that sort of thing very agreeably. They were amiable to me when I last was in London and I was sorry to do no more—but I stick to seclusion on the theory of letting my heart regain its strength (if it hasn't). Upon rather urgent solicitation I looked in at a meeting of illustrious lawyers the other day. They are bent on a 'restatement of the law.' I just came in while Root was flamboyant, took a back seat, wagged my head at Learned Hand and one or two others and slid out for Court. I suppose my name will go in as also present—which I take it is what was wanted—but I don't care much for the business. As Brandeis said "I am restating the law every day. It's my job." You don't get originality or genius by saying that you want to do something particular—and I don't quite see where the desired restatement is to come from, unless from the fresh minds that from time to time sing their song. In spite of the German Code, whatever its merits may be, I should not expect [much] from committees. The general function of committees is to take the personality out of discourse. I dare say it has been just as well to have McKenna, Day and others cut out some of my exuberances from opinions of the Court—but in general I think that what I have said is true. I must stop and go down to solitaire—so I will send this off—though if you were here I should have a thousand things to say (if I got a chance). Don't overwork. I ought to put this into every letter—like *delenda est Carthago.* I am so afraid you run the machine too hard—but I have confidence in your wife.                *Affectionately yours, O. W. Holmes*

*PRIVATE*                                *16 Warwick Gardens, 12.III.23*
*My dear Justice:* You will be puzzled by my long silence; but you will, I know, be generous, and not attribute it to negligence. The truth is that I have had a queer adventure which has involved three weeks cessation from work. I have a German student who, as you can imagine, has been persistently undernourished for some years. He took ill with pernicious anaemia and the doctors decided that it was a case for transfusion; the poor fellow hadn't, of course, a relative in this country, so I naturally volunteered and a pint of my blood now flows in German veins. It was a most queer business. For about a week it left me as weak as a cat; then a fortnight of quite glorious lethargy, when gazing at the ceiling seemed work. Now I'm on the job again and as fit as can be. Please don't mention this anywhere; I merely tell it to you to show that only *saeva necessitas* stood in the way of continuity. . . .

My warm love to you both.                      *Ever yours, H. J. L.*

---

[1] Presumably Ernest Willoughby (1847-1924), tenth Baron Middleton.

*Washington, D.C., March 27, 1923*

*Dear Laski:* Your letter with some private information about yourself has just arrived. It is a noble tale—but I should have thought that your Missus would have shrieked in protest. You certainly try your machine in every possible way. Of course I shall keep quiet, but I should damn well like to say to the Boston gents, "That's the kind of a hairpin the lad is." Well, I will turn to other themes. We are in adjournment and (bar one case that I ought to study but that I wish was in Hell and am neglecting for a day or two of freedom) I am entitled to leisure. I shall tell the brethren on Saturday that I have one lame leg and the other cut off—*i.e.,* I had two cases[1]—one to which four disagree—the other a decision on motion to dismiss which after writing and getting the concurrence of all, made up my mind ought to be set down for argument —and I have got agreement to that.

Tomorrow a.m. I anticipate my long deferred visit to Rice at the Congressional Library, Print Department. Meantime I have been reading (yesterday and today) S. Reinach's volume 4, *Cultes, mythes et religions* which has been published for 10 or a dozen years but I got only recently. He is a delightful creature (although he believes Frazer and Totems and Magic &c. too much for me) and gives one a series of interesting excursions from the Inquisition to the drawing on a prehistoric bone. He almost persuaded me to read a book by that beast Andrew Lang—whom to my regret he respects. Did I ever tell you of my only *rencontre* with A.L.? Introduced. "Are you the son of Oliver Wendell Holmes?" "Yes." "Well, I don't like him." Exit. How I have regretted that I was not quick enough with rapier or bludgeon to hand him one back before he vanished. I had read some of his books and thought them dull before. Since, I have taken pleasure in thinking his *Joan of Arc* poor stuff. But he may be more of a man on Religion and Magic. I have a volume that came from my father but I never looked into it. I should like to read some of Lea's book[2] but I doubt if I get the chance—especially as Frankfurter writes that he is sending me a volume to read and return (which is a trial to friendship when one doesn't ask for it—but he told me about it when he was here —and I believe excited my interest, but I forget the theme). . . . The spring is on us. Mists of brown and green in the trees— crocuses by the river side. And for a simple lark a visit to the zoo— and luncheon at Rauscher's—where we are always welcomed by a very pleasing waitress. The doctor called this morning to relieve my wife from some anxiety about me—and said my heart was a

---

[1] The cases have not been identified.

[2] The reference is, perhaps, to Henry Charles Lea's *Superstition and Force* (1866) or his *History of the Inquisition* (3 vols., 1888).

good pump and that there are very few men of my age as well off as I—to which I replied that most of them were dead.

28th/ Frankfurter's book has come and as I might have known is one that I am eager to read: Plucknett's *Statutes and their Interpretation in the 14th Century*. I almost could fist from going to the Congressional Library or finishing S. Reinach (for I don't read a book in a flash of gun powder, like you). The editor, Hazeltine,[3] seems to be an intelligent, not very original man—but doing his work with pleasant unction. Like Cato with his *delenda est Carthago* I always want to end with: Don't drive the machine too hard. I think I have referred to Cato before and probably shall again. Tarde says repetition is a mark of love—and applies it I believe by way of suggestion to the cosmos. The starting point is safer.                                    *Aff'ly yours, O. W. Holmes*

*April 14, 1923*

*Dear Laski:* A letter from you 29.III.23 [1]—if that is intelligible— doubly delightful that you seem in such good spirits. I also am cheerful enough after the first week of renewed sitting. We started off with a lot of decisions. I had only one and that not interesting,[2] but one by Sutherland was against the minimum wage law[3]—F.F. losing his case—and in that I wrote a dissent. The C.J. and Sanford seemed to think I said something dangerous or too broad so they dissented separately. I sent you the opinions as soon as they were printed—I think that what I said was plain common sense. It was intended *inter alia* to dethrone Liberty of Contract from its ascendancy in the Liberty business. I am curious to see what the enthusiasts for liberty of contract will say with regard to liberty of speech under a State law punishing advocating the overthrow of government—by violence. The case was argued this week.[4]

---

[3] Harold Dexter Hazeltine (1871-1960); legal historian and general editor of the Cambridge Studies in Legal History; since 1919 he had been Downing Professor of the Laws of England at Cambridge University.

[1] Omitted from this edition.

[2] *Gardner* v. *Chicago Title & Trust Co.*, 261 U.S. 453 (April 9, 1923).

[3] In *Adkins* v. *Children's Hospital*, 261 U.S. 525, in which Felix Frankfurter had been counsel for the appellants, Sutherland, J., for a majority of the Court held that the statute fixing minimum wages for women in the District of Columbia was unconstitutional. Holmes wrote a dissenting opinion; Taft, C. J., wrote another in which Sanford, J., concurred. Brandeis took no part in the consideration of the case.

[4] *Gitlow* v. *New York*, 268 U.S. 652 (argued April 12, 1923; reargued November 23, 1923; decided June 8, 1925). The Court subsumed freedom of speech in the liberty secured against state action by the Fourteenth Amendment. A majority of the Court, however, with Holmes and Brandeis dissenting, found that the defendant's rights had not been unconstitutionally destroyed.

Before the sitting began I had a day or two—say two days—in which I had no duty on my mind, or, what is as bad, some damned book that I thought I ought to read for improvement's sake, so I said to myself what shall I do—and looking round took down Montaigne. He never had hit me before—indeed I hadn't looked into him for a long time. It happened that our rhythms were in harmony and I sat reading him all day long. I am the richer for it and have had a lot of amusement. Curious—that business of harmony of rhythms. If you give a great man a chance probably he will compel it after a while—but it is very pleasant when the hour is favorable and you don't have to wait. I think I haven't told you of my modest adventure in the Print Department, the most expensive was Dürer's "Death's Head Coat of Arms"—a good impression. Item, long desired by me, Rembrandt's portrait of himself in a felt hat sitting by a window looking at you. Not a bright impression and with a slight tear, but as I have noticed before with some of R's later states—modified and more interesting than the brilliant first state—though the difference in cost is between a modest sum and hundreds or thousands of dollars. Item, "The Morning Ploughman," companion to the Evening one I had before —by Samuel Palmer. Do you know him? He got the unearthly (perhaps from Blake) and though it doesn't seem to me a proper use of etching he moves me. Finally two of the Mantegna procession series—plates thought not to be from his hand and therefore cheaper than some others of the set. I got the two for $25 which was cheap. I buy no books—I am too old. My wife buys some to amuse our evenings—but I delight to read the catalogues I get— often if not always thanks to you. I get amusing letters from time to time. One a printed diatribe vs. Prohibition with "How could you do it?" written—as if I were responsible for the 18th Amendment. Another today, enclosing articles from the *American* with a dig at the minimum wage decision, the letter beginning "Your writ of error for the rich is no *supprise* to us ex-heroes of the World War." *Il faut souffrir pour être belle.* On the whole there has been more tedium from dull arguments than interest in the question. . . . Mrs. Codman[5] took luncheon with us today and just as she was leaving we had the fire department here over my chimney on fire. Nice fellows the firemen. This is the third time it has happened since we have lived in this house. Luckily the house is old and well built. This is all my news.

*Aff'ly yours, O. W. Holmes*

Apropos of Emerson—I took down his essay on Montaigne and thought it admirable beyond my expectations.

[5] Mrs. Russell Codman of Boston was a summer neighbor and close friend of Holmes's.

*16 Warwick Gardens, 26.IV.23*

*My dear Justice:* . . . Much has happened since I wrote last. First of all Frida and I hopped over to France for a week and had pleasant hours. A visit to Anatole France was as always a great occasion and I excerpt one or two passages. He asked me if I had read a novel *Ulysses* by James Joyce which contained much about excretory functions. I said no and asked if he had. "I do not believe in the lavatory school of fiction" he said; and I wish I could reproduce that exquisite French wave of the hand. He was very down on Paul Bourget—"Rome in a lady's scent bottle" and on Huysmans "who washes his mind in public" and as ever enthusiastic about the *Provinciales* of Pascal, and Voltaire. He thought Rousseau wrote the most perfect French prose and said that Flaubert was simply a waste of time. He was marvellously active and though he talks *pour produire des drames* there is always something that is more than worth the price of admission. We had dinner with Aulard, the historian of the Revolution and he talked for two hours like a great master of his craft. Incidentally he was one of the few Frenchmen we met who was politically sane. We went to a sitting of the Chamber but came out soon enough; it was like an hour in the monkey-house at the zoo. . . . I was amused and amazed that when I mentioned Nathaniel Hawthorne to Anatole France he had never heard of him; and that, similarly, Aulard had never read the *Federalist*. They are the least universal race of scholars I have encountered, especially in their economics. . . .                             *Ever yours affectionately, H. J. L.*

*Washington, D.C., May 5, 1923*
*Saturday, 8 p.m.*

*Dear Laski:* Nearly a week has gone by since I received your letter of the 13th[1] and until now I haven't had a free moment—I doubt if I ever waited so long before. And now on coming home from the Conference I get another dated 26.IV and my cup runneth over. You are the most delightful of correspondents and I am haunted by the thought that I don't give you *quid pro quo*. I should have sat down at once to reply (at 5 p.m.) but I was so tired that as soon as I could put my papers in order I lay down and slept like a dog till close to 7 when we dine. The tension has not been in vain as one of my cases was on a reargument in which we stood 4 to 4 and this will go without a dissent; Sutherland privily disagrees but will say nothing.[2] I take credit only for convincing

---

[1] Omitted from this edition.
[2] *United States* v. *Sischo*, 262 U.S. 165 (May 7, 1923).

one or two, but I think I made a pretty good job and there is always a satisfaction when the hitches are over and you have cleared the obstacles. Also it always is pleasant to finish a thing— even if you then are keen to begin another. The event of the week has been the opening of the Freer gallery in the Smithsonian grounds—a beautiful building—with a square in the middle a patch of green, a little fountain and two peacocks and a peahen. The lady it is said will have nothing to do with one of them and he flocked apart and took the sunlight. The other displayed his fan and shivered with amorous anticipations. The show itself is distinguished, yet I think disappointing to most. Oriental objects which require an expert eye to distinguish them from many others in many other museums—and Whistler—painting—etchings and peacock room (a room or so of A. Thayer[3]—not better I should think than many other painters). Whistler has been seen so much that it requires reflection to realize this as a treasure house. I should explain that my wife came for me after Court and we took in the show on the way back. We then went on, and on the other side of the road by the Potomac basin—lately framed in cherry blossoms—at just a picturesque distance was a long bed of tulips— embowered with avenues of trees through which shone the de- clining sun—while maidens cantered by the side of it and three mocking birds sang the poetry of the moment. Nature can do some things that man can't quite reproduce. . . . (6th) The other day I had a visit from Winfield [4] whose book you sent me—and much pleasant talk. He inspected my Statham's *Abridgment* and after pronouncing it a perfect copy called my attention to the only bit of humor in the book. Sub *Tolle* 'A Miller of Tatlock took double toll because he had heard the rector of that town say on Palm Sunday: Tolle, Tolle.' Also we had an agreeable evening with an etcher-man, who had managed to get most of the illustrious who took part in the disarmament conference to let him do them, gen- erally in dry point, the result somewhat like Sargent's charcoal sketches, and had got their signatures on the copies. These I believe are my only outside experiences. My inside ones are mainly in the law. Last night and this morning there are two letters from my young Chinese friend, as yet unseen, Mr. Wu. I am a little em- barrassed by his enthusiasm for me. I told him in my last letter that it would abate as he grew older—but he persists and it is a pretty thing in a young fellow of just 24. I don't want to damp his confidence in life, at the same time he speaks so very frankly about

<hr>

[3] The work of Abbott Thayer (1849-1921), vigorous American painter, is fully represented in the Freer Gallery.

[4] Percy Winfield (1878-1953), teacher of law at Cambridge, in 1923 was lecturer in English Legal History at Harvard. See, *supra*, p. 276.

himself that I hesitate as to what cautions I ought to interpose. He
hopes to come to Cambridge in August in which event I dare say
I shall see him as he promises. My mind turns back to the Whistler
(Freer) show. When you see the results of a life gathered together
it is a little hard to avoid the feeling I used to have in the old
Court House in Court Square when on the morning after some
illusion upon the Museum stage I saw the scenes slid out and piled
upon a wagon—but it isn't right. Perhaps the moral is that it is
better to show jewels separately and not *en masse* as at the Palais
Royal in former days. With this I close. I have received an assignment of two cases[5] that will require some fine sewing, as old
C. J. Morton[6] used to say. Not profoundly interesting except for the
pleasure of untying knots. After them I don't suppose I shall have
much more to do—we have taken our stateroom for Boston on the
train for the night of June 18—as we don't adjourn till June 11.
Farewell for the moment.        *Affectionately yours, O. W. Holmes*

*16 Warwick Gardens, 18.V.23*

*My dear Justice:* . . . I have read immensely since I wrote last—
all I think in French 18th century literature. First with immense
interest and complete conviction, Rocquain's *Esprit révolution-
naire.* That is a first-rate job. Rousseau and Co. did not make the
Revolution, they did not even create the revolutionary temper.
That grew out of economic discontent on the one hand and the
results of the struggle over *Unigenitus*[1] on the other. The big men
when they come are influential in intensification not origination. If
the book lies to your hand I think it would interest you much. I
would send it on but it is unfortunately out of print. Then I read
Aubertin *L'esprit public au XVIIIme siècle,* not so good as Rocquain because merely skilful elaboration of the obvious, but still
quite attractive. They gave me a line and from them I went back
to the men themselves. First to Helvétius amusing and very
shrewd but no *fond;* then Holbach much bigger in every way than
he is given credit for; then a vast dose of Voltaire who for all his
quite damnable tricks and gestures is as big as you like, especially
in the correspondence where he emerges as a real giant; and finally
Grimm's letters, he being the nodus of the group. I can't avoid the
conviction that the fifty years '38-89 are as valuable an epoch as
any in modern history. Men cared deeply for intelligence and got
a good perspective of life. . . .

---

[5] On May 21, Holmes delivered the Court's opinion in *Stevens v. Arnold,*
262 U.S. 266; *Hart* v. *B. F. Keith Exchange, id.* 271.

[6] Marcus Morton (1819-1891); Associate Justice, Supreme Judicial Court
of Massachusetts, 1869-1882; Chief Justice, 1882-1890.

[1] The Bull of Clement XI, *Unigenitus,* was issued in 1713, and virtually
read the Jansenists out of the Church.

Frida has been in the country this last fortnight so I have been
dining out much. An amusing dinner at the Webbs with Ramsay
MacDonald as the *prima donna*. They all feel near office; and I
enjoyed urging upon them that suburban England is a race of
snobs which would far rather be misgoverned by its social superiors than well-governed by its inferiors. I am sure that is right
here; though I add that it seems very untrue of America where
brains and power do not seem to attract each other. A good dinner,
too, with Sankey to meet three or four judges, of whom Atkin and
Scrutton struck me as the best. They had just worked off the great
decision in *Ex parte O'Brien*[2] about which I felt great joy as
(strictly *entre nous*) I had written MacDonald's speech urging that
the Irish deportations were illegal and Simon had told the House
they were not. Atkin was very impressive—keen, alert, modern-
minded; and when he denounced McReynolds J. on the basis of
some recent U.S. decisions he had just read my heart warmed to
him on the spot. . . .

My love to you both.               *Ever yours affectionately, H. J. L.*


*Washington, D.C., May 31, 1923*
*Dear Laski:* A longed for letter has come. As to Rocquain probably
I shan't be ready for him before Beverly and then I fear I shall
have forgotten his name, unless I take a memo along. A day or two
ago Brandeis was saying to me that Kropotkin (I think) on the
French Revolution gives you the theory of the Russian—that what
that really did was to dispossess the nobles from the land, at first
on a theory of repayment, but ultimately without repayment—
that the evil to be feared was a counterrevolution started by the
*émigrés*. Therefore the Russians said we will take the land and
will exterminate the possible counter-revolvants—and they done
it—wholesale.

At present, apart from preparing a couple of dissents,[1] attending
to the out of Court work, *certioraris* &c., and reading such opinions
as come around, I am idling. That is I didn't offer to relieve any-

---

[2] *Ex parte O'Brien*, [1923] 2 K.B. 361. In March the Home Office had
directed that a number of suspected conspirators against the Irish Free State
should be seized and deported to Ireland for internment. Ramsay MacDonald,
in the House of Commons, had been Labour's spokesman in attacking the
government's action as highhanded and arbitrary. Mr. Aet O'Brien, one of the
men deported, on March 23 brought *habeas corpus* proceedings in the King's
Bench, which denied relief. On May 19, however, the Court of Appeal had
reversed the King's Bench. On a subsequent appeal to the House of Lords,
that body decided that it had no jurisdiction to review the case. See *Secretary
of State* v. *O'Brien*, [1923] A.C. 603.

[1] On June 11, Holmes delivered a brief dissenting opinion in *Pennsylvania*
v. *West Virginia*, 262 U.S. 553, 600. He concurred in a dissent of Brandeis,
J., in *Kentucky Co.* v. *Paramount Exchange, id.* 544, 551 but delivered no
other dissenting opinion than that in *Pennsylvania* v. *West Virginia*.

one and with real sorrow even declined to write an introduction
or personal letter for a volume of essays by Mrs. King[2] that Walter
Lippmann is interested in getting out. I said, and I think rightly,
that I couldn't tell how narrow my margin might be and that I had
made an absolute rule that I could do nothing outside. When I
wrote my little introduction for Wigmore's book I said never again.
The doctor says it is a miracle that I have been able to get through
my regular work and I don't want to take any chances. I am tired
and languid and the grasshopper is a burden. But I hated to say
no to anything that Lippmann asked. You will smile in scorn when
I admit that I am still powdering along on Montaigne. But I
haven't had a great deal of time and this is a solemn task—begin
at the beginning and read to the end. My! What a collection of
sayings there is in the old boy. He knew all I know, bar later discoveries. You don't love him perhaps but you like him wonderfully.
I think it is interesting to see what succulence he got from a few
classics—by taking them seriously and believing them. It is like
people brought up on the Bible. Judge Hoar[3] always had some
hammer of a sentence with which he drove in his point, whatever
it was. But I long have thought that if you knew a column of
advertisements by heart, you could achieve unexpected felicities
with them. You can get a happy quotation anywhere if you have
the eye.

. . . The afternoon brings a request (*entre nous*) from Holdsworth for a letter advocating the grant of a subsidiary allowance
in aid of publishing his history. I can't for the life of me read
what the name of the fund to which he applies is—but I shall
write a letter gladly. He has done a big job—if I can judge by
what I read in former days.

I end a little abruptly in order to catch the mail tonight—forgive
a tired old man for doing no better. The mocking birds are here in
the park now. And the town is filling up with Shriners—some kind
of Masons I believe. The shops and Penn. Avenue are decorated
and I expect general discomfort for a week or more. Also a man
asked me to join in a petition to have this block put into the
business zone—horror! Only five of us hold out I believe—but I
don't suppose anything will happen in my lifetime that will make
it impossible to live here. Alas, I have dreamed of repose all my
life and never have had it yet.          *Aff'ly yours, O. W. Holmes*

---

[2] Walter Lippmann ultimately did an introduction to the posthumous collection of Gertrude Besse King's essays and reviews, *Alliances of the Mind*
(1924).

[3] Ebenezer Rockwood Hoar (1816-1895); Associate Justice, Supreme Judicial Court of Massachusetts, 1859-1869; Attorney General of the United
States, 1869-1870.

*16 Warwick Gardens, 6.VI.23*
*My dear Justice:* You will pardon this long silence when I say that
I have been working furiously and joyously at my book on the
state[1]—the first chapter almost done after those endless efforts at
getting a start which you will know not less bitterly than I. But
now it is really under weigh [*sic*] and I feel less discontented with
the result than I shall probably be a year from now. But the thesis
I am sure is pretty right. It is a discussion anent the purpose of the
State with the answer (I) that you cannot make any final answer
since the purpose grows as science gives us different mechanisms
(II) that the philosophic theory of the State is, so far as it tries to
build a logical whole hopelessly contradicted by the facts of any
given state (III) that the business of the state is to satisfy demand
and the question what demand is answered by saying those demands which as a matter of history (a) make the state strong (b)
fit the conventions of the time. It results of course in complete
scepticism, which will not, I imagine, displease you. I think it is a
real gain to political science to get rid of all the nonsense about the
good life—doing something worth doing in concert with one's
fellows, or the modern tendency to list a vast range of separate
instincts which don't differ except in name from the old faculty-
psychology of the XVIIIth century. Well! You know what I am at.

And I have bought books mightily. I got some pounds on
account from my edition of the *Vindiciae* (to come out in September) and set to work. (1) A complete Voltaire. This was idiotically
cheap, 80 volumes for three guineas. I got it for the correspondence
mainly and the pamphlets anent the *Encyclopedia*. Of course one
gets a raft of rubbish thrown in but when I come to write my
Social Ideas in the 18th Century it is impossible to work without
a Voltaire perpetually at hand. Which reminds me that while
searching for this I was shown a Voltaire into which the owner had
bound 400 original unpublished letters of Voltaire to such people
as Rousseau, Hume, Frederic the Great. The man wanted fifteen
hundred pounds for it and I don't think that was beyond the mark.
(2) The works of d'Alembert. A delightful copy in five charm-
ingly-bound volumes. I have dipped in, butterfly-fashion, and the
*éloges* at the Academy struck me as being in the really grand
manner. (3) The *Causeries du lundi* of Sainte-Beuve in fifteen
volumes bound in half-morocco. This, my dear Justice, I bought at
a country sale near our cottage for 12/6 and I feel godlike over it.
For it really is the greatest brain-book in the world. I take down a
volume each weekend to the cottage and the twenty odd essays
give me discourses of every shape and form of letters. So every
taste is satisfied. If I get bored with reading about Bonald I can

---

[1] *The Grammar of Politics* (1925).

turn to Montaigne. (4) A set of Diderot. This, I fear, on the same
low principle as my purchase of Voltaire, that I would rather work
at home than in the Museum. But it has been great fun buying
them and the sense of a great company about me as I write confers
a satisfaction that you will share.

Of reading much and little because chiefly in the light way. The
cottage at week-ends makes for *belles-lettres*. It is wonderful there,
a spur of the Chiltern hills with nightingales in the early evening
and a thrush that wakes us at dawn just above the eaves. And a
garden full of larkspur and hollyhocks and great rambler roses—
for what more could one ask. . . .

We have been out a little—not overmuch. We gave a dinner for
the Eugene Meyers,[2] mainly talk between him and some economists
on reparations; and we dined with them to see the first night of
Drinkwater's *Oliver Cromwell*. Why, oh why, does the historical
dramatist always assume that his hero always had a vision of the
illimitable future? Cromwell prays at Ely and seems almost to en-
visage the Rent Restriction Act of 1919. Still a beautifully written
thing by dint of making skilful use of Cromwell's own superb
dispatches. You remember that great one after Marston Moor.
Cromwell and Lincoln, (if I may be pardoned) are blood-brothers
at bottom. Also a jolly dinner at Haldane's to meet the new Prime
Minister.[3] Not a big intelligence, I judged, but a man of determination and energy. He remind [*sic*] me a good deal of Hughes in a
certain quiet simplicity and obvious depth of character. And I
liked his sense of oppression at the bigness of his task. It was a
relief beyond words after the debonair lightheartedness of Lloyd
George. . . .

What of you both? I direct this to Beverly Farms on the suspicion that it will about greet you on arrival. Our plans are a little
vague. Here, I think, until the end of July, then a month at the
sea on the Belgian coast. I told you, I think, that I had been re-
appointed lecturer at Cambridge for another year. That, with my
new importance as Wallas's successor, removes all my financial
problems, and though I do not yet save, at least I do not accumulate debts. And if reparations are settled and the American people
rejects Henry Ford for the presidency[4] I shall almost feel that the

---

[2] Eugene Meyer (1875-1959), banker who in 1918 had turned public
servant; he became director of the War Finance Corporation, thereafter had
many important government posts, and later became publisher and editor of
the Washington *Post*.

[3] Bonar Law, for reasons of health, had resigned as Prime Minister on May
20, and his Chancellor of the Exchequer, Stanley Baldwin (1867-1947),
succeeded him on May 25.

[4] In the spring of 1923 there was considerable discussion of the possibility
that Henry Ford might become the Democratic candidate for President in the
next year's elections, and that if he did not secure that nomination he would
become an independent candidate.

world is on the mend. This perhaps because term ends in a fortnight.

My love to you; and please remember that I wait eagerly to see
your dissent in the Nebraska language case.[5]

*Yours affectionately, H. J. L.*

*Beverly Farms, Sunday, June 24, 1923*
*Dear Laski:* Your letter met me here on our arrival last night and
gave me joy. We got to the Touraine Tuesday morning and were
so tired by the night journey with jolts that nearly threw you to the
floor, that we did absolutely nothing until we came here—I played
solitaire, eat, lay down, and slept. One exception was that on the
last evening we went to a movie across the way—*The Covered
Wagon*—a picture of crossing the plains in '48 and '49—artistically
*nil*, but really wonderful presentations of the trains of wagons moving—or fording rivers—real Indians attacking &c &c—the first
show I have gone to for two years. I am not going to bother about
improving my mind—at my age it is like the fear of acquiring bad
habits. But, by a happy coincidence, I also bought the whole of
Sainte-Beuve's *Causeries* (in paper however) and see idle amusement ahead—if it civilizes one a little there is no objection—but
that is not the object. I am afraid I shall not get hold of the other
things you recommend—but I may.

I didn't think the dissent on teaching languages worth sending.
I agree with the Court that an Ohio law excluding German only (I
believe an ebullition of Cox when he wanted to be President) was
bad [1]—but said that it was legitimate to try to make the young
citizens speak English and that if a legislature thought that the
best way to do that for children who could hear only Polish or
German or French at home, was to make them talk only English
during school hours I was not prepared to say that it was an unconstitutional limitation of the liberty of the school master. I have
little else to tell. I have been pretty tired as I said—and am thankful to have got through my work without a breakdown—the
doctor said it was a miracle—so I am pleased—but I endeavour
to look on whatever happens coolly. I suppose it is the windup
before very long—but I want to keep producing as long as I can

[5] In *Meyer* v. *Nebraska*, 262 U.S. 390, and *Bartels* v. *Iowa*, *id.* 404, a
majority of the Court held that state statutes forbidding the instruction of
children in foreign modern languages were unconstitutional. Holmes wrote a
dissenting opinion, Sutherland, J., concurring.

[1] Among the cases disposed of in connection with *Meyer* v. *Nebraska*, 262
U.S. 390, was an appeal in *Bohning* v. *Ohio* (*id.* 404), in which a majority
of the Court sustained an Ohio decision that a state statute of 1919 prohibiting the teaching of German in public schools was unconstitutional. James
M. Cox (1870-1950), who was Democratic candidate for the Presidency in
1920, was Governor of Ohio when the statute was enacted.

and as it is well to have an aim—I will put it at 90, without expectation, or disappointment if the fury with the accursed shears snips the thread. I love to hear about what you are writing—reading—buying—doing—and although you won't get a *quid pro quo* from me I don't doubt it is chalked down on your credit side in heaven when you write.						*Affectionately yours, O. W. Holmes*

*16 Warwick Gardens, 16.VI.23*

*My dear Justice:* . . . I have written little these last ten days; I have, however, read a great deal and been out much. In the last department, above all a wonderful dinner with Morley where we laid our minds on the table and fought amicably over my career. This, said he, is an age not of doctrine but of occasions; you can seize them only in the House of Commons. The constituency you need can be addressed only from a platform and that must needs be the place where the great decisions are made. I answer that occasions are only moments charged with doctrine; and it is more important to furnish the doctrine than to seize the pith of other men's thought. M. was very unconvinced. It is better, he insisted, to be Cromwell than Rousseau. Bad examples; but it is surely better to be Voltaire than the Duc de Choiseul.[1] The statesman on the modern stage is inevitably a pigmy; the writer who knows his business, even more the teacher, watches hundreds who never heard of him rediscover the truths he has uttered. Like all feminine temperaments Morley has a feverish zest for the market-place; and in my view he first unduly exalts its charm and second fails to see that what is a commonplace of the study is a discovery of the statesman. Then a long talk with Haldane who is in great form these days. He told me the inner history of the King's refusal to have Curzon as Prime Minister.[2] All agreed that he deserved the job; all said that his conscious knowledge of superior powers was fatal to the management of men. He had been too contemptuous of ordinary mortals to be loved by them; and they took their revenge. Who was it said of statesmen that they should at least appear to love their fellows and that the better to secure the appearance, it is wise to love them in reality? Haldane is gloomy about the Courts just now, lacking in minds like Watson and Blackburn; he added, where I cannot judge, that they used to have much help from Massachusetts decisions, especially in tort

[1] The Duc de Choiseul (1719-1785); his rise as statesman was largely owing to Madame de Pompadour, his fall, to Madame du Barry; at the height of his career he was Foreign Minister and friend of the Encyclopedists.

[2] On the resignation of Bonar Law in May it had commonly been supposed that he would be succeeded by Lord Curzon, Foreign Minister, and leader of the House of Lords.

cases, but that this day has passed. Then a fascinating dinner with
Tawney the economist to meet some Austrialians, including their
Prime Minister.[3] I had never met them as of the top before, only
in student form; and I thought them in general very like what you
get from Minnesota or Winnipeg—no historic sense, something of
the charm of sincerity, the go-ahead confidence in manifest destiny, the belief in mechanisms and statistics of new volume as the
tests of civilisation. I asked questions—why good law but no political science? Why no architects, artists, poets? A serene confidence
that these must come. I make choking references to a great essay
of Hume's; but only Tawney and an Australian professor had heard
of Hume. The latter, rather neatly I thought, countered my acidity
by suggesting that Hume was a great sceptic. But I was given
neither facts nor hopes. I add a dinner with young Mosley, Curzon's son-in-law and a warm friend of mine, to meet some German
journalists. Your good German mind is really very good. Here a
journalist who quotes Goethe to explain the Peace of Versailles,
and asks me if Vergennes[4] is honoured in America. The men who
will save Europe are the men who have the historic sense and
use it to penetrate the *fond* of these difficult hours. One fellow,
Edwards,[5] of a great Berlin paper, I thought of [*sic*] real statesman,
painting the mind of his countrymen *vis à vis* France with clear,
bold stroke in a manner that made you feel that French blindness
was really criminal.

. . . An English book I want to add from gratitude is Farbman's
*Bolshevism in Retreat*—quite the best discussion of the Russian
revolution I have seen. I hope you will send for it. Quite short, and
the work of an observer on the spot, it has the air of accuracy and
truth. It convinces me all over again first that great political
catastrophes are ultimately uncreative and second that they never
occur save after a preparation of essentially moral decline. It is
1715-1789 all over again. Here and here and here you can arrest
the corruption—here the chance grows feebler—here at last there
is no remedy save the knife. A man who would do for Russia
what Burke did for France, omitting the invective, would do a
great service. I don't want to push comparisons too far; but Moscow
sets the perspective of today as Paris in 1789 and I am sure that
now, as then, reformation in order to preserve is the watchword of
great events. It is thrilling to see how the Bolshevists go through
all the gestures of the Jacobins—the same useless end. They wish

---

[3] Stanley Melbourne Bruce, Viscount Bruce of Melbourne (1883-        ),
was Prime Minister of Australia from 1923 to 1929.

[4] The Comte de Vergennes (1717-1787). As foreign minister of Louis
XVI he showed his hatred of England by providing French support to the
Americans in the War of Independence.

[5] Not identified.

to make an international confraternity and they make a national state. . . .

My love longingly to you both.

*Ever affectionately yours, H. J. L.*


*Beverly Farms, June 29, 1923*

*Dear Laski:* You have straw for your bricks—I have little or none and therefore shall write but a postscript to my letter of a few days ago, but must write that to acknowledge another charmer from you "(16.VI.23)." I say I have no straw because I am idling, and my chief events have been no more than getting my annual volume of opinions from the binder and reading volume 1 of Sainte-Beuve's *Causeries*—I recur to the coincidence of our purchases. I had no idea that I should get so much pleasure, whether in reading about important people of whom I never heard or about the well known. His exquisiteness comes near to the squeamish perhaps at moments, but it is a good razor strop—and I like to plunge into the French literary tradition expounded by one who revered it and yet in 1849 was already able to appreciate the English. He keeps opening vistas. And I put down books to be read on a list, though I fear I shall not carry my homage further. I blush to confess certain chasms in my knowledge, although I make no bones of admitting general ignorance on a large scale. But I will whisper to you that I never have entered into Thucydides or read more than little fragments—and how should one dare to die before one has appreciated him? And that I can't recite on Tacitus although in times past I have read a little more of him. Commines[1] perhaps can wait for better days. When the cat is away the mouse will play—and, as I have not you present for a conscience, my present intent is not to go outside of literature and to amuse myself at least until I feel the need of a greater tension. Also I am going to try to get stronger on my legs. I hardly walked at all while I was working—and I don't know whether I can get back an elasticity that I have not now. Of course I agree with you as *vs.* Morley on ideas as against politics. If a man can put an idea into the world he may leave it to the retail dealers to make it popular. Though I agree, as I needs must in view of my life, that it isn't bad to put one's ideas to a practical test. I am in very good condition and enjoy the mere breathing of the country air. In the midst of scorching heat round-about we are liable to be almost too cool from ice off the coast.

*Ever affectionately yours, O. W. Holmes*

---

[1] Philippe de Commines (1445-1509); chronicler of Louis XI and Charles VIII; he revived the classical tradition in writing of history critically and philosophically.

*16 Warwick Gardens, 8.VII.23*

*My dear Justice:* A glorious letter from you tells me that you are at your ease, and with Sainte-Beuve as an elbow companion; there isn't, I think, a better way of taking instruction pleasantly. I have meanwhile been clearing up to get rid of the term. Setting exam papers, making speeches to departing students, sitting on the endless committees which accumulate at this time of year—not until the end of this week can I hope to reach peace. And your genial countrymen have turned up in their hundreds. Some of them like Mack[1] and your attractive young secretary Benjamin are both attractive and welcome; others like the mother of a bloody infant prodigy who, at sixteen, was a Ph.D. of Columbia and spoke nine languages were incredible. She came to ask my advice about his future, and I fear that she thought me merely flippant when I urged her to teach him how to play. Another good soul from Iowa wandered in with a letter from Walter Lippmann and merely wanted me to arrange a dinner at which she could meet all the Labour leaders. They make one a little angry, the more so because they are so incurably well-meaning. I feel pretty sure that the well-meaning of this world have quite a special place in hell.

But more pleasant things have happened. We went to a jolly reception at Sir John Hall's[2] where there was much that would have pleased you. First a collection of portraits by Raeburn, Kneller, Vandyck, Lely that were amazing—especially the Raeburn; and Hall showed me a receipt for the two of them at four guineas apiece. It makes one think a little about the supposed merits of the aristocratic patronage of art. The people there interested me a lot, especially Kipling. His talk has not a sparkle of wit or perception about it. He is like a rather well-to-do grocer who has all the right sentiments about the interests of trade, the well-being of the empire, and the wickedness of the Germans. You wonder if the Kipling who wrote half a dozen unforgettable things was really this man or an accidental emanation from him. I liked hugely Garvin,[3] the journalist; self-assertive, confident, generous and warm-hearted. In most of what he said he was wrong, and almost always he was wrong for the right reasons. Noyes[4] the poet was an artist in attitudes, posing even for the little debutantes and explaining how passionately one felt the poetry one wrote. Then

---

[1] Julian Mack (1866-1943); Federal Circuit judge in Chicago, 1911-1941.
[2] Sir John Richard Hall, Bart. (1865-1928), author of *The Bourbon Restoration* (1909) and *England and the Orleans Monarchy* (1912).
[3] J. L. Garvin (1868-1947); conservative journalist and editor of the London *Observer*; biographer of Joseph Chamberlain; editor of the fourteenth edition of the *Encyclopaedia Britannica*.
[4] Alfred Noyes (1880-1958); British poet of American fame; best known, unfortunately, for "The Highwayman."

a dinner with the Dighton Pollocks,[5] he a warm friend of yours and of Beatrice Chamberlain's and full of pleasant memories for which I was very grateful. And he was not taken in by the well-organised greatness of that incredible person Beck, the U.S. Solicitor-General, who comes here with great *éclat* to explain the Supreme Court to us. One with Haldane with Lady Horner to give it the spice of penetration she always brings, and a lunch with young Oswald Mosley to meet some Germans one of whom, an economist Kessler,[6] I sent along with a note to you as he seemed to me in every way a remarkable person. . . .

I have read some jolly things of late. Paul [*sic*] Masson's *La religion de Rousseau*, a little long, but in the mass the most illuminating study of Rousseau I have ever read. . . . And I reread Pound's *Interpretations of Legal History* which I still thought excellent but this time with the definite sense that most of its classifications are entirely unreal and that the explanation offered of the fellow servant doctrine is simply silly. He is overburdened by his knowledge and that makes him, I think, search for schematization where what is really evident is individuality. But the learning is on the Actonian scale. . . .

My love to you both. From now on I shall be a frequent correspondent much at my ease.    *Ever yours affectionately, H. J. L.*


*Beverly Farms, July 18* [?], *1923*
*Dear Laski:* A letter from you yesterday put the *comble* to my desires. Yesterday also I went to Boston by train—the first time that I have done it for two years—without ill effects. But I realize more or less that I am not as strong as I was—and am confirmed in my resolution to take this vacation very easily and very idly. I haven't quite finished volume 5 of Sainte-Beuve. I dare say that in the same time you would have engolubated the whole lot. (The word is made for the occasion. Pronounce that *u* as in tub.) I don't infinitely admire him. He is just (usually), and learned—and interesting—but I don't think that he has charm or that he opens vistas—of thought that is. He does in the way of suggesting lines of reading that would be entertaining, although not necessary to salvation. I envy you the variety of interesting people that you see and talk with but I fear that my time for that has pretty much gone by. I was tickled to note what you say about Beck. He seems to me to be more engaged upon the glories of No. 1 than any other

---

[5] Dighton Nicholas Pollock (1864-1927); chancery barrister; cousin of Sir Frederick Pollock.

[6] Count Harry Kessler (1868-1932), biographer of Walter Rathenau, lectured at the Institute of Politics at Williams College in August 1923.

subject. You remember the story of Theodore Hook[1] crossing Bond Street to where an unknown was occupying the side-walk, "Pray Sir, are you anybody in particular?" We meet, when we do, pleasantly enough, but I feel as if we lived in different worlds of interest. What you say about Pound's classifications I think strikes most of us. I wrote to him that I thought he rather overticketed the different eras but that perhaps it helped to make the movement clear and intelligible. Pollock wrote that he didn't believe the judges knew much about the different schools or cared for them[2] —and of course I quite agree—but still it is a Paul Veronese panorama. I don't remember his explanation of the fellow-servant doctrine. I am glad you liked Benjamin. He has not many goods in his shop window but I found him a most faithful, accurate and attentive secretary, and he was always and usefully suggestive to a remarkable degree. Mack I haven't got near enough to know much about—but my predispositions are favorable. How pleasant it is in Sainte-Beuve to come on some chap you never heard of and get a delightful picture—like Gourville in volume 5 to mention one of the last I've read. G's description of his own last days made me think of myself—hoping at the beginning of the year that he might be able to eat strawberries and when they are over aspiring to peaches—and so on so long as it pleases God. Sainte-Beuve so hates the violent man of the Terror that he makes me doubt if he is just—but the doubt is rare. By way of distraction I have listened to a murder story—*The Mystery of the Middle Temple*—or some such name—and other trifles—and so you have my life. I send you both my love and hope that you won't get tired of writing to me.　　　　　　　　　*Affectionately yours, O. W. Holmes*

I praise your always putting your address on your letters.


*16 Warwick Gardens, 14.VII.23*

*My dear Justice:* . . . It's been a difficult week, for the average temperature has been ninety and that, as you know, is not a dispensation for which we are well-prepared in England. But I have managed a little sightseeing. We had a pleasant dinner here on Tuesday—Hirst the economist, Bernstorff[1] of the German embassy, Drake[2] a lawyer with his very clever wife. It was a boiling night, but we all fell on Hirst who preaches the pure milk of the

---

[1] Theodore Edward Hook (1788-1841); novelist, wit, and carefree man of letters.

[2] 2 *Holmes-Pollock Letters* 112.

[1] Count Albrecht von Bernstorff, secretary in the German Embassy, was nephew of Count Johann Heinrich von Bernstorff, German Ambassador to the United States, 1914-1917.

[2] Not identified.

Cobdenite word and has a leaning for Herbert Spencer who (forgive me) was really a very vague old gentleman whose Nonconformist assertiveness beguiled his generation into thinking that a loud voice speaks important truths. We went also to dinner to Wells, as ever delightful, rolling in paradoxes and building Utopias over the salad-plates. Plato wouldn't have liked him for he would never have got Wells to analyse his terms; but I suspect that Aristophanes would have muttered that despite his radicalism the fellow was a good companion at table. . . . Nor must I omit to tell you of a jolly dinner with four clever Japanese from which I cull two remarks. (1) Englishmen, thinks the Japanese financier, are never aware of a world outside their own. They speak always as though you have lived to learn the family relationships. I think that is very true. You go to dinner here and hear a serene tale of the two maiden aunts say of Lord Curzon about whom you neither know nor care and with whom you are supposed to visit. (2) My Japanese professor of politics, a very wise and liberal-minded person, avers that the central institution of England is the committee. "Politics, business, charity, sport," he says "you run all in committee. When I discovered you were theists I thought your religion had escaped the system until I found you had adopted the dogma of the Trinity so as to give God a casting vote." I like this pretty blasphemy; and I refer you to Pollock's *Essays in the Law* for an admirable proof of its substance.[3] Pollock by the way is I hear quite recovered[4] and his nephew spoke of him to me as well and active-minded. . . .

*Ever yours affectionately, H. J. L.*

*Beverly Farms, July 29, 1923*

*Dear Laski:* Your letter of the 14th has waited two days for an answer, as I had written in the week, and yesterday when I was expecting to write Reginald Foster[1] came in early and spent the morning in delightful jaw. He is an accomplished lad of 60—reads as you do—down the page instead of across it (as he put it) and has gobbled up an appalling lot. He had just been seeing an uncle of 91 at Vevey[2]—still, he said, funny and walking and eating like

---

[3] Sir Frederick Pollock, "Government by Committees in England," *Essays in the Law* (1922), p. 110.

[4] Sir Frederick Pollock in May had been injured when struck by a bicyclist. 2 *Holmes-Pollock Letters* 116.

[1] Reginald Foster (1863-1944), Boston lawyer, was the son of Dwight Foster and Henrietta Baldwin Foster.

[2] George William Baldwin (1832-1930); Civil War veteran and lawyer who practiced in Boston from 1863 until 1880 and then retired, spending his remaining years in Europe.

a young man—the descendants of Roger Sherman[3] all have the gift of saying short sharp witty things—from Evarts[4] and Judge Hoar[5] to Arthur Hill. Not quite all—I never heard that Sim. Baldwin,[6] ex-C.J. and governor of Connecticut, said anything funny but his brother, the uncle in question, did and it seems still does —though 91 is really old. Several things that you say need answer, or suggest one. 1. Sainte-Beuve's paper on the reception of Lacordaire implies rather more knowledge than I have to appreciate it—though in other essays I get tickling allusions to their present things and people. 2. We have had it cold after a few days of heat, and the electricity being off for the moment I have a wood fire burning in my room at this moment. 3. What you say of Wells agrees with my impressions. . . .

5. The Japs talked rightly about the English, but when Englishmen are here I often have noticed that the conversation is apt to be local and unintelligible to them. The first time I was in England I dined with Harcourt and a lot of delightful people—I thought I was going to hear wonderful talk—but hardly understood a word. Probably I have told you of my wife's reply to a visitor who disposed of something by saying we don't do that in England —"That's why we came to this country."

6. Pound's article[7] that you mention struck me the same way. I wrote to F.F. saying that I didn't see that he told us anything on a first glance—and since then on reading more carefully got nothing from it.

7. Finally I shall try to get hold of *Pride and Prejudice* and reread it—but I grieve to confess that the last time I tackled Saint Jane as Pollock calls her I found her—I whisper it—a bore.

I have heard again from my young Chinaman in Berlin—he was thinking of giving a year to Spinoza which I rather dissuaded. If he is going to make law his theme, clearly he had better descend to the concrete and if philosophy I told him that I thought present views of life and the world were more subtle, manifold in points of contact and profound than those of any of the ancients—although of course you can read into them what you like. This

[3] Roger Sherman (1726-1793); lawyer and merchant; delegate to the First Continental Congress and to the Constitutional Convention of 1787; Congressman and Senator from Connecticut; father of fifteen children.

[4] William Maxwell Evarts (1818-1901), son of Roger Sherman's daughter; a distinguished lawyer; Attorney General in Johnson's administration; Secretary of State under Hayes; Senator from New York.

[5] Ebenezer Rockwood Hoar (1816-1895), *supra*, p. 362, was first cousin of Evarts.

[6] Simeon Baldwin (1840-1927) was the son of Roger Sherman Baldwin and Emily Baldwin; his career as practicing lawyer, Professor of Law at the Yale Law School, Associate Justice and Chief Justice of the Supreme Court of Connecticut, and Governor of Connecticut made him for many years the first citizen of Connecticut.

[7] "The Theory of Judicial Decision" (part III), *Harv. L. Rev.* 940.

without prejudice to regarding some of Spinoza's grand *aperçus* as fundamental. Foster also had been in Corsica—he said you saw Letitia Bonaparte in the women everywhere and the people lived in little settlements separated by mountains or ravines and disliked their neighbors. His Corsican chauffeur was mighty careful not to run down a hen—he said that to run down a hobbled animal meant three weeks in jail—and if he ran down a hen there would be trouble which Foster interpreted as a possible knife in your back. Also delightful perfume from aromatic thickets which Napoleon said he could shut his eyes and recall. He was a glimpser of the past.                                 *Affectionately yours, O. W. H.*

*16 Warwick Gardens, 1.VIII.23*

*My dear Justice:* A perfect day on which to write to you, for to-day I have been married twelve years, and I feel as though I were still in the faint early flush of an idyll. You can guess what such years of perfect comradeship have meant. Certainly I have been blessed as few others in these matters.

. . . Also a party here for H. G. Wells—Arnold Bennett, Nevinson, Massingham and Haldane. Grand talk, what of all moving me being the unanimous agreement that no man ever had the critical perception of Goethe. Bennett said that the *Conversations* were for him a supreme experience, and Wells said he first learned from Goethe that you could make Hogsville a mirror of universal life. . . . And I went to a dinner at the House of Commons where I heard Birrell make the most perfect after-dinner speech I have ever heard. The best thing was his description of Wilson's *Congressional Government* as "Bagehot played on a penny whistle," and of Taine who reduced the world to psychological laws and was indifferent to the unimportant problem of whether psychology existed. It was a great *tour de force;* and, good heavens, I must not forget his definition of the Balliol man as a person who exhibited "a conscious knowledge of effortless superiority."

. . . Also I have written—a long article for Coolidge comparing Lenin and Mussolini[1] and arguing that if you want to preserve civilisation you must decide to tread the path of reason and not of violence. . . .                    *Ever affectionately yours, H. J. L.*

*Beverly Farms, August 12, 1923*
*Anniversary of my final operation last year.*

*Dear Laski:* Your letters are a liberal education and a constant delight—more than ever the one coming this morning—"1.VIII.23."

---

[1] "Lenin and Mussolini," 2 *Foreign Affairs* 43 (September 1923). Professor Archibald Cary Coolidge (1866-1928), of Harvard University, was editor, at the time, of *Foreign Affairs.*

I couldn't do that! Birrell's judgment on Wilson's *Congressional Government* is exactly the one I formed except that I didn't have his wit in expressing it. Well I have reread *Pride and Prejudice*—in view of your recent expression. I am not with you. Of course, the author is an artist in her way of telling a simple story. But it seems to me that to introduce bores, snobs and fools into literature one must be able to transfigure them. Dickens transfigures Mrs. Nickleby adorably—but I don't think Miss Austen transfigures Mrs. Bennet (if that is the name of the heroine's mother) or the incredible parson, and only by making the heroine a *deus ex machina* does she save the provincial prig of a lover. I delight in the bloom and first intention of much modern English speech —but the first intentions of a century ago were simply brutal. Of course Little Pedlington is everywhere—I thought I saw it among the Souls[1] in their day—but the profound ignorance of and indifference to anything but local standards, of which no doubt there is a good deal still, is in too large a dose for me to swallow. I was interested—I am in any story—but when I think of the myriad books that even when unsuccessful explore depths of the human soul—when I think that the Gioconda was painted and Hamlet written centuries before, I can't get out a very high note on Fred Pollock's Saint Jane. So, that's that. I do but little—I have read only 8 volumes of Sainte-Beuve. I do hope that he was a hypocrite and a dirty fellow. As probably I have said before, his prudery about things that we shouldn't fear to mention to grown women, and his attitude to unbelievers, sound hollow to me. I hope he merely was dressing in the fashion—but if so—I don't like him. He is good reading—but it is time for me to change the diet. You talk of progress—of course in a specific matter. People talk of it in general terms—who knows what he means when he speaks of it? I understand and agree when it is said that there has been progress in philosophy—or mathematics—but when they speak of the world I'm blowed if I know. I suppose Aristotle's brain was as good as the modern ones. I was told years ago that the mediaeval popular music was happier than ours. I do not regard the great multiplication of the species as a benefit—*Que scai je?* Let me repeat a chestnut of mine, merely because it came up in talk a day or two ago. I said to a dame that my ideal man never would think about morality. He naturally would do the kind, generous, splendid thing—but that while in all other departments we prefer native gifts to industry—(which also is a gift of a less specialized

---

[1] "The Souls" was the name given to the small and fashionable group, including Balfour, Curzon, and Margot Tennant, which met for week-end conversation, wit, and, mutual admiration in the 1890's. See 2 *Margot Asquith: An Autobiography* (1920), Chapter I; Haldane, *Richard Burdon Haldane: An Autobiography* (1929), pp. 129-131.

sort) we have a queer notion that in morality industry is better
than genius. . . .

I had more to say but have been interrupted—this p.m. by a
call from the man who is the great gospel critic at Harvard—
coming I think originally from Oxford. You used to blow his horn.
We spoke of you with high appreciation but he said that in some
way, he didn't know what, he feared that he had offended you
before you left. Is the name Kersop [*sic*] Lake?[2] Something like
that. I liked him and wondered what the trouble had been. He
professed to, also.

Naturally I am with you on your anniversary. We have been
fortunate and I read in Ste. B. Madame de Maintenon's statement
that three quarters of the marriages were failures. My love to you
both.                                              *Yours, O. W. H.*

> *Grand Hotel, Oostduinkerke-Sur-Mer,*
> *Belgium, 10.VIII.23*

*My dear Justice:* . . . I was very moved by Harding's death.[1] I
met him three or four times in Washington. I thought him medio-
cre in ability but with a real and generous goodwill to his fellow-
men, a quality I am still sentimental enough to think important.
Though it is difficult to say of any one man that he will be disastrous to the republic, I should guess that Coolidge will come as
near to success in that venture as anyone. He is dull, illiterate,
stupid and obstinate. The whole of his reputation is poor mythology. I wish to heaven that Americans would realise that a constitution built on the historic dogmas of the XVIIIth century has
very little application to our own time. If ever an office needed
revision it is that of the Vice-President. No people ought to have
inflicted on it a man chosen either for his complete lack of qualities (as Coolidge) or because his suppression is desired (as Roosevelt). But this is to ask for reason in politics, which, outside of
books, is, I know, a dark and difficult adventure. But if I began
to state my feelings about the American Constitution I should ex-
haust both your patience and the vocabulary of vituperation. . . .

Our love to you both from a full heart.

> *Ever yours affectionately, H. J. L.*

> *Grand Hotel, Oostduinkerke-Bains 21.VIII.23*

*My dear Justice:* . . . I have talked art until I feel like generalis-
ing about it. What has interested me exceedingly is that half the

---

[2] *Supra,* p. 40.
[1] President Harding had died in office on August 2 and Calvin Coolidge
succeeded to the Presidency.

artists round here, particularly Ensor[1] whose work is beyond praise
from me, have, since the war, taken to still life. I don't profess to
understand and they don't profess to explain; but where eight
years ago they wanted movement now they seem to want repose.
One wonders where [sic] it is the unconscious expression of a
physiological rhythm. Where they do paint life they run to violent
gestures, brilliant colours, brutal contrast—red sails and blue skies,
as though the war had knocked harmony out of them. I'm interested very much in their general sympathy for revolution. They all
regard the present order as finished. They seek, so to say, a new
balance of things. Ensor, who talks like a God, makes you think
of Turgot prophesying on the eve of the Revolution. Nothing
unites peasant and man of business. Parliament no longer debates.
Statesmen are deaf to the voices about them. The scale of civilisation is too large for the human mind to manipulate. There are
no solutions while man competes with the cow as a multiplier of
his kind. I give you extracts of what they are thinking. Few of
them read; all of them reflect. All of them reflect on lines that the
eighteenth century would have called philanthropic. They are bitterly hostile to politicians and priests. They loathe business men.
They are passionately curious about China, Persia, Japan. It all
seems to me as I watch it like the pageant of declining Rome before the Huns of Attila swept down upon it. And when you turn
from them to the peasant with his endless toil, a machine ploughing the fields by day and breeding these endless children by night,
you cannot help wondering why men have ever been so crude as
to see a design in things. Self-preservation, and a limited number
with unending curiosity; but progress surely simply a happy piece
of skilful mythopoeisis to make men perpetuate the race. Indeed I
offer you the hypothesis that progress is simply a secularisation
of the kingdom of heaven with God anthropomorphised into the
member of a salon à la Mme. du Deffand. And one feels all this
the more as the news comes daily—deadlock between England
and France, the German mark so much wastepaper.[2] . . .

*Ever affectionately yours, H. J. L.*


*Beverly Farms, August 25, 1923*
*My dear Laski:* A good one from you from Belgium. I should think
that you were right about Harding—which would account for

---

[1] James Ensor (1860-1942), son of a British father and Belgian mother; he
became a distinguished expressionist painter, poet, and writer, was made a
Baron in 1929, and died during the German occupation of Belgium.

[2] During August the British government had taken firm positions in opposition both to the Franco-Belgian claims for German reparations, and to the
legality of the Franco-Belgian occupation of the Ruhr. In the meanwhile
inflation in Germany had virtually destroyed the value of the mark.

what seems the genuine sorrow of the country over his death. Coolidge is getting the advantage of his silence and of the unknown. I am not without hopes since I saw the other day that he was magnanimous enough in former times to say in a public speech that he didn't want credit that he didn't deserve and that the credit, that which was given to him on account of the police strike, belonged to Curtis.[1] (This without prejudice to ulterior questions. It was magnanimous from his point of view.) I wish you would develop more at length your grounds for disliking our constitution. Of course it has the 18th century emphasis and Bagehot criticised forcibly the division of powers—but I suspect that you don't like the bill of rights of former days—whereas I have been rather led to the belief that we have grown so accustomed to the enjoyment of those rights that we forget that they had to be fought for and may have to be fought for again. As I have no plan for reconstructing society at all costs I am inclined to stand by them. To turn. I wonder what you think of Carlyle's *French Revolution*. I can't get the books you recommend without going to town which I have done but twice, to get my hair cut &c with no time for the Athenaeum or Schoenhof. So I read Carlyle for an hour or two. I like a spoonful of highly seasoned hash—but three volumes of it are too much. Ejaculation is not the form for narrative—but what eloquence and what insight. I notice that he preceded Ruskin as to the bogus modesty of *Paul and Virginia*. I haven't read the last for more than fifty years but I am quite sure that I should think the sentiment like that of the 18th century painting, *e.g.* Greuze. The time was when my father asking what book I would take to a desert island, if but one, I answered C's *French Revolution*. I shouldn't say so now—but what should I? If I were allowed a dictionary, perhaps the *Iliad* or *Odyssey*— perhaps a book that lies on the outer edge of one's knowledge and powers like Analytical Geometry. If one were of that belief, perhaps something like the *Imitation* that one would end by knowing by heart—I never read it. I blush to say that Sainte-Beuve still hangs on. I have read but ten volumes. My only notion of your beloved Mlle. de Lespinasse is what I got from him. I think I

---

[1] At the time of the Boston Police strike, Edwin U. Curtis was Police Commissioner and stubbornly resisted the demands of the police for improved wages and working conditions. The Mayor of Boston at the time was Andrew J. Peters. Under his guidance a compromise had been suggested, but was rejected by Curtis. Coolidge, sympathizing with Curtis, had rejected Peters' request for the mobilization of the militia. When the strike occurred and rioting broke out, Coolidge finally acceded to Peters' request that the guardsmen should be called out, but coupled that action with the reinstatement of Curtis to a position of authority. The reference to Coolidge's rejection of personal credit for his part in controlling the strike is probably to an address which he delivered in January 1921; see Coolidge, *The Price of Freedom* (1924), 29.

should like a better-looking girl—but they are all sausage to me
—in Brooks Adams's phrase. Oh, how often do I wish you were
still in Rockport or nearer. My summer would be much richer and
it would warm my aged heart.                    *Aff'ly yours, O. W. H.*

                                        *Grand Hotel, Oostduinkerke-Bains,*
                                                        *Belgium 29.VIII.23*
*My dear Justice:* . . . I have written a good deal since I wrote
you last; actually since I came here I have eighty pages done; and
even granted that I shall rewrite it twice at least I feel *in medias
res.* It is curious how setting out one's convictions revises them.
I came back for instance to a much greater regard for the Mon-
tesquieu-Tocqueville-Mill school than ever before. I felt, that is,
how much more political questions are moral questions, I mean of
character, of *esprit,* and how little questions of machinery and
formulae. I don't belittle the latter. But I suspect that a guild
chairman under guild socialism would not be very different from
a cabinet minister of today. I have been writing about responsibility and as I have written it has become incredibly more urgent
to me to find the secret of the moral tradition which builds responsibility than of the political machinery which secures it; *e.g.*
the King in Parliament could always decide that the present House
of Commons should sit permanently. It doesn't, not because of a
fear of revolution, but because it really wants, within the limit of
its knowledge, to act decently. I agree that there are governments,
the France of the *Ancien régime,* the Russia of 1903, of which
this is untrue. But I should be inclined to guess that few governments can live long without acquiring a tradition that it is worth
while to seek the right. Certainly if they don't no considerations
of machinery can really prevent them from seeking the wrong. . . .
    What you say of the localism of English conversation is, I think,
even more true today. I have dined a dozen times at the Asquiths
and heard names discussed with awe that I had not even heard
of. It isn't true of Morley or Haldane or Birrell; but you must
know the gossip or you merely peer over the world. The cultivation of the abstract seems to ruin their talk.
    My love to you both and Frida's. I needn't say, at this distance,
what a joy I have in all you write.
                                        *Ever affectionately yours, H. J. L.*

                                        *Beverly Farms, September 4, 1923*
*My dear Laski:* So many things occur to me that I want to talk
about with you, between letters, but when one comes from you as

now and I start to answer it, I have forgotten them. I will not
speak of Japan—except to say that I have written to the Ambassador and am anxious about my dear friend Kaneko,[1] whom I
have known from his small boyhood. I went on and read Carlyle's
*French Revolution,* having looked into it—and hardly can imagine
you would value it highly. As a grotesque imaginative poem on
the emotional side I can admire it—and dividing mankind around
the two poles of emotion and thought—the poets at one end and
the philosophers at the other—I don't expect serious thought from
Carlyle. There is more thought in one inadequate sentence of another inadequate book—to the effect that the world had come to
demand wheat bread and that there wasn't enough to go round—
the English having the first take, the Germans the second, the
French only the third, and thereupon a row. A Scotch gardener
said to my wife that you couldn't understand Carlyle's domestic
relations unless you realized that he was a Scotch peasant. I think
you feel it here in all his talk about ending a lie. I am indebted
to Sainte-Beuve, volume 11 for having led me to read a little of
Cowper. They talk about the lucidity and conciseness of French
—read Cowper where S.B. translates him and see how many more
words it takes S.B. to turn his poetry into prose. But of course no
poet can be read in a translation. I thank S.B. also for a passage
from Monluc[2] [*sic*] which expresses in a slightly different form
what for years I have quoted from a character in a novel by
Frédéric Soulié[3]—Valor never is proved—but always is to be
proved. With Monluc it becomes a general moral that you never
can say I have done the trick, but must go on to the end, trying
to do better. I accept the moral, at least for the next term. I don't
attempt to look farther ahead than that, for though I am in much
better condition than when I came here my walks grow pretty
short. You make me miserable about Thucydides. Am I to die
without ever having really read him? As to progress of the world,
I don't know what it means. I believe that there has been progress
in mathematics and philosophy—but as to the world? I was told
years ago that the popular music of the mediaeval ages was much
more joyful than ours. I envy your sights—and don't sympathize

---

[1] Count Kentaro Kaneko (1853-1942), Japanese statesman, had been a
student at Harvard in 1872, was a frequent visitor to the United States, and
was a lifelong friend of Holmes's. His house in Japan was destroyed by fire
and his daughter was killed in the earthquake of September 1, 1923.

[2] The sketch of Blaire de Montluc (1502-1577), Marshal of France, included this quotation: "*Si vous désirez monter au bout de l'échelle d'honneur,
ne vous arrêtez pas au milieu, ains, degré par degré, tâchez à gagner le bout,
sans penser que votre renom durera tel que vous l'avez acquis: vous vous
trompez, quelque nouveau venu le vous emportera, si vous ne le gardez bien
et ne tâchez à faire de mieux en mieux.*" 11 *Causeries* (1856) 85.

[3] Frédéric Soulié (1800-1847); playwright and novelist; author, *inter alia,*
of *Le Vicomte de Béziers* (1834).

with your artist friends in their loathing for business men. It seems
to me merely an illustration of the inability of men to appreciate
other forms of energy than that which is natural to them. I am
not, and I fear could not be a business man—but the types that
I have in mind seem to me among the greatest. This is a disinterested appreciation of what generally is disagreeable to me. I am
distraught with business myself at this moment, in the way of
paying bills &c. &c. I have asked a man to buy tickets &c. to
Washington for the night of Wednesday the 26th. Tell me not
that I could not be happy off the Bench. I shall give up my busy
idleness with regret—but the files of *certioraris* that I shall find
waiting for me begin to loom into a mountain. Let me forget it
for this and the following weeks. Oh, how gladly would I run
over to Rockport, now unvisited, for a jaw with you. My love to
you both.                                    *Affectionately yours, O. W. Holmes*


                                        *Beverly Farms, September 11, 1923*
*Dear Laski:* This ought to be a short and more than usually unworthy reply to your last from Belgium 29.VIII.23 (I like to copy
what I couldn't do). For this is the last week but one here and
there is competition for every moment of my time. Half an hour
that I had intended for you has just been snatched away by two
callers—dear people to whom I grudged the interruption. You
will despise me when I confess that I don't expect to finish Sainte-
Beuve before I go—I have read eleven volumes with excursions
and alarums. I think I mentioned Carlyle's *French Revolution* and
now I am in the middle of *Lettres choisies* de Mme. de Sévigné.
I ought to be able to recite on her at the day of judgment but a
little is enough, though I don't mind more. One perhaps would
have liked to know her in life for the easier moments. She could
give you small change for a dollar bill—she couldn't have changed
a ten. But last night came *Chance, Love and Logic* by Charles S.
Peirce with introduction by Cohen and supplement by Dewey.
Averse as I am to improvement right now I at once read Cohen's
masterly little discourse and I think I must read the book at once.
It suggests an image. More than ten years ago we had a flower
bed on the bank in front of this house—including certain poppies
that my wife's father gave her with the warning that she never
would get rid of them. The bed was obliterated as I have intimated ten or more years ago—but a few days back my wife had
some turf turned up to allow some creeping roses to expand and
lo! up came the old poppies—the seeds must have been waiting
their time. So these obscure geniuses drop a few seeds that no one
notices and when they are dead their seeds sprout and blossom

into one's most valued flowers. How much more impressive than "our most highly gifted men."

We were stirred by the Japanese disaster—although I did not mention it in my last. I hear of poverty and starvation in other parts of the world and remain unmoved, preferring in spite of your scorn for patriotism to turn my money to good of my own country. But a misfortune like this that comes from nature I think calls for a certain amount of mutual insurance—just as people in a remote settlement turn out to help one of them to repair damage if his house is struck by lightning. So I forked out—though less than I at first intended to. I excited the wrath of my ex sister-in-law[1] (she married again) by saying that the gifts of the very rich to public purposes—like Carnegie's Libraries—raised the only doubt I ever felt about the regime of private ownership—that they could be justified only after a most careful consideration of the immediate detriment &c &c. She said, "Then I shan't tell you the nice things I have been doing for the Art Museum." "Don't," quoth I. "Well, you had better take your walk." "I will." We have met since with effusion. In fact an art museum is one of the objects of rich men's gifts that I have least doubt about and most believe in—whether I should admire my sister-in-law's gifts or not. I have run on as long as time permits. Now I must walk—and then be polite to a dame at luncheon—a friend of my wife's—and perhaps later I may read until interrupted by sleep.

*Aff'ly yours, O. W. H.*

*Beverly Farms, September 21, 1923*
*Friday, p.m.*

*Dear Laski:* Another superlative letter[1]—after your return to London. This is my last from Beverly Farms. Will go to Boston on Monday—Washington Wednesday night and on Thursday morning cubic yards of cases to be examined (*certioraris*). Idleness is ending. I will not recur to Constitution, Carlyle, and Coolidge all of which themes would lend themselves to jaw, though perhaps without much difference of opinion—except that the last is still *sub judice*. I will only add as to Sainte-Beuve that when he talks as a pious Catholic he makes me want to puke—though I won't swear that it isn't my prejudice rather than his fault. I forget whether I had received and read Peirce, *Chance, Love and Logic,* ed. Cohen—which put a momentary edge on to my mind. But Peirce thinks his ultimates are cosmic ultimates, whereas I think they couldn't be assumed to be more than his intellectual limita-

---

[1] Mrs. Walter Scott Fitz was first married to Holmes's brother, Edward Jackson Holmes.

[1] Omitted from this edition.

tions. The professional philosophers hate to end with an *ignoramus*. Another book sent to me—Bédier, *Le roman de Tristan et Yseult* is a modern French version made by a scholar with something of the poet in him from the old fragments. The early middle ages whether seen in the older parts of Winchester or in their literature make my heart shake. They seem more supernatural than other things. Did I ever tell you of the top of the Aletsch glacier passed in coming down the Mönch? I won't now—I never saw my impressions indicated elsewhere except in the *Pêcheur d'Islande* —or did I ever moralize to you on Pharaoh's head? feelings which again Pierre Loti understood—or on the total eclipse of the sun? These all stir the mind at the bottom of one's brain. So did the dark corners of Winchester. That damned Sainte-Beuve keeps coming up in my mind—this time because he criticises careless expressions in private letters as if they had occurred in academic orations. However, he has given me a lot of pleasure and some incidental instruction—unsought but not objected to. Charley Curtis called the other evening after his return from lion hunting in Africa. He told me that there were a lot of letters from Franklin to his wife's grandmother or great grandmother—one on her approaching or recent marriage—in which he adverted to having had to do with her education and her instruction in addition, subtraction, and division and gallantly regretted that he could not have included multiplication.[2] I gathered that the honored patriarch had not lived in France in vain. I think Frankfurter is really at work on the 14th Amendment and his book—at which I rejoice. He seems to have been having a happy summer. If Bertrand Russell should call I should be most happy as I want to see and talk with him. I don't think I ever have—I am afraid it was your suggestion rather than his—but it was a good one from whomsoever it came and I hope will realize itself. I still have difficulty with philosophic as with economic language. As I have told you before that seems to me the chief trouble. Ideas are not often hard but words are the devil. On the chance of getting a boat this week I stop and shall start for the village at once. Why don't you find out when the mails go—it isn't in me to discover. The country grows enchanting just as I have to leave it. Love to you both.                                    *Aff'ly yours, O. W. H.*

*Antietam*

   *61 years ago*
      *September 17*

---

[2] See *Benjamin Franklin and Catherine Ray Greene: Their Correspondence, 1755-1790* (Roelker, ed., 1949), p. 20: "You must practise *addition* to your Husband's Estate, by Industry and Frugality; *Subtraction* of all unnecessary Expences; *Multiplication* (I would gladly have taught you that myself, but you thought it was time enough and wouldn't learn). . . ."

*16 Warwick Gardens, 26.IX.23*

*My dear Justice:* The main thing in my mind, as you will imagine,
is dear old Morley's death.[1] Conventionally I do not regret it at
all. He was very tired and fragile and he had a singularly happy
life. But he leaves a big gap for me to whom he had been these
last years a dear and warm friend. Politically, I suppose he was
very far from me, and some of his Gods I hope never to revere.
But he always talked from a full mind and a full heart. He liked
the men who really count and the lamp of reason burned the more
brightly for his presence. Some of his work seems to me very first
rate—in literary criticism the essays on Macaulay and Carlyle, in
political criticism those on Maine and Condorcet; the biographies
of Voltaire and Diderot, the essays on Machiavelli and Robespierre.
I have always liked the life of Cobden as a great picture of that
era, and disliked the Gladstone as a tombstone rather than a
book, though it has great occasions. As I look back the striking
thing about the long hours I used to spend there was his wide
and generous attitude to life. And many of his heroes were mine
—especially Cromwell, Voltaire and Mill. And I think he did some
great political work—Ireland, India and South Africa are all trib-
utes to his insight. I heard from him only on Friday, full of talk
and requests for books. Today I should have lunched with him;
tomorrow I follow his funeral. Life is like a harlequinade written
by a madman. I wish I could give you and Felix, Morley and
Haldane the power of immortality; but then I should want also
to get rid of Nicholas Butler and Coolidge, so perhaps it is best
as it is. . . .

For the rest, the main thing is that we are the proud possessors
of a little motor-car given us by my father. Neither of us drives it
yet . . .

My love to you both. Keep well and remember that there is
the image of God even in McReynolds.

*Ever affectionately yours, Harold*

*Washington, D.C., September 28, 1923*

*Dear Laski:* Your letter reached us yesterday just after we arrived
and was most welcome. As expected I went to work at once as
soon as we could get some breakfast and worked like a horse
being dirty as a pig until I had got my things into order and 16
*certioraris* examined. Then I took a bath and a nap—night travel
not being ideal repose. Today (a.m.) bank business, Secretary[1]—

---

[1] Viscount Morley died on September 23.
[1] James M. Nicely had graduated from the Harvard Law School in June
1923.

nice chap he seems etc. etc., with luncheon at Rauscher's. Then
return, and as soon as I have scribbled a few lines to you and
examined the books and pamphlets that Nicely is sorting, to the
*certioraris* again. The multitude of little things to be attended to,
each taking time, I cannot recount but you can guess. I gather
that Wigmore's book to which I wrote an introduction,[2] is out,
but my secretary has not discovered a copy for me—if not, I shall
write a sarcastic note offering to pay for the volume but I feel
free to enclose a copy of my part with this. You will note the
misprint. I wrote to Wigmore exhorting him to set it right but the
proof reading of my galley proofs of the book leaves me apprehensive.

Naturally I am in such a drive that I can't expatiate—take the
print as excuse for more MS. though it has little that I haven't
said before.

Rejoice at the thought of ever possibly seeing you.

*Aff'ly yours, O. W. Holmes*

*16 Warwick Gardens, 6.X.23*

*My dear Justice:* Much has happened since your delightful letter
of Monday—mainly reflections upon the art of driving my car. . . .
I went . . . to hear Gooch on Franco-German relations since
1870[1]—a quite admirable lecture which I enjoyed greatly. He
showed beyond dispute . . . that given the temper engendered
by 1870-1 war was inevitable . . . I add that Gooch like all the
people one meets has a profound respect for Thiers which I find
myself quite unable to share. A second-rate historian, a politician
who never did himself a great act and in the destruction of the
Commune acted like Haynau[2] after 1848.

. . . for work I had to reread the *Republic*. I think honestly I
admired it as a work of art more than ever I did; but also I felt
that I could have given Socrates some posers rather more abstruse
than those of simple-minded Thrasymachus. I like the *Laws* better and the *Phaedo* better still—the conclusion of the last ranking,
I think, with the choruses of *Oedipus Coloneus* as the peak of
Greek literature.

You, I take it, are at the end of *certioraris* and watching the
clans assemble. At least you will have the company of Brandeis
—a great solace. Your new men, of course, I do not know, though

<hr />

[2] "Law and the Social Factor," an Introduction to *Rational Basis of Legal
Institutions* (1923; Modern Legal Philosophy Series, Wigmore, ed.).

[1] Gooch's Creighton Lecture at the University of London was published
under the title, *Franco-German Relations, 1871-1914* (1923).

[2] Julius Haynau (1786-1853); Austrian General whose hostility to revolution in Italy and Hungary was nearly as effective as it was savage.

evil things have been said to me of Butler. Has it ever struck you that you, Felix, Morris Cohen, Brandeis and I with, I think, Johnny Palfrey and Hand, J. for makeweights would be an admirable supreme court. We should never dissent; we should merely want arguments in labour cases; and we would devise endless novelties.

My love to you both.      *Ever yours affectionately, Harold J. Laski*

*Washington, D.C., October 11, 1923*

*Dear Laski:* On the principle that whenever you write one of your precious letters you are to have a reply though it be only an acknowledgment I write now, but I am working all I can and have done two opinions also this week, *per quod,* as my wife thinks, in addition to which at all events, I now have a brisk cold and am coughing and sneezing. So I am no good. Your letter speaks of Morley's death. I thought at once of you when I heard of it. My own emotions were moderate, but you make me want and intend to read more of him if I ever read again. Also I received a day or two ago *The Way Out*—and have glanced at your essay —as yet I could no more. I love your generous attitude, but I don't see how a rich life is possible for many so long as we have the wholesale machine production made necessary by the great population, which in turn it reacts to increase. However, I am old and I told the C.J. I was only a ghost—not that I quite believe that—but I am pretty well out of the problems for the future. I can't do more for the moment than send you my love. I am not ill but simply no good until I can let a little water run into the cistern—now it has all run out (a good deal through my nose). I hope I shall see Bertrand Russell if he comes here. I expect about Xmas a visit from my little Chinaman, Mr. Wu, of whom I have told you. He is now at Cambridge, Mass. For the time being he has set me on a pedestal. I smile and tell him he will get over it—but it is pretty while it lasts. A new edition of Pollock on *Torts* comes this p.m. Oh, would that I could gut a book by a simple movement of finger and thumb like you. Did I speak of Sir J. Reynolds's *Discourses on Art* which I read coming on. It fortified reflections of ancient date, and tickled me no little.

*Aff'ly yours, O. W. H.*

You received I presume my poor little last peep—the last I shall utter except from the Bench.

*16 Warwick Gardens, 13.X.23*

*My dear Justice:* Not merely a delightful letter from you, but a copy of your introduction to the law volume which I read eagerly

and, save in detail, I think without dissent. All change—I reject
the word progress—has to be paid for; and regulations deemed
necessary *e.g.* Factory Acts are the exchange of a bulge in one
direction of the circle for a bulge considered more advisable in
another.[1] The test, I take it, of adequacy is never quantitative
once one moves from material conditions; and until we know far
more of the terms of mental improvement than now, it is advisable
to confine changes very largely to avenues *e.g.* housing, preventive
medicine, education, where change of a particular kind seems to
secure a definite return. Does this outrage you?

. . . I re-read Zimmern's *Greek Commonwealth.* It is, I think,
quite unquestionably the best book an Englishman has ever written on Greece; and it left me with a despairing sense that the
transformation of the scale of life has really made most political
problems insoluble. I put it to my class that you could pull Pericles by the sleeve in the Agora in the fifth century; if you pulled
Baldwin by the sleeve in Downing Street, you would, I think, get
forty shillings and costs. It is horrible to go into a London tube
at six at night and to remember that good government means
translating the inarticulate wills of those rows on rows of tired
faces into something like reality. And there is the other side.
Gladstone, after all, spoke to an audience of a million most of
whom were trained to the point of weighing the meaning of
words. Today one speaks to twenty millions to whom words in an
exact sense are often counters without meaning. . . .

Our love unitedly to you both. *Macte antiquae virtutis.*

*Ever yours affectionately, H. J. L.*

*16 Warwick Gardens, 23.X.23*

*My dear Justice:* A delightful letter from you this morning[1] has
warmed my heart; though, I add, that I do not like you to have
colds. And if, as you told Taft, C.J., you are a ghost it is greatly
to be wished that you would persuade your brethren to follow
your example. I read yesterday a host of U.S. decisions of last
year, and I felt that you were a lonely figure on that Court especially in this that you were the only figure on it who consciously

---

[1] In his Introduction to *The Rational Basis of Legal Institutions* (1923)
Holmes had written as follows (p. xxxi): "The notion that we can secure an
economic paradise by changes in property alone seems to me twaddle. I can
understand better legislation that aims rather to improve the quality than to
increase the quantity of the population. I can understand saying, whatever the
cost, so far as may be, we will keep certain strains out of our blood. . . .
I can understand a man's saying in any case I want this or that and I am
willing to pay the price, if he realizes what the price is. What I most fear
is saying the same thing when those who say it do not know and have
made no serious effort to find out what it will cost, as I think we in this
country are rather inclined to do."

[1] *Supra,* p. 386.

took care to watch your own intellectual prepossessions. All of them, I thought, had a yardstick of good and bad by which they measured (especially in the minimum wage case)[2] the constitutionality of legislation; and none of them realised that his yardstick was merely the fruit of his very limited and special experience. Brandeis, I think, can transcend it; but even he is more the statesman than the judge. I hope this is not jaundiced heresy.

. . . I dined the other night with Arnold Bennett and he told me that a novel *Ulysses* by James Joyce was a most important portent in modern letters. Conscientious as I am, I got hold of a copy. I make only two remarks. First, that no two consecutive pages were ever intelligible to me, and, second, that I can only conceive it to have been written in a lavatory. I remarked this to one of the younger poets and he answered that it was the biggest thing in a generation. My head is, consequently, bloody, but I fear quite unbowed. I swear that I have intelligence enough to read a great novel and say—this has the divine spark in it; but if a novel leaves me as bewildered as a man would be who had tried to grasp the mathematical theory of relativity in a sewer I say there is something wrong with the novel. . . .

*Ever yours affectionately, H. J. L.*

*Washington, D.C., October 19, 1923*
*Dear Laski:* It is Friday, the last day of our sitting for three weeks. I have three opinions written that I think will go on Monday.[1] My work is more or less done up to this moment. My cold has ceased to bother me, and your letter of 6.X.23 has just come and has been read (sometimes with difficulty) the instant before I set pen to paper. My spirit is free and my head empty. I am tickled with your proposed Supreme Court—like Chicago we would make culture hum. But I want to say a deprecatory word as to some of your implications past and present. McReynolds has improved wonderfully and I think is a useful and quite suggestive man. He has some special knowledge and experience and his doubts and difficulties are always worth considering. He controls his impulses much more than at first and now that Clarke has gone, with whom he couldn't get along (queer, for they both are kindly men), and with the present C.J. things go as smoothly as possible. Butler has shown none of the difficult qualities that were attributed to him and Sanford is a very pleasant chap with valuable experiences

[2] *Adkins* v. *Children's Hospital, supra,* p. 353.
[1] On October 22, Holmes delivered the Court's opinions in *United States* v. *Walter*, 263 U.S. 15; *American Railway Express* v. *Levee, id.,* 19, and *Davis* v. *Wechsler, id.,* 22.

from the Circuit bench. All that you say makes me wish that I knew Sankey and hope that I shall see Bertrand Russell. You are right in calling Brandeis a great solace. We walked home the last part of the way last night after driving through the Smithsonian to the foot of Paul Jones's statue by the River, and he was wonderfully pleasant. As to your activities with your motor I revere but do not emulate. In these days I am taking in sail rather than letting more out. I like too the problems suggested by the difference between dictatorship *in vacuo* and in actual circumstances. If free from considerations of the *milieu,* and with a warranty that the policy inaugurated should continue say 1000 years, one might start a movement that would make many of the godly howl. I infer that you haven't seen Wigmore's book to which I wrote a short introduction (sent to you the other day), *Rational Basis of Legal Institutions.* Extracts showing the diverse opinions upon fundamentals. I thought the effort one of the most desirable that could be imagined—but I own that the galley proofs disappointed me sadly and I thought most of the talk pretty thin. However my condition when I read them and the haste and pressure may have made me unjust. My notions of Thiers are mainly derived from Sainte-Beuve last summer. S.B. also shows him great respect. I remember that when I read Napier's *Peninsular War* (during our Civil War) I got the idea that he had French inaccuracies which Napier went for—but that is sometime ago. I can't recite on the *Republic* though I read it a few summers back. You always feel in Plato's dialogues that you could have put a good deal more difficult questions than the simpler minded interlocutors. I once was up on his *Phaedo* but 'tis sixty years since. I used to delight in it. I am glad that you put John Palfrey on your list of judges. I long have wished to see him on the bench. His goods are not in his shop window but he is a thinking man. Also, as I may have told you, he is the most generous of friends. When I was in trouble last summer he took charge for my wife of all my accounts, checks &c. Kept everything in first rate order, turned up to her every two or three days, and was a main anchor. He specially excluded all thought of pay or present and all so quietly with such unobtrusive delicacy that if I hadn't loved him before I could not have helped it then.

How about adding Cardozo to your list? All that I have seen or heard of him leads me to think he is one of the elect. L. Hand of course I accept. It is time for me to start for court so I wind up rather suddenly—leaving the undone vast.

*Affectionately yours, O. W. Holmes*

*Washington, D.C., November 5, 1923*

*Dear Laski:* Alongside of your last letter a day or two ago[1] came a dear little note from your daughter—but as it held out that she was sending a photograph of you and Mrs. Laski and her I await the arrival of the portrait before answering her. Yours suggests a remark or two—apropos of Brandeis. I told him once that when he had strong economic convictions I thought that he sometimes became the advocate and ceased to be detached—but it isn't often. Then as to James Joyce I read his first book—I suppose—autobiographical of his own youth, and was struck by his use of dirty words as well as by his telling things that I hardly regarded as a gift to mankind, though I suppose he felt like Rousseau. I have seen that and *Ulysses* taken solemnly—but thus far have felt free to wait for *Ulysses*. On the other hand, having a fit of coughing one night and remembering what you said, I lit the light and took up Zimmern's *Greek Commonwealth*—with the result that I have reread it and again think it not only the best English book about Greece, as you say, but one of the best books I ever read. Only very lately could a work be produced that so expressed the resultant of real economic insight, geographic knowledge, familiarity with the Greek writers, intimacy with the land, aesthetic perception and a general world view at once penetrating and exquisite. He always is fine but I grieve with you that he should have turned to mere occasional writing. Zimmern done, this p.m. I took up the *Medea* of Euripides. Again I howl to you that the Loeb edition instead of a critical translation of the text should have allowed the worthy Arthur S. Way, whoever he may be, to give his notion of a poetical parallel, not so good as Gilbert Murray, and no closer to the plain actualities of the original. The outburst about women, 410-430, to which Zimmern calls attention, is striking, even though it has not Murray's 'hard, hating voices'—which gives you an extra but modern thrill. It takes a good deal of adjustment to read it with even a conjecture of the Greek feeling. In the evening I have listened to various things.

Sea stories by Bill Adams (I think the title is $\left\{\begin{array}{l}\text{Fenceless}\\\text{Unfenced}\end{array}\right\}$? Meadows)[2] that have the sea in them. Some parts of a Clarendon Press book of Contemporary Men—about people by John Aubrey—to which an article in the *New Republic* by one of the Stracheys, I forget which,[3] called our attention &c. &c. but I don't get much day time. There is always something to be done other than read-

---

[1] See, *supra*, p. 387.

[2] Bill Adams, *Fenceless Meadows* (1923).

[3] Lytton Strachey, in an essay, "John Aubrey," 36 *New Republic* 176 (Oct. 10, 1923), had commended Aubrey's *Brief Lives* (Clark ed., 2 vols., 1898).

ing. One morning a visit to the Zoo, and inspection of cats, monkeys, birds, deer and bears, followed by a sort of a ghost of a lark in lunching at Rauscher's—in memory of the days when such excursions ended with a dinner and a bottle of wine. I don't want to drink wine nowadays, but the feeling that I can't takes away one element of the picturesque. On Monday we shall be at it again—and this Friday, horrid thought, we have a Conference at 10 a.m. I shall prepare for it by fasting and prayer. I have written to Brandeis today that I don't intend to write a dissent to which he spurred me. And so I am free except as opinions come in. My little Chinese friend Mr. Wu, hitherto known by correspondence only, expects to turn up here about Christmas. He has a generous enthusiasm for me that makes me smile a little sadly—I tell him he will get over it when he is a little older—but it is generous while it lasts and is all right to a young man. Indeed he sometimes says things to which in my heart I agree, though I shouldn't dare admit it to anyone. It is as much as ever if we old ones are able to keep up our courage—but on the other hand we don't think it matters so much as we once did. You certainly have done much to keep me in heart.              *Affectionately yours, O. W. Holmes*

*Washington, D.C., November 10, 1923*
*Dear Laski:* Another ripper from you 30.X.23.[1] Would that I had matters of equal interest to tell. But I have only a few items. After all I succumbed and have written a short dissent in a case which still hangs fire.[2] I do not expect to convince anyone as it is rather a statement of my convictions than an argument, although it indicates my grounds. Brandeis is with me, but I had written a note to him saying that I did not intend to write when the opinion came and stirred my fighting blood. Not of course that I refer to that, which I think is the worst possible form—but I think it will be gathered that I don't agree with it. I dislike even the traditional 'Holmes *Dissenting*.' We are giving our views on a question of law, not fighting with another cock.

After finishing Zimmern's *Greek Commonwealth*, as to which I wrote to you, I read the *Medea* (Euripides) which I think I hadn't got to in my last. I am not sure. Did I speak of his state-

---

[1] Omitted from this edition.

[2] On November 19, Holmes, with Brandeis concurring, delivered a short dissenting opinion in *Craig* v. *Hecht*, 269 U.S. 255, 280. The majority of the Court held that an order of a District Judge committing the author of libelous criticisms of the Judge for contempt of court could not be reviewed in *habeas corpus* proceedings. Holmes and Brandeis believed that under a federal statute the District Judge had no power to punish the publisher by the process of contempt and that therefore *habeas corpus* was an appropriate remedy.

ment of women's wrongs, or of how G. Murray first gives it a modern intensification with his 'hard, hating voices.' I thought I noticed in E. a tendency at the end of a feeling or passionate outburst to sum up with a *quasi* axiomatic line that rather settles the coffee grounds with a dash of cold water—but on a hasty attempt to verify I find no more than these. Line 49—the nurse after saying that the boys approach 'all careless of their mother's wrongs' as the *bête noir* puts it[3]—adds νέα γὰρ φροντὶς οὐκ ἀλγεῖν φιλεῖ.[4] 810: Medea after telling how she is going to let hell loose, and that people may know that she is a bad man to her foes but kind to her friends winds up τῶν γὰρ τοιούτων εὐκλεέστατος βίος,[5] and 1080 also 'passion overmastereth sober thought': ὅσπερ μεγίστων αἴτιος κακῶν βροτοῖς.[6]

Perhaps none of these is convincing but I think probably there is something in it. Then the Greeks were nearer akin to rustic manners of the present day. There is no indirection in their speech —I don't know Euripides more than very slightly. I think I notice the recurrence of favorite collocations and rhythms, but don't challenge me—along with great magic power a suggestion of formula. All said there is a lot of tremendosity in it.

I think I haven't mentioned a second visit to Rice and the acquisition of yet another Nanteuil—three of the portraits by Rubens's scholars. 1 Vandyke—1 Pontius, 1 Vorsterman—and two more yankee etchings. With the prospect of a little A. Durer copperplate, Descent into Hell, that I rather admire—$15. Also I have sought a pleasant spot to be buried in—but that between ourselves. In short I have had a few hours that have felt like leisure. I looked into Macaulay's Notice of Barère's *Memoirs,* with amusement at the swashing way in which after assuming that he had taken up the book in a judicial spirit he proceeded to obliterate him with the blackness of ink.

Sunday a.m. 11th/ To return to Euripides a moment, have I not to the point of tediousness spoken of a parallel though superior tendency in the Bard? Shakespeare had such a sense of the mystery of life and the universe that everything pulls the trigger for a magnificent explosion. Whether it be Macbeth when told of his wife's death, or R. II when he realizes his downfall or Percy when run through. They say great things, but I hardly think that people in those situations would have said them. We forget what seems to me the dramatic incongruity in his splendor of the phrase. This morning I have another long letter from my little Chinese friend. He goes back to China next summer. I can't but wonder how he

---

[3] The translation is that of Arthur S. Way.
[4] "For the young heart loves not to brood in grief" (Way, tr.).
[5] "Most glorious is the life of such as I" (Way, tr.).
[6] "And this is cause of direst ills in men" (Way, tr.).

will find himself in that atmosphere, and remember that my first
Japanese student wrote that he didn't know whether to bless me or
curse me, and later went crazy and killed himself. However I
haven't shaped this one's course.

I have grown stouter during the vacation and the breeches that
I have donned for Sunday and the ensuing days are rather a
torture round the Equator, but I will smile and smile and be a
villain.                        *Affectionately yours, O. W. Holmes . . .*

*16 Warwick Gardens, 16.XI.23*
*My dear Justice:* My humble apologies for this interval of silence.
This sudden general election has multiplied my work heavily.[1]
First, speaking on behalf of party candidates such as Russell, H. G.
Wells *et al;* then the work of colleagues away fighting for their
seats; then some dutiful journalism for the party. I have hardly
known where to turn; but now, except for a few speeches this next
month, my duties are done, and I hope to get back to peace again.
. . . Then a most amusing (this strictly *entre nous*) lunch at
the Asquiths. They wanted me to organise an electoral arrangement between liberals and labour. I said keep out L-George and
Winston Churchill from your party; give us the capital levy and
the nationalisation of the mines together with compulsory education up to sixteen and there is a basis. But he wanted to go on
with his old program on the basis that we ultimately meant the
same thing. Her passion to be back in Downing Street is incredible.
You would have thought that the hope of the world lay in Asquith's return to power. She cursed all his enemies, laughed at the
trade unions, sneered at the Tories, and when I asked her what
she had to offer the working class she talked just like a *grande
dame* of the 18th century who has heard with amazement that
there is an *émeute* at the palace-gates. Another queer adventure
was a speech I had to make to the Pan-African Congress.[2] It was
a most queer feeling to address four hundred black people. Luckily I was talking about a purely technical subject, and except your
very able . . . Dubois, I don't think many understood me so I
was spared more than a formal discussion.

---

[1] On November 13, the Prime Minister, Stanley Baldwin, informed the
House of Commons that he had advised the King to dissolve Parliament on
Friday, November 16, in order that a general election might be held on
December 6. The central issue at stake in the election was the newly-
developed Unionist program of Protection in place of Free Trade. The Liberal
Party, led by Asquith and Lloyd George, and the Labour Party, under
Ramsay MacDonald, were agreed in opposing the Unionist plan of Protection.
[2] Laski had addressed the Pan-African Congress in London on November
8. W. E. Burghardt DuBois (1868-      ), author and editor, founder of
the Pan-African Congress, reported on the Congress in 37 *New Republic* 145
(Jan. 2, 1924).

. . . But really and truly exquisite—I know no other word—
is Goncourt's *La femme au XVIIIme siècle* which made me feel
that Talleyrand's 'he has not lived who did not live before '89'
was not entirely untrue. . . . For Morris Cohen's sake I bought
and read the essays of Charles Peirce, but I cannot say I was
greatly impressed. He had a gift for clarity of statement and, now
and again, for the telling phrase. But in general I thought them
at about the level of the article in a philosophic magazine and not
really meriting republication. . . .

I have bought some pretty things, too, which I wish much I
could show you. The correspondence of Frederic the Great in an
attractive 18th century edition—ten volumes for half-a-crown (so
have the mighty fallen). And you remember the Comte de Guibert
who was one of de Lespinasse's lovers, and wrote a now rare book
on military tactics with a preface to show that military reform in
France involved political reform—that, to my joy, I picked up
last week in Cambridge for five shillings in quite perfect condition.
Also more of Linguet's pamphlets including his *Théorie des lois
civiles* which is long but has repaid my excursions into since he
turns out to be another who anticipated Karl Marx and has down
the whole materialist interpretation of history. Also I picked up
(you would have shared my thrill) Hazlitt's copy of Burke's
*Reflections* with many pencil-scorings against passages he especially hated. Some of the exclamations are so emphatic that he has
gone right through the paper to the other side; I can imagine that
murkily passionate nature of Hazlitt's banging down his fist upon
some especially obnoxious phrase and against the passage which
deals with Marie Antoinette ("The age of chivalry . . .") he
writes "O sink of snobbery." I paid ten shillings for it, and thought
I had a very real bargain. . . .    *Ever affectionately yours, H. J. L.*

*Washington, D.C., November 29, 1923*
*My dear Laski:* A wonderful account of your activities up to
16.XI.23 came just at the right moment. Up to today, Thanks-
giving, I have been so busy that it would have been hard to
write but now we are adjourned till next Monday December 3.
I don't know whether I shall be allowed to fire off a case that interested me and in which I have a majority.[1] If I do I will send it
unless I forget, and I enclose herewith a case on which B. and I
dissented.[2] Why did my taking up Euripides intrigue you? I agree

---

[1] Perhaps *National Association of Window Glass Manufacturers* v. *United
States*, 263 U.S. 403 (Dec. 10, 1923), in which Holmes for a unanimous
court wrote the opinion holding that an agreement between manufacturers
and a union did not violate the Sherman Anti-Trust law.
[2] *Craig* v. *Hecht, supra*, p. 391.

with you that he is the most human of the three—but Aeschylus
in his *Prometheus* has always hit me where I lived since I was a
boy and could only read a translation. Perhaps you mean that you
didn't see anything in my criticism—I submitted it—but I adhere.
For pathos E. is the boy. Did I ever say that I think *Anthony and
Cleopatra* has perhaps more of that in simple human form than
anything of the bard's? "Unarm Eros: the long day's task is done,"
seems to me heart-breaking. I am rather relieved by what you
say about Charles Peirce. It seemed to me that he was rather overrated especially allowing for what he owed to Chauncey Wright[3]
—(I remember old James, the father,[4] who had the Irish impatience of logic, which William inherited, saying once: "There was
Chauncey Wright like a great brass pot listening to the sound of
his own emptiness.") Chauncey Wright taught me that you
couldn't affirm necessity of the Universe. I have read almost
nothing—a good article by M. Cohen on the logic of Fiction,[5]
which was read hurriedly seems to me to give new lights and to
show that $\sqrt{-1}$ has its place in the Universe, and some stories,
&c. listened to at solitaire. I don't greatly cater to the Goncourts,
but when I was young I thought I got a considerable something
from *Les maitresses de Louis Quinze*. Trollope also must wait for
better days, with me. L. Hand dined with us at the tavern last
Sunday night and we had much pleasant talk here afterwards.
The next night we had Lepaulle,[6] a young Frenchman whom you
may remember, lecturing now at Harvard and I believe Columbia,
interested in the philosophical side of law and a very good nar-
rator. *Inter alia* he told of a dinner at Paris where his friend simply
called up random numbers by telephone and invited them. One of
the guests, apprehensive of what it might be, brought a policeman
—all right, have him in—and there was a dame well dressed in a
fashion of 25 years before, who when asked where were you on
such a day last year, answered, On the back of a camel coming
from the —— mountains in the Sahara—and being cross-ques-
tioned by another who had been a soldier in those parts answered
with precision and turned out to be an authoritative writer on that
part of the world. They had a great success. I should think it took
Paris to do it. Otherwise I keep to my usual repose. On December

---

[3] Chauncey Wright (1830-1875), philosophical essayist and lecturer whose
association with William James, Holmes, and others in the so-called Metaphysical Club significantly affected the direction of their thought. See Wiener,
*Evolution and the Founders of Pragmatism* (1949).
[4] Henry James (1811-1882), speculative, if not philosophical father of
Henry and William James.
[5] Morris Cohen, "On the Logic of Fiction," 20 *Journal of Philosophy* 20;
reprinted as Chapter V, *A Preface to Logic* (1944).
[6] Pierre Lepaulle (see, *supra*, p. 306) was currently Lecturer on Comparative Law at the Harvard Law School.

20 I expect my young Chinaman and have arranged for him to go to the Cosmos Club. Lepaulle as well as Pound seems to have been struck by his intelligence. That's all, now.

*Aff'ly yours, O. W. Holmes*

*16 Warwick Gardens, December 1, 1923*
*My dear Justice:* A delightful letter from you comes as an oasis in the midst of this electoral turmoil. Night after night I tramp forth to tell the electors that in a choice between Adam Smith and F. E. Smith[1] I prefer the old Adam. One meeting I had for Bertrand Russell which was full of interest. Neither of us spoke about current politics at all, but of the kind of life erect-minded men would wish to lead, and for two hours two thousand men and women sat without stirring; it was a most moving sight. I had one great meeting with Bernard Shaw who made one of the cleverest and wittiest speeches I have ever heard; and a jolly meeting for young Oswald Mosley in which he and I competed in invective against his father-in-law Lord Curzon.[2] After that meeting we went on to supper to Curzon with whom I spent an hour. He is most amusing. He has real learning, real dignity of mind, and, most truly, the grand manner. But he has no consciousness that others exist, criticism seems to him an insult, and he limits the world that counts to a few families with whom he has been accustomed to mingle. He is very properly anti-French; and there is a very human contempt running through him for his colleagues. I should judge that he is capable of great sympathy for individuals, but that the spectacle *e.g.* of a Germany literally starving does not move him very profoundly. He said one thing that I thought true and just. "The Prime Minister protests that he is a simple man; no simple man ever became Prime Minister of England." I met there another whom you may have met in your English *wanderjahre*— Lord Long[3] who used to be Walter Long. He interested me profoundly. He is quite obviously a really stupid man. He emits opinions about which he becomes quite inarticulate as soon as you ask him to explain them. His favourite book is the Stud Book and he would rather die than read a labour newspaper yet there was a kind of *justesse* about his opinions (or prejudices) which was astonishing. He always wanted to do the right thing and always (equally) in the wrong way. It was an amusing supper which I left feeling that Burke was right when he said that aristocracy

---

[1] Lord Birkenhead.

[2] Lord Curzon was Foreign Minister in Baldwin's Cabinet.

[3] Walter Hume Long (1854-1924), Viscount Long, had been Secretary of State for the Colonies, 1916-1919, and first Lord of the Admiralty, 1919-1921.

needs to be protected against talent. One other dinner I must mention when I went with Frida to Arnold Bennett's to meet Thomas Hardy. He was a great man indeed, carved out of granite, with that calm stoicism of outlook which comes from the power to accept the most bitter blows without repining. He was, I thought, unduly pessimistic about the world. But you could not be in his presence an hour without the sense that you had seen as good a thing as is made. It was a striking contrast that between his calm quiet majesty of outlook, and H. G. Wells skipping eagerly and hurriedly from subject to subject, quickly angry and as quickly pleased, making opinions on the spur of the moment and contradicting himself in the next breath while Hardy was the agnostic on all things save where the reflection of years had given him the power to judge.

I have been reading chiefly about work and I therefore reserve your Euripidean points until the week after next and the end of term brings leisure. But I have re-read Maitland's *Domesday Book* with infinite joy as on the whole the most perfect economic-legal book in the language. Also those very clever *Lettres écrites de la montagne* of Rousseau in which there occurs the reference to Althusius which Gierke used as the proof that Rousseau had read and profited by Althusius.[4] But I note with amusement that the letter is based upon a chapter of Pufendorf in the Barbeyrac edition of which the same reference to Althusius occurs. Now no other leading 18th century writer refers to Althusius; I don't believe that Rousseau read the eight hundred folio pages of a forgotten if distinguished pedant; and I should like to bet my books that Rousseau deliberately faked the reference to produce a false impression of learning. . . . Lastly I read *Goethe* by Croce the Italian critic which I frankly thought (how angry it would make Roscoe Pound) piffle of the most third-rate kind. Nearly all that Goethe wrote has a specifically autobiographic context; all this Croce decides to ignore. He will build up a Goethe from the writings independent of fact. The result is nonsense; the Goethe who emerges is unrecognizable and could never have lived in the Romantic movement.

. . . I also bought a glorious Augustine *De Civitate Dei* (1505) —a miracle of printing for ten shillings. It lacked the back; and for ten shillings I have had a rough pigskin put on which makes it resemble an old monastic book. . . .

Our love and homage to you both. Take care and prosper.

*Ever affectionately yours, H. J. L.*

---

[4] Otto von Gierke, *Johannes Althusius* (2nd ed., 1913).

*Washington, D.C., December 15, 1923*

*Dear Laski:* This will come late to wish you a Merry Christmas
but I am wishing it. A bully long one from you December 1. You
speak of Curzon. I saw him once or twice with the Souls[1] when
they were in full blast. I mainly remember thinking that Little
Peddlington was everywhere, from the interest taken in some
verses of his in which he chaffed some of them—or somebodies'
else. His 'Simple Man' remark is A-1, if perhaps obvious. Hardy
is a deity whom I have not worshipped. I have not read his later
books, and the earlier ones read long, long ago with pleasure but
without so far as I remember adoration. Croce I think a pretty
big chap—at least I read his *Aesthetics* (tr. Ainslie) with that impression—before I knew you. I glanced at his *Goethe* in the Boston
Athenaeum with impressions similar to yours so far as they went.
I have just finished volume I of Ferrero, *Greatness etc. of Rome*
of which I think I spoke heretofore. I read (present tense) no
more of that—though it gave me some pleasure and suggestion.
Also *Ariel ou la vie de Shelley*—lightly touched—just—but giving
that impression of squalor in Shelley's points of contact with the
world that is disagreeable. I always have believed that he could
not have made his adorable excursions into the fourth dimension if
he hadn't been something of a damned fool. I am on the point of
having a little time for reading and wish you were here to give me
a tip—for I can't remember those that you have given me in the
past. I envy you your Augustine *De Civitate Dei*. W. Lippmann
dined here a couple of nights back—and was most agreeable. He
told me of a man speaking to another on the train—"Did I meet
you in Albany?" "No, I never was there"—"Neither was I—it
must have been two other men." My work is done—substantially.
My cases were disposed of on Monday[2]—I was given but one new
one which was written and has been approved by the brethren.[3]
The dentist and a morning of business are my only preoccupation
for the next two weeks, except my expected young Chinaman and
an afternoon to hear Mme. Duze [*sic*] in *Ghosts.*[4] But it is astonishing how many fool letters one has to answer and fool books to
acknowledge. Yesterday *inter alia* it was a young woman who
wanted to paint my portrait—later in the morning another who

[1] See, *supra*, p. 375; concerning Curzon's association with the Souls, and
his verses written for their informal gatherings, see 1 Ronaldshay, *Life of
Lord Curzon* (1928), 163 *et seq.*

[2] *Diaz* v. *Patterson*, 263 U.S. 399; *National Association of Window Glass
Manufacturers* v. *United States*, id. 403 (Dec. 10, 1923).

[3] On January 7, 1924, Holmes delivered the Court's opinion in two cases:
*Queen Insurance Co.* v. *Globe Insurance Co.*, 263 U.S. 487; *New York* v.
*Jersawit*, id. 493.

[4] Eleonora Duse was on her final American tour, which ended with her
death in Pittsburgh, in April 1924.

found me in the street said I had better wait till she could paint me, then at luncheon a chap, from whom I once bought an etching that I never have known what to do with, had me from the luncheon table to the telephone to know if he could do an etching of me—to which I, "No!" "Oh, but I want to do it for myself." (hum-hum) "I am afraid that I am too busy." As I write there comes a copy of my opinion on an alleged conspiracy, anti-trust, which I enclose.[5] Not that it is anything remarkable but the Solicitor-General (Beck) fulminated on the wickedness of the combination, misquoted Shakespeare, unless I greatly err, and I regretfully fear was disappointed.

I think I must have written since Learned Hand dined here— also very pleasant. Pursuant to my plan of not going out I stayed away from the reception at the White House, the other evening. I am in good shape except coughing especially at night—an ancient trouble—but which makes my eyelids now droop—so I will leave your most agreeable society for a half hour slumber. Homage to your missus.                           *Aff'ly yours, O. W. Holmes*

*16 Warwick Gardens, December 13, 1923*
*My dear Justice:* The electoral battle is over, and we have won an amazing victory.[1] Probably within six weeks a Labour ministry will be in power for the first time in English history; and though I do not think the situation will admit of great changes, it will be satisfactory because it will produce on the elector the atmosphere of labour as a government. I wish I could reproduce for you the excitement the new situation has created. The *rentier* is in despair; the trade-unionist holds his head a little higher; the clubs discuss the probable destination of offices with that air of secret knowledge which makes clubs intolerable to me. I spend hours each day with Ramsay MacDonald, Webb, and the rest trying to discover the outlines of a policy. It is all very thrilling; but I prefer the quietude of my books. *Very strictly entre nous* MacDonald offered me a cabinet post if I would fight an election; and I found myself —what a tribute to the attractiveness of learning—barely tempted. To be behind the fight as an observer without duties is, I think,

---

[5] *National Association of Window Glass Manufacturers* v. *United States,* 263 U.S. 403 (Dec. 10, 1923).

[1] In the general election the Conservatives lost 88 seats, Labour gained 47, and the Liberal party gained 41, resulting in total returns, respectively, of 258, 191, and 158. No party having a majority, but the Conservatives having a plurality of seats, Mr. Baldwin on December 11 had determined to retain office. On the 12th the Executive of the Labour Party turned down the possibility of Coalition and assumed the obligation, should the necessity arise, of forming a Labour government.

better for a disinterested judgment; and this period of confusion I can, I think, well afford to leave. I hope to heaven we shall go back to a two-party system, for at present the prospects are towards an indefinite series of general elections. The real triumph, I think, is for Sidney Webb who had worked and dreamed and hoped for this for over forty years—another proof, were one needed, of the power of the man of thought. I do wish Morley had lived a few months longer to see MacDonald Prime Minister. The old man had talked of it so eagerly and so often.

*Minora canamus.* I have just finished term and you can imagine that freedom from such trammels is a relief after these long weeks of energetic fighting. Now for a month at least I can go back to my book in peace. But the time since I wrote last has been lightened by two jolly dinners. One with Haldane to meet, *inter alia,* Barrie and Bernard Shaw. The contrast between them was startling—Shaw, dogmatic, impulsive, eloquent, full of the flashing phrase and the denial direct, Barrie, timid, gentle, sceptical, making himself felt by insinuation rather than statement. I found him very humanly attractive but, I think, devoid of intellectual power —a feminine mind full of intuitive subtlety but not capable of logical argument. Then a dinner at the Asquiths' where they discussed the election; she full of energy and vigour, finding consolation for the small numbers in the fact that they held the balance; guessing that the nation even yet must turn to him; contemptuous of all their opponents and prepared only to defend her suppliants. He, on the other hand, weary of politics, turning to me with eagerness to know why I preferred Catullus to Horace, insisting that (you would agree) the majesty of *Prometheus Vinctus* is unapproachable and urging, *me dissentiente,* that Lytton Strachey is the greatest thing since Sainte-Beuve. It was like stepping into an XVIIIth century salon before the Revolution. There was talk of power and a skilled observer could detect that the door without had meanwhile been slowly barred. She has no consciousness of the degree to which Asquith has lost his hold. Lloyd-George was there but plainly out of courtesy alone—he was distressed and subdued and ill at ease; contrary to his usual custom he did not seem to have the energy even to answer my genial jibes. He kept muttering about a new generation like an old man who cannot grasp new ways. . . . *Ever affectionately yours, Harold J. Laski*


*16 Warwick Gardens, 23.XII.23*
*My dear Justice:* Days, thank heaven, of peace! Reading and writing have passed the hours more pleasantly than I can say. A good dinner with the Webbs to talk out policy with Ramsay Mac-

Donald—the chief point of interest to you being that probably
Haldane will be asked to take the Foreign Office, the Admiralty,
or Education, and Sankey, J. to be Lord Chancellor.[1] That would
be a great appointment. It is very exhilarating to watch the process
of government from the inside, and especially to note its accidental character. I am struck, for instance, by the large degree to
which things depend on accident. I suggest a line of policy, Mac-
Donald, to whom that idea at the moment is strange, indicates
receptiveness, and in a trice the idea has legs and arms and moves
like a living thing on its way. I respect MacDonald more and
more. It is, after all, a great thing to be prospectively the first
labour Prime Minister in English history; but he takes it with
soberness and dignity and with a full sense of the arduous work
involved. And he has a reading mind—the ethos of life matters
much to him. He sees the significance of things like research and
enquiry, and he will use the non-political expert, I think, to a
greater degree than ever before. Webb in this atmosphere is at
his very best—a perfect mine of ideas and suggestions with an
insight into the manipulation of affairs that is astounding.

. . . Then *Candide* which I had not read for years. It really
is a delight. How anyone can compare *Rasselas* with it I can't
imagine, for its delicacy of touch and its sidewise satire are worlds
beyond the heavy bludgeon Johnson had to use. Then the *Dictionnaire philosophique* which is adorable. Pray look in it for the
word *Contradiction* as an instance of Voltaire at his very best. . . .
In a very different line I read the *Life of Charles Lamb* by E. V.
Lucas—quite undiluted delight. It's funny how you can have no
other attitude to Lamb except sheer affection. It doesn't seem
possible to write a bad book about him. His sheer loveableness
transcends the stupidity of all biographers; but Lucas, in a much
smaller way, has a kindred temperament, a love of little traits, a
winsomeness of character, that make him something near the ideal
biographer. Also I have had a great dose of Trollope—the Barset-
shire novels—for the God knows whath time and I find myself
loving him as I love only the divine Jane, Hardy and Balzac. On
Birrell's advice I had a shot at George Sand, but I cannot say I
was tempted—I tried *Consuelo*—to persevere. And, lastly, to criticise the new book Wallas is writing I went into some of the bye-
ways of Hobbes and fairly convinced myself that no philosopher
ever came near to having so good a style. That reminds me to ask
you if you have ever reflected why Descartes is the only French
philosopher of the first eminence. If you take the Renascence as

---

[1] Lord Haldane became Lord Chancellor in the first Labour ministry, in
January 1924. Mr. Justice Sankey continued as judge of the King's Bench
Division of the High Court.

the starting point him apart—you have to take as the great names
either Anglo-Saxons or Germans. . . .

*Ever affectionately yours, H. J. L.*


*16 Warwick Gardens, 28.XII.23*

*My dear Justice:* We go this evening to Antwerp, and I therefore
write now in case the pressure of guesthood makes letters difficult
abroad. . . . I do want badly to find the *Testament du Père
Meslier*. Did you ever read that—either in the Voltairean extracts
or in its complete form? A proud Catholic priest converted by the
experience of a rural parish to passionate anti-clericalism? It is a
thrilling record, and expresses much of my own dislike of religions
with fair accuracy. I spent the other night with G. P. Gooch the
historian—the most learned man in England today. He is an
orthodox Christian and I asked him how he reconciled that belief
with his sense of evidence. His answer, I think, will interest you.
First, it had never occurred to him to question it. Second, ever
since he had read William James's *Will to Believe* he had realised
that his faith stood on a pinnacle where logic was incapable of
touching it, and thirdly, that the universal desire of men for immortality convinced him there must be a God. I urged that (1)
was of course illegitimate; that (2) meant he had a private revelation inapplicable to any other person and (3) was to argue that
the world must be the centre of the universe because until Coper-
nicus everyone thought so. I was astonished at the distress it
caused him to learn that I was both agnostic and anti-clerical. He
really believed that Christianity, for instance, induced kindliness
in men. I asked if he meant in individuals *e.g.* Francis of Assisi
or on a balance of the world and he insisted on the latter; but he
refused my invitation to consider the history of Christian intolerance. It was great discussion, though I found it bewildering that a
man who could handle evidence so superbly as Gooch did not
think his canons applicable to his own beliefs. . . . Let me add
that Birrell was there and we walked home together. He amused
me much by his emphatic assertion that scholarship did not interest him at all. He wanted to be pleased, and he would give
Mommsen ten times over for two new essays by Hazlitt; but he
added that many years ago he was given Renan on M. Aurelius to
review and was so enthralled that he spent the guineas he got for
the review on buying Renan's complete works. We all, I may say,
agreed in condemning Carlyle, but agreed also that one wants
today a preacher with the same mind and fervour. Birrell told me
he knew Matt Arnold well in his last days and that beneath a
supercilious exterior he had one of the most sensitive natures
imaginable and that Matt in the street when approached by a

beggar would give him tuppence and rave rhetorically against the injustice of the social order. Birrell was very good on Ruskin. When he was young Ruskin was regarded as a great art critic and a bad economist; today he is a great economist and a bad art critic. There is, I think, a real truth in that, though it is stated *à la* Birrell. He regretted the absence of a great jurisprudence in England. I argued that you needed instruments like the Harvard Law School for that and that the Inns of Court could make the foundations tomorrow if they wished. "Ah!" said Birrell, "When I balance a law school against Grand Night at the Inner Temple, my stomach rebels against scholarship." A profound saying which explains better than most that solid port wine fed reality which men in the eighteenth century called Oxford. . . .

*Ever affectionately yours, H. J. L.*

# IV

## 1924

*Washington, D.C., January 7, 1924*
*Dear Laski:* Some days have gone by since I received your last delightful letter because I have been driven.[1] Yesterday, Sunday, I had a case that frightened me and that I loathed, but when it was tackled it turned out to be the usual old donkey in the lion's skin and it has gone to the printer. I am glad that you keep out of politics for the present. The *Vindiciae* has not come yet. I was disappointed in my hopes of reading while we were adjourned. I believe I have told you about that but I must recur to Aubrey's *Brief Lives*—2 volumes, Clarendon Press, as one of the most delightful of books for leisure moments. I must break off for Court where I have two little opinions to deliver.[2] 6 p.m.—I fired them off, but my throat is in such bad condition in these days that I hardly could articulate the last sentences. Nothing serious, only annoying, but as soon as I talk I cough. Our friend the Solicitor General (Beck) has just published a diary kept while he was in England at the time of the armistice.[3] His name is one that he will not willingly let die. If Brandeis is right in thinking him perfectly naif and ingenuous there are worse people in the world. I have heard reports of mutual comments upon conceit by him and Lord Birkenhead. Have you ever seen the latter? He used to help Leslie Scott, and when I last was staying with L.S. I saw him amusingly as I saw his subsequent Chancellorship amazedly. Isn't Asquith as old as I am or nearly so? Why should he not have lost his hold?

---

[1] *Supra,* p. 402.

[2] *Queen Insurance Co.* v. *Globe Insurance Co.,* 263 U.S. 487; *New York* v. *Jersawit, id.,* 493.

[3] James M. Beck, *A Diary of Armistice Days* (1923).

I should like to read Keynes if I get a chance. Fired by you I
did read Tocqueville's *Ancient Regime* with responsive emotions,
and when my friend Wu was here and I had talk with him I
begged him to read the book, in view of his return to China and
probable influence there. Anything that will discourage men from
believing general propositions I welcome only less than anything
that will encourage them to make them. I forget whether I told
you of Wu's coming down here. He more than satisfied my hopes
and seems as far as one can judge of a different race a very remarkable young man.

Frankfurter wrote some time ago naming a Secretary for next
year.[4] It seems odd when life is still vivid to feel bound to suggest that the lad takes a risk, but it came over me that he ought
to be cautioned. We are having a very fairly interesting run of
cases and the C.J. inclines more than Fuller or White to stop the
other side when the matter seems clear to all of us, which I think,
is a good thing. Fuller hated to change anything—even to adjourn
half an hour for luncheon instead of two JJ. leaving the bench at
a time and clashing their knives and forks behind his screen. White
favored that (just before my time) but was no less set in a lot
of hobbies that I didn't believe in—one being that in a *per curiam*,
you mustn't say anything, only cite some cases and say dismissed,
affirmed, or reversed. I wish I could write more at length but this
much suffices to carry you once more all good wishes for the year.
*Aff'ly yours, O. W. H.*

*Washington, D.C., January 11, 1924*
*Dear Laski:* Two letters from you came last night burgeoning with
points on which I should like to talk with you. *Imprimis*—Mac-
Donald—I had an impression that I had had a book by him in the
Home University Library[1] but a rapid glance does not show him
on the list and if I am wrong I have no impressions. I didn't think
much of the book I have in mind. An occasional correspondent of
mine expressed distrust, but the judgment comes from a different
party. 2. I turned at once to *Contradictions* and was as amused as
you predicted. I should advise one who wants to belittle Voltaire
to go on to *Coquilles*—I only glanced at it but got a notion of V's
confident way of talking about things he didn't know about. Comparing *Rasselas* with *Candide* strikes me as being the speech of a
true Briton. Lucas I have a friendly liking for (not that I know
him). I should not think *Consuelo* was the handle to take hold of
for G. Sand—I read a translation when I was a boy. But some of

---

[4] W. Barton Leach, later Story Professor of Law at the Harvard Law
School, was Holmes's secretary at the October 1924 term of Court.

[1] Probably *The Socialist Movement* (1911).

her shorter stories left a deep impression on me. As to the philosophers of different countries—I take very little stock in Bergson
—he seems to me to want to please the ladies. I remember that
Davidson[2] used to be enthusiastic about Rosmini on whom I can't
recite. As I said the other day I think Croce is a good deal of a
man *non obstant* his shortcomings. I am glad you have a foothold
in Japan and only hope that you won't lead them astray. I am
much interested in what you say of Gooch and Christianity. I can
but come back to my formula that property, friendship, and truth
have a common root in time. A man is shaped to beliefs long held
however uncritically—as the roots of a tree that has grown in the
crevices of a rock. If a man approached the preliminary historical
question with an unbiased mind (and even Newman agreed that
in that field reason was lawful) and professed to be satisfied, I
should simply regard him as wanting in intelligence. All I know of
the testament of the Père[3]—I forget his name—is what Voltaire
tells. I note what Birrell said of M. Arnold to his credit. I didn't
get behind a philistine dogmatism which I didn't care for. I told
you the other day of reading some Ruskin. I think the truth is that
he had insights both in art and even in economics—but I no more
should think him a great economist than I should think him the
voice of God in morals and art. I believe that concludes my recita-
tion. I have little variety to offer. I listen to arguments, note my
opinions and pass on to the next. But I have absolutely given up
the world. I didn't go to the judicial reception at the White House
last night to which I ought to go if to anything. I have a little
whiff of novelty when the *Print Collector's Quarterly* comes in
as it did this morning. And my wife reads stories and funny things.
A definition of jeopardy: the act of behaving like a jeopard—led
me to look at the derivation of the word as it suggests for English
equivalent *ibigod*—but it seems to be *jeu perdu* or *parti*—which
I didn't know before.

I have done my opinion for the week.[4] The case scared me but
came out easy and short and Brandeis who was the other way said
he'd agree if I'd cut off its tail. So it is shorter still. Among the
funny do you know Leacock? He makes me laugh. Not consumedly but pleasantly.                    *Aff'ly yours, O. W. Holmes*
How I envy your skip over to Antwerp. But I take short views
now. And you are still young. I am content. The struggle is pretty
well over.

---

[2] See, *supra,* p. 139.

[3] Père Meslier, *supra,* p. 402.

[4] Presumably *Wilson v. Illinois Southern Railway,* 263 U.S. 574 (Jan. 14,
1924).

*16 Warwick Gardens, 20.1.24*

*My dear Justice:* We got back on Monday last from an adorable holiday abroad.

. . . I see with great joy that J. W. Davis,[1] your late ambassador here, is a candidate for the Presidency. May I hope for his success? I always thought him one of the ablest people I saw in America. By the way, if your delightful-sounding Chinee is coming to England, please see that he visits me.

Our love to you both. Henceforward I threaten regular weekly budgets.                              *Ever yours affectionately, H. J. L.*
*Vindiciae* not yet out.


*Warwick Gardens, 27.1.24*

*My dear Justice:* . . . We have, as you will have seen, lived through exciting days since I wrote last week.[1] Last Monday, Frida and I dined with MacDonald at the House to see the last of the government. We heard a great speech from Asquith, a moderate but pleasing one from Baldwin, and one from MacDonald himself which I thought admirable in tone and temper. And the scene in the Lobby was indescribable—the labour people sober and stern, the Liberals bewildered, the Tories gloomy beyond words, save for Austen Chamberlain who looked very happy.[2] Then government-making began. Haldane is as I told you back as chancellor and most happy therein; and of the others I think you know Webb only. It has all been taken most calmly and with common luck ought to do some good. There will be no new era; but I seem to think that we can make people see that a new social order has arrived in power. I lunched with MacDonald on Thursday and found him in the proper mood; and the disappointment of those not elevated to office is, I think, a sign that our revolution does not need barricades for its accomplishment; chiefly, I add, because

---

[1] John W. Davis (1873-1955), who had been United States Ambassador in London from 1918 to 1921, secured the Democratic nomination to the Presidency in July 1924.

[1] On January 15, after the reading of the King's Speech to the new Parliament, MacDonald had indicated that his Party would move to amend the address by expressing a lack of confidence in the Conservative government. When the motion was made on the 17th, Asquith had indicated that he would support the motion and that his Party would become the ally of Labour and refuse partnership with the Unionists in a coalition government. The motion to amend was sustained on the 21st and on the 22nd Baldwin resigned, with MacDonald becoming Prime Minister and Minister of Foreign Affairs.

[2] Austen Chamberlain had been leader of the Conservative Party in the House of Commons from 1921 until the fall of 1922, when his view that coalition should be continued was overridden. He had not held office during the government of Bonar Law and Baldwin.

despite the outcries of the Tory dames it cannot make great changes. On Friday night at Cambridge I was switched to a very different atmosphere. I dined with Rutherford the physicist and heard from him something of what the new trend in physics means. I cannot say I grasped it all—but I did get the sense of a new world as arresting to those who grasp its essentials as the world of the Renaissance. In this catalogue of meals let me mention two more. A dinner last Wednesday for Walter Lippmann—Russell and Massingham. Walter, as always, grimly silent; Russell like nothing so much as a fighting cock except for ten wonderful minutes when he summarised for us his meeting with Lenin in 1920. And last night we dined with Lady Horner—the McKennas, Violet Asquith and Haldane the other guests. McKenna talked excellently on the financial outlook, Haldane and he had a fight I enjoyed on the proper relation between the civil service and the minister. I held the scales and voted against both. Another who has drifted this way is Garfield,[3] the President of Williams College. A very pleasant fellow I thought, not indecently oppressed by intelligence. . . .

Our love to you both. Russell will soon be bringing you my salute.                             *Ever yours affectionately, H. J. L.*

*Washington, D.C., February 1, 1924*
*Dear Laski:* Welcome back. Now my turn for leisure has come and this time I hope not illusory. We adjourned Monday for three weeks. All my opinions up to then were delivered—the one case given me to write is distributed and seems to be meeting approval, and all the *certioraris,* etc. examined. I began, yesterday, by reading *The Cid* and Racine's *Phèdre* to see if [I] could distinguish between smoked herring in a box. I saw the romantic of Corneille but still find it hard to come up to him or Racine. In that connection I read part of Strachey's *Landmarks of French Literature*—in the Home University Library. I think, by the by, that he undervalues Montaigne's philosophical significance. Not many men it seems to me have had so much insight but he didn't pose and make a row about it or look solemn. Not that pose and solemnity would humbug Strachey but I suspect that Montaigne's *sans gène* did make him think more lightly of the old man, especially as I see that he uses superlatives about Pascal—who I agree merited say one or two—but I humbly think while he knew one or two deep things didn't know as much about man or life or the rational use of thought as Montaigne. "If this be treason make the most of

---

[3] Harry A. Garfield (1863-1942); son of President James A. Garfield; President of Williams College, 1908-1934.

it." A few sublime passages make people forget the sophistical or
inadequate reasoning in a large part of the *Pensées*. I think that
I shall dabble in French a little longer, and then look around
among my books for a further descent from philosophy to literature. If you were here, you would tell me of something that was
necessary to my salvation but unless I wire "Cable me something
serious to read right off" I must shift for myself—and I dare say it
is just as well to take off the pressure and dawdle in amusement
for a couple of weeks. I told you that I followed your lead to
Tocqueville's *Ancient Regime* and of recommending it to my young
Chinaman. I repeat my recommendation of Aubrey's *Brief Lives*—
and I mention that Knopf sent me *The Old and The New Germany* which impressed and moved me—as an ignorant outsider
(by John P. Coar, once, it says, a member of the Massachusetts
bar, but I don't remember him). He, like you, seems to think that
we (the United States) ought to do something damned particular
and be quick about it—but I don't gather from a too rapid reading
exactly what. I am too old to be in the great stream, and try to
be serene. A Baltimore paper this morning illustrated what it
conceived as a parallel to your government, by La Follette-Mac-
Donald—and Justice Holmes-Haldane! But I think my writing has
kept up to the mark. Each of my last four cases has frightened me
when it was assigned—but they all have satisfied me more than I
expected. That often happens when a writer has just turned off
something—but I gather from the brethren that they are pleased.
I should have some hesitation about Davis—he makes beautiful
arguments—but I don't feel sure that I haven't had glimpses of a
weaker side. Nothing very tangible—some expressions in his face
—possibly an economic divagation—I know not—and may be
quite wrong—as all that I have seen I have liked very much. Your
letters always give me joy.                *Aff'ly yours, O. W. Holmes*

*16 Warwick Gardens, 4.II.24*

*My dear Justice:* A quiet but fruitful week! First I have written a
long pamphlet for the Fabian Society on the right to dissolve
Parliament.[1] As you can imagine, this is a hot subject with us just
now as an early defeat of the government is not unlikely. I found
it a fascinating job, especially in working out the impact of precedents on the present situation. I hope it will be out early next
month, and then I shall wait patiently for your remarks. For the
rest, no gaieties except a hard business talk with MacDonald on

[1] *The Position of Parties and the Right of Dissolution* (Fabian Tract, No.
210; 1924).

the American situation.[2] I told him that in my judgment American co-operation was in any case unlikely, and that this oil business had made it more so;[3] for no President faced with re-election under these difficult conditions would risk antagonising any further sections of public opinion. MacDonald, I thought, took it rather hard. Your blessed Europeanised Americans come over here and fill our statesmen up with the notion that you are dying with anxiety to intervene; and poor fellows like Robert Cecil, who saw only the pro-leaguers, of course come back with the notion that it is a holy cause to America as it is to themselves. It is so difficult to make them see that Kansas and Dakota are thinking about the price of crops and that most of them think of Europe as a place from which all honest, democratic people have moved away.

Poor Wilson! I was stirred by his death for it is a grim irony.[4] I saw him half-a-dozen times, never with liking, but two or three times with some real admiration; above all, he liked Felix which was a title to my regard. But he had the most unpliable mind I ever met, with a kind of intellectual hubris which I found very distasteful. I was surprised at the narrow range of knowledge upon which he made generalisations and his complete inability to judge men. But I think that in 1917-19 he better expressed the emotions of the common people than any other man, and, if rhetorically, in a way that stirred them to thought. The end was a great tragedy. . . .

I must add one or two minor delights. Our new secretary of war—a miner[5]—opened his first Army Council with the words, "Well, gents, I hope we shall all pull well together for our King and country, and the dear old flag." Another causes consternation because his wife sits all day in his room. The other day confidential papers had to be read and the secretary looked a little doubtfully at the lady. "Oh," said the new minister, "don't mind Mother; we always tell her everything." I add that the King—the King, mark you—has sent the Webbs three brace of pheasants; when the Fabian Society was founded forty years ago that was hardly

---

[2] The American drift towards isolation which had marked her foreign policy in 1923 had been somewhat retarded when Charles G. Dawes and Owen D. Young joined the Reparations Commission in Paris in January. The efforts which Lord Robert Cecil and Lloyd George had made in their American lectures in 1923 to persuade the United States to join the League of Nations had not, however, been notably successful.

[3] On January 24 the Senate Committee investigating transfers of oil lands had revealed the details of the scandalous transactions in which Harding's Secretary of the Interior, Albert B. Fall, had been involved.

[4] Woodrow Wilson had died on February 3.

[5] Stephen Walsh (1859-1929) had been a member of Parliament since 1906 and an important figure in the Miner's Federation for many years.

expected. I do wish I could tell you the amusing inside stories of all these changes. They have an epic quality.

Our love to you both.      *Ever affectionately yours, H. J. L.*

*Washington, D.C., February 13, 1924*

*Dear Laski:* Your letter (February 1?) gives me the usual pleasure. I meantime have not been as idle as I hoped to be. Last week I had some inward misery that the doctor attributed to my having walked two miles—one way up hill. It is disgusting but necessary to recognize old age. The result was that I couldn't go to Wilson's funeral—which the doctor if consulted would have forbidden anyhow. Then the C.J. asked me to write a case in which he decided that he ought not to sit[1] and I had a partial dissent from Brandeis to write.[2] These were distributed yesterday. Meantime my only reading has been Rousseau's *Confessions*. It is wonderful that a book written a hundred and fifty years ago can be so interesting. Of course I don't believe in the plots and spies that he saw everywhere, and I think he was *naif* enough not to realize that his writings threatened the thing that then was, too much for governments not to kick him out. I should call him one of the great martyrs to free speech, and honor him with the more joy that he seemed to take his literary fame so lightly, didn't get his hand into his waistcoat, and was so far from statuesque. I have turned now to *Faust*—which I read slowly even with Bayard Taylor's blunt edged translation along side. Some business affairs make momentary incursions including the income tax to be paid. But my secretary has to bother about that more than I. I ought to explain "the thing that then was." In some MS notes of trials—by Increase Sumner, a judge in Massachusetts just after the revolution—are indictments laying acts "against the peace of the thing that then was." I suppose this means of the King or the State or whatever then may have been the sovereign power—not a vituperative reminiscence. All goes well here—although when I get a pull down —all over now—I can't help wondering whether I am finished and ought to say so—but I can't see that my work has fallen off. I go forth with the secretary for a morning walk—to do some jobs and will post this.                *Aff'ly yours, O. W. Holmes*

*16 Warwick Gardens, 12.II.24*

*My dear Justice:* . . . Last night Frida and I went to dine with MacDonald. He made me feel what a tragedy politics really is. He

---

[1] *Edwards* v. *Slocum*, 264 U.S. 61 (Feb. 18, 1924).

[2] The case has not been identified. Apparently Holmes ultimately concurred in the Brandeis opinion in question; see, *infra*, p. 415.

had been in office a month and had obviously aged and wearied. He is at his desk at nine, and rarely in bed before midnight. And the day is a constant stream of visitors and reports, endless decisions on papers he has hardly had time to read, and cabinet troubles to harmonise. The way of the statesman is hard; and now that fighting has begun in the House there is added the complication of debate. The glory seems to me very meretricious. He asked me about one or two books that have just appeared and when I said what I thought of them he said sadly, "Ah, Laski, I shall have to wait until I am out of office before I can turn over the pages of a book again.". . .

I have read much too. . . . Item, *New Viewpoints* (detestable word!) *in American History* by A. M. Schlesinger. It isn't really first rate but I enjoyed it immensely. It takes all the salient features in American historiography in the last twenty years and explains how they have shifted the perspective of interpretation. Some of the chapters *e.g.* immigration and that on Charles Beard's work I found both sane and illuminating. . . .

Our love to you both. Keep clear of the oil companies.

*Ever affectionately yours, H. J. L.*


*Washington, D.C., February 17, 1924*
*Dear Laski:* Your letter of February 4 finds the adjournment at an end. We come in tomorrow. There will be considerable outpouring. What you say about Wilson interests me. I wish I could see a rational statement by someone who believes in him of his supposed intellectual or moral achievements. Of course, as I once said about Marshall, you can't really separate a man from the place he filled. His environment is part of him and Wilson was the nominal head of a great nation in a great war. But I never read anything of his that seemed to me anywhere near first rate—and I can't help surmising that his supposed idealism was No. 1. But I was prejudiced early by stories told me by White (C.J.) and I don't feel quite the confidence in them that I did at the time— also I have forgotten them. I should like to revise my opinion. I have been meaning to ask Brandeis to expound. In the way of reading, after Rousseau's *Confessions* the first part of *Faust* filled my time. Every line of Margaret seems to me the tenderest pathos, without a flaw, and of course, there are fine lines or passages elsewhere—but it seems to me in the rest rather a hocus pocus. I don't like Goethe, I am afraid, as well as the poor ragamuffin Rousseau. He poses as the universal wise man in statuesque attitude with a star on his breast. Perhaps at bottom it is that he is on the side of the poets and I prefer the philosophers. Goethe could not explain and so he said theory was gray.

Yesterday eve I looked into Shaftesbury's *Characteristics* and read the *Letter on Enthusiasm*. It is a b c to us, but still not to a large part of the world and wonderfully rational, serene, and well written. I suppose he had a good deal of influence at or a little before the time of Hume. But when a man disregards current conventions he must wait for the future. I notice that Allibone[1] evidently regards him as a noxious outsider—as late as 1858. Queer that Allibone and Lea[2] should have been providing works of such massive labor in their several corners in Philadelphia at about the same time. Philadelphia hardly seems the natural home of scholars—but they were world men. I wonder if they had any relations with each other. I think I have A. F.'s *Penguins* and will look for it in a moment. But books except reports will be shut for a month. I must tuck in some odd ends to be ready for tomorrow. So *adieu* for the moment.          *Affectionately yours, O. W. Holmes*
Frankfurter sent me a discourse of Santayana's on the Unknowable. It needs reading twice. In a general way his thinking more than that of other philosophers coincides with mine. But he has a patronizing tone—as of one who saw through himself but didn't expect others to.

*16 Warwick Gardens, 24.II.24*
*My dear Justice:* A delightful letter from you this morning[1] tells me that you are reading Goethe, stimulating Brandeis to dissent, and thinking of resignation. The last is definitely impossible. Everyone agrees that your judicial work is as good as ever—if it is not better than ever; and frankly I think it would be fatal to the cause of judicial scepticism if you went just now. You are laying the foundations of the next age in jurisprudence; and I frankly think that what you are doing is to deposit a liberal tradition the influence of which may well be the salvation of the United States in the next period. Don't desert your post until you have convinced yourself that it is essential. Every liberal mind in America would despair if you resigned. . . .

I have had a busy time since I wrote last. I agreed to work out the detailed case for the Dockers who have been on strike here.[2]

---

[1] Samuel Austin Allibone (1816-1889); author of *A Critical Dictionary of English Literature* (3 vols., 1858-71).

[2] Henry Charles Lea (1825-1909); author of *A History of the Inquisition of the Middle Ages* (3 vols., 1888).

[1] The letter of February 13, *supra*, p. 411.

[2] In early February the Transport and General Workers' Union, representing the dock laborers, gave notice that a strike would occur on February 16, its objective being a wage increase of two shillings a day and a guaranteed work week. When the strike occurred, the government appointed a Court of Inquiry, and on February 26 a settlement, satisfactory to the dockers, was reached.

414 )                                              ( 1924

I did that and though it took time and effort, the men to my great
joy have won the 2/-a day they asked for and a commission to
attempt decasualisation. The one sense I got was of distress at the
almost speechless gratitude they feel when a non-manual worker
treats them as human beings. Some of them were quite extraordinary, and their leader,[3] I think, would have made a very great
advocate at the bar. Otherwise I have been about but little—a
dinner with Haldane, a lunch with the Webbs, and the Pepys
dinner at Magdalene. The latter was decorated by the presence of
Gosse the critic who took an hour to say that Pepys was a great
civil servant who kept a diary for ten years some parts of which
were quite unprintable. I thought Gosse a poseur without feeling,
with mostly an appetite for small beer. We were talking of 17th
century drama and he told me he had a complete collection of
Etherege's plays. I asked him if E. was any good and he said
"none whatever." I did not push the point but we left each other
in no doubt of dissimilar tastes. . . .

Our love to you both.        *Ever affectionately yours, H. J. L.*


                                    *Washington, D.C., March 1, 1924*
*Dear Laski:* Another week has gone by and another letter from
you has come[1]—to my ever recurrent happiness. As I read one
line I said to myself, good Lord—Laski says *Viewpoint,* but the
next line brought peace. Also this p.m., after conference, brought
*Daedalus* and *Microcosmographia*[2]—I assume from you. I have
rushed through them—especially the former, with no little amusement and pleasure. Is Haldane a biologist—and any relation to
the Chancellor?[3] Also pricked by you I read *L'isle des penguins,*
which had lain by me too long—but I am not quite with you about
it. Irony is not a sufficient energizer for a volume—also I think
there is a swinish element—a sort of nastiness, in A. F. His sex
talk has none of the charm of really felt lubricity. Also many, as
I suppose, allusions miss fire with me because I don't understand
them. The passage p. 244 on the faculty of doubting is A-1, and
of course there are other good things. But I feel about this somewhat as I used to feel about his miracle stories. As to them I said
a man has no right to tell you a story with a sneer that says of

---

[3] Ernest Bevin ( 1881-1951 ).

[1] *Supra,* p. 411.

[2] *Microcosmographia Academica,* Francis MacDonald Cornford (2nd ed.,
1922).

[3] John Bendon Sanderson Haldane ( 1892-      ), author of *Daedalus,* in
1924 was Reader in Biochemistry at Cambridge. Later he became Weldon
Professor of Biometry at University College, London. His uncle was Lord
Haldane, and his father John Scott Haldane ( 1860-1936 ), physiologist and
philosopher.

course I am not such a damned fool as to believe this. When
Flaubert tells of a miracle he tells it as a monk would have told
it—and you believe and are interested. With A. F. I used to say,
damn his eyes, what right has he to take my time with his. Of
course this book is not parallel but I give my point of view. *Les
dieux ont soif* I thought a great story, the best picture yet of the
French Revolution. One of his later ones on the fall of an angel—
I forget the exact title—I thought swill. Your book has not come
yet.

Sunday 11:30. I have just finished breakfast—which means a
sleep from 1:15. I have a case to write in which Brandeis is the
other way[4]—and that of last week awaits the doubts of McKenna
to determine whether it shall be a dissent or the opinion of the
Court.[5] Brandeis and Van Devanter are with me and the C.J. not
strongly against. The only events out of the routine last week were
(1) attendance in the House at a joint session of House and
Senate to hear Hughes eulogize Harding. It was a difficult matter
and I thought he made it interesting and extricated himself with
taste and tact. (2) a call from Meiklejohn,[6] the deposed president
of Amherst, and Hamilton[7] his friend, an economist which I enjoyed but did too much of the talking, as they were both rather
inclined to silence. I was pleased when Hamilton in answer to my
suggestion that I took no stock in a socialism that did not begin
by taking life in hand, said that he agreed with me. How I
thank you for having directed me to the volume of Malthus in
the 17th Street Shop—although I never have read that edition.
Apropos of the French Revolution I always was pleased with the
tradition that man went on fishing in the Seine just as if there were
nothing doing. I have seen [the] incident or something like it used
in a play. Following the suggestion of the last word, like Mrs.
Nickelby, I was interested to hear of a radio play—which is made
up of the sounds in a mine where men have been buried. Hearers
are requested to turn out the lights in their room to heighten the
effect. It's a thrilling notion—you hear the pick pick of the reliev-
ing party working to dig them out &c.&c. F. is reading to me a
book by Beebe about a visit to the Gallapagos—science and

---

[4] Probably *The Chicago Junction Case,* 264 U.S. 258 (March 3, 1924),
in which Brandeis wrote the Court's opinion. See, *infra,* p. 416.

[5] Probably *Western Union* v. *Czizek,* 264 U.S. 281 (March 10, 1924), in
which McKenna, J., dissented without opinion.

[6] Alexander Meiklejohn (1872-    ) began his academic career in the
field of philosophy. He was President of Amherst College from 1912 to June
1923, when, after disagreements with the trustees of the college on questions
of policy, he resigned the Presidency.

[7] Walton Hale Hamilton (1881-1958) was Professor of Economics at Amherst from 1915 to 1923. Subsequently he became Professor of Law at Yale
and a member of the Georgia bar.

literary charm combined. And she has up her sleeve a life of Wilberforce with whom she seems charmed *non obstant* what I tell her of his obstinate resistance to any relief from the oppression practiced on working men. I hope you remember my objection to the book on the laborer of that time that you put me on to.[8] The whole innuendo is that the rich classes were keeping large funds from the laborers—which I see nothing to indicate—and ignoring except in a note to which no consequences were attached, the very rapid growth of the population, and the expense of the war with Napoleon. I must go to work—and try to armor my vessel against possible projectiles from Mr. B. He generally drives home with me and we have much pleasant talk.

*Affectionately yours, O. W. Holmes*

*Washington, D.C., March 9, 1924*

*Dear Laski:* It is too bad but this must be a mere memorandum and I hardly know which way to turn. Yesterday was my birthday, 83, and I received many letters and flowers—some charming and touching things. Your letter too came at the happy moment and was full of encouragement. I was not thinking *of* resigning—only *about* it—and anxiously wondering if I was right. At present things seem to be going well. I did not dissent from Brandeis in a case when I thought of it[1]—and he came in with me in one of mine when at first he was the other way. But in yet another when he, Vandevanter and Sanford came with me, McKenna had oscillated to the other side—so I shall be a dissentient in a case assigned to me.[2]

I received yesterday from Girard the latest edition of his *Manuel de droit Romain,* an admirable book, which pleased me. I was glad to know that he had survived the troubles of late years.

In one week now we adjourn and then I hope for some leisure. Meantime I thank you more than I have expressed for your letter.

*Affectionately yours, O. W. Holmes*

*16 Warwick Gardens, 4.III.24*

*My dear Justice:* First, our warmest greetings for your birthday. I hope it will bring you all that we who love you wish. I need not say how much I would give to be spending it with you. The

---

[8] Hammond, *The Skilled Labourer, supra,* p. 155.

[1] On March 3 Brandeis delivered the Court's opinion in *The Chicago Junction Case,* 264 U.S. 258. Mr. Justice Sutherland wrote a dissenting opinion in which McReynolds and Sanford, JJ., concurred.

[2] The case has not been identified.

publisher will be sending you my offering of the *Vindiciae*. Please accept it with my very warm affection.

But little news since I wrote last week. On Tuesday a jolly time at Downing Street. MacDonald took me all over the house; and that is certainly, with its engravings, the most admirable part of the office. But I was oppressed by the weight of responsibility it entails. He showed me the cabinet agenda for a meeting; it seemed appalling even to imagine that creative decisions were possible on the range of problems involved. He had read no book since coming into office. He had often been interrupted in the midst of a most important interview to go down into the House and make a speech in a debate most of which he had not heard. And he emphasised to me what a relief it was to see someone who could speak of other things than politics. I went into his room with admiration and I came out with pity. On Sunday we dined alone with Haldane and had a good long talk. He is very happy—full of projects, working endlessly, and with that zest for the moment which makes his temperament such an enviable one. He told me much of the technical way in which the government does its business which I found it useful to know. We spoke much of you and Brandeis and Taft. The latter he likes for his good nature, though (*entre nous*) he complained that there is no *fond* in Taft's mind. Yesterday I lunched with an old school fellow and had that queer sense one has in going into an old ruin you somehow feel you know. He spoke so much of men and events that have become wan ghosts to me. Things were to him living—religious dogma for instance—I had long ago buried without tears. He hated London because it disturbed the mind. He wanted a niche into which he could crawl and let the great world go by. He realised, he said, that one ought not to let one's mind rust, and so he had taken up conchology. If I would go down to Lichfield he would show me a great collection of fossil-shells, which, however, he took only from such strata; he was not interested in a period after neolithic. It was like playing a part in a dainty 18th century comedy in which when the play is over you dust the actors delicately and put them back in the box with tissue-paper. I found him adorable. He had published one paper—methods of fishing in Homeric times, and with his Greek verse class and his conchology he was deliriously happy. He envied only one person, and that was a mutual school-friend who had had the luck to be at the Bodleian and so specialise in Greek palaeography. He frankly thought my life horrible, though he liked my Baskerville *Virgil*. I was too remote for him from the things that endure, "building my life," he said, "on impermanences." Can't you imagine what a glorious afternoon I had by letting him just ramble on? I must not forget to add that he wore his grandfather's watch—a heavy gold hunter carefully kept in a washleather case, which struck in the night so that you could know the time without the pain of getting out of bed. He knew it was rather clumsy and old-fashioned, but he thought his grandfather would like to feel that it was being used. Altogether old lace and lavender! . . .

Our love to you both. *Ever affectionately yours, H. J. L.*

*Washington, D.C., March 16, 1924*

*Dear Laski:* A birthday letter from you for which affectionate thanks. The previous one came on my birthday and I wrote a short answer. I am delighted with your friend who would have no fossil shells after the neolithic period. I don't think Byron the person interests me greatly—and I think rather better of his poetry than you do though I feel the force of (I believe) Emerson's remark that some day we all should talk as well as B. wrote. He was A-1 in letter writing according to my rather ancient recollections. Things are going well with me. I have a decision tomorrow on the right claimed by the Trade Commission to go through all the books, correspondence, and papers of a corporation engaged in interstate commerce to see if they couldn't find out something to its disadvantage.[1] Also one to write[2]—and that is all in sight when we adjourn tomorrow for three weeks. There is an article in the *Harvard Law Review* by Hough, J.[3] which has some hits at me—and says I am *hors concours* in hurdling a difficulty and treats me as if I searched for epigrams. I think I see deeper than he does in the matter he refers to—a lien asserted on vessels sold by the U.S. for a collision while owned by the U.S.—and I swear I don't hunt for epigrams. Hough is somewhat in the same line —and I quoted him the other day that "algebraic formulae are not lightly to be attributed to legislators."[4] I seem to act as something of an irritant to his mind—though he said kind things. *Per contra* a telegram this morning, signed Hermann Hagedorn, Director, says that I have been awarded the gold medal of honor of the Roosevelt Memorial Association for distinguished service to the American people in the development of public law. I don't suppose it is a sell—but I have no idea beyond the telegram of its significance. I have read nothing—beyond dipping at odd moments into Hansi's *Colmar en France.* You know Hansi's de-

---

[1] *Federal Trade Commission* v. *American Tobacco Company,* 264 U.S. 298. The Court held that the Commission was not empowered to demand production of the papers.

[2] Probably *Prestonettes, Inc.* v. *Coty,* 264 U.S. 359 (April 7, 1924).

[3] In "Admiralty Jurisdiction—of Late Years," 37 *Harv. L. Rev.* 529 (March 1924), Judge Hough criticized Holmes's opinion in *The Western Maid,* 257 U.S. 419 (1922).

[4] Quoted by Holmes in *Edwards v. Slocum,* 264 U.S. 61, 63 (Feb. 18, 1924).

lightful little colored sketches in former days of Alsace. So anti-
German that it was said that there was a price upon him once.
This is just a pretty, charming book full of pictures, colored and
not, that makes one wish he could see the old place. By and by
I may improve my mind. Now it is more than time that I turned
to considering the declaration of Congress that the emergency
still continues in Washington that requires it to meddle with rents
&c. there.[5]                          *Affectionately yours, O. W. Holmes*
How would I like to have a day in Paris with you!

                                        *16 Warwick Gardens, 18.III.24*
*My dear Justice:* . . . Since I wrote last I have been very
busy. . . . Then, in the long catalogue of meals, a dinner with
young Mosley to meet Curzon. The latter was in a dignified mood
and we pricked him wickedly by criticisms of Oxford, Toryism,
the aristocracy, and he tried to maintain that the world was built
on manner which was unattainable in a democracy. He added
that taste was possible only in a leisured society and speculated
on what should be sacrificed to leave room for taste. But when
I discovered that he worshipped the art of Rossetti and Burne-
Jones and that he did not think Méryon knew how to etch I told
him that I preferred the chromolithographs of a Xmas number to
the best Rossetti ever painted. I wish you could have seen his
face. It was a kind of compromise between horror-struck surprise
and amused toleration of youthful audacity. And when we discussed Tolstoy's novels, and I praised *Anna Karenina* with some
excusable extravagance he looked just like a Marquis who has
learned the bad news that his heir *will* marry the daughter of a
newly-created earl. He is a delight if you have a good temper.
Not an atom of humour, dignity as carefully arranged as a papal
procession, and a mind as closed to novelty as that of an Inquisitor. But also a great stock of knowledge and very real practical
wisdom. He talked about India, I thought, with much insight
and a real power to arrange his ideas.
    . . . the Testament of the Abbé Meslier which I had only read
before in the truncated form in which Voltaire published it.
Really a most astounding performance. If an articulate priest
could feel this, the rage of the dumb peasant in the provinces
must have been beyond words and I only wonder that the revolution was not more bloody. Most of it, of course, is simply invective, but it is great invective; and the picture of the Church

---

⁵ In *Chastleton Corporation* v. *Sinclair*, 264 U.S. 543 (April 21, 1924),
Holmes wrote the Court's opinion holding that the judicial power could be
exercised to determine whether an emergency justifying rent controls still
continued.

as a conspiracy organised by the rich against the poor is etched in fire. The kind of document, I think, that is worth a hundred histories. . . .

Well—I go to Paris on Sunday and I shall hope to go on writing. Our love, warmly, to you both.

*Ever affectionately yours, H. J. L.*

*Washington, D.C., March 28, 1924*
*Dear Laski:* Before another letter comes from you let me emit a little steam. I have had a few days with not much to do and have turned with vacuous mind toward unknown regions in the classics. First, coming on a volume of Seneca that hitherto had escaped me among my books, I spent a very few hours in turning the pages. It seemed to me that a little went a good way, but I picked up an impression. When you see a Roman gentleman praising a younger man for letting his slaves eat with him and suggesting that he should look for the gentleman in them as they may see the slave in him and laying down the maxim, treat your inferiors as you would like your superiors to treat you, you begin to suspect that the lesson of cosmopolitan humanity came to the Christian churches from the Romans rather than to the Romans from the Christians. And when, just after, I read a little Plutarch the impression was confirmed, adding of course Greeks to Romans for the total thought. But I have begun with my exceptions before laying down my rule. The starting point is a blasphemy. The literature of the past is a bore. When it is not so, it is because it is an object of present reflection and scientific study and the interest is in your thought about it, not in it—or because it is presented with illusion as in Gilbert Murray's Euripides—where what pleases the ladies is what is not in Euripides—or because an occasional student has got himself into an artificial attitude by study and preparation. But you can get impressions that are worth while if you don't waste too much time on them. There are passages in Euripides that moved me when a school boy and move me still. The glance into Seneca paid, I then took a play of Plautus—having read that the *precieux* of the time of M. Aurelius affected his speech. The ease of the Latin and the rudimentariness of the emotion made it worth while. There is little to please the sophisticated intellect until modern times. So at least I said as I read Plautus but then never having read—(I blush to say) Tacitus I took up his history. I stand by my general proposition, but there is a cove who is alive today as ever. The intensity of his speech is enough—little though you care for Galba or Otho. He is an eternal lesson in writing. I don't spend a great deal of

time on him so I have read only one book—but it was worth the price of admission. Before I leave you for the day and drop the subject let me repeat if I have said it before that I think the biggest thing in antiquity is "Father forgive them—they know not what they do." There is the modern transcending of a moral judgment in the most dramatic of settings—and purporting to come from the mouth of one who has been supposed authority for the Athanasian Creed.

March 29. Your letter delightful as ever has come—only the immediate preoccupation of yesterday prevented my saying first that I had received the *Vindiciae* and read your introduction. I thought it admirable—but I still complain that you take for granted knowledge of things not generally known when a word of explanation would make it easier. You may reply, as I have to similar complaints, that you are writing for experts, but I think a little more consideration of the general reader would be an advantage. I let the *Vindiciae*—the *corpus*—wait for better days. I remember Lord Curzon in the days of the Souls[1]—but have not seen him since. Your judgment does not surprise me—although I remember some verses of his were thought humorous by the parties interested. They seemed to me average. Rossetti, still more Burne-Jones, always seemed to me to have something nasty in them—although that is not the popular view—perhaps the word is too strong. Carlyle, as I told you last summer, fell in my estimation when I reread the *French Revolution*. I sometimes think that his interest in truth was mainly aesthetic. He seems to me a poet not a thinker. I have listened to some levities—Wodehouse—*Leave it to Psmith* made me roar. Conrad's *Rover*—I think it is, not quite finished. Also I have read Sedgwick's *Life of Marcus Aurelius*—my reflections omitted—and reread G. Willis—*Philosophy of Speech*—to my limited judgment an original and stimulating book that I don't remember ever hearing mentioned. The time to go to a conference draws near—I unexpectedly expect my opinions to go through. I wish I could have a jaw with you.

*Affectionately yours, O. W. Holmes*

*16 Warwick Gardens, 6.IV.24*
*My dear Justice:* . . . I went for one afternoon to Anatole France. He was in great form and we had a tremendous fight over the virtues of seventeenth and eighteenth century literature in France. Like most of the mighty he sees endless beauty in Racine and Corneille; I told him, to his horror, that I would gladly give them both for another *Persian Letters* by Montesquieu. He was, I was

[1] See, *supra*, p. 398.

glad to find, hostile to Marcel Proust and warmly appreciative of
H. G. Wells. Hardy he did not seem to like; and I got the sense
from his talk that I always get on the continent that Hardy must
somehow miss universalism for the Europeans, perhaps because
the dialect does not penetrate through translation. Once again he
showed me his really glorious library, his Tanagra statues, and
his Méryon etchings. He is 85 last week, and as he said cheerfully more sceptical than ever. I put to him your point about his
description of miracles and he urged strongly that you were able
to say that in America where you did not feel the Roman Church
as the vastest of social forces, controlling the whole intellectual
life of the people. Only by ridicule could you make them aware
that legends were to be examined. . . .

My love warmly to you both.

*Ever affectionately yours, H. J. L.*

*Washington, D.C., April 18, 1924*
*Dear Laski:* This is Good Friday—do you know what that is? I
remember the times when I didn't. Your letter after Paris has
arrived and been read this moment and thanks to the breathing
space that this holy day has given me, I turn to you with a peaceful face. The first event to be told, the only, but a great one, is
that Bertrand Russell called the other afternoon. He had but one
day in Washington, arriving I think in the morning and leaving
for Cincinnati after a dinner and a lecture. So I hardly dared expect him—but we started in and had a jaw that delighted my
soul. I had just read Santayana's *Scepticism and Animal Faith.*
(By the way I think our starting point put in plain words would
be similar or the same, but there is such a mass of literary ara-
besques and variations that though the book may gain as literature,
I think it is diminished in philosophical significance.) I spoke of
the tone of patronising irony—and thought it an echo of Catholicism. He said: more of the Latin—Santayana thinks the English
good for football, but thinks that speculation should be left to
the Latin races. Whereas we agreed that most of the improvements since Descartes had come from England. Well I can't remember all that we talked of but he gave me unmixed joy. I felt
alive all over. I have two decisions written but whether I shall be
allowed to deliver either on Monday I don't yet know.[1] Sutherland may hold up one for a dissent but unless he makes converts
he will have only McReynolds with him. Yesterday morning my

---

[1] On April 21, Holmes delivered the Court's opinion in *Charleston Corporation* v. *Sinclair,* 264 U.S. 543. On April 28 he delivered the Court's
opinion in *Burns National Bank* v. *Duncan,* 265 U.S. 17; Sutherland and
McReynolds, JJ., dissented.

friend Rice of the Print Department came up with 3 Dürers.
Middling or less impressive and therefore cheap. "The Knight and
Death"—"Pirkheimer"—and "The Elector of Saxony." He said he
would rather have a reproduction of the best state than an original of a poorer one. Aesthetically he is right, but I like that actual
association with the past—and the look of the past that a reproduction can't have—and on the other hand I don't want at my
age and in my circumstances treasures that make me feel, as John
Murray[2] said, when he showed me his family things (Byron, Scott,
and all the rest) a trustee for the future. I like to have enough
to tickle and stimulate me without worrying. If all my things
burned it would be sad for me, and something of a loss to the
world but not irreparable. And my best Dürer wood-cuts I leave
at the library, to which I have given a number of things that I
thought better for them to have than for me. Rice carried off the
"Knight" and "Pirkheimer" to have some wrinkles smoothed out.
I have wanted them ever since I was a boy. I should like to add
the "Melancholia"—but I am not likely to, I fear. I once had
Goltzius's[3] reproduction—only distinguishable by the vulgar
through the absence of one word in one of the keys—and also
some sort (a copy I presume) of the "Knight and Death"—but
I must have given them away when I thought I was leaving prints
forever. Several of my early possessions have disappeared I suppose in that way. Most of Callot's "Miseries of War" and two
or three early mezzotints *inter alia.* I envy you your talk with A.
France. His appreciation of Racine and Corneille shows how vain
it is for most people to seek the inner delights of a foreign language. Jusserand, talking with my wife, didn't seem to see any
superiority in "Hark, Hark, The Lark at Heaven's Gate Sings"
over the translation. On the other hand the outsider can mark
limitations that the insider doesn't feel. So I think we are entitled
to our reserves about R. and C. as France is to his affirmations.
He ought to be ready to accept a sceptical view of absolute aesthetic judgments. He has professed it in former days. My wife is
reading to me a good story, *Justice of the Peace* by Nivens [*sic*]
(or some such name) revived after 10 years quiescence by Hugh
Walpole—C. Morley *et al.*[4] I dare say the feminists didn't like it,
but so far, I think it quite unusually good. I think I told you that
*Leave it to Psmith* made me roar—another liberating blasphemy
that brings peace of mind as to the literature of the past. I must
shut up and go downstairs to solitaire—Conference tomorrow—

[2] John Murray (1808-1892), British publisher and man of letters, and
successor to his father, the publisher of the same name.

[3] Hendrik Goltzius (1558-1617); painter and engraver, and masterful
copyist of Dürer, Albrecht, and Van Leyden.

[4] Frederick Niven, *Justice of the Peace,* with Introductions by Hugh Walpole and Christopher Morley (1923).

and I fear me some cases for me that I don't want—there were several this week of the kind I hate—rate cases and what not.

*Affectionately yours, O. W. Holmes*

Russell pleased me by saying that he didn't think you were running the machine too hard.

*16 Warwick Gardens, 19.IV.24*

*My dear Justice:* . . . Then a visit from the German jurist Kantorowicz, some of whose work (admirable work it is) you may have read. He is a brilliant fellow, who in manner and temperament reminded me all the time of Felix, and with Felix's omnivorous appetite for omniscience. I amused myself by putting to him all Pound's Gods, and getting his opinions. Gierke he thought learned but pointless; Stammler simply muddle-headed; Kohler ridiculous; his two admirations were Max Weber and Eugen Ehrlich, both of whom I am prepared to revere this side idolatry. He saw my Tourtolon [*sic*] (whom I like) and solemnly cursed him with bell, book, and candle. Then, yesterday, a good lunch with the Webbs and much political talk. I gather that a general election is probably impending. The liberals are restless, and MacDonald feels that he has exploited all the good there is in this minority situation. Really I think he has done very well; and it is very amusing to watch him being courted by people who, two years ago, would not have sat in the same room with him. You must not miss the great joke that Curzon's son-in-law, a clever and eloquent fellow,[1] has joined the Labour party; so does time bring its revenges. I should dearly like ten minutes of Curzon's undiluted views on that change. Churchill, whom I saw the other day, takes the simple and childlike view that any aristocrat who joins the Labour party is a traitor to his class; and then goes on to denounce the Labour party on the ground, God save the mark, that it is essentially a class-organisation. I wish it were anything so coherent as that would imply. Some people are in it because they really have a considered social philosophy; others because they have a vague pity for the working-class; others again on religious grounds. It is a queer mixture, and I have sat through many a meeting which made me feel with Halifax that "ignorance maketh a man enter into a party, and shame preventeth him from leaving it." But it's the best of the lot and liberalism today in England is so completely void of influence or meaning that to dwell even casually in its halls is like spending your time in the archaeological section of the British Museum. . . .

I must add that I had a delightful note from Brandeis who told

---

[1] Sir Oswald Mosley.

me that your companionship was the crown of his life. As you know, he does not waste words.

My love to you both. Tell Mrs. Holmes that last night I found Diana explaining who you were to Alexander, the philosopher, and adding, for your reputation's sake, that you never hang people.

*Ever yours affectionately, H. J. L.*


*16 Warwick Gardens, 3.V.24*

*My dear Justice:* . . . I have been overwhelmed since I wrote last. I was sucked into the vortex of jury-duty, just at the beginning of term. The case is, by good luck, an historic one—turning on libels in connection with the Punjab rebellion of 1919.[1] It is a magnificent spectacle; but I find five hours a day in Court very tiring, and the effort to explain to the rest of the jury what it is all about is not an easy one. I have been very impressed—this is all stale to you—by three things—1. the magnificent impartiality of the judge, McCardie, J. It is an object lesson in helpful discretion. 2. The queer strands of thought which pass through and influence a jury's mind. It is clearly impressed less by the weight of facts than by a kind of composite total impression gained from watching what I may call the flow of the drama. 3. The value, compared to America, of the rigorous control of counsel by the judge. Rhetoric, bullying, insinuation, are reduced to their minimum. Few questions of a recondite nature fail to evoke from the judge the remark, "You must tell the witness where you are trying to lead him." Traps are simply prohibited. I am enjoying the experience immensely. . . .     *Ever yours affectionately, H. J. L.*


*Washington, D.C., May 4, 1924*

*Dear Laski:* Your letter[1] has waited longer than they often do, but this last week I haven't known which way to turn, and I don't yet. It was the last week of regular sitting and there was a lot of work as well as two cases to write. One of them, that I care noth-

---

[1] Sir Michael O'Dwyer, Lieutenant Governor of the Punjab in 1919, had brought an action of libel against Sir Sankaran Nair for statements in his *Gandhi and Anarchy* (1922) concerning Sir Michael's part in events leading up to the Amritsar massacre—the shooting of Indian civilians by British troops under the command of General Dyer. The trial ended with eleven of the jury voting to award Sir Michael £500 in damages, plus costs, with Laski dissenting. Counsel ultimately agreed to accept the verdict of the majority. Criticism of McCardie, J., was principally addressed to his charge to the jury in which he stated that General Dyer, who had ordered the shooting of civilians had acted rightly—despite the fact that he had been found at fault in earlier proceedings by the Secretary of State for India. See 35 *Nation and Athenaeum* 342 (June 14, 1924); 23 *New Statesman* 273, 282 (June 14, 1924).

[1] *Supra,* p. 424.

ing about, I found that a majority could not stomach and I have
taken it back to see if I can't soften it so that it can be swallowed.[2] It really is a question of Alabama state law and therefore
only a bet as to which way the Supreme Court of that state will
decide when they come to this question—although these parties
will be finished even if we go wrong. I am interested at your
German's estimate of different jurists. Ehrlich I think he is all
right about though E's last book, *Die Juristische Logik* I cared
less for. He labored the obvious I thought. Max Weber I know
nothing about—(give information hereafter). I am tickled as to
Stammler (whom my Chinese lad studied with and adores) and
think as to Tourtoulon he is very wrong. He is d'd lucky if he is
half so clever—though Tourtoulon also abounds in directions when
brevity would have been wit and I believe talks drool about justice.

Have I told you that Bertrand Russell spent an hour of his day
in Washington up here with me? I think so. I took to him greatly
and we jawed steadily. I wonder if French is any better for analytic statement, as you say, than English? I will hear argument
but don't believe it at present. I think a good many Frenchmen
are better analysts of the moral or intellectual state of A or B
than most others—but as to the language, *quaere*. Wells, I agree
is stimulating but his thought doesn't generally strike me as important. But he is an artist and he can give you a moral atmosphere as well as any *mussoo* ever hatched.

Someone sent me *The Romance of the Last Crusade*—a striking account (I guess from a short peek) of the campaign with
Allenby. But it led me to the reflection (that didn't impress my
wife—as much as it does me, I fear) that ultimates—the biggest
things—are not romantic. That campaign offered sufficient danger
to prove their courage, and enough hardship to try their strength.
The place where you got killed was in the trenches in the main
battle. Romance is not the word for them. So in our war. The
staff and cavalry had romance. The infantry of the line stood the
great slaughter.

I scrabble off this line—better luck next time. We adjourn June
9 and I shall go to Beverly Farms very shortly thereafter.

*Aff'ly yours, O. W. Holmes*

B. Russell seems to hold sound opinions about you.

---

[2] *Opelika* v. *Opelika Sewer Co.*, 265 U.S. 215 (May 26, 1924). The
question in issue concerned the irrevocability under state law of a contract
between a sewer company and a municipality. The Court unanimously held
that state decisions indicating that the contract was irrevocable were binding
on it, though enforcement of the contract meant that rates charged by the
sewer company were no longer remunerative.

*16 Warwick Gardens, 11.V.24*
*My dear Justice:* I am, after a fortnight, still a juryman on the
same case; and at a guess I should hazard the opinion that the
case will last another ten days. It is, of course, very tiring; but
I believe it is the biggest thing of its kind since Warren Hastings,
and I am not sorry to devote time to it. Also I have learned much.
I am sure of the following things. (1) The average juryman is
quite incapable of appreciating the technique of evidence. (2)
He is moved by curiously irrelevant things—*e.g.* the appearance
of counsel, the remarks *obiter* of the judge, the length of the case,
etc. (3) He is hopelessly at sea immediately the locale of a case
involves imagination; India is to him as devoid of meaning as
Laputa. If a Viceroy appears in the box to say that the Lieutenant
Governor of the Punjab did his duty he thinks further discussion
useless. (4) He cannot even begin to grasp points of law. I have
spent hours in the box trying to explain to the others why hearsay
evidence is not admissible, but utterly in vain. On the other hand,
I think he is most eager to do the right thing. Unless special
prejudices are involved (like the colour difficulty in this case) his
general impression of the evidence is not broadly inaccurate. His
main defect is his intense servility. He literally cannot grasp the
fact that an official can lie. If evidence is brought to show that
men were tortured in the Punjab to make them enlist and the
British official said he never heard of it, my jury man promptly
insists that it didn't occur. I enjoy the whole experience immensely,
and there are some lively incidents each day which are worth
the price of admission. One I must not fail to record. McCardie,
J. is rather proud of his knowledge of political science. Counsel
mentioned James Mill and added "the father of Stuart Mill, my
Lord;" McCardie, J. testily: "You may take it, Mr. Charles, that
I have read all important political works," then, catching my eye,
"that a normal judge would have read." Then even he could not
maintain seriousness and we both roared with laughter. . . .
My love to you both—                          *Ever yours, H. J. L.*


*Washington, D.C., May 22, 1924*
*Dear Laski:* This will be a languid and seedy letter in reply to
11.V.24 and the last I believe was a hurried one. We have had
a great deal of rain to interfere with the beauties of May, our
best month—and I have been having a cough and a cold that
have taken the stuffing out of me. So I haven't been making the
most of my leisure. I loll and slumber more or less every day.
Always some opinions to read and letters to be written—the item
of thanks for books that I don't want and wish were at the devil

is an appreciable one. I won't include in that list Mrs. Gertrude
King's (Felix's friend) *Alliances for the Mind*. W. Lippmann's
introduction gives rather an impressive picture of her activities.
The essays are clever and have the feminine gift of words and
allusions that import familiarity with the arcana but *between ourselves* I didn't see that she had more than a sympathetic and intelligent welcome to ideas to contribute. It is not uncommon for
women to seem at home in structures that they did not help to
build and couldn't. How say you? My latest excursion was the
*Chanson de Roland*. I never had read it—and expected a chore
—but it was a short matter and impressed me much more than
I expected. I was particularly interested in recalling Homer. Two
books about fighting—rather savage persons talking tall in both—
but how different in manners. I thought of a Greek statue and
Michelangelo's "Captive." That reminds me—did we ever talk of
M. Arnold's illustrations of supreme poetry,

> ὣς φάτο τους δ ἤδη κατέχεν φυσίζοος αἶα
> ἐν Λακεδαίμονι αὖθι, φίλῃ εν πατρίδι γαίῃ[1]

I wonder whether he would have said what he did but for the
φίλῃ—the dear fatherland. Homer may have had that feeling—
but could one say of him that φίλος was more than a possessive
pronoun? A man is hit in his dear lives etc. I have wondered this
for years but don't remember that we ever talked on it. Have you
light? Cohen and his wife lunched here on Sunday—and his remarks led me to take down Santayana's *Life of Reason*, volume
IV, *Reason in Art* and I am rereading it and also (on the same
stimulus) *Huckleberry Finn*. There is such a dilution of literature
in Santayana—so much pork for a shilling when he philosophises,
that it makes me think by way of reaction how many mathematically compacted sentences would it take to give us all that is
important. Yet I believe that I am more in accord with the *motif*
of his arabesque than perhaps with any other philosopher—who
has expressed his system. The doctor came to see me this p.m.
and seemed to think that I had done pretty well not to die this
winter or last—but eased my conscience by telling me not to offer
to do extra work. I hope to feel all right in a day or two—but
just now I am not a centre of radiant energy.

*Aff'ly yours, O. W. H.*

---

[1] See "The Study of Poetry, in *Essays in Criticism, Second Series* (1903),
16. Arnold puts the following translation by Dr. Hawtrey in his footnote:

> "So said she; they long since in Earth's soft arms
>       were reposing,
> There, in their own dear land, their fatherland,
>       Lacedaemon."—*Iliad*, III, 243, 244.

*16 Warwick Gardens, 25.V.24*

*My dear Justice:* You must forgive my not writing last week. My duties as a juryman go on—tomorrow is the twentieth day—and with college work as well I have a load it is well nigh impossible to carry. But I don't grudge the time, for I have learned enormously from the experience. First, I know the depths of colour-prejudice, and I think a good deal of political science needs rewriting to meet it. Secondly, I can, I think, recite fairly fully on the habits of bureaucracy. The things which distinguish it are these: 1. Its members all say the same thing. 2. They cannot understand that their expert knowledge is open to independent enquiry. If I may so phrase [it] they do not see that the business of an expert is to be on tap and not on top. 3. They have complete contempt for all outside their charmed circle. I realise now the agony Kipling's Pagett, M.P., must have caused when he arrived in Calcutta. 4. They do not realise how many people there are who want a share, however small, in deciding their own destiny. They know that their rules are the result of experience; they cannot see why people should want to make their own rules. Hardly less interesting is the jury. I note some points. 1. They cannot grasp the significance of martial law. A dispute arose between counsel as to whether martial law dates from the Viceroy's proclamation or from the start of the condition which made it necessary. I was fascinated, but the result on my colleagues was a state of angry boredom. I tried to make them see that a century of English history was largely concerned with putting martial law in its proper place, but all in vain. 2. Reading is very difficult as a vehicle of evidence. We have now some witnesses on commission from India, and their testimony is read. But it doesn't convey a tithe of what was meant when a dull colonel struggled in the box to explain what he did. 3. They don't even bestir themselves to grasp legal points. They assume the ultimate direction of the judge on all these matters and simply leave them out as irrelevant. 4. When they are baffled by evidence they are much too terrified to ask what it means. Sooner than raise their voices in the open court they would prefer to remain completely in the dark. But with two exceptions, they are the most decent persons imaginable; and they accept what is, after all, a very trying ordeal for most of them with quite amazing good humour.

This job, and work, apart, I have not had the time to go about much. I had a jolly dinner with Massingham and the old *Nation* crowd when we stripped the universe to pieces, and Tomlinson (the critic)[1] and I maintained against all comers that Marcel

[1] H. M. Tomlinson (1873-1958) had been Literary Editor of *The Nation and Athenaeum* from 1917 to 1923.

Proust was a third-rate snob of no importance except as showing that third-rate snobs would in self-protection hail him as first rate. We also scrapped happily over Carlyle's judgment of Lamb; and that ended in my backing up Massingham in the insistence that Carlyle, with a million defects, purified and elevated his age and that the million defects were largely irrelevant. But I can't say there was enthusiasm for our view. And I was mentally attacked, especially by old Birrell, for insisting that the bicentenary of Kant was to the centenary of Byron as infinity to a third-rate negative quantity. That is exaggeration; but I swore and will swear that except as interesting evidence of *Weltschmerz* and a few dozen beautiful short poems Byron is quite negligible—as surely negligible as Keats and Shelley are first-rate. The man who thought Pope a great poet damns himself without any aid from me; but old Birrell charged me with blasphemy in his finest style. The path to reconciliation came over our joint maintenance that Hazlitt is the greatest of English essayists. But that, of course, is almost excessively easy.

I have read a good deal, for over-work has meant the need to be soothed a little. In sheer interest the thing I have liked best is Leslie Stephen's recollections[2]—a belated reprint of some old magazine articles. They are quite beautiful—and Leslie Stephen at its Leslieest. . . .

I send this on to Beverly Farms. Do have a happy and restful summer. If some unexpected increment arrives I shall suddenly turn up. But the hope, I fear, is faint.

Our love warmly to you both.                    *Ever yours, H. J. L.*

*Beverly Farms, June 15, 1924*

*Dear Laski:* Two delightful letters[1] welcomed me to this place yesterday afternoon. Of course I agree with you as to the relative importance of Kant and Byron—I am in suspense as to Proust, and I do not quite see the ground for your superlatives about Hazlitt. I have not read L. Stephen's *Recollections*. It would be immense if you should turn up here. So much for your letters. . . . For my part the end of the term, receipt of the Roosevelt medal, and moving have taken most of my time. I read the *Persae* (Aeschylus) and thought how it must have stirred the Greeks—but remained composed. Mrs. Grant La Farge sent me *Tertium Organum* by Ouspensky of which I have read a quarter with grow-

---

[2] *Some Early Impressions* (1924).

[1] The second has been omitted from this edition.

ing conviction that it will say damned little to me. Also I have
received from Cohen, Spengler, *Der Untergang des Abendlandes*
which I should think would prove stimulating—but being in German is a task. I think, however, that in these last years German
and Greek come a little easier to me than they did. If you have
ever looked at Ouspensky, which I don't believe, remind me to
tell you—No, I will tell you now. When the Grand Duke was in
Boston before you were born Count Schouvaloff and I had some
philosophic discourse and more wine.[2] He worked off several
things—which I do not now suppose to have been original. One
was the notion of a being knowing only the plane (Helmholz?).
Another that has often recurred to me was that the point multiplied by infinity gave a new form inconceivable to the point—
the line, and so the line x ∞ gave the surface and the surface the
solid—infinity marking always the transition to a new mode of
being inconceivable at the lower stage. Whether he got the 4th
dimension (wherein Ouspensky dwells—Cohen says ignorantly)
as the next step, I don't remember. I have increased in girth and
all my clothes are tight which makes a bother only partially cured
by letting everything out. It now is Monday and if the eternal
rain doesn't prevent I shall go to Beverly to try how it would do
to get shirts with an additional ¼ inch in the neck and drawers
that I can button comfortably. I have recurred to the unfinished
*Causeries* of Sainte-Beuve. I have still a volume and a half—and
though I don't like the man I must say that I got great pleasure
in reading about the Marechal de Villars[3] than which it would
be hard to find a subject to which I am more indifferent. Also I
slept like a pig for an hour or two of day time. You will gather
that I hardly have settled down to a regular pace. I suppose it is
well for an old fellow not to be too strenuous but I am avaricious
of time and uneasy if I don't invest it well. Talking of investments
I have sold a house belonging to a trust under my sister's will
and am now trying to talk with the Old Colony Trust Company
about investing the proceeds. So there is one fly in my ointment,
but I recur to the anticipation of Bergson, that no doubt I have
mentioned more than once, in *Rejected Addresses*—"Thinking is
but an idle waste of thought." The telephone has enabled me to
dispose of $2000 since the last word—so part of the trouble is
over. I will drool on no longer—I hope your jury experience came
out satisfactorily.          *Ever affectionately yours, O. W. Holmes*
Don't you think that these square pointed pens are stinking?

---

[2] Count Piotr Andreyevich Schouvaloff [Shuvalov] (1827-1899) accompa-
nied Grand Duke Alexis of Russia on his trip to America in 1871-1872.

[3] The Duc de Villars (1653-1734), Marshal of France, made his name as
one of the great generals of France in the War of the Spanish Succession.

*16 Warwick Gardens, 21.VI.24*

*My dear Justice:* . . . I cannot see any indicia of permanent greatness about Gladstone. Every social idea of importance in his age he misunderstood; every political idea he adopted he had to be driven into seeing; usually adopting it for party advantage. He was by nature a High Churchman whose other convictions were all the convictions of tactic except for a belief in nationalism most of which was misplaced sentimentalism. Doubtless a great orator and a great party leader—but how morally inferior to Bright and how intellectually inferior to Disraeli. . . . I add that Birrell came to see me and got off two perfect remarks. 1. The colonial Secretary, Thomas,[1] is a great snob and likes nothing so much as to be seen about with royalty. "He is becoming" said Birrell, "a younger brother of the Albert Memorial." 2. We discussed Newman and the Church of England. "The Church of England is wonderful. What more beautiful than a silent English village, the magic of her bells catching your ear as you walk on the green grass, in *the opposite direction from the Church.*" He was adorable beyond words. We talked much of L. Stephen. He had, said Birrell, a most honest mind. If he wrote that Shakespeare was a very great man, he took out the "very" lest people should say he was praising his friends. He told me that when the great Lord Acton died and Carnegie gave his library to Morley the latter told the new Lord Acton that he could keep any volumes he pleased: the new Lord kept a set of *Punch* and said he saw no others that he wanted.

. . . Finally, a novel by E. M. Forster, *A Passage to India,* which is the biggest novel this country has produced in fifteen years. Pray read it and tell me if the problem of racial contact has ever been more exquisitely observed than there. Not a word of comment, not a line to show bias, but the whole thing in perfect solution. A masterpiece indeed, with a style exactly to the purpose.

Well, I must stop. We begin dining out again tomorrow and I hope next week to have a more varied chronicle.

*Ever affectionately yours, H. J. L.*

*16 Warwick Gardens, 1.VII.24*

*My dear Justice:* . . . Then a dinner at Haldane's with Ramsay MacDonald—almost entirely political talk, but to me most inter-

---

[1] James Henry Thomas (1874-1949); Secretary of State for Colonies, 1924 and 1931; Secretary of State for the Dominions 1930-1935; author of *When Labour Rules* (1920), *My Story* (1937).

esting. MacDonald told me that the job takes, on an average
fifteen hours a day; that he has had to take decisions on seventeen
subjects totally unconnected with each other; that if he read all
the papers sent in to be read he would go through over a thousand
foolscap pages a day. Even Haldane, whose own job is no sine-
cure, was appalled at the sheer volume of work revealed. Mac-
Donald said that if you stopped to go much beyond the surface
of things, you got caught up in doubts that were like nightmares
and that the only thing to do was to plunge boldly in the knowledge that the next man would have to do the same. Both he and
Haldane were most interesting on the types of men you get in a
Cabinet. There are some who literally cannot do any business at
all and merely repeat the advice of their permanent officials.
There are some, again, who do their own work most competently
but refuse to budge an inch beyond purely departmental questions. There are others who carry their weight on all subjects.
There are others also who insist on butting in with the clearest
inability to understand. I gathered that in a cabinet of twenty
you can expect four or five who are really generally useful; that
ten will bear their own burdens so long as they are not expected
to go beyond their province; and the remainder are deadweights
who are there for political reasons not justified in the event. Mac-
Donald told me that the interesting things to him were first the
absolute loyalty of the Civil Service which had worked in amazing harmony under entirely novel circumstances, and secondly the
degree to which the Prime Minister is the general maid of all
work in the cabinet. In that respect we seem to come nearer to
presidential government than the strict classicists would like to
admit. One other interesting meal was a lunch with a most able
Indian judge. We talked for hours over the whole range of the
Indian question. He left me with three clear impressions. 1. We
have permanently lost our moral hold of India. 2. There is nothing near the necessary degree of moral unity in India to enable
us to withdraw. 3. The real reason of our failure is not so much
the growth of Indian nationalism—still a very tender and dubious
plant—but our own sheer lack of good manners. I add that I have
never seen in any human being a more perfect courtesy than this
old Brahman displayed. He had thought out each detail of the
lunch like a Lucullus. He was as gravely respectful to my blun-
dering generalisations about India as if I had been an expert
thereon of long standing. He criticised this country with a gentle
solicitude about my own feelings that was really as exquisite a
performance as I have seen. He told me stories of ill-behaviour
especially by the wives of the Anglo-Indians—an intolerable third
sex—without a trace of bitterness and with a real desire not to

attack but to explain. I would have given much for you to have been there.

. . . I read Rousseau's *Confessions* which I thought absolutely first-class—as honest a piece of egoism as there is in literature. And the style is sheer magic—a musical quality that I don't know elsewhere. . . . I have read—and you both must read—*Saint Joan* by Bernard Shaw. To say that it is a masterpiece literally isn't enough. The scene between Warwick and the Bishop, and the trial-scene are in the tradition of the great and permanent things of life. The preface I thought good; but I warmly dissent (and so wrote Shaw) from the doctrine that we are as credulous as the middle ages, having merely changed the objects of credulity. For, obviously, it is not credulity for me to accept J. J. Thomson's account of atomic structure when I know that I am in the realm of verifiable hypothesis. But it is credulity for me to accept the Angelic Doctor's computation of the number of angels capable of standing on the head of a pin. But these are trifles besides the *tout ensemble*. It is a terrific achievement and there is a nervous strength about the style which makes it a joy to read. Please order at once from Charles Lauriat and tell me your views.

At last I have found a complete Bentham—cheap, I think, as I only paid five pounds for it and Lowdermilk in Washington used to want $85. My copy is weak about the joints, but when I next get a cheque I shall have it rebound in pigskin. . . .

Our warm love to you both.

*Ever affectionately yours, H. J. L.*

*Beverly Farms, Monday, July 6, 1924*
*Dear Laski:* A good one from you telling of influenza after jury duty and your reading in bed. You don't tell whether the result of the jury trial was satisfactory.[1] I should think you were right about Gladstone. You hardly can remember when H. Spencer spoke of him as a man for a moment of transition and without philosophic significance and provoked Gladstone to a reply to show that he was philosophically important. I thought Spencer was O.K. I don't doubt either that you are right about Voltaire. But Sainte-Beuve makes me dislike him and other Frenchmen more than my wont. I think I have mentioned Spengler, *Der Untergang des Abendlandes*—on which I am slowly making my way with a dictionary. I wish he was dead and damned but he makes Sainte-Beuve seem pretty light—little as I am inclined to do more than get from him stimulus and hints. Space (of two dimensions) is the realm of death—Euclidean geometry—meas-

---

[1] See, *supra*, p. 425, note 1.

urement—concepts—cause and effect. Time and the sense of distance from us is life—destiny—transcending reason—only *to be*
lived and felt especially by the poet and *par excellence*—the
musician. The Greeks had no horizon—only definite things, and
distances and the naught: τὸ μὴ ὄν. The Northern race, imperious
and intolerant of limit had the sense of the infinite—hence Rembrandt, non-Euclidean geometry, the infinitesimal calculus—the
music of Parsifal which I infer, though I am only half through
the book, is the end. For each *kult* has its life. It is unintelligible
to any other. Excursions and alarums on Arabic art and thought
treated with great respect—Egyptian and Chinese—both I should
think preferred to the Greek as nearer to the Northern. It is silly,
perhaps, to try to give an impression of the book in a sentence,
when I am so generally ignorant of what he deals with and bothered by the language into the boot. I don't have much time for
reading and just now is a moment of paying bills and accounts—
so that I have less than ever. I am not growing haggard with
intellectual effort—unless it be the attempt to make a sum come
out right. I shall try to get *A Passage to India*. Fred Pollock mentioned it also, the other day. Obedient to your suggestion also I
laid open on my table Carlyle, *Chartism*, "Impossible," distracted
as I did so by adjoining passages, "Sinking of the Vengeur" etc.
He is fly paper—if you get foot or hand upon his pages you stick
—even when you damn him. Must go downstairs for a caller. My
love to you.                                          *Aff'ly, O. W. H.*

*Beverly Farms, July 10, 1924*
*Dear Laski:* Your letter—July 1—incredible—is so good that I sit
down at once to answer it—stopping only to tell the *New Republic*, of which it reminded me, to come here instead of Washington. I also stop now to order *Saint Joan*—and resume. My
work is done, but my task, that damned German book, with the
dictionary, is not—although the end draws nearer. One doesn't
often meet a book so abounding in suggestion, very generally not
believed but none the less stimulating. But even while summing
up every truth as simply the way a given crowd thought and felt
and saw, he has the German dogmatism and patronizes the Greeks
as if he were in the Kathedra—at least *quoad* them. "A most good
play—would 'twere done"—
Your impressions of Rousseau (*Confessions*) are similar to those
I felt when I read him some months back. My Bentham I think
cost $30 so we're not far apart. I especially note your reflection
on good manners. I long have said that half the labor trouble is
due to bad manners—and used to say in Boston that the way
some of the ladies in Beacon Street treated their servants and

employees was enough to start a socialist revolt. I am far from
surprised at the reflection applying to India. I shall have no novelties until I am through with the Spengler. The accursed beast
makes Sainte-Beuve seem pretty thin when I take him up. You
mention Brandeis who gives me as much pleasure as it is possible
that I should give to him. From time to time I hear talk of a third
party—La Follette and Brandeis. Do you suppose it possible that
he has political *velléités* underneath? I shouldn't be surprised if
judging didn't satisfy him—taking all the conditions. This is but
a bulletin.                    *Affectionately yours, O. W. Holmes*

*Beverly Farms, July 23, 1924*
*Dear Laski:* Your letter of the 15th[1] delightful, as usual, has come
and as usual provokes a remark or two. 1. I am glad that you
stick to your path and don't try for the House of Commons at
present. 2. I should think that Webb, with all his knowledge and
great achievements, was but moderately interesting (rather an
impertinent comment perhaps, but I should not take him to be a
great thinker). 3. I am surprised at the word accountancy, but
am inclined to agree with you on the subject, although I haven't
felt prepared to criticize Harvard College for adding a business
college with special endowments. Some people have. 4. I have
made similar remarks to myself about the great French nobles
with all their charm to those whom they were interested to charm.
5. I never read *Daniel Deronda* or have forgotten it pretty thoroughly—probably the latter. 6. *The Pluralistic Universe* is not
fresh in my mind—my general remark would be the same that I
should make about Cause and Effect—or necessity. I don't know
that causes produce equivalent effects—or whether the cosmos is
merely having a transitory whim of orderly sequence, but discoveries are made on the assumptions of continuity &c. and therefore those assumptions seem best for practical purposes. Chauncy
Wright long ago pointed out to me the impossibility of assuming
necessity as an ultimate cosmic fact. I don't know anything about
ultimate or absolute truth and all the rest follows. 7. At your
imaginary dinner who is Br. or Dr. Thorne? I blush not to know.
8. After reading *Der Untergang des Abendlandes,* any comparison
of Greek with modern plays from a literary point of view seems
impossible. I found the book very suggestive on that as on many
other matters, though it seemed to me extreme and dogmatic.
The author, Oswald Spengler, reinforced my belief of the difficulties if not as he says the impossibilities of our getting inside
their ways of feeling and thinking. I was pleased to see their

[1] Omitted from this edition.

absence of horizon dwelt upon. I often have illustrated it from Symonds, *Greek Poets*: "Fair the tranquil reaches of the sea"; he translates Greek that literally is "the quiet flood of the sea"—*i.e.*, he takes in the horizon.

I have little to tell on my own account. I get up latish and when the morning business is attended to (there generally is something) we go out for a motor drive from 11 to 1, then luncheon, then a little reading interrupted by a nap, a walk, quite short now, a little more reading or writing of letters, and supper at seven. I don't worry at not doing much but I wish I could idle with gusto. I can't feel quite right if I haven't added something in the course of the day. Perhaps the enchanting drives ought to be enough, but they hardly are. The other day I received a letter signed "Member of the Bar" saying that dispassionate people all believed that La Follette would be the next President; that he hates the Supreme Court, and that I could ensure the execration if I gave him a chance to appoint a new judge. In my innocence I didn't see the point until my wife said that it was an oblique recommendation to resign. My wife has been much interested in reading about MacDonald and his wife. If there is in the shop windows a cheap little photograph of Mrs. MacDonald and also of her monument[2] I should like to get them—only cheap ones and if you get them *a bill strictly to be sent for the amount.* I have read *Saint Joan* that you praised latterly. I think the story is admirably brought out and the conception of Joan what I should think any sensible man would have found were I not warned by the book of that animal Andrew Lang[3] what fool things could be thought. The usual criticism that he draws no characters but makes everyone talk Shaw seems to me correct—and I have a less opinion of his general wisdom than perhaps you have. He seems to me to dogmatize in an illbred way on his personal likes and dislikes. Of course I delight in his wit. Spengler seemed to think *Man and Superman* one of the expiring flashes of the old culture that he thinks is dead before the civilization of great cities with their rootless populations. Spengler tickles me by his magnificent waving aside of all the later 'isms as all expressions of the end of a *kult*. It wouldn't cost you the trouble it did me to read him, *i.e.*, volume 1. If you do, tell me what you think. He bullies the world from the standpoint of the higher mathematics. I wish that I might believe that he knows little about them. I should doubt if he knew much about the physical sciences, but he seems all

[2] Mrs. MacDonald (Margaret Gladstone) was the great-niece of Lord Kelvin, with whom Holmes was acquainted. It is not impossible that Holmes had known her before her marriage to MacDonald in 1896. She had died in 1911.

[3] *The Maid of France* (1908).

there on sculpture, architecture, painting and music. He thinks the end was in the music of *Parsifal*.

*Affectionately yours, O. W. Holmes*

*16 Warwick Gardens, 22.VII.24*
*My dear Justice:* A delightful note from you tells me of your struggles with Spengler. I deeply sympathise, adding that I doubt he is worth the labour. I dislike his dogmatism and his air of confident self-assertion about things that are really dubious. I agree that he is suggestive, but I should incline to the view that an expert would say that he has driven an hypothesis through the material without much regard to what the material is. . . .

*Ever affectionately yours, H. J. L.*

*16 Warwick Gardens, 29.VII.24.*
*My dear Justice:* . . . at Haldane's on Sunday his sister[1] said that she remembered you most perfectly in the 'nineties as the most perfect flirt in London. It was all, she said, in a way you had of cocking your eye that they found quite ravishing. She remembered writing to Margot Asquith to say she couldn't go into the country as she was meeting you at dinner and she would not miss the thrill. I do not draw conclusions from the fact of Miss Haldane's spinsterhood—I leave the fact there in its naked coldness. . . .

My love to you both.            *Ever affectionately yours, H. J. L.*

*Beverly Farms, July 31, 1924*
*Dear Laski:* What you say about Spengler in your letter (22d) just received is quite in accord with my conclusions except that he seems to have been rather more a stimulus to me than you found him. And what do you think I am up to now? The last of my Day of Judgment books: Thucydides. In the last edition with a translation alongside to save trouble and give you the hint. I don't find the Greek difficult and am interested to discover how few words I need to look out. I either know them or divine by the root. A good many axioms or sentences that might be modern texts, and in short a more modern tone than I expected. I have just time for Book 1. I don't think the arrangement very good and don't admire the style, but I go on with interest. The last two days when I was below par and kept the house gave me more time for him than usual. This morning I shall go out for a drive

---
[1] Elizabeth S. Haldane (1862-1937); author of *Descartes* (1905); *George Eliot and Her Times* (1927); *From One Century to Another* (1937).

but I have come to the conclusion that two hours rather rapid driving is too much for me. It is a lesson when one feels much as one always has felt to be pulled up on a very slight excess. One feels as if one could do all that one ever did, and walk ten miles without too much trouble. But a mile and a quarter would be apt to seek revenge—and so I keep to about half a mile, and I fear must cut my drives down to an hour. Luckily the desk does not have the same limits. Poor Cabot Lodge is in the hospital as no doubt you have seen. I imagine with the same trouble that I had. I have the friendship of lifelong association with him. I got a pleasant (dictated) letter from him this morning in answer to a line from me. If I am right he has not come to the trial, the second and principal operation. They made me wait three weeks while they poured water into me. I suppose to wash me out. Can you tell me where a Greek line that has been running in my head comes from. I risk the chance of some errors that your eye will detect: τις δ'οἶδεν ἐι το ζῆν μεν κατθανεῖν το κατθανεῖν δε ζῆν —.[1] I am glad to hear about the progress of your book and am wondering whether you will give me new light on the state and law. I am much interested. My days go so quietly and swiftly that I have nothing to tell.                    *Aff'ly yours, O. W. H.*

I forgot to mention that Beveridge called the day before yesterday and explained my not seeing him before by his having been hard at work. He will send me his first Chapter (*Life of Lincoln*). As to Pope Joan the talk of Cauchon and Warwick is of course very clever, and dramatically effective, but I take less pleasure in 20th century interpretations put into 18th century mouths than in some other things. No—the play brings tears and ever present amusement at Shaw's cunning wit, but I never read anything of his yet that seemed to me to have great thought or great anything else above wit in it. And there y'are, as Mr. Dooley says. I am afraid we are not at one on that theme.

*Beverly Farms, August 8, 1924*

Dear Laski: A letter from you[1] takes my breath away with its many reflections and its account of things seen and heard and reading done. I think you hardly give Story credit enough. Grant, if you like, that he was rather a *vulgarisateur,* he was one on a

---

[1] The full quotation, which is from Fragment 639 of Euripides (Nauck, ed.), is as follows:

τίς δ'οἶδεν εἰ τὸ ζῆν μέν ἐστι κατθανεῖν
τὸ κατθανεῖν δὲ ζῆν κ.'τω νομίσεται

("Who knoweth if to live be but to die
While death be held as life in the world below.")

[1] Most of Laski's letter of July 29, 1924, to which this is a reply has been omitted from this edition.

great scale—did much to make the law accessible and intelligible
and in short was voluminous. Volume is usually in inverse ratio to
intensity, but is itself a gift like the others. I think Pound is somewhat of the same class. He impresses me more by the mass of his
writing and the army of knowledge that he commands than by
the poignancy of any particular insight. But I am not surprised
that he struck you more than the others. I delight in Bernouilli's
*Ex ungue leonem* apropos of Newton's solution—the more that in
those volumes of 17th century lives by I forget whom, there was
a chap who intimated that Newton got much from him and gave
no credit. Montaigne seems to me much more than companionable.
I think he had profound philosophic insights and covers much
more ground than Pascal who often is exalted to a far higher place
in the history of thought. Macaulay does not hit me hard and an
essay or two of his that I read within a year or two disgusted me,
but still he was a pretty big man. When you consider in addition
to his work in parliament, his history and essays, that he made an
early and illuminating application of Bentham in the penal code
for India, (I speak from a memory of 50 years ago) and wrote
some good poems in spite of M. Arnold (the verses about the old
Jacobite buried abroad and the battle of (Naseby?) I think it
hard to deny. I have been taken up with Thucydides. I don't quite
share your enthusiasms. He was the first. I don't forget it. But
considered apart from that I find it a moderate pleasure, hardly
that, for just as I hate to read about our civil war I don't like to
read of the blunders and misfortunes of those one loves of 2000
years ago. Then the great part of it is tupenny skirmishes, and I
reflect with satisfaction that while that was going on Socrates was
firing away and that the political fall of Athens was the beginning
of her leadership in philosophy. I read Books 1 & 2 and 7 in the
Greek, the rest, not quite finished in the translation with only an
occasional eye to the original. I have about a day more to read,
the time for reading is not long, and then I mean to drop improvement and the Day of Judgment.

I want to post this this morning and in a moment I am off to
Ipswich to show my cousin the tablet for Ann Bradstreet (our
10th muse in the 1600's) an ancestor of ours. I uncovered the
tablet and made a speech (in my book of speeches) that I thought
not bad.[1] The machine is here. My love to you both.

*Aff'ly yours, O. W. H.*

*Beverly Farms, August 16, 1924*
*Dear Laski:* Your letter[1] excites my envy by its accounts of your

[1] *Speeches*, 92.
[1] Omitted from this edition.

surroundings—because you have the old all about you—the occasional hints of a reasonably remote past that one finds scattered
here are not the same as being surrounded by palpable remains.
As far as the country goes I would not change, for the mixture of
sea and inland here, easily accessible in these days of motors, fills
the bill. But I think that by nature I belong in the old. I am
amused by your correspondents. Doesn't it strike you as pretty
cheeky for unknown persons to ask you to send what here they
call an autographed photograph? I always say I haven't any.
Cranks continue with me. One, who said she was a cousin, ended
after I had paid no attention to her requests that I investigate her
alleged failure to receive her letters through the post and her
suggestions of kinship, wrote that I should resign and hand back
the Roosevelt medal. Another one wanted me to secure what she
called a beautiful life for her niece who she said was betrayed by
her mother. Last night also I got an irritated letter based on my
failure to reply to an earlier one asking me to back up some
damned peace projects. There is something doing most of the
time. I am pleased to hear it said that Spengler (*Untergang des
Abendlandes*) doesn't know so much as he assumed to know and
from another source that Croce has made a delicious review of
his book and poked fun at him.[2] I think that when I last wrote I
hadn't read *Marius the Epicurean*—to my view an unsatisfactory
product of the old unearned Oxford exquisiteness. I don't believe
Pater ever had had the hard teaching of affairs. And I eternally
dislike the putting of 19th century doubts and discriminations
into some century of the past and a different race, when I devoutly
believe that it is impossible for the writer to think the thoughts
of that time and place. I believe I let out slack about Thucydides
and won't run the risk of repeating. Now I am in the middle of
Tolstoi, *La guerre et la paix.* If a man writes a long novel it ought
to be *thin*—so that a chapter melts in the mouth. I resent a man's
taking so much of my time on his fiction and the more that Tolstoi
is thick and all that he says matters. Not that I care what he
thinks, but he makes a panorama like Paul Veronese with the
intensity of Rembrandt. Frankfurter was here two days ago—in
excellent form. I found him delightful and we talked from 12 N
to 9 PM. I thought his essay[3] admirable—I don't remember about
the last sentence, which you criticise.

I am glad at what you say of Pound—and pleased at his praise
of Wu (and myself—as I never am quite sure how he feels about
me, although all our relations have been pleasant and friendly).
Wu certainly is a remarkable and very agreeable young man.

---

[2] The review has not been located.

[3] Frankfurter and Landis, "Power of Congress over Procedure in Criminal
Contempts," 37 *Harv. L. Rev.* 1010 (June 1924).

Frankfurter was equally warm about him. I don't remember your opinion of Wambaugh—I never have known what his contributions might be—but I understand that he will leave and that a very good man will take his place.[4] You advert to the *dicta* in dissents. One of the advantages of a dissent is that one can say what one thinks without having to blunt the edges and cut off the corners to suit someone else. As to the wise writer who puts you on a level with Plato, Kant and Leacock, the last name is known to me only as that of a writer of very funny things. If your correspondent had put *him* high I should have agreed but hardly should have expected light on political science. Tell me of the other. You speak of inconsistencies about Sherlock Holmes. I seem to remember in Scott, the hump back and hideous red head of Campo Basso in one novel and in another, a tall handsome swart man, the ladies' favourite—Campo Basso—but I can't verify off hand.[5] I have seen one or two ladies for transitory jaws—but in the main am as quiet as ever—and always ready for a letter from you.

*Affectionately yours, O. W. Holmes*

*Beverly Farms, August 24, 1924*
*Dear Laski:* Your letter,[1] like Hume for Kant, awakens me from my dogmatic slumber. This is not a compliment but a figurative expression of the puddle of repose into which your letter splashes. After I got through *La guerre et la paix* with some admiration and not great pleasure I turned for ease of mind to Pound's *Law and Morals* which I gobbled up with comfort. But again I was led to agree with your remark that he brings his categories ready made instead of finding them in the *res.* I always blow Pound's horn. I admire and am overwhelmed by his learning, but I rarely find that unexpectedness which as you say is the most attractive thing. It worries me to think that perhaps or probably I don't do him justice but few of his own thoughts about the law seem to me important contributions. I say this in the most private confidence, and ask you to correct me if you can. I often find things I didn't know and am glad to know—but they are old facts not new theories—I beg you to teach me to qualify this impression—I want to admire more. As to your Latin dramas, I wrote to you last winter of the effect of Plautus on me. *The Way of All Flesh* which I am reading now has an amusing essay supposed to be by

---

[4] In 1925 Thomas Reed Powell was appointed Professor of Law at Harvard and took over the course in Constitutional Law from Professor Wambaugh.
[5] The Count of Campo-Basso appears in *Quentin Durward* and *Anne of Geierstein.*
[1] Omitted from this edition.

a Cambridge student, the hero, to the effect that the Greek trage-
dians are also bores, and that Aristophanes thought and said so.
I always am moved by the *Prometheus* and find passages in the
others—but I think we hardly realize on what a different plane
they are from modern drama. I agree with you about Montesquieu,
but think that we must give Rousseau credit for his echoes—I
thought I was reading a first sketch of Hegel when I read his
*Contrat social.* I was pleased in a lecture of Santayana on the
unknowable[2] to see another man now out of fashion, Herbert
Spencer, given a certain credit. If I may quote myself we must
correct the judgment of posterity by that of the time.[3] He was in
fashion once, therefore he filled a need. Our fashion is no more
respectable than any other. If a man has his time of being in
fashion he has all that anyone has, and has proved his claim to
be a force shaping the future.

As to onomatopoeia in poetry—hm—taking onomatopoeia in
the strict sense—but I agree to and assert that the main feature
of style properly so called is sound—what I have called an under-
song in the words. Thackeray has it to a marked degree. I don't
see how you can doubt that modern poetry is more subtile, taken
in the mass, than any earlier verse. This Butler (*Way of All Flesh*)
is a queer chap—over-valued I think by those who discovered
him. (I first did for myself in *The New Quarterly,*[4] a short-lived
periodical for which I subscribed because I had staid at the home
of the man who kept it going—at Bury St. Edmonds where they
had the pageant.) But he was a clever, original-minded man with
*aperçus* that I suspect were not quite penetrating enough to give
him a coherent view of the world. I have some philosophical books
sent me by Cohen which I hope to plunge into tomorrow—after
finishing *The Way of All Flesh.* Lord how I like this irresponsible
leisure. My love to you both.   *Affectionately yours, O. W. Holmes*


*Beverly Farms, August 31, 1924*
*Dear Laski:* Your letter[1] comes at a happy moment when I fain
would talk with you, even though it be from afar. As to Story,
let me add, only apropos of your remark, that I don't mind his
writing being diffuse and thin—as I think I wrote that a three
volume novel ought to be. The conclusion may be, don't write
three volume novels, and certainly I have no ambition to write like

[2] George Santayana, *The Unknowable* (1923).
[3] *Speeches,* p. 73.
[4] Portions of Samuel Butler's Notes, later published as the *Note-Books*
(1912) were printed in the *New Quarterly Review* in 1910.
[1] Omitted from this edition.

Story. What I said about Macaulay was only to do justice to a considerable power, not to express a personal liking—I have read nothing of his with pleasure for years, except the verses which I still praise. I can't verify the references to Thucydides as I have returned him but don't doubt I should agree. I think I admitted as much as that.

Since finishing *War and Peace* and Butler's *Way of All Flesh* which I think I have mentioned, and Pound's little book that I know I did, I have read a careful study of Nietzsche by W. M. Salter (question, is he a gentleman mentioned in philosophic circles?) which, without changing my conviction that he made too much row about himself, and that he tells me little that I didn't know, nevertheless moves some sympathy in me. Before I knew him if not before him I used to say that equality between individuals, as a moral formula, was too rudimentary. If you said equality between human foot pounds I could understand it. In that case if a philosopher and a fool were at the two ends of a plank at sea, the former might say, "Tommy, I am more than you, therefore let go." I do not say that Tommy would be bound by the consideration, as I don't think morals quite so important in the world as the philosophers teach—(as an anchor for other dogmatisms). I suppose Nietzsche wrote in or at least came from a more theological atmosphere than ours—and so got that tiresome tone of fluttering the dovecotes and was himself so fluttered. I think he might have died silent and the world not have been appreciably worse off. After him I took up another book sent by Cohen, G. Simmel, *Mélanges de philosophie relativiste* translated from German. I don't see why any one wanted to translate him— he seems to me a dull maker of categories. One observation of his gives me pleasure as confirming an old one of mine—that with the child generally (which I suppose is conjecture) and with the adult at certain moments (which we know to be true) there is no differentiation of me and not me—but just a homogenous content of consciousness. The content is all sound, or rapture or pain. I have wondered long but never have impressed anyone with the suggestion whether this fact is not at least a partial explanation of sympathy. The suggestion of pain begins to occupy the field. Later, if by a second, we say this is not my pain—but already we have been disturbed. I throw it out *valeat quantum*.

Also yesterday or the day before I took up Birrell's *Hazlitt*— which you sent me and have nearly finished rereading it, with renewed pleasure. What is more agreeable than a bookish man talking sympathetically about another bookish man, and how clear is Birrell and how moving in some of his quotations, Hazlitt. I am now having the comfort akin to that which Birrell speaks of in a volume of miscellaneous essays—I have dropped the sense

of duty and took to my room the last mentioned volumes and one
of Scott and one of Kipling's short stories—irresponsible browsing
—and I have declined to write an introduction to a volume of a
work called *Outline of Christianity!*, the theme suggested being the
world of today and yesterday. I shouldn't write, whatever the
theme suggested—but if the good friend who wrote had known
me better I hardly think he would have wanted my company
there. This is about all. I have been feeling a little pale as I
usually do at this time, perhaps a reminiscence of early cholera
morbus and later dysenteries of which more than once I nearly
died. This time it has been merely a hint, that has led me to keep
pretty quiet, the best remedy, and allowed me the joy of taking
to a couch at 11 a.m. Today all right again.

*Affectionately yours, O. W. Holmes*


*Beverly Farms, September 16, 1924*
*Tomorrow is Antietam 62 years ago!*

*My dear Laski:* Massingham's death, of which you speak, I
supposed would be a loss to you, but I hardly knew how great
before your letter.[1] *Contra* Birrell I am a devout Malthusian as you
know. I don't remember details, but that he stated a most important principle I have no doubt, and one that socialists generally
ignore. Someone was telling me of a recent book estimating that
in a hundred years the world would be full—in the sense that
population would press on the total means of subsistence. Such
estimates are speculative of course—but as they used to say in
Chemistry the experiment fails but the principle remains the
same. You speak of novels—Scott, Trollope, Thackeray &c. Alas,
my gusto for them has diminished, and as I believe I wrote it
was a relief to turn from *La guerre et la paix* and *The Way of
All Flesh* to a book on Nietzsche, some German essays translated
into French (I wondered why) and Santayana's *Scepticism and
Animal Faith.* Santayana's opinions I should think and my own on
the fundamentals agree more than of others in the trade—but as
I think I said, his desire to make literature leads him to put every
thought in arabesque that sometimes takes more time than it is
worth to unravel. I have read a few tales hardly worth mentioning
—though Cabot Lodge in a recent article mentioned one, Birming-
ham's *Spanish Gold*, as delighting hospital days.[2] I called at his
house last week and was told that he was doing well, but he has
not yet had the second operation (like mine) which is the trial.

---

[1] Omitted from this edition.

[2] In July, Senator Lodge was in the hospital in Boston. He returned to
Nahant in August. Following a second operation, in October, he died on
November 9, 1924.

At the present moment as leisure permits I am reading the *New Testament*—i.e., I haven't yet finished Matthew. I wish that I knew of a comment by a great scholar who was also a rationalist. In the words attributed to Jesus there are sentences that seem to come from such different sources. I suppose the writer, or those from whom he gathered, put in all the things that seemed to him or them especially nice whencesoever their *provenance*—just as within my memory, when he was alive, all current indecent stories were attributed to Mr. Lincoln. Yesterday Mr. Justice Higgins (of Australia) and his wife took luncheon with us—he was simple and intelligent—not on the hair trigger, but pleasant. You speak of Rousseau as belonging to the class that write perorations. It is most common. I remember that when I read *Progress and Poverty* I thought that H. George took to the wings of rhetoric just when I wanted the direct fact. We leave here September 29—going to Washington Wednesday, October 1.

*Affectionately yours, O. W. H.*

*Beverly Farms, September 21, 1924*
*Dear Laski:* Your letter[1] comes this Sunday morning as I have come to expect it. We seem to agree pretty exactly about Butler —also about Simmel. As to Ethics I recur to my book—a body of imperfect social generalizations expressed in terms of emotion.[1] I should quite willingly meet you by enlarging my formula to social demands based upon tacit generalizations &c. Of course time and place largely affect them. I read a book by Giddings—probably the same that you mention and remember getting little nourishment from it. As to your question why is A a natural rebel &c— (formulated by Gilbert in one of his operettas)—I don't see why you mightn't as well ask why has one red hair and another black— or any other born difference. The ideal of some of your socialist friends would abolish all such, at least I was deeply tickled at one of your French friends declaring difference of gifts an injustice. He must have been in a hurry for the imagined ultimate of a cosmos of equal wavelets and naught else—a conception that encourages me in a surmise that time is a form of the finite consciousness. To that extent I incline with Kant. Pound's book on *Law and Morals* was the text that started my writing about him to you. It seems to have made the same impression on us both. My last serious reading was the Gospels. I get some new impressions on rereading—one is of more amazement than ever that they should be thought evidence of the miracles. The mere way in

---

[1] Omitted from this edition.
[1] In "Ideals and Doubts," *Collected Legal Papers* 303, 306.

which they are told I should think would show that the tales could
not be relied upon. I observe in running my eye over what I have
written that if I use a word in one sentence I am pretty likely
to use it again in a later one—a natural infirmity of the aged mind.
If I were writing for print I would correct it—here—not.

A week from tomorrow we go to the Touraine and on Wednesday evening, October 1 expect to make the night journey to Washington putting up at first at the Powhatan for meals and slumber.
But as soon as I have breakfasted on Thursday morning I intend
to go hell-bent to the house and plunge into work. The new
secretary[2] as usual instructed to appear on Friday at 11 a.m. That
gives me a day clear—and a start on the morning of his coming. I
haven't seen him and forget his name. We expect a call from
Frankfurter and Mrs. this afternoon. They take luncheon with
Beveridge who no doubt will talk about his *Lincoln.* I was glancing this morning at Gray's letters—I have read them in times past
—they are pleasant browsing. The vacation has almost inverted
time and ended before it has begun.        *Aff'ly yours, O. W. H.*

*16 Warwick Gardens, 26.IX.24*
*My dear Justice:* I have had a dazzling ten days in the North, full
of more genuine pleasure than I can remember in a long time. First
I went to Ashington, a miners' village in Northumberland. I stayed
with a miner who began by discussing Kant with me, with a
knowledge and an insight which must be rare outside a group of
dons. I gave four lectures to about 200 miners and their questions
and arguments were as searching as I have ever met, particularly
when, as in the discussion on industrial organisation, we touched
on questions where they had special experience. Each evening I
was there my host had in a dozen men for talk, and I frankly can
rarely remember such talk. What was the value of Lester Ward's
work?[1] Where did Hardy stand in the pageant of English literature? Was security, as Bentham said, more important than freedom? What were the proper limits of consumers' co-operation? You
imagine a dozen men furiously smoking round a fire, and the
questions beginning almost before I could think of the answers.
And it was all done with the courtesy and modesty of really great
gentlemen. Many of them had not had a day's schooling after
fourteen. They all belonged to a little society where week by week
for ten years they had met to discuss intellectual problems. One
man, the oldest of them, was a passionate Carlylian, and to hear

[2] W. Barton Leach; see, *supra,* 405.
[1] Lester Ward (1841-1913); evolutionary sociologist; author, *inter alia,*
of *Dynamic Sociology* (1883) and *Pure Sociology* (1903).

him quote rolling sentences from *Chartism* with the pleasant burr
of a Northumbrian accent and his great gnarled hands making
passionate gestures of approval was an experience I shall not easily
forget. It reminded me all the time of that fine sentence of
Carlyle: "Education is like light—from a chaos it makes a world."
From Ashington I went to Manchester where I had two days of
grand talk with Tout the historian[2] and Alexander the philosopher.
Tout is something of a hero. For fifteen years he has worked at a
vast book on English medieval administration. It has all been
done in the Record Office on the documents, in the midst of
teaching. Practically, there is only one other man in England who
really knows the problems and could offer the fellowship of equal
learning. I asked him if he thought it had been worth it and he
said that so many medieval civil servants seemed to have become
his friends that at times he felt as though they were his real
friends and the people about him pale wraiths of unsubstantial
character. There is something fine about devotion of that kind.
Alexander has just retired and is settling down to finish his *Space,
Time and Deity*. We agreed to dismiss Croce and Bergson as
ultimately unimportant. He thought Spinoza incomparable, and
Hume and Bradley the two most significant people in English
philosophy. Then two days of our annual conference on adult
education.[3] A charming presidential address from Haldane, who
was quite at his best. A first-rate paper from a trade-unionist on
the motives which lead the workman into adult classes. He begins,
he said, from discontent. He wants either a way of escape from a
sordid environment, or else the knowledge with which to be
armed for the industrial conflict. Then intelligence begins to exert
its fascination, and he is compelled to give allegiance to the subject for its own sake. One speech in the discussion attracted me
when a working-man made a plea for greater attention to abstract
studies like mathematics and logic. He said he had been working
ten years at the former and to follow the significance of the
calculus was to win a new respect for the human mind. I read a
paper which gave me at least one happy moment. I explained the
importance of providing working-men with a meeting-ground
where apart from any formal teaching they could talk over the
universe in comfort. I pointed out that at Oxford what was im-

---

[2] Thomas Frederick Tout (1855-1929); Professor of Medieval and Modern
History at Manchester, 1890-1925; his most distinguished piece of historical
work was his monumental *Chapters in the Administrative History of Medieval
England* (6 vols., 1920-31).

[3] Lord Haldane told of his and Laski's work in organizing and directing
the activities of the British Institute of Adult Education in his *Autobiography*
(1929), p. 310 *et seq.*

portant was not the lectures which were usually abominable, nor
even the tutors since only a few could be either distinguished or
inspiring. What was really urgent was the group of undergraduates in a quiet room who between eleven and two in the morning
found that they had discovered eternal truth. In the discussion
which followed Conway the great Latin scholar[4] said his experience at Cambridge had been different. He had never discovered
eternal truth there and even when he seemed to have his hand on
her skirt, she whisked away around the corner. There was vast
laughter against me, especially from Haldane to whom I whis-
pered, like Huxley to old Brodie,[5] that the Lord had delivered
Conway into my hand. When I replied I thanked him warmly for
the best definition of the difference between Oxford and Cambridge I had ever heard; and he left me the field. . . .

*Ever yours, H. J. L.*

*Washington, D.C., October 9, 1924*
*Dear Laski:* A bulletin is all that is possible in the crowding rush
of work at the beginning of this term. Your account of your discourse to and with the miners is most interesting. I am all law
now. I reread Renan's *Vie de Jesus* coming on. Good to make
one realize the situation—the relation of Romans and Jews etc.,
and I should think a possible source of pleasure to those who find
consolation in the thought of Christ's having preceded them in
suffering, and his sympathy, without believing the miracles—but
I should suppose they would not be many. I dislike his rhetoric
especially his pronouncing various sayings and doings "delicious"
—and though I assume him to be sincere the words seem to me a
sentimental performance assuming more as to the character and
words of Christ than is warranted. Just before coming on I reread
some of Fitzgerald's letters with much delight—though he has the
usual English characteristic of assuming that British standards are
final. Did I mention *Endymion?* I don't know when I read that
before the other day. Many lines that only Keats could have
written—but not impressing me as a whole except that it was the
work of a young man who wants to let off some of his energy upon

---

[4] Robert Seymour Conway (1864-1933); Hulme Professor of Latin at
Manchester, 1903-1929.

[5] Sir Benjamin Brodie (1783-1862), physiologist and surgeon to William
IV, was the neighbor of Huxley on the platform at the 1860 meeting of the
Association for the Advancement of Science during the famous attack of
Bishop Wilberforce on Darwin. During the course of the Bishop's address,
and before delivering his reply, Huxley turned to Sir Benjamin, saying,
"The Lord has delivered him into my hands." See 1 *Life and Letters of
T. H. Huxley* (1890), 202.

a woman. I can no more. But I hope you will write even when I
fail.                                                                    *O. W. H.*


*16 Warwick Gardens, 4.X.24*

*My dear Justice:* . . . as you will know, we are in the midst of a
first-rate political crisis which will, I think, result in a general
election.[1] So I have been dining on it with Haldane and Mac-
Donald and having the peculiar thrill which comes from knowing
news about a day before anyone else. Haldane, I think, will not
like leaving office; he is gratified by the amplitude of the Chancellorship. And I thought J. M. Barrie, who was there, said a not
untrue thing when he remarked that Haldane would have been
very happy as a cardinal. Yet I admired H. for going off in the
middle of these hectic events to give a presidential address to a
working-men's club on the scientific mind. MacDonald is tired, and
I imagine that the surrender of responsibility will not irk him
greatly. He asked me quite pathetically about books, and insisted
that the life of the thinker is the only one which has really final
compensations. We talked over the chances and agreed that the
Tories will come back with Birkenhead as Chancellor.[2] I was
amused to find that all of us regarded him as the most brilliant
charlatan of the day with one redeeming quality only, that he was
loyal to his friends. But one there said as a footnote that he had
few friends which is I believe true. He reminds me tremendously
of Brougham, the same amazing energy, the same restless vanity,
the same love of third-rate omniscience, and, I think, the same
jealousy and love of fifth-rate company. Balfour once said to me
that Birkenhead cannot converse, he can only orate, and that is a
true index to what he is. On the way back from Haldane's I met
Baldwin and we walked over the Green Park together. He told me
that he viewed with horror the prospect of office, and that it
would be a happy day for him if MacDonald decided to go on
despite defeat. I said that he could always retire from politics. No,
he said, its curse is the curse of alcohol; you must go on, and
when you are not in office you miss the sense of power. It is only
in office that retirement looks attractive. I wish you could meet

---

[1] Both opposition parties had opened October with vigorous attacks on
Labor policies with respect to the Russian treaty and the withdrawal of
charges which had been preferred against the editor of the Communist publication, *Workers Weekly*. Losing what he considered a vote of confidence on
the latter issue MacDonald on October 10 requested a dissolution of Parliament, and a general election was scheduled for October 29.

[2] The Conservative Party gained a sweeping victory in the General Election
on the 29th. Mr. Baldwin, the new Prime Minister, appointed Lord Birkenhead Secretary for India and Viscount Cave Lord Chancellor.

Baldwin. He isn't a profound person, but he is one of the most loveable people I have met since I came home. . . .

*Ever affectionately yours, H. J. L.*


*Washington, D.C., October 24, 1924*
*Dear Laski:* Nearly a week has gone by since your last stimulating letter came, and some days since the arrival of Mill's *Autobiography.*[1] I have been so pressed with work at the beginning of the term that I haven't even read your introduction. The whole book will be the first to be read when I can breathe—probably next week when we adjourn for three weeks. I must stick in a word about Lord Birkenhead. Your general tone I agree to but as I used to see him with Leslie Scott it is only fair to say that he is very witty and amusing. I wish I could tell you of books, but I can read nothing but records and briefs. In the evenings when my wife's eyes let her read I have listened to Archie Butt's letters to his mother while he was at the White House with Roosevelt. Simple, kindly, innocently admiring, but I think, indiscreetly published, as he talks of the living or lately dead. Also *Professor How Could You* or some such title, which makes me laugh. A chap who is bound by his wife's bossing, without quite saying so to himself, and slides off to extravagant adventures. I can't yet imagine the end, but there is a very comical mixture of simple acceptance of ordinary conventions with moral insensibility to arson and slaughter of his kind. Such things are a relief when one has done about as much as one can in the course of work. I am bothered from time to time by the question whether I ought to resign, but I should like to keep on to 85, and if I reach that point in as good condition as now to aim at a further point. I live from day to day or month to month, however, and am prepared, I think, for the accursed shears. I scrabble off this bulletin as better than silence. My love to you both. *Affectionately yours, O. W. Holmes*


*Washington, D.C., November 2, 1924—Sunday*
*Dear Laski:* This will be brief in my turn—in answer to yours[1] while electioneering. For I have just emerged from a month's high pressure and slept late this morning and again this afternoon and haven't much to tell. I sent round three opinions last week that seemed to satisfy the boys and shall print a dissent tomorrow that

---

[1] Laski contributed a preface to the World's Classics edition of Mill's *Autobiography* (1924).
[1] Omitted from this edition.

I hope will give pain to some of them.[2] Not a burning theme. By an odd accident I believe that Sutherland who writes for the majority is engaged on a dissent from one of mine which has a precarious five for it—McKenna absent—also not on a burning theme. True to my promise, as soon as free I read Mill's *Autobiography* and your good introduction. I think it gives one a gentle warmth and friendly liking to hear the just man tell about himself. Do you know about his wife—I have a general notion that the world didn't rate her as highly as he did. It hardly could have —but I imagine that it was not ever enthusiastic about her. How was it?

At the end of the afternoon an hour ago I took up *The Newcomes*—which I have here in larger type than at Beverly—though I wish it was larger still. The first chapter again made me cry. I think I will go on and read it, though that is more of a job for me than for you. Also I had out my prints and glanced them over— pleasant roots in the past, as I have said before—and I have taken in the Zoo—and a chrysanthemum show (the overfed clubmen of blossoms don't please me as much as the original flower), and paid my tax on my house and am waiting for my bill to pay the main tax and see what money I have left. As I may have remarked a mild and regulated avarice is a vice to be recommended to the old. But it is 7—I must to the Powhatan to sup—and post this. Wherefore *adieu*. Birrell was not the only reader.

*Affectionately yours, O. W. Holmes*

*16 Warwick Gardens, 3.XI.24*

My dear Justice: Well! The thing is over and we have had a damned good licking. As MacDonald said to me on Friday, we have now at least four years to devote ourselves to political science. Yet there are some comforting features. We lost only one cabinet minister—a record since 1900. Practically we have wiped out the liberal party, so that we are back again at the two-party system which I regard as essential to political stability, and our total poll is one million larger than it was a year ago. So that I remain incurably optimistic about the future; for if in 25 years we can increase our voting strength from sixty thousand to five and a

<hr>

[2] On November 17, Holmes delivered the Court's opinion in five relatively unimportant cases. Mr. Justice McKenna retired from the Court in January 1925, and had participated only intermittently in the Court's work during the opening months of the October term, 1924. In *Mackenzie* v. *Engelhard Co.*, 266 U.S. 131, McReynolds, Sutherland and Sanford, JJ., dissented without opinion. In *Panama Railroad* v. *Rock, id.* 209, 215, Holmes, with Taft, C.J., and McKenna and Brandeis, JJ., concurring, dissented from the opinion of Sutherland, J., for the majority that the Code of Panama did not recognize a cause of action for wrongful death.

half millions, it is obvious that the process of political education is slow but sure.

. . . my main joy this last fortnight has been in La Bruyère and Vauvenargues. The former is not only politically important but I think as a moralist he makes Seneca *et al.* in the expressive idiom of your country look like five cents . . .

*Ever affectionately yours, H. J. L.*

*Washington, D.C., November 13, 1924*

*Dear Laski:* Your letter of the 3d comes at a happy moment—or rather came just before it, for yesterday when it arrived I was bothered with little things. The certificate of a somewhat important purchase that I made nearly a month ago had not arrived —a tooth had broken off—another step of commandant up the stairs and I had to go to the dentist to have the root taken out— and I knew that there was something that I had had it in my mind to do but couldn't remember what. Now, the certificate has come —the root is pulled out—and the errand which I feared might be important but wasn't is attended to. I have got all my opinions in shape to deliver. I have had pleasant words from my brethren and the sky is clear. Apropos of W. Lippmann he had an article in the *New Republic:* "Why I shall vote for Davis"[1] that I thought contrasted very advantageously with Croly's "Why I shall vote for LaFollette."[2] If I had had a vote I should have voted for Coolidge —quite apart from the fact that his election relieves my conscience from the doubt whether I ought to resign so as to give the appointment to him. I think your judgment of Coolidge is prejudiced—and while I don't expect anything very astonishing from him I don't want anything very astonishing—and am far from sympathising with Croly's ratiocinatory warnings to do something —God knows what—pretty quick or look out. By a mistake I missed Felix's article on the same side[3] much to my regret. . . . Felix sent me the Henderson book also but I have had no time to look into it. I am still in the middle of *These Eventful Years* which I believe I dilated upon to you. It takes the place of many newspapers. The Germans in it—Ludendorff, Tirpitz and Scheer remind me so of the Confederates after our war—the same boasting that they were the better men. My old friend McCabe[4] of Richmond used to give me so much of it that one day I said to him, "You licked us clean up to Appomattox, didn't you." I never for a moment have believed that Birkenhead was first rate—as your

---

[1] 40 *New Republic* 218 (Oct. 29, 1924).

[2] *Id.* 221.

[3] *Id.* 199 (Oct. 22, 1924).

[4] *Supra,* p. 253.

letter would seem to imply—but the contrary—*non obstant* the praise I heard of him as chancellor. I fully agree with you as to Ehrlich's *Juristische Logik*. It doesn't seem to me comparable to the *Sociology* if that was the name—alas I have it not—only a chapter or so that he sent to me, but I read it with admiration. Finally I don't think we say look like 5 cents—but like 35 cents—a figure that always has excited my questioning wonder. Five would be easier but I suspect less subtle. My leisure draws to a close— there hasn't been a great deal of it—but I come back refreshed and the great burden of stuff at the beginning of the term is disposed of. The work comes as easy as ever—but physical exertion is more difficult and limited. When I told my wife of a walk along a narrow path at the top of a bank and overing a stone wall at the end she seemed horrified and called my secretary and me Wander- lust and the Pied Piper—but I walked up three flights of stairs this morning without trouble. The trouble with that damned *Eventful Years* is that there is so much of it in such plebeian form—no— not plebeian—lower middle class—the names and the theme are fit for romance—but the look of the thing makes you want to send it to a library of the upward and onward. The hour of 9 p.m. has come. I must to solitaire and listen to a foolish tale or Mark Twain's *Autobiography* (an unlovely man—with some great- ness in him). My love to you both—and thanks for your letters which are a permanent joy.    *Affectionately yours, O. W. Holmes* The soft white shirt with stiff cuffs is the greatest comfort of modern times.

*16 Warwick Gardens, 9.XI.24*
*My dear Justice:* . . . Well, we are back again in peaceful times. A Tory government with us (not a bad cabinet especially in its demotion of Curzon)[1] and a Coolidge government with you. The latter I expected, though not with that immense majority. America must have an immense self-confidence to entrust the executive power for four years to a man without mind or heart. I do not ob- ject to mediocrity *in se* but I do object strongly to complacent mediocrity. Coolidge seems to me a natural churchwarden in a rural parish who has by accident strayed into great affairs. You will have seen that Eustace Percy has become Education Minister. It's an interesting appointment. He has lots of brains, but an over- emphasised *hauteur* and literally no sense of humour. In part he owes the place to Baldwin's liking for young men, and in part to

[1] Lord Curzon, who had been Foreign Minister in Baldwin's earlier govern- ment, had just been appointed Lord President of the Council.

the belief that it placates the Duke of Northumberland [2] who rules the extreme reactionaries in the Tory party. I thought he would make Leslie Scott at least S-G. But that does not appear likely, and his power is so great at the moment that he can pretty well do as he likes.

We have not been out much since I wrote last, except to a jolly dinner at Haldane's. He was in great form and told us interesting tales of Bain and his memories of Stuart Mill. Also of Acton at the Club, sententious, full of weird knowledge, and yet always succumbing in argument because he quoted authorities of whose significance he alone could judge. . . .

*Ever affectionately yours, Harold J. L.*

*Washington, D.C., November 21, 1924*

*Dear Laski:* An admirably keen letter from you, 9th, deserves more of a reply than you will get. "Story, God bless you, I have none to tell, Sir," as doubtless I have had to say more than once before now. I told you the other day that I think you are pre-judiced against the President—though I do not suggest that he is a great man. I am surprised at what you say of Eustace Percy's *hauteur.* He kept it to himself when here, though I thought I noticed that some of your young friends were attracted to the Lorrd Eustace. I was told that he united to his godliness a ca-pacity to drive a sharp bargain in his official doings. I liked what I saw of him. I am sorry that Scott gets no appointment if he wanted one. I haven't heard from him for ages. I should have liked to hear Haldane tell of Bain and Mill. Bain struck me as of a much coarser grain than Mill. We have been reading your *White Monkey,* but last night my wife handed it over to me to finish by myself as she thought it disagreeable. It seems to belong to the small change of literature, but the talk in its assumptions and short cuts and refinements of intelligences is sadly superior to what I have read lately in American novels. I notice however, there as in *Punch,* American slang &c are to be observed. . . . I agree with you in liking Quakers. Their discipline gives them much better manners than most people have. Brandeis generally drives home with me. I am the last leaf in keeping to my old one horse coupé. I agree with you as to form in B's opinions. I told him once, but don't nag about it, that I don't think an opinion should be like an essay with footnotes, but rather should be *quasi* an oral utterance. If, however, you are to go the other way I greatly

---

[2] Alan Ian Percy (1880-1930), eighth Duke of Northumberland, was elder brother of Lord Eustace Percy, and inflexible in his loyalty to conservatism. The Duke's mother was daughter of the Duke of Argyll (1823-1900), of whose family Holmes was an intimate friend.

respect the knowledge and thoroughness with which he gathers together all manner of reports and documents.

Time to scuttle for court. I will stop and post this in hopes to catch the supposed mail.    *Affectionately yours, O. W. Holmes*


                                            *16 Warwick Gardens, 16.XI.24*
*My dear Justice:* A delight of a letter from you, with news of dissents on the Court which I always await with a calm joy. I was glad the Mill interested you. Despite its defects, I don't believe a man interested in ideas could read it unmoved. You ask about Mrs. Mill. I believe that he was literally the only person who was in the least impressed by her. Mrs. Grote said briefly that she was a stupid woman; Bain said she had a knack of repeating prettily what J. S. M. said and that he told her it was wonderful; Morley told me that Louis Blanc told him he once sat for an hour with her and that she repeated to him what afterwards turned out to be an article Mill had just finished for the *Edinburgh*. I should guess that she was a comfortable and sympathetic person and that Mill, brought up to fight Austin, Praed,[1] Macaulay and Grote, had never met a really soft cushion before. If she was what he thought, someone else at least should have given us indications.

. . . Poor Lodge—a career of frustration; no man can live by eating his own bile.[2] The Lodge I shall want to remember is a Lodge who brightened up one day at Mrs. Jack Gardiner's[3] [*sic*] when I told him that the ancient Anglo-Saxon essays were still read.[4] A queer compound of inhibitions, and too little power to make human attachments for political success. I see they have appointed the biggest blackguard in Mass. to succeed him in the Senate. What a puppet-show it all is! . . .

My love to you both.        *Ever affectionately yours, H. J. L.*


                                            *Washington, D.C., November 29, 1924*
*Dear Laski:* You confirm my impressions about Mrs. Mill. Trevelyan I remember as a boy and very young man. When first I went to his father's house the children had been told that I was a

---

[1] Winthrop Mackworth Praed (1802-1839); poet, lawyer, and conservative member of Parliament.

[2] Senator Henry Cabot Lodge of Massachusetts had died on November 9. William M. Butler (1861-1937) was appointed to fill the Lodge vacancy in the Senate.

[3] Isabella Stewart Gardner (1840-1924), art collector, and Boston's most exuberant hostess.

[4] Lodge's Ph.D. thesis, "The Anglo-Saxon Land Law," had been published in *Essays in Anglo-Saxon Law* (Adams, ed., 1876).

soldier and were keen to see a "bang-y" man but disappointed as
I wore ordinary clothes—so old Trevelyan told me. The disappearance of Lodge leaves another blank for me though I saw him
little and rarely got talk that hit me where I lived. We had been
thrown together from time to time since I went with him to Illinois to try to shoot prairie chickens in 1867. At one time he came
to suggest that I should run for Governor and dangled a possible
senatorship before me—not then knowing his own destiny, but I
told him the law was my line. When he stuck by Blaine after
Blaine's nomination, he having gone out to oppose him, many
people cut him. I made a point of stopping him and saying that
in his position on the Republican Committee I didn't think that as
a gentleman he could have done otherwise.[1] When he came to
tell me that Roosevelt would nominate me he recurred to this fact
with feeling. His local associations were strong and he could be
very agreeable. I rather regretted that somehow he rather froze
my spontaneity. But the old associations counted with me as I
think they did with him. He read a great deal and remembered.

The Conference is over and I propose as soon as this draws to
an end to recumb and slumber. I maintain my enthusiasm for
*These Eventful Years.* I feel as if I was making up for not having
read the newspapers and so, *non obstant* difficulties, have finished
volume 1 and read a little of volume 2. *The White Monkey* at
odd minutes, a chapter at a time, the small change of literature,
but a very clever transcript of daily cackle, more civilized and
more on the hair trigger than ours but not much more important.
I notice the incursion of American slang. At intervals I have
listened to Mark Twain's *Autobiography*—a disagreeable man
with greatness in him. I have just declined to go to Chicago University and deliver an address and receive a degree. I should have
liked to go but age and infirmities seem to forbid. Also a cuss—
two cusses—caught me at my front door and wanted to photograph me in my study, as they did it seems with the others, bar
Brandeis whom they got walking. They came in for a few minutes
and made the best if not the only one I have had for many years
except with the Court. This I believe ends my simple story. Why
are you so savage about Massachusetts politicians? Is it memories
of the police strike? I noticed a pompous article by a woman the
other day in the *New Republic* on Women's Sense of Humour[2]
founded, I gathered from a glance, on the theorem that man is
the offshoot created by woman for her amusement but that she

---

[1] James G. Blaine (1830-1893) had been the Republican nominee for
President in 1884.

[2] Mary Austin, "Sense of Humor in Women," 41 *New Republic* 10 (Nov.
26, 1924).

was IT. Rum lot when they become publicly articulate. Also an address from your colleague Jenks's Inaugural, *Sources of the Law,* that I regretted to think not as valuable as other contributions of his. I could expatiate but refrain. If you keep on about Thackeray I shall have to reread, whatever the difficulties of print. Of course he comes nearer home than Dickens, but I think not to be compared with him for creative imagination.

So, skirting the edge of possible controversies,

*Affectionately yours, O. W. H.*


*16 Warwick Gardens, 7.XII.24*
*My dear Justice:* First of all my two triumphs. I have finished my book—like Gibbon I could tell you time and place. It is fearfully long—five to six hundred pages of print, I should judge. But I think it has new things to say and also practical things. I hope to get it out early in March.[1] Yet I part with it with regret. Do you know that feeling? It's been a constant companion for the last three years, and I have become intimate with it. Now, I am going to take six months rest from writing except for two Fabian tracts[2] and a chapter for the *Cambridge Medieval History* on political philosophy from Dante to the Reformation.[3] I rather look forward to that; it is pleasant to be able to say one's say briefly on Ockham and Marsilius, Augustino Trionfo and Nicholas of Cusa. I always enjoy proving that there were great men before Agamemnon, especially for the sake of friends like Walter Lippmann who really believe that modern history began with Theodore Roosevelt. Then the second triumph. You know by repute at least Mariana's *De Rege*—which is, I believe, except for Althusius's *Politica Methodice Digesta* the rarest book in modern political theory. It was burnt everywhere for its approval of assassination; and there is no copy either in the Museum or the Bodleian. I have seen one in Paris, and there is one at Corpus Christi Cambridge; but I know no others at all accessible. I got a catalogue of an auction sale of the books of an old teacher of Spanish in Liverpool in which it listed a number of things by Cervantes *et al.* and said "No. 172. A book by Mariana (Professor Kelly inserts the note 'the famous book')." I tumbled to it that this might be *De Rege,* trained at once for Liverpool and the sale, found practically no competition and bought it (a perfect copy with the vellum binding as white as on the day of issue), for seventeen shillings. . . .

*Ever affectionately yours, H. J. L.*

---

[1] *A Grammar of Politics* was published in the summer of 1925.

[2] *The Problem of a Second Chamber* (Fabian Tract, No. 213; 1925); *Socialism and Freedom* (Fabian Tract, No. 216; 1925).

[3] 8 *Cambridge Medieval History* (1936) 620.

*Washington, D.C., [Thursday] December 18, 1924*

*Dear Laski:* Your last, received yesterday, announced the finishing of your book. I congratulate you, but know the blank that comes when the pressure is taken off. I feel the same today for a relatively infinitesimal cause. I have just sent to the printer the first draft of a decision on a case of frightful importance given to me on Monday and on which I have been concentrated with fierce intensity.[1] I fear that my brethren or some of them will think that I should have taken a month. But I always say that it is impact not dead pull that drives a pile and I think I have seen and stated the points. Naturally I have read nothing—but I have half listened at night to *The Green Hat*—by Michael Arlen—of whom I should like to hear anything that you know. It is a very fishy story, only redeemed by a rather remarkable style and subtlety. (Is there a faint distinction between subtle and subtile—the latter being slightly more friendly in its implication?) I have heard that the author was not an Englishman but an Armenian or some thing— the foreign blood often gives a smack to the style—witness Conrad, Santayana, this man? *et al.* At this point I took a drive with my wife to the zoo and saw two baby lions and two puma cubs— not to speak of the monkey that seemed to rage when we clapped our hands and then skipped on to a shelf and whacked that in like manner, a beautiful mild day, and the buzzards wheeling nobly high over head. I delight in going to this or any zoo—apart from intrinsic interest I always feel, probably from old association, as if I were beginning a spree that would end with a show in the evening and a bottle or more of champagne. How far away are such delights now—when I would rather not drink than drink—alas— but the regret is only for departed criminal propensity.

The other day two chaps caught me by my door and asked to photograph me in my library—one of the results appeared in the paper—as per enclosure—a better one got me sitting as I am now at my desk. It is the first time for years except with the other justices. About a year ago a very good etching of me was published but it is large and costs money. I gather that some people buy it, as I have been asked to add my autograph though I signed a number in pencil—which is more preferred to ink as more lasting—to my surprise. I ought to be at work, but here I am dawdling and saying nothing. I have noticed of old that the mind spontaneously insists on a little idleness after a strain. Have you?

What do you know about Ockham of whom you speak of talking? Gents of that kidney are known to me only at second hand.

---

[1] *Sanitary District of Chicago* v. *United States*, 266 U.S. 405 (Jan. 5, 1925). The Court sustained the action of the lower court in granting an injunction to the United States against the division of waters of Lake Michigan by the State of Illinois.

I took Cohen's word for it that I needn't read Thomas Aquinas. I note also your pleasure at the *Iliad*. I must confess that to me it is picking into the remote corners of a shagbark (if you know the nut) for better morsels—when I can get more and just as good with less trouble from a modern book. I do indeed sympathize with your triumphs in getting the *De Rege* by an author, Manana [*sic*] if I read you rightly, that I know not of and do not find either in Larousse or Holtzendorff—the only works that seem likely to tell of him in my shelves. . . . Did you get anything new from the critical edition of *Ecclesiastes*? I have just looked into the Macaulay's essay on Sir William Temple to see whether I wanted to get Dorothy Osborne's letters—it looks as if they might be worth while—but you see how paralyzing to all other matters the law is. I have to rely upon you for my themes—no matter—if the boys think I have punched my case I am content to be dull for a fortnight. And perhaps I may pick up some improvement when all my work is done—in a day or two. With two weeks adjournment beside this.          *Affectionately yours, O. W. Holmes*

*16 Warwick Gardens, 14.XII.24*
*My dear Justice:* . . . a bright evening here with Emma Goldman the anarchist whom I found a simple and charming woman whose faith I denied but whose *bona fides* I found beyond doubt. I listened for hours to her account of her adventures in Soviet Russia—a tale like a narrative out of Phillips Oppenheim. Lenin she made out to be what would happen if you added a great organising mind like that of Brandeis to the cold-blooded Jesuitry of a Grand Inquisitor. And (*entre nous*) in view of her American past I was a little amused at her eagerness to start a campaign against Russia's treatment of its political prisoners. The Bastille, clearly, must fall afresh in every revolution. But of course Bolshevism must be anathema to a philosophic anarchist.

Of reading this week I have done but little. Some Balzac, and a new translation of the *Old Testament* by one Moffatt,[1] which, with certain crudities, really had its points *e.g.* it made the Song of Songs genuinely like an authentic Arab love-poem and the Elijah-saga really read like a piece out of Herodotus. In general the result was to make the whole thing the natural epic of a barbaric tribe and David especially the mean little skunk that he obviously was. I came to see that the very stateliness of the prose in the authorised version does clearly destroy the true atmosphere of the

---

[1] Rev. James Moffatt (1870-1944), Scottish-born church historian who, following an academic career in Scotland and England, in 1927 became Washburn Professor of Church History at Union Theological Seminary in New York.

original and that, I take it, justifies the man's effort. The translator is one Moffatt, a theologian in Edinburgh and I rather wonder if he knows the true effect he produces. . . .

Our love to you both,      *Ever affectionately yours, H. J. L.*

                              *Washington, D.C., December 28, 1924*
*Dear Laski:* Your letter that came yesterday makes me ashamed to write—for I have nothing to show for my day except that I have had my hair cut. I got up late, had to send off Judge Augustus Hand because of the barber—and after luncheon and a brief episode of listening to the amusing and smart article by George Harvey on the French debt[1] (apropos of poor dear Jusserand's recent conversation and speech) and a brief delighted dawdle over some of the book catalogues that I suppose I owe to you went off to sleep again. Perhaps I have sufficiently accounted for myself in this life by having read every word of *These Eventful Years.* I am interested by the effect on you of the new translation of the Old Testament. My father long ago spoke of the need of "depolarizing" the customary language—I have succeeded in doing it for myself in spots—but I think I should rather like to see the new book. You remember Renan's translation of the Song of Solomon—with *dramatis personae*—chorus of old men—chorus of women of the harem—*"une danseuse"* &c? I believe his theory of the book of Job is not the accepted one.

You made me pause again by speaking of a great organizing mind like that of Brandeis. I never thought of him in that light— and am quite blank as to whether you are right or not. Of course he has a great mind. What you say of China pretty well hits my level. I have talked with and read enthusiasts on Chinese art but they seem to me to have hypnotized themselves into a mode of thought—as men can and do with almost anything capable of being reduced to propositions—if not more with things that are not. In the artistic and literary chapters of the Big Book (*These E. Y.*) I was shocked to see how many illustrious names were not known to me. Doughty, an English poet, who is called a giant, for one, Péguy[2] another and Paul Claudel who is called the greatest living French poet—but I *felt* quite out of it with the French— and of course with the Germans and Italians. However when I am

---

[1] In an editorial in the Washington *Post* on December 28, 1923, George Harvey had charged that Jusserand, the retiring French ambassador, had spoken disingenuously when he indicated to the Secretary of the Treasury, Andrew Mellon, that France intended to pay her war debts to the United States.

[2] Charles Péguy (1873-1914), French poet, passionately concerned for justice and spiritual purity, died in the first World War.

crushed by your incessant activity I console myself by repeating a sentence from an admired American writer—"Go to the slug, thou ant."

What adorable things those catalogues are. It is a swindle to tell booksellers to send them to me for I never buy anything nowadays, but I am lost in the first that I take up and mark things that I should like—and then throw it away. I stopped with the first that I took up this afternoon (A. Maurice & Co.) and marked books that I never should do more than look into if I had them—like Sir Harry Vane's *The Retired Man's Meditations*—but they look so good when you are in the spirit world of titles. I used to think I would write a library of titles and leave to weaker hands to fill them out. I must leave you for solitaire—it is past my usual hour. Conference tomorrow, Monday, with possibly another case for me —and next week a probably hard month of sitting.

My poor friend Rice of the print department is in the hospital —so I have had no day off with him. If I could remember which book had about Elijah I would send for it while at the Capitol tomorrow. I don't believe I should care much for Emma Goldman —I had my belly full of isms when young. A happy New Year to you all.

*Affectionately yours, O. W. Holmes*


*Washington, D.C., December 29, 1924*

P.S. to yesterday's letter:

Why do you put Bradley so high? I never read his works, as I never read Thomas Aquinas—but I inferred from what I knew that he wouldn't say much to me. Answer this. Of course you understood that my mention of Sir Harry Vane was merely naming the first that I happened to come on in the catalogue—there are lots that I mark in this way before I throw the catalogue away. I hate to throw them away—but I think it wise not to keep masses of stuff after the pleasure of running through them.

This morning I have grasped that it is David not Elijah that you pronounce a mean little skunk—which is more intelligible. Did Russell in telling of America say anything about Cohen? I should like to know what he thinks of him—though B. R.'s judgments have something of his eccentricity. I told you how much I enjoyed seeing him—I should have liked to have long jaws.

*Yours, O. W. H.*

# Biographical Appendix

**Adams, Brooks** (1848-1927), descendant of Presidents. His forebodings of doom found justification in a cyclical and cynical interpretation of history which he formulated in *The Law of Civilization and Decay* (1895). He was as distinctively a Bostonian and as uncompromisingly an Adams as his better-known brother, Henry, whom he idolized—in that devotion rising above the rebellious skepticism which sharpened his judgment of his own world and its aspirations.

**Alexander, Samuel** (1859-1938), beloved Professor of Philosophy at Manchester from 1893 to 1924. Save for his one large work, *Space, Time, and Deity* (2 vols., 1920), Alexander's distinguished contributions to philosophy were principally in essays and lectures. His metaphysical affiliations were with Spinoza, with the realists and theists; in his ethics he was an evolutionist, and in aesthetics he was greatly concerned with the psychology of artistry.

**Ames, James Barr** (1846-1910), beloved Dean and Professor of the Harvard Law School. As teacher he made of the case method of instruction a success which its founder, Langdell, never achieved. As scholar he is best known for his numerous essays on English legal history and his many case-books on various branches of the law.

**Astor, Nancy** (1879- ), Viscountess. American zest, Virginian charm, and marriage to Lord Astor facilitated an energetic career as suffragette, conservative member of Parliament, explosive friend of the great, and intemperate enemy of intemperance. With humor and pride she has told her own story under the somewhat possessive title *My Two Countries* (1923).

**Aulard, François Alphonse** (1849-1928), founder of the *Société de l'histoire de la Révolution* and masterful editor of forgotten records of the Revolution. His own interpretations of the Revolution, though frankly partisan, were so infused with enthusiasm and so firmly grounded in scholarship that they commenced a new era in the historiography of the Revolution. His greatest single work was the *Histoire politique de la Révolution française* (1901). His passionate disagreement with Taine's despairing interpretation of the Revolution was most fully expressed in his *Taine: Historien de la Révolution française* (1907).

**Austin, John** (1790-1859), follower of Bentham and father of the modern school of analytical jurisprudence. In *The Province of Jurisprudence Determined* (1832) he sought to define the boundaries between "law strictly so-called" and "law by analogy." By his process of definition he determined that his province of jurisprudence should be that of "law strictly so-called," wherein every positive law may be seen to be a direct or circuitous command of a sovereign. This discarding of morality and the law of nature was, needless to say, a repudiation which critics of the analytical school have been unwilling to accept.

Bagehot, Walter (1826-1877) economist, whose training in the law and intimate relations with leaders in political and intellectual affairs gave to his writing in political science (*The English Constitution* and *Physics and Politics*) and economics (*Lombard Street*) an effective vitality. Admiring the deferential strain in British character and seeing the social value of dullness as contrasted with originality, he was no radical in his politics and was an ardent and able spokesman for that political liberalism and institutional conservatism which marked the age of Victoria.

Bain, Alexander (1818-1903), Scottish logician and psychologist who, as friend and biographer of John Stuart Mill, was faithful to the utilitarian tradition in ethics and to Mill's principles of logic. He was a founder of the philosophical journal, *Mind*. His principal contributions to the intellectual history of his time were in psychology. Though he made no major additions to psychological theory, his insistence that the methods of psychology should be scientific influenced the direction of later psychological research, particularly that of William James. It has been suggested that he was the grandfather of pragmatism.

Bayle, Pierre (1647-1706), French philosopher who turned from Calvinism to Catholicism and returned again from whence he started. His *Dictionnaire historique et critique* (1696) became the model of Diderot's *Encyclopédie* in an age of enlightenment for which Bayle might have had small sympathy. Though he rejected the all-sufficiency of reason, considered that man's nature is essentially evil, and in politics was timidly conservative, in his *Dictionnaire* he indulged an ingenious talent

for irreverent paradox which was the admiration of the *philosophes* of the eighteenth century. Voltaire spoke fairly of him: "Bayle is the first of logicians and sceptics. His greatest enemies must confess that there is not a line in his works which contains an open aspersion of Christianity; but his warmest apologists must acknowledge that there is not a page in his controversial writings which does not lead the reader to doubt, and often to scepticism." See, herein, Jurieu, Pierre.

Beck, James Montgomery (1861-1936), lawyer and politician whose service as Solicitor General of the United States in the Harding administration was followed by a career in Congress from 1927 to 1934. His most pretentious work, *The Constitution of the United States* (1922), stimulated Thomas Reed Powell's devastating sketch of constitutional pontification in 33 *New Republic* 297 (Feb. 7, 1923).

Becker, Carl (1873-1945), Professor of History at Cornell. His greatest contributions to the history of ideas were *The Declaration of Independence* (1922) and *The Heavenly City of the Eighteenth Century Philosophers* (1932).

Berenson, Bernard (1865-1959), American-born art critic, whose life in Italy contributed to the distinction of his many works on the Italian painters. He has told the story of his life in art in *Sketch for a Self Portrait* (1949).

Beveridge, Albert J. (1862-1927). Following his energetic career as Senator from Indiana and leader of the Progressive Republicans, he professionalized an aptitude for history and wrote his monumental *Life of John Marshall* (4 vols., 1918-19). Thereafter he turned to the task of writing a four-volume biography of Lincoln, but died when his work was but half completed. Holmes's association with him was as a summer neighbor on the North Shore of Massachusetts.

Beveridge, Sir William (1879-    ), later first Baron Beveridge; economist, civil servant and, from 1919 to 1937, Director of the London

# Biographical Appendix

School of Economics. His lifelong concern with problems of unemployment led to his most famous achievement—the Beveridge Report of 1942, in which he set forth proposals for a scheme of social insurance, a plan which in many of its essentials was adopted by the Labor Government between 1945 and 1947.

Birrell, Augustine (1850-1933), lawyer, statesman, and essayist. In public life he was a loyal supporter of Gladstone and held the presidency of the Board of Education in the Campbell-Bannerman government. As Chief Secretary for Ireland from 1907 to 1916 he followed the succession of Morley and Bryce, doing his duties charmingly but so casually that he failed entirely to foresee the Easter rebellion. His political career ended, he returned to a quiet life of letters in Chelsea. He told his own story in *Things Past Redress* (1937).

Boissier, Gaston (1823-1908), Latinist, critic, and archaeologist who was Sainte-Beuve's successor at the College of France. His principal historical works were *La religion romaine d'Auguste aux Antonins* (2 vols., 1874) and *La fin du paganisme* (1891). In literary criticism his most important volumes were *Cicéron et ses amis* (1865) and *Madame de Sévigné* (1887).

Bosanquet, Bernard (1848-1923), philosopher and political theorist who gave a Hegelian interpretation to Rousseau's "general will." Through metaphysical inquiry he discovered the moral person of the state and assigned to it an unlimited authority by which it compelled the individual to realize his freedom. In coloring the supremacy of a state's authority with the virtue of moral truth he believed that he had not taken from the individual liberties which he might legitimately seek to retain. His most important work in political theory was *The Philosophical Theory of the State* (1899).

Bossuet, Jacques Bénigne (1627-1704), Catholic theologian who believed that the drift of his age toward rationalism must be stopped by restoring the philosophical credit of Providence and of miracle, and by the reconversion of Protestants. In his political writing, while denying to Louis XIV the special grace of arbitrary power and to the people any natural rights, he acknowledged that the King's authority was as absolute as were his rights divine. As theological controversialist he succeeded in effecting the Papal condemnation of Fénelon's quietism. His fame as preacher rests principally on the magniloquence of his funeral orations.

Bowen, Charles (1835-1894), Baron Bowen. At the bar and on the bench he retained the graceful literary talent which marked his early contributions to the *Saturday Review*. His subtle and sensitive genius was largely wasted on the jurymen of the Queen's Bench, on which he sat from 1879 to 1882, but refreshed and vivified the Court of Appeal, to which he was advanced in 1882. The opinions which perhaps most fully reveal the quality of his mind and of his style were those which he delivered in *Mogul Steamship Company* v. *McGregor*, 23 Q.B.D. 598 (1889) and *Maxim Nordenfeldt Gas and Ammunition Co.* v. *Nordenfeldt* [1893] Ch. 630.

Bradlaugh, Charles (1833-1891), self-made atheist and missionary of doubt who saw a natural alliance between political republicanism and theological radicalism. He succeeded in his effort to force a respectable society to make itself ridiculous by prosecuting and persecuting him. Elected to Parliament in 1880 he finally prevailed, five years later, in his effort to be seated despite his atheism.

Bradley, Francis Herbert (1846-1924), principal figure in the English philosophical movement away from empiricism and utilitarianism towards an idealism largely Kantian and Hegelian in inspiration. In metaphysics his inquiries led him to the Absolute, a superrelational reality beyond the reach of experience yet imperfectly manifested in the appearance with which experience is concerned. His metaphysics and his distrust of an optimistic empiricism led him in political theory to the belief that the individual must recognize his social station and find his freedom in participation in the life of the moral organism known as the state.

Brandeis, Louis Dembitz (1856-1941). His service on the bench of the Supreme Court of the United States from 1916 to 1939 followed a distinguished, successful, and vigorous career at the Boston bar. The high morality of his mind and his deep concern that the state's efforts to improve the lot of man should not be frustrated by constitutional abstractions made him an influence of profound importance. Frequently associated in dissent from the views of a majority of their Brethren, Holmes and Brandeis differed greatly in their temperaments, their political convictions, and their basic interests, yet were devoted friends and allies in their search for truth.

Brissaud, Jean-Baptiste (1854-1904), Professor of Law at Toulouse. Brissaud's greatest work of historical scholarship was Cours d'histoire générale du droit français (1904). His philosophic inclinations were utilitarian and scientific, and his concern as legal historian was with the institutions which surround and shape the law, rather than with its content. His perspective was European, not merely French, and he did much to further the comparative method in the study of legal history.

Brunetière, Ferdinand (1849-1906), militant critic, historian of ideas in French literature, and champion of the classical tradition. Brunetière discovered the sources of modern pollution in the Enlightenment, and made it his special responsibility to assault its progeny, the scientific naturalism of Zola and Anatole France. His ultimate conversion to Catholicism concluded a lifelong search for the security of a disciplined tradition. His greatest work was Études critiques sur l'histoire de la littérature française (8 vols., 1880-1907). Laski included a telling summary of Brunetière's traditionalism in Authority in the Modern State (1919) 171 et seq.

Buchanan, George (1506-1562). Scottish by birth, he was so French in the humanistic bias of his thought and mood that he has been described as the Scots Rabelais. His principal work, De jure regni apud Scotos (1578), was a dialogue in which, over somewhat flabby opposition, he was able to develop the thesis that royal authority is limited by a body of law made by the majority of the people, and, in doing this, to justify the dethronement of Mary, Queen of Scots.

Cardozo, Benjamin N. (1870-1938), one of the greatest of American common-law judges. He sat on the New York Court of Appeals from 1914 to 1932, when he was named Holmes's successor on the Supreme Court of the United States by President Hoover. The sensitivity of his temperament, the delicacy of his mind, and his profound concern with the philosophy of law and the responsibility of judges were shown not only in his judicial opinions but in his extrajudicial writings, such as The Nature of the Judicial Process (1922) and The Paradoxes of Legal Science (1928).

Cecil, Lord Robert (1864-1958), first Viscount Cecil of Chalwood; conservative statesman whose greatest efforts were in the cause of world peace and the League of Nations. In 1937 he was awarded the Nobel Peace Prize.

Clarke, John Hessin (1857-1945). Following a career at the Ohio bar he was appointed United States District Judge for the Northern District of Ohio by Woodrow Wilson in 1914. In 1916 President Wilson elevated him to the Supreme Court of the United States to fill the vacancy resulting from the resignation of Charles Evans Hughes. Mr. Justice Clarke resigned from the Court in 1922 in order to devote his energies to the cause of world peace and the League of Nations.

Cohen, Morris Raphael (1880-1947), American philosopher whose devoted friends Holmes, Laski, and Felix Frankfurter found in him the same qualities which made him a profoundly influential teacher of many generations of students at City College, New York. His skeptical bent in metaphysics did not destroy a passionate conviction that man's ultimate reliance must be on reason or qualify the conviction that logical and mathematical relations have reality. His *Law and the Social Order* (1933) contained his essays on legal philosophy, a group of writings which had greatly influenced the thinking of American judges and lawyers. The story of his personal and intellectual life is told in his autobiography, *A Dreamer's Journey* (1949).

Cole, G. D. H. (1889-1959), economist and political scientist whose innumerable writings on economic and political problems have had a significant influence on socialist thought and the policies of the Labour Party in the last thirty years. Neither these works nor his teaching at Oxford prevented him from collaborating with his wife, Margaret, in the writing of a five-foot shelf of mystery stories.

Curzon, George Nathaniel (1859-1925), Marquess Curzon of Kedleston. His arrogant conservatism combined with political ambition made him see British imperialism as a "majestic responsibility." As Viceroy of India he took the vision seriously and exercised his responsibilities with such majestic luxury and administrative capacity that he antagonized nearly all with whom he had dealings. Foreign Secretary in the Coalition Government of Lloyd George and in Bonar Law's cabinet, he ended his career having, in the words of Harold Nicolson, "achieved successes rather than success."

Dicey, Albert Venn (1835-1922), Vinerian Professor of English Law at Oxford. Through him Stephen blood and personal friendship he was closely associated with the intellectual and political leaders of his day. His notable contributions to law and jurisprudence include his Introduction to the *Study of the Law of the Constitution* (1885) and *Lectures on the Relation between Law and Public Opinion in England during the Nineteenth Century* (1905).

Dickinson, G. Lowes (1862-1932), historian, political scientist, and philosopher whose academic post at Cambridge was the center from which his humane and sensitive intelligence made its influence felt throughout the world of letters. He was intimately associated with the London School of Economics as lecturer on political science from 1896 until 1920. E. M. Forster has painted an unforgettable portrait of his friend in *Goldsworthy Lowes Dickinson* (1934).

Dilke, Sir Charles Wentworth (1843-1911), Second Baronet; politician and author, whose political loyalties embraced both radicalism and imperialism. As President of the Local Government Board from 1882 to 1885 he rendered invaluable service to Gladstone, but his effective public career was brought to an end by a notorious divorce case in which he, without justice, was implicated.

Duguit, Léon (1859-1928), Professor of Constitutional Law at Bordeaux. In a series of volumes on public law and jurisprudence Duguit developed the thesis that the state is beneath the law, has no claim to sovereignty, and lacks the personality attributed to it by classical legal theory. On the basis of these principles Duguit asserted that the state is legally responsible for its wrongful acts and that the stuff of law is to be found not in rights, but in duties. He found that the requirement of social solidarity was the driving influence in modern law by means of which the interests of state and individual were reconciled and adjusted. In 1919 Laski and his wife published a translation of Duguit's *Les transformations du droit public* (1913) under the title, *Law in the Modern State*. Laski's later, somewhat more critical estimate of Duguit's philosophy of law is to be found in *Modern Theories of Law* (Jennings, ed., 1933) 52.

Ehrlich, Eugen (1862-1922), Professor of Roman Law at the University of Czernowitz. Ehrlich was the European leader of the modern sociological movement in jurisprudence. His most influential books were *Grundelung der Soziologie des Rechts* (1913) and *Die juristische Logik* (1918). He found in the inner order of such social institutions as the family, the corporation, and the labor union the basic facts of law which, through the state's legislation and the decisions of courts, takes on the form of legal propositions. His emphasis upon the dichotomy between the living law, created by society, and the rules established by statute or decision for deciding lawsuits had considerable influence on English and American jurisprudence and methods of legal study. Ehrlich's philosophy of law was related, of course, both in fact and in theory, to the pluralistic strain in modern political theory as represented by Hauriou in France and Laski in England. The *Grundelung* was published in translation as *Fundamental Principles of the Sociology of Law* (Moll, tr., 1936). Einstein, Lewis (1877-1949), American diplomat and scholar. His most important foreign post was that of Minister to Czechoslovakia from 1921 to 1930. His principal historical works are *Tudor Ideals* (1920) and *Divided Loyalties* (1933). His intimate friendship with Holmes is recorded in their extensive unpublished correspondence.

Faguet, Émile (1847-1916), critic and literary historian whose sympathies were those of a cool-headed liberal and whose insights into the character of the great writers of France made his criticism as useful to the historians of ideas as to the historians of letters. His great works of criticism were his *Histoire de la littérature française* (2 vols., 1900-1901) and *Politiques et moralistes du XIXᵉ siècle* (3 vols., 1890-1899). In his later years his concern was principally with the political and intellectual problems of his own day, as in his *Le liberalisme* (1902) and *L'anticléricalisme* (1906), in which he sought to defend the middle way between Traditionalism and Jacobinism.

Figgis, John Neville (1866-1919), churchman and historian. Concerned primarily with assuring churches adequate freedom, Figgis insisted, with Gierke, that each group in society has a personality of its own and an inherent liberty of growth. He had great influence on the movement in English political theory towards pluralism. His most important works were *From Gerson to Grotius* (1907) and *Churches in the Modern State* (1913).

Garvin, J. L. (1868-1947), thunderous editor of the London *Observer* and a forceful influence on British conservatism. His achievements, outside journalism, were principally those of writing the official biography of Joseph Chamberlain and editing the fourteenth edition of the *Encyclopaedia Brittanica*.

Geny, François (1861-1959), author of *Méthode d'interprétation et sources en droit privé positif* (1899) and *Science et technique en droit privé positif* (4 vols., 1913-24). A realist to some and a neoscholastic to others, Geny attacked the assumption that logic was a sufficient instrument of interpreting the code, insisted that the solution of legal questions requires "free scientific research," and urged that the creative responsibility of judges necessitates frequent reference to the law of nature and to standards of justice and utility.

Gierke, Otto von (1844-1921). His great concept of *Genossenschaft*, as a Germanic principle of coöperative association, was at the foundation of his theory that the corporate body is not, as the Roman law considered it to be, a *persona ficta* but a real group person, created not by the state but by social action. Made familiar to English and American scholars by Maitland, Gierke had great influence on pluralistic theories of the state, though those who admired the depth of his scholarship and the massiveness of his *Genossenschafts theorie* did not accept his ultimately Hegelian view that all groups in a society are subordinate to the will of the state.

Girard, Paul Frédéric (1852-1926), Professor of Law at Paris. He was a great Romanist who did much to encourage the study of Roman law in France and to introduce to that study the methods of German scholarship. His most important work was his *Manuel de droit romain* (1895), one of Holmes's favorites among Continental studies of law.

Gray, John Chipman (1839-1915), Professor of Law at the Harvard Law School from 1869 to 1913. A master of the law of property and an active practitioner, Gray concerned himself, somewhat impatiently, with the larger problems of jurisprudence in his *Nature and Sources of the Law* (1909). He there insisted that all theories of sovereignty are inadequate which deny or do not recognize that judges are makers of the law and as such exercise a larger share of sovereign power than do legislators. "The law of a great nation," he said, "means the opinions of half-a-dozen old gentlemen . . ."; a proposition which played a significant part in initiating the American movement towards a so-called "realist" school of jurisprudence.

Green, Thomas Hill (1836-1882). Rebel against English empiricism, he taught a doubting generation that idealism in philosophy does not, of necessity, mean conservatism in politics. His political theory emphasized the dependence of the individual upon the whole and found that the ideal of freedom may be achieved only in fulfillment of the general will as expressed in the authority of the state, and, so expressed, sanctioned by the inherited tradition of morality. His most important work in political theory was *The Principles of Moral Obligation* (1888).

Grote, George (1794-1871), banker, philosopher, radical, and Whig M.P., who in 1843 abandoned affairs for history and published his *History of Greece* (8 vols., 1846-56). His enthusiasm for democracy, his understanding of philosophy, and his experience in affairs made his *History* one of the classics of modern historical writing and did much to make the traditions of Athenian democracy a creative force in nineteenth-century thought.

Hackett, Francis (1883-1962). Irish by birth and education, he came to the United States in 1901, where he drifted into journalism. He was on the editorial board of *The New Republic* in its early years. After 1922 he was a free-lance writer. He has written of certain aspects of his life in *I Chose Denmark* (1940).

Hammond, John Lawrence (1872-1949), journalist, biographer, and historian. With his wife, Barbara Hammond (1873-1961), he told the tragic history of the industrial revo-lution in a notable trilogy, *The Village Labourer, 1760-1832* (1911), *The Town Labourer, 1760-1832* (1917), and *The Skilled Labourer, 1760-1832* (1919). In journalism his most memorable writing was for the Manchester *Guardian*, to which for many years he contributed unsigned leaders.

Hand, Learned (1872-1961), Federal District Judge from 1909 to 1924 and Circuit Judge in the Second Circuit from 1924 to 1951. One of the great figures in American law, his special distinctions were not dissimilar to those of Holmes, in their graceful mingling of literary gifts with a philosophical if skeptical enthusiasm.

Harrison, Frederic (1831-1923), critic and man of letters. The Positivism of Comte became his religion and he its leading British missionary. His active pen and multifarious interests produced a series of short biographies; a historical romance, *Theophano: The Crusade of the Tenth Century* (1904); and a volume of critical essays, *Studies in Early Victorian Literature* (1895).

Hauriou, Maurice (1856-1929), Professor of Public Law at Toulouse. Mixing the preconceptions of Catholicism with the premises of pluralistic sociology, he contributed largely to the institutional theory of law which he first suggested in his *Précis de droit administratif* (1910) and more fully developed in his *Principes de droit public* (1916) and in his essay *"La théorie de l'institution et de la fondation"* (*Cahiers de la journée*, No. 4, 1925). That theory conceived of society as an aggregate of institutions of which the State was but one, lacking any legitimate claim to supremacy over other institutions.

Henderson, Arthur (1863-1935), labour leader and statesman. In his early years Henderson played a critical part in the formation of the Labour Party, and later became Home Secretary in MacDonald's first government. His greatest concern then and thereafter was with international affairs and led to his becoming MacDonald's Foreign Secretary in 1929. When the National government was formed in 1931, Henderson joined the opposition. In

1934 he was awarded the Nobel Peace Prize.

Hill, James J. (1838-1916), efficient organizer and voracious purchaser of railroads. The first great result of his acquisitions was the Great Northern Railway. Hill's later efforts to utilize the holding company as a means of making monopoly effective were brought to a halt by the decision of the Supreme Court (with Holmes dissenting) that the Northern Securities Company had been organized in violation of the Sherman Anti-Trust Act. Hill's program for creative capitalism was described in his *Highways of Progress* (1910).

Hirst, Francis W. (1873-1953), publicist and economist, long associated with the London School of Economics. His enthusiastic Liberalism is recorded in his *Early Life and Letters of John Morley* (2 vols., 1927). His recollections of his friendships and youthful association are found in his volume of reminiscences, *In the Golden Days* (1947).

Holbach, Baron von (1723-1789), German-born contributor of scientific articles to the *Encyclopédie*. His most vigorous philosophical energies, in *Le système de la nature* (1770) and *Christianisme dévoilé* (1767), were devoted to attacking not only Christianity but the natural religion of Voltaire. It was not surprising, perhaps, that Voltaire described *Le système de la nature* as execrable in morality and absurd in physics.

Horner, Sir John (1842-1927). He and his wife, Lady Horner, were the intimate friends of many of the leading figures in British political and intellectual affairs, and members of that elect circle known as "The Souls." Their daughter Katherine in 1907 married Raymond Asquith. There are frequent references to Sir John and Lady Horner in Spender and Asquith, *Life of Lord Oxford and Asquith* (2 vols., 1932) and *Richard Bendon Haldane, an Autobiography* (1929).

House, Edward M. (1858-1938). Carrying the Texan title of Colonel, he became the intimate adviser to Woodrow Wilson in all matters, both domestic and foreign. His greatest fame is for the part which he played in Europe in the postwar settlements after the First World War. His efforts to persuade Wilson to secure confirmation of the Versailles Treaty by compromise with the Senate failed and led to a final breach between him and the President.

Hughes, Charles Evans (1862-1948). After serving with distinction as Governor of New York, he became an Associate Justice of the Supreme Court of the United States in 1910. In 1916 he resigned from the Court to become Republican nominee for the Presidency, being defeated by a narrow margin when Wilson was reëlected. In 1930 he was named Chief Justice of the United States by President Hoover, retiring in 1941. A great judge, and among the greatest of Chief Justices, his strength of character and intellect made an indelible impression on his times and on the institutions with which he was associated.

Hunt, William Morris (1824-1879). Born in Vermont, he nurtured his artistic spirit in Europe, where he became a disciple of Millet. Returning to the United States in 1855, he became the Newport teacher and friend of William and Henry James and of Holmes. His later years in Boston found him the inspiring teacher of the young and the ardent supporter of modernism in art.

Inge, William Ralph (1860-1954), Dean of St. Paul's, 1911-1934, teacher, scholar, and essayist. In 1911 Asquith, then Prime Minister, persuaded Inge to move from his academic post as Professor of Divinity at Cambridge to the Deanship of St. Paul's Cathedral. Thereafter his pithy observations on affairs brought upon him, and perhaps earned for him the title of "the gloomy Dean." His studies of mysticism and of Plotinus were his greatest achievements in scholarship.

Jenks, Edward (1861-1939), teacher and historian of law. His academic career began at the University of Melbourne and took him successively to Liverpool, Oxford, and London. From 1903 to 1924 he was Principal and Director of Legal Studies of the

Law Society and from 1924 to 1929 held the chair of English Law at the University of London. His most useful book was *A Short History of English Law* (1912).

Jusserand, Jean Jules (1855-1932), diplomat and scholar who was French Ambassador to the United States from 1902 to 1915. His principal works of literary criticism concerned English literature.

Ker, William Paton (1855-1923), Professor of English Literature at University College, London, from 1889 to 1922, and Fellow of All Souls from 1879 until his death. Ker's learning in comparative literature was extraordinarily wide and his relatively short list of published works only suggests the breadth of scholarship of which innumerable students were the beneficiaries. Author, *inter alia*, of *Epic and Romance* (1897) and *Collected Essays of W. P. Ker* (Whibley, ed., 1925).

La Bruyère, Jean de (1645-1696), essayist and defender of the ancients whose barbed portraits of his contemporaries in his *Caractères* (1688) gave pain to the subjects as intense as the pleasure which it gave to the audience. Master of style, he preserved in his method and his mood the tradition of the seventeenth century and satisfied the taste of the eighteenth.

Lamennais, Félicité de (1782-1854). His earliest distinctions were achieved as leader of the Ultramontane party, when he claimed total freedom for the Roman church and insisted that toleration was blasphemy. His great works of this period were *De l'état et l'église au 18e siècle et à l'heure actuelle* (1808) and *De l'indifférence en matière de religion* (1817-24). Bitter experience with a state which had secured the vigorous support of a Gallican hierarchy led him to believe that religious liberty could be found only in a society which saw freedom as the source of truth and the people as the custodians of liberty. The Church's answer to his plea for freedom was excommunication and disgrace for Liberal Catholicism, of which Lammenais had come,

through the pages of *L'avenir,* to be the leader. Laski wrote of Lamennais in Chapter III of *Authority in the Modern State* (1919).

Lang, Andrew (1844-1912), knowledgeable journalist and man of letters whose archaeological wanderings were more those of a folklorist than of a scientist. His talent for fugitive verse grew into a fugitive competence in many fields—fiction, history, psychical research, and sport all engaged his versatile enthusiasm.

Langdell, Christopher Columbus (1826-1906), Dean of the Harvard Law School, 1870-1895. His conviction that the life of the law was logic, not experience, led him to his great discovery—the case-method of legal education. In the hands of his successors the method contributed strength to the conviction of Holmes that the life of the law has not been logic; it has been experience.

Leroy, Maxime (1873-1957), sociologist and historian of French socialism. His important works include *La loi, essai sur le théorie de l'autorité dans la démocratie* (1908) and *Histoire des idées sociales en France* (2 vols., 1946, 1949).

Mack, Julian W. (1866-1943), Federal judge whose distinguished services on the District Courts and Circuit Courts of Appeal covered the thirty years between 1911 and 1941. For many years he was an active leader of American Zionism, and in numerous public offices advanced the cause of civil liberty and the public's welfare.

McKenna, Joseph (1843-1926), Associate Justice of the Supreme Court of the United States, 1898-1926. A Catholic, he came to the Court after a political career in Congress, a Federal circuit judgeship, and a brief term as President McKinley's Attorney General. If settled conviction which may form the basis for predicting a judge's decision is a fault in the judicial temperament McKenna could escape that criticism, for his constitutional opinions, though frequently strong, were constantly variable. The occasional flowering of his conservatism into an effulgent fear of change—as when he determined that the Federal Employers'

Liability Act was unconstitutional—did not prevent an independent mind from showing statesmanship.

McReynolds, James Clark (1862-1941). Appointed to the Supreme Court of the United States by Wilson in 1914, he contributed little wisdom, much conservatism, and unparalleled ill temper to the deliberations of the Court. Holmes, however, found lovable qualities behind the jagged and irascible surface.

Maitland, Frederic William (1850-1906). Trained in the law, Maitland in 1884 abandoned his career as conveyancer to become Reader in the History of English Law at Cambridge, and four years later Downing Professor. His contributions to the legal and institutional history of England were of unequaled brilliance, mingling literary style, philosophic insight, and detailed learning with such graceful ease that few of his readers have failed to fall victims to his charm. He influenced Laski's political thought principally through his Introduction to a substantial portion of Gierke's *Political Theories of the Middle Age* (1900).

Massingham, H. W. (1860-1924), journalist and critic, who edited *The Nation* from 1907 until 1923 and in doing so made it a powerful journal of liberal opinion. His notable qualities as a journalist are described by his associates in *H.W.M.: A Selection from the Writings of H. W. Massingham* (H. J. Massingham, ed., 1926).

Masterman, C. F. G. (1874-1927), journalist and liberal politician. He successively was literary editor of *The Speaker* and of *The Nation,* and held important posts in the government before the First World War.

Mommsen, Theodor (1817-1903), historian of ancient Rome, active liberal politician, and Professor of Ancient History at Berlin. All of a scholar's learning and much of a journalist's enthusiasm combined to make his *Roman History* a great achievement. His later works, even more monumental in their scholarly dimensions, were a vast edition of the *Corpus inscriptionum latinarum* and his *Römischen Staatsrechts* (a part of the *Handbook of Roman*

*Antiquities,* written with Joachim Marquardt, 1812-1882). The latter work has been described as "the greatest historical treatise on political institutions ever written."

Nevinson, Henry Woodd (1856-1941), traveler, man of letters, and journalist. His talents as war correspondent were far greater than those of a mere reporter and made him a military historian of considerable stature. The record of his life in journalism and pursuit of lost causes is found in his trilogy of *Changes and Chances.*

Pitney, Mahlon (1858-1924), Associate Justice of the Supreme Court of the United States, 1912-1922, appointed by Taft. The Presidential expectations that Pitney would prove himself on the Federal bench the conservative which his practice, political career, and chancellorship in New Jersey had indicated him to be were not disappointed.

Primrose, Archibald Philip (1847-1927), fifth Earl of Rosebery; statesman who was Gladstone's Foreign Secretary and briefly succeeded his chief as Prime Minister in 1894. Thereafter he became the leader of the imperialist wing of the Liberal Party, but when the policies of that wing were overridden and Campbell-Bannerman became Prime Minister in 1905 he retired from politics. Thereafter he gave his energies to public address and to the pursuits of a cultivated leisure.

Proudhon, Pierre Joseph (1809-1865), French socialist who stirred Marx with his declaration that "property is theft" and antagonized him by repudiating the dictatorship of the proletariat. His conviction that federalism would be the greatest instrument for achieving justice was the reflection of his dislike of strong state authority. His theories became an important element in the dogma of the syndicalists of a later generation.

Pufendorf, Samuel (1632-1694). In his efforts to formulate a theory of the law of nature he so skillfully mixed the divergent views of Grotius and Hobbes that a view of his own was the result. He pictured the world with which the law is concerned as peopled with moral beings acting not only in response to the instinct of self-preservation but by reason of sociability, and emphasized the rights of the individual against the state. The source of international law he discovered neither in treaties nor in custom, but in a law of nature more rational than divine.

Redlich, Josef (1869-1936), Professor of Public Law at the University of Vienna, statesman, and learned student of the English government. His greatest contributions to scholarship were *The Procedure of the House of Commons* (1908) and *Local Government in England* (Hirst, tr., 1907). In 1925 he came to the Harvard Law School as Professor of Comparative Public Law. His qualities as teacher and scholar are described by Felix Frankfurter and Charles C. Burlingham in 50 *Harv. L. Rev.* 389, 392 (January 1937).
Rice, Richard A. (1846-1924), Professor of Art at Williams College until 1911. He then moved to Washington and in 1912 became Chief of the Division of Prints in the Library of Congress.

Rivers, William Halse Rivers (1864-1922), experimental psychologist and ethnologist long associated with Cambridge University. In ethnology his most important work was a *History of Melanesian Society* (1914) and in psychology, *Instinct and the Unconscious* (1920) and *Social Organization* (1924). Arnold Bennett wrote with feeling of him in "W. H. R. Rivers: Some Recollections," 19 *New Statesman* 290 (June 17, 1922).

Root, Elihu (1845-1937), lawyer and statesman. He was Secretary of War and Secretary of State under Theodore Roosevelt and Republican Senator from New York from 1909 to 1915. In his later years his great preoccupation was with problems of world peace.

Rosebery, Lord. *See* Primrose, Archibald Philip.

Rutherford, Sir Ernest (1871-1937), Baron Rutherford. Born and educated in New Zealand he became one of the great physicists of his times. His academic career was at McGill, Manchester, and Cambridge. His great discoveries in physics concerned radioactivity and the structure of atoms.

Sanford, Edward Terry (1865-1930). Advanced by President Harding to the Supreme Court of the United States from the Federal District Court in Tennessee, Sanford was a colorless colleague of Holmes's from 1923 to 1930. His tranquil inclinations were conservative, yet he joined with Holmes and Brandeis in a number of their important opinions on free speech.

Sankey, John (1866-1948), first Viscount Sankey; successively Judge of the King's Bench and of the Court of Appeal between 1914 and 1929; and Lord Chancellor from 1929 to 1935. At the bar he had been a master in the field of workmen's compensation and by his distinguished service as Chairman the Coal Mining Commission of 1919 had shown the capacity to make an acute intelligence the instrument of progress. It was no surprise, therefore, when he became Chancellor in the Labour Government of 1929.

Scott, James Brown (1866-1943), Professor of Law at Illinois, Columbia, and Chicago, and authority on international law. He held many governmental posts in connection with foreign affairs, and from 1907 to 1924 was editor of the *American Journal of International Law*.

Scott, Sir Leslie (1869-1950), Lord Justice of Appeal from 1935 to 1948. His life was devoted more to professional than to political affairs, but his professional services to the state were many. He and Lady Scott were intimate friends of Holmes.

Scrutton, Thomas Edward (1856-1934), Justice of the King's Bench, 1910-1916, and of the Court of Appeal, 1916 to 1934. His genius as practitioner and as judge was in the field of commercial law; an irascible, ill-mannered temperament was somewhat softened with the years and at no time was so dominant as to prevent his being a great lawyer and a great judge.

Simon, Sir John (1873-1954), first Viscount Simon; conservative Liberal, who held many high offices of state and served as Lord Chancellor from 1940 to 1945. His legal capacities were acknowledged by all; his political judgment was mistrusted by those who thought appeasement of Hitler a mistake and doubted whether the rearmament of Germany would make for peace.

Smuts, Jan Christiaan (1870-1951), South African soldier, statesman, and philosopher. His youth was spent in the military service of the Boers, his maturity in the service both of Great Britain and of his own people, with the public's gratitude for these latter services more prevalent abroad than at home. Following the First World War he put his hopes in the League of Nations. His lifelong interest in philosophy produced one piece of work of some importance—*Holism and Evolution* (1926).

Sorel, Georges (1847-1922), most famous for his *Reflections on Violence* (1908) and for his espousal of syndicalism. His lifelong search was for an ethical principie which would guarantee the development of morality. The search led him down many divergent paths. He accepted the leadership of Proudhon and of Marx, identified democracy with mediocrity, and ultimately hailed, in succession, Fascism and Bolshevism as preferable to socialism.

Soto, Domingo de (1494-1560), Spanish jurist, who sought, in his most important work, *De justicia et jure* (2 vols., 1553-54), to translate Thomistic ethics into principles of the legal order.

Stammler, Rudolf (1856-1938), whose neo-Kantian philosophy of law emphasized the collective interests in a community of free-willing men and accepted as absolute "the principles of just law." If, as Geny charged, he failed to inform us what law is "just" and showed a greater skill in juggling abstractions than in establishing criteria of judgment, he did, despite the sterility of his basic effort, succeed in reminding judges of their creative responsibilities in guiding the judicial process. He also persuasively supported the thesis that

the content of the law of nature is variable and changing. His most important works were *Lehre von dem richtigen Recht* (1902), (published in an English translation under the title *The Theory of Justice,* Husik, tr., 1925), *Wirtschaft und Recht* (1896), and *Lehrbuch der Rechtsphilosophie* (1922).

Stephen, Sir James Fitzjames (1829-1894). Lawyer, judge, and publicist, he was the forceful brother of Sir Leslie Stephen. In affairs his greatest achievement was as successor to Sir Henry Maine as legal member of the Council in India. That experience converted him to the cause of codification and nourished the doubt whether the optimism of Mill, in so far as it affected political principles, was acceptable. The result was the publication of his *Liberty, Equality, Fraternity* (1873). That work, together with his *History of the Criminal Law* (3 vols., 1883), reveal more fully than any other of his writings the vigor of his mind and the breadth of his scholarship.

Story, Joseph (1779-1845), Associate Justice of the Supreme Court of the United States from 1811 to 1845. Appointed to the Court by Madison he became as ardent a defender of national power as his Chief, John Marshall. His extraordinary energies were such that while serving on the Court he was also a member of the law faculty at Harvard and the author of ten large treatises on various subjects in the law. The utility of these volumes as reasoned, if somewhat uncritical compendia of cases and principles, was enormous and they had an influence equal to if not greater than Story's judicial opinions.

Suárez, Francisco (1548-1617). In answering such Protestant theorists of the Reformation as Althusius, he revivified the Thomistic version of the law of nature and made the last great contributions to scholastic philosophy. His political theory reëmphasized the medieval doctrine of popular sovereignty as a limitation on the power of kings.

Taine, Hippolyte (1828-1893), critic and historian whose misanthropic positivism led him to see man as a "dismal gorilla" and whose respect for the fruitfulness of inequality led him to condemn the objectives and the achievements of the French Revolution. In his chief historical work, *Les origines de la France contemporaine* (6 vols., 1876-94), he was immersed in the tragedies of a modern France which had not enjoyed the buoyant successes of Victorian England, and became in the words of Professor Gooch, "a pessimist in a passion." The greatest influence in the views of Taine as historian was on the conservatives who, abandoning his positivism, shared his regret that the Revolution had occurred.

Tarde, Gabriel (1843-1904), French social psychologist. In his best known work, *Les lois de l'imitation* (1890), he sought to uncover the laws of repetition, by which he conceived that most actions of most men are determined. In all his work he was more concerned with concrete instances than with large abstractions.

Tawney, R. H. (1880-1962), economic historian and publicist, long associated with London University and frequently called to the public service. Of his many works the best known, perhaps, are *Religion and the Rise of Capitalism* (1926) and *The Acquisitive Society* (1920).

Vauvenargues, Marquis de (1715-1747), soldier, moralist, and epigrammatist. It was largely owing to the friendship of Voltaire that the Marquis, becoming an invalid, turned to letters as his occupation. The most important result was his *Introduction à la connaissance de l'esprit humain* (1746) with its accompanying maxims.

Vinogradoff, Sir Paul (1854-1925), legal historian of Russian birth who became Professor of Jurisprudence at Oxford in 1903, succeeding Sir Frederick Pollock. His greatest discovery was the manuscript of Bracton's *Notebook* and his most important piece of historical writing was *Villainage in England* (1892). His Oxford seminar produced the Oxford *Studies in Social and Legal History* (9 vols., 1908-27), under his editorship.

Viollet, Paul (1840-1914), legal historian whose major work was his *Droit public: Histoire des institutions politiques et administratives de la France* (3 vols., 1889-1903).

Wallas, Graham (1858-1932). In his early years Wallas was intimately associated with Shaw and Webb in the Fabian Society. Later he became one of the organizers of and early lecturers at the London School of Economics and Political Science, filling its first chair of political science from 1914 to 1923. His earliest book, *The Life of Francis Place* (1898), was an important addition to knowledge of the history of the British labor movement. In his later works he endeavored to build a science of social psychology in the hope that political theory might be freed from the grip of intellectualism. *The Great Society* (1914) was a book of enormous influence in revealing the relationships between psychology and political science and in suggesting how fruitful the scientific temper might be when applied to the problems of political theory.

Ward, Lester Frank (1841-1913), American sociologist whose most important work, *Dynamic Sociology* (2 vols., 1883), was written while he was a civil servant in Washington engaged in scientific research and before his appointment as Professor of Sociology at Brown University. His sociological theory emphasized the capacity of man by conscious effort to improve the human lot and through that emphasis served effectively to refute the evolutionary determinism of Spencer. From an early date Holmes was an admirer of Ward's writing.

Wigmore, John Henry (1863-1943), learned Dean of the Law School of Northwestern University. His monumental treatise on *The Law of Evidence* (3rd ed., 10 vols., 1940) is one of the great classics of Anglo-American law. His close friendship with Holmes survived the strain to which it was subjected by Wigmore's petulant postwar patriotism which found Holmes's tolerant views on free speech intolerable.

Wister, Owen (1860-1938), lawyer, novelist, grandson of Fanny Kemble, and, above all, Philadelphian. A vigorous admirer of Theodore Roosevelt's vigor, he was best known, perhaps, for his novel *The Virginian* (1902). His friendship with Holmes began when Holmes was on the Massachusetts bench and Wister was a law student at Harvard.

Wu, John C. H. (1899-      ), jurist, judge, and intimate friend of Holmes. The original story of their intimacy is revealed in the letters of Holmes to Wu, first published in the *T'ien Hsia Monthly* for October 1935, later reprinted in Shriver, *Justice Oliver Wendell Holmes, His Book Notices and Uncollected Letters and Papers* (1936), 151 *et seq.* Dr. Wu has written of his own life, of his friendship with Holmes, and of his conversion to Roman Catholicism in *Beyond East and West* (1951).

Zimmern, Sir Alfred (1879-1957), historian, classicist, and student of foreign affairs. He held many academic posts in Great Britain and the United States, and participated in such international enterprises as the League of Nations and UNESCO. His most important piece of scholarship is *The Greek Commonwealth* (1911).

# Index

MARK DEWOLFE HOWE is Professor of Law, Harvard Law School. Mr. Howe has for many years made the life and work of Justice Holmes the object of his scholarship. He has in progress the definitive biography of the Justice, of which two volumes have appeared: *The Shaping Years 1847-1870; The Proving Years 1870-1882.* Mr. Howe has also edited the *Holmes-Pollock Letters,* Holmes' *The Common Law,* and *The Occasional Speeches of Justice Holmes.* In addition to the numerous works relating to Holmes, Mr. Howe is also the compiler of *Cases on Church and State in the United States.*

# Atheneum Paperbacks

## Government and Public Affairs

## Economics and Business

## History and Societal Studies

## Literature and the Arts

## Philosophy and Religion

## Physical Sciences and Mathematics

## Life Sciences

## The Worlds of Nature and of Man